Contents

Preface   v
To the Student   vi
Using this Study Guide and Selected Solutions Manual   vii

Chapter 1   Chemistry in Our Lives   1
Study Guide   1
Selected Answers and Solutions to Text Problems   9

Chapter 2   Chemistry and Measurements   13
Study Guide   13
Selected Answers and Solutions to Text Problems   30

Chapter 3   Matter and Energy   41
Study Guide   41
Selected Answers and Solutions to Text Problems   55
Selected Answers to Combining Ideas from Chapters 1 to 3   68

Chapter 4   Atoms   70
Study Guide   70
Selected Answers and Solutions to Text Problems   87

Chapter 5   Nuclear Chemistry   97
Study Guide   97
Selected Answers and Solutions to Text Problems   108

Chapter 6   Ionic and Molecular Compounds   115
Study Guide   115
Selected Answers and Solutions to Text Problems   139
Selected Answers to Combining Ideas from Chapters 4 to 6   150

Chapter 7   Chemical Reactions and Quantities   152
Study Guide   152
Selected Answers and Solutions to Text Problems   175

Chapter 8   Gases   192
Study Guide   192
Selected Answers and Solutions to Text Problems   207
Selected Answers to Combining Ideas from Chapters 7 and 8   219

Chapter 9   Solutions   220
Study Guide   220
Selected Answers and Solutions to Text Problems   243

Chapter 10   Reaction Rates and Chemical Equilibrium   256
Study Guide   256
Selected Answers and Solutions to Text Problems   267

Chapter 11   Acids and Bases   272
Study Guide   272
Selected Answers and Solutions to Text Problems   290
Selected Answers to Combining Ideas from Chapters 9 to 11   301

iii

Contents

Chapter 12 **Introduction to Organic Chemistry: Hydrocarbons** **303**
Study Guide 303
Selected Answers and Solutions to Text Problems 323

Chapter 13 **Alcohols, Phenols, Thiols, and Ethers** **332**
Study Guide 332
Selected Answers and Solutions to Text Problems 343

Chapter 14 **Aldehydes, Ketones, and Chiral Molecules** **351**
Study Guide 351
Selected Answers and Solutions to Text Problems 366
Selected Answers to Combining Ideas from Chapters 12 to 14 373

Chapter 15 **Carbohydrates** **375**
Study Guide 375
Selected Answers and Solutions to Text Problems 386

Chapter 16 **Carboxylic Acids and Esters** **391**
Study Guide 391
Selected Answers and Solutions to Text Problems 402

Chapter 17 **Lipids** **410**
Study Guide 410
Selected Answers and Solutions to Text Problems 425

Chapter 18 **Amines and Amides** **431**
Study Guide 431
Selected Answers and Solutions to Text Problems 444
Selected Answers to Combining Ideas from Chapters 15 to 18 450

Chapter 19 **Amino Acids and Proteins** **451**
Study Guide 451
Selected Answers and Solutions to Text Problems 460

Chapter 20 **Enzymes and Vitamins** **468**
Study Guide 468
Selected Answers and Solutions to Text Problems 477

Chapter 21 **Nucleic Acids and Protein Synthesis** **482**
Study Guide 482
Selected Answers and Solutions to Text Problems 494
Selected Answers to Combining Ideas from Chapters 19 to 21 501

Chapter 22 **Metabolic Pathways for Carbohydrates** **502**
Study Guide 502
Selected Answers and Solutions to Text Problems 510

Chapter 23 **Metabolism and Energy Production** **515**
Study Guide 515
Selected Answers and Solutions to Text Problems 521

Chapter 24 **Metabolic Pathways for Lipids and Amino Acids** **525**
Study Guide 525
Selected Answers and Solutions to Text Problems 536
Selected Answers to Combining Ideas from Chapters 22 to 24 541

Preface

This Study Guide and Selected Solutions Manual is intended to accompany *General, Organic, and Biological Chemistry: Structures of Life*, Fifth Edition. The purpose of this Study Guide is to provide you with additional learning resources that will increase your understanding of the concepts. Each section in this Study Guide is correlated with a chapter section in the text. Within each section, there are Learning Goals, Guides to Problem Solving, and Learning Exercises and Answers that focus on problem solving and promote an understanding of the chemical principles of each Learning Goal. A checklist of Learning Goals and a multiple-choice Practice Test provide a review of the entire chapter content.

The Answers and complete Solutions to the odd-numbered problems in the text are provided in the Selected Solutions Manual, which is included with each chapter of the Study Guide.

I hope that this Study Guide and Selected Solutions Manual will help you in the learning of chemistry. If you wish to make comments or corrections, or ask questions, you can send me an e-mail message at khemist@aol.com.

Karen C. Timberlake

To the Student

*"One must learn by doing the thing;
though you think you know it, you have
no certainty until you try."*
—*Sophocles*

Here you are in a chemistry class with your textbook in front of you. Perhaps you have already been assigned some reading or some problems to do in the book. Looking through the chapter, you may see words, terms, and pictures that are new to you. This may very well be your first experience with a science class like chemistry. At this point, you may have some questions about what you can do to learn chemistry. This Study Guide is written with that consideration in mind.

Learning chemistry is similar to learning a new skill such as tennis or skiing or driving. If I asked you how you would learn to play tennis or ski or drive a car, you would probably tell me that you would need to practice often. It is the same with learning chemistry; understanding the chemical ideas and successfully solving the problems depends on the time and effort you invest. If you practice every day, you will find that learning chemistry is an exciting experience and a way to understand the current issues of the environment, health, and medicine.

Manage Your Study Time

I often recommend a study system to students: read one section of the text, and immediately do the questions and problems that are at the end of that section. In this way, you concentrate on a small amount of information and actively use what you learned to answer questions. This helps you to organize and review the information without being overwhelmed by the entire chapter. It is important to understand each section because the sections build like steps. Information presented in each chapter proceeds from the basic to the more complex. Perhaps you can study only three or four sections of the chapter. As long as you also practice doing some problems at the same time, the concepts and problem-solving strategies will stay with you.

Form a Study Group

I highly recommend that you form a study group in the first week of your chemistry class. Working with your peers will help you use the language of chemistry. Scheduling a time to meet each week will help you study and prepare to discuss problems. You will be able to teach some things to the other students in the group, and sometimes they will help you understand a topic that puzzles you. You won't always understand a concept right away. Your group will help you see your way through it. Most of all, a study group creates a strong support system as students help each other complete the class successfully.

Go to Office Hours

Attend your instructor's office hours. Your instructor wants you to understand and enjoy learning this material. Often a tutor is assigned to a class, or there are tutors available at your college. Don't be intimidated. Going to see your instructor, or tutor is one of the best ways to clarify what you need to learn in chemistry.

Using this Study Guide and Selected Solutions Manual

Now you are ready to sit down and learn chemistry. Let's go over some methods that can help you study chemistry. This Study Guide and the Selected Solutions Manual is written specifically to help you understand and practice the chemical concepts that are presented in your class and in your text. Some of the exercises teach basic skills; others encourage you to extend your scientific curiosity. The following features are part of this Study Guide and the Selected Solutions Manual:

1. Learning Goals

The Learning Goals give you an overview of what each section in the chapter is about and what you can expect to accomplish when you complete your study and learning of that section.

2. Key Terms

Key Terms appear throughout each chapter in the Study Guide. As you review the definitions of the Key Terms, you will have an overview of the topics you have studied in that chapter. Because many of the Key Terms may have been new to you, this is an opportunity to review their meaning.

3. Key Concepts

Each section of each chapter begins with the Key Concepts that summarize the important ideas in that section. The summary of concepts is written to guide you through each of the learning activities. When you are ready to begin your study, read the matching section in the textbook and review the Guides to Problem Solving and the Sample Problems in the text.

4. Learning Exercises

The Learning Exercises give you an opportunity to practice problem solving related to the chemical principles in the chapter. Each set of Learning Exercises reviews one chemical principle. At various times, you will notice some essay questions that illustrate the concepts. These have been included because I believe that writing out your ideas is a very important way of learning new content. The answers are found immediately following each Learning Exercise. Check your answers right away. If they don't match the answers in the Study Guide, review that section of the text again. It is important to make corrections before you go on. Chemistry involves a layering of skills such that each one must be mastered before the next one can be learned.

5. Checklists

Use the Checklists to check your understanding of the Learning Goals. The checklists give you an overview of the major topics in each section. If something does not sound familiar, go back and review it. One aspect of being a strong problem-solver is the ability to check your knowledge and understanding as you study.

6. Practice Tests

A Practice Test is found at the end of each chapter. When you feel you have learned the material in a chapter, you can check your understanding by taking the Practice Test. Answers for all of the questions are included at the end of each Practice Test. The Practice Test questions are keyed to the Learning Goals, which allows you to identify the sections you may need to review. If the results of this test indicate that you know the material, you are ready to proceed to the next chapter.

7. Selected Answers and Solutions

The Selected Answers and Solutions include the Learning Goals, Chapter Outline, Key Math Skills, Core Chemistry Skills, and Answers and Solutions to the odd-numbered problems in the text. For certain chapters, Selected Answers to the Combined Ideas for groups of chapters are included.

Resources

General, Organic, and Biological Chemistry: Structures of Life, fifth edition, provides an integrated teaching and learning package of support material for both students and professors.

Name of Supplement	Available in Print	Available Online	Instructor or Student Supplement	Description
Study Guide and Selected Solutions Manual (ISBN 0133891917)	✓		Resource for Students	The **Study Guide and Selected Solutions Manual**, by Karen Timberlake and Mark Quirie, promotes active learning through a variety of exercises with answers as well as practice tests that are connected directly to the learning goals of the textbook. Complete solutions to odd-numbered problems are included.
MasteringChemistry® (www.masteringchemistry.com) (ISBN 0133858375)		✓	Resource for Students and Instructors	MasteringChemistry® from Pearson is the leading online teaching and learning system designed to improve results by engaging students before, during, and after class with powerful content. Ensure that students arrive ready to learn by assigning educationally effective content before class, and encourage critical thinking and retention with in-class resources such as Learning Catalytics. Students can further master concepts after class through traditional homework assignments that provide hints and answer-specific feedback. The Mastering gradebook records scores for all automatically graded assignments while diagnostic tools give instructors access to rich data to assess student understanding and misconceptions.
MasteringChemistry with Pearson eText (ISBN 0133899306)		✓	Resource for Students	The fifth edition of *General, Organic, and Biological Chemistry: Structures of Life* features a Pearson eText enhanced with media within Mastering. In conjunction with Mastering assessment capabilities, Interactive Videos and 3D animations will improve student engagement and knowledge retention. Each chapter will contain a balance of interactive animations, videos, sample calculations, and self-assessments/quizzes embedded directly in the eText. Additionally, the Pearson eText offers students the power to create notes, highlight text in different colors, create bookmarks, zoom, and view single or multiple pages.
Instructor's Solutions Manual–Download Only (ISBN 0133891909)		✓	Resource for Instructors	Prepared by Mark Quirie, the solutions manual highlights chapter topics, and includes answers and solutions for all questions and problems in the text.
Instructor Resource Materials–Download Only (ISBN 0133891887)		✓	Resource for Instructors	Includes all the art, photos, and tables from the book in JPEG format for use in classroom projection or when creating study materials and tests. In addition, the instructors can access modifiable PowerPoint™ lecture outlines. Also available are downloadable files of the Instructor's Solutions Manual and a set of "clicker questions" designed for use with classroom-response systems. Also visit the Pearson Education catalog page for Timberlake's *General, Organic, and Biological Chemistry: Structures of Life* fifth Edition, at www.pearsonhighered.com to download available instructor supplements.
TestGen Test Bank–Download Only (ISBN 0133891895)		✓	Resource for Instructors	Prepared by William Timberlake, this resource includes more than 2000 questions in multiple-choice, matching, true/false, and short-answer format.

Name of Supplement	Available in Print	Available Online	Instructor or Student Supplement	Description
Laboratory Manual by Karen Timberlake (ISBN 0321811852)	✓		Resource for Students	This best-selling lab manual coordinates 35 experiments with the topics in *General, Organic, and Biological Chemistry: Structures of Life* fifth edition, uses laboratory investigations to explore chemical concepts, develop skills of manipulating equipment, reporting data, solving problems, making calculations, and drawing conclusions.
Online Instructor Manual for Laboratory Manual (ISBN 0321812859)		✓	Resource for Instructors	This manual contains answers to report sheet pages for the *Laboratory Manual* and a list of the materials needed for each experiment with amounts given for 20 students working in pairs, available for download at www.pearsonhighered.com.

Chemistry in Our Lives

When a female victim was found dead in her home, samples of her blood and stomach contents were sent to Sarah, who works as a forensic scientist. After using a variety of chemical tests, Sarah concluded that the victim was poisoned when she ingested ethylene glycol. Since the initial symptoms of ethylene glycol poisoning are similar to those of intoxication, the victim was unaware of the poisoning. When ethylene glycol is oxidized, the products can cause renal failure and may be toxic to the body. Two weeks later, police arrested the victim's husband after finding a bottle of ethylene glycol in the kitchen of the couple's home. How does this result show the use of the scientific method?

Credit: nyaivanova / Shutterstock

1.1   Chemistry and Chemicals

Learning Goal: Define the term chemistry and identify substances as chemicals.

* Chemistry is the study of the composition, structure, properties, and reactions of matter.
* A chemical is a substance containing one type of material that has the same composition and properties wherever it is found.

♦ **Learning Exercise 1.1**

Indicate if each of the following is a chemical or not:

a. _____ ascorbic acid (vitamin C)

b. _____ time for a radioisotope to lose half its activity

c. _____ sodium fluoride in toothpaste

d. _____ amoxicillin, an antibiotic

e. _____ distance of 2.5 mi on a treadmill during exercise

f. _____ carbon nanotubes used to transport medication to cancer cells

Answers   **a.** yes   **b.** no   **c.** yes   **d.** yes   **e.** no   **f.** yes

1.2   Scientific Method: Thinking Like a Scientist

Learning Goal: Describe the activities that are part of the scientific method.

Scientific Method

- The scientific method is a process of making observations, writing a hypothesis, and testing the hypothesis with experiments.

The hypothesis is modified if the results of the experiments do not support it.

- When the results of the experiments are analyzed, a conclusion is made as to whether the hypothesis is true or false.

The scientific method develops conclusions using observations, hypotheses, and experiments.

♦ **Learning Exercise 1.2A**

Identify each of the following as an observation (O), a hypothesis (H), or an experiment (E):

a. _____ Sunlight is necessary for the growth of plants.

b. _____ Plants in the shade are shorter than plants in the sun.

c. _____ Plant leaves are covered with aluminum foil and their growth is measured.

d. _____ Fertilizer is added to plants.

e. _____ Ozone slows plant growth by interfering with photosynthesis.

f. _____ Ozone causes brown spots on plant leaves.

Answers   **a.** H   **b.** O   **c.** E   **d.** E   **e.** H   **f.** O

Nurses make observations in the hospital.
Credit: Pressmaster / Shutterstock

♦ **Learning Exercise 1.2B**

Identify each of the following as an observation (O), a hypothesis (H), an experiment (E), or a conclusion (C):

a. _____ One half-hour after eating a wheat roll, Cynthia experiences stomach cramps.

b. _____ The next morning, Cynthia eats a piece of toast, and one half-hour later has an upset stomach.

c. _____ Cynthia thinks she may be gluten intolerant.

d. _____ Cynthia tries a gluten-free roll and does not have any stomach cramps.

e. _____ Because Cynthia does not have an upset stomach after eating a gluten-free roll, she believes that she is gluten intolerant.

Answers   **a.** O   **b.** O   **c.** H   **d.** E   **e.** C

1.3   Learning Chemistry: A Study Plan

Learning Goal: Develop a study plan for learning chemistry.

- Components of the text that promote learning include: *Looking Ahead, Learning Goals, Chapter Readiness, Key Math Skills, Core Chemistry Skills, Analyze the Problems, Sample Problems, Study Checks with Answers, Guides to Problem Solving (GPS), Chemistry Link to Health, Chemistry Link to the Environment, Questions and Problems, Clinical Applications, Clinical Updates, Concept Maps, Chapter Reviews, Key Terms, Review of Key Math Skills, Review of Core Chemistry Skills,*

Understanding the Concepts, Additional Questions and Problems, Challenge Problems, Answers to Selected Questions and Problems, Combining Ideas, and *Glossary/Index.*

- An active learner continually interacts with chemical concepts while reading the text and attending class.
- Working with a study group clarifies ideas and facilitates problem solving.

♦ **Learning Exercise 1.3**

Which of the following activities would be included in a successful study plan for learning chemistry?

    a. ____ attending class once in a while

    b. ____ working problems with friends from class

    c. ____ attending review sessions

    d. ____ planning a regular study time

    e. ____ not doing the assigned problems

    f. ____ visiting the instructor during office hours

Answers   **a.** no   **b.** yes   **c.** yes   **d.** yes   **e.** no   **f.** yes

1.4   Key Math Skills for Chemistry

Learning Goal: Review math concepts used in chemistry: place values, positive and negative numbers, percentages, solving equations, interpreting graphs, and writing numbers in scientific notation.

- Basic math skills are important in learning chemistry.
- In a number, we identify the place value of each digit.
- A positive number is *greater* than zero and has a positive sign ($+$); a negative number is *less* than zero and has a negative sign ($-$).
- A percentage is calculated as the parts divided by the whole, then multiplied by 100%.
- A linear equation is solved by rearranging it to place the unknown value on one side.
- A graph represents the relationship between two variables, which are plotted on perpendicular axes.
- A number written in scientific notation consists of a coefficient and a power of 10.

Key Terms for Sections 1.1–1.4

Match each of the following key terms with the correct definition:

    a. scientific method   **b.** experiment   **c.** scientific notation
    d. conclusion   **e.** chemistry   **f.** hypothesis

1. ____ an explanation of nature validated by many experiments

2. ____ the study of substances and how they interact

3. ____ a possible explanation of a natural phenomenon

4. ____ the process of making observations, writing a hypothesis, and testing with experiments

5. ____ a procedure used to test a hypothesis

6. ____ a form of writing large and small numbers using a coefficient that is at least 1 but less than 10, followed by a power of 10

Answers   **1.** d   **2.** e   **3.** f   **4.** a   **5.** b   **6.** c

Study Note

On your calculator, there are four keys that are used for basic mathematical operations. The change sign $\boxed{+/-}$ key is used to change the sign of a number.

To practice these basic calculations on the calculator, work through the problem going from left to right doing the operations in the order they occur. If your calculator has a change sign $\boxed{+/-}$ key, a negative number is entered by pressing the number and then pressing the change sign $\boxed{+/-}$ key. At the end, press the equals $\boxed{=}$ key or ANS or ENTER.

Addition and Subtraction

Example 1: $15 - 8 + 2 =$

Solution: $15 \boxed{-} 8 \boxed{+} 2 \boxed{=} 9$

Example 2: $4 + (-10) - 5 =$

Solution: $4 \boxed{+} 10 \boxed{+/-} \boxed{-} 5 \boxed{=} -11$

Multiplication and Division

Example 3: $2 \times (-3) =$

Solution: $2 \boxed{\times} 3 \boxed{+/-} \boxed{=} -6$

Example 4: $\dfrac{8 \times 3}{4} =$

Solution: $8 \boxed{\times} 3 \boxed{\div} 4 \boxed{=} 6$

♦ Learning Exercise 1.4A

 KEY MATH SKILL

Identifying Place Values

1. Identify the place value for each of the digits in the number 825.10.

Digit	Place Value
8	
2	
5	
1	
0	

Answer

Digit	Place Value
8	hundreds
2	tens
5	ones
1	tenths
0	hundredths

2. A tablet contains 0.325 g of aspirin. Identify the place value for each of the digits in the number 0.325 g.

Digit	Place Value
3	
2	
5	

Answer

Digit	Place Value
3	tenths
2	hundredths
5	thousandths

♦ Learning Exercise 1.4B

 KEY MATH SKILL

Using Positive and Negative Numbers in Calculations

Solve the following:

$$\frac{-14 + 22}{-4} = ?$$

Answer

$$\frac{-14 + 22}{-4} = -2$$

♦ Learning Exercise 1.4C

 KEY MATH SKILL

Calculating Percentages

There are 20 patients on the 3rd floor of a hospital. If 4 patients were discharged today, what percentage of patients were discharged?

Answer

$$\frac{4 \text{ patients discharged}}{20 \text{ patients}} \times 100\% = 20\% \text{ patients discharged}$$

Study Note

1. Solve an equation for a particular variable by performing the same mathematical operation on *both* sides of the equation.
2. If you eliminate a symbol or number by subtracting, you need to subtract that same symbol or number on the opposite side.
3. If you eliminate a symbol or number by adding, you need to add that same symbol or number on the opposite side.
4. If you cancel a symbol or number by dividing, you need to divide both sides by that same symbol or number.
5. If you cancel a symbol or number by multiplying, you need to multiply both sides by that same symbol or number.

♦ **Learning Exercise 1.4D**

Solve the following equation for *y*:

$$3y - 8 = 22$$

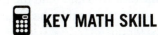

KEY MATH SKILL

Solving Equations

Answer

$$3y - 8 = 22$$
$$3y - 8 \, (+8) = 22 \, (+8)$$
$$3y = 30$$
$$\frac{3y}{3} = \frac{30}{3}$$
$$y = 10$$

♦ **Learning Exercise 1.4E**

Use the following graph to answer questions **a** and **b**:

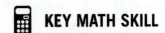

KEY MATH SKILL

Interpreting Graphs

Time for Cooling of Coffee versus Temperature

a. How many minutes elapse when coffee cools from 100 °C to 65 °C?

b. What is the temperature after the coffee has cooled for 15 min?

Time for Cooling of Coffee versus Temperature

Time for Cooling of Coffee versus Temperature

Answers

a. Draw a horizontal line from 65 °C on the temperature axis to intersect the curved line. Then drop a vertical line to the time axis and read the time where it crosses the *x* axis, which is estimated to be 9 min.

b. Draw a vertical line from 15 min on the time axis to intersect the curved line. Draw a horizontal line from the intersect to the temperature axis and read the temperature where it crosses the *y* axis, which is estimated to be 57 °C.

	Guide to Writing a Number in Scientific Notation
STEP 1	Move the decimal point to obtain a coefficient that is at least 1 but less than 10.
STEP 2	Express the number of places moved as a power of 10.
STEP 3	Write the product of the coefficient multiplied by the power of 10.

⬛ KEY MATH SKILL

Writing Numbers in Scientific Notation

♦ **Learning Exercise 1.4F**

Write each of the following numbers in scientific notation:

a. 240 000 _____

b. 825 _____

c. 2300 _____

d. 53 000 _____

e. 0.002 _____

f. 0.000 001 5 _____

g. 0.08 _____

h. 0.000 24 _____

Answers
a. 2.4×10^5 **b.** 8.25×10^2 **c.** 2.3×10^3 **d.** 5.3×10^4
e. 2×10^{-3} **f.** 1.5×10^{-6} **g.** 8×10^{-2} **h.** 2.4×10^{-4}

Checklist for Chapter 1

You are ready to take the Practice Test for Chapter 1. Be sure you have accomplished the following learning goals for this chapter. If not, review the section listed at the end of the goal. Then, apply your new skills and understanding to the Practice Test.

After studying Chapter 1, I can successfully:

_____ Describe a substance as a chemical. (1.1)

_____ Identify the steps of the scientific method. (1.2)

_____ Design a study plan for successfully learning chemistry. (1.3)

_____ Use math skills needed for chemistry: place values, positive and negative numbers, percentages, solving equations, interpreting graphs, and writing numbers in scientific notation. (1.4)

Practice Test for Chapter 1

The chapter sections to review are shown in parentheses at the end of each question.

1. Which of the following would be described as a chemical? (1.1)
   A. sleeping   B. salt   C. singing
   D. listening to a concert   E. energy

2. Which of the following is not a chemical? (1.1)
   A. aspirin   B. sugar   C. feeling cold
   D. glucose   E. vanilla

For questions 3 through 7, identify each statement as an observation (O), a hypothesis (H), or an experiment (E): (1.2)

3. _____ More sugar dissolves in 50 mL of hot water than in 50 mL of cold water.

4. _____ Samples containing 20 g of sugar each are placed separately in a glass of cold water and a glass of hot water.

5. _____ Sugar consists of white crystals.

6. _____ Water flows downhill.

7. _____ Drinking 10 glasses of water a day will help me lose weight.

For questions 8 through 12, answer yes or no. (1.3)

To learn chemistry, I will:

8. _____ work the problems in the chapter and check answers

9. _____ attend some classes but not all

10. _____ form a study group

11. _____ set up a regular study time

12. _____ wait until the night before the exam to start studying

13. Solve for the value of a in the equation $5a + 11 = 36$. (1.4)
    A. 1   B. 5   C. 15   D. 25   E. 30

14. Give the answer for the problem $\dfrac{22 + 23}{1 - 4}$. (1.4)
    A. 5   B. −5   C. −7   D. −15   E. 15

15. At the zoo, there are 8 lions, 6 tigers, and 2 panthers. What percentage of the animals at the zoo are lions? (1.4)
    A. 50%   B. 30%   C. 20%   D. 10%   E. 5%

16. Use the following graph to determine the solubility of carbon dioxide in water, in g CO_2/100 g water, at 40 °C: (1.4)

Solubility of Carbon Dioxide in Water

A. 0.10   **B.** 0.15   **C.** 0.20   **D.** 0.25   **E.** 0.30

17. The number 24 000 written in scientific notation is (1.4)
    A. 24   **B.** 24×10^3 **C.** 2.4×10^3 **D.** 2.4×10^{-3} **E.** 2.4×10^4

18. The number 0.005 written in scientific notation is (1.4)
    A. 5   **B.** 5×10^{-3} **C.** 5×10^{-2} **D.** 0.5×10^{-4} **E.** 5×10^3

19. The contents found in a container at a victim's home were identified as 65.0 g of ethylene glycol in 182 g of solution. What is the percentage of ethylene glycol in the solution? (1.4)
    A. 15.3%   **B.** 28.0%   **C.** 35.7%   **D.** 48.0%   **E.** 65.0%

20. For breakfast, a patient has a tray with 55 g of eggs, 65 g of banana, and 85 g of milk. What percentage of the breakfast was milk? (1.4)
    A. 85%   **B.** 65%   **C.** 41%   **D.** 32%   **E.** 27%

Answers to the Practice Test

1. B	**2.** C	**3.** O	**4.** E	**5.** O
6. O	**7.** H	**8.** yes	**9.** no	**10.** yes
11. yes	**12.** no	**13.** B	**14.** D	**15.** A
16. A	**17.** E	**18.** B	**19.** C	**20.** C

Chemistry in Our Lives

Learning Goals

- Define the term chemistry and identify substances as chemicals.
- Describe the activities that are part of the scientific method.
- Develop a study plan for learning chemistry.
- Review math concepts used in chemistry: place values, positive and negative numbers, percentages, solving equations, interpreting graphs, and writing numbers in scientific notation.

Chapter Outline

Chapter Opener: Forensic Scientist

1.1 Chemistry and Chemicals

1.2 Scientific Method: Thinking Like a Scientist

Explore Your World: Nobel Prize Winners in Chemistry
Chemistry Link to Health: Early Chemist: Paracelsus

1.3 Learning Chemistry: A Study Plan

1.4 Key Math Skills for Chemistry

Clinical Update: Forensic Evidence Solves the Murder

🖩 Key Math Skills

- Identifying Place Values (1.4A)
- Using Positive and Negative Numbers in Calculations (1.4B)
- Calculating Percentages (1.4C)
- Solving Equations (1.4D)
- Interpreting Graphs (1.4E)
- Writing Numbers in Scientific Notation (1.4F)

Selected Answers and Solutions to Text Problems

1.1 **a.** Chemistry is the study of the composition, structure, properties, and reactions of matter.
b. A chemical is a substance that has the same composition and properties wherever it is found.

1.3 Many chemicals are listed on a vitamin bottle such as vitamin A, vitamin B_3, vitamin B_{12}, vitamin C, and folic acid.

1.5 Typical items found in a medicine cabinet and some of the chemicals they contain are as follows:
Antacid tablets: calcium carbonate, cellulose, starch, stearic acid, silicon dioxide
Mouthwash: water, alcohol, thymol, glycerol, sodium benzoate, benzoic acid
Cough suppressant: menthol, beta-carotene, sucrose, glucose

1.7 **a.** An observation (O) is a description or measurement of a natural phenomenon.
b. A hypothesis (H) proposes a possible explanation for a natural phenomenon.
c. An experiment (E) is a procedure that tests the validity of a hypothesis.

   d. An observation (O) is a description or measurement of a natural phenomenon.
   e. An observation (O) is a description or measurement of a natural phenomenon.
   f. A conclusion (C) is an explanation of an observation that has been validated by repeated experiments that support a hypothesis.

1.9 **a.** An observation (O) is a description or measurement of a natural phenomenon.
   b. A hypothesis (H) proposes a possible explanation for a natural phenomenon.
   c. An experiment (E) is a procedure that tests the validity of a hypothesis.
   d. An experiment (E) is a procedure that tests the validity of a hypothesis.

1.11 There are several things you can do that will help you successfully learn chemistry, including forming a study group, going to lecture, working *Sample Problems* and *Study Checks*, working *Questions and Problems* and checking answers, reading the assignment ahead of class, going to the instructor's office hours, and keeping a problem notebook.

1.13 Ways you can enhance your learning of chemistry include:
   a. forming a study group.
   c. visiting the professor during office hours.
   e. being an active learner.

1.15 **a.** The bolded 8 is in the thousandths place.
   b. The bolded 6 is in the ones place.
   c. The bolded 6 is in the hundreds place.

1.17 **a.** $15 - (-8) = 15 + 8 = 23$
   b. $-8 + (-22) = -30$
   c. $4 \times (-2) + 6 = -8 + 6 = -2$

1.19 **a.** $\dfrac{21 \text{ flu shots}}{25 \text{ patients}} \times 100\% = 84\%$ received flu shots
   b. total grams of alloy = 56 g silver + 22 g copper = 78 g of alloy
   $\dfrac{56 \text{ g silver}}{78 \text{ g alloy}} \times 100\% = 72\%$ silver
   c. total number of coins = 11 nickels + 5 quarters + 7 dimes = 23 coins
   $\dfrac{7 \text{ dimes}}{23 \text{ coins}} \times 100\% = 30\%$ dimes

1.21 **a.**
$$4a + 4 = 40$$
$$4a + \cancel{4} - \cancel{4} = 40 - 4$$
$$4a = 36$$
$$\frac{\cancel{4}a}{\cancel{4}} = \frac{36}{4}$$
$$a = 9$$

   b.
$$\frac{a}{6} = 7$$
$$\cancel{6}\left(\frac{a}{\cancel{6}}\right) = 6(7)$$
$$a = 42$$

1.23 **a.** The graph shows the relationship between the temperature of a cup of tea and time.
   b. The vertical axis measures temperature, in °C.
   c. The values on the vertical axis range from 20 °C to 80 °C.
   d. As time increases, the temperature decreases.

1.25 a. Move the decimal point four places to the left to give 5.5×10^4.
   b. Move the decimal point two places to the left to give 4.8×10^2.
   c. Move the decimal point six places to the right to give 5×10^{-6}.
   d. Move the decimal point four places to the right to give 1.4×10^{-4}.
   e. Move the decimal point three places to the right to give 7.2×10^{-3}.
   f. Move the decimal point five places to the left to give 6.7×10^5.

1.27 a. 7.2×10^3, which is also 72×10^2, is larger than 8.2×10^2.
   b. 3.2×10^{-2}, which is also 320×10^{-4}, is larger than 4.5×10^{-4}.
   c. 1×10^4 or 10 000 is larger than 1×10^{-4} or 0.0001.
   d. 6.8×10^{-2} or 0.068 is larger than 0.000 52.

1.29 $\dfrac{120 \text{ g ethylene glycol}}{450 \text{ g liquid}} \times 100\% = 27\%$ ethylene glycol

1.31 No. All of these ingredients are chemicals.

1.33 Yes. Sherlock's investigation includes making observations (gathering data), formulating a hypothesis, testing the hypothesis, and modifying it until one of the hypotheses is validated.

1.35 a. Describing the appearance of a patient is an observation (O).
   b. Formulating a reason for the extinction of dinosaurs is a hypothesis (H).
   c. Measuring the completion time of a race is an observation (O).

1.37 a. When two negative numbers are added, the answer has a negative sign.
   b. When a positive and negative number are multiplied, the answer has a negative sign.

1.39 a. An observation (O) is a description or measurement of a natural phenomenon.
   b. A hypothesis (H) proposes a possible explanation for a natural phenomenon.
   c. A conclusion (C) is an explanation of an observation that has been validated by repeated experiments that support a hypothesis.

1.41 If experimental results do not support your hypothesis, you should:
   b. modify your hypothesis.

1.43 A successful study plan would include:
   b. working the *Sample Problems* as you go through a chapter.
   c. going to your professor's office hours.

1.45 a. $4 \times (-8) = -32$
   b. $-12 - 48 = -12 + (-48) = -60$
   c. $\dfrac{-168}{-4} = 42$

1.47 total number of gumdrops = 16 orange + 8 yellow + 16 black = 40 gumdrops
   a. $\dfrac{8 \text{ yellow gumdrops}}{40 \text{ total gumdrops}} \times 100\% = 20\%$ yellow gumdrops
   b. $\dfrac{16 \text{ black gumdrops}}{40 \text{ total gumdrops}} \times 100\% = 40\%$ black gumdrops

1.49 a. Move the decimal point five places to the left to give 1.2×10^5.
   b. Move the decimal point seven places to the right to give 3.4×10^{-7}.
   c. Move the decimal point two places to the right to give 6.6×10^{-2}.
   d. Move the decimal point three places to the left to give 2.7×10^3.

1.51 a. An observation (O) is a description or measurement of a natural phenomenon.
   b. A hypothesis (H) proposes a possible explanation for a natural phenomenon.
   c. An experiment (E) is a procedure that tests the validity of a hypothesis.
   d. A hypothesis (H) proposes a possible explanation for a natural phenomenon.

1.53 a.

$$2x + 5 = 41$$
$$2x + 5 - 5 = 41 - 5$$
$$2x = 36$$
$$\frac{2x}{2} = \frac{36}{2}$$
$$x = 18$$

b.

$$\frac{5x}{3} = 40$$
$$3\left(\frac{5x}{3}\right) = 3(40)$$
$$5x = 120$$
$$\frac{5x}{5} = \frac{120}{5}$$
$$x = 24$$

1.55 a. The graph shows the relationship between the solubility of carbon dioxide in water and temperature.
   b. The vertical axis measures the solubility of carbon dioxide in water ($g\ CO_2/100\ g$ water).
   c. The values on the vertical axis range from 0 to 0.35 $g\ CO_2/100\ g$ water.
   d. As temperature increases, the solubility of carbon dioxide in water decreases.

Chemistry and Measurements

Greg has been on Inderal for high blood pressure. Every two months, he has his blood pressure taken by a registered nurse. During his last visit, his blood pressure was lower, 130/85. Thus, the dosage of Inderal was reduced to 45 mg to be taken twice daily. If one tablet contains 15 mg of Inderal, how many tablets does Greg need to take in one day?

Credit: AVAVA / Shutterstock

CHAPTER READINESS*

🖩 Key Math Skills

- Identifying Place Values (1.4A)
- Using Positive and Negative Numbers in Calculations (1.4B)

- Calculating Percentages (1.4C)
- Writing Numbers in Scientific Notation (1.4F)

*These Key Math Skills from the previous chapter are listed here for your review as you proceed to the new material in this chapter.

2.1   Units of Measurement

Learning Goal: Write the names and abbreviations for the metric or SI units used in measurements of length, volume, mass, temperature, and time.

- In science, physical quantities are described in units of the metric or International System of Units (SI).
- Some important units of measurement are meter (m) for length, liter (L) for volume, gram (g) and kilogram (kg) for mass, degree Celsius (°C) and kelvin (K) for temperature, and second (s) for time.

Key Terms for Section 2.1

Match each of the following key terms with the correct definition:

  a. International System of Units   **b.** volume
  c. gram   **d.** second
  e. meter   **f.** liter
  g. mass

1 L = 1.06 qt
946 mL = 1 qt

1. _____ the metric unit for volume that is slightly larger than a quart

2. _____ the metric unit used in measurements of mass

3. _____ the amount of space occupied by a substance

4. _____ the metric and SI unit for time

5. _____ a measure of the quantity of material in an object

6. _____ the official system of measurement used by scientists and used in most countries of the world

7. _____ the metric unit for length that is slightly longer than a yard

Volume is the space occupied by a substance. In the metric system, volume is based on the liter (L), which is equal to 1.06 quarts (qt).
Credit: Pearson Education

Answers   **1.** f   **2.** c   **3.** b   **4.** d   **5.** g   **6.** a   **7.** e

♦ **Learning Exercise 2.1**

Match the measurement with the quantity in each of the following:

1. length   **2.** mass   **3.** volume   **4.** temperature   **5.** time

  a. _____ 45 g   **b.** _____ 8.2 m   **c.** _____ 215 °C   **d.** _____ 45 L

  e. _____ 825 K   **f.** _____ 8.8 s   **g.** _____ 140 g   **h.** _____ 50 s

Answers   **a.** 2   **b.** 1   **c.** 4   **d.** 3
          e. 4   **f.** 5   **g.** 2   **h.** 5

2.2   Measured Numbers and Significant Figures

Learning Goal: Identify a number as measured or exact; determine the number of significant figures in a measured number.

On an electronic balance, the digital readout gives the mass of a nickel, which is 5.01 g.
Credit: Richard Megna / Fundamental Photographs, NYC

- A measured number is obtained when you use a measuring device.

- An exact number is obtained by counting items or from a definition within the same measuring system.

- There is uncertainty in every measured number but not in exact numbers.

- Significant figures in a measured number are all the digits, including the estimated digit.

- A number is a significant figure if it is

  a. not a zero

  b. a zero between nonzero digits

  c. a zero at the end of a decimal number

  d. in the coefficient of a number written in scientific notation

- A zero is not significant if it is
  - **a.** at the beginning of a decimal number
  - **b.** used as a placeholder in a large number without a decimal point

♦ Learning Exercise 2.2A

Are the numbers in each of the following statements measured (M) or exact (E)?

- **a.** _____ There are 7 days in 1 week.
- **b.** _____ A pulmonary treatment lasts for 25 min.
- **c.** _____ There are 1000 g in 1 kg.
- **d.** _____ A nurse pours 10. mL of cough syrup.
- **e.** _____ There are 4 bags of glucose IV solution for a patient.
- **f.** _____ The height of a patient is 1.5 m.

A volume of 10. mL of cough syrup is measured for a patient.

Answers   **a.** E (definition)   **b.** M (use a watch)   **c.** E (metric definition)
d. M (use a measuring cup)   **e.** E (counted)   **f.** M (use a metric ruler)

Study Note

Significant figures (abbreviated SFs) are all the numbers reported in a measurement, including the estimated digit. Zeros are significant unless they are placeholders appearing at the beginning of a decimal number or in a large number without a decimal point.

4.255 g (four SFs)   0.0040 m (two SFs)   46 500 L (three SFs)   150. mL (three SFs)

♦ Learning Exercise 2.2B

State the number of significant figures in each of the following measured numbers:

a. 35.24 g _____	**b.** 0.000 080 m _____	
c. 55 000 m _____	**d.** 600. mL _____	
e. 5.025 L _____	**f.** 0.006 kg _____	
g. 268 200 mm _____	**h.** 25.0 °C _____	

⊛ **CORE CHEMISTRY SKILL**

Counting Significant Figures

Answers   **a.** 4   **b.** 2   **c.** 2   **d.** 3   **e.** 4   **f.** 1   **g.** 4   **h.** 3

2.3 Significant Figures in Calculations

Learning Goal: Adjust calculated answers to give the correct number of significant figures.

- In multiplication or division, the final answer is written so that it has the same number of significant figures as in the measurement with the fewest significant figures.
- In addition or subtraction, the final answer is written so that it has the same number of decimal places as the measurement with the fewest decimal places.
- To evaluate a calculator answer, count the significant figures in the measurements and round off the calculator answer properly.
- Answers for chemical calculations rarely use all the numbers that appear in the calculator display. Exact numbers are not included in the determination of the number of significant figures (SFs).

Study Note

1. To round off a number when the first digit to be dropped is *less* than 5, keep the digits you need and drop all the digits that follow.

    Round off 42.8254 to three SFs → 42.8 (drop 254)

2. To round off a number when the first digit to be dropped is 5 or *greater*, keep the proper number of digits and increase the last retained digit by 1.

    Round off 8.4882 to two SFs → 8.5 (drop 882; increase final digit by 1)

3. When rounding off large numbers without decimal points, maintain the value of the answer by adding nonsignificant zeros as placeholders.

    Round off 356 835 to three SFs → 357 000 (drop 835; increase final digit by 1; add placeholder zeros)

♦ **Learning Exercise 2.3A**

KEY MATH SKILL

Round off each of the following to give two significant figures:

Rounding Off

    a. 88.75 m _____
    b. 0.002 923 g _____
    c. 50.525 g _____

    d. 1.672 m _____
    e. 0.001 055 8 kg _____
    f. 82 080 mL _____

Answers   **a.** 89 m   **b.** 0.0029 g   **c.** 51 g   **d.** 1.7 m   **e.** 0.0011 kg   **f.** 82 000 mL

Study Note

1. An answer obtained from multiplying and dividing has the same number of significant figures as the measurement with the fewest significant figures.

    $$1.5 \times 32.546 = 48.819 \rightarrow 49 \quad \textit{Answer rounded off to two SFs}$$
      Two SFs   Five SFs

2. An answer obtained from adding or subtracting has the same number of decimal places as the measurement with the fewest decimal places.

    $$82.223 + 4.1 = 86.323 \rightarrow 86.3 \quad \textit{Answer rounded off to the tenths place}$$
    Thousandths place   Tenths place

♦ **Learning Exercise 2.3B**

⚛ CORE CHEMISTRY SKILL

Solve each problem and give the answer with the correct number of significant figures or decimal places:

Using Significant Figures in Calculations

    a. $1.3 \times 71.5 =$
    b. $\dfrac{8.00}{4.00} =$

    c. $\dfrac{0.082 \times 25.4}{0.116 \times 3.4} =$
    d. $\dfrac{3.05 \times 1.86}{118.5} =$
    e. $\dfrac{376}{0.0073} =$

    f. $38.520 - 11.4 =$
    g. $4.2 + 8.15 =$
    h. $102.56 + 8.325 - 0.8825 =$

Answers   **a.** 93   **b.** 2.00   **c.** 5.3   **d.** 0.0479
             e. 52 000 (5.2×10^4) **f.** 27.1   **g.** 12.4   **h.** 110.00

2.4   Prefixes and Equalities

Learning Goal: Use the numerical values of prefixes to write a metric equality.

- In the metric system, larger and smaller units use prefixes to change the size of the unit by factors of 10. For example, a prefix such as *centi* or *milli* preceding the unit meter gives a smaller length than a meter. A prefix such as *kilo* added to gram gives a unit that measures a mass that is 1000 times *greater* than a gram.
- An equality contains two units that measure the *same quantity* such as length, volume, mass, or time.
- Some common metric equalities are: 1 m = 100 cm; 1 L = 1000 mL; 1 kg = 1000 g.
- Some useful metric–U.S. equalities are: 2.54 cm = 1 in.; 1 kg = 2.205 lb; 1 L = 1.057 qt.

Some metric (SI) prefixes are:

Prefix	Symbol	Numerical Value	Scientific Notation	Equality
Prefixes That Increase the Size of the Unit				
peta	P	1 000 000 000 000 000	10^{15}	1 Pg = 1×10^{15} g 1 g = 1×10^{-15} Pg
tera	T	1 000 000 000 000	10^{12}	1 Tg = 1×10^{12} g 1 g = 1×10^{-12} Tg
giga	G	1 000 000 000	10^{9}	1 Gm = 1×10^{9} m 1 m = 1×10^{-9} Gm
mega	M	1 000 000	10^{6}	1 Mg = 1×10^{6} g 1 g = 1×10^{-6} Mg
kilo	k	1 000	10^{3}	1 km = 1×10^{3} m 1 m = 1×10^{-3} km
Prefixes That Decrease the Size of the Unit				
deci	d	0.1	10^{-1}	1 dL = 1×10^{-1} L 1 L = 10 dL
centi	c	0.01	10^{-2}	1 cm = 1×10^{-2} m 1 m = 100 cm
milli	m	0.001	10^{-3}	1 ms = 1×10^{-3} s 1 s = 1×10^{3} ms
micro	μ*	0.000 001	10^{-6}	1 μg = 1×10^{-6} g 1 g = 1×10^{6} μg
nano	n	0.000 000 001	10^{-9}	1 nm = 1×10^{-9} m 1 m = 1×10^{9} nm
pico	p	0.000 000 000 001	10^{-12}	1 ps = 1×10^{-12} s 1 s = 1×10^{12} ps
femto	f	0.000 000 000 000 001	10^{-15}	1 fs = 1×10^{-15} s 1 s = 1×10^{15} fs

*In medicine and nursing, the abbreviation mc for the prefix micro is used because the symbol μ may be misread, which could result in a medication error. Thus, 1 μg would be written as 1 mcg.

♦ Learning Exercise 2.4A

Match the items in column A with those from column B.

A		B	
1. ____ megameter		**a.** nanometer	
2. ____ 0.1 m		**b.** decimeter	
3. ____ millimeter		**c.** 10^{-6} m	
4. ____ centimeter		**d.** 0.01 m	
5. ____ 10^{-9} m		**e.** 1000 m	
6. ____ micrometer		**f.** 10^{-3} m	
7. ____ kilometer		**g.** 10^{6} m	

Answers   **1.** g   **2.** b   **3.** f   **4.** d
5. a   **6.** c   **7.** e

Some Typical Laboratory Test Values

Substance in Blood	Typical Range
Albumin	3.5–5.0 g/dL
Ammonia	20–150 mcg/dL
Calcium	8.5–10.5 mg/dL
Cholesterol	105–250 mg/dL
Iron (male)	80–160 mcg/dL
Protein (total)	6.0–8.0 g/dL

Laboratory results for blood work are often reported in mass per deciliter (dL).

♦ Learning Exercise 2.4B

Complete each of the following metric relationships:

a. 1 L = _____ mL   **b.** 1 L = _____ dL

c. 1 m = _____ cm   **d.** 1 s = _____ ms

e. 1 kg = _____ g   **f.** 1 m = _____ mm

g. 1 mg = _____ mcg   **h.** 1 dL = _____ L

Answers   **a.** 1000   **b.** 10   **c.** 100   **d.** 1000
e. 1000   **f.** 1000   **g.** 1000   **h.** 0.1

The metric length of 1 m is the same length as 10 dm, 100 cm, or 1000 mm.

CHASSENET / BSIP SA / Alamy

♦ Learning Exercise 2.4C

For each of the following pairs, which is the larger unit?

a. milliliter or microliter _____   **b.** g or kg   _____

c. nm or m   _____   **d.** centimeter or decimeter _____

e. kilosecond or second _____   **f.** PL or pL   _____

Answers   **a.** milliliter   **b.** kg   **c.** m   **d.** decimeter   **e.** kilosecond   **f.** PL

2.5   Writing Conversion Factors

Learning Goal: Write a conversion factor for two units that describe the same quantity.

- A conversion factor represents an equality expressed in the form of a fraction.
- Two conversion factors can be written for any relationship between equal quantities.

   For example, the metric–U.S. equality 2.54 cm = 1 in. can be written as follows:

$$\frac{2.54 \text{ cm}}{1 \text{ in.}} \quad \text{and} \quad \frac{1 \text{ in.}}{2.54 \text{ cm}}$$

- A percentage is written as a conversion factor by expressing matching units in the relationship as the parts of a specific substance in 100 parts of the whole.
- An equality may also be stated that applies only to a specific problem.
- Equalities stated within dosage problems for medications can be written as conversion factors.
- The ratio of parts per million (ppm) is the same as the milligrams of a substance per kilogram (mg/kg).
- The ratio of parts per billion (ppb) equals the micrograms per kilogram (mcg/kg, μg/kg).

Study Note

Metric conversion factors are obtained from metric prefixes. For example, the metric equality 1 m = 100 cm is written as two factors:

$$\frac{1 \text{ m}}{100 \text{ cm}} \quad \text{and} \quad \frac{100 \text{ cm}}{1 \text{ m}}$$

♦ **Learning Exercise 2.5A**

Write the equality and two conversion factors for each of the following pairs of units:

⚛ **CORE CHEMISTRY SKILL**

Writing Conversion Factors from Equalities

- **a.** millimeters and meters
- **b.** kilogram and grams
- **c.** kilograms and pounds
- **d.** seconds and minutes
- **e.** centimeters and meters
- **f.** milliliters and quarts
- **g.** deciliters and liters
- **h.** millimeters and centimeters

Answers

a. 1 m = 1000 mm

$$\frac{1000 \text{ mm}}{1 \text{ m}} \quad \text{and} \quad \frac{1 \text{ m}}{1000 \text{ mm}}$$

b. 1 kg = 1000 g

$$\frac{1000 \text{ g}}{1 \text{ kg}} \quad \text{and} \quad \frac{1 \text{ kg}}{1000 \text{ g}}$$

c. 1 kg = 2.20 lb

$$\frac{2.20 \text{ lb}}{1 \text{ kg}} \quad \text{and} \quad \frac{1 \text{ kg}}{2.20 \text{ lb}}$$

d. 1 min = 60 s

$$\frac{60 \text{ s}}{1 \text{ min}} \quad \text{and} \quad \frac{1 \text{ min}}{60 \text{ s}}$$

e. $1 \text{ m} = 100 \text{ cm}$

$$\frac{100 \text{ cm}}{1 \text{ m}} \quad \text{and} \quad \frac{1 \text{ m}}{100 \text{ cm}}$$

f. $1 \text{ qt} = 946 \text{ mL}$

$$\frac{946 \text{ mL}}{1 \text{ qt}} \quad \text{and} \quad \frac{1 \text{ qt}}{946 \text{ mL}}$$

g. $1 \text{ L} = 10 \text{ dL}$

$$\frac{10 \text{ dL}}{1 \text{ L}} \quad \text{and} \quad \frac{1 \text{ L}}{10 \text{ dL}}$$

h. $1 \text{ cm} = 10 \text{ mm}$

$$\frac{10 \text{ mm}}{1 \text{ cm}} \quad \text{and} \quad \frac{1 \text{ cm}}{10 \text{ mm}}$$

Study Note

1. Sometimes, a statement within a problem gives an equality that is true only for that problem. Then conversion factors can be written that are true only for that problem. For example, a problem states that there are 50 mg of vitamin B in a tablet. The equality and its conversion factors are

    50 mg of vitamin B = 1 tablet

    $$\frac{1 \text{ tablet}}{50 \text{ mg vitamin B}} \quad \text{and} \quad \frac{50 \text{ mg vitamin B}}{1 \text{ tablet}}$$

2. If a problem gives a percentage (%), it can be stated as parts per 100 parts. For example, a candy bar contains 45% by mass chocolate. This percentage (%) equality and its conversion factors are written using the same unit.

    45 g of chocolate = 100 g candy bar

    $$\frac{45 \text{ g chocolate}}{100 \text{ g candy bar}} \quad \text{and} \quad \frac{100 \text{ g candy bar}}{45 \text{ g chocolate}}$$

♦ **Learning Exercise 2.5B**

Write the equality and two conversion factors for each of the following statements:

a. A cheese contains 55% fat by mass.

b. The Daily Value (DV) for zinc is 15 mg.

c. A 125-g steak contains 45 g of protein.

d. An iron tablet contains 65 mg of iron.

Answers

a. 100 g of cheese = 55 g of fat

$$\frac{55 \text{ g fat}}{100 \text{ g cheese}} \quad \text{and} \quad \frac{100 \text{ g cheese}}{55 \text{ g fat}}$$

b. 15 mg of zinc = 1 day

$$\frac{15 \text{ mg zinc}}{1 \text{ day}} \quad \text{and} \quad \frac{1 \text{ day}}{15 \text{ mg zinc}}$$

c. 125 g of steak = 45 g of protein

$$\frac{45 \text{ g protein}}{125 \text{ g steak}} \quad \text{and} \quad \frac{125 \text{ g steak}}{45 \text{ g protein}}$$

d. 1 tablet = 65 mg of iron

$$\frac{65 \text{ mg iron}}{1 \text{ tablet}} \quad \text{and} \quad \frac{1 \text{ tablet}}{65 \text{ mg iron}}$$

One tablet contains 65 mg of iron.

Credit: Editorial Image, LLC / Alamy

♦ **Learning Exercise 2.5C**

Write the equality and two conversion factors, and identify the numbers as exact or give the number of significant figures for each of the following:

a. A low-dose aspirin has 81 mg in each tablet.

b. The EPA level for fluoride in drinking water is 4 ppm.

c. One tablespoon of cough syrup contains 15 mL of cough syrup.

Answers

a. 1 tablet = 81 mg of aspirin

$$\frac{1 \text{ tablet}}{81 \text{ mg aspirin}} \text{ and } \frac{81 \text{ mg aspirin}}{1 \text{ tablet}}$$

The 81 mg is measured: It has two SFs. The 1 tablet is exact.

b. 1 kg of water = 4 mg of fluoride

$$\frac{1 \text{ kg water}}{4 \text{ mg fluoride}} \text{ and } \frac{4 \text{ mg fluoride}}{1 \text{ kg water}}$$

The 4 mg is measured: It has one SF. The 1 kg is exact.

c. 1 tablespoon of syrup = 15 mL of syrup

$$\frac{1 \text{ tablespoon syrup}}{15 \text{ mL syrup}} \text{ and } \frac{15 \text{ mL syrup}}{1 \text{ tablespoon syrup}}$$

The 15 mL is measured: It has two SFs. The 1 tablespoon is exact.

2.6 Problem Solving Using Unit Conversion

Learning Goal: Use conversion factors to change from one unit to another.

- Conversion factors can be used to change a quantity expressed in one unit to a quantity expressed in another unit.
- In the process of problem solving, a given unit is multiplied by one or more conversion factors until the needed unit is obtained.

Guide to Problem Solving Using Conversion Factors	
STEP 1	State the given and needed quantities.
STEP 2	Write a plan to convert the given unit to the needed unit.
STEP 3	State the equalities and conversion factors.
STEP 4	Set up the problem to cancel units and calculate the answer.

Example: A patient receives 2850 mL of saline solution. How many liters is 2850 mL?

STEP 1 State the given and needed quantities.

Analyze the Problem	Given	Need
	2850 mL	liters

STEP 2 Write a plan to convert the given unit to the needed unit.

$$\text{milliliters} \xrightarrow{\text{Metric factor}} \text{liters}$$

STEP 3 State the equalities and conversion factors.

$$1\ L = 1000\ mL$$

$$\frac{1\ L}{1000\ mL} \quad \text{and} \quad \frac{1000\ mL}{1\ L}$$

STEP 4 Set up the problem to cancel units and calculate the answer.

$$2850\ \cancel{mL} \times \frac{1\ L}{1000\ \cancel{mL}} = 2.85\ L$$

Three SFs   Exact   Three SFs

♦ **Learning Exercise 2.6A**

Use metric conversion factors to solve each of the following problems:
For **e** to **h**, complete boxes for Given and Need.

a. 189 mL = _____ L   **b.** 2.7 cm = _____ mm

c. 0.274 m = _____ cm   **d.** 76 mg = _____ g

e. How many meters tall is a person whose height is 175 cm?

Analyze the Problem	Given	Need

CORE CHEMISTRY SKILL

Using Conversion Factors

f. There are 0.646 L of water in a teapot. How many milliliters is that?

Analyze the Problem	Given	Need

g. If a ring contains 13 500 mg of gold, how many grams of gold are in the ring?

Analyze the Problem	Given	Need

h. You walked a distance of 1.5 km on the treadmill at the gym. How many meters did you walk?

Analyze the Problem	Given	Need

Answers **a.** 0.189 L   **b.** 27 mm   **c.** 27.4 cm   **d.** 0.076 g

e.

Analyze the Problem	Given	Need	Answer
	175 cm	meters (m)	1.75 m

f.

Analyze the Problem	Given	Need	Answer
	0.646 L	milliliters (mL)	646 mL

g.

Analyze the Problem	Given	Need	Answer
	13 500 mg	grams (g)	13.5 g

h.

Analyze the Problem	Given	Need	Answer
	1.5 km	meters (m)	1500 m

Study Note

1. When the setup for a calculation requires a series of conversion factors, it is helpful to write a plan first. In the plan, we start with the given unit and proceed to the needed unit. Then we use a conversion factor to make each unit change.

    Plan: Given unit $\longrightarrow$ unit (1) $\longrightarrow$ unit (2) (needed unit)

2. To convert from one unit to another, select conversion factors that cancel the given unit and provide the needed unit for the problem.

$$\text{Given unit} \times \frac{\text{unit (1)}}{\text{given unit}} \times \frac{\text{unit (2)}}{\text{unit (1)}} = \text{unit (2) (needed unit)}$$

♦ **Learning Exercise 2.6B**

Use metric–U.S. conversion factors to solve each of the following problems:

a. 8.10 in. = _____ mm

b. 4.6 qt = _____ mL

c. 1.50 ft = _____ cm

d. 880 g = _____ lb

Answers   **a.** 208 mm   **b.** 430 mL   **c.** 45.7 cm   **d.** 1.9 lb

♦ **Learning Exercise 2.6C**

Use conversion factors to solve each of the following problems:

a. A piece of plastic tubing measures 120 mm. What is the length of the tubing in inches?

b. A dialysis patient weighs 245 lb. What is the mass of the patient in kilograms?

c. Your friend has a height of 6 ft 3 in. What is your friend's height in meters?

d. In a triple-bypass surgery, a patient requires 3.00 pt of whole blood. How many milliliters of blood were given?

1 pt of blood contains 473 mL.

Credit: Syner-Comm / Alamy

e. A doctor orders 0.450 g of a sulfa drug. On hand are 150-mg tablets. How many tablets of the sulfa drug are needed?

f. A mouthwash contains 62% alcohol by volume. How many milliliters of alcohol are in a 1.18-L bottle of mouthwash?

Answers   **a.** 4.7 in.   **b.** 111 kg   **c.** 1.9 m   **d.** 1420 mL   **e.** 3 tablets   **f.** 730 mL

2.7 Density

Learning Goal: Calculate the density of a substance; use the density to calculate the mass or volume of a substance.

• The density of a substance is the ratio of its mass to its volume, usually in units of g/mL or g/cm³.

$$\text{Density} = \frac{\text{mass of substance}}{\text{volume of substance}}$$

• The volume of 1 mL is equal to the volume of 1 cm³.

Key Terms for Sections 2.2–2.7

Match each of the following key terms with the correct description:

    a. equality   **b.** conversion factor   **c.** measured number   **d.** exact number
    e. density   **f.** prefix   **g.** significant figures

1. ____ number obtained by counting

2. ____ part of the name of a metric unit that precedes the base unit and specifies the size of the measurement

3. ____ ratio in which the numerator and denominator are quantities from an equality

4. ____ relationship between two units that measure the same quantity

5. ____ digits recorded in a measurement

6. ____ number obtained when a quantity is determined by using a measuring device

7. ____ relationship of the mass of an object to its volume expressed as grams per cubic centimeter (g/cm^3) or grams per milliliter (g/mL)

Answers   **1.** d   **2.** f   **3.** b   **4.** a   **5.** g   **6.** c   **7.** e

♦ **Learning Exercise 2.7A**

Calculate the density for each of the following:

    a. What is the density, in grams per milliliter, of glycerol if a 200.0-mL sample has a mass of 252 g?

    b. A person with diabetes may produce 5 to 12 L of urine per day. Calculate the density, in grams per milliliter, of a 100.0 mL-urine sample that has a mass of 100.2 g.

Answers   **a.** 1.26 g/mL   **b.** 1.002 g/mL

Guide to Using Density	
STEP 1	State the given and needed quantities.
STEP 2	Write a plan to calculate the needed quantity.
STEP 3	Write the equalities and their conversion factors including density.
STEP 4	Set up the problem to calculate the needed quantity.

Example: Density can be used as a factor to convert between the mass (g) and volume (mL) of a substance. The density of silver is 10.5 g/mL. What is the mass, in grams, of 6.0 mL of silver?

    STEP 1 State the given and needed quantities.

Analyze the Problem	Given	Need
	6.0 mL of silver; density 10.5 g/mL	grams of silver

    STEP 2 Write a plan to calculate the needed quantity.

$$\text{milliliters} \xrightarrow{\text{Density factor}} \text{grams}$$

STEP 3 Write the equalities and their conversion factors including density.

$$1 \text{ mL} = 10.5 \text{ g}$$

$$\frac{1 \text{ mL}}{10.5 \text{ g}} \quad \text{and} \quad \frac{10.5 \text{ g}}{1 \text{ mL}}$$

STEP 4 Set up the problem to calculate the needed quantity.

$$6.0 \text{ mL silver} \times \frac{10.5 \text{ g silver}}{1 \text{ mL silver}} = 63 \text{ g of silver}$$

Density factor

◆ **Learning Exercise 2.7B**

⚛ **CORE CHEMISTRY SKILL**

Use density as a conversion factor to solve each of the following:

Using Density as a Conversion Factor

a. A sugar solution has a density of 1.20 g/mL. What is the mass, in grams, of 0.225 L of the solution?

b. A piece of pure gold weighs 0.26 lb. If gold has a density of 19.3 mL, what is the volume, in milliliters, of the piece of gold?

c. A salt solution has a density of 1.15 g/mL and a volume of 425 mL. What is the mass, in grams, of the solution?

d. A 50.0-g sample of a glucose solution has a density of 1.28 g/mL. What is the volume, in liters, of the sample?

Answers   **a.** 270. g   **b.** 6.1 mL   **c.** 489 g   **d.** 0.0391 L

Checklist for Chapter 2

You are ready to take the Practice Test for Chapter 2. Be sure that you have accomplished the following learning goals for this chapter. If not, review the section listed at the end of the goal. Then apply your new skills and understanding to the Practice Test.

After studying Chapter 2, I can successfully:

_____ Write the names and abbreviations for the metric (SI) units of measurement. (2.1)

_____ Identify a number as a measured number or an exact number. (2.2)

_____ Count the number of significant figures in measured numbers. (2.2)

_____ Report a calculated answer with the correct number of significant figures. (2.3)

_____ Write an equality from the relationship between two equal quantities. (2.4)

_____ Write two conversion factors for an equality. (2.5)

_____ Use conversion factors to change from one unit to another unit. (2.6)

_____ Calculate the density of a substance or use density to calculate the mass or volume. (2.7)

Practice Test for Chapter 2

The chapter sections to review are shown in parentheses at the end of each question.

1. Which of the following is a metric measurement of volume? (2.1)
   A. kilogram   B. kilowatt   C. kiloliter   D. kilometer   E. kiloquart

2. Which of the following is a metric measurement of length? (2.1)
   A. centiliter   B. centigram   C. centiyard   D. centifoot   E. centimeter

3. The exact number in the following is (2.2)
   A. 4.5 L   B. 4 syringes   C. 6 qt   D. 15 g   E. 2.0 m

4. The measured number in the following is (2.2)
   A. 1 book   B. 2 cars   C. 4 flowers   D. 5 rings   E. 45 g

5. The number of significant figures in 105.4 m is (2.2)
   A. 1   B. 2   C. 3   D. 4   E. 5

6. The number of significant figures in 0.000 82 g is (2.2)
   A. 1   B. 2   C. 3   D. 4   E. 5

7. The calculator answer 5.7805 rounded to two significant figures is (2.2)
   A. 5   B. 5.7   C. 5.8   D. 5.78   E. 6.0

8. The calculator answer 3486.512 rounded to three significant figures is (2.2)
   A. 4000   B. 3500   C. 349   D. 3487   E. 3490

9. The answer for 16.0 ÷ 8.0 with the correct number of significant figures is (2.3)
   A. 2   B. 2.0   C. 2.00   D. 0.2   E. 5.0

10. The answer for 58.5 + 9.158 with the correct number of decimal places is (2.3)
    A. 67   B. 67.6   C. 67.7   D. 67.66   E. 67.658

11. The answer for $\dfrac{2.5 \times 3.12}{4.6}$ with the correct number of significant figures is (2.3)

    A. 0.54   B. 7.8   C. 0.85   D. 1.7   E. 1.69

12. Which of these prefixes has the largest value? (2.4)
    A. centi   B. deci   C. milli   D. kilo   E. micro

13. What is the decimal equivalent of the prefix *centi*? (2.4)
    A. 0.001   B. 0.01   C. 0.1   D. 10   E. 100

14. Which of the following is the smallest unit of mass measurement? (2.4)
    A. gram   **B.** milligram   **C.** kilogram   **D.** decigram   **E.** centigram

15. Which volume is the largest? (2.4)
    A. mL   **B.** dL   **C.** cm³   **D.** L   **E.** kL

16. Which of the following is a conversion factor? (2.5)
    A. 12 in.   **B.** 3 ft   **C.** 20 m   **D.** $\dfrac{1000\text{ g}}{1\text{ kg}}$ **E.** 2 cm³

17. Which is the correct conversion factor that relates milliliters to liters? (2.5)
    A. $\dfrac{1000\text{ mL}}{1\text{ L}}$ **B.** $\dfrac{100\text{ mL}}{1\text{ L}}$ **C.** $\dfrac{10\text{ mL}}{1\text{ L}}$ **D.** $\dfrac{0.01\text{ mL}}{1\text{ L}}$ **E.** $\dfrac{0.001\text{ mL}}{1\text{ L}}$

18. Which is the conversion factor for millimeters and centimeters? (2.5)
    A. $\dfrac{1\text{ mm}}{1\text{ cm}}$ **B.** $\dfrac{10\text{ mm}}{1\text{ cm}}$ **C.** $\dfrac{100\text{ cm}}{1\text{ mm}}$ **D.** $\dfrac{100\text{ mm}}{1\text{ cm}}$ **E.** $\dfrac{10\text{ cm}}{1\text{ mm}}$

19. A doctor orders 20 mg of prednisone. If a tablet contains 5 mg of prednisone, how many tablets should be given? (2.5)
    A. 1   **B.** 2   **C.** 3   **D.** 4   **E.** 5

20. 294 mm is equal to (2.6)
    A. 2940 m   **B.** 29.4 m   **C.** 2.94 m   **D.** 0.294 m   **E.** 0.0294 m

21. A doctor orders 200 mg of penicillin to be injected. If it is available as 1000 mg of penicillin per 5 mL, how many milliliters should be given? (2.6)
    A. 1 mL   **B.** 2 mL   **C.** 3 mL   **D.** 4 mL   **E.** 5 mL

22. What is the volume, in liters, of 800. mL of blood plasma? (2.6)
    A. 0.8 L   **B.** 0.80 L   **C.** 0.800 L   **D.** 8.0 L   **E.** 80.0 L

23. What is the mass, in kilograms, of a 22-lb toddler? (2.6)
    A. 10. kg   **B.** 48 kg   **C.** 10 000 kg   **D.** 0.048 kg   **E.** 22 000 kg

24. The number of milliliters in 2 dL of an antiseptic liquid is (2.6)
    A. 20 mL   **B.** 200 mL   **C.** 2000 mL   **D.** 20 000 mL   **E.** 500 000 mL

25. What is the height, in meters, of a person who is 5 ft 4 in. tall? (2.6)
    A. 64 m   **B.** 25 m   **C.** 14 m   **D.** 1.6 m   **E.** 1.3 m

26. How many ounces are in 1500 grams of carrots? (1 lb = 16 oz) (2.6)
    A. 94 oz   **B.** 53 oz   **C.** 24 000 oz   **D.** 33 oz   **E.** 3.3 oz

27. How many quarts of orange juice are in 255 mL of juice? (2.6)
    A. 0.255 qt   **B.** 270 qt   **C.** 236 qt   **D.** 0.270 qt   **E.** 0.400 qt

28. Your doctor places you on a 2200-kcal diet, with 19% of the kilocalories from fat. How many kilocalories are you allowed from fat? (2.6)
    A. 19 kcal   **B.** 2200 kcal   **C.** 1900 kcal   **D.** 420 kcal   **E.** 4200 kcal

29. How many milliliters of a salt solution with a density of 1.8 g/mL are needed to provide 450 g of salt solution? (2.7)
    A. 250 mL   **B.** 25 mL   **C.** 720 mL   **D.** 450 mL   **E.** 45 mL

30. Three liquids have densities of 1.15 g/mL, 0.79 g/mL, and 0.95 g/mL. When the liquids, which do not mix, are poured into a graduated cylinder, the liquid at the top is the one with a density of (2.7)
    A. 1.15 g/mL   **B.** 1.00 g/mL   **C.** 0.95 g/mL   **D.** 0.79 g/mL   **E.** 0.16 g/mL

31. A sample of oil has a mass of 65 g and a volume of 80.0 mL. What is the density of the oil? (2.7)
    A. 1.5 g/mL   **B.** 1.4 g/mL   **C.** 1.2 g/mL   **D.** 0.90 g/mL   **E.** 0.81 g/mL

32. What is the mass, in grams, of a 10.0-mL sample of an antihistamine solution with a density of 1.04 g/mL? (2.7)
    A. 104 g   **B.** 10.4 g   **C.** 1.04 g   **D.** 1.40 g   **E.** 9.62 g

33. Ethanol has a density of 0.785 g/mL. What is the mass, in grams, of 0.250 L of ethanol? (2.7)
    A. 196 g   **B.** 158 g   **C.** 3.95 g   **D.** 0.253 g   **E.** 0.160 g

34. 1.5 ft is the same length, in centimeters, as (2.6)
    A. 46 cm   **B.** 7.1 cm   **C.** 18 cm   **D.** 3.8 cm   **E.** 0.59 cm

35. A patient has a blood volume of 6.8 qt. If the density of blood is 1.06 g/mL, what is the mass, in grams, of the patient's blood? (2.7)
    A. 1060 g   **B.** 6400 g   **C.** 6800 g   **D.** 1500 g   **E.** 990 g

Answers to the Practice Test

1. C	**2.** E	**3.** B	**4.** E	**5.** D
6. B	**7.** C	**8.** E	**9.** B	**10.** C
11. D	**12.** D	**13.** B	**14.** B	**15.** E
16. D	**17.** A	**18.** B	**19.** D	**20.** D
21. A	**22.** C	**23.** A	**24.** B	**25.** D
26. B	**27.** D	**28.** D	**29.** A	**30.** D
31. E	**32.** B	**33.** A	**34.** A	**35.** C

2

Chemistry and Measurements

Learning Goals

- Write the names and abbreviations for the metric or SI units used in measurements of length, volume, mass, temperature, and time.
- Identify a number as measured or exact; determine the number of significant figures in a measured number.
- Adjust calculated answers to give the correct number of significant figures.
- Use the numerical values of prefixes to write a metric equality.
- Write a conversion factor for two units that describe the same quantity.
- Use conversion factors to change from one unit to another.
- Calculate the density of a substance; use the density to calculate the mass or volume of a substance.

Chapter Outline

Chapter Opener: Registered Nurse

2.1 Units of Measurement

Explore Your World: Units Listed on Labels

2.2 Measured Numbers and Significant Figures

2.3 Significant Figures in Calculations

2.4 Prefixes and Equalities

2.5 Writing Conversion Factors

Explore Your World: SI and Metric Equalities on Product Labels

2.6 Problem Solving Using Unit Conversion

Chemistry Link to Health: Toxicology and Risk–Benefit Assessment

2.7 Density

Explore Your World: Sink or Float

Chemistry Link to Health: Bone Density

Clinical Update: Greg's Follow-Up Visit with His Doctor

🖩 Key Math Skill

- Rounding Off (2.3)

⚛ Core Chemistry Skills

- Counting Significant Figures (2.2)
- Using Significant Figures in Calculations (2.3)
- Using Prefixes (2.4)
- Writing Conversion Factors from Equalities (2.5)
- Using Conversion Factors (2.6)
- Using Density as a Conversion Factor (2.7)

Selected Answers and Solutions to Text Problems

2.1 **a.** A liter is a unit of volume.
    b. A centimeter is a unit of length.
    c. A kilometer is a unit of length.
    d. A second is a unit of time.

2.3 **a.** The unit is a meter, which is a unit of length.
    b. The unit is a gram, which is a unit of mass.
    c. The unit is a milliliter, which is a unit of volume.
    d. The unit is a second, which is a unit of time.
    e. The unit is a degree Celsius, which is a unit of temperature.

2.5 **a.** A second is a unit of time.
    b. A kilogram is a unit of mass.
    c. A gram is a unit of mass.
    d. A degree Celsius is a unit of temperature.

2.7 Measured numbers are obtained using some type of measuring device. Exact numbers are numbers obtained by counting items or using a definition that compares two units in the same measuring system.
    a. The value 67.5 kg is a measured number; measurement of mass requires a measuring device.
    b. The value 2 tablets is obtained by counting, making it an exact number.
    c. The values in the metric definition 1 L = 1000 mL are exact numbers.
    d. The value 1720 km is a measured number; measurement of distance requires a measuring device.

2.9 Measured numbers are obtained using some type of measuring device. Exact numbers are numbers obtained by counting items or using a definition that compares two units in the same measuring system.
    a. 6 oz of hamburger meat is a measured number (3 hamburgers is a counted/exact number).
    b. Neither are measured numbers (both 1 table and 4 chairs are counted/exact numbers).
    c. Both 0.75 lb of grapes and 350 g of butter are measured numbers.
    d. Neither are measured numbers (the values in a definition are exact numbers).

2.11 **a.** Zeros at the beginning of a decimal number are not significant.
    b. Zeros between nonzero digits are significant.
    c. Zeros at the end of a decimal number are significant.
    d. Zeros in the coefficient of a number written in scientific notation are significant.
    e. Zeros used as placeholders in a large number without a decimal point are not significant.

2.13 **a.** All five numbers are significant figures (5 SFs).
    b. Only the two nonzero numbers are significant (2 SFs); the preceding zeros are placeholders.
    c. Only the two nonzero numbers are significant (2 SFs); the zeros that follow are placeholders.
    d. All three numbers in the coefficient of a number written in scientific notation are significant (3 SFs).
    e. All four numbers to the right of the decimal point, including the last zero, in a decimal number are significant (4 SFs).
    f. All three numbers, including the zeros at the end of a decimal number, are significant (3 SFs).

2.15 Both measurements in part **b** have three significant figures, and both measurements in part **c** have two significant figures.

2.17 **a.** 1.607 kg has four significant figures.
    b. 130 mcg has two significant figures.
    c. 4.02×10^6 red blood cells has three significant figures.

2.19 A calculator often gives more digits than the number of significant figures allowed in the answer.

2.21 **a.** 1.85 kg; the last digit is dropped since it is 4 or less.
  b. 88.2 L; since the fourth digit is 4 or less, the last three digits are dropped.
  c. 0.004 74 cm; since the fourth significant digit (the first digit to be dropped) is 5 or greater, the last retained digit is increased by 1 when the last four digits are dropped.
  d. 8810 m; since the fourth significant digit (the first digit to be dropped) is 5 or greater, the last retained digit is increased by 1 when the last digit is dropped (a nonsignificant zero is added at the end as a placeholder).
  e. 1.83×10^5 s; since the fourth digit is 4 or less, the last digit is dropped. The $\times 10^5$ is retained so that the magnitude of the answer is not changed.

2.23 **a.** As written, 5080 L only has three significant figures; this can be shown in scientific notation as 5.08×10^3 L.
  b. As written, 37 400 g only has three significant figures; this can be shown in scientific notation as 3.74×10^4 g.
  c. To round off 104 720 m to three significant figures, drop the final digits 720 and increase the last retained digit by 1 and add placeholder zeros to give 105 000 m or 1.05×10^5 m.
  d. To round off 0.000 250 82 s to three significant figures, drop the final digits 82 and increase the last retained digit by 1 to give 0.000 251 s or 2.51×10^{-4} s.

2.25 **a.** $45.7 \times 0.034 = 1.6$ Two significant figures are allowed since 0.034 has 2 SFs.
  b. $0.002\,78 \times 5 = 0.01$ One significant figure is allowed since 5 has 1 SF.
  c. $\dfrac{34.56}{1.25} = 27.6$ Three significant figures are allowed since 1.25 has 3 SFs.
  d. $\dfrac{(0.2465)(25)}{1.78} = 3.5$ Two significant figures are allowed since 25 has 2 SFs.

2.27 **a.** $45.48 \text{ cm} + 8.057 \text{ cm} = 53.54 \text{ cm}$ Two decimal places are allowed since 45.48 cm has two decimal places.
  b. $23.45 \text{ g} + 104.1 \text{ g} + 0.025 \text{ g} = 127.6 \text{ g}$ One decimal place is allowed since 104.1 g has one decimal place.
  c. $145.675 \text{ mL} - 24.2 \text{ mL} = 121.5 \text{ mL}$ One decimal place is allowed since 24.2 mL has one decimal place.
  d. $1.08 \text{ L} - 0.585 \text{ L} = 0.50 \text{ L}$ Two decimal places are allowed since 1.08 L has two decimal places.

2.29 The km/h markings indicate how many kilometers (how much distance) will be traversed in 1 hour's time if the speed is held constant. The mph (mi/h) markings indicate the same distance traversed *but measured in miles* during the 1 hour of travel.

2.31 **a.** mg   **b.** dL   **c.** km   **d.** fg

2.33 **a.** centiliter   **b.** kilogram   **c.** millisecond   **d.** gigameter

2.35 **a.** 0.01   **b.** 1 000 000 000 000 (or 1×10^{12})
  c. 0.001 (or 1×10^{-3})   **d.** 0.1

2.37 **a.** 1 decigram   **b.** 1 microgram
  c. 1 kilogram   **d.** 1 centigram

2.39 **a.** 1 m = 100 cm   **b.** $1 \text{ m} = 1 \times 10^9$ nm
  c. 1 mm = 0.001 m   **d.** 1 L = 1000 mL

2.41 **a.** kilogram, since 10^3 g is greater than 10^{-3} g
b. milliliter, since 10^{-3} L is greater than 10^{-6} L
c. km, since 10^3 m is greater than 10^0 m
d. kL, since 10^3 L is greater than 10^{-1} L
e. nanometer, since 10^{-9} m is greater than 10^{-12} m

2.43 **a.** 100 cm = 1 m; $\dfrac{100 \text{ cm}}{1 \text{ m}}$ and $\dfrac{1 \text{ m}}{100 \text{ cm}}$

b. 1000 mg = 1 g; $\dfrac{1000 \text{ mg}}{1 \text{ g}}$ and $\dfrac{1 \text{ g}}{1000 \text{ mg}}$

c. 1 L = 1000 mL; $\dfrac{1 \text{ L}}{1000 \text{ mL}}$ and $\dfrac{1000 \text{ mL}}{1 \text{ L}}$

d. 1 dL = 100 mL; $\dfrac{1 \text{ dL}}{100 \text{ mL}}$ and $\dfrac{100 \text{ mL}}{1 \text{ dL}}$

2.45 **a.** 1 yd = 3 ft; $\dfrac{3 \text{ ft}}{1 \text{ yd}}$ and $\dfrac{1 \text{ yd}}{3 \text{ ft}}$; the 1 yd and 3 ft are both exact (U.S. definition).

b. 1 kg = 2.20 lb; $\dfrac{2.20 \text{ lb}}{1 \text{ kg}}$ and $\dfrac{1 \text{ kg}}{2.20 \text{ lb}}$; the 2.20 lb is measured: it has 3 SFs; the 1 kg is exact.

c. 1 min = 60 s; $\dfrac{60 \text{ s}}{1 \text{ min}}$ and $\dfrac{1 \text{ min}}{60 \text{ s}}$; the 1 min and 60 s are both exact.

d. 1 gal of gasoline = 27 mi; $\dfrac{27 \text{ mi}}{1 \text{ gal gasoline}}$ and $\dfrac{1 \text{ gal gasoline}}{27 \text{ mi}}$; the 27 mi is measured: it has 2 SFs; the 1 gal is exact.

e. 100 g of sterling = 93 g of silver; $\dfrac{93 \text{ g silver}}{100 \text{ g sterling}}$ and $\dfrac{100 \text{ g sterling}}{93 \text{ g silver}}$; the 93 g is measured: it has 2 SFs; the 100 g is exact.

2.47 **a.** 1 s = 3.5 m; $\dfrac{1 \text{ s}}{3.5 \text{ m}}$ and $\dfrac{3.5 \text{ m}}{1 \text{ s}}$; the 3.5 m is measured: it has 2 SFs; the 1 s is exact.

b. 4700 mg of potassium = 1 day; $\dfrac{4700 \text{ mg potassium}}{1 \text{ day}}$ and $\dfrac{1 \text{ day}}{4700 \text{ mg potassium}}$; the 4700 mg is measured: it has 2 SFs; the 1 day is exact.

c. 1 gal of gasoline = 46.0 km; $\dfrac{1 \text{ gal gasoline}}{46.0 \text{ km}}$ and $\dfrac{46.0 \text{ km}}{1 \text{ gal gasoline}}$; the 46.0 km is measured: it has 3 SFs; the 1 gal is exact.

d. 1 kg of plums = 29 mcg of pesticide; $\dfrac{1 \text{ kg plums}}{29 \text{ mcg pesticide}}$ and $\dfrac{29 \text{ mcg pesticide}}{1 \text{ kg plums}}$; the 29 mcg is measured: it has 2 SFs; the 1 kg is exact.

2.49 **a.** 1 tablet = 630 mg of calcium; $\dfrac{630 \text{ mg calcium}}{1 \text{ tablet}}$ and $\dfrac{1 \text{ tablet}}{630 \text{ mg calcium}}$; the 630 mg is measured: it has 2 SFs; the 1 tablet is exact.

b. 60 mg of vitamin C = 1 day; $\dfrac{60 \text{ mg vitamin C}}{1 \text{ day}}$ and $\dfrac{1 \text{ day}}{60 \text{ mg vitamin C}}$; the 60 mg is measured: it has 1 SF; the 1 day is exact.

c. 1 tablet = 50 mg of atenolol; $\dfrac{50 \text{ mg atenolol}}{1 \text{ tablet}}$ and $\dfrac{1 \text{ tablet}}{50 \text{ mg atenolol}}$; the 50 mg is measured: it has 1 SF; the 1 tablet is exact.

d. 1 tablet = 81 mg of aspirin; $\dfrac{81 \text{ mg aspirin}}{1 \text{ tablet}}$ and $\dfrac{1 \text{ tablet}}{81 \text{ mg aspirin}}$; the 81 mg is measured: it has 2 SFs; the 1 tablet is exact.

2.51 **a.** 5 mL of syrup $=$ 10 mg of Atarax; $\dfrac{10 \text{ mg Atarax}}{5 \text{ mL syrup}}$ and $\dfrac{5 \text{ mL syrup}}{10 \text{ mg Atarax}}$

b. 1 tablet $=$ 0.25 g of Lanoxin; $\dfrac{0.25 \text{ g Lanoxin}}{1 \text{ tablet}}$ and $\dfrac{1 \text{ tablet}}{0.25 \text{ g Lanoxin}}$

c. 1 tablet $=$ 300 mg of Motrin; $\dfrac{300 \text{ mg Motrin}}{1 \text{ tablet}}$ and $\dfrac{1 \text{ tablet}}{300 \text{ mg Motrin}}$

2.53 **a.** **Given** 175 cm **Need** meters

Plan cm $\rightarrow$ m $\qquad \dfrac{1 \text{ m}}{100 \text{ cm}}$

Set-up 175 cm $\times \dfrac{1 \text{ m}}{100 \text{ cm}} = 1.75$ m (3 SFs)

b. **Given** 5500 mL **Need** liters

Plan mL $\rightarrow$ L $\qquad \dfrac{1 \text{ L}}{1000 \text{ mL}}$

Set-up 5500 mL $\times \dfrac{1 \text{ L}}{1000 \text{ mL}} = 5.5$ L (2 SFs)

c. **Given** 0.0018 kg **Need** grams

Plan kg $\rightarrow$ g $\qquad \dfrac{1000 \text{ g}}{1 \text{ kg}}$

Set-up 0.0018 kg $\times \dfrac{1000 \text{ g}}{1 \text{ kg}} = 1.8$ g (2 SFs)

2.55 **a.** **Given** 0.500 qt **Need** milliliters

Plan qt $\rightarrow$ mL $\qquad \dfrac{946 \text{ mL}}{1 \text{ qt}}$

Set-up 0.500 qt $\times \dfrac{946 \text{ mL}}{1 \text{ qt}} = 473$ mL (3 SFs)

b. **Given** 175 lb **Need** kilograms

Plan lb $\rightarrow$ kg $\qquad \dfrac{1 \text{ kg}}{2.20 \text{ lb}}$

Set-up 175 lb $\times \dfrac{1 \text{ kg}}{2.20 \text{ lb}} = 79.5$ kg (3 SFs)

c. **Given** 74 kg body mass, 15% body fat **Need** pounds of body fat

Plan kg of body mass $\rightarrow$ kg of body fat $\rightarrow$ lb of body fat

$$\dfrac{15 \text{ kg body fat}}{100 \text{ kg body mass}} \qquad \dfrac{2.20 \text{ lb body fat}}{1 \text{ kg body fat}}$$

Set-up 74 kg body mass $\times \dfrac{15 \text{ kg body fat}}{100 \text{ kg body mass}} \times \dfrac{2.20 \text{ lb body fat}}{1 \text{ kg body fat}}$

$= 24$ lb of body fat (2 SFs)

d. **Given** 10.0 oz of fertilizer, 15% nitrogen **Need** grams of nitrogen

Plan oz of fertilizer $\rightarrow$ lb of fertilizer $\rightarrow$ g of fertilizer $\rightarrow$ g of nitrogen
(percent equality: 100 g of fertilizer $=$ 15 g of nitrogen)

$$\dfrac{1 \text{ lb}}{16 \text{ oz}} \qquad \dfrac{454 \text{ g}}{1 \text{ lb}} \qquad \dfrac{15 \text{ g nitrogen}}{100 \text{ g fertilizer}}$$

Set-up 10.0 oz fertilizer $\times \dfrac{1 \text{ lb}}{16 \text{ oz}} \times \dfrac{454 \text{ g}}{1 \text{ lb}} \times \dfrac{15 \text{ g nitrogen}}{100 \text{ g fertilizer}} = 43$ g of nitrogen (2 SFs)

2.57 **a.** **Given** 250 L of water **Need** gallons of water

Plan $L \rightarrow qt \rightarrow gal$ $\dfrac{1.06 \text{ qt}}{1 \text{ L}}$ $\dfrac{1 \text{ gal}}{4 \text{ qt}}$

Set-up $250 \text{ L} \times \dfrac{1.06 \text{ qt}}{1 \text{ L}} \times \dfrac{1 \text{ gal}}{4 \text{ qt}} = 66 \text{ gal } (2 \text{ SFs})$

b. **Given** 0.024 g of sulfa drug, 8-mg tablets **Need** number of tablets

Plan g of sulfa drug $\rightarrow$ mg of sulfa drug $\rightarrow$ number of tablets

$\dfrac{1000 \text{ mg}}{1 \text{ g}}$ $\dfrac{1 \text{ tablet}}{8 \text{ mg sulfa drug}}$

Set-up $0.24 \text{ g sulfa drug} \times \dfrac{1000 \text{ mg}}{1 \text{ g}} \times \dfrac{1 \text{ tablet}}{8 \text{ mg sulfa drug}} = 3 \text{ tablets } (1 \text{ SF})$

c. **Given** 34-lb child, 115 mg of ampicillin/kg of body mass **Need** milligrams of ampicillin

Plan lb of body mass $\rightarrow$ kg of body mass $\rightarrow$ mg of ampicillin

$\dfrac{1 \text{ kg}}{2.20 \text{ lb}}$ $\dfrac{115 \text{ mg ampicillin}}{1 \text{ kg body mass}}$

Set-up $34 \text{ lb body mass} \times \dfrac{1 \text{ kg body mass}}{2.20 \text{ lb body mass}} \times \dfrac{115 \text{ mg ampicillin}}{1 \text{ kg body mass}}$

$= 1800 \text{ mg of ampicillin } (2 \text{ SFs})$

d. **Given** 4.0 oz of ointment **Need** grams of ointment

Plan $oz \rightarrow lb \rightarrow g$ $\dfrac{1 \text{ lb}}{16 \text{ oz}}$ $\dfrac{454 \text{ g}}{1 \text{ lb}}$

Set-up $4.0 \text{ oz} \times \dfrac{1 \text{ lb}}{16 \text{ oz}} \times \dfrac{454 \text{ g}}{1 \text{ lb}} = 110 \text{ g of ointment } (2 \text{ SFs})$

2.59 **a.** **Given** 500. mL of IV saline solution, 80. mL/h **Need** infusion time in hours

Plan mL of IV saline solution $\rightarrow$ hours $\dfrac{1 \text{ h}}{80. \text{ mL saline solution}}$

Set-up $500. \text{ mL saline solution} \times \dfrac{1 \text{ h}}{80. \text{ mL saline solution}} = 6.3 \text{ h } (2 \text{ SFs})$

b. **Given** 72.6-lb child, 1.5. mg of Medrol/kg of body mass, 20. mg of Medrol/mL of solution **Need** milliliters of Medrol solution

Plan lb of body mass $\rightarrow$ kg of body mass $\rightarrow$ mg of Medrol $\rightarrow$ mL of solution

$\dfrac{1 \text{ kg}}{2.20 \text{ lb}}$ $\dfrac{1.5 \text{ mg Medrol}}{1 \text{ kg body mass}}$ $\dfrac{1 \text{ mL solution}}{20. \text{ mg Medrol}}$

Set-up $72.6 \text{ lb body mass} \times \dfrac{1 \text{ kg body mass}}{2.20 \text{ lb body mass}} \times \dfrac{1.5 \text{ mg Medrol}}{1 \text{ kg body mass}} \times \dfrac{1 \text{ mL solution}}{20. \text{ mg Medrol}}$

$= 2.5 \text{ mL of Medrol solution } (2 \text{ SFs})$

2.61 **a.** **Given** 175 lb of body weight, $LD_{50} = 3300$ mg/kg **Need** grams of table salt

Plan lb of body weight $\rightarrow$ kg of body mass $\rightarrow$ mg of table salt $\rightarrow$ g of table salt

$\dfrac{1 \text{ kg body mass}}{2.20 \text{ lb body weight}}$ $\dfrac{3300 \text{ mg table salt}}{1 \text{ kg body mass}}$ $\dfrac{1 \text{ g table salt}}{1000 \text{ mg table salt}}$

Set-up

$175 \text{ lb body weight} \times \dfrac{1 \text{ kg body mass}}{2.20 \text{ lb body weight}} \times \dfrac{3300 \text{ mg table salt}}{1 \text{ kg body mass}} \times \dfrac{1 \text{ g table salt}}{1000 \text{ mg table salt}}$

$= 260 \text{ g of table salt } (2 \text{ SFs})$

b. **Given** 175 lb of body weight, $LD_{50} = 6$ mg/kg **Need** grams of sodium cyanide

Plan lb of body weight $\rightarrow$ kg of body mass $\rightarrow$ mg of sodium cyanide $\rightarrow$ g of sodium cyanide

$$\frac{1 \text{ kg body mass}}{2.20 \text{ lb body weight}} \qquad \frac{6 \text{ mg sodium cyanide}}{1 \text{ kg body mass}} \qquad \frac{1 \text{ g sodium cyanide}}{1000 \text{ mg sodium cyanide}}$$

Set-up

$$175 \text{ lb body weight} \times \frac{1 \text{ kg body mass}}{2.20 \text{ lb body weight}} \times \frac{6 \text{ mg sodium cyanide}}{1 \text{ kg body mass}} \times \frac{1 \text{ g sodium cyanide}}{1000 \text{ mg sodium cyanide}}$$

$$= 0.5 \text{ g of sodium cyanide (1 SF)}$$

c. **Given** 175 lb of body weight, LD_{50} = 1100 mg/kg **Need** grams of aspirin

Plan lb of body weight → kg of body mass → mg of aspirin → g of aspirin

$$\frac{1 \text{ kg body mass}}{2.20 \text{ lb body weight}} \qquad \frac{1100 \text{ mg aspirin}}{1 \text{ kg body mass}} \qquad \frac{1 \text{ g aspirin}}{1000 \text{ mg aspirin}}$$

Set-up $175 \text{ lb body weight} \times \frac{1 \text{ kg body mass}}{2.20 \text{ lb body weight}} \times \frac{1100 \text{ mg aspirin}}{1 \text{ kg body mass}} \times \frac{1 \text{ g aspirin}}{1000 \text{ mg aspirin}}$

$$= 88 \text{ g of aspirin (2 SFs)}$$

2.63 Density is the mass of a substance divided by its volume. $\text{Density} = \dfrac{\text{mass (grams)}}{\text{volume (mL)}}$

The densities of solids and liquids are usually stated in g/mL or g/cm^3, so in some problems the units will need to be converted.

a. **Given** 1.65 lb, 170 mL **Need** density (g/mL)

Plan lb → g then calculate density $\qquad \dfrac{454 \text{ g}}{1 \text{ lb}}$

Set-up $1.65 \text{ lb} \times \dfrac{454 \text{ g}}{1 \text{ lb}} = 749 \text{ g (3 SFs)}$

$$\therefore \text{Density} = \frac{\text{mass}}{\text{volume}} = \frac{749 \text{ g}}{170 \text{ mL}} = 4.4 \text{ g/mL (2 SFs)}$$

b. **Given** 20.0 mL initial volume, 21.45 mL final volume, 4.50 g **Need** density (g/mL)

Plan calculate volume by difference, then calculate density

Set-up volume of gem: 21.45 mL total – 20.0 mL water = 1.45 mL

$$\therefore \text{Density} = \frac{\text{mass}}{\text{volume}} = \frac{4.50 \text{ g}}{1.45 \text{ mL}} = 3.10 \text{ g/mL (3 SFs)}$$

c. **Given** 514.1 g, 114 cm^3 **Need** density (g/mL)

Plan convert volume cm^3 → mL then calculate the density $\qquad \dfrac{1 \text{ mL}}{1 \text{ cm}^3}$

Set-up $114 \text{ cm}^3 \times \dfrac{1 \text{ mL}}{1 \text{ cm}^3} = 114 \text{ mL}$

$$\therefore \text{Density} = \frac{\text{mass}}{\text{volume}} = \frac{514.1 \text{ g}}{114 \text{ mL}} = 4.51 \text{ g/mL (3 SFs)}$$

2.65 In these problems, the density is used as a conversion factor.

a. **Given** 150 mL of liquid, density 1.4 g/mL **Need** grams of liquid

Plan mL → g $\qquad \dfrac{1.4 \text{ g}}{1 \text{ mL}}$

Set-up $150 \text{ mL} \times \dfrac{1.4 \text{ g}}{1 \text{ mL}} = 210 \text{ g of liquid (2 SFs)}$

b. **Given** 0.500 L of glucose solution, density 1.15 g/mL **Need** grams of solution

Plan L → mL → g $\qquad \dfrac{1000 \text{ mL}}{1 \text{ L}} \qquad \dfrac{1.15 \text{ g}}{1 \text{ mL solution}}$

Set-up $0.500 \text{ L solution} \times \dfrac{1000 \text{ mL}}{1 \text{ L}} \times \dfrac{1.15 \text{ g}}{1 \text{ mL solution}} = 575 \text{ g of solution (3 SFs)}$

c. Given 225 mL of bronze, density 7.8 g/mL   **Need** ounces of bronze

Plan mL → g → lb → oz $\dfrac{7.8\ \text{g}}{1\ \text{mL}}\quad\dfrac{1\ \text{lb}}{454\ \text{g}}\quad\dfrac{16\ \text{oz}}{1\ \text{lb}}$

Set-up $225\ \cancel{\text{mL}} \times \dfrac{7.8\ \cancel{\text{g}}}{1\ \cancel{\text{mL}}} \times \dfrac{1\ \cancel{\text{lb}}}{454\ \cancel{\text{g}}} \times \dfrac{16\ \text{oz}}{1\ \cancel{\text{lb}}} = 62\ \text{oz of bronze (2 SFs)}$

2.67 **a.** Specific gravity $= \dfrac{\text{density of substance}}{\text{density of water}} = \dfrac{1.030\ \cancel{\text{g/mL}}}{1.00\ \cancel{\text{g/mL}}} = 1.03\ (3\ \text{SFs})$

b. Density $= \dfrac{\text{mass of glucose solution}}{\text{volume of glucose solution}} = \dfrac{20.6\ \text{g}}{20.0\ \text{mL}} = 1.03\ \text{g/mL (3 SFs)}$

c. Specific gravity $= \dfrac{\text{density of substance}}{\text{density of water}}$

∴ Density of substance = specific gravity × density of water
= 0.85 × 1.00 g/mL = 0.85 g/mL (2 SFs)

d. Density $= \dfrac{\text{mass of HDL}}{\text{volume of HDL}} = \dfrac{0.230\ \text{g}}{0.200\ \text{mL}} = 1.15\ \text{g/mL (3 SFs)}$

2.69 **a.** 42 mcg of iron = 1 dL of blood; $\dfrac{42\ \text{mcg iron}}{1\ \text{dL blood}}$ and $\dfrac{1\ \text{dL blood}}{42\ \text{mcg iron}}$

b. Given 8.0 mL blood sample, 42 mcg of iron/dL   **Need** micrograms of iron

Plan mL of blood → dL of blood → mcg of iron $\dfrac{1\ \text{dL blood}}{100\ \text{mL blood}}\quad\dfrac{42\ \text{mcg iron}}{1\ \text{dL blood}}$

Set-up $8.0\ \cancel{\text{mL blood}} \times \dfrac{1\ \cancel{\text{dL blood}}}{100\ \cancel{\text{mL blood}}} \times \dfrac{42\ \text{mcg iron}}{1\ \cancel{\text{dL blood}}} = 3.4\ \text{mcg of iron (2 SFs)}$

2.71 Both measurements in part **c** have two significant figures, and both measurements in part **d** have four significant figures.

2.73 **a.** The number of legs is a counted number; it is exact.
b. The height is measured with a ruler or tape measure; it is a measured number.
c. The number of chairs is a counted number; it is exact.
d. The area is measured with a ruler or tape measure; it is a measured number.

2.75 **a.** length $= 38.4\ \cancel{\text{in.}} \times \dfrac{2.54\ \text{cm}}{1\ \cancel{\text{in.}}} = 97.5\ \text{cm (3 SFs)}$

b. length $= 24.2\ \cancel{\text{in.}} \times \dfrac{2.54\ \text{cm}}{1\ \cancel{\text{in.}}} = 61.5\ \text{cm (3 SFs)}$

c. There are three significant figures in the length measurement.
d. Area = length × width = 97.5 cm × 61.5 cm = $6.00 \times 10^3\ \text{cm}^2$ (3 SFs)

2.77 **Given** 18.5 mL initial volume, 23.1 mL final volume, 8.24 g mass   **Need** density (g/mL)
Plan calculate volume by difference, then calculate density
Set-up The volume of the object is 23.1 mL − 18.5 mL = 4.6 mL

∴ Density $= \dfrac{\text{mass}}{\text{volume}} = \dfrac{8.24\ \text{g}}{4.6\ \text{mL}} = 1.8\ \text{g/mL (2 SFs)}$

2.79 The liquid with the highest density will be at the bottom of the cylinder; the liquid with the lowest density will be at the top of the cylinder:

A is vegetable oil (D = 0.92 g/mL), **B** is water (D = 1.00 g/mL), **C** is mercury
(D = 13.6 g/mL)

2.81 **a.** To round off 0.000 012 58 L to three significant figures, drop the final digit 8 and increase the last retained digit by 1 to give 0.000 012 6 L or 1.26×10^{-5} L.

b. To round off 3.528×10^2 kg to three significant figures, drop the final digit 8 and increase the last retained digit by 1 to give 3.53×10^2 kg.

c. To round off 125 111 m to three significant figures, drop the final digits 111 and add three zeros as placeholders to give 125 000 m (or 1.25×10^5 m).

2.83 **a.** The total mass is the sum of the individual components of the dessert.
137.25 g + 84 g + 43.7 g = 265 g. No places to the right of the decimal point are allowed since the mass of the fudge sauce (84 g) has no digits to the right of the decimal point.

b. Given grams of dessert from part **a** **Need** pounds of dessert

Plan $g \rightarrow lb \quad \dfrac{1 \text{ lb}}{454 \text{ g}}$

Set-up 265 g dessert (total) $\times \dfrac{1 \text{ lb}}{454 \text{ g}}$ = 0.584 lb of dessert (3 SFs)

2.85 **Given** 1.75 Euros/kg of grapes, \$1.36/Euro **Need** cost in dollars per pound

Plan Euros/kg $\rightarrow$ Euros/lb $\rightarrow$ \$/lb $\quad \dfrac{1.75 \text{ Euros}}{1 \text{ kg grapes}} \quad \dfrac{1 \text{ kg}}{2.20 \text{ lb}} \quad \dfrac{\$1.36}{1 \text{ Euro}}$

Set-up $\dfrac{1.75 \text{ Euros}}{1 \text{ kg grapes}} \times \dfrac{1 \text{ kg}}{2.20 \text{ lb}} \times \dfrac{\$1.36}{1 \text{ Euro}}$ = \$1.08/lb of grapes (3 SFs)

2.87 **Given** 4.0 lb of onions **Need** number of onions

Plan lb $\rightarrow$ g $\rightarrow$ number of onions $\quad \dfrac{454 \text{ g}}{1 \text{ lb}} \quad \dfrac{1 \text{ onion}}{115 \text{ g}}$

Set-up 4.0 lb onions $\times \dfrac{454 \text{ g}}{1 \text{ lb}} \times \dfrac{1 \text{ onion}}{115 \text{ g}}$ = 16 onions (2 SFs)

2.89 **Given** 215 mL initial, 285 mL final volume, density of lead 11.3 g/mL **Need** grams of lead

Plan calculate the volume by difference and mL $\rightarrow$ g $\quad \dfrac{11.3 \text{ g}}{1 \text{ mL}}$

Set-up The difference between the initial volume of the water and its volume with the lead object will give us the volume of the lead object: 285 mL total $-$ 215 mL water = 70. mL of lead, then

70. mL lead $\times \dfrac{11.3 \text{ g lead}}{1 \text{ mL lead}}$ = 790 g of lead (2 SFs)

2.91 **Given** 1.50 L of gasoline **Need** cm^3 of olive oil

Plan L of gasoline $\rightarrow$ mL of gasoline $\rightarrow$ g of gasoline $\rightarrow$ g of olive oil $\rightarrow$ cm^3 of olive oil
(equality from question: 1 g olive oil = 1 g of gasoline)
$\dfrac{1000 \text{ mL gasoline}}{1 \text{ L gasoline}} \quad \dfrac{0.74 \text{ g gasoline}}{1 \text{ mL gasoline}} \quad \dfrac{1 \text{ cm}^3 \text{ olive oil}}{0.92 \text{ g olive oil}}$

Set-up 1.50 L gasoline $\times \dfrac{1000 \text{ mL}}{1 \text{ L}} \times \dfrac{0.74 \text{ g gasoline}}{1 \text{ mL gasoline}}$ = 1110 g of gasoline

1110 g olive oil $\times \dfrac{1 \text{ cm}^3 \text{ olive oil}}{0.92 \text{ g olive oil}}$ = 1200 cm^3 ($1.2 \times 10^3 \text{ cm}^3$) of olive oil (2 SFs)

2.93 **a. Given** 8.0 oz **Need** number of crackers

Plan oz $\rightarrow$ number of crackers $\quad \dfrac{6 \text{ crackers}}{0.50 \text{ oz}}$

Set-up 8.0 oz $\times \dfrac{6 \text{ crackers}}{0.5 \text{ oz}}$ = 96 crackers (2 SFs)

b. Given 10 crackers, 4 g of fat/serving   **Need** ounces of fat

  Plan number of crackers → servings → g of fat → lb of fat → oz of fat

$$\frac{1 \text{ serving}}{6 \text{ crackers}} \quad \frac{4 \text{ g fat}}{1 \text{ serving}} \quad \frac{1 \text{ lb}}{454 \text{ g}} \quad \frac{16 \text{ oz}}{1 \text{ lb}}$$

  Set-up $10 \text{ crackers} \times \dfrac{1 \text{ serving}}{6 \text{ crackers}} \times \dfrac{4 \text{ g fat}}{1 \text{ serving}} \times \dfrac{1 \text{ lb}}{454 \text{ g}} \times \dfrac{16 \text{ oz}}{1 \text{ lb}} = 0.2 \text{ oz of fat } (1 \text{ SF})$

c. Given 2300 mg of sodium, 140 mg of sodium/serving   **Need** number of servings

  Plan mg of sodium → servings $\dfrac{1 \text{ serving}}{140 \text{ mg sodium}}$

  Set-up $2300 \text{ mg sodium} \times \dfrac{1 \text{ serving}}{140 \text{ mg sodium}} = 16 \text{ servings } (2 \text{ SFs})$

2.95 Given 10 days, 4 tablets/day, 250-mg tablets   **Need** ounces of amoxicillin

  Plan days → tablets → mg of amoxicillin → g → lb → oz of amoxicillin

$$\frac{4 \text{ tablets}}{1 \text{ day}} \quad \frac{250 \text{ mg amoxicillin}}{1 \text{ tablet}} \quad \frac{1 \text{ g}}{1000 \text{ mg}} \quad \frac{1 \text{ lb}}{454 \text{ g}} \quad \frac{16 \text{ oz}}{1 \text{ lb}}$$

  Set-up $10 \text{ days} \times \dfrac{4 \text{ tablets}}{1 \text{ day}} \times \dfrac{250 \text{ mg amoxicillin}}{1 \text{ tablet}} \times \dfrac{1 \text{ g}}{1000 \text{ mg}} \times \dfrac{1 \text{ lb}}{454 \text{ g}} \times \dfrac{16 \text{ oz}}{1 \text{ lb}}$

  $= 0.35 \text{ oz of amoxicillin } (2 \text{ SFs})$

2.97 Given 5.0 mL of elixir, 30. mg of phenobarbital/7.5 mL

  Need milligrams of phenobarbital

  Plan mL of elixir → mg of phenobarbital $\dfrac{30. \text{ mg phenobarbital}}{7.5 \text{ mL elixir}}$

  Set-up $5.0 \text{ mL elixir} \times \dfrac{30. \text{ mg phenobarbital}}{7.5 \text{ mL elixir}} = 20. \text{ mg of phenobarbital } (2 \text{ SFs})$

2.99 Because the balance can measure mass to 0.001 g, the mass should be reported to 0.001 g. You should record the mass of the object as 31.075 g.

2.101 Given 3.0-h trip   **Need** gallons of gasoline

  Plan h → mi → km → L → qt → gal $\dfrac{55 \text{ mi}}{1 \text{ h}} \quad \dfrac{1 \text{ km}}{0.621 \text{ mi}} \quad \dfrac{1 \text{ L}}{11 \text{ km}} \quad \dfrac{1.06 \text{ qt}}{1 \text{ L}} \quad \dfrac{1 \text{ gal}}{4 \text{ qt}}$

  Set-up $3.0 \text{ h} \times \dfrac{55 \text{ mi}}{1 \text{ h}} \times \dfrac{1 \text{ km}}{0.621 \text{ mi}} \times \dfrac{1 \text{ L}}{11 \text{ km}} \times \dfrac{1.06 \text{ qt}}{1 \text{ L}} \times \dfrac{1 \text{ gal}}{4 \text{ qt}}$

  $= 6.4 \text{ gal of gasoline } (2 \text{ SFs})$

2.103 Given 1.50 g of silicon, 3.00 in. diameter, density 2.33 g/cm^3 **Need** thickness (mm)

  Plan g → cm^3 $\dfrac{1 \text{ cm}^3}{2.33 \text{ g silicon}}$ and $d(\text{in.}) \to r(\text{in.}) \to r(\text{cm})$ $r = \dfrac{d}{2} \quad \dfrac{2.54 \text{ cm}}{1 \text{ in.}}$

  then rearrange the volume equation for thickness (cm) → thickness (mm)

  $$V = \pi r^2 h \to h = \dfrac{V}{\pi r^2} \quad \dfrac{10 \text{ mm}}{1 \text{ cm}}$$

  Set-up Volume of wafer: $1.50 \text{ g} \times \dfrac{1 \text{ cm}^3}{2.33 \text{ g}} = 0.644 \text{ cm}^3$

  Radius of wafer: $\dfrac{3.00 \text{ in.}}{2} \times \dfrac{2.54 \text{ cm}}{1 \text{ in.}} = 3.81 \text{ cm}$

  $\therefore h = \dfrac{V}{\pi r^2} = \dfrac{0.644 \text{ cm}^3}{\pi (3.81 \text{ cm})^2} = 0.0141 \text{ cm} \times \dfrac{10 \text{ mm}}{1 \text{ cm}} = 0.141 \text{ mm } (3 \text{ SFs})$

2.105 a. Given   180 lb of body weight   **Need**   cups of coffee

    Plan

    lb of body weight → kg of body mass → mg of caffeine → fl oz of coffee → cups of coffee

$$\frac{1\ kg\ body\ mass}{2.20\ lb\ body\ weight} \quad \frac{192\ mg\ caffeine}{1\ kg\ body\ mass} \quad \frac{6\ fl\ oz\ coffee}{100.\ mg\ caffeine} \quad \frac{1\ cup\ coffee}{12\ fl\ oz\ coffee}$$

    Set-up $180\ \cancel{lb\ body\ weight} \times \dfrac{1\ \cancel{kg\ body\ mass}}{2.20\ \cancel{lb\ body\ weight}} \times \dfrac{192\ mg\ caffeine}{1\ \cancel{kg\ body\ mass}}$

        $= 1.571 \times 10^4\ mg$ of caffeine (2 SFs allowed)

        $1.571 \times 10^4\ \cancel{mg\ caffeine} \times \dfrac{6\ \cancel{fl\ oz\ coffee}}{100.\ \cancel{mg\ caffeine}} \times \dfrac{1\ cup\ coffee}{12\ \cancel{fl\ oz\ coffee}}$

        $= 79$ cups of coffee (2 SFs)

  b. Given   milligrams of caffeine from part **a**   **Need**   cans of cola

    Plan   mg of caffeine → cans of cola $\dfrac{1\ can\ cola}{50.\ mg\ caffeine}$

    Set-up $1.571 \times 10^4\ \cancel{mg\ caffeine} \times \dfrac{1\ can\ cola}{50.\ \cancel{mg\ caffeine}} = 310$ cans of cola (2 SFs)

  c. Given   milligrams of caffeine from part **a**   **Need**   number of No-Doz tablets

    Plan   mg of caffeine → No-Doz tablets $\dfrac{1\ No\text{-}Doz\ tablet}{100.\ mg\ caffeine}$

    Set-up $1.571 \times 10^4\ \cancel{mg\ caffeine} \times \dfrac{1\ No\text{-}Doz\ tablet}{100.\ \cancel{mg\ caffeine}} = 160$ No-Doz tablets (2 SFs)

2.107 a. Given   65 kg of body mass, 3.0% fat   **Need**   pounds of fat

    Plan   kg of body mass → kg of fat → lb of fat

        (percent equality: 100 kg of body mass = 3.0 kg of fat)

$$\frac{3.0\ kg\ fat}{100\ kg\ body\ mass} \quad \frac{2.20\ lb\ fat}{1\ kg\ fat}$$

    Set-up $65\ \cancel{kg\ body\ mass} \times \dfrac{3.0\ \cancel{kg\ fat}}{100\ \cancel{kg\ body\ mass}} \times \dfrac{2.20\ lb\ fat}{1\ \cancel{kg\ fat}} = 4.3$ lb of fat (2 SFs)

  b. Given   3.0 L of fat   **Need**   pounds of fat

    Plan   L → mL → g → lb $\dfrac{1000\ mL}{1\ L} \quad \dfrac{0.94\ g}{1\ mL} \quad \dfrac{1\ lb}{454\ g}$

    Set-up $3.0\ \cancel{L} \times \dfrac{1000\ \cancel{mL}}{1\ \cancel{L}} \times \dfrac{0.94\ \cancel{g}}{1\ \cancel{mL}} \times \dfrac{1\ lb}{454\ \cancel{g}} = 6.2$ lb of fat (2 SFs)

Credit: Network Photographer / Alamy

Since Charles had a visit with Daniel, a dietitian, Charles and his mother have been preparing healthier foods with smaller serving sizes. Charles has lost 6 lb. Yesterday he had a blood glucose test that showed his blood glucose level was normal. One of the meals that Charles likes consists of rice, chicken, and carrots. If Charles consumes 6 g of carbohydrate, 4 g of fat, and 12 g of protein, what is the energy content of the meal, in kilojoules and kilocalories?

CHAPTER READINESS*

📠 Key Math Skills

- Using Positive and Negative Numbers in Calculations (1.4B)
- Solving Equations (1.4D)
- Interpreting Graphs (1.4E)
- Writing Numbers in Scientific Notation (1.4F)
- Rounding Off (2.3)

⚛ Core Chemistry Skills

- Counting Significant Figures (2.2)
- Using Significant Figures in Calculations (2.3)
- Writing Conversion Factors from Equalities (2.5)
- Using Conversion Factors (2.6)

* These Key Math Skills and Core Chemistry Skills from previous chapters are listed here for your review as you proceed to the new material in this chapter.

3.1   Classification of Matter

Learning Goal: Classify examples of matter as pure substances or mixtures.

- Matter is anything that has mass and occupies space.
- A pure substance, whether it is an element or compound, has a definite composition.
- Elements are the simplest type of matter.
- A compound consists of atoms of two or more elements always chemically combined in the same proportion.
- Mixtures contain two or more substances that are physically, not chemically, combined.
- Mixtures are classified as homogeneous or heterogeneous.

Key Terms for Section 3.1

Match the following terms with the descriptions:

    a. element   **b.** mixture   **c.** pure substance
    d. matter   **e.** compound

1. _____ anything that has mass and occupies space

2. _____ an element or a compound that has a definite composition

An aluminum can consists of many atoms of the element aluminum.

Credit: Norman Chan / Fotolia

3. ____ the physical combination of two or more substances that does not change the identities of the substances

4. ____ a pure substance consisting of two or more elements with a definite composition that can be broken down into simpler substances only by chemical methods

5. ____ a pure substance containing only one type of matter that cannot be broken down by chemical methods

Answers   **1.** d   **2.** c   **3.** b   **4.** e   **5.** a

♦ Learning Exercise 3.1A

Identify each of the following as an element (E) or a compound (C):

⚛ CORE CHEMISTRY SKILL

Classifying Matter

1. ____ iron   2. ____ carbon dioxide
3. ____ potassium iodide   4. ____ gold
5. ____ aluminum   6. ____ table salt (sodium chloride)

Answers   **1.** E   **2.** C   **3.** C   **4.** E   **5.** E   **6.** C

♦ Learning Exercise 3.1B

Identify each of the following as a pure substance (P) or mixture (M):

1. ____ bananas and milk   2. ____ sulfur
3. ____ silver   4. ____ a bag of raisins and nuts
5. ____ pure water   6. ____ sand and water

Answers   **1.** M   **2.** P   **3.** P   **4.** M   **5.** P   **6.** M

Water consists of many molecules of H_2O, each containing two H atoms and one O atom.

Credit: Bomshtein / Shutterstock

♦ Learning Exercise 3.1C

Identify each of the following mixtures as homogeneous (Ho) or heterogeneous (He):

1. ____ chocolate milk   2. ____ sand and water
3. ____ orange soda   4. ____ a bag of raisins and nuts
5. ____ air   6. ____ vinegar

Answers   **1.** Ho   **2.** He   **3.** Ho   **4.** He   **5.** Ho   **6.** Ho

3.2   States and Properties of Matter

Learning Goal: Identify the states and the physical and chemical properties of matter.

- The states of matter are solid, liquid, and gas.
- Physical properties are those characteristics of a substance that can change without affecting the identity of the substance.
- A substance undergoes a physical change when its shape, size, or state changes, but its composition does not change.

- Chemical properties are those characteristics of a substance that change when a new substance is produced.
- Melting, freezing, boiling, and condensing are typical changes of state.

♦ Learning Exercise 3.2A

State whether the following statements describe a gas (G), a liquid (L), or a solid (S):

1. _____ There are no attractions among the particles.

2. _____ The particles are held close together in a definite pattern.

3. _____ This substance has a definite volume but no definite shape.

4. _____ The particles are moving extremely fast.

5. _____ This substance has no definite shape and no definite volume.

6. _____ The particles in this substance are vibrating slowly in fixed positions.

7. _____ This substance has a definite volume and a definite shape.

Answers   1. G   2. S   3. L   4. G   5. G   6. S   7. S

♦ Learning Exercise 3.2B

Classify each of the following as a physical (P) or chemical (C) property:

a. _____ Silver is shiny.

b. _____ Water is a liquid at 25 °C.

c. _____ Wood burns.

d. _____ Mercury is a very dense liquid.

e. _____ Helium is not reactive.

f. _____ Ice cubes float in water.

Answers   a. P   b. P   c. C   d. P   e. C   f. P

♦ Learning Exercise 3.2C

Classify each of the following changes as physical (P) or chemical (C):

⚛ CORE CHEMISTRY SKILL

Identifying Physical and Chemical Changes

a. _____ Sodium melts at 98 °C.

b. _____ Iron forms rust in air and water.

c. _____ Water condenses on a cold window.

d. _____ Fireworks explode when ignited.

e. _____ Gasoline burns in a car engine.

f. _____ Paper is cut to make confetti.

Answers   a. P   b. C   c. P   d. C   e. C   f. P

3.3   Temperature

Learning Goal: Given a temperature, calculate a corresponding temperature on another scale.

- Temperature is measured in degrees Celsius (°C) or kelvins (K). In the United States, the Fahrenheit scale (°F) is still in use.
- The equation $T_F = 1.8T_C + 32$ is used to convert a Celsius temperature to a Fahrenheit temperature.

- When rearranged for T_C, this equation is used to convert a Fahrenheit temperature to a Celsius temperature.

$$T_C = \frac{(T_F - 32)}{1.8}$$

- The temperature on the Celsius scale is related to the temperature on the Kelvin scale: $T_K = T_C + 273$.

Guide to Calculating Temperature	
STEP 1	State the given and needed quantities.
STEP 2	Write a temperature equation.
STEP 3	Substitute in the known values and calculate the new temperature.

♦ **Learning Exercise 3.3**

Calculate the temperature in each of the following problems:

a. To prepare yogurt, milk is warmed to 185 °F. What Celsius temperature is needed to prepare the yogurt?

b. A heat-sensitive vaccine is stored at −12 °C. What is that temperature on a Fahrenheit thermometer?

c. A patient has a temperature of 39.5 °C. What is that temperature on the Fahrenheit scale?

d. A patient in the emergency room with hyperthermia has a temperature of 105 °F. What is the temperature on the Celsius scale?

e. The temperature in an autoclave used to sterilize surgical equipment is 253 °F. What is that temperature on the Celsius scale?

f. Liquid nitrogen at −196 °C is used to freeze and remove precancerous skin growths. What temperature will this be on the Kelvin scale?

Answers   **a.** 85.0 °C   **b.** 10 °F   **c.** 103.1 °F
            d. 41 °C   **e.** 123 °C   **f.** 77 K

🞿 **CORE CHEMISTRY SKILL**

Converting between Temperature Scales

Very high temperatures (hyperthermia) can lead to convulsions and brain damage.

Credit: Digital Vision / Alamy

3.4 Energy

Learning Goal: Identify energy as potential or kinetic; convert between units of energy.

- Energy is the ability to do work.
- Potential energy is stored energy, which is determined by position or composition; kinetic energy is the energy of motion.
- The SI unit of energy is the joule (J), the metric unit is the calorie (cal). One calorie (cal) is equal to exactly 4.184 joules (J).

$$\frac{4.184 \text{ J}}{1 \text{ cal}} \quad \text{and} \quad \frac{1 \text{ cal}}{4.184 \text{ J}}$$

Key Terms for Sections 3.2–3.4

Match the following terms with the statements:

    a. potential energy   **b.** joule   **c.** kinetic energy
    d. calorie   **e.** energy   **f.** physical change

1. _____ the SI unit of energy

2. _____ the energy of motion

3. _____ the amount of heat energy that raises the temperature of exactly 1 g of water exactly 1 °C

4. _____ a change in physical properties of a substance with no change in its identity

5. _____ the ability to do work

6. _____ a type of energy that is stored for future use

Answers   **1.** b   **2.** c   **3.** d   **4.** f   **5.** e   **6.** a

♦ **Learning Exercise 3.4A**

State whether each of the following statements describes potential (**P**) or kinetic (**K**) energy:

1. _____ a potted plant sitting on a ledge   **2.** _____ your breakfast cereal

3. _____ logs sitting in a fireplace   **4.** _____ a piece of candy

5. _____ an arrow shot from a bow   **6.** _____ a ski jumper standing at the top of the ski jump

7. _____ a jogger running   **8.** _____ a skydiver waiting to jump

9. _____ water flowing down a stream   **10.** _____ a bowling ball striking the pins

Answers   **1.** P   **2.** P   **3.** P   **4.** P   **5.** K
                 6. P   **7.** K   **8.** P   **9.** K   **10.** K

♦ **Learning Exercise 3.4B**

Match the words in column A with the descriptions in column B.

  A   **B**

1. _____ calorie   **a.** the SI unit of work and energy

2. _____ kilocalorie   **b.** the heat needed to raise 1 g of water by 1 °C

3. _____ joule   **c.** 1000 cal

Answers   **1.** b   **2.** c   **3.** a

♦ **Learning Exercise 3.4C**

Calculate each of the following conversions:

    a. 58 000 cal to kcal   **b.** 3450 J to cal

    c. 2.8 kJ to cal   **d.** 15 200 cal to kJ

⚛ **CORE CHEMISTRY SKILL**

Using Energy Units

Answers   **a.** 58 kcal   **b.** 825 cal   **c.** 670 cal   **d.** 63.6 kJ

3.5   Energy and Nutrition

Learning Goal: Use the energy values to calculate the kilocalories (kcal) or kilojoules (kJ) for a food.

*   The nutritional calorie (Cal) is the same amount of energy as 1 kcal, or 1000 calories.
*   When a substance is burned in a calorimeter, the water that surrounds the reaction chamber absorbs the heat given off. The heat absorbed by the water is calculated, and the energy value for the substance (energy per gram) is determined.
*   The energy values for three food types are: carbohydrate 4 kcal/g (17 kJ/g), fat 9 kcal/g (38 kJ/g), protein 4 kcal/g (17 kJ/g).
*   The energy content of a food is the sum of kilocalories or kilojoules from carbohydrate, fat, and protein.

Guide to Calculating the Energy from a Food	
STEP 1	State the given and needed quantities.
STEP 2	Use the energy value for each food type and calculate the kcal or kJ rounded off to the tens place.
STEP 3	Add the energy for each food type to give the total energy from the food.

♦ **Learning Exercise 3.5A**

Calculate the kilojoules (kJ) for each food using the following data (round off the kilojoules for each food type to the tens place):

Food	Carbohydrate	Fat	Protein	kJ
a. green peas, cooked, 1 cup	19 g	1 g	9 g	_____
b. potato chips, 10 chips	10 g	8 g	1 g	_____
c. cream cheese, 8 oz	5 g	86 g	18 g	_____
d. lean hamburger, 3 oz	0	10 g	23 g	_____
e. banana, 1	26 g	0	2 g	_____

Answers	**a.** 510 kJ	**b.** 490 kJ	**c.** 3670 kJ
	d. 770 kJ	**e.** 470 kJ	

♦ **Learning Exercise 3.5B**

Use energy values to solve each of the following:

1. Complete the following table listing ingredients for a peanut butter sandwich (round off the kilocalories for each food type to the tens place):

	Carbohydrate	Fat	Protein	kcal
bread, 2 slices	30 g	0 g	5 g	_____
peanut butter, 2 tbsp	10 g	13 g	8 g	_____
jelly, 2 tsp	10 g	0 g	0 g	_____
margarine, 1 tsp	0 g	7 g	0 g	_____

Total kcal in sandwich _____

2. How many kilocalories are in a single serving of pudding that contains 31 g of carbohydrate, 5 g of fat, and 5 g of protein (round off the kilocalories for each food type to the tens place)?

3. One serving of peanut butter (2 tbsp) has an energy value of 190 kcal. If there are 10 g of carbohydrate and 8 g of protein, how many grams of fat are in one serving of peanut butter (round off the kilocalories for each food type to the tens place)?

4. A serving of breakfast cereal provides 220 kcal. In this serving, there are 6 g of fat and 8 g of protein. How many grams of carbohydrate are in the cereal (round off the kilocalories for each food type to the tens place)?

Answers

1. bread = 140 kcal; peanut butter = 190 kcal; jelly = 40 kcal; margarine = 60 kcal
   total kcal in sandwich = 430 kcal
2. carbohydrate = 120 kcal; fat = 50 kcal; protein = 20 kcal total = 190 kcal
3. carbohydrate = 40 kcal; protein = 30 kcal
   190 kcal − 30 kcal − 40 kcal = 120 kcal of fat

$$120 \text{ kcal} \times \frac{1 \text{ g fat}}{9 \text{ kcal}} = 13 \text{ g of fat}$$

4. fat = 50 kcal; protein = 30 kcal 30 kcal + 50 kcal = 80 kcal from fat and protein
   220 kcal − 80 kcal = 140 kcal from carbohydrate

$$140 \text{ kcal} \times \frac{1 \text{ g carbohydrate}}{4 \text{ kcal}} = 35 \text{ g of carbohydrate}$$

3.6 Specific Heat

Learning Goal: Use specific heat to calculate heat loss or gain.

* Specific heat is the amount of energy required to raise the temperature of 1 g of a substance by 1 °C.
* The specific heat for liquid water is 1.00 cal/g °C or 4.184 J/g °C.
* The heat lost or gained can be calculated using the mass of the substance, temperature difference, and its specific heat (SH): Heat = mass $\times \Delta T \times SH$

Guide to Calculations Using Specific Heat	
STEP 1	State the given and the needed quantities.
STEP 2	Calculate the temperature change (ΔT).
STEP 3	Write the heat equation and needed conversion factors.
STEP 4	Substitute in the given values and calculate the heat, making sure units cancel.

♦ **Learning Exercise 3.6**

The specific heat for water is 1.00 cal/g °C or 4.184 J/g °C. Calculate the kilocalories (kcal) and kilojoules (kJ) gained or released during the following:

CORE CHEMISTRY SKILL

Using the Heat Equation

1. heating 20.0 g of water from 22 °C to 77 °C

2. heating 10.0 g of water from 12.4 °C to 67.5 °C

3. cooling 0.450 kg of water from 80.0 °C to 35.0 °C

4. cooling 125 g of water from 72.0 °C to 45.0 °C

Answers   **1.** 1.1 kcal, 4.6 kJ (gained)   **2.** 0.551 kcal, 2.31 kJ (gained)
                 3. 20.3 kcal, 84.7 kJ (released)   **4.** 3.38 kcal, 14.1 kJ (released)

3.7 Changes of State

Learning Goal: Describe the changes of state between solids, liquids, and gases; calculate the energy involved.

* A substance melts and freezes at its melting (freezing) point. During the process of melting or freezing, the temperature remains constant.
* The heat of fusion is the energy required to change 1 g of solid to liquid at the melting point. For ice to melt at 0 °C, 80. cal/g or 334 J/g, is required. This is also the amount of heat lost when 1 g of water freezes at 0 °C.
* A substance boils and condenses at its boiling point. During the process of boiling or condensing, the temperature remains constant.
* The heat of vaporization is the energy required to change 1 g of liquid to 1 g of gas at the boiling point. For water to boil at 100 °C, 540 cal/g or 2260 J/g, is required to change 1 g of liquid to 1 g of gas (steam); it is also the amount of heat released when 1 g of water vapor condenses at 100 °C.
* Evaporation is a surface phenomenon, while boiling occurs throughout the liquid.

- Sublimation is the change of state from a solid directly to a gas. Deposition is the opposite process.
- A heating or cooling curve illustrates the changes in temperature and state as heat is added to or removed from a substance.
- When a substance is heated or cooled, the energy gained or released is the total of the energy involved in temperature changes as well as the energy involved in changes of state.

Key Terms for Sections 3.5–3.7

Match the following terms with the descriptions:

    a. energy value   **b.** specific heat   **c.** Calorie (Cal)   **d.** kilojoule   **e.** heat of vaporization

1. _____ a nutritional unit of energy equal to 1000 cal or 1 kcal

2. _____ a quantity of heat that changes the temperature of exactly 1 g of a substance by exactly 1 °C

3. _____ the number of kilocalories or kilojoules obtained per gram of carbohydrate, fat, or protein

4. _____ a unit of energy equal to 1000 J

5 _____ energy required to convert exactly 1 g of a liquid to vapor at its boiling point

Answers   **1.** c   **2.** b   **3.** a   **4.** d   **5.** e

♦ **Learning Exercise 3.7A**

Identify each of the following as

    1. melting   **2.** freezing   **3.** sublimation   **4.** condensation

a. _____ A liquid changes to a solid.

b. _____ Ice forms on the surface of a lake in winter.

c. _____ Dry ice in an ice cream cart changes to a gas.

d. _____ Butter in a hot pan turns to liquid.

e. _____ A gas changes to a liquid.

Melting and freezing are reversible processes.

Credit: John A. Rizzo / Photodisc / Getty Images

Answers   **a.** 2   **b.** 2   **c.** 3   **d.** 1   **e.** 4

Guide to Calculations Using a Heat Conversion Factor	
STEP 1	State the given and needed quantities.
STEP 2	Write a plan to convert the given quantity to the needed quantity.
STEP 3	Write the heat conversion factor and any metric factor.
STEP 4	Set up the problem and calculate the needed quantity.

♦ **Learning Exercise 3.7B**

Calculate each of the following when a substance melts or freezes:

    a. How many joules of heat are needed to melt 24.0 g of ice at 0 °C?

b. How much heat, in kilojoules, is released when 325 g of water freezes at 0 °C?

c. How many kilocalories of heat are required to melt 120 g of ice in an ice bag at 0 °C?

d. How many grams of ice would melt when 1200 cal of heat is absorbed?

An ice bag is used to treat a sports injury.
Credit: wsphotos / Getty Images

Answers   **a.** 8020 J   **b.** 109 kJ   **c.** 9.6 kcal   **d.** 15 g

◆ **Learning Exercise 3.7C**

Calculate each of the following when a substance boils or condenses:

a. How many joules are needed to completely change 5.00 g of water to vapor at 100 °C?

b. How many kilocalories are released when 42 g of steam at 100 °C condenses to form liquid water at 100 °C?

c. How many grams of water can be converted to steam at 100 °C when 155 kJ of energy is absorbed?

d. How many grams of steam condense if 24 kcal is released at 100 °C?

Answers   **a.** 11 300 J   **b.** 23 kcal   **c.** 68.6 g   **d.** 44 g

◆ **Learning Exercise 3.7D**

On each heating or cooling curve, indicate the portion that corresponds to a solid, liquid, or gas and the changes in state.

1. Draw a heating curve for water that begins at −20 °C and ends at 120 °C.

2. Draw a heating curve for bromine from −25 °C to 75 °C. Bromine has a melting point of −7 °C and a boiling point of 59 °C.

Copyright © 2015 Pearson Education, Inc.

3. Draw a cooling curve for sodium from 1000 °C to 0 °C. Sodium has a freezing point of 98 °C and a boiling (condensation) point of 883 °C.

Answers

1.

2.

3.

♦ **Learning Exercise 3.7E**

Calculate the energy change in each of the following:

   a. How many kilojoules are released when 35.0 g of water at 65.0 °C cools to 0.0 °C and completely changes to solid? (*Hint*: Two steps are needed.)

   b. How many kilocalories are needed to melt 15 g of ice at 0. °C, heat the water to 100. °C, and convert the water to gas at 100. °C? (*Hint*: Three steps are needed.)

Answers   **a.** 21.2 kJ   **b.** 11 kcal

Checklist for Chapter 3

You are ready to take the Practice Test for Chapter 3. Be sure you have accomplished the following learning goals for this chapter. If not, review the section listed at the end of the goal. Then apply your new skills and understanding to the Practice Test.

After studying Chapter 3, I can successfully:

_____ Identify matter as a pure substance or mixture. (3.1)

_____ Identify a mixture as homogeneous or heterogeneous. (3.1)

_____ Identify the physical state of a substance as a solid, liquid, or gas. (3.2)

_____ Calculate a temperature in degrees Fahrenheit, degrees Celsius, or kelvins. (3.3)

_____ Describe some forms of energy. (3.4)

_____ Change a quantity in one energy unit to another energy unit. (3.4)

_____ Using the energy values, calculate the energy, in kilocalories (Cal) or kilojoules (kJ), for a food sample. (3.5)

_____ Given the mass of a sample, specific heat, and the temperature change, calculate the heat lost or gained. (3.6)

_____ Calculate the heat change for a change of state for a specific amount of a substance. (3.7)

_____ Calculate the total heat for a combination of change of temperature and change of state for a specific amount of a substance. (3.7)

_____ Draw heating and cooling curves using the melting and boiling points of a substance. (3.7)

Practice Test for Chapter 3

For questions 1 through 4, classify each of the following as a pure substance (P) *or a mixture* (M): (3.1)

1. toothpaste _____

2. platinum _____

3. chromium _____

4. mouthwash _____

For questions 5 through 8, classify each of the following mixtures as homogeneous (Ho) *or heterogeneous* (He): (3.1)

5. noodle soup _____

6. salt water _____

7. chocolate chip cookie _____

8. mouthwash _____

9. Which of the following is a chemical property? (3.2)
   A. dynamite explodes
   B. a shiny metal
   C. a melting point of 110 °C
   D. rain on a cool day
   E. breaking up cement

For questions 10 through 12, answer with solid (S), *liquid* (L), *or gas* (G): (3.2)

10. _____ has a definite volume but takes the shape of a container

11. _____ does not have a definite shape or definite volume

12. _____ has a definite shape and a definite volume

13. Which of the following is a chemical property of silver? (3.2)
   A. density of 10.5 g/mL
   B. shiny
   C. melts at 961 °C
   D. good conductor of heat
   E. reacts to form tarnish

14. Which of the following is a physical property of silicon? (3.2)
- **A.** burns in chlorine
- **B.** has a black to gray color
- **C.** reacts with nitric acid
- **D.** reacts with oxygen to form sand
- **E.** used to form silicone

For questions 15 through 19, answer as physical change (P) *or chemical change* (C): (3.2)

15. _____ Butter melts in a hot pan.

16. _____ Iron forms rust with oxygen.

17. _____ Baking powder forms bubbles (CO_2) as a cake is baking.

18. _____ Water boils.

19. _____ Propane burns in a camp stove.

20. 105 °F = _____ °C (3.3)
- **A.** 73 °C
- **B.** 41 °C
- **C.** 58 °C
- **D.** 90 °C
- **E.** 189 °C

21. The melting point of gold is 1064 °C. The Fahrenheit temperature needed to melt gold would be (3.3)
- **A.** 129 °F
- **B.** 623 °F
- **C.** 1031 °F
- **D.** 1913 °F
- **E.** 1947 °F

22. The average daytime temperature on the planet Mercury is 683 K. What is this temperature on the Celsius scale? (3.3)
- **A.** 956 °C
- **B.** 715 °C
- **C.** 680. °C
- **D.** 410. °C
- **E.** 303 °C

23. Which of the following would be described as potential energy? (3.4)
- **A.** a car going around a racetrack
- **B.** a rabbit hopping
- **C.** oil in an oil well
- **D.** a moving merry-go-round
- **E.** a bouncing ball

24. Which of the following would be described as kinetic energy? (3.4)
- **A.** a car battery
- **B.** a can of tennis balls
- **C.** gasoline in a car fuel tank
- **D.** a box of matches
- **E.** a tennis ball crossing over the net

For questions 25 through 27, consider a cup of milk that is 3.5% butterfat with an energy value of 690 kJ. In the cup of milk, there are 12 g of carbohydrate 9.0 g of fat and protein: (3.5)

25. The number of kilocalories provided by the carbohydrate is
- **A.** 4 kcal
- **B.** 9 kcal
- **C.** 36 kcal
- **D.** 48 kcal
- **E.** 81 kcal

26. The number of kilojoules provided by the fat is
- **A.** 9.0 kJ
- **B.** 38 kJ
- **C.** 150 kJ
- **D.** 200 kJ
- **E.** 340 kJ

27. Using your answers to questions 25 and 26, the number of kcal provided by the protein is
- **A.** 4 kcal
- **B.** 9 kcal
- **C.** 36 kcal
- **D.** 48 kcal
- **E.** 81 kcal

28. The number of joules needed to raise the temperature of 5.0 g of water from 25 °C to 55 °C is (3.6)
- **A.** 5.0 J
- **B.** 36 J
- **C.** 30.0 J
- **D.** 335 J
- **E.** 630 J

29. The number of kilojoules released when 15 g of water cools from 58 °C to 22 °C is (3.6)
- **A.** 0.13 kJ
- **B.** 0.54 kJ
- **C.** 2.3 kJ
- **D.** 63 kJ
- **E.** 150 kJ

For questions 30 through 34, match items A *to* E *with one of the statements*: (3.7)

- **A.** melting
- **B.** evaporation
- **C.** heat of fusion
- **D.** heat of vaporization
- **E.** boiling

30. _____ the energy required to convert a gram of solid to liquid

31. _____ the heat needed to convert a gram of liquid to gas

32. _____ the conversion of liquid molecules to gas at the surface of a liquid

33. _____ the conversion of solid to liquid

34. _____ the formation of a gas within the liquid as well as on the surface

35. The number of joules needed to convert 15.0 g of ice to liquid at 0 °C is (3.7)
   A. 73 J   **B.** 334 J   **C.** 2260 J   **D.** 4670 J   **E.** 5010 J

36. The number of calories released when 2.0 g of water at 50. °C is cooled and frozen at 0. °C is (3.7)
   A. 80. cal   **B.** 160 cal   **C.** 260 cal   **D.** 440 cal   **E.** 1100 cal

37. What is the total number of kilojoules required to convert 25 g of ice at 0. °C to gas at 100. °C? (3.7)
   A. 8.4 kJ   **B.** 19 kJ   **C.** 59 kJ   **D.** 67 kJ   **E.** 75 kJ

For questions 38 through 41, consider the heating curve for p-toluidine. Answer the following questions when heat is added to p-toluidine at −20 °C, where toluidine is below its melting point: (3.7)

38. On the heating curve, segment **BC** indicates
   A. solid   **B.** melting   **C.** liquid   **D.** boiling   **E.** gas

39. On the heating curve, segment **CD** shows toluidine as
   A. solid   **B.** melting   **C.** liquid   **D.** boiling   **E.** gas

40. The boiling point of toluidine is
   A. 20 °C   **B.** 45 °C   **C.** 100 °C   **D.** 200 °C   **E.** 250 °C

41. On the heating curve, segment **EF** shows toluidine as
   A. solid   **B.** melting   **C.** liquid   **D.** boiling   **E.** gas

42. A patient on a diet has a lunch of 3 oz of salmon (8 g of fat, 16 g of protein), 1 cup of nonfat milk (12 g of carbohydrate, 9 g of protein), and 1 cup of raw carrots (11 g of carbohydrate, 2 g of protein). What is the total kilocalories for the lunch? (_Round off the kilocalories for each food type to the tens place._) (3.5)
   A. 270 kcal   **B.** 200 kcal   **C.** 110 kcal   **D.** 90 kcal   **E.** 50 kcal

43. For the lunch in problem 42, how many hours of swimming are needed to expend the same energy, in kilocalories, if swimming requires 2100 kJ/h? (3.5)
   A. 5.7 h   **B.** 5.0 h   **C.** 2.8 h   **D.** 1.6 h   **E.** 0.54 h

Answers to the Practice Test

1. M	**2.** P	**3.** P	**4.** M	**5.** He
6. Ho	**7.** He	**8.** Ho	**9.** A	**10.** L
11. G	**12.** S	**13.** E	**14.** B	**15.** P
16. C	**17.** C	**18.** P	**19.** C	**20.** B
21. E	**22.** D	**23.** C	**24.** E	**25.** D
26. E	**27.** C	**28.** E	**29.** C	**30.** C
31. D	**32.** B	**33.** A	**34.** E	**35.** E
36. C	**37.** E	**38.** B	**39.** C	**40.** D
41. E	**42.** A	**43.** E		

Matter and Energy

Learning Goals

- Classify examples of matter as pure substances or mixtures.
- Identify the states and the physical and chemical properties of matter.
- Given a temperature, calculate a corresponding temperature on another scale.
- Identify energy as potential or kinetic; convert between units of energy.
- Use the energy values to calculate the kilocalories (kcal) or kilojoules (kJ) for a food.
- Use specific heat to calculate heat loss or gain.
- Describe the changes of state between solids, liquids, and gases; calculate the energy involved.

Chapter Outline

Chapter Opener: Dietitian

3.1 Classification of Matter

Chemistry Link to Health: Breathing Mixtures

3.2 States and Properties of Matter

3.3 Temperature

Chemistry Link to Health: Variation in Body Temperature

3.4 Energy

Chemistry Link to the Environment: Carbon Dioxide and Climate Change

3.5 Energy and Nutrition

Explore Your World: Counting Calories

Chemistry Link to Health: Losing and Gaining Weight

3.6 Specific Heat

3.7 Changes of State

Chemistry Link to Health: Steam Burns

Clinical Update: A Diet and Exercise Program for Charles

❀ Core Chemistry Skills

- Classifying Matter (3.1)
- Identifying Physical and Chemical Changes (3.2)
- Converting between Temperature Scales (3.3)
- Using Energy Units (3.4)
- Using the Heat Equation (3.6)

Selected Answers and Solutions to Text Problems

3.1 A *pure substance* is matter that has a fixed or definite composition: either elements or compounds. In a *mixture*, two or more substances are physically mixed but not chemically combined.

  a. Baking soda is composed of one type of matter ($NaHCO_3$), which makes it a pure substance.
  b. A blueberry muffin is composed of several substances mixed together, which makes it a mixture.
  c. Ice is composed of one type of matter (H_2O molecules), which makes it a pure substance.
  d. Zinc is composed of one type of matter (Zn atoms), which makes it a pure substance.
  e. Trimix is a physical mixture of oxygen, nitrogen, and helium gases, which makes it a mixture.

3.3 *Elements* are the simplest type of pure substance, containing only one type of atom. *Compounds* contain two or more elements chemically combined in a specific proportion.

  a. A silicon (Si) chip is an element since it contains only one type of atom (Si).
  b. Hydrogen peroxide (H_2O_2) is a compound since it contains two elements (H, O) chemically combined.
  c. Oxygen (O_2) is an element since it contains only one type of atom (O).
  d. Rust (Fe_2O_3) is a compound since it contains two elements (Fe, O) chemically combined.
  e. Methane (CH_4) in natural gas is a compound since it contains two elements (C, H) chemically combined.

3.5 A *homogeneous mixture* has a uniform composition; a *heterogeneous mixture* does not have a uniform composition throughout the mixture.

  a. Vegetable soup is a heterogeneous mixture since it has chunks of vegetables.
  b. Seawater is a homogeneous mixture since it has a uniform composition.
  c. Tea is a homogeneous mixture since it has a uniform composition.
  d. Tea with ice and lemon slices is a heterogeneous mixture since it has chunks of ice and lemon.
  e. Fruit salad is a heterogeneous mixture since it has chunks of fruit.

3.7 **a.** A gas has no definite volume or shape.
  b. In a gas, the particles do not interact with each other.
  c. In a solid, the particles are held in a rigid structure.

3.9 A *physical property* is a characteristic of the substance such as color, shape, odor, luster, size, melting point, and density. A *chemical property* is a characteristic that indicates the ability of a substance to change into a new substance.

  a. Color and physical state are physical properties.
  b. The ability to react with oxygen is a chemical property.
  c. The temperature of a substance is a physical property.
  d. Milk souring describes chemical reactions and is thus a chemical property.
  e. Burning butane gas in oxygen forms new substances, which makes it a chemical property.

3.11 When matter undergoes a *physical change*, its state or appearance changes, but its composition remains the same. When a *chemical change* occurs, the original substance is converted into a new substance, which has different physical and chemical properties.

  a. Water vapor condensing is a physical change since the physical form of the water changes, but the composition of the substance does not.
  b. Cesium metal reacting is a chemical change since new substances form.
  c. Gold melting is a physical change since the physical state changes, but not the composition of the substance.

d. Cutting a puzzle results in a physical change since the size and shape change, but not the composition of the substance.

e. Grating cheese results in a physical change since the size and shape change, but not the composition of the substance.

3.13 **a.** The high reactivity of fluorine is a chemical property since it allows for the formation of new substances.

b. The physical state of fluorine is a physical property.

c. The color of fluorine is a physical property.

d. The reactivity of fluorine with hydrogen is a chemical property since it allows for the formation of new substances.

e. The melting point of fluorine is a physical property.

3.15 The Fahrenheit temperature scale is still used in the United States. A normal body temperature is 98.6 °F on this scale. To convert her 99.8 °F temperature to the equivalent reading on the Celsius scale, the following calculation must be performed:

$$T_C = \frac{(99.8 - 32)}{1.8} = \frac{67.8}{1.8} = 37.7 \,°C \,(3 \,\text{SFs}) \,(1.8 \text{ and } 32 \text{ are exact numbers})$$

Because a normal body temperature is 37.0 on the Celsius scale, her temperature of 37.7 °C would indicate a mild fever.

3.17 To convert Celsius to Fahrenheit: $T_F = 1.8(T_C) + 32$

To convert Fahrenheit to Celsius: $T_C = \dfrac{(T_F - 32)}{1.8}$ (1.8 and 32 are exact numbers)

To convert Celsius to Kelvin: $T_K = T_C + 273$

To convert Kelvin to Celsius: $T_C = T_K - 273$

a. $T_F = 1.8(T_C) + 32 = 1.8(37.0) + 32 = 66.6 + 32 = 98.6 \,°F$

b. $T_C = \dfrac{(T_F - 32)}{1.8} = \dfrac{(65.3 - 32)}{1.8} = \dfrac{33.3}{1.8} = 18.5 \,°C$

c. $T_K = T_C + 273 = -27 + 273 = 246 \,K$

d. $T_K = T_C + 273 = 62 + 273 = 335 \,K$

e. $T_C = \dfrac{(T_F - 32)}{1.8} = \dfrac{(114 - 32)}{1.8} = \dfrac{82}{1.8} = 46 \,°C$

3.19 **a.** $T_C = \dfrac{(T_F - 32)}{1.8} = \dfrac{(106 - 32)}{1.8} = \dfrac{74}{1.8} = 41 \,°C$

b. $T_C = \dfrac{(T_F - 32)}{1.8} = \dfrac{(103 - 32)}{1.8} = \dfrac{71}{1.8} = 39 \,°C$

No, there is no need to phone the doctor. The child's temperature is less than 40.0 °C.

3.21 When the roller-coaster car is at the top of the ramp, it has its maximum potential energy. As it descends, potential energy is converted into kinetic energy. At the bottom, all of its energy is kinetic.

3.23 **a.** Potential energy is stored in the water at the top of the waterfall.

b. Kinetic energy is displayed as the kicked ball moves.

c. Potential energy is stored in the chemical bonds in the coal.

d. Potential energy is stored when the skier is at the top of the hill.

3.25 **a.** **Given** 3.0 h, 270 kJ/h   **Need** joules

Plan $h \rightarrow kJ \rightarrow J$ $\dfrac{1000 \text{ J}}{1 \text{ kJ}}$

Set-up $3.0 \, \cancel{h} \times \dfrac{270 \, \cancel{kJ}}{1.0 \, \cancel{h}} \times \dfrac{1000 \, J}{1 \, \cancel{kJ}} = 8.1 \times 10^5 \, J \ (2 \, SFs)$

b. Given 3.0 h, 270 kJ/h   **Need** kilocalories

Plan $h \rightarrow kJ \rightarrow J \rightarrow cal \rightarrow kcal$ $\dfrac{1000 \, J}{1 \, kJ} \quad \dfrac{1 \, cal}{4.184 \, J} \quad \dfrac{1 \, kcal}{1000 \, cal}$

Set-up $3.0 \, \cancel{h} \times \dfrac{270 \, \cancel{kJ}}{1.0 \, \cancel{h}} \times \dfrac{1000 \, \cancel{J}}{1 \, \cancel{kJ}} \times \dfrac{1 \, \cancel{cal}}{4.184 \, \cancel{J}} \times \dfrac{1 \, kcal}{1000 \, \cancel{cal}} = 190 \, kcal \ (2 \, SFs)$

3.27 a. Given 125 kJ   **Need** kilocalories

Plan $kJ \rightarrow J \rightarrow cal \rightarrow kcal$ $\dfrac{1000 \, J}{1 \, kJ} \quad \dfrac{1 \, cal}{4.184 \, J} \quad \dfrac{1 \, kcal}{1000 \, cal}$

Set-up $125 \, \cancel{kJ} \times \dfrac{1000 \, \cancel{J}}{1 \, \cancel{kJ}} \times \dfrac{1 \, \cancel{cal}}{4.184 \, \cancel{J}} \times \dfrac{1 \, kcal}{1000 \, \cancel{cal}} = 29.9 \, kcal \ (3 \, SFs)$

b. Given 870. kJ   **Need** kilocalories

Plan $kJ \rightarrow J \rightarrow cal \rightarrow kcal$ $\dfrac{1000 \, J}{1 \, kJ} \quad \dfrac{1 \, cal}{4.184 \, J} \quad \dfrac{1 \, kcal}{1000 \, cal}$

Set-up $870. \, \cancel{kJ} \times \dfrac{1000 \, \cancel{J}}{1 \, \cancel{kJ}} \times \dfrac{1 \, \cancel{cal}}{4.184 \, \cancel{J}} \times \dfrac{1 \, kcal}{1000 \, \cancel{cal}} = 208 \, kcal \ (3 \, SFs)$

3.29 a. Given 1 cup of orange juice that contains 26 g of carbohydrate, 2 g of protein, and no fat
Need total energy in kilojoules

Food Type	Mass		Energy Value		Energy (rounded off to the tens place)
Carbohydrate	26 $\cancel{g}$	$\times$	$\dfrac{17 \, kJ}{1 \, \cancel{g}}$	$=$	440 kJ
Protein	2 $\cancel{g}$	$\times$	$\dfrac{17 \, kJ}{1 \, \cancel{g}}$	$=$	30 kJ
			Total energy content	$=$	470 kJ

b. Given one apple that provides 72 kcal of energy and contains no fat or protein
Need grams of carbohydrate

Plan kcal $\rightarrow$ g of carbohydrate $\dfrac{1 \, g \text{ of carbohydrate}}{4 \, kcal}$

Set-up $72 \, \cancel{kcal} \times \dfrac{1 \, g \text{ carbohydrate}}{4 \, \cancel{kcal}} = 18 \, g \text{ of carbohydrate } (2 \, SFs)$

c. Given 1 tablespoon of vegetable oil that contains 14 g of fat, and no carbohydrate or protein
Need total energy in kilocalories

Food Type	Mass		Energy Value		Energy (rounded off to the tens place)
Fat	14 $\cancel{g}$	$\times$	$\dfrac{9 \, kcal}{1 \, \cancel{g}}$	$=$	130 kcal

d. Given 1 avocado that provides 405 kcal in total, and contains 13 g of carbohydrate and 5 g of protein
Need grams of fat

Food Type	Mass		Energy Value		Energy (rounded off to the tens place)
Carbohydrate	13 g	×	$\dfrac{4 \text{ kcal}}{1 \text{ g}}$	=	50 kcal
Fat	? g	×	$\dfrac{9 \text{ kcal}}{1 \text{ g}}$	=	? kcal
Protein	5 g	×	$\dfrac{4 \text{ kcal}}{1 \text{ g}}$	=	20 kcal
			Total energy content	=	405 kcal

∴ Energy from fat = 405 kcal − (50 kcal + 20 kcal) = 335 kcal

∴ 335 kcal $\times \dfrac{1 \text{ g fat}}{9 \text{ kcal}}$ = 37 g of fat

3.31 **Given** one cup of clam chowder that contains 16 g of carbohydrate, 12 g of fat, and 9 g of protein
Need total energy in kilocalories and kilojoules

Food Type	Mass		Energy Value		Energy (rounded off to the tens place)
Carbohydrate	16 g	×	$\dfrac{4 \text{ kcal (or 17 kJ)}}{1 \text{ g}}$	=	60 kcal (or 270 kJ)
Fat	12 g	×	$\dfrac{9 \text{ kcal (or 38 kJ)}}{1 \text{ g}}$	=	110 kcal (or 460 kJ)
Protein	9 g	×	$\dfrac{4 \text{ kcal (or 17 kJ)}}{1 \text{ g}}$	=	40 kcal (or 150 kJ)
			Total energy content	=	210 kcal (or 880 kJ)

3.33 3.2 L glucose solution $\times \dfrac{1000 \text{ mL solution}}{1 \text{ L solution}} \times \dfrac{5.0 \text{ g glucose}}{100. \text{ mL solution}} \times \dfrac{4 \text{ kcal}}{1 \text{ g glucose}}$

= 640 kcal (rounded off to the tens place)

3.35 Copper, which has the lowest specific heat of the samples, would reach the highest temperature.

3.37 **a. Given** $SH_{\text{water}} = 1.00 \text{ cal/g} \,°\text{C}$; mass = 8.5 g; $\Delta T = 36\,°\text{C} - 15\,°\text{C} = 21\,°\text{C}$
Need heat in calories
Plan Heat = mass × ΔT × SH

Set-up Heat = 8.5 g × 21 °C × $\dfrac{1.00 \text{ cal}}{\text{g} \,°\text{C}}$ = 180 cal (2 SFs)

b. Given $SH_{\text{water}} = 4.184 \text{ J/g} \,°\text{C}$; mass = 25 g; $\Delta T = 61\,°\text{C} - 86\,°\text{C} = -25\,°\text{C}$
Need heat in joules
Plan Heat = mass × ΔT × SH

Set-up Heat = 25 g × (−25 °C) × $\dfrac{4.184 \text{ J}}{\text{g} \,°\text{C}}$ = −2600 J (2 SFs)

c. Given $SH_{\text{water}} = 1.00 \text{ cal/g} \,°\text{C}$; mass = 150 g; $\Delta T = 77\,°\text{C} - 15\,°\text{C} = 62\,°\text{C}$
Need heat in kilocalories

Plan   Heat = mass × ΔT × *SH*   then cal → kcal $\dfrac{1\ \text{kcal}}{1000\ \text{cal}}$

Set-up   Heat = 150 g × 62 °C × $\dfrac{1.00\ \text{cal}}{\text{g °C}}$ × $\dfrac{1\ \text{kcal}}{1000\ \text{cal}}$ = 9.3 kcal (2 SFs)

d. Given SH_{copper} = 0.385 J/g °C; mass = 175 g; ΔT = 188 °C − 28 °C = 160. °C
    Need heat in kilojoules

Plan   Heat = mass × ΔT × *SH*   then J → kJ $\dfrac{1\ \text{kJ}}{1000\ \text{J}}$

Set-up   Heat = 175 g × 160. °C × $\dfrac{0.385\ \text{J}}{\text{g °C}}$ × $\dfrac{1\ \text{kJ}}{1000\ \text{J}}$ = 10.8 kJ (3 SFs)

3.39 **a. Given** SH_{water} = 4.184 J/g °C = 1.00 cal/g °C; mass = 25.0 g;
           ΔT = 25.7 °C − 12.5 °C = 13.2 °C
    Need heat in joules and calories
    Plan Heat = mass × ΔT × *SH*

Set-up   Heat = 25.0 g × 13.2 °C × $\dfrac{4.184\ \text{J}}{\text{g °C}}$ = 1380 J (3 SFs)

or Heat = 25.0 g × 13.2 °C × $\dfrac{1.00\ \text{cal}}{\text{g °C}}$ = 330. cal (3 SFs)

b. Given SH_{copper} = 0.385 J/g °C = 0.0920 cal/g °C; mass = 38.0 g;
           ΔT = 246 °C − 122 °C = 124 °C
    Need heat in joules and calories
    Plan Heat = mass × ΔT × *SH*

Set-up   Heat = 38.0 g × 124 °C × $\dfrac{0.385\ \text{J}}{\text{g °C}}$ = 1810 J (3 SFs)

or Heat = 38.0 g × 124 °C × $\dfrac{0.0920\ \text{cal}}{\text{g °C}}$ = 434 cal (3 SFs)

c. Given SH_{ethanol} = 2.46 J/g °C = 0.588 cal/g °C; mass = 15.0 g;
           ΔT = −42.0 °C − 60.5 °C = −102.5 °C
    Need heat in joules and calories
    Plan Heat = mass × ΔT × *SH*

Set-up   Heat = 15.0 g × (−102.5 °C) × $\dfrac{2.46\ \text{J}}{\text{g °C}}$ = −3780 J (3 SFs)

or Heat = 15.0 g × (−102.5 °C) × $\dfrac{0.588\ \text{cal}}{\text{g °C}}$ = −904 cal (3 SFs)

d. Given SH_{iron} = 0.452 J/g °C = 0.108 cal/g °C; mass = 125 g;
           ΔT = 55 °C − 118 °C = −63 °C
    Need heat in joules and calories
    Plan Heat = mass × ΔT × *SH*

Set-up   Heat = 125 g × (−63 °C) × $\dfrac{0.452\ \text{J}}{\text{g °C}}$ = −3600 J (2 SFs)

or Heat = 125 g × (−63 °C) × $\dfrac{0.108\ \text{cal}}{\text{g °C}}$ = −850 cal (2 SFs)

3.41 **a.** The change from solid to liquid state is melting.
     b. Coffee is freeze-dried using the process of sublimation.
     c. Liquid water turning to ice is freezing.
     d. Ice crystals form on a package of frozen corn due to deposition.

3.43 **a.** $65 \ \cancel{\text{g ice}} \times \dfrac{80. \ \text{cal}}{1 \ \cancel{\text{g ice}}} = 5200 \ \text{cal} \ (2 \ \text{SFs});$ heat is absorbed

b. $17.0 \ \cancel{\text{g ice}} \times \dfrac{334 \ \text{J}}{1 \ \cancel{\text{g ice}}} = 5680 \ \text{J} \ (3 \ \text{SFs});$ heat is absorbed

c. $225 \ \cancel{\text{g water}} \times \dfrac{80. \ \cancel{\text{cal}}}{1 \ \cancel{\text{g water}}} \times \dfrac{1 \ \text{kcal}}{1000 \ \cancel{\text{cal}}} = 18 \ \text{kcal} \ (2 \ \text{SFs});$ heat is released

d. $50.0 \ \cancel{\text{g water}} \times \dfrac{334 \ \cancel{\text{J}}}{1 \ \cancel{\text{g water}}} \times \dfrac{1 \ \text{kJ}}{1000 \ \cancel{\text{J}}} = 16.7 \ \text{kJ} \ (3 \ \text{SFs});$ heat is released

3.45 **a.** Water vapor in clouds changing to rain is an example of condensation.
b. Wet clothes drying on a clothesline involves evaporation.
c. Steam forming as lava flows into the ocean involves boiling.
d. Water droplets forming on a bathroom mirror after a hot shower involves condensation.

3.47 **a.** $10.0 \ \cancel{\text{g water}} \times \dfrac{540 \ \text{cal}}{1 \ \cancel{\text{g water}}} = 5400 \ \text{cal} \ (2 \ \text{SFs});$ heat is absorbed

b. $5.00 \ \cancel{\text{g water}} \times \dfrac{2260 \ \text{J}}{1 \ \cancel{\text{g water}}} = 11 \ 300 \ \text{J} \ (3 \ \text{SFs});$ heat is absorbed

c. $8.0 \ \cancel{\text{kg steam}} \times \dfrac{1000 \ \cancel{\text{g}}}{1 \ \cancel{\text{kg}}} \times \dfrac{540 \ \cancel{\text{cal}}}{1 \ \cancel{\text{g steam}}} \times \dfrac{1 \ \text{kcal}}{1000 \ \cancel{\text{cal}}} = 4300 \ \text{kcal} \ (2 \ \text{SFs});$ heat is released

d. $175 \ \cancel{\text{g steam}} \times \dfrac{2260 \ \cancel{\text{J}}}{1 \ \cancel{\text{g steam}}} \times \dfrac{1 \ \text{kJ}}{1000 \ \cancel{\text{J}}} = 396 \ \text{kJ} \ (3 \ \text{SFs});$ heat is released

3.49

3.51 **a.** Two calculations are needed:

(1) ice $0 \ °\text{C} \rightarrow$ water $0 \ °\text{C}$: $50.0 \ \cancel{\text{g ice}} \times \dfrac{334 \ \text{J}}{1 \ \cancel{\text{g ice}}} = 16 \ 700 \ \text{J}$

(2) water $0 \ °\text{C} \rightarrow 65.0 \ °\text{C}$: $\Delta T = 65.0 \ °\text{C} - 0 \ °\text{C} = 65.0 \ °\text{C}$

$50.0 \ \cancel{\text{g water}} \times 65.0 \ \cancel{°\text{C}} \times \dfrac{4.184 \ \text{J}}{\cancel{\text{g water}} \ \cancel{°\text{C}}} = 13 \ 600 \ \text{J}$

$\therefore$ Total heat needed $= 16 \ 700 \ \text{J} + 13 \ 600 \ \text{J} = 30 \ 300 \ \text{J} \ (3 \ \text{SFs})$

b. Two calculations are needed:

(1) steam $100 \ °\text{C} \rightarrow$ water $100 \ °\text{C}$: $15.0 \ \cancel{\text{g steam}} \times \dfrac{-540 \ \cancel{\text{cal}}}{1 \ \cancel{\text{g steam}}} \times \dfrac{1 \ \text{kcal}}{1000 \ \cancel{\text{cal}}} = -8.1 \ \text{kcal}$

(2) water $100 \ °\text{C} \rightarrow 0 \ °\text{C}$: $15.0 \ \cancel{\text{g water}} \times -100. \ \cancel{°\text{C}} \times \dfrac{1.00 \ \cancel{\text{cal}}}{\cancel{\text{g}} \ \cancel{°\text{C}}} \times \dfrac{1 \ \text{kcal}}{1000 \ \cancel{\text{cal}}} = -1.50 \ \text{kcal}$

$\therefore$ Total heat released $= 8.1 \ \text{kcal} + 1.50 \ \text{kcal} = 9.6 \ \text{kcal} \ (2 \ \text{SFs})$

c. Three calculations are needed:

(1) ice $0 \,^\circ C \rightarrow$ water $0 \,^\circ C$: $24.0 \text{ g ice} \times \dfrac{334 \text{ J}}{1 \text{ g ice}} \times \dfrac{1 \text{ kJ}}{1000 \text{ J}} = 8.02 \text{ kJ}$

(2) water $0 \,^\circ C \rightarrow 100 \,^\circ C$: $24.0 \text{ g water} \times 100.\,^\circ C \times \dfrac{4.184 \text{ J}}{\text{g} \,^\circ C} \times \dfrac{1 \text{ kJ}}{1000 \text{ J}} = 10.0 \text{ kJ}$

(3) water $100 \,^\circ C \rightarrow$ steam $100 \,^\circ C$: $24.0 \text{ g water} \times \dfrac{2260 \text{ J}}{1 \text{ g water}} \times \dfrac{1 \text{ kJ}}{1000 \text{ J}} = 54.2 \text{ kJ}$

$\therefore$ Total heat needed $= 8.02 \text{ kJ} + 10.0 \text{ kJ} + 54.2 \text{ kJ} = 72.2 \text{ kJ (3 SFs)}$

3.53 Two calculations are needed:

(1) steam $100. \,^\circ C \rightarrow$ water $100. \,^\circ C$: $18.0 \text{ g steam} \times \dfrac{540 \text{ cal}}{1 \text{ g steam}} \times \dfrac{1 \text{ kcal}}{1000 \text{ cal}} = 9.7 \text{ kcal}$

(2) water $100. \,^\circ C \rightarrow 37.0 \,^\circ C$: $18.0 \text{ g water} \times 63 \,^\circ C \times \dfrac{1.00 \text{ cal}}{\text{g} \,^\circ C} \times \dfrac{1 \text{ kcal}}{1000 \text{ cal}} = 1.1 \text{ kcal}$

$\therefore$ Total heat released $= 9.7 \text{ kcal} + 1.1 \text{ kcal} = 10.8 \text{ kcal (3 SFs)}$

3.55 a. Using the energy totals from Table 3.8:

Breakfast	Energy
Banana, 1 medium	110 kcal
Milk, nonfat, 1 cup	90 kcal
Egg, 1 large	70 kcal
Total =	270 kcal

Lunch	Energy
Carrots, 1 cup	50 kcal
Beef, ground, 3 oz	220 kcal
Apple, 1 medium	60 kcal
Milk, nonfat, 1 cup	90 kcal
Total =	420 kcal

Dinner	Energy
Chicken, no skin, 6 oz	2 × 110 kcal
Potato, baked	100 kcal
Broccoli, 3 oz	30 kcal
Milk, nonfat, 1 cup	90 kcal
Total =	440 kcal

b. total kilocalories for one day $= 270 \text{ kcal} + 420 \text{ kcal} + 440 \text{ kcal} = 1130 \text{ kcal}$
c. Since Charles will maintain his weight if he consumes 1800 kcal per day, he will lose weight on this new diet (1130 kcal/day).
d. For Charles, his energy balance is 1130 kcal/day − 1800 kcal/day = −670 kcal/day.

$$5.0 \text{ lb} \times \dfrac{3500 \text{ kcal}}{1.0 \text{ lb}} \times \dfrac{1 \text{ day}}{670 \text{ kcal}} = 26 \text{ days (2 SFs)}$$

3.57 a. The diagram shows two different kinds of atoms chemically combined in a definite 2:1 ratio; it represents a compound.
b. The diagram shows two different kinds of matter (atoms and molecules) physically mixed, not chemically combined; it represents a mixture.
c. The diagram contains only one kind of atom; it represents an element.

3.59 A *homogeneous mixture* has a uniform composition; a *heterogeneous mixture* does not have a uniform composition throughout the mixture.

    a. Lemon-flavored water is a homogeneous mixture since it has a uniform composition (as long as there are no lemon pieces).

    b. Stuffed mushrooms are a heterogeneous mixture since there are mushrooms and chunks of filling.

    c. Eye drops are a homogeneous mixture since they have a uniform composition.

3.61 61.4 °C

$$T_F = 1.8(T_C) + 32 = 1.8(61.4) + 32 = 111 + 32 = 143 \,°F \text{ (3 SFs)}$$

3.63 $T_C = \dfrac{(T_F - 32)}{1.8} = \dfrac{(155 - 32)}{1.8} = \dfrac{123}{1.8} = 68.3 \,°C \text{ (3 SFs)}$

(1.8 and 32 are exact numbers)

$$T_K = T_C + 273 = 68.3 + 273 = 341 \text{ K (3 SFs)}$$

3.65 **Given**   10.0 cm³ cubes of gold ($SH_{gold} = 0.129 \text{ J/g °C}$), and

               aluminum ($SH_{aluminum} = 0.897 \text{ J/g°C}$); $\Delta T = 25\,°C - 15\,°C = 10.\,°C$

   Need   energy in joules and calories

   Plan   cm³ → g   Heat = mass × ΔT × SH $\dfrac{19.3 \text{ g gold}}{1 \text{ cm}^3}$ $\dfrac{2.70 \text{ g aluminum}}{1 \text{ cm}^3}$

   Set-up   <u>for gold:</u> $10.0 \text{ cm}^3 \times \dfrac{19.3 \text{ g}}{1 \text{ cm}^3} \times 10.\,°C \times \dfrac{0.129 \text{ J}}{\text{g °C}} = 250 \text{ J (2 SFs)}$

               $10.0 \text{ cm}^3 \times \dfrac{19.3 \text{ g}}{1 \text{ cm}^3} \times 10.\,°C \times \dfrac{0.129 \text{ J}}{\text{g °C}} \times \dfrac{1 \text{ cal}}{4.184 \text{ J}} = 60. \text{ cal (2 SFs)}$

        <u>for aluminum:</u> $10.0 \text{ cm}^3 \times \dfrac{2.70 \text{ g}}{1 \text{ cm}^3} \times 10.\,°C \times \dfrac{0.897 \text{ J}}{\text{g °C}} = 240 \text{ J (2 SFs)}$

               $10.0 \text{ cm}^3 \times \dfrac{2.70 \text{ g}}{1 \text{ cm}^3} \times 10.\,°C \times \dfrac{0.897 \text{ J}}{\text{g °C}} \times \dfrac{1 \text{ cal}}{4.184 \text{ J}} = 58 \text{ cal (2 SFs)}$

      Thus, the energy needed to heat each of the metals is almost the same.

3.67 **a.** **Given**   a meal consisting of: cheeseburger: 46 g of carbohydrate, 40. g of fat, 47 g of protein

                       french fries: 47 g of carbohydrate, 16 g of fat, 4 g of protein

                       chocolate shake: 76 g of carbohydrate, 10. g of fat, 10. g of protein

   Need   energy from each food type in kilocalories

   Plan   total grams of each food type, then g → kcal

   Set-up   total carbohydrate = 46 g + 47 g + 76 g = 169 g

            total fat = 40. g + 16 g + 10. g = 66 g

            total protein = 47 g + 4 g + 10. g = 61 g

Food Type	Mass		Energy Value		Energy (rounded off to the tens place)
Carbohydrate	169 g	×	$\dfrac{4 \text{ kcal}}{1 \text{ g}}$	=	680 kcal
Fat	66 g	×	$\dfrac{9 \text{ kcal}}{1 \text{ g}}$	=	590 kcal
Protein	61 g	×	$\dfrac{4 \text{ kcal}}{1 \text{ g}}$	=	240 kcal

   b. total energy for the meal = 680 kcal + 590 kcal + 240 kcal = 1510 kcal

c. Given 1510 kcal from meal   **Need** hours of sleeping to "burn off"

Plan kcal → h $\dfrac{1 \text{ h sleeping}}{60 \text{ kcal}}$

Set-up 1510 ~~kcal~~ $\times \dfrac{1 \text{ h sleeping}}{60 \text{ ~~kcal~~}} = 25$ h of sleeping (2 SFs)

d. Given 1510 kcal from meal   **Need** hours of running to "burn off"

Plan kcal → h $\dfrac{1 \text{ h running}}{750 \text{ kcal}}$

Set-up 1510 ~~kcal~~ $\times \dfrac{1 \text{ h running}}{750 \text{ ~~kcal~~}} = 2.0$ h of running (2 SFs)

3.69 *Elements* are the simplest type of pure substance, containing only one type of atom. *Compounds* contain two or more elements chemically combined in a definite proportion. In a *mixture*, two or more substances are physically mixed but not chemically combined.
   a. Carbon in pencils is an element since it contains only one type of atom (C).
   b. Carbon monoxide is a compound since it contains two elements (C, O) chemically combined.
   c. Orange juice is composed of several substances physically mixed together (e.g. water, sugar, citric acid), which makes it a mixture.

3.71 A *homogeneous mixture* has a uniform composition; a *heterogeneous mixture* does not have a uniform composition throughout the mixture.
   a. A hot fudge sundae is a heterogeneous mixture since it has ice cream, fudge sauce, and perhaps a cherry.
   b. Herbal tea is a homogeneous mixture since it has a uniform composition.
   c. Vegetable oil is a homogeneous mixture since it has a uniform composition.

3.73 a. A vitamin tablet is a solid.
   b. Helium in a balloon is a gas.
   c. Milk is a liquid.
   d. Air is a mixture of gases.
   e. Charcoal is a solid.

3.75 A *physical property* is a characteristic of the substance such as color, shape, odor, luster, size, melting point, and density. A *chemical property* is a characteristic that indicates the ability of a substance to change into a new substance.
   a. The luster of gold is a physical property.
   b. The melting point of gold is a physical property.
   c. The ability of gold to conduct electricity is a physical property.
   d. The ability of gold to form a new substance with sulfur is a chemical property.

3.77 When matter undergoes a *physical change*, its state or appearance changes, but its composition remains the same. When a *chemical change* occurs, the original substance is converted into a new substance, which has different physical and chemical properties.
   a. Plant growth produces new substances, so it is a chemical change.
   b. A change of state from solid to liquid is a physical change.
   c. Chopping wood into smaller pieces is a physical change.
   d. Burning wood, which forms new substances, results in a chemical change.

3.79 a. $T_C = \dfrac{(T_F - 32)}{1.8} = \dfrac{(134 - 32)}{1.8} = \dfrac{102}{1.8} = 56.7 \,°C$

   $T_K = T_C + 273 = 56.7 + 273 = 330.$ K

   b. $T_C = \dfrac{(T_F - 32)}{1.8} = \dfrac{(-69.7 - 32)}{1.8} = \dfrac{-101.7}{1.8} = -56.50 \,°C$

   $T_K = T_C + 273 = -56.50 + 273 = 217$ K

3.81 $T_C = \dfrac{(T_F - 32)}{1.8} = \dfrac{(-15 - 32)}{1.8} = \dfrac{-47}{1.8} = -26\,°C$

$T_K = T_C + 273 = -26 + 273 = 247\,K$

3.83 Sand must have a lower specific heat than water since the same amount of heat causes a greater temperature change in the sand than in the water.

3.85 **Given** mass $= 0.50$ g of oil; 18.9 kJ produced

Need energy value (kcal/g)

Plan kJ → kcal $\quad \dfrac{1000\text{ J}}{1\text{ kJ}} \quad \dfrac{1\text{ cal}}{4.184\text{ J}} \quad \dfrac{1\text{ kcal}}{1000\text{ cal}}$

then energy value $= \dfrac{\text{heat in kcal}}{\text{mass in g}}$

Set-up $18.9\,\cancel{\text{kJ}} \times \dfrac{1000\,\cancel{\text{J}}}{1\,\cancel{\text{kJ}}} \times \dfrac{1\,\text{cal}}{4.184\,\cancel{\text{J}}} \times \dfrac{1\text{ kcal}}{1000\,\cancel{\text{cal}}} = 4.52\text{ kcal}\;(3\text{ SFs})$

$\therefore$ energy value $= \dfrac{\text{heat produced}}{\text{mass of oil}} = \dfrac{4.52\text{ kcal}}{0.50\text{ g oil}} = 9.0\text{ kcal/g of vegetable oil }(2\text{ SFs})$

3.87 **a.** The melting point of chloroform is about $-60\,°C$.

b. The boiling point of chloroform is about $60\,°C$.

c. The diagonal line **A** represents the solid state as temperature increases. The horizontal line **B** represents the change from solid to liquid or melting of the substance. The diagonal line **C** represents the liquid state as temperature increases. The horizontal line **D** represents the change from liquid to gas or boiling of the liquid. The diagonal line **E** represents the gas state as temperature increases.

d. At $-80\,°C$, it is solid; at $-40\,°C$, it is liquid; at $25\,°C$, it is liquid; at $80\,°C$, it is gas.

3.89

a. Dibromomethane is a solid at $-75\,°C$.

b. At $-53\,°C$, solid dibromomethane melts (solid → liquid).

c. Dibromomethane is a liquid at $-18\,°C$.

d. At $110\,°C$, dibromomethane is a gas.

e. Both solid and liquid dibromomethane will be present at the melting temperature of $-53\,°C$.

3.91 **Given** 1 lb of body fat; 15% (m/m) water in body fat

Need kilocalories to "burn off"

Plan Because each gram of body fat contains 15% water, a person actually loses 85 grams of fat per hundred grams of body fat. (We considered 1 lb of fat as exactly 1 lb.)

$$lb \text{ of body fat} \rightarrow g \text{ of body fat} \rightarrow g \text{ of fat} \rightarrow kcal$$

$$\frac{454 \text{ g body fat}}{1 \text{ lb body fat}} \quad \frac{85 \text{ g fat}}{100 \text{ g body fat}} \quad \frac{9 \text{ kcal}}{1 \text{ g fat}}$$

Set-up $\quad 1 \text{ lb body fat} \times \dfrac{454 \text{ g body fat}}{1 \text{ lb body fat}} \times \dfrac{85 \text{ g fat}}{100 \text{ g body fat}} \times \dfrac{9 \text{ kcal}}{1 \text{ g fat}} = 3500 \text{ kcal (2 SFs)}$

3.93 **Given** $\quad$ mass $= 725$ g of water; $SH_{water} = 4.184 \text{ J/g} \,^{\circ}C$; $\Delta T = 37\,^{\circ}C - 65\,^{\circ}C = -28\,^{\circ}C$
Need $\quad$ heat in kilojoules

Plan $\quad$ Heat $=$ mass $\times \Delta T \times SH$, then J $\rightarrow$ kJ $\quad \dfrac{1 \text{ kJ}}{1000 \text{ J}}$

Set-up $\quad$ Heat $= 725 \text{ g} \times (-28\,^{\circ}C) \times \dfrac{4.184 \text{ J}}{\text{g} \,^{\circ}C} \times \dfrac{1 \text{ kJ}}{1000 \text{ J}} = -85 \text{ kJ (2 SFs)}$

$\therefore$ 85 kJ are lost from the water bottle and are transferred to the muscles.

3.95 **Given** $\quad$ 0.66 g of olive oil; 370 g of water; $SH_{water} = 1.00 \text{ cal/g} \,^{\circ}C$;
$\quad\quad\quad\quad \Delta T = 38.8\,^{\circ}C - 22.7\,^{\circ}C = 16.1\,^{\circ}C$
Need $\quad$ energy value (in kcal/g)

Plan $\quad$ Heat $=$ mass $\times \Delta T \times SH \quad$ then cal $\rightarrow$ kcal $\quad \dfrac{1 \text{ kcal}}{1000 \text{ cal}}$

Set-up $\quad$ Heat $= 370 \text{ g} \times 16.1\,^{\circ}C \times \dfrac{1 \text{ cal}}{\text{g} \,^{\circ}C} \times \dfrac{1 \text{ kcal}}{1000 \text{ cal}} = 6.0 \text{ kcal}$

$\therefore$ energy value $= \dfrac{\text{heat produced}}{\text{mass of oil}} = \dfrac{6.0 \text{ kcal}}{0.66 \text{ g oil}} = 9.1 \text{ kcal/g of olive oil (2 SFs)}$

3.97 **a. Given** $\quad 2.4 \times 10^7 \text{ J}/1.0$ lb of oil; mass $= 150$ kg of water; $SH_{water} = 4.184 \text{ J/g} \,^{\circ}C$;
$\quad\quad\quad\quad\quad\quad \Delta T = 100\,^{\circ}C - 22\,^{\circ}C = 78\,^{\circ}C$
$\quad\quad$ **Need** $\quad$ kilograms of oil needed

$\quad\quad$ **Plan** $\quad$ Heat $=$ mass $\times \Delta T \times SH \quad$ then J $\rightarrow$ lb of oil $\rightarrow$ kg of oil $\quad \dfrac{1 \text{ kg}}{2.20 \text{ lb}}$

$\quad\quad$ **Set-up** $\quad$ Heat $= 150 \text{ kg water} \times \dfrac{1000 \text{ g}}{1 \text{ kg}} \times 78\,^{\circ}C \times \dfrac{4.184 \text{ J}}{\text{g} \,^{\circ}C} = 4.9 \times 10^7 \text{ J (2 SFs)}$

$\quad\quad \therefore$ mass of oil $= 4.9 \times 10^7 \text{ J} \times \dfrac{1.0 \text{ lb oil}}{2.4 \times 10^7 \text{ J}} \times \dfrac{1.0 \text{ kg oil}}{2.20 \text{ lb oil}} = 0.93 \text{ kg of oil (2 SFs)}$

$\quad\quad$ **b. Given** $\quad 2.4 \times 10^7 \text{ J}/1.0$ lb of oil; mass $= 150$ kg of water; water $100\,^{\circ}C \rightarrow$ steam $100\,^{\circ}C$
$\quad\quad$ **Need** $\quad$ kilograms of oil needed

$\quad\quad$ **Plan** $\quad$ heat for water $100\,^{\circ}C \rightarrow$ steam $100\,^{\circ}C$; $\quad$ then J $\rightarrow$ lb of oil $\rightarrow$ kg of oil $\quad \dfrac{1 \text{ kg}}{2.20 \text{ lb}}$

$\quad\quad$ **Set-up** $\quad$ Heat $= 150 \text{ kg water} \times \dfrac{1000 \text{ g}}{1 \text{ kg}} \times \dfrac{2260 \text{ J}}{1 \text{ g water}} = 3.4 \times 10^8 \text{ J (2 SFs)}$

$\quad\quad \therefore$ mass of oil $= 3.4 \times 10^8 \text{ J} \times \dfrac{1.0 \text{ lb oil}}{2.4 \times 10^7 \text{ J}} \times \dfrac{1.0 \text{ kg oil}}{2.20 \text{ lb oil}} = 6.4 \text{ kg of oil (2 SFs)}$

3.99 $\quad$ Two calculations are required:

$\quad$ (1) $\quad$ ice $0\,^{\circ}C \rightarrow$ water $0\,^{\circ}C$: $275 \text{ g ice} \times \dfrac{334 \text{ J}}{1 \text{ g ice}} \times \dfrac{1 \text{ kJ}}{1000 \text{ J}} = 91.9 \text{ kJ}$

$\quad$ (2) $\quad$ water $0\,^{\circ}C \rightarrow 24.0\,^{\circ}C$: $\Delta T = 24.0\,^{\circ}C - 0\,^{\circ}C = 24.0\,^{\circ}C$;

$\quad\quad\quad 275 \text{ g water} \times 24.0\,^{\circ}C \times \dfrac{4.184 \text{ J}}{\text{g} \,^{\circ}C} \times \dfrac{1 \text{ kJ}}{1000 \text{ J}} = 27.6 \text{ kJ}$

$\therefore$ Total heat absorbed $= 91.9 \text{ kJ} + 27.6 \text{ kJ} = 119.5 \text{ kJ}$

3.101 Given

Copper	Water
mass = 70.0 g	mass = 50.0 g
initial temperature = 54.0 °C	initial temperature = 26.0 °C
final temperature = 29.2 °C	final temperature = 29.2 °C
SH = ? J/g °C	SH = 4.184 J/g °C

Need specific heat (SH) of copper (J/g °C)

Plan heat lost by copper = −heat gained by water

For both, heat = mass $\times \Delta T \times SH$

Set-up For water:

$$\text{heat gained} = \text{mass} \times \Delta T \times SH = 50.0 \; \cancel{g} \times (29.2 \; \cancel{°C} - 26.0 \; \cancel{°C}) \times \frac{4.184 \; J}{\cancel{g} \; \cancel{°C}} = 669 \; J$$

For copper:

$$\therefore \text{heat lost by copper} = -669 \; J$$

$$SH = \frac{\text{heat lost}}{\text{mass} \times \Delta T} = \frac{-669 \; J}{70.0 \; g \times (29.2 \; °C - 54.0 \; °C)} = \frac{0.385 \; J}{g \; °C} \; (3 \; SFs)$$

3.103 a. Given heat = 11 J; mass = 4.7 g; ΔT = 4.5 °C

Need specific heat (J/g °C)

Plan $SH = \dfrac{\text{heat}}{\text{mass} \times \Delta T}$

Set-up specific heat (SH) = $\dfrac{11 \; J}{4.7 \; g \times 4.5 \; °C} = \dfrac{0.52 \; J}{g \; °C} \; (2 \; SFs)$

b. By comparing this calculated value to the specific heats given in Table 2.8, we would identify the unknown metal as titanium (SH = 0.523 J/g °C) rather than aluminum (SH = 0.897 J/g °C).

Selected Answers to Combining Ideas from Chapters 1 to 3

CI.1 **a.** There are 4 significant figures in the measurement 20.17 lb.

b. $20.17 \text{ lb} \times \dfrac{1 \text{ kg}}{2.20 \text{ lb}} = 9.17 \text{ kg (3 SFs)}$

c. $9.17 \text{ kg} \times \dfrac{1000 \text{ g}}{1 \text{ kg}} \times \dfrac{1 \text{ cm}^3}{19.3 \text{ g}} = 475 \text{ cm}^3 \text{ (3 SFs)}$

d. $T_F = 1.8(T_C) + 32 = 1.8(1064) + 32 = 1947\,°F \text{ (4 SFs)}$
$T_K = T_C + 273 = 1064 + 273 = 1337 \text{ K (4 SFs)}$

e. $\Delta T = T_{\text{final}} - T_{\text{initial}} = 1064\,°C - 500.\,°C = 564\,°C = \text{temperature change}$

$9.17 \text{ kg} \times \dfrac{1000 \text{ g}}{1 \text{ kg}} \times \dfrac{0.129 \text{ J}}{\text{g} °C} \times \dfrac{1 \text{ cal}}{4.184 \text{ J}} \times 564\,°C \times \dfrac{1 \text{ kcal}}{1000 \text{ cal}} = 159 \text{ kcal}$
to raise the temperature

$9.17 \text{ kg} \times \dfrac{1000 \text{ g}}{1 \text{ kg}} \times \dfrac{63.6 \text{ J}}{\text{g}} \times \dfrac{1 \text{ cal}}{4.184 \text{ J}} \times \dfrac{1 \text{ kcal}}{1000 \text{ cal}} = 139 \text{ kcal to melt}$

Total energy $= 159 \text{ kcal} + 139 \text{ kcal} = 298 \text{ kcal (3 SFs)}$

f. $9.17 \text{ kg} \times \dfrac{1000 \text{ g}}{1 \text{ kg}} \times \dfrac{\$45.98}{1 \text{ g}} = \$422\,000 \text{ (3 SFs)}$

CI.3 **a.** The water has its own shape in sample **B**.

b. Water sample **A** is represented by diagram **2**, which shows the particles in a random arrangement but close together.

c. Water sample **B** is represented by diagram **1**, which shows the particles fixed in a definite arrangement.

d. The state of matter indicated in diagram **1** is a <u>solid</u>; in diagram **2**, it is a <u>liquid</u>; and in diagram **3**, it is a <u>gas</u>.

e. The motion of the particles is slowest in diagram <u>**1**</u>.

f. The arrangement of particles is farthest apart in diagram <u>**3**</u>.

g. The particles fill the volume of the container in diagram <u>**3**</u>.

h. water $45\,°C \rightarrow 0\,°C$: $\Delta T = 0\,°C - 45\,°C = -45\,°C$

$\text{Heat} = 19 \text{ g} \times (-45\,°C) \times \dfrac{4.184 \text{ J}}{\text{g} °C} \times \dfrac{1 \text{ kJ}}{1000 \text{ J}} = -3.6 \text{ kJ (2 SFs)}$

$\therefore 3.6 \text{ kJ of heat is removed.}$

CI.5 **a.** $0.250 \text{ lb} \times \dfrac{454 \text{ g}}{1 \text{ lb}} \times \dfrac{1 \text{ cm}^3}{7.86 \text{ g}} = 14.4 \text{ cm}^3 \text{ (3 SFs)}$

b. $30 \text{ nails} \times \dfrac{14.4 \text{ cm}^3}{75 \text{ nails}} = 5.76 \text{ cm}^3 = 5.76 \text{ mL (3 SFs)}$

New water level $= 17.6 \text{ mL water} + 5.76 \text{ mL} = 23.4 \text{ mL (3 SFs)}$

c. $\Delta T = T_f - T_i = 125\,°C - 16\,°C = 109\,°C$

$\text{mass of iron nails } = 0.250 \text{ lb} \times \dfrac{454 \text{ g}}{1 \text{ lb}} = 113 \text{ g (3 SFs)}$

$\text{Heat } = \text{ mass} \times \Delta T \times SH$

$= 0.250 \text{ lb} \times \dfrac{454 \text{ g}}{1 \text{ lb}} \times 109\,°C \times \dfrac{0.452 \text{ J}}{\text{g} °C} = 5590 \text{ J (3 SFs)}$

d. Two calculations are needed:

(1) iron $25\,°C \rightarrow 1535\,°C$: $\Delta T = 1535\,°C - 25\,°C = 1510\,°C$

$$1\ \text{nail} \times \frac{0.250\ \text{lb-Fe}}{75\ \text{nails}} \times \frac{454\ \text{g Fe}}{1\ \text{lb Fe}} \times \frac{0.452\ \text{J}}{\text{g}\,°C} \times 1510.\,°C = 1030\ \text{J}$$

(2) solid iron $1535\,°C \rightarrow$ liquid iron $1535\,°C$:

$$1\ \text{nail} \times \frac{0.250\ \text{lb Fe}}{75\ \text{nails}} \times \frac{454\ \text{g Fe}}{1\ \text{lb Fe}} \times \frac{272\ \text{J}}{1\ \text{g Fe}} = 412\ \text{J}$$

$\therefore$ Total heat required $= 1030\ \text{J} + 412\ \text{J} = 1440\ \text{J}\ (3\ \text{SFs})$

4

Atoms

Credit: Martin Harvey /Alamy

John is preparing to plant a new crop in his fields. Although the element nitrogen in the soil is important, he will also check the soil levels of the elements phosphorus and potassium, which are also important for a good yield. Tests show that the level of phosphorus in the soil is below 15 mg/kg, which is low. Tests also show that the potassium level in the soil is in the optimal range from 150 to 200 mg/kg. Thus, John will apply a fertilizer that contains phosphorus but no potassium. What are the symbols of the elements potassium, phosphorus, and nitrogen found in fertilizers?

CHAPTER READINESS*

🖩 Key Math Skills

- Using Positive and Negative Numbers in Calculations (1.4B)
- Calculating Percentages (1.4C)
- Rounding Off (2.3)

⚛ Core Chemistry Skills

- Counting Significant Figures (2.2)
- Using Significant Figures in Calculations (2.3)

*These Key Math Skills and Core Chemistry Skills from previous chapters are listed here for your review as you proceed to the new material in this chapter.

4.1 Elements and Symbols

Learning Goal: Given the name of an element, write its correct symbol; from the symbol, write the correct name.

- Chemical symbols are one- or two-letter abbreviations for the names of the elements; only the first letter of a chemical symbol is a capital letter.
- Element names are derived from planets, mythology, and names of geographical locations and famous scientists.
- Of all the elements, only about 20 are essential for the well-being of the human body. Oxygen, carbon, hydrogen, and nitrogen make up 96% of human body mass.

♦ **Learning Exercise 4.1A**

Write the symbol for each of the following elements that are essential to health:

1. carbon _____

2. iron _____

3. sodium _____

4. phosphorus _____

5. oxygen _____

6. nitrogen _____

7. iodine _____

8. sulfur _____

9. potassium _____

10. cobalt _____

11. calcium _____

12. selenium _____

Answers   **1.** C   **2.** Fe   **3.** Na   **4.** P   **5.** O   **6.** N
7. I   **8.** S   **9.** K   **10.** Co   **11.** Ca   **12.** Se

♦ **Learning Exercise 4.1B**

Write the name of the element represented by each of the following symbols:

1. Mg _____

2. H _____

3. Ag _____

4. F _____

5. Cr _____

6. Be _____

7. Si _____

8. Br _____

9. Zn _____

10. Al _____

The element silver is used for dental fillings.
Credit: Pearson Science / Pearson Education

Answers   **1.** magnesium   **2.** hydrogen   **3.** silver   **4.** fluorine   **5.** chromium
6. beryllium   **7.** silicon   **8.** bromine   **9.** zinc   **10.** aluminum

4.2   The Periodic Table

Learning Goal: *Use the periodic table to identify the group and the period of an element; identify the element as a metal, a nonmetal, or a metalloid.*

- The periodic table is an arrangement of the elements into vertical columns and horizontal rows.
- Each vertical column is a group of elements that have similar properties.
- A horizontal row of elements is called a *period*.
- On the periodic table, the metals are located on the left of the heavy zigzag line, the nonmetals are to the right, and metalloids are found along the heavy zigzag line.
- The element hydrogen (H) located on the top left of the periodic table is a nonmetal.
- Main group, or representative, elements are found in Groups 1A (1), 2A (2), and 3A (13) to 8A (18). Transition elements are B-group elements (3–12).

Periodic Table of Elements

Representative elements

Alkali metals
Alkaline earth metals

Halogens Noble gases

Transition elements

| Metals | Metalloids | Nonmetals |

Study Note

1. The periodic table consists of horizontal rows called *periods* and vertical columns called *groups*, which are also called *families*.

2. Group 1A (1) contains the *alkali metals*, Group 2A (2) contains the *alkaline earth metals*, Group 7A (17) contains the *halogens*, and Group 8A (18) contains the *noble gases*.

Key Terms for Sections 4.1–4.2

Match each of the following key terms with the correct definition:

a. nonmetal	b. period	c. chemical symbol	d. metal
e. group number	f. halogen	g. periodic table	h. transition element

1. _____ a horizontal row of elements on the periodic table

2. _____ an element with little or no luster that is a poor conductor of heat and electricity

3. _____ a number that appears at the top of each vertical column (group) in the periodic table

4. _____ an element that is shiny, malleable, ductile, and a good conductor of heat and electricity

5. _____ an element in the center of the periodic table that has a group number of 3 through 12

6. ____ an arrangement of elements by increasing atomic number

7. ____ a one- or two-letter abbreviation that represents the name of an element

8. ____ an element in Group 7A (17)

Answers **1.** b   **2.** a   **3.** e   **4.** d
            5. h   **6.** g   **7.** c   **8.** f

♦ **Learning Exercise 4.2A**

Indicate whether the following elements are part of the same group (G), the same period (P), or neither (N):

a. Li, C, and O _____   b. Br, Cl, and F _____

c. Al, Si, and Cl _____   d. C, N, and O _____

e. Mg, Ca, and Ba _____   f. C, S, and Br _____

g. Li, Na, and K _____   h. K, Ca, and Br _____

Answers   **a.** P   **b.** G   **c.** P   **d.** P
            e. G   **f.** N   **g.** G   **h.** P

♦ **Learning Exercise 4.2B**

Complete the list of some elements important in the body, symbols, group numbers, period numbers, and whether it is a metal, nonmetal, or metalloid in the following table:

Element and Symbol	Group Number	Period Number	Type of Element
	2A (2)	3	
Carbon, C			
	5A (15)	2	
Sulfur, S			
	5A (15)	5	
	1A (1)	1	

Answers

Element and Symbol	Group Number	Period Number	Type of Element
Magnesium, Mg	2A (2)	3	metal
Carbon, C	4A (14)	2	nonmetal
Nitrogen, N	5A (15)	2	nonmetal
Sulfur, S	6A (16)	3	nonmetal
Antimony, Sb	5A (15)	5	metalloid
Hydrogen, H	1A (1)	1	nonmetal

♦ **Learning Exercise 4.2C**

Identify each of the following elements as a metal (M), a nonmetal (NM), or a metalloid (ML):

1. Cl _____   2. P _____   3. Fe _____   4. Si _____   5. Al _____

6. O _____   7. Ca _____   8. Zn _____   9. Ge _____   10. Ag _____

Answers   1. NM   2. NM   3. M   4. ML   5. M
             6. NM   7. M   8. M   9. ML   10. M

♦ **Learning Exercise 4.2D**

Match the name of each of the following chemical groups with the elements K, Cl, He, Fe, Mg, Ne, Li, Cu, and Br:

1. halogen   _____

2. noble gas   _____

3. alkali metal   _____

4. alkaline earth metal _____

5. transition element _____

Answers   1. Cl, Br   2. He, Ne   3. K, Li   4. Mg   5. Fe, Cu

4.3   The Atom

Learning Goal: Describe the electrical charge and location in an atom for a proton, a neutron, and an electron.

- An atom is the smallest particle that retains the characteristics of an element.
- Atoms are composed of three subatomic particles. Protons have a positive charge (+), electrons carry a negative charge (−), and neutrons are electrically neutral.
- The protons and neutrons, with masses of about 1 amu, are found in the tiny, dense nucleus.
- The electrons are located outside the nucleus and have masses much smaller than the mass of a neutron or proton.

Dalton's Atomic Theory

1. All matter is made up of tiny particles called atoms.

2. All atoms of a given element are similar to one another and different from atoms of other elements.

3. Atoms of two or more different elements combine to form compounds. A particular compound is always made up of the same kinds of atoms and the same number of each kind of atom.

4. A chemical reaction involves the rearrangement, separation, or combination of atoms. Atoms are neither created nor destroyed during a chemical reaction.

◆ **Learning Exercise 4.3A**

True (T) or false (F): Each of the following statements is consistent with current atomic theory:

1. All matter is composed of atoms.

2. All atoms of an element are similar.

3. Atoms can combine to form compounds.

4. Most of the mass of the atom is outside of the nucleus.

Answers   **1.** T   **2.** T   **3.** T   **4.** F

◆ **Learning Exercise 4.3B**

Match the following terms with the correct statements:

   a. proton   **b.** neutron   **c.** electron   **d.** nucleus

1. _____ is found in the nucleus of an atom

2. _____ has a 1− charge

3. _____ is found outside the nucleus

4. _____ has a mass of about 1 amu

5. _____ is the small, dense center of the atom

6. _____ is neutral

Aluminum foil consists of atoms of aluminum.
Credit: Russ Lappa / Pearson Education / Prentice Hall

Answers   **1.** a and b   **2.** c   **3.** c   **4.** a and b   **5.** d   **6.** b

4.4   Atomic Number and Mass Number

Learning Goal: Given the atomic number and the mass number of an atom, state the number of protons, neutrons, and electrons.

• The atomic number, which can be found on the periodic table, is the number of protons in a given atom of an element.

• In a neutral atom, the number of protons is equal to the number of electrons.

• The mass number is the total number of protons and neutrons in an atom.

Study Note

1. The *atomic number* is the number of protons in every atom of an element. In neutral atoms, the number of electrons equals the number of protons.
2. The *mass number* is the total number of neutrons and protons in the nucleus of an atom.
3. The number of neutrons is *mass number − atomic number.*

Example: How many protons and neutrons are in the nucleus of a strontium atom with a mass number of 89?

Solution: The atomic number of Sr is 38. Thus, an atom of Sr has 38 protons.
Mass number − atomic number = number of neutrons: 89 − 38 = 51 neutrons

---

♦ **Learning Exercise 4.4A**

Give the number of protons in each of the following neutral atoms:

⚛ **CORE CHEMISTRY SKILL**

Counting Protons and Neutrons

   a. an atom of carbon   ____

   b. an atom of the element with atomic number 15   ____

   c. an atom with a mass number of 40 and atomic number 19   ____

   d. an atom with 9 neutrons and a mass number of 19   ____

   e. a neutral atom that has 18 electrons   ____

Answers   **a.** 6   **b.** 15   **c.** 19   **d.** 10   **e.** 18

♦ **Learning Exercise 4.4B**

Determine the number of neutrons in each of the following atoms:

   a. a mass number of 42 and atomic number 20   _____

   b. a mass number of 10 and 5 protons   _____

   c. a silicon atom with a mass number of 30   _____

   d. a mass number of 9 and an atomic number of 4 _____

   e. a mass number of 22 and 10 protons   _____

   f. a zinc atom with a mass number of 66   _____

Answers   **a.** 22   **b.** 5   **c.** 16   **d.** 5   **e.** 12   **f.** 36

4.5   Isotopes and Atomic Mass

Learning Goal: Determine the number of protons, neutrons, and electrons in one or more of the isotopes of an element; calculate the atomic mass of an element using the percent abundance and mass of its naturally occurring isotopes.

- *Isotopes* are atoms of the same element that have the same number of protons but different numbers of neutrons.

- The atomic mass of an element is the weighted average mass of all the isotopes in a naturally occurring sample of that element.

Key Terms for Sections 4.3–4.5

Match each of the following key terms with the correct definition:

   a. electron   **b.** atom   **c.** atomic mass   **d.** mass number   **e.** neutron
   f. isotope   **g.** atomic number   **h.** nucleus   **i.** proton

1. ____ the total number of neutrons and protons in the nucleus of an atom

2. ____ the smallest particle of an element that retains the characteristics of the element

3. ____ a negatively charged subatomic particle having a minute mass

4. _____ a neutral subatomic particle found in the nucleus of an atom

5. _____ a number that is equal to the number of protons in an atom

6. _____ the compact, extremely dense center of an atom where the protons and neutrons are located

7. _____ a positively charged subatomic particle found in the nucleus of an atom

8. _____ the weighted average mass of all the naturally occurring isotopes of an element

9. _____ an atom that differs in mass number from another atom of the same element

Answers   **1.** d   **2.** b   **3.** a   **4.** e   **5.** g
            6. h   **7.** i   **8.** c   **9.** f

Study Note

In the atomic symbol for a particular atom, the mass number appears in the upper left corner and the atomic number in the lower left corner of the atomic symbol. $\begin{array}{l}\text{Mass number} \rightarrow \\ \text{Atomic number} \rightarrow\end{array} {}^{32}_{16}\text{S}$

This isotope is also written several other ways including sulfur-32, S-32, and ^{32}S.

♦ **Learning Exercise 4.5A**

Complete the following table for neutral atoms:

Atomic Symbol	Atomic Number	Mass Number	Number of Protons	Number of Neutrons	Number of Electrons
	12			12	
			20	22	
		55		29	
	35			45	
		35	17		
$^{120}_{50}$Sn					

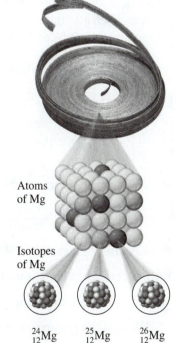

Atoms of Mg

Isotopes of Mg

$^{24}_{12}$Mg $^{25}_{12}$Mg $^{26}_{12}$Mg

Answers

Atomic Symbol	Atomic Number	Mass Number	Number of Protons	Number of Neutrons	Number of Electrons
$^{24}_{12}$Mg	12	24	12	12	12
$^{42}_{20}$Ca	20	42	20	22	20
$^{55}_{26}$Fe	26	55	26	29	26
$^{80}_{35}$Br	35	80	35	45	35
$^{35}_{17}$Cl	17	35	17	18	17
$^{120}_{50}$Sn	50	120	50	70	50

The nuclei of three naturally occurring magnesium isotopes have the same number of protons but different numbers of neutrons.
Credit: Pearson Science / Pearson Education

♦ **Learning Exercise 4.5B**

Identify the sets of atoms that are isotopes.

A. $^{20}_{10}X$ **B.** $^{20}_{11}X$ **C.** $^{21}_{11}X$ **D.** $^{19}_{10}X$ **E.** $^{19}_{9}X$

Answer   Atoms A and D are isotopes (atomic number 10); atoms B and C are isotopes (atomic number 11).

♦ **Learning Exercise 4.5C**

Essay   Copper has two naturally occurring isotopes, $^{63}_{29}Cu$ and $^{65}_{29}Cu$. If that is the case, why is the atomic mass of copper listed as 63.55 on the periodic table?

Answer   Copper in nature consists of two isotopes that have different atomic masses. The atomic mass is the weighted average of the individual masses of the two isotopes, which takes into consideration their percent abundance in the sample. The atomic mass does not represent the mass of any individual atom.

Study Note

To calculate the atomic mass of an element, multiply the mass of each isotope by its percentage abundance. Then add these values together. For example, a large sample of naturally occurring chlorine atoms consists of 75.76% of Cl-35 atoms (mass 34.97 amu) and 24.24% of Cl-37 atoms (mass 36.97 amu).

Isotope	Mass	×	Abundance (%)	=	Contribution to Atomic Mass
Cl-35	34.97	×	$\dfrac{75.76}{100}$	=	26.49 amu
Cl-37	36.97	×	$\dfrac{24.24}{100}$	=	8.962 amu
			Atomic mass of Cl	=	35.45 amu

♦ **Learning Exercise 4.5D**

Rubidium is the element with atomic number 37.

1. What is the symbol for rubidium? _____

2. What is the group number for rubidium? _____

3. What is the name of the family that includes rubidium? _____

4. Rubidium has two naturally occurring isotopes, $^{85}_{37}Rb$ and $^{87}_{37}Rb$. How many protons, neutrons, and electrons are in each isotope?

5. In naturally occurring rubidium, 72.17% is $^{85}_{37}$Rb with a mass of 84.91 amu; 27.83% is $^{87}_{37}$Rb with a mass of 86.91 amu. Calculate the atomic mass for rubidium using the weighted average mass method.

Answers

1. Rb

2. Rubidium is in Group 1A (1).

3. Rubidium is in the family called the alkali metals.

4. The isotope $^{85}_{37}$Rb has 37 protons, 48 neutrons, and 37 electrons. The isotope $^{87}_{37}$Rb has 37 protons, 50 neutrons, and 37 electrons.

5. 84.91 amu (72.17/100) + 86.91 amu (27.83/100) = 61.28 amu + 24.19 amu = 85.47 amu for the atomic mass of Rb.

4.6 Electron Energy Levels

Learning Goal: Describe the energy levels, sublevels, and orbitals for the electrons in an atom.

- Energy levels, which are indicated by the principal quantum number n, contain electrons of similar energies, and increase in order of energy ($n = 1 < 2 < 3 < 4 < 5 < 6 < 7$).
- Within each energy level, electrons with identical energy are grouped in sublevels s, p, d, f.
- An orbital is a region around the nucleus in which an electron with a specific energy is most likely to be found. Each orbital holds a maximum of two electrons.
- An s orbital is spherical, and a p orbital has two lobes along an axis. The d and f orbitals have more complex shapes.
- An s sublevel contains one s orbital; a p sublevel contains three p orbitals; a d sublevel contains five d orbitals; and an f sublevel contains seven f orbitals.

♦ Learning Exercise 4.6

State the maximum number of electrons for each of the following:

a. 3p sublevel _____ **b.** 3d sublevel _____ **c.** 2s orbital _____

d. energy level 4 _____ **e.** 1s sublevel _____ **f.** 4p orbital _____

g. 5p sublevel _____ **h.** 4f sublevel _____

Answers **a.** 6 **b.** 10 **c.** 2 **d.** 32

e. 2 **f.** 2 **g.** 6 **h.** 14

4.7 Electron Configurations

Learning Goal: Draw the orbital diagram and write the electron configuration for an element.

- The orbital diagram for an element shows the orbitals as boxes that are occupied by paired and unpaired electrons.
- Within a sublevel, electrons enter orbitals in the same energy level one at a time until all the orbitals are half-filled.
- Additional electrons enter with opposite spins until the orbitals in that sublevel are filled with two electrons each.
- The electron configuration for an element such as silicon shows the number of electrons in each sublevel: $1s^2 2s^2 2p^6 3s^2 3p^2$.

- An abbreviated electron configuration for an element such as silicon places the symbol of a noble gas in brackets to represent the filled sublevels: $[Ne]3s^23p^2$.
- The periodic table consists of *s, p, d,* and *f* sublevel blocks.
- Beginning with 1*s*, an electron configuration is obtained by writing the sublevel blocks in order going across each period on the periodic table until the element is reached.

Guide to Drawing Orbital Diagrams	
STEP 1	Draw boxes to represent the occupied orbitals.
STEP 2	Place a pair of electrons with opposite spins in each filled orbital.
STEP 3	Place the remaining electrons in the last occupied sublevel in separate orbitals.

♦ **Learning Exercise 4.7A**

Draw the orbital diagram for each of the following elements:

   a. beryllium _____   **b.** carbon   _____

   c. sodium   _____   **d.** nitrogen _____

   e. fluorine _____   **f.** magnesium _____

Answers

a. 1s [↑↓] 2s [↑↓]

b. 1s [↑↓] 2s [↑↓] 2p [↑][↑][ ]

c. 1s [↑↓] 2s [↑↓] 2p [↑↓][↑↓][↑↓] 3s [↑]

d. 1s [↑↓] 2s [↑↓] 2p [↑][↑][↑]

e. 1s [↑↓] 2s [↑↓] 2p [↑↓][↑↓][↑]

f. 1s [↑↓] 2s [↑↓] 2p [↑↓][↑↓][↑↓] 3s [↑↓]

♦ **Learning Exercise 4.7B**

Write the electron configuration ($1s^22s^22p^6$, etc.) for each of the following elements:

   a. carbon   _____   **b.** magnesium _____

   c. iron   _____   **d.** silicon _____

   e. chlorine _____   **f.** phosphorus _____

⚛ **CORE CHEMISTRY SKILL**

Writing Electron Configurations

Answers   **a.** $1s^22s^22p^2$ **b.** $1s^22s^22p^63s^2$
   c. $1s^22s^22p^63s^23p^64s^23d^6$ **d.** $1s^22s^22p^63s^23p^2$
   e. $1s^22s^22p^63s^23p^5$ **f.** $1s^22s^22p^63s^23p^3$

⚛ **CORE CHEMISTRY SKILL**

Using the Periodic Table to Write Electron Configurations

♦ **Learning Exercise 4.7C**

Write the abbreviated electron configuration for each of the elements in 4.7B:

   a. carbon _____   **b.** magnesium _____   **c.** iron   _____

   d. silicon _____   **e.** chlorine _____   **f.** phosphorus _____

Answers   **a.** $[He]2s^22p^2$ **b.** $[Ne]3s^2$ **c.** $[Ar]4s^23d^6$
   d. $[Ne]3s^23p^2$ **e.** $[Ne]3s^23p^5$ **f.** $[Ne]3s^23p^3$

♦ **Learning Exercise 4.7D**

Name the element with an electron configuration that ends with each of the following notations:

a. $3p^5$ _____   **b.** $2s^1$ _____

c. $3d^8$ _____   **d.** $4p^1$ _____

e. $5p^5$ _____   **f.** $3p^2$ _____

g. $1s^1$ _____   **h.** $6s^2$ _____

Answers   **a.** chlorine   **b.** lithium   **c.** nickel   **d.** gallium
            e. iodine   **f.** silicon   **g.** hydrogen   **h.** barium

Guide to Writing Electron Configurations Using Sublevel Blocks	
STEP 1	Locate the element on the periodic table.
STEP 2	Write the filled sublevels in order, going across each period.
STEP 3	Complete the configuration by counting the electrons in the last occupied sublevel block.

♦ **Learning Exercise 4.7E**

Use the sublevel blocks on the periodic table to write the electron configuration for each of the following elements:

a. S _____

b. As _____

c. Tc _____

d. Br _____

e. Sr _____

f. V _____

Answers   **a.** S $1s^22s^2\,2p^63s^23p^4$ **b.** As $1s^22s^2\,2p^63s^23p^64s^23d^{10}4p^3$
            c. Tc $1s^22s^2\,2p^63s^23p^64s^23d^{10}4p^65s^24d^5$ **d.** Br $1s^22s^2\,2p^63s^23p^64s^23d^{10}4p^5$
            e. Sr $1s^22s^2\,2p^63s^23p^64s^23d^{10}4p^65s^2$ **f.** V $1s^22s^2\,2p^63s^23p^64s^23d^3$

4.8   Trends in Periodic Properties

⚛ **CORE CHEMISTRY SKILL**

Learning Goal: Use the electron configurations of elements to explain the trends in periodic properties.

Identifying Trends in Periodic Properties

- The physical and chemical properties of the elements change in a periodic manner going across each period and are repeated in each successive period.

- Representative elements in a group have similar behavior.

- The group number of a representative element gives the number of valence electrons in the atoms of that group.

- A Lewis symbol is a convenient way to represent the valence electrons, which are shown as dots on the sides, top, or bottom of the symbol for an element. For beryllium, a Lewis symbol is:

Be ·

- The atomic size of representative elements generally increases going down a group and decreases going across a period.
- The ionization energy of representative elements generally decreases going down a group and increases going across a period.
- The metallic character of representative elements generally increases going down a group and decreases going across a period.

Key Terms for Sections 4.6–4.8

Match each of the following key terms with the correct definition:

a. *f* block **b.** *s* block **c.** sublevel **d.** electron configuration
e. *d* block **f.** orbital **g.** ionization energy **h.** valence electrons
i. group number **j.** Lewis symbol

1. _____ the block of 14 elements in the rows at the bottom of the periodic table

2. _____ a list of the number of electrons in each sublevel within an atom, arranged by increasing energy

3. _____ the elements in groups 1A (1) and 2A (2) in which electrons fill the *s* orbitals

4. _____ contains electrons of identical energy

5. _____ the block of 10 elements from Groups 3B (3) to 2B (12)

6. _____ the representation of an atom that shows valence electrons as dots around the symbol of the element

7. _____ a measure of how easily an element loses a valence electron

8. _____ the electrons in the highest energy level of an atom

9. _____ the number at the top of each vertical column in the periodic table

10. _____ a region around the nucleus where electrons are most likely to be found

Answers   **1.** a   **2.** d   **3.** b   **4.** c   **5.** e
6. j   **7.** g   **8.** h   **9.** i   **10.** f

♦ **Learning Exercise 4.8A**

⚛ CORE CHEMISTRY SKILL

Drawing Lewis Symbols

State the number of valence electrons, the group number of each element, and draw the Lewis symbol for each of the following:

Element	Valence Electrons	Group Number	Lewis Symbol
sulfur			
oxygen			
magnesium			
hydrogen			
fluorine			
aluminum			

Answers

Element	Valence Electrons	Group Number	Lewis Symbol
sulfur	6 e^-	Group 6A (16)	$\ddot{\underset{\cdot\cdot}{S}}\cdot$
oxygen	6 e^-	Group 6A (16)	$\cdot\ddot{\underset{\cdot\cdot}{O}}:$
magnesium	2 e^-	Group 2A (2)	$\dot{Mg}\cdot$
hydrogen	1 e^-	Group 1A (1)	H·
fluorine	7 e^-	Group 7A (17)	$\cdot\ddot{\underset{\cdot\cdot}{F}}:$
aluminum	3 e^-	Group 3A (13)	$\cdot\dot{Al}\cdot$

♦ **Learning Exercise 4.8B**

Indicate the element that has the larger atomic size.

1. _____ Mg or Ca   **2.** _____ Si or Cl

3. _____ Sr or Rb   **4.** _____ Br or Cl

5. _____ Li or Cs   **6.** _____ Li or N

7. _____ N or P   **8.** _____ As or Ca

Answers   **1.** Ca   **2.** Si   **3.** Rb   **4.** Br
             5. Cs   **6.** Li   **7.** P   **8.** Ca

♦ **Learning Exercise 4.8C**

Indicate the element in each of the following that has the lower ionization energy:

1. _____ Mg or Na   **2.** _____ P or Cl

3. _____ K or Rb   **4.** _____ Br or F

5. _____ Li or O   **6.** _____ Sb or N

7. _____ K or Br   **8.** _____ S or Na

Answers   **1.** Na   **2.** P   **3.** Rb   **4.** Br
             5. Li   **6.** Sb   **7.** K   **8.** Na

Ionization energy decreases going down a group and increases going from left to right across a period.

♦ **Learning Exercise 4.8D**

Indicate the element that has more metallic character.

1. _____ K or Na   **2.** _____ O or Se

3. _____ Ca or Br   **4.** _____ I or F

5. _____ Li or N   **6.** _____ Pb or Ba

Answers   **1.** K   **2.** Se   **3.** Ca
             4. I   **5.** Li   **6.** Ba

Metallic character increases going down a group and decreases going from left to right across a period.

Checklist for Chapter 4

You are ready to take the Practice Test for Chapter 4. Be sure that you have accomplished the following learning goals for this chapter. If not, review the section listed at the end of each goal. Then apply your new skills and understanding to the Practice Test.

_____ Write the correct symbol or name for an element. (4.1)

_____ Use the periodic table to identify the group and period of an element. (4.2)

_____ Identify an element as a metal, nonmetal, or metalloid. (4.2)

_____ State the electrical charge, mass, and location in an atom for a proton, a neutron, and an electron. (4.3)

_____ Given the atomic number and mass number of an atom, state the number of protons, neutrons, and electrons. (4.4)

_____ State the number of protons, neutrons, and electrons in an isotope of an element. (4.5)

_____ Calculate the atomic mass of an element using the abundance and mass of its naturally occurring isotopes. (4.5)

_____ Describe the energy levels, sublevels, and orbitals for the electrons in an atom. (4.6)

_____ State the maximum number of electrons in orbitals and sublevels. (4.6)

_____ Draw the orbital diagram for an element. (4.7)

_____ Write the electron configuration for an element using sublevel notation or abbreviated notation. (4.7)

_____ Predict the periodic trends in valence electrons, group numbers, atomic size, ionization energy, and metallic character going down a group or across a period. (4.8)

_____ Draw the Lewis symbol for a representative element. (4.8)

Practice Test for Chapter 4

For questions 1 through 5, write the correct symbol for each of the elements listed: (4.1)

1. potassium _____   **2.** phosphorus _____   **3.** calcium _____

4. carbon _____   **5.** sodium _____

For questions 6 through 10, write the correct element name for each of the symbols listed: (4.1)

6. Fe _____   **7.** Cu _____   **8.** Cl _____

9. Pb _____   **10.** Ag _____

11. Some important elements in the body C, N, and O are part of a (4.2)
   A. period   **B.** group   **C.** neither

12. Some important elements in the body Li, Na, and K are part of a (4.2)
   A. period   **B.** group   **C.** neither

13. What is the classification of an atom with 15 protons and 17 neutrons? (4.2)
   A. metal   **B.** nonmetal   **C.** transition element   **D.** noble gas   **E.** halogen

14. What is the group number of the element with atomic number 3? (4.2)
   A. 1A (1)   **B.** 2A (2)   **C.** 3B (3)   **D.** 3A (13)   **E.** 5A (15)

For questions 15 through 17, indicate whether the statement is True or False: (4.3)

15. _____ The electrons of an atom are located in the nucleus.

16. _____ Most of the mass of an atom is due to the protons and neutrons.

17. _____ All matter is composed of atoms.

For questions 18 through 21, consider an atom with 12 protons and 13 neutrons: (4.4)

18. This atom has an atomic number of
    A. 12   **B.** 13   **C.** 23   **D.** 24   **E.** 25

19. This atom has a mass number of
    A. 12   **B.** 13   **C.** 23   **D.** 24   **E.** 25

20. This is an atom of
    A. carbon   **B.** sodium   **C.** magnesium   **D.** aluminum   **E.** manganese

21. The number of electrons in this atom is
    A. 12   **B.** 13   **C.** 23   **D.** 24   **E.** 25

For questions 22 through 25, consider an atom of calcium with a mass number of 42: (4.4)

22. This atom of calcium has an atomic number of
    A. 20   **B.** 22   **C.** 40   **D.** 41   **E.** 42

23. The number of protons in this atom of calcium is
    A. 20   **B.** 22   **C.** 40   **D.** 41   **E.** 42

24. The number of neutrons in this atom of calcium is
    A. 20   **B.** 22   **C.** 40   **D.** 41   **E.** 42

25. The number of electrons in this atom of calcium is
    A. 20   **B.** 22   **C.** 40   **D.** 41   **E.** 42

26. A platinum atom, $^{195}_{78}$Pt, has (4.4)
    A. 78 p^+, 78 e^-, 78 n^0 **B.** 195 p^+, 195 e^-, 195 n^0
    C. 78 p^+, 78 e^-, 195 n^0 **D.** 78 p^+, 78 e^-, 117 n^0
    E. 78 p^+, 117 e^-, 117 n^0

For questions 27 and 28, use the following list of atoms: (4.5)

    $^{14}_{7}$G $^{16}_{8}$J $^{19}_{9}$M $^{16}_{7}$Q $^{18}_{8}$R

27. Which atom(s) is (are) isotopes of an atom with 8 protons and 9 neutrons?
    A. J   **B.** J, R   **C.** M, Q   **D.** M   **E.** Q

28. Which atom(s) are isotopes of an atom with 7 protons and 8 neutrons?
    A. G   **B.** J   **C.** G, Q   **D.** J, R   **E.** none

29. How many sublevels are in the $n = 3$ energy level? (4.6)
    A. 1   **B.** 2   **C.** 3   **D.** 4   **E.** 5

30. How many *d* orbitals are in each *d* sublevel? (4.6)
    A. 1   **B.** 2   **C.** 3   **D.** 4   **E.** 5

31. The electron configuration for oxygen is (4.7)
    A. $2s^2 2p^4$ **B.** $1s^2 2s^4 2p^4$ **C.** $1s^2 2s^6$ **D.** $1s^2 2s^2 2p^2 3s^2$ **E.** $1s^2 2s^2 2p^4$

32. The electron configuration for aluminum is (4.7)
    A. $1s^2 2s^2 2p^9$ **B.** $1s^2 2s^2 2p^6 3p^5$ **C.** $1s^2 2s^2 2p^6 3s^2 3p^1$ **D.** $1s^2 2s^2 2p^8 3p^1$ **E.** $1s^2 2s^2 2p^6 3p^3$

33. The number of valence electrons in gallium is (4.8)
  A. 1   **B.** 2   **C.** 3   **D.** 13   **E.** 31

34. An atom of oxygen is larger than an atom of (4.8)
  A. lithium   **B.** sulfur   **C.** fluorine   **D.** boron   **E.** argon

35. Of Li, Na, K, Rb, and Cs, the element with the most metallic character is (4.8)
  A. Li   **B.** Na   **C.** K   **D.** Rb   **E.** Cs

36. Of C, Si, Ge, Sn, and Pb, the element with the greatest ionization energy is (4.8)
  A. C   **B.** Si   **C.** Ge   **D.** Sn   **E.** Pb

37. The Lewis symbol $\cdot X \cdot$ would be correct for an element in (4.8)
  A. Group 1A (1)   **B.** Group 2A (2)   **C.** Group 4A (14)
  D. Group 6A (16)   **E.** Group 7A (17)

38. The Lewis symbol $X \cdot$ would be correct for (4.8)
  A. magnesium   **B.** chlorine   **C.** sulfur
  D. cesium   **E.** nitrogen

For questions 39 through 43, match the final notation in the electron configuration with the following elements: (4.7)

  A. As   **B.** Rb   **C.** Na   **D.** N   **E.** Xe

39. $4p^3$ _____   **40.** $5s^1$ _____   **41.** $3s^1$ _____

42. $5p^6$ _____   **43.** $2p^3$ _____

44. Which element has a larger atomic size, Mg or P? (4.8)

45. Which element has a larger atomic size, Ar or Xe? (4.8)

46. Which element has a higher ionization energy, N or F? (4.8)

47. Which element has a lower ionization energy, Br or F? (4.8)

48. Which element is more metallic, Li or K? (4.8)

49. Which element is more metallic, Mg or P? (4.8)

Answers to the Practice Test

1. K	**2.** P	**3.** Ca	**4.** C	**5.** Na
6. iron	**7.** copper	**8.** chlorine	**9.** lead	**10.** silver
11. A	**12.** B	**13.** B	**14.** A	**15.** False
16. True	**17.** True	**18.** A	**19.** E	**20.** C
21. A	**22.** A	**23.** A	**24.** B	**25.** A
26. D	**27.** B	**28.** C	**29.** C	**30.** E
31. E	**32.** C	**33.** C	**34.** C	**35.** E
36. A	**37.** B	**38.** D	**39.** A	**40.** B
41. C	**42.** E	**43.** D	**44.** Mg	**45.** Xe
46. F	**47.** Br	**48.** K	**49.** Mg	

4
Atoms

Learning Goals

- Given the name of an element, write its correct symbol; from the symbol, write the correct name.
- Use the periodic table to identify the group and the period of an element; identify the element as a metal, a nonmetal, or a metalloid.
- Describe the electrical charge and location in an atom for a proton, a neutron, and an electron.
- Given the atomic number and the mass number of an atom, state the number of protons, neutrons, and electrons.
- Determine the number of protons, neutrons, and electrons in one or more of the isotopes of an element.
- Calculate the atomic mass of an element using the percent abundance and mass of its naturally occurring isotopes.
- Describe the energy levels, sublevels, and orbitals for the electrons in an atom.
- Draw the orbital diagram and write the electron configuration for an element.
- Use the electron configurations of elements to explain the trends in periodic properties.

Chapter Outline

Chapter Opener: Farmer

4.1   Elements and Symbols

Chemistry Link to Health: Latin Names for Elements in Clinical Usage

Chemistry Link to Health: Toxicity of Mercury

4.2   The Periodic Table

Chemistry Link to Health: Elements Essential to Health

4.3   The Atom

Explore Your World: Repulsion and Attraction

4.4   Atomic Number and Mass Number

Chemistry Link to the Environment: Many Forms of Carbon

4.5   Isotopes and Atomic Mass

4.6   Electron Energy Levels

Chemistry Link to Health: Biological Reactions to UV Light

Chemistry Link to the Environment: Energy-Saving Fluorescent Bulbs

4.7   Electron Configurations

4.8   Trends in Periodic Properties

Clinical Update: Improving Crop Production

⚛ Core Chemistry Skills

- Counting Protons and Neutrons (4.4)
- Writing Atomic Symbols for Isotopes (4.5)
- Writing Electron Configurations (4.7)
- Using the Periodic Table to Write Electron Configurations (4.7)
- Identifying Trends in Periodic Properties (4.8)
- Drawing Lewis Symbols (4.8)

Selected Answers and Solutions to Text Problems

4.1   **a.** Cu is the symbol for copper.
        b. Pt is the symbol for platinum.
        c. Ca is the symbol for calcium.
        d. Mn is the symbol for manganese.
        e. Fe is the symbol for iron.
        f. Ba is the symbol for barium.
        g. Pb is the symbol for lead.
        h. Sr is the symbol for strontium.

4.3   **a.** Carbon is the element with the symbol C.
        b. Chlorine is the element with the symbol Cl.
        c. Iodine is the element with the symbol I.
        d. Selenium is the element with the symbol Se.
        e. Nitrogen is the element with the symbol N.
        f. Sulfur is the element with the symbol S.
        g. Zinc is the element with the symbol Zn.
        h. Cobalt is the element with the symbol Co.

4.5   **a.** Sodium (Na) and chlorine (Cl) are in NaCl.
        b. Calcium (Ca), sulfur (S), and oxygen (O) are in $CaSO_4$.
        c. Carbon (C), hydrogen (H), chlorine (Cl), nitrogen (N), and oxygen (O) are in $C_{15}H_{22}ClNO_2$.
        d. Lithium (Li), carbon (C), and oxygen (O) are in Li_2CO_3.

4.7   **a.** C, N, and O are in Period 2.
        b. He is the element at the top of Group 8A (18).
        c. The alkali metals are the elements in Group 1A (1).
        d. Period 2 is the horizontal row of elements that ends with neon (Ne).

4.9   **a.** C is Group 4A (14), Period 2.
        b. He is the noble gas in Period 1.
        c. Na is the alkali metal in Period 3.
        d. Ca is Group 2A (2), Period 4.
        e. Al is Group 3A (13), Period 3.

4.11 On the periodic table, *metals* are located to the left of the heavy zigzag line, *nonmetals* are elements to the right, and *metalloids* (B, Si, Ge, As, Sb, Te, Po, and At) are located along the line.
        a. Ca is a metal.
        b. S is a nonmetal.
        c. Metals are shiny.
        d. An element that is a gas at room temperature is a nonmetal.

    e. Group 8A (18) elements are nonmetals.

    f. Br is a nonmetal.

    g. B is a metalloid.

    h. Ag is a metal.

4.13 **a.** Ca, an alkaline earth metal, is needed for bones and teeth, muscle contraction, and nerve impulses.

    b. Fe, a transition element, is a component of the oxygen carrier hemoglobin.

    c. K, an alkali metal, is the most prevalent ion (K^+) in cells, and is needed for muscle contraction and nerve impulses.

    d. Cl, a halogen, is the most prevalent negative ion (Cl^-) in fluids outside cells, and is a component of stomach acid (HCl).

4.15 **a.** A macromineral is an element essential to health that is present in the human body in amounts from 5 to 1000 g.

    b. Sulfur is a component of proteins, liver, vitamin B_1, and insulin.

    c. 86 g is a typical amount of sulfur in a 60.-kg adult.

4.17 **a.** The electron has the smallest mass.

    b. The proton has a 1+ charge.

    c. The electron is found outside the nucleus.

    d. The neutron is electrically neutral.

4.19 Rutherford determined that positively charged particles called protons are located in a very small, dense region of the atom called the nucleus.

4.21 **a.** True

    b. True

    c. True

    d. False; since a neutron has no charge, it is not attracted to a proton (a proton is attracted to an electron).

4.23 In the process of brushing your hair, strands of hair become charged with like charges that repel each other.

4.25 **a.** The atomic number is the same as the number of protons in an atom.

    b. Both are needed since the number of neutrons is the (mass number) − (atomic number).

    c. The mass number is the number of particles (protons + neutrons) in the nucleus.

    d. The atomic number is the same as the number of electrons in a neutral atom.

4.27 The atomic number defines the element and is found above the symbol of the element in the periodic table.

    a. Lithium, Li, has an atomic number of 3.

    b. Fluorine, F, has an atomic number of 9.

    c. Calcium, Ca, has an atomic number of 20.

    d. Zinc, Zn, has an atomic number of 30.

    e. Neon, Ne, has an atomic number of 10.

    f. Silicon, Si, has an atomic number of 14.

    g. Iodine, I, has an atomic number of 53.

    h. Oxygen, O, has an atomic number of 8.

4.29 The atomic number gives the number of protons in the nucleus of an atom. Since atoms are neutral, the atomic number also gives the number of electrons in the neutral atom.

    a. There are 18 protons and 18 electrons in a neutral argon atom.

    b. There are 25 protons and 25 electrons in a neutral manganese atom.

    c. There are 53 protons and 53 electrons in a neutral iodine atom.

    d. There are 48 protons and 48 electrons in a neutral cadmium atom.

4.31 The atomic number is the same as the number of protons in an atom and the number of electrons in a neutral atom; the atomic number defines the element. The number of neutrons is the (mass number) − (atomic number).

Name of the Element	Symbol	Atomic Number	Mass Number	Number of Protons	Number of Neutrons	Number of Electrons
Zinc	Zn	30	66	30	$66 - 30 = 36$	30
Magnesium	Mg	12	$12 + 12 = 24$	12	12	12
Potassium	K	19	$19 + 20 = 39$	19	20	19
Sulfur	S	16	$16 + 15 = 31$	16	15	16
Iron	Fe	26	56	26	$56 - 26 = 30$	26

4.33 a. Since the atomic number of strontium is 38, every Sr atom has 38 protons. An atom of strontium (mass number 89) has 51 neutrons ($89 - 38 = 51 \, n$). Neutral atoms have the same number of protons and electrons. Therefore, 38 protons, 51 neutrons, 38 electrons.

b. Since the atomic number of chromium is 24, every Cr atom has 24 protons. An atom of chromium (mass number 52) has 28 neutrons ($52 - 24 = 28 \, n$). Neutral atoms have the same number of protons and electrons. Therefore, 24 protons, 28 neutrons, 24 electrons.

c. Since the atomic number of sulfur is 16, every S atom has 16 protons. An atom of sulfur (mass number 34) has 18 neutrons ($34 - 16 = 18 \, n$). Neutral atoms have the same number of protons and electrons. Therefore, 16 protons, 18 neutrons, 16 electrons.

d. Since the atomic number of bromine is 35, every Br atom has 35 protons. An atom of bromine (mass number 81) has 46 neutrons ($81 - 35 = 46 \, n$). Neutral atoms have the same number of protons and electrons. Therefore, 35 protons, 46 neutrons, 35 electrons.

4.35 a. Since the number of protons is 15, the atomic number is 15 and the element symbol is P. The mass number is the sum of the number of protons and the number of neutrons, $15 + 16 = 31$. The atomic symbol for this isotope is $^{31}_{15}\text{P}$.

b. Since the number of protons is 35, the atomic number is 35 and the element symbol is Br. The mass number is the sum of the number of protons and the number of neutrons, $35 + 45 = 80$. The atomic symbol for this isotope is $^{80}_{35}\text{Br}$.

c. Since the number of electrons is 50, there must be 50 protons in a neutral atom. Since the number of protons is 50, the atomic number is 50, and the element symbol is Sn. The mass number is the sum of the number of protons and the number of neutrons, $50 + 72 = 122$. The atomic symbol for this isotope is $^{122}_{50}\text{Sn}$.

d. Since the element is chlorine, the element symbol is Cl, the atomic number is 17, and the number of protons is 17. The mass number is the sum of the number of protons and the number of neutrons, $17 + 18 = 35$. The atomic symbol for this isotope is $^{35}_{17}\text{Cl}$.

e. Since the element is mercury, the element symbol is Hg, the atomic number is 80, and the number of protons is 80. The mass number is the sum of the number of protons and the number of neutrons, $80 + 122 = 202$. The atomic symbol for this isotope is $^{202}_{80}\text{Hg}$.

4.37 a. Since the element is argon, the element symbol is Ar, the atomic number is 18, and the number of protons is 18. The atomic symbols for the isotopes with mass numbers of 36, 38, and 40 are $^{36}_{18}\text{Ar}$, $^{38}_{18}\text{Ar}$, and $^{40}_{18}\text{Ar}$, respectively.

b. They all have the same atomic number (the same number of protons and electrons).

c. They have different numbers of neutrons, which gives them different mass numbers.

d. The atomic mass of argon listed on the periodic table is the weighted average atomic mass of all the naturally occurring isotopes of argon.

e. The isotope Ar-40 ($^{40}_{18}\text{Ar}$) is the most prevalent in a sample of argon because its mass is closest to the average atomic mass of argon listed on the periodic table (39.95 amu).

4.39 $^{69}_{31}$Ga $68.93 \times \dfrac{60.11}{100} = 41.43$ amu

$^{71}_{31}$Ga $70.92 \times \dfrac{39.89}{100} = 28.29$ amu

Atomic mass of Ga $= 69.72$ amu $(4\,\text{SFs})$

4.41   **a.** A $1s$ orbital is spherical.
     b. A $2p$ orbital has two lobes.
     c. A $5s$ orbital is spherical.

4.43   **a.** **1 and 2**; $1s$ and $2s$ orbitals have the same shape (spherical) and can contain a maximum of two electrons.
     b. **3**; $3s$ and $3p$ sublevels are in the same energy level ($n = 3$).
     c. **1 and 2**; $3p$ and $4p$ sublevels contain orbitals with the same two-lobed shape and can contain the same maximum number of electrons (six).
     d. **1, 2, and 3**; all of the $3p$ orbitals have two lobes, can contain a maximum of two electrons, and are in energy level $n = 3$.

4.45   **a.** There are five orbitals in the $3d$ sublevel.
     b. There is one sublevel in the $n = 1$ energy level.
     c. There is one orbital in the $6s$ sublevel.
     d. There are nine orbitals in the $n = 3$ energy level: one $3s$ orbital, three $3p$ orbitals, and five $3d$ orbitals.

4.47   **a.** Any orbital can hold a maximum of two electrons. Thus, a $2p$ orbital can have a maximum of two electrons.
     b. The $3p$ sublevel contains three p orbitals, each of which can hold a maximum of two electrons, which gives a maximum of six electrons in the $3p$ sublevel.
     c. Using $2n^2$, the calculation for the maximum number of electrons in the $n = 4$ energy level is $2(4)^2 = 2(16) = 32$ electrons.
     d. The $5d$ sublevel contains five d orbitals, each of which can hold a maximum of two electrons, which gives a maximum of 10 electrons in the $5d$ sublevel.

4.49 The electron configuration shows the number of electrons in each sublevel of an atom. The abbreviated electron configuration uses the symbol of the preceding noble gas to show completed sublevels.

4.51 Determine the number of electrons and then fill orbitals in the following order: $1s^2 2s^2 2p^6 3s^2 3p^6$
     a. Boron is atomic number 5 and so it has 5 electrons. Fill orbitals as

       $1s$ $2s$ $2p$
       [↑↓] [↑↓] [↑ | |]

     b. Aluminum is atomic number 13 and so it has 13 electrons. Fill orbitals as

       $1s$ $2s$ $2p$ $3s$ $3p$
       [↑↓] [↑↓] [↑↓|↑↓|↑↓] [↑↓] [↑ | |]

     c. Phosphorus is atomic number 15 and so it has 15 electrons. Fill orbitals as

       $1s$ $2s$ $2p$ $3s$ $3p$
       [↑↓] [↑↓] [↑↓|↑↓|↑↓] [↑↓] [↑ |↑ |↑]

     d. Argon is atomic number 18 and so it has 18 electrons. Fill orbitals as

       $1s$ $2s$ $2p$ $3s$ $3p$
       [↑↓] [↑↓] [↑↓|↑↓|↑↓] [↑↓] [↑↓|↑↓|↑↓]

4.53   **a.** B $1s^2 2s^2 2p^1$ **b.** Na $1s^2 2s^2 2p^6 3s^1$
     c. Li $1s^2 2s^1$ **d.** Mg $1s^2 2s^2 2p^6 3s^2$

4.55 **a.** C $[\text{He}]2s^22p^2$

       b. Si $[\text{Ne}]3s^23p^2$

       c. P $[\text{Ne}]3s^23p^3$

       d. F $[\text{He}]2s^22p^5$

4.57 **a.** Li is the element with one electron in the $2s$ sublevel.

       b. S is the element with two electrons in the $3s$ and four electrons in the $3p$ sublevels.

       c. Si is the element with two electrons in the $3s$ and two electrons in the $3p$ sublevels.

       d. F is the element with two electrons in the $2s$ and five electrons in the $2p$ sublevels.

4.59 **a.** Al has three electrons in the energy level $n = 3$, $3s^23p^1$.

       b. C has two $2p$ electrons, $2p^2$.

       c. Ar completes the $3p$ sublevel, $3p^6$.

       d. Be completes the $2s$ sublevel, $2s^2$.

4.61 On the periodic table, the s sublevel block is on the left, the p sublevel block is on the right, and the d sublevel block is in the center between the s and p blocks.

       a. As $1s^22s^22p^63s^23p^64s^23d^{10}4p^3$ $[\text{Ar}]4s^23d^{10}4p^3$

       b. Fe $1s^22s^22p^63s^23p^64s^23d^6$ $[\text{Ar}]4s^23d^6$

       c. In $1s^22s^22p^63s^23p^64s^23d^{10}4p^65s^24d^{10}5p^1$ $[\text{Kr}]5s^24d^{10}5p^1$

       d. I $1s^22s^22p^63s^23p^64s^23d^{10}4p^65s^24d^{10}5p^5$ $[\text{Kr}]5s^24d^{10}5p^5$

       e. Ti $1s^22s^22p^63s^23p^64s^23d^2$ $[\text{Ar}]4s^23d^2$

4.63 **a.** Ga has three electrons in energy level $n = 4$; two are in the $4s$ block, and one is in the $4p$ block.

       b. N is the third element in the $2p$ block; it has three $2p$ electrons.

       c. Xe is the final element (6 electrons) in the $5p$ block.

       d. Zr is the second element in the $4d$ block; it has two $4d$ electrons.

4.65 **a.** Zn is the tenth element in the $3d$ block; it has 10 $3d$ electrons.

       b. Na has one electron in the $3s$ block; the $2p$ block in Na is complete with six electrons.

       c. As is the third element in the $4p$ block; it has three $4p$ electrons.

       d. Rb is the first element in the $5s$ block; Rb has one $5s$ electron.

4.67 **a.** Aluminum in Group 3A (13) has three valence electrons.

       b. Any element in Group 5A (15) has five valence electrons.

       c. Barium in Group 2A (2) has two valence electrons.

       d. Each halogen in Group 7A (17) has seven valence electrons.

4.69 The number of dots is equal to the number of valence electrons, as indicated by the group number.

       a. Sulfur is in Group 6A (16); $\cdot\ddot{\underset{\cdot}{\text{S}}}\colon$

       b. Nitrogen is in Group 5A (15); $\cdot\underset{\cdot}{\overset{\cdot\cdot}{\text{N}}}\cdot$

       c. Calcium is in Group 2A (2); $\overset{\cdot}{\text{Ca}}\cdot$

       d. Sodium is in Group 1A (1); Na$\cdot$

       e. Gallium is in Group 3A (13); $\cdot\overset{\cdot}{\text{Ga}}\cdot$

4.71 The atomic size of representative elements decreases going across a period from Group 1A to 8A and increases going down a group.

       a. In Period 3, Na, which is on the left, is larger than Cl.

       b. In Group 1A (1), Rb, which is farther down the group, is larger than Na.

       c. In Period 3, Na, which is on the left, is larger than Mg.

       d. In Period 5, Rb, which is on the left, is larger than I.

4.73 **a.** The atomic size of representative elements decreases from Group 1A to 8A: Mg, Al, Si.

       b. The atomic size of representative elements increases going down a group: I, Br, Cl.

c. The atomic size of representative elements decreases from Group 1A to 8A: Sr, Sb, I.

d. The atomic size of representative elements decreases from Group 1A to 8A: Na, Si, P.

4.75 a. In Br, the valence electrons are closer to the nucleus, so Br has a higher ionization energy than I.

b. In Mg, the valence electrons are closer to the nucleus, so Mg has a higher ionization energy than Sr.

c. Attraction for the valence electrons increases going from left to right across a period, giving P a higher ionization energy than Si.

d. Attraction for the valence electrons increases going from left to right across a period, giving Xe a higher ionization energy than I.

4.77 a. Br, Cl, F; ionization energy decreases going down a group.

b. Na, Al, Cl; going across a period from left to right, ionization energy increases.

c. Cs, K, Na; ionization energy decreases going down a group.

d. Ca, As, Br; going across a period from left to right, ionization energy increases.

4.79 Ca, Ga, Ge, Br; since metallic character decreases from left to right across a period, Ca, in Group 2A (2), will be the most metallic, followed by Ga, then Ge, and finally Br, in Group 7A (17).

4.81 Sr has a <u>lower</u> ionization energy and <u>more</u> metallic character than Sb.

4.83 Going down Group 6A (16),

a. 1; the ionization energy <u>decreases</u>

b. 2; the atomic size <u>increases</u>

c. 2; the metallic character <u>increases</u>

d. 3; the number of valence electrons <u>remains the same</u>

4.85 a. False; N has a smaller atomic size than Li.

b. True

c. True

d. False; N has less metallic character than Li.

e. True

4.87 a. Group 1A (1), alkali metals

b. metal

c. 19 protons

d. The most prevalent isotope is K-39, $^{39}_{19}K$.

e. $^{39}_{19}K$ $38.964 \times \dfrac{93.26}{100}$ = 36.34 amu

$^{40}_{19}K$ $39.964 \times \dfrac{0.0117}{100}$ = 0.00468 amu

$^{41}_{19}K$ $40.962 \times \dfrac{6.73}{100}$ = 2.76 amu

Atomic mass of K = 39.10 amu (4 SFs)

4.89 a. False; all atoms of a given element are identical to one another but different from atoms of other elements.

b. True

c. True

d. False; atoms are never created or destroyed during a chemical reaction.

4.91 a. The atomic mass is the weighted average of the masses of all of the naturally occurring isotopes of the element. Isotope masses are based on the masses of all subatomic particles in the atom: protons (1), neutrons (2), and electrons (3), although almost all of that mass comes from the protons (1) and neutrons (2).

b. The number of protons (1) is the atomic number.

c. The protons (1) are positively charged.

d. The electrons (3) are negatively charged.

e. The number of neutrons (2) is the (mass number) − (atomic number).

4.93 a. $^{16}_{8}X$, $^{17}_{8}X$, and $^{18}_{8}X$ all have an atomic number of 8, so all have 8 protons.

b. $^{16}_{8}X$, $^{17}_{8}X$, and $^{18}_{8}X$ all have an atomic number of 8, so all are isotopes of oxygen.

c. $^{16}_{8}X$ and $^{16}_{9}X$ have mass numbers of 16, whereas $^{18}_{8}X$ and $^{18}_{10}X$ have mass numbers of 18.

4.95

	Atomic Symbol		
	$^{70}_{32}Ge$	$^{73}_{32}Ge$	$^{76}_{32}Ge$
Atomic Number	32	32	32
Mass Number	70	73	76
Number of Protons	32	32	32
Number of Neutrons	70 − 32 = 38	73 − 32 = 41	76 − 32 = 44
Number of Electrons	32	32	32

4.97 a. The diagram shows 4 protons and 5 neutrons in the nucleus of the element. Since the number of protons is 4, the atomic number is 4, and the element symbol is Be. The mass number is the sum of the number of protons and the number of neutrons, 4 + 5 = 9. The atomic symbol is $^{9}_{4}Be$.

b. The diagram shows 5 protons and 6 neutrons in the nucleus of the element. Since the number of protons is 5, the atomic number is 5, and the element symbol is B. The mass number is the sum of the number of protons and the number of neutrons, 5 + 6 = 11. The atomic symbol is $^{11}_{5}B$.

c. The diagram shows 6 protons and 7 neutrons in the nucleus of the element. Since the number of protons is 6, the atomic number is 6, and the element symbol is C. The mass number is the sum of the number of protons and the number of neutrons, 6 + 7 = 13. The atomic symbol is $^{13}_{6}C$.

d. The diagram shows 5 protons and 5 neutrons in the nucleus of the element. Since the number of protons is 5, the atomic number is 5, and the element symbol is B. The mass number is the sum of the number of protons and the number of neutrons, 5 + 5 = 10. The atomic symbol is $^{10}_{5}B$.

e. The diagram shows 6 protons and 6 neutrons in the nucleus of the element. Since the number of protons is 6, the atomic number is 6, and the element symbol is C. The mass number is the sum of the number of protons and the number of neutrons, 6 + 6 = 12. The atomic symbol is $^{12}_{6}C$.

Representations **B** ($^{11}_{5}B$) and **D** ($^{10}_{5}B$) are isotopes of boron; **C** ($^{13}_{6}C$) and **E** ($^{12}_{6}C$) are isotopes of carbon.

4.99 a. This orbital diagram is possible. The orbitals up to $3s^2$ are filled with electrons having opposite spins. The element represented would be magnesium.

b. Not possible. The $2p$ sublevel would fill completely before the $3s$, and only 2 electrons are allowed in an orbital (not 3 as shown in the $3s$).

4.101 Atomic size increases going down a group. Li is **D** because it would be smallest. Na is **A**, K is **C**, and Rb is **B**.

4.103 a. Na has the largest atomic size.

b. Cl is a halogen.

c. Si has the electron configuration $1s^2 2s^2 2p^6 3s^2 3p^2$.

d. Ar, a noble gas, has the highest ionization energy.

e. S is in Group 6A (16).

f. Na, in Group 1A (1), has the most metallic character.

g. Mg, in Group 2A (2), has two valence electrons.

4.105 a. Br is in Group 7A (17), Period 4.

b. Ar is in Group 8A (18), Period 3.

c. Li is in Group 1A (1), Period 2.

d. Ra is in Group 2A (2), Period 7.

4.107 On the periodic table, *metals* are located to the left of the heavy zigzag line, *nonmetals* are located to the right of the line, and *metalloids* (B, Si, Ge, As, Sb, Te, Po, and At) are located along the line.

a. Zn is a metal.

b. Co is a metal.

c. Mn is a metal.

d. I is a nonmetal.

4.109 a. False; the proton is a positively charged particle.

b. False; the neutron has about the same mass as a proton.

c. True

d. False; the nucleus is the tiny, dense central core of an atom.

e. True

4.111 a. Since the atomic number of cadmium is 48, every Cd atom has 48 protons. An atom of cadmium (mass number 114) has 66 neutrons ($114 - 48 = 66\,n$). Neutral atoms have the same number of protons and electrons. Therefore, 48 protons, 66 neutrons, 48 electrons.

b. Since the atomic number of technetium is 43, every Tc atom has 43 protons. An atom of technetium (mass number 98) has 55 neutrons ($98 - 43 = 55\,n$). Neutral atoms have the same number of protons and electrons. Therefore, 43 protons, 55 neutrons, 43 electrons.

c. Since the atomic number of gold is 79, every Au atom has 79 protons. An atom of gold (mass number 199) has 120 neutrons ($199 - 79 = 120\,n$). Neutral atoms have the same number of protons and electrons. Therefore, 79 protons, 120 neutrons, 79 electrons.

d. Since the atomic number of radon is 86, every Rn atom has 86 protons. An atom of radon (mass number 222) has 136 neutrons ($222 - 86 = 136\,n$). Neutral atoms have the same number of protons and electrons. Therefore, 86 protons, 136 neutrons, 86 electrons.

e. Since the atomic number of xenon is 54, every Xe atom has 54 protons. An atom of xenon (mass number 136) has 82 neutrons ($136 - 54 = 82\,n$). Neutral atoms have the same number of protons and electrons. Therefore, 54 protons, 82 neutrons, 54 electrons.

4.113

Name	Atomic Symbol	Number of Protons	Number of Neutrons	Number of Electrons
Selenium	$^{80}_{34}\text{Se}$	34	$80 - 34 = 46$	34
Nickel	$^{28+34}_{28}\text{Ni}$ or $^{62}_{28}\text{Ni}$	28	34	28
Magnesium	$^{12+14}_{12}\text{Mg}$ or $^{26}_{12}\text{Mg}$	12	14	12
Radium	$^{228}_{88}\text{Ra}$	88	$228 - 88 = 140$	88

4.115 a. The 3*p* sublevel starts to fill after completion of the 3*s* sublevel.

b. The 5*s* sublevel starts to fill after completion of the 4*p* sublevel.

c. The 4*p* sublevel starts to fill after completion of the 3*d* sublevel.

d. The 4*s* sublevel starts to fill after completion of the 3*p* sublevel.

4.117 a. Iron is the sixth element in the 3*d* block; iron has six 3*d* electrons.

b. Barium has a completely filled 5*p* sublevel, which is six 5*p* electrons.

c. Iodine has a completely filled 4*d* sublevel, which is 10 4*d* electrons.

d. Radium has a filled 7*s* sublevel, which is two 7*s* electrons.

4.119 a. Phosphorus in Group 5A (15) has an electron configuration that ends with $3s^23p^3$.

   b. Lithium is the alkali metal that is highest in Group 1A (1) and has the smallest atomic size (H in Group 1A (1) is a nonmetal).

   c. Cadmium in Period 5 has a complete $4d$ sublevel with 10 electrons.

   d. Nitrogen at the top of Group 5A (15) has the highest ionization energy in that group.

   e. Sodium, the first element in Period 3, has the largest atomic size of that period.

4.121 a. Na on the far left of the heavy zigzag line on the periodic table is a metal.

   b. P is in Group 5A (15).

   c. F at the top of Group 7A (17) and to the far right in Period 2 has the highest ionization energy.

   d. Na has the lowest ionization energy and loses an electron most easily.

   e. Cl is found in Period 3 in Group 7A (17).

4.123 a. Since the element is lead (Pb), the atomic number is 82, and the number of protons is 82. In a neutral atom, the number of electrons is equal to the number of protons, so there will be 82 electrons. The number of neutrons is the (mass number) − (atomic number) = 208 − 82 = 126 n. Therefore, 82 protons, 126 neutrons, 82 electrons.

   b. Since the element is lead (Pb), the atomic number is 82, and the number of protons is 82. The mass number is the sum of the number of protons and the number of neutrons, 82 + 132 = 214. The atomic symbol for this isotope is $^{214}_{82}\text{Pb}$.

   c. Since the mass number is 214 (as in part **b**) and the number of neutrons is 131, the number of protons is the (mass number) − (number of neutrons) = 214 − 131 = 83 p. Since there are 83 protons, the atomic number is 83, and the element symbol is Bi (bismuth). The atomic symbol for this isotope is $^{214}_{83}\text{Bi}$.

4.125 a. Atomic size increases going down a group, which gives O the smallest atomic size in Group 6A (16).

   b. Atomic size decreases going from left to right across a period, which gives Ar the smallest atomic size in Period 3.

   c. Ionization energy decreases going down a group, which gives C the highest ionization energy in Group 4A (14).

   d. Ionization energy increases going from left to right across a period, which gives Na the lowest ionization energy in Period 3.

   e. Metallic character increases going down a group, which gives Ra the most metallic character in Group 2A (2).

4.127 $^{28}_{14}\text{Si}$ $27.977 \times \dfrac{92.23}{100} = 25.80 \text{ amu}$

       $^{29}_{14}\text{Si}$ $28.976 \times \dfrac{4.68}{100} = 1.36 \text{ amu}$

       $^{30}_{14}\text{Si}$ $29.974 \times \dfrac{3.09}{100} = 0.926 \text{ amu}$

       Atomic mass of Si = 28.09 amu (4 SFs)

4.129 a. X is a metal; Y and Z are nonmetals.

   b. X has the largest atomic size.

   c. Because Y and Z have six valence electrons (ns^2np^4) and are in Group 6A (16), they will have similar properties.

   d. Y has the highest ionization energy.

   e. Y has the smallest atomic size.

Nuclear Chemistry

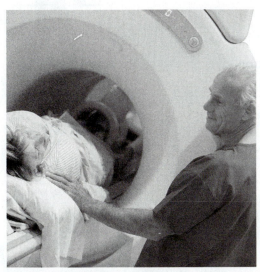

During a nuclear stress test, Simone walks on a treadmill until she reaches the maximum level. Then she is given an injection of Tl-201 and placed under a scanner that will take images of her heart muscle under stress. The comparison of her scans at rest and under stress shows that she has normal blood flow to her heart muscle. If the half-life of Tl-201 is 3.0 days, how many days will pass for the activity to decrease to one-fourth the activity of the dose she received?

Credit: Konstantin Sutyagin / Shutterstock

CHAPTER READINESS*

 Key Math Skills

- Using Positive and Negative Numbers in Calculations (1.4B)
- Solving Equations (1.4D)
- Interpreting a Graph (1.4E)

Core Chemistry Skills

- Using Conversion Factors (2.6)
- Counting Protons and Neutrons (4.4)
- Writing Atomic Symbols for Isotopes (4.5)

*These Key Math Skills and Core Chemistry Skills from previous chapters are listed here for your review as you proceed to the new material in this chapter.

5.1   Natural Radioactivity

Learning Goal: Describe alpha, beta, positron, and gamma radiation.

- Radioactive isotopes have unstable nuclei that break down (decay), spontaneously emitting alpha (α), beta (β), positron (β^+), or gamma (γ) radiation.
- An alpha particle is the same as a helium nucleus; it contains 2 protons and 2 neutrons.
- A beta particle is a high-energy electron, and a positron is a high-energy positive particle. A gamma ray is very high-energy radiation.
- Because radiation can damage cells in the body, proper protection must be used: shielding, time limitation, and distance.

Study Note

It is important to learn the symbols for the radiation particles in order to describe the different types of radiation:

^1_1H or p	^1_0n or n	$^{\ 0}_{-1}e$ or β	^4_2He or α	$^{\ 0}_{+1}e$ or β^+	$^0_0\gamma$ or γ
proton	neutron	beta particle	alpha particle	positron	gamma ray

---

♦ **Learning Exercise 5.1A**

Match the description in column B with the terms in column A.

A	B
1. ___ $^{18}_{8}O$	**a.** symbol for a beta particle
2. ___ γ	**b.** symbol for an alpha particle
3. ___ β^+	**c.** an atom that emits radiation
4. ___ radioisotope	**d.** symbol for a positron
5. ___ $^{4}_{2}He$	**e.** symbol for an isotope of oxygen
6. ___ β	**f.** symbol for gamma radiation

Answers　　　**1.** e　　**2.** f　　**3.** d　　**4.** c　　**5.** b　　**6.** a

Different types of radiation penetrate the body to different depths.

Credit: 4x6 / Getty Images

♦ **Learning Exercise 5.1B**

Essay　Discuss some things you can do to minimize the amount of radiation received if you work with a radioactive substance. Describe how each method helps to limit the amount of radiation you would receive.

Answer

Three ways to minimize exposure to radiation are: (1) use shielding, (2) keep time short in the radioactive area, and (3) keep as much distance as possible from the radioactive materials. Shielding such as clothing and gloves stop alpha and beta particles from reaching your skin, whereas lead or concrete will absorb gamma rays. Limiting the time spent near radioactive samples reduces exposure time. Increasing the distance from a radioactive source reduces the intensity of radiation. Wearing a film badge will monitor the amount of radiation you receive.

♦ **Learning Exercise 5.1C**

What type(s) of radiation (alpha, beta, and/or gamma) would each of the following shielding materials protect you from?

　　a. heavy clothing _____　　　**b.** skin _____

　　c. paper _____　　　**d.** concrete _____

　　e. lead wall _____

Answers　　　**a.** alpha, beta　　　　**b.** alpha　　　　**c.** alpha
　　　　　　　　d. alpha, beta, gamma　　**e.** alpha, beta, gamma

　　　　　Copyright © 2015 Pearson Education, Inc.

5.2 Nuclear Reactions

Learning Goal: Write a balanced nuclear equation showing mass numbers and atomic numbers for radioactive decay.

- A balanced nuclear equation represents the changes in the nuclei of radioisotopes.
- In all nuclear equations, the sum of the mass numbers for the reactants and the products is equal and the sum of the atomic numbers for the reactants and the products is equal.
- The new isotopes and the type of radiation emitted can be determined from the symbols that show the mass numbers and atomic numbers of the isotopes in the nuclear reaction.

$$\text{Radioisotope} \longrightarrow \text{new nucleus} + \text{radiation}$$

Total of the mass numbers is equal on both sides of the equation.

$$^{11}_{6}\text{C} \longrightarrow {}^{7}_{4}\text{Be} + {}^{4}_{2}\text{He}$$

Total of the atomic numbers is equal on both sides of the equation.

- A new radioactive isotope is produced when a nonradioactive isotope is bombarded by a small particle such as a proton, an alpha particle, a beta particle, or a neutron.

$^{10}_{5}\text{B}$	$+$	$^{4}_{2}\text{He}$	$\longrightarrow$	$^{13}_{7}\text{N}$	$+$	$^{1}_{0}n$
Stable nucleus		*Bombarding particle* (α)		*New nucleus*		*Neutron emitted*

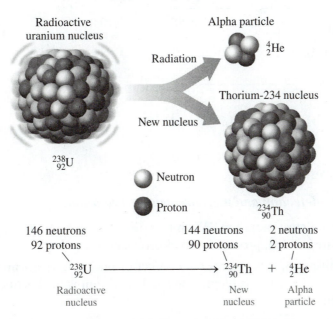

In the nuclear equation for alpha decay, the mass number of the new nucleus decreases by 4, and its atomic number decreases by 2.

Guide to Completing a Nuclear Equation	
STEP 1	Write the incomplete nuclear equation.
STEP 2	Determine the missing mass number.
STEP 3	Determine the missing atomic number.
STEP 4	Determine the symbol of the new nucleus.
STEP 5	Complete the nuclear equation.

♦ **Learning Exercise 5.2A**

⚛ CORE CHEMISTRY SKILL

Writing Nuclear Equations

Write a nuclear symbol that completes each of the following nuclear equations:

a. $^{66}_{29}Cu \longrightarrow {}^{66}_{30}Zn + ?$ _____

b. $^{127}_{53}I \longrightarrow ? + {}^{1}_{0}n$ _____

c. $^{238}_{92}U \longrightarrow ? + {}^{4}_{2}He$ _____

d. $^{24}_{11}Na \longrightarrow ? + {}^{0}_{-1}e$ _____

e. $? \longrightarrow {}^{30}_{14}Si + {}^{0}_{-1}e$ _____

Answers   **a.** $^{0}_{-1}e$ **b.** $^{126}_{53}I$ **c.** $^{234}_{90}Th$ **d.** $^{24}_{12}Mg$ **e.** $^{30}_{13}Al$

♦ **Learning Exercise 5.2B**

Complete each of the following equations for bombardment reactions:

a. $? + {}^{40}_{20}Ca \longrightarrow {}^{40}_{19}K + {}^{1}_{1}H$ _____

b. $^{1}_{0}n + {}^{27}_{13}Al \longrightarrow {}^{24}_{11}Na + ?$ _____

c. $^{1}_{0}n + {}^{10}_{5}B \longrightarrow ? + {}^{4}_{2}He$ _____

d. $? + {}^{23}_{11}Na \longrightarrow {}^{23}_{12}Mg + {}^{1}_{0}n$ _____

e. $^{1}_{1}H + {}^{197}_{79}Au \longrightarrow ? + {}^{1}_{0}n$ _____

Answers   **a.** $^{1}_{0}n$ **b.** $^{4}_{2}He$ **c.** $^{7}_{3}Li$ **d.** $^{1}_{1}H$ **e.** $^{197}_{80}Hg$

5.3   Radiation Measurement

Learning Goal: Describe the detection and measurement of radiation.

- A Geiger counter is used to detect radiation. When radiation passes through the gas in the counter tube, some atoms of gas are ionized, producing an electrical current.
- The activity of a radioactive sample measures the number of nuclear transformations per second. The curie (Ci) is equal to 3.7×10^{10} disintegrations/s. The SI unit is the becquerel (Bq), which is equal to 1 disintegration/s.
- The radiation dose absorbed by a gram of body tissue is measured in the unit rad (radiation absorbed dose) or the SI unit gray (Gy), which is equal to 100 rad.
- The biological damage to the body caused by different types of radiation is measured in the unit rem (radiation equivalent) or the SI unit sievert (Sv), which is equal to 100 rem.

♦ **Learning Exercise 5.3A**

Match each type of measurement unit with the radiation process measured.

a. curie   **b.** becquerel   **c.** rad   **d.** gray   **e.** rem

1. _____ an activity of 1 disintegration/s

2. _____ the amount of radiation absorbed by 1 g of material

3. _____ an activity of 3.7×10^{10} disintegrations/s

4. _____ a unit measuring the biological damage caused by different kinds of radiation

5. _____ a unit that measures the absorbed dose of radiation, which is equal to 100 rad

Answers   **1.** b   **2.** c   **3.** a   **4.** e   **5.** d

♦ **Learning Exercise 5.3B**

a. A sample of Ir-192 used in brachytherapy to treat breast and prostate cancers has an activity of 35 μCi. What is its activity in becquerels?

b. If an absorbed dose is 15 mrem, what is the absorbed dose in sieverts?

Answers   **a.** 1.3×10^6 Bq   **b.** 1.5×10^{-4} Sv

5.4   Half-Life of a Radioisotope

Learning Goal: Given the half-life of a radioisotope, calculate the amount of radioisotope remaining after one or more half-lives.

- The half-life of a radioactive sample is the time required for one-half of the sample to decay (emit radiation).

- Most radioisotopes used in medicine, such as Tc-99m and I-131, have short half-lives. By comparison, many naturally occurring radioisotopes, such as C-14, Ra-226, and U-238, have long half-lives. For example, potassium-42 has a half-life of 12 h, whereas potassium-40 takes 1.3×10^9 yr for one-half of the radioactive sample to decay.

Guide to Using Half-Lives	
STEP 1	State the given and needed quantities.
STEP 2	Write a plan to calculate the unknown quantity.
STEP 3	Write the half-life equality and conversion factors.
STEP 4	Set up the problem to calculate the needed quantity.

Example: Chromium-51, which is used to measure blood volume, has a half-life of 28 days. How many micrograms of a 16-μg sample of chromium-51 will remain active after 84 days?

Solution:

Step 1: State the given and needed quantities.

	Given	Need
Analyze the Problem	16 μg of Cr-51, 84 days elapsed, half-life = 28 days	micrograms of Cr-51 remaining

Step 2: Write a plan to calculate the unknown quantity.

Plan 84 days $\xrightarrow{\text{half-life}}$ Number of half-lives

16 μg of Cr-51 $\xrightarrow{\text{Number of half-lives}}$ μg of Cr-51 remaining

Step 3: Write the half-life equality and conversion factors.

1 half-life of Cr-51 = 28 days

$$\frac{28 \text{ days}}{1 \text{ half-life}} \quad \text{and} \quad \frac{1 \text{ half-life}}{28 \text{ days}}$$

Step 4: Set up the problem to calculate the needed quantity.

$$\text{Number of half-lives} = 84 \text{ days} \times \frac{1 \text{ half-life}}{28 \text{ days}} = 3 \text{ half-lives}$$

Now, we can calculate the quantity of Cr-51 that remains active.

$$16 \text{ μg} \xrightarrow{\text{1 half-life}} 8.0 \text{ μg} \xrightarrow{\text{2 half-lives}} 4.0 \text{ μg} \xrightarrow{\text{3 half-lives}} 2.0 \text{ μg}$$

♦ **Learning Exercise 5.4**

1. Suppose you have an 80.-mg sample of iodine-125, which is used to treat prostate cancer. If iodine-125 has a half-life of 60. days, how many milligrams are radioactive

   a. after one half-life?

   b. after two half-lives?

   c. after 240 days?

⚛ **CORE CHEMISTRY SKILL**

Using Half-Lives

2. $^{99m}_{43}\text{Tc}$, which is used to image the heart, brain, and lungs, has a half-life of 6.0 h. If a technician picked up a 16-mg sample at 8 A.M., how many milligrams of the radioactive sample will remain active at 8 P.M. that same day?

3. Phosphorus-32, which is used to treat leukemia, has a half-life of 14.3 days. How many micrograms of a 240-μg sample will be radioactive after 71.5 days?

4. Iodine-131, which is used for the treatment of thyroid cancer, has a half-life of 8.0 days. How many days will it take for 80. mg of I-131 to decay to 5.0 mg?

5. An archaeologist finds some pieces of a wooden boat at an ancient site. When a sample of the wood is analyzed for C-14, one-eighth of the original amount of C-14 remains. If the half-life of carbon-14 is 5730 yr, how many years ago was the boat made?

Answers　　**1. a.** 40. mg　**b.** 20. mg　**c.** 5.0 mg　**2.** 4.0 mg
　　　　　　　3. 7.5 μg　　**4.** 32 days　**5.** 17 200 yr

5.5　Medical Applications Using Radioactivity

Learning Goal: Describe the use of radioisotopes in medicine.

- Nuclear medicine uses radioactive isotopes that go to specific sites in the body.
- For diagnostic work, radioisotopes are used that emit gamma rays and produce nonradioactive products.
- By detecting the radiation emitted by medical radioisotopes, evaluations can be made about the location and extent of an injury, disease, tumor, blood flow, or level of function of a particular organ.

♦ **Learning Exercise 5.5**

Write the nuclear symbol for each of the following radioactive isotopes:

　a. _____ iodine-131, used to study thyroid gland activity

　b. _____ phosphorus-32, used to locate and treat brain tumors

　c. _____ sodium-24, used to determine blood flow and to locate a blood clot or embolism

　d. _____ nitrogen-13, used in positron emission tomography

Answers　　**a.** $^{131}_{53}\text{I}$　　**b.** $^{32}_{15}\text{P}$　　**c.** $^{24}_{11}\text{Na}$　　**d.** $^{13}_{7}\text{N}$

5.6 Nuclear Fission and Fusion

Learning Goal: Describe the processes of nuclear fission and fusion.

- In fission, a large nucleus breaks apart into smaller nuclei, releasing one or more types of radiation and a great amount of energy.
- A chain reaction is a fission reaction that will continue once initiated.
- In fusion, small nuclei combine to form a larger nucleus, which releases great amounts of energy.
- Nuclear fission is currently used to produce electrical power while nuclear fusion applications are still in the experimental stage.

Key Terms for Sections 5.1–5.6

Match each of the following key terms with the correct definition:

    a. radiation   **b.** half-life   **c.** curie   **d.** nuclear fission
    e. alpha particle   **f.** positron   **g.** rem

1. _____ a particle identical to a helium nucleus produced in a radioactive nucleus

2. _____ the time required for one-half of a radioactive sample to undergo radioactive decay

3. _____ a unit of radiation measurement equal to 3.7×10^{10} disintegrations per second

4. _____ a process in which large nuclei split into smaller nuclei with the release of energy

5. _____ energy or particles released by radioactive atoms

6. _____ a measure of biological damage caused by radiation

7. _____ produced when a proton is transformed into a neutron

Answers   **1.** e   **2.** b   **3.** c   **4.** d   **5.** a   **6.** g   **7.** f

♦ Learning Exercise 5.6A

Essay   Discuss the nuclear processes of fission and fusion for the production of energy.

Answer

Nuclear fission is a splitting of the atom into two or more nuclei accompanied by the release of large amounts of energy and radiation. In the process of *nuclear fusion*, two or more nuclei combine to form a heavier nucleus and release a large amount of energy. However, fusion requires a considerable amount of energy to initiate the process. Because the extremely high temperatures are difficult to maintain, fusion technology is still in the experimental stage.

♦ Learning Exercise 5.6B

Balance each of the following nuclear equations by writing the nuclear symbol for the missing particle and state if each is a fission or fusion reaction:

a. $^{235}_{92}\text{U} + ^{1}_{0}n \longrightarrow ^{143}_{54}\text{Xe} + ? + 3^{1}_{0}n$ _____

b. $^{2}_{1}\text{H} + ^{2}_{1}\text{H} \longrightarrow ? + ^{1}_{0}n$ _____

c. $^3_1H + ? \longrightarrow {}^4_2He + {}^1_0n$ _____

d. $^{235}_{92}U + {}^1_0n \longrightarrow {}^{91}_{36}Kr + ? + 3{}^1_0n$ _____

Answers   **a.** $^{90}_{38}Sr$, fission   **b.** ^3_2He, fusion   **c.** ^2_1H, fusion   **d.** $^{142}_{56}Ba$, fission

Checklist for Chapter 5

You are ready to take the Practice Test for Chapter 5. Be sure you have accomplished the following learning goals for this chapter. If not, review the section listed at the end of the goal. Then apply your new skills and understanding to the Practice Test.

After studying Chapter 5, I can successfully:

_____ Describe alpha, beta, and gamma radiation. (5.1)

_____ Write a nuclear equation showing mass numbers and atomic numbers for radioactive decay. (5.2)

_____ Write a nuclear equation for the formation of a radioactive isotope. (5.2)

_____ Describe the detection and measurement of radiation. (5.3)

_____ Calculate the amount of radioisotope remaining after one or more half-lives. (5.4)

_____ Calculate the amount of time for a specific amount of a radioisotope to decay given its half-life. (5.4)

_____ Describe the uses of radioisotopes in medicine. (5.5)

_____ Describe the processes of nuclear fission and fusion. (5.6)

Practice Test for Chapter 5

1. The correctly written symbol for an isotope of sulfur is (5.1)
   A. $^{30}_{16}Su$ **B.** $^{14}_{30}Si$ **C.** $^{30}_{16}S$ **D.** $^{30}_{16}Si$ **E.** $^{16}_{30}S$

2. Alpha particles are composed of (5.1)
   A. protons   **B.** neutrons   **C.** electrons
   D. protons and electrons   **E.** protons and neutrons

3. Gamma radiation is a type of radiation that (5.1)
   A. originates in the electron shells
   B. is most dangerous
   C. is least dangerous
   D. is the heaviest
   E. travels the shortest distance

4. The charge on an alpha particle is (5.1)
   A. -1 **B.** $+1$ **C.** -2 **D.** $+2$ **E.** $+4$

5. Beta particles are (5.1)
   A. protons   **B.** neutrons   **C.** electrons
   D. protons and electrons   **E.** protons and neutrons

For questions 6 through 10, select from the following: (5.1)

A. $_{-1}^{0}X$ **B.** $_{2}^{4}X$ **C.** $_{1}^{1}X$ **D.** $_{0}^{1}X$ **E.** $_{0}^{0}X$

6. an alpha particle

7. a beta particle

8. a gamma ray

9. a proton

10. a neutron

11. Shielding from gamma rays is provided by (5.1)
    A. skin   **B.** paper   **C.** clothing   **D.** lead   **E.** air

12. The skin will provide shielding from (5.1)
    A. alpha particles   **B.** beta particles   **C.** gamma rays
    D. ultraviolet rays   **E.** X-rays

13. The radioisotope iodine-131 is used as a radioactive tracer for studying thyroid activity. The symbol for iodine-131 is (5.5)
    A. I   **B.** $_{131}I$ **C.** $_{53}^{131}I$ **D.** $_{131}^{53}I$ **E.** $_{53}^{78}I$

14. When an atom emits an alpha particle, its mass number will (5.2)
    A. increase by 1   **B.** increase by 2   **C.** increase by 4
    D. decrease by 4   **E.** not change

15. When a nucleus emits a positron, the atomic number of the new nucleus (5.2)
    A. increases by 1   **B.** increases by 2   **C.** decreases by 1
    D. decreases by 2   **E.** does not change

16. When a nucleus emits a gamma ray, the atomic number of the new nucleus (5.2)
    A. increases by 1   **B.** increases by 2   **C.** decreases by 1
    D. decreases by 2   **E.** does not change

For questions 17 through 20, select the particle that completes each of the following equations: (5.2)

A. neutron   **B.** alpha particle   **C.** beta particle   **D.** gamma ray

17. $_{50}^{126}Sn \longrightarrow _{51}^{126}Sb + ?$

18. $_{30}^{69}Zn \longrightarrow _{31}^{69}Ga + ?$

19. $_{43}^{99m}Tc \longrightarrow _{43}^{99}Tc + ?$

20. $_{62}^{149}Sm \longrightarrow _{60}^{145}Nd + ?$

21. What symbol completes the following reaction? (5.2)
    $_{0}^{1}n + _{7}^{14}N \longrightarrow ? + _{1}^{1}H$
    A. $_{8}^{15}O$ **B.** $_{6}^{15}C$ **C.** $_{8}^{14}O$ **D.** $_{6}^{14}C$ **E.** $_{7}^{15}N$

22. To complete this nuclear equation, you need to write (5.2)
    $? + _{26}^{54}Fe \longrightarrow _{28}^{57}Ni + _{0}^{1}n$
    A. an alpha particle   **B.** a beta particle   **C.** gamma
    D. neutron   **E.** proton

23. The name of the unit used to measure the number of disintegrations per second is (5.3)
    A. curie   **B.** rad   **C.** rem   **D.** gray   **E.** sievert

24. The rem and the sievert are units used to measure (5.3)
   A. activity of a radioactive sample
   B. biological damage of different types of radiation
   C. radiation absorbed
   D. background radiation
   E. half-life of a radioactive sample

25. Radiation can cause (5.3)
   A. nausea   **B.** a lower white cell count   **C.** fatigue
   D. hair loss   **E.** all of these

26. Radioisotopes used in medical diagnosis (5.5)
   A. have short half-lives   **B.** emit only gamma rays   **C.** locate in specific organs
   D. produce nonradioactive nuclei   **E.** all of these

27. The time required for a radioisotope to decay is measured by its (5.4)
   A. half-life   **B.** protons   **C.** activity   **D.** fusion   **E.** radioisotope

28. Oxygen-15, used in imaging brain function and blood flow, has a half-life of 2 min. How many half-lives have occurred in the 10 min it takes to prepare the sample? (5.4)
   A. 2   **B.** 3   **C.** 4   **D.** 5   **E.** 6

29. Iodine-131, used to treat Graves' disease as well as thyroid and prostate cancers, has a half-life of 8.0 days. How many days will it take for a 160-mg sample to decay to 10 mg? (5.4)
   A. 8.0 days   **B.** 16 days   **C.** 32 days   **D.** 40. days   **E.** 48 days

30. Phosphorus-32, used to treat leukemia and pancreatic cancer, has a half-life of 14.3 days. After 28.6 days, how many milligrams of a 120-mg sample will still be radioactive? (5.4)
   A. 240 mg   **B.** 120 mg   **C.** 60. mg   **D.** 30. mg   **E.** 15 mg

31. The "splitting" of a large nucleus to form smaller particles accompanied by a release of energy is called (5.6)
   A. radioisotope **B.** nuclear fission   **C.** nuclear fusion   **D.** bombardment   **E.** half-life

32. The process of combining small nuclei to form larger nuclei is (5.6)
   A. radioisotope **B.** fission   **C.** fusion   **D.** bombardment   **E.** half-life

33. A fusion reaction (5.6)
   A. occurs in the Sun
   B. forms larger nuclei from smaller nuclei
   C. requires extremely high temperatures
   D. releases a large amount of energy
   E. all of these

Answers to the Practice Test

1. C	**2.** E	**3.** B	**4.** D	**5.** C
6. B	**7.** A	**8.** E	**9.** C	**10.** D
11. D	**12.** A	**13.** C	**14.** D	**15.** C
16. E	**17.** C	**18.** C	**19.** D	**20.** B
21. D	**22.** A	**23.** A	**24.** B	**25.** E
26. E	**27.** A	**28.** D	**29.** C	**30.** D
31. B	**32.** C	**33.** E		

5

Nuclear Chemistry

Learning Goals

- Describe alpha, beta, positron, and gamma radiation.
- Write a balanced nuclear equation showing mass numbers and atomic numbers for radioactive decay.
- Describe the detection and measurement of radiation.
- Given the half-life of a radioisotope, calculate the amount of radioisotope remaining after one or more half-lives.
- Describe the use of radioisotopes in medicine.
- Describe the processes of nuclear fission and fusion.

Chapter Outline

Chapter Opener: Nuclear Medicine Technologist

5.1   Natural Radioactivity

5.2   Nuclear Reactions

  Chemistry Link to Health: Radon in Our Homes

5.3   Radiation Measurement

  Chemistry Link to Health: Radiation and Food

5.4   Half-Life of a Radioisotope

  Chemistry Link to the Environment: Dating Ancient Objects

5.5   Medical Applications Using Radioactivity

  Chemistry Link to Health: Brachytherapy

5.6   Nuclear Fission and Fusion

  Chemistry Link to the Environment: Nuclear Power Plants

  Clinical Update: Cardiac Imaging Using a Radioisotope

⚛ Core Chemistry Skills

- Writing Nuclear Equations (5.2)
- Using Half-Lives (5.4)

Selected Answers and Solutions to Text Problems

5.1   **a.** ^4_2He is the symbol for an alpha particle.
  b. $^0_{+1}e$ is the symbol for a positron.
  c. $^0_0\gamma$ is the symbol for gamma radiation.

5.3   **a.** Since the element is potassium, the element symbol is K and the atomic number is 19. The potassium isotopes with mass number 39, 40, and 41 will have the atomic symbol $^{39}_{19}\text{K}$, $^{40}_{19}\text{K}$, and $^{41}_{19}\text{K}$, respectively.

    b. Each isotope has 19 protons and 19 electrons, but they differ in the number of neutrons present. Potassium-39 has $39 - 19 = 20$ neutrons, potassium-40 has $40 - 19 = 21$ neutrons, and potassium-41 has $41 - 19 = 22$ neutrons.

5.5 **a.** beta particle (β, $_{-1}^{0}e$)
    b. alpha particle (α, $_{2}^{4}He$)
    c. neutron (n, $_{0}^{1}n$)
    d. argon-38 ($_{18}^{38}Ar$)
    e. carbon-14 ($_{6}^{14}C$)

5.7 **a.** Since the element is copper, the element symbol is Cu and the atomic number is 29. The copper isotope with mass number 64 will have the atomic symbol $_{29}^{64}Cu$.
    b. Since the element is selenium, the element symbol is Se and the atomic number is 34. The selenium isotope with mass number 75 will have the atomic symbol $_{34}^{75}Se$.
    c. Since the element is sodium, the element symbol is Na and the atomic number is 11. The sodium isotope with mass number 24 will have the atomic symbol $_{11}^{24}Na$.
    d. Since the element is nitrogen, the element symbol is N and the atomic number is 7. The nitrogen isotope with mass number 15 will have the atomic symbol $_{7}^{15}N$.

5.9

Medical Use	Atomic Symbol	Mass Number	Number of Protons	Number of Neutrons
Heart imaging	$_{81}^{201}Tl$	201	81	120
Radiation therapy	$_{27}^{60}Co$	60	27	33
Abdominal scan	$_{31}^{67}Ga$	67	31	36
Hyperthyroidism	$_{53}^{131}I$	131	53	78
Leukemia treatment	$_{15}^{32}P$	32	15	17

5.11 **a.** 1. <u>Alpha particles</u> do not penetrate the skin.
     b. 3. <u>Gamma radiation</u> requires shielding protection that includes lead or thick concrete.
     c. 1. <u>Alpha particles</u> can be very harmful if ingested.

5.13 The mass number of the radioactive atom is reduced by four when an alpha particle ($_{2}^{4}He$) is emitted. The unknown product will have an atomic number that is two less than the atomic number of the radioactive atom.
     a. $_{84}^{208}Po \longrightarrow {}_{82}^{204}Pb + {}_{2}^{4}He$
     b. $_{90}^{232}Th \longrightarrow {}_{88}^{228}Ra + {}_{2}^{4}He$
     c. $_{102}^{251}No \longrightarrow {}_{100}^{247}Fm + {}_{2}^{4}He$
     d. $_{86}^{220}Rn \longrightarrow {}_{84}^{216}Po + {}_{2}^{4}He$

5.15 The mass number of the radioactive atom is not changed when a beta particle ($_{-1}^{0}e$) is emitted. The unknown product will have an atomic number that is one greater than the atomic number of the radioactive atom.
     a. $_{11}^{25}Na \longrightarrow {}_{12}^{25}Mg + {}_{-1}^{0}e$
     b. $_{8}^{20}O \longrightarrow {}_{9}^{20}F + {}_{-1}^{0}e$
     c. $_{38}^{92}Sr \longrightarrow {}_{39}^{92}Y + {}_{-1}^{0}e$
     d. $_{26}^{60}Fe \longrightarrow {}_{27}^{60}Co + {}_{-1}^{0}e$

5.17 The mass number of the radioactive atom is not changed when a positron ($_{+1}^{0}e$) is emitted. The unknown product will have an atomic number that is one less than the atomic number of the radioactive atom.
     a. $_{14}^{26}Si \longrightarrow {}_{13}^{26}Al + {}_{+1}^{0}e$
     b. $_{27}^{54}Co \longrightarrow {}_{26}^{54}Fe + {}_{+1}^{0}e$

c. $^{77}_{37}\text{Rb} \longrightarrow ^{77}_{36}\text{Kr} + ^{0}_{+1}e$

d. $^{93}_{45}\text{Rh} \longrightarrow ^{93}_{44}\text{Ru} + ^{0}_{+1}e$

5.19 Balance the mass numbers and the atomic numbers in each nuclear equation.

    a. $^{28}_{13}\text{Al} \longrightarrow ^{28}_{14}\text{Si} + ^{0}_{-1}e$ $? = ^{28}_{14}\text{Si}$ beta decay

    b. $^{180m}_{73}\text{Ta} \longrightarrow ^{180}_{73}\text{Ta} + ^{0}_{0}\gamma$ $? = ^{0}_{0}\gamma$ gamma emission

    c. $^{66}_{29}\text{Cu} \longrightarrow ^{66}_{30}\text{Zn} + ^{0}_{-1}e$ $? = ^{0}_{-1}e$ beta decay

    d. $^{238}_{92}\text{U} \longrightarrow ^{234}_{90}\text{Th} + ^{4}_{2}\text{He}$ $? = ^{238}_{92}\text{U}$ alpha decay

    e. $^{188}_{80}\text{Hg} \longrightarrow ^{188}_{79}\text{Au} + ^{0}_{+1}e$ $? = ^{188}_{79}\text{Au}$ positron emission

5.21 Balance the mass numbers and the atomic numbers in each nuclear equation.

    a. $^{1}_{0}n + ^{9}_{4}\text{Be} \longrightarrow ^{10}_{4}\text{Be}$ $? = ^{10}_{4}\text{Be}$

    b. $^{1}_{0}n + ^{131}_{52}\text{Te} \longrightarrow ^{132}_{53}\text{I} + ^{0}_{-1}e$ $? = ^{132}_{53}\text{I}$

    c. $^{1}_{0}n + ^{27}_{13}\text{Al} \longrightarrow ^{24}_{11}\text{Na} + ^{4}_{2}\text{He}$ $? = ^{27}_{13}\text{Al}$

    d. $^{4}_{2}\text{He} + ^{14}_{7}\text{N} \longrightarrow ^{17}_{8}\text{O} + ^{1}_{1}\text{H}$ $? = ^{17}_{8}\text{O}$

5.23   **a.** 2. <u>Absorbed dose</u> can be measured in rad.

    b. 3. <u>Biological damage</u> can be measured in mrem.

    c. 1. <u>Activity</u> can be measured in mCi.

    d. 2. <u>Absorbed dose</u> can be measured in Gy.

5.25 $8 \text{ mGy} \times \dfrac{1 \text{ Gy}}{1000 \text{ mGy}} \times \dfrac{100 \text{ rad}}{1 \text{ Gy}} = 0.8 \text{ rad (1 SF)}$

Thus, a technician exposed to a 5-rad dose of radiation received more radiation than one exposed to 8 mGy (0.8 rad) of radiation.

5.27   **a.** $70.0 \text{ kg body mass} \times \dfrac{4.20 \text{ }\mu\text{Ci}}{1 \text{ kg body mass}} = 294 \text{ }\mu\text{Ci (3 SFs)}$

    b. from 50 rad of gamma radiation (we use a biological damage factor of 1, so 1 rad of gamma radiation = 1 rem):

       $50 \text{ rad} \times \dfrac{1 \text{ Gy}}{100 \text{ rad}} = 0.5 \text{ Gy (1 SF)}$

5.29   **a.** 2. two half-lives:

       $34 \text{ days} \times \dfrac{1 \text{ half-life}}{17 \text{ days}} = 2.0 \text{ half-lives}$

    b. 1. one half-life:

       $20 \text{ min} \times \dfrac{1 \text{ half-life}}{20 \text{ min}} = 1 \text{ half-life}$

    c. 3. three half-lives:

       $21 \text{ h} \times \dfrac{1 \text{ half-life}}{7 \text{ h}} = 3 \text{ half-lives}$

5.31   **a.** After one half-life, one-half of the sample would be radioactive:

       $80.0 \text{ mg of } ^{99m}_{43}\text{Tc} \xrightarrow{\text{1 half-life}} 40.0 \text{ mg of } ^{99m}_{43}\text{Tc (3 SFs)}$

    b. After two half-lives, one-fourth of the sample would still be radioactive:

       $80.0 \text{ mg of } ^{99m}_{43}\text{Tc} \xrightarrow{\text{1 half-life}} 40.0 \text{ mg of } ^{99m}_{43}\text{Tc} \xrightarrow{\text{2 half-lives}} 20.0 \text{ mg of } ^{99m}_{43}\text{Tc (3 SFs)}$

    c. $18 \text{ h} \times \dfrac{1 \text{ half-life}}{6.0 \text{ h}} = 3.0 \text{ half-lives}$

$$80.0 \text{ mg of } {}^{99m}_{43}\text{Tc} \xrightarrow{\text{1 half-life}} 40.0 \text{ mg of } {}^{99m}_{43}\text{Tc} \xrightarrow{\text{2 half-lives}}$$

$$20.0 \text{ mg of } {}^{99m}_{43}\text{Tc} \xrightarrow{\text{3 half-lives}} 10.0 \text{ mg of } {}^{99m}_{43}\text{Tc} \text{ (3 SFs)}$$

d. $24 \text{ h} \times \dfrac{1 \text{ half-life}}{6.0 \text{ h}} = 4.0 \text{ half-lives}$

$$80.0 \text{ mg of } {}^{99m}_{43}\text{Tc} \xrightarrow{\text{1 half-life}} 40.0 \text{ mg of } {}^{99m}_{43}\text{Tc} \xrightarrow{\text{2 half-lives}} 20.0 \text{ mg of } {}^{99m}_{43}\text{Tc} \xrightarrow{\text{3 half-lives}}$$

$$10.0 \text{ mg of } {}^{99m}_{43}\text{Tc} \xrightarrow{\text{4 half-lives}} 5.00 \text{ mg of } {}^{99m}_{43}\text{Tc} \text{ (3 SFs)}$$

5.33 The radiation level in a radioactive sample is cut in half with each half-life; the half-life of Sr-85 is 65 days.

a. For the radiation level to drop to one-fourth of its original level, $\frac{1}{4} = \frac{1}{2} \times \frac{1}{2}$ or two half-lives

$$2 \text{ half-lives} \times \frac{65 \text{ days}}{1 \text{ half-life}} = 130 \text{ days (2 SFs)}$$

b. For the radiation level to drop to one-eighth of its original level, $\frac{1}{8} = \frac{1}{2} \times \frac{1}{2} \times \frac{1}{2}$ or three half-lives

$$3 \text{ half-lives} \times \frac{65 \text{ days}}{1 \text{ half-life}} = 195 \text{ days (2 SFs)}$$

5.35 **a.** Since the elements calcium and phosphorus are part of bone, any calcium or phosphorus atom, regardless of isotope, will be carried to and become part of the bony structures of the body. Once there, the radiation emitted by any radioactive isotope can be used to diagnose or treat bone diseases.

b. Strontium (Sr) acts much like calcium (Ca) because both are Group 2A (2) elements. The body will accumulate radioactive strontium in bones in the same way that it incorporates calcium. Radioactive strontium is harmful to children because the radiation it produces causes more damage in cells that are dividing rapidly.

5.37 $4.0 \text{ mL solution} \times \dfrac{45 \,\mu\text{Ci}}{1 \text{ mL solution}} = 180 \,\mu\text{Ci of selenium-75 (2 SFs)}$

5.39 Nuclear fission is the splitting of a large atom into smaller fragments with a simultaneous release of large amounts of energy.

5.41 $ {}^{1}_{0}n + {}^{235}_{92}\text{U} \longrightarrow {}^{131}_{50}\text{Sn} + {}^{103}_{42}\text{Mo} + 2{}^{1}_{0}n + \text{energy} \quad ? = {}^{103}_{42}\text{Mo}$

5.43 **a.** Neutrons bombard a nucleus in the <u>fission</u> process.
b. The nuclear process that occurs in the Sun is <u>fusion</u>.
c. <u>Fission</u> is the process in which a large nucleus splits into smaller nuclei.
d. <u>Fusion</u> is the process in which small nuclei combine to form larger nuclei.

5.45 **a.** $74 \text{ MBq} \times \dfrac{1 \times 10^6 \text{ Bq}}{1 \text{ MBq}} \times \dfrac{1 \text{ Ci}}{3.7 \times 10^{10} \text{ Bq}} = 2.0 \times 10^{-3} \text{ Ci (2 SFs)}$

b. $74 \text{ MBq} \times \dfrac{1 \times 10^6 \text{ Bq}}{1 \text{ MBq}} \times \dfrac{1 \text{ Ci}}{3.7 \times 10^{10} \text{ Bq}} \times \dfrac{1 \times 10^3 \text{ mCi}}{1 \text{ Ci}} = 2.0 \text{ mCi (2 SFs)}$

5.47 For the activity to drop to one-eighth of its original level, $\dfrac{1}{8} = \dfrac{1}{2} \times \dfrac{1}{2} \times \dfrac{1}{2}$ or three half-lives

$$3 \text{ half-lives} \times \frac{3.0 \text{ days}}{1 \text{ half-life}} = 9.0 \text{ days (2 SFs)}$$

5.49

5.51

5.53   Half of a radioactive sample decays with each half-life:

6.4 μCi of $^{14}_{6}$C $\xrightarrow{\text{1 half-life}}$ 3.2 μCi of $^{14}_{6}$C $\xrightarrow{\text{2 half-lives}}$ 1.6 μCi of $^{14}_{6}$C $\xrightarrow{\text{3 half-lives}}$ 0.80 μCi of $^{14}_{6}$C

∴ the activity of carbon-14 drops to 0.80 μCi in three half-lives or 3 × 5730 years, which makes the age of the painting 17 200 years.

5.55   **a.** $^{25}_{11}$Na has 11 protons and 25 − 11 = 14 neutrons.

   b. $^{61}_{28}$Ni has 28 protons and 61 − 28 = 33 neutrons.

   c. $^{84}_{37}$Rb has 37 protons and 84 − 37 = 47 neutrons.

   d. $^{110}_{47}$Ag has 47 protons and 110 − 47 = 63 neutrons.

5.57   **a.** gamma emission

   b. positron emission

   c. alpha decay

5.59   **a.** $^{225}_{90}$Th $\longrightarrow$ $^{221}_{88}$Ra + $^{4}_{2}$He

   b. $^{210}_{83}$Bi $\longrightarrow$ $^{206}_{81}$Tl + $^{4}_{2}$He

   c. $^{137}_{55}$Cs $\longrightarrow$ $^{137}_{56}$Ba + $^{0}_{-1}e$

   d. $^{126}_{50}$Sn $\longrightarrow$ $^{126}_{51}$Sb + $^{0}_{-1}e$

   e. $^{18}_{9}$F $\longrightarrow$ $^{18}_{8}$O + $^{0}_{+1}e$

5.61   **a.** $^{4}_{2}$He + $^{14}_{7}$N $\longrightarrow$ $^{17}_{8}$O + $^{1}_{1}$H   ? = $^{17}_{8}$O

   b. $^{4}_{2}$He + $^{27}_{13}$Al $\longrightarrow$ $^{30}_{14}$Si + $^{1}_{1}$H   ? = $^{1}_{1}$H

   c. $^{1}_{0}n$ + $^{235}_{92}$U $\longrightarrow$ $^{90}_{38}$Sr + $3^{1}_{0}n$ + $^{143}_{54}$Xe   ? = $^{143}_{54}$Xe

   d. $^{23m}_{12}$Mg $\longrightarrow$ $^{23}_{12}$Mg + $^{0}_{0}\gamma$? = $^{23}_{12}$Mg

5.63   **a.** $^{16}_{8}$O + $^{16}_{8}$O $\longrightarrow$ $^{28}_{14}$Si + $^{4}_{2}$He

   b. $^{18}_{8}$O + $^{249}_{98}$Cf $\longrightarrow$ $^{263}_{106}$Sg + $4^{1}_{0}n$

   c. $^{222}_{86}$Rn $\longrightarrow$ $^{218}_{84}$Po + $^{4}_{2}$He

   d. $^{80}_{38}$Sr $\longrightarrow$ $^{80}_{37}$Rb + $^{0}_{+1}e$

5.65   First, calculate the number of half-lives that have elapsed:

$$24 \text{ h} \times \frac{1 \text{ half-life}}{6.0 \text{ h}} = 4.0 \text{ half-lives}$$

Now we can calculate the number of milligrams of technicium-99m that remain:

120 mg of $^{99m}_{43}$Tc $\xrightarrow{\text{1 half-life}}$ 60. mg of $^{99m}_{43}$Tc $\xrightarrow{\text{2 half-lives}}$ 30. mg of $^{99m}_{43}$Tc $\xrightarrow{\text{3 half-lives}}$ 15 mg of $^{99m}_{43}$Tc $\xrightarrow{\text{4 half-lives}}$ 7.5 mg of $^{99m}_{43}$Tc (2 SFs)

5.67 In the fission process, an atom splits into smaller nuclei with a simultaneous release of large amounts of energy. In fusion, two (or more) small nuclei combine (fuse) to form a larger nucleus, with a simultaneous release of large amounts of energy.

5.69 Fusion occurs naturally in the Sun and other stars.

5.71 $120 \; \cancel{nCi} \times \dfrac{1 \times 10^{-9} \; \cancel{Ci}}{1 \; \cancel{nCi}} \times \dfrac{3.7 \times 10^{10} \; Bq}{1 \; \cancel{Ci}} = 4400 \; Bq = 4.4 \times 10^3 \; Bq \; (2 \; SFs)$

5.73 Half of a radioactive sample decays with each half-life:

$1.2 \; mg \; of \; {}^{32}_{15}P \xrightarrow{\text{1 half-life}} 0.60 \; mg \; of \; {}^{32}_{15}P \xrightarrow{\text{2 half-lives}} 0.30 \; mg \; of \; {}^{32}_{15}P$

$\therefore$ two half-lives must have elapsed during this time (28.6 days), yielding the half-life for phosphorus-32:

$\dfrac{28.6 \; days}{2 \; half\text{-}lives} = 14.3 \; days/half\text{-}life \; (3 \; SFs)$

5.75 **a.** ${}^{47}_{20}Ca \longrightarrow {}^{47}_{21}Sc + {}^{0}_{-1}e$

b. First, calculate the number of half-lives that have elapsed:

$18 \; \cancel{days} \times \dfrac{1 \; half\text{-}life}{4.5 \; \cancel{days}} = 4.0 \; half\text{-}lives$

Now we can calculate the number of milligrams of calcium-47 that remain:

$16 \; mg \; of \; {}^{47}_{20}Ca \xrightarrow{\text{1 half-life}} 8.0 \; mg \; of \; {}^{47}_{20}Ca \xrightarrow{\text{2 half-lives}} 4.0 \; mg \; of \; {}^{47}_{20}Ca \xrightarrow{\text{3 half-lives}}$

$2.0 \; mg \; of \; {}^{47}_{20}Ca \xrightarrow{\text{4 half-lives}} 1.0 \; mg \; of \; {}^{47}_{20}Ca$

c. Half of a radioactive sample decays with each half-life:

$4.8 \; mg \; of \; {}^{47}_{20}Ca \xrightarrow{\text{1 half-life}} 2.4 \; mg \; of \; {}^{47}_{20}Ca \xrightarrow{\text{2 half-lives}} 1.2 \; mg \; of \; {}^{47}_{20}Ca$

$\therefore$ two half-lives have elapsed.

$2 \; \cancel{half\text{-}lives} \times \dfrac{4.5 \; days}{1 \; \cancel{half\text{-}life}} = 9.0 \; days \; (2 \; SFs)$

5.77 **a.** ${}^{180}_{80}Hg \longrightarrow {}^{176}_{78}Pt + {}^{4}_{2}He$

b. ${}^{198}_{79}Au \longrightarrow {}^{198}_{80}Hg + {}^{0}_{-1}e$

c. ${}^{82}_{37}Rb \longrightarrow {}^{82}_{36}Kr + {}^{0}_{+1}e$

5.79 ${}^{1}_{0}n + {}^{238}_{92}U \longrightarrow {}^{239}_{93}Np + {}^{0}_{-1}e$

5.81 Half of a radioactive sample decays with each half-life:

$64 \; \mu Ci \; of \; {}^{201}_{81}Tl \xrightarrow{\text{1 half-life}} 32 \; \mu Ci \; of \; {}^{201}_{81}Tl \xrightarrow{\text{2 half-lives}} 16 \; \mu Ci \; of \; {}^{201}_{81}Tl \xrightarrow{\text{3 half-lives}}$

$8.0 \; \mu Ci \; of \; {}^{201}_{81}Tl \xrightarrow{\text{4 half-lives}} 4.0 \; \mu Ci \; of \; {}^{201}_{81}Tl$

$\therefore$ four half-lives must have elapsed during this time (12 days), yielding the half-life for thallium-201:

$\dfrac{12 \; days}{4 \; half\text{-}lives} = 3.0 \; days/half\text{-}life \; (2 \; SFs)$

5.83 First, calculate the number of half-lives that have elapsed:

$27 \; \cancel{days} \times \dfrac{1 \; half\text{-}life}{4.5 \; \cancel{days}} = 6.0 \; half\text{-}lives$

Because the activity of a radioactive sample is cut in half with each half-life, the activity must have been double its present value before each half-life. For 6.0 half-lives, we need to double the value six times:

$$1.0 \ \mu\text{Ci of } ^{47}_{20}\text{Ca} \xleftarrow{\text{1 half-life}} 2.0 \ \mu\text{Ci of } ^{47}_{20}\text{Ca} \xleftarrow{\text{2 half-lives}} 4.0 \ \mu\text{Ci of } ^{47}_{20}\text{Ca} \xleftarrow{\text{3 half-lives}} 8.0 \ \mu\text{Ci of } ^{47}_{20}\text{Ca}$$

$$\xleftarrow{\text{4 half-lives}} 16 \ \mu\text{Ci of } ^{47}_{20}\text{Ca} \xleftarrow{\text{5 half-lives}} 32 \ \mu\text{Ci of } ^{47}_{20}\text{Ca} \xleftarrow{\text{6 half-lives}} 64 \ \mu\text{Ci of } ^{47}_{20}\text{Ca}$$

∴ the initial activity of the sample was 64 μCi (2 SFs).

5.85 $^{48}_{20}\text{Ca} + ^{244}_{94}\text{Pu} \longrightarrow ^{292}_{114}\text{Fl}$

5.87 First, calculate the number of half-lives that have elapsed since the technician was exposed:

$$36 \ \cancel{h} \times \frac{1 \text{ half-life}}{12 \ \cancel{h}} = 3.0 \text{ half-lives}$$

Because the activity of a radioactive sample is cut in half with each half-life, the activity must have been double its present value before each half-life. For 3.0 half-lives, we need to double the value three times:

$$2.0 \ \mu\text{Ci of } ^{42}_{19}\text{K} \xleftarrow{\text{1 half-life}} 4.0 \ \mu\text{Ci of } ^{42}_{19}\text{K} \xleftarrow{\text{2 half-lives}} 8.0 \ \mu\text{Ci of } ^{42}_{19}\text{K} \xleftarrow{\text{3 half-lives}} 16 \ \mu\text{Ci of } ^{42}_{19}\text{K}$$

∴ the activity of the sample when the technician was exposed was 16 μCi (2 SFs).

Ionic and Molecular Compounds

Sarah, a pharmacy technician, talked with her customer regarding questions about stomach upset from the low-dose aspirin, $C_9H_8O_4$, he was taking to prevent a heart attack or stroke. Sarah explained that when he takes a low-dose aspirin, he needs to drink a glass of water. If his stomach is still upset, he can take the aspirin with food or milk each time. A few days later, Sarah talked with her customer again. He told her he followed her suggestions and that he no longer had any upset stomach from the low-dose aspirin. Is aspirin an ionic or a molecular compound?

Credit: Design Pics Inc./Alamy

CHAPTER READINESS*

🖩 Key Math Skills

- Using Positive and Negative Numbers in Calculations (1.4B)
- Solving Equations (1.4D)

⚛ Core Chemistry Skills

- Writing Electron Configurations (4.7)
- Drawing Lewis Symbols (4.8)

*These Key Math Skills and Core Chemistry Skills from previous chapters are listed here for your review as you proceed to the new material in this chapter.

6.1   Ions: Transfer of Electrons

Learning Goal: Write the symbols for the simple ions of the representative elements.

- The stability of the noble gases is associated with a stable electron configuration of 8 electrons, an octet, in their outermost energy level. Helium is stable with 2 electrons in the $n = 1$ energy level.

- Atoms of elements other than the noble gases achieve stability by losing, gaining, or sharing valence electrons with other atoms in the formation of compounds.

- Metals of the representative elements in Groups 1A (1), 2A (2), and 3A (13) achieve a noble gas electron configuration by losing their valence electron(s) to form positively charged cations with a charge of 1+, 2+, or 3+, respectively.

- Nonmetals in Groups 5A (15), 6A (16), and 7A (17) gain valence electrons to achieve an octet forming negatively charged anions with a charge of 3−, 2−, or 1−, respectively.

- *Ionic bonds* occur when the valence electrons of atoms of a metal are transferred to atoms of nonmetals. For example, sodium atoms lose electrons and chlorine atoms gain electrons to form the ionic compound NaCl.

- *Covalent bonds* form when atoms of nonmetals share valence electrons. In the molecular compounds H_2O and C_3H_8, atoms share electrons.

Study Note

When an atom loses or gains electrons, it acquires the electron configuration of the nearest noble gas. For example, sodium loses 1 electron, which gives the Na^+ ion the electron configuration of neon. Oxygen gains 2 electrons to give an oxide ion, O^{2-}, the electron configuration of neon.

♦ **Learning Exercise 6.1A**

⚛ **CORE CHEMISTRY SKILL**

The following metals, which are essential to health, lose electrons when they form ions. Indicate the group number, the number of electrons lost, and the ion (symbol and charge) for each of the following:

Writing Positive and Negative Ions

Metal	Group Number	Electrons Lost	Ion Formed
magnesium			
sodium			
calcium			
potassium			
zinc			

Answers

Metal	Group Number	Electrons Lost	Ion Formed
magnesium	2A (2)	2	Mg^{2+}
sodium	1A (1)	1	Na^+
calcium	2A (2)	2	Ca^{2+}
potassium	1A (1)	1	K^+
zinc	2B (12)	3	Zn^{2+}

♦ **Learning Exercise 6.1B**

The following nonmetals, which are essential to health, gain electrons when they form ions. Indicate the group number, the number of electrons gained, and the ion (symbol and charge) for each of the following:

Nonmetal	Group Number	Electrons Gained	Ion Formed
chlorine			
oxygen			
nitrogen			
iodine			
sulfur			

Answers

Nonmetal	Group Number	Electrons Gained	Ion Formed
chlorine	7A (17)	1	Cl^-
oxygen	6A (16)	2	O^{2-}
nitrogen	5A (15)	3	N^{3-}
iodine	7A (17)	1	I^-
sulfur	6A (16)	2	S^{2-}

6.2 Writing Formulas for Ionic Compounds

Learning Goal: Using charge balance, write the correct formula for an ionic compound.

- In the formulas of ionic compounds, the total positive charge is equal to the total negative charge. For example, the compound magnesium chloride, $MgCl_2$, contains Mg^{2+} and two Cl^-. The sum of the charges is zero: $(2+) + 2(1-) = 0$.
- When two or more ions are needed for charge balance, that number is indicated by subscripts in the formula.
- A subscript of 1 is understood and not written.

For the following exercises, you may want to cut pieces of paper that represent typical positive and negative ions, as shown. To determine an ionic formula, place the smallest number of positive and negative pieces together to complete a geometric shape. Write the number of positive ions and negative ions as the subscripts for the formula.

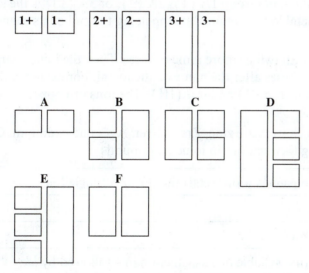

CORE CHEMISTRY SKILL

Writing Ionic Formulas

♦ **Learning Exercise 6.2A**

Write the letter (A to F) that matches the arrangement of ions in the following compounds:

Compound	Combination	Compound	Combination
1. $MgCl_2$	_____	**2.** Na_2S	_____
3. LiCl	_____	**4.** CaO	_____
5. K_3N	_____	**6.** $AlBr_3$	_____
7. MgS	_____	**8.** $BaCl_2$	_____

Answers   **1.** C   **2.** B   **3.** A   **4.** F   **5.** E   **6.** D   **7.** F   **8.** C

Study Note

You can check that the ionic formula you write is electrically neutral by multiplying each ionic charge by its subscript. When added together, their sum should equal zero. For example, the formula Na_2O gives $2(1+) + 1(2-) = (2+) + (2-) = 0$.

♦ **Learning Exercise 6.2B**

Write the correct formula for the ionic compound formed from each of the following pairs of ions:

1. Na^+ and Cl^- _____   2. K^+ and S^{2-} _____

3. Al^{3+} and O^{2-} _____   4. Mg^{2+} and Cl^- _____

5. Ca^{2+} and S^{2-} _____   6. Al^{3+} and Cl^- _____

7. Li^+ and N^{3-} _____   8. Ba^{2+} and P^{3-} _____

Answers   1. $NaCl$ 2. K_2S 3. Al_2O_3 4. $MgCl_2$
           5. CaS 6. $AlCl_3$ 7. Li_3N 8. Ba_3P_2

6.3   Naming and Writing Ionic Compounds

Learning Goal: Given the formula of an ionic compound, write the correct name; given the name of an ionic compound, write the correct formula.

- In naming ionic compounds, the positive ion is named first, followed by the name of the negative ion. The name of a representative metal ion in Group 1A (1), 2A (2), or 3A (13) is the same as its element name. The name of a nonmetal ion is obtained by replacing the end of its element name with *ide*.

- Most transition elements form cations with two or more ionic charges. Then the ionic charge must be written as a Roman numeral in parentheses after the name of the metal. For example, the cations of iron, Fe^{2+} and Fe^{3+}, are named iron(II) and iron(III). The ions of copper are Cu^+, copper(I), and Cu^{2+}, copper(II).

- The only transition elements with fixed charges are zinc, Zn^{2+}; silver, Ag^+; and cadmium, Cd^{2+}; no Roman numerals are used when naming their cations in ionic compounds.

Guide to Naming Ionic Compounds with Metals that Form a Single Ion	
STEP 1	Identify the cation and anion.
STEP 2	Name the cation by its element name.
STEP 3	Name the anion by using the first syllable of its element name followed by *ide*.
STEP 4	Write the name for the cation first and the name for the anion second.

♦ **Learning Exercise 6.3A**

Write the ions and the correct formula for each of the following ionic compounds:

Formula	Ions		Name
1. Cs_2O	_____	_____	_____
2. $BaBr_2$	_____	_____	_____

3. Mg_3P_2 _____ _____ _____

4. Na_2S _____ _____ _____

Answers
1. Cs^+, O^{2-}, cesium oxide
2. Ba^{2+}, Br^-, barium bromide
3. Mg^{2+}, P^{3-}, magnesium phosphide
4. Na^+, S^{2-}, sodium sulfide

Guide to Naming Ionic Compounds with Variable Charge Metals	
STEP 1	Determine the charge of the cation from the anion.
STEP 2	Name the cation by its element name and use a Roman numeral in parentheses for the charge.
STEP 3	Name the anion by using the first syllable of its element name followed by *ide*.
STEP 4	Write the name for the cation first and the name for the anion second.

♦ **Learning Exercise 6.3B**

Write the name for each of the following ions:

1. Cl^- _____ **2.** Fe^{2+} _____ **3.** Cu^+ _____

4. Ag^+ _____ **5.** O^{2-} _____ **6.** Ca^{2+} _____

7. S^{2-} _____ **8.** Al^{3+} _____ **9.** Fe^{3+} _____

10. Ba^{2+} _____ **11.** Cu^{2+} _____ **12.** N^{3-} _____

Answers
1. chloride
2. iron(II)
3. copper(I)
4. silver
5. oxide
6. calcium
7. sulfide
8. aluminum
9. iron(III)
10. barium
11. copper(II)
12. nitride

♦ **Learning Exercise 6.3C**

Write the symbol for each of the following ions:

Name	Symbol
1. chromium(III) ion	_____
2. cobalt(II) ion	_____
3. zinc ion	_____
4. lead(IV) ion	_____
5. gold(I) ion	_____
6. silver ion	_____
7. potassium ion	_____
8. nickel(III) ion	_____

Some Metals That Form More Than One Positive Ion

Element	Possible Ions	Name of Ion
Bismuth	Bi^{3+}	Bismuth(III)
	Bi^{5+}	Bismuth(V)
Chromium	Cr^{2+}	Chromium(II)
	Cr^{3+}	Chromium(III)
Cobalt	Co^{2+}	Cobalt(II)
	Co^{3+}	Cobalt(III)
Copper	Cu^+	Copper(I)
	Cu^{2+}	Copper(II)
Gold	Au^+	Gold(I)
	Au^{3+}	Gold(III)
Iron	Fe^{2+}	Iron(II)
	Fe^{3+}	Iron(III)
Lead	Pb^{2+}	Lead(II)
	Pb^{4+}	Lead(IV)
Manganese	Mn^{2+}	Manganese(II)
	Mn^{3+}	Manganese(III)
Mercury	Hg_2^{2+}	Mercury(I)*
	Hg^{2+}	Mercury(II)
Nickel	Ni^{2+}	Nickel(II)
	Ni^{3+}	Nickel(III)
Tin	Sn^{2+}	Tin(II)
	Sn^{4+}	Tin(IV)

*Mercury(I) ions form an ion pair with a 2+ charge.

Answers
1. Cr^{3+}
2. Co^{2+}
3. Zn^{2+}
4. Pb^{4+}
5. Au^+
6. Ag^+
7. K^+
8. Ni^{3+}

♦ **Learning Exercise 6.3D**

Write the ions and a correct name for each of the following ionic compounds:

⚛ CORE CHEMISTRY SKILL

Naming Ionic Compounds

Formula	Ions		Name
1. $CrCl_2$	_____	_____	_____
2. $SnBr_4$	_____	_____	_____
3. Na_3P	_____	_____	_____
4. Ni_2O_3	_____	_____	_____
5. CuO	_____	_____	_____
6. Mg_3N_2	_____	_____	_____

Answers
1. Cr^{2+}, Cl^-, chromium(II) chloride
2. Sn^{4+}, Br^-, tin(IV) bromide
3. Na^+, P^{3-}, sodium phosphide
4. Ni^{3+}, O^{2-}, nickel(III) oxide
5. Cu^{2+}, O^{2-}, copper(II) oxide
6. Mg^{2+}, N^{3-}, magnesium nitride

Guide to Writing Formulas from the Name of an Ionic Compound	
STEP 1	Identify the cation and anion.
STEP 2	Balance the charges.
STEP 3	Write the formula, cation first, using subscripts from the charge balance.

♦ **Learning Exercise 6.3E**

Write the ions and the correct ionic formula for each of the following ionic compounds:

Compound	Positive Ion	Negative Ion	Formula of Compound
aluminum sulfide			
copper(II) chloride			
magnesium oxide			
gold(III) bromide			
silver oxide			

Answers

Compound	Positive Ion	Negative Ion	Formula of Compound
aluminum sulfide	Al^{3+}	S^{2-}	Al_2S_3
copper(II) chloride	Cu^{2+}	Cl^-	$CuCl_2$
magnesium oxide	Mg^{2+}	O^{2-}	MgO
gold(III) bromide	Au^{3+}	Br^-	$AuBr_3$
silver oxide	Ag^+	O^{2-}	Ag_2O

6.4 Polyatomic Ions

Learning Goal: Write the name and formula for an ionic compound containing a polyatomic ion.

- A polyatomic ion is a group of nonmetal atoms that carries an electrical charge, usually negative, $1-$, $2-$, or $3-$. The polyatomic ion NH_4^+, ammonium ion, has a positive charge.
- Polyatomic ions cannot exist alone but are combined with an ion of the opposite charge.
- The names of ionic compounds containing polyatomic anions often end with *ate* or *ite*.
- When there is more than one polyatomic ion in the formula for a compound, the entire polyatomic ion formula is enclosed in parentheses and the subscript written outside the parentheses.

Key Terms for Sections 6.1–6.4

Match each of the following key terms with the correct definition:

a. ion	**b.** cation	**c.** anion
d. polyatomic ion	**e.** ionic bond	

1. _____ a positively charged ion

2. _____ a negatively charged ion

3. _____ a group of covalently bonded nonmetal atoms that has an overall charge

4. _____ an atom or group of atoms having an electrical charge

5. _____ the attraction between positively charged and negatively charged ions

Answers   **1.** b   **2.** c   **3.** d   **4.** a   **5.** e

---

Study Note

By learning the most common polyatomic ions such as nitrate NO_3^-, carbonate CO_3^{2-}, sulfate SO_4^{2-}, and phosphate PO_4^{3-}, you can derive their related polyatomic ions. For example, the nitrite ion, NO_2^-, has one oxygen atom less than the nitrate ion: NO_3^-, nitrate, and NO_2^-, nitrite.

Names and Formulas of Some Common Polyatomic Ions

Nonmetal	Formula of Ion*	Name of Ion
Hydrogen	OH^-	Hydroxide
Nitrogen	NH_4^+	Ammonium
	NO_3^-	**Nitrate**
	NO_2^-	Nitrite
Chlorine	ClO_4^-	Perchlorate
	ClO_3^-	**Chlorate**
	ClO_2^-	Chlorite
	ClO^-	Hypochlorite
Carbon	**CO_3^{2-}**	**Carbonate**
	HCO_3^-	Hydrogen carbonate (or bicarbonate)
	CN^-	Cyanide
	$C_2H_3O_2^-$	Acetate
Sulfur	**SO_4^{2-}**	**Sulfate**
	HSO_4^-	Hydrogen sulfate (or bisulfate)
	SO_3^{2-}	Sulfite
	HSO_3^-	Hydrogen sulfite (or bisulfite)
Phosphorus	**PO_4^{3-}**	**Phosphate**
	HPO_4^{2-}	Hydrogen phosphate
	$H_2PO_4^-$	Dihydrogen phosphate
	PO_3^{3-}	Phosphite

*Formulas and names in bold type indicate the most common polyatomic ion for that element.

♦ **Learning Exercise 6.4A**

Write the polyatomic ion (symbol and charge) for each of the following:

1. sulfate ion ____

2. hydroxide ion ____

3. carbonate ion ____

4. sulfite ion ____

5. ammonium ion ____

6. phosphate ion ____

7. nitrate ion ____

8. nitrite ion ____

Answers
1. SO_4^{2-} 2. OH^- 3. CO_3^{2-} 4. SO_3^{2-}
5. NH_4^+ 6. PO_4^{3-} 7. NO_3^- 8. NO_2^-

Plaster cast
$CaSO_4$

Ca^{2+} SO_4^{2-}
Sulfate ion

The sulfate ion in $CaSO_4$ is a poly-atomic ion, which is a group of atoms that have an ionic charge.

Credit: Pearson Education / Pearson Science

Guide to Writing Formulas with Polyatomic Ions	
STEP 1	Identify the cation and polyatomic ion (anion).
STEP 2	Balance the charges.
STEP 3	Write the formula, cation first, using the subscripts from charge balance.

♦ **Learning Exercise 6.4B**

Write the formula for the ions and the correct formula for each of the following compounds:

Compound	Positive Ion	Negative Ion	Formula
sodium phosphate			
iron(II) hydroxide			
ammonium carbonate			
silver bicarbonate			
chromium(III) sulfate			
lead(II) nitrate			
potassium sulfite			
barium phosphate			

Answers

Compound	Positive Ion	Negative Ion	Formula
sodium phosphate	Na^+	PO_4^{3-}	Na_3PO_4
iron(II) hydroxide	Fe^{2+}	OH^-	$Fe(OH)_2$
ammonium carbonate	NH_4^+	CO_3^{2-}	$(NH_4)_2CO_3$
silver bicarbonate	Ag^+	HCO_3^-	$AgHCO_3$
chromium(III) sulfate	Cr^{3+}	SO_4^{2-}	$Cr_2(SO_4)_3$
lead(II) nitrate	Pb^{2+}	NO_3^-	$Pb(NO_3)_2$
potassium sulfite	K^+	SO_3^{2-}	K_2SO_3
barium phosphate	Ba^{2+}	PO_4^{3-}	$Ba_3(PO_4)_2$

Guide to Naming Ionic Compounds with Polyatomic Ions	
STEP 1	Identify the cation and polyatomic ion (anion).
STEP 2	Name the cation using a Roman numeral, if needed.
STEP 3	Name the polyatomic ion.
STEP 4	Write the name for the compound, cation first and the polyatomic ion second.

♦ **Learning Exercise 6.4C**

Write the ions and a correct name for each of the following ionic compounds:

Formula	Ions	Name
1. $Ba(NO_3)_2$	_____ _____	_____
2. $Fe_2(SO_4)_3$	_____ _____	_____
3. Na_3PO_3	_____ _____	_____
4. $Al(ClO_3)_3$	_____ _____	_____
5. $(NH_4)_2CO_3$	_____ _____	_____
6. $Cr(OH)_2$	_____ _____	_____

Answers
1. Ba^{2+}, NO_3^-, barium nitrate
3. Na^+, PO_3^{3-}, sodium phosphite
5. NH_4^+, CO_3^{2-}, ammonium carbonate
2. Fe^{3+}, SO_4^{2-}, iron(III) sulfate
4. Al^{3+}, ClO_3^-, aluminum chlorate
6. Cr^{2+}, OH^-, chromium(II) hydroxide

6.5 Molecular Compounds: Sharing Electrons

Learning Goal: Given the formula of a molecular compound, write its correct name; given the name of a molecular compound, write its formula.

- Molecular compounds are composed of nonmetals bonded together to give discrete units called *molecules*.
- The name of a molecular compound is written using the element name of the first nonmetal and the first syllable of the second nonmetal name followed by the suffix *ide*.
- Prefixes are used to indicate the number of atoms of each nonmetal in the formula: mono (1), di (2), tri (3), tetra (4), penta (5), hexa (6), hepta (7), octa (8), nona (9), deca (10).
- In the name of a molecular compound, the prefix *mono* is usually omitted, as in NO, nitrogen oxide. Traditionally, however, CO is named carbon monoxide.
- If the vowels *o* and *o* or *a* and *o* appear together, the first vowel is omitted.
- The formula of a molecular compound is written using the symbols of the nonmetals in the name followed by subscripts determined from the prefixes.

Guide to Naming Molecular Compounds	
STEP 1	Name the first nonmetal by its element name.
STEP 2	Name the second nonmetal by using the first syllable of its element name followed by *ide*.
STEP 3	Add prefixes to indicate the number of atoms (subscripts).

♦ **Learning Exercise 6.5A**

Use the appropriate prefixes to name the following molecular compounds:

Writing the Names and Formulas for Molecular Compounds

1. CS_2 _____

2. CCl_4 _____

3. CO _____

4. SO_3 _____

5. N_2O_4 _____

6. PCl_3 _____

7. P_4S_6 _____

8. IF_7 _____

9. ClO_2 _____

10. S_2O _____

Answers
1. carbon disulfide
2. carbon tetrachloride
3. carbon monoxide
4. sulfur trioxide
5. dinitrogen tetroxide
6. phosphorus trichloride
7. tetraphosphorus hexasulfide
8. iodine heptafluoride
9. chlorine dioxide
10. disulfur oxide

Guide to Writing Formulas for Molecular Compounds	
STEP 1	Write the symbols in the order of the elements in the name.
STEP 2	Write any prefixes as subscripts.

♦ **Learning Exercise 6.5B**

Write the formula for each of the following molecular compounds:

1. dinitrogen oxide _____

2. silicon tetrabromide _____

3. bromine pentafluoride _____

4. carbon dioxide _____

5. sulfur hexafluoride _____

6. oxygen difluoride _____

7. phosphorus octasulfide _____

8. selenium hexafluoride _____

9. iodine chloride _____

10. xenon trioxide _____

Answers
1. N_2O
2. $SiBr_4$
3. BrF_5
4. CO_2
5. SF_6
6. OF_2
7. PS_8
8. SeF_6
9. ICl
10. XeO_3

Summary of Writing Formulas and Names

- In compounds containing two different elements, the first takes its element name. The ending of the name of the second element is replaced by *ide*. For example, $BaCl_2$ is named *barium chloride*. If the metal forms two or more positive ions, a Roman numeral is added to its name to indicate the ionic charge in the compound. For example, $FeCl_3$ is named *iron(III) chloride*.

- In ionic compounds with three or more elements, a group of atoms is named as a polyatomic ion. The names of negative polyatomic ions end in *ate* or *ite*, except for hydroxide and cyanide. For example, Na_2SO_4 is named *sodium sulfate*. No prefixes are used.

- When a polyatomic ion occurs two or more times in a formula, its formula is placed inside parentheses, and the number of ions is shown as a subscript after the parentheses $Ca(NO_3)_2$. If the subscript is 1, it is not written.

- In naming molecular compounds, a prefix before the name of one or both nonmetal names indicates the numerical value of a subscript. For example, N_2O_3 is named *dinitrogen trioxide*.

♦ **Learning Exercise 6.5C**

Indicate the type of compound (ionic or molecular). Then give the formula and name for each.

Formula	Ionic or Molecular?	Name
MgCl₂		
		nitrogen trichloride
		potassium sulfate
Li₂O		
CCl₄		
Na₃PO₄		
		dihydrogen sulfide
		calcium hydrogen carbonate (bicarbonate)

Answers

MgCl₂	ionic	magnesium chloride
NCl₃	molecular	nitrogen trichloride
K₂SO₄	ionic	potassium sulfate
Li₂O	ionic	lithium oxide
CCl₄	molecular	carbon tetrachloride
Na₃PO₄	ionic	sodium phosphate
H₂S	molecular	dihydrogen sulfide
Ca(HCO₃)₂	ionic	calcium hydrogen carbonate (bicarbonate)

6.6   Lewis Structures for Molecules and Polyatomic Ions

Learning Goal: Draw the Lewis structures for molecular compounds or polyatomic ions.

- In a covalent bond, atoms of nonmetals share electrons to achieve an octet.
- In a double bond, two pairs of electrons are shared between the same two atoms to complete octets.
- In a triple bond, three pairs of electrons are shared to complete octets.
- Bonding pairs of electrons are shared between atoms. Nonbonding electrons are also called lone pairs.

♦ **Learning Exercise 6.6A**

List the number of bonds typically formed by the following atoms in molecular compounds:

a. N _____   b. S _____   c. P _____   d. C _____

e. Cl _____   f. O _____   g. H _____   h. F _____

Answers   a. 3   b. 2   c. 3   d. 4   e. 1   f. 2   g. 1   h. 1

	Guide to Drawing Lewis Structures
STEP 1	Determine the arrangement of atoms.
STEP 2	Determine the total number of valence electrons.
STEP 3	Attach each bonded atom to the central atom with a pair of electrons.
STEP 4	Place the remaining electrons using single or multiple bonds to complete the octets (two for H).

Example: A Lewis formula for SCl_2 can be drawn as follows:

STEP 1 Determine the arrangement of atoms.

Cl   S   Cl

STEP 2 Determine the total number of valence electrons.

1 S and 2 Cl = $1(6\,e^-) + 2(7\,e^-)$ = 20 valence electrons

STEP 3 Attach each bonded atom to the central atom with a pair of electrons.

Cl—S—Cl $20\,e^- - 4\,e^-$ = 16 remaining valence electrons (8 pairs)

STEP 4 Place the remaining electrons using single or multiple bonds to complete the octets.

:C̈l—S̈—C̈l:

⚛ CORE CHEMISTRY SKILL

Drawing Lewis Structures

♦ **Learning Exercise 6.6B**

Draw the Lewis structure for each of the following molecular compounds:

a. H_2 b. NCl_3 c. HCl

d. Cl_2 e. H_2S f. CCl_4

Answers

a. H:H   b. :C̈l:N̈:C̈l: c. H:C̈l: d. :C̈l:C̈l: e. H:S̈:   f. :C̈l:
              :C̈l: H   :C̈l:C:C̈l:
                                                                            :C̈l:

Study Note

A Lewis structure for CO_2 can be drawn with double bonds as follows:

STEP 1   **Determine the arrangement of atoms.**

        O   C   O

STEP 2   **Determine the total number of valence electrons.**

        1 C and 2 O $= 1(4\,e^-) + 2(6\,e^-) = 16$ valence electrons

STEP 3   **Attach each bonded atom to the central atom with a pair of electrons.** Each bonding pair can be represented by a bond line.

        O—C—O $16\,e^- - 4\,e^- = 12$ remaining valence electrons (6 pairs)

STEP 4   **Place the remaining electrons using single or multiple bonds to complete octets.**

        :Ö—C—Ö:

When octets cannot be completed with available valence electrons, one or more lone pairs are shared between the central atom and the bonded atoms to form double or triple bonds.

        :Ö=C=Ö:

♦ **Learning Exercise 6.6C**

Each of the following compounds contains a multiple bond. Draw the Lewis structures.

    a. CS_2 **b.** HCN

    c. H_2CCH_2 **d.** HONO

Answers   **a.** :S̈::C::S̈: or :S̈=C=S̈:   **b.** H:C⋮⋮N: or H—C≡N:

                          H H

       H H | |

   c. H:C̈::C̈:H   or   H—C=C—H   **d.** H:Ö:N::Ö: or H—Ö—N=Ö:

Study Note

A Lewis structure for the polyatomic ion ClO_2^- can be drawn as follows:

STEP 1 **Determine the arrangement of atoms.**

$$[O \quad Cl \quad O]^-$$

STEP 2 **Determine the total number of valence electrons.**

$1\ Cl$ and $2\ O = 1(7\ e^-) + 2(6\ e^-) + 1\ e^-$ (negative charge) $= 20$ valence electrons

STEP 3 **Attach each bonded atom to the central atom with a pair of electrons.** Each bonding pair can be represented by a bond line.

$$[O{:}Cl{:}O]^- \quad \text{or} \quad [O{-}Cl{-}O]^-$$

STEP 4 **Place the remaining electrons using single or multiple bonds to complete octets.**

20 valence $e^- - 4$ bonding $e^- = 16$ remaining valence electrons (8 pairs)

Thus, 8 lone pairs of electrons are placed on the Cl and O atoms.

$$\left[\ddot{\underset{\cdot\cdot}{O}}{:}\ddot{\underset{\cdot\cdot}{Cl}}{:}\ddot{\underset{\cdot\cdot}{O}}{:}\right]^- \quad \text{or} \quad \left[\ddot{\underset{\cdot\cdot}{O}}{-}\ddot{\underset{\cdot\cdot}{Cl}}{-}\ddot{\underset{\cdot\cdot}{O}}{:}\right]^-$$

♦ **Learning Exercise 6.6D**

Draw a Lewis structure for each of the following ions:

a. CO_3^{2-}

b. NO_3^-

Answers

a. $\left[\ddot{\underset{\cdot\cdot}{O}}{:}{-}\underset{\overset{\displaystyle |}{\overset{\displaystyle :\ddot{O}:}{}}}{C}{=}\ddot{\underset{\cdot\cdot}{O}}{:}\right]^{2-}$

b. $\left[\ddot{\underset{\cdot\cdot}{O}}{:}{=}\underset{\overset{\displaystyle |}{\overset{\displaystyle :\ddot{O}:}{}}}{N}{-}\ddot{\underset{\cdot\cdot}{O}}{:}\right]^-$

6.7 Electronegativity and Bond Polarity

Learning Goal: Use electronegativity to determine the polarity of a bond.

- Electronegativity values indicate the ability of an atom to attract electrons in a chemical bond. In general, metals have low electronegativity values and nonmetals have high values.

Electronegativity Increases →

H 2.1							18 Group 8A

Electronegativity Decreases ↓

1 Group 1A	2 Group 2A		13 Group 3A	14 Group 4A	15 Group 5A	16 Group 6A	17 Group 7A	
Li 1.0	Be 1.5		B 2.0	C 2.5	N 3.0	O 3.5	F 4.0	
Na 0.9	Mg 1.2		Al 1.5	Si 1.8	P 2.1	S 2.5	Cl 3.0	
K 0.8	Ca 1.0		Ga 1.6	Ge 1.8	As 2.0	Se 2.4	Br 2.8	
Rb 0.8	Sr 1.0		In 1.7	Sn 1.8	Sb 1.9	Te 2.1	I 2.5	
Cs 0.7	Ba 0.9		Tl 1.8	Pb 1.9	Bi 1.9	Po 2.0	At 2.1	

- When atoms sharing electrons have the same or similar electronegativity values, electrons are shared equally and the bond is *nonpolar covalent*.

- Electrons are shared unequally in *polar covalent* bonds because they are attracted to the more electronegative atom.

- An electronegativity difference of 0 to 0.4 indicates a nonpolar covalent bond, whereas a difference of 0.5 to 1.8 indicates a polar covalent bond.

- An electronegativity difference greater than 1.8 indicates a bond that is ionic.

- A polar bond has a charge separation, which is called a *dipole*; the positive end of the dipole is marked as δ^+ and the negative end as δ^-.

$$\overset{\delta^+}{H} \text{—} \overset{\delta^-}{Cl}$$

Electrons are shared unequally in the polar covalent bond of HCl.

♦ **Learning Exercise 6.7A**

⚛ CORE CHEMISTRY SKILL

Using Electronegativity

Using the electronegativity values, determine the following:

1. the electronegativity difference for each pair

2. the type of bonding as (I) ionic, (PC) polar covalent, or (NC) nonpolar covalent

Elements	Electronegativity Difference	Bonding	Elements	Electronegativity Difference	Bonding
a. H and O	_____	_____	**b.** N and S	_____	_____
c. Al and O	_____	_____	**d.** Li and F	_____	_____
e. H and Cl	_____	_____	**f.** Cl and Cl	_____	_____
g. S and F	_____	_____	**h.** H and C	_____	_____

Answers   **a.** 1.4, PC   **b.** 0.5, PC   **c.** 2.0, I   **d.** 3.0, I
                 e. 0.9, PC   **f.** 0.0, NP   **g.** 1.5, PC   **h.** 0.4, NP

♦ **Learning Exercise 6.7B**

Write the symbols δ^+ and δ^- over the appropriate atoms in polar bonds.

1. H—O   2. N—H   3. C—Cl

4. O—F   5. N—F   6. P—Cl

Answers

$\quad\;\delta^+\;\;\delta^-$ $\quad\;\delta^-\;\;\delta^+$ $\quad\;\delta^+\;\;\delta^-$
1. H—O   2. N—H   3. C—Cl

$\quad\;\delta^+\;\;\delta^-$ $\quad\;\delta^+\;\;\delta^-$ $\quad\;\delta^+\;\;\delta^-$
4. O—F   5. N—F   6. P—Cl

6.8   Shapes and Polarity of Molecules

Learning Goal: Predict the three-dimensional structure of a molecule, and classify it as polar or nonpolar.

- The VSEPR theory predicts the geometry of a molecule by placing the electron groups around a central atom as far apart as possible. One electron group may be a single, double, or triple bond, or a lone pair.

- A central atom with two electron groups has a linear geometry (180°); three electron groups give a trigonal planar geometry (120°); and four electron pairs give a tetrahedral geometry (109°).

- The atoms bonded to the central atom determine the shape of a molecule or polyatomic ion, which may be linear, trigonal planar, trigonal pyramidal, or tetrahedral.

180°

Linear shape

- A trigonal planar molecule has a central atom bonded to three atoms and no lone pairs. A bent molecule with a bond angle of 120° has a central atom bonded to two atoms and one lone pair.

120°

Trigonal planar shape   Bent shape

- A tetrahedral molecule has a central atom bonded to four atoms and no lone pairs. In a trigonal pyramidal molecule, a central atom is bonded to three atoms and one lone pair. In a bent molecule with a bond angle of 109°, a central atom is bonded to two atoms and two lone pairs.

109°

Tetrahedral   Trigonal pyramidal   Bent
shape   shape   shape

- Nonpolar molecules can have polar bonds if their dipoles are in a symmetric arrangement and the bond dipoles cancel each other.
- In polar molecules, the bond dipoles do not cancel each other.

Guide to Predicting Shape (VSEPR Theory)	
STEP 1	Draw the Lewis structure.
STEP 2	Arrange the electron groups around the central atom to minimize repulsion.
STEP 3	Use the atoms bonded to the central atom to determine the shape.

♦ **Learning Exercise 6.8A**

⚛ **CORE CHEMISTRY SKILL**

Match the shape of a molecule with the following descriptions:

Predicting Shapes

    a. linear   **b.** trigonal planar   **c.** tetrahedral

    d. trigonal pyramidal   **e.** bent (120°)   **f.** bent (109°)

Shape of Molecule

1. three electron groups with three bonded atoms   _____

2. two electron groups with two bonded atoms   _____

3. four electron groups with three bonded atoms   _____

4. three electron groups with two bonded atoms   _____

5. four electron groups with four bonded atoms   _____

6. four electron groups with two bonded atoms   _____

Answers   **1.** b   **2.** a   **3.** d   **4.** e   **5.** c   **6.** f

♦ **Learning Exercise 6.8B**

For each of the following, draw the Lewis structure, state the number of electron groups and bonded atoms, and predict the shape and angle of the molecule:

Molecule or Ion	Lewis Structure	Number of Electron Groups	Number of Bonded Atoms	Shape and Angle
CH_4				
H_2CO (C is the central atom)				
SO_3^{2-}				
H_2S				

Answers

Molecule or Ion	Lewis Structure	Number of Electron Groups	Number of Bonded Atoms	Shape and Angle
CH_4	H:C:H with H above and H below	4	4	Tetrahedral, 109°
H_2CO	H:C::O: with H below	3	3	Trigonal planar, 120°
SO_3^{2-}	[:O:S:O: with :O: below]$^{2-}$	4	3	Trigonal pyramidal, 109°
H_2S	H:S: with H below	4	2	Bent, 109°

Guide to Determining the Polarity of a Molecule	
STEP 1	Determine if the bonds are polar covalent or nonpolar covalent.
STEP 2	If the bonds are polar covalent, draw the Lewis structure and determine if the dipoles cancel.

♦ **Learning Exercise 6.8C**

⚛ **CORE CHEMISTRY SKILL**

Identifying Polarity of Molecules

Using the dipole arrows, draw the bond dipoles in each of the following molecules and determine whether the molecule is polar or nonpolar:

1. CF_4 **2.** HCl

3. NH_3 **4.** OF_2

Answers

1. CF_4 bond dipoles cancel, nonpolar

2. HCl   H→Cl   ⟶   bond dipole does not cancel, polar

3. NH_3 H→N̈←H   ↑   bond dipoles do not cancel, polar
                      ↑
                      H

4. OF_2 :Ö→F   ⤬   bond dipoles do not cancel, polar
                    ↓   ⤢
                    F

6.9   Attractive Forces in Compounds

Learning Goal: Describe the attractive forces between ions, polar covalent molecules, and nonpolar covalent molecules.

- The interactions between particles in solids and liquids determine their melting points.
- Ionic solids have high melting points due to strong ionic interactions between positive and negative ions.
- In polar substances, dipole–dipole attractions occur between the positive end of one molecule and the negative end of another.

Dipole–dipole
attraction

- Hydrogen bonding, a particularly strong type of dipole–dipole attraction, occurs between partially positive hydrogen atoms and the strongly electronegative atoms F, O, or N.

Hydrogen bond

- Dispersion forces occur when temporary dipoles form within the nonpolar molecules, causing weak attractions to other nonpolar molecules. Dispersion forces are the only attractive force that occur in nonpolar molecules. Dispersion forces occur in polar molecules, but they are not the strongest type of attractive force.

Key Terms for Sections 6.5–6.9

Match each of the following key terms with the correct definition:

    a. polar covalent bond   **b.** multiple bond   **c.** VSEPR theory
    d. nonpolar covalent bond   **e.** dipole–dipole attraction **f.** dispersion forces

1. _____ equal sharing of valence electrons by two atoms

2. _____ the unequal attraction for shared electrons in a covalent bond

3. _____ the atoms in a molecule are arranged to minimize repulsion between electrons

4. _____ weak dipoles attractions from momentary polarization of nonpolar molecules

5. _____ the sharing of two or three pairs of electrons by two atoms

6. _____ interaction between the positive end of a polar molecule and the negative end of another

Answers   **1.** d   **2.** a   **3.** c   **4.** f   **5.** b   **6.** e

♦ Learning Exercise 6.9

Indicate the major type of attractive force that occurs in each of the following substances:

CORE CHEMISTRY SKILL

Identifying Attractive Forces

    a. ionic bonds   **b.** dipole–dipole attractions   **c.** hydrogen bonds   **d.** dispersion forces

1. _____ KCl   **2.** _____ NF_3 **3.** _____ SCl_2 **4.** _____ Cl_2

5. _____ HF   **6.** _____ H_2O **7.** _____ C_4H_{10} **8.** _____ Na_2O

Answers   **1.** a   **2.** b   **3.** b   **4.** d   **5.** c   **6.** c   **7.** d   **8.** a

Checklist for Chapter 6

You are ready to take the Practice Test for Chapter 6. Be sure you have accomplished the following learning goals for this chapter. If not, review the section listed at the end of the goal. Then apply your new skills and understanding to the Practice Test.

After studying Chapter 6, I can successfully:

_____ Illustrate the octet rule for the formation of ions. (6.1)

_____ Write the formulas for ionic compounds containing the ions of metals and nonmetals of representative elements. (6.2)

_____ Use charge balance to write an ionic formula. (6.2)

_____ Write the name for an ionic compound. (6.3)

_____ Write the formula for a compound containing a polyatomic ion. (6.4)

_____ Write the names and formulas for molecular compounds. (6.5)

_____ Draw the Lewis structures for molecular compounds or polyatomic ions. (6.6)

_____ Classify a bond as nonpolar covalent, polar covalent, or ionic. (6.7)

_____ Use the VSEPR theory to determine the shape of a molecule. (6.8)

_____ Classify a molecule as polar or nonpolar. (6.8)

_____ Identify the attractive forces between particles. (6.9)

Practice Test for Chapter 6

For questions 1 through 4, consider an atom of phosphorus: (6.1)

1. Phosphorus is in Group
   A. 2A (2)   **B.** 3A (13)   **C.** 5A (15)   **D.** 7A (17)   **E.** 8A (18)

2. How many valence electrons does an atom of phosphorus have?
   A. 2   **B.** 3   **C.** 5   **D.** 8   **E.** 15

3. To achieve an octet, a phosphorus atom in an ionic compound will
   A. lose 1 electron   **B.** lose 2 electrons   **C.** lose 5 electrons
   D. gain 2 electrons   **E.** gain 3 electrons

4. A phosphide ion has a charge of
   A. 1+   **B.** 2+   **C.** 5+   **D.** 2−   **E.** 3−

5. To achieve an octet, a calcium atom (6.1)
   A. loses 1 electron   **B.** loses 2 electrons   **C.** loses 3 electrons
   D. gains 1 electron   **E.** gains 2 electrons

6. To achieve an octet, a chlorine atom (6.1)
   A. loses 1 electron   **B.** loses 2 electrons   **C.** loses 3 electrons
   D. gains 1 electron   **E.** gains 2 electrons

7. Another name for a positive ion is (6.1)
   A. anion   **B.** cation   **C.** proton   **D.** positron   **E.** sodium

8. The correct ionic charge for a calcium ion is (6.1)
   A. 1+   **B.** 2+   **C.** 1−   **D.** 2−   **E.** 3−

9. The correct ionic charge for a silver ion is (6.1)
   A. 1+   **B.** 2+   **C.** 1−   **D.** 2−   **E.** 3−

10. The correct ionic charge for a phosphate ion is (6.1)
    A. 1+   **B.** 2+   **C.** 1−   **D.** 2−   **E.** 3−

11. The correct ionic charge for a fluoride ion is (6.1)
    A. 1+   **B.** 2+   **C.** 1−   **D.** 2−   **E.** 3−

12. The correct ionic charge for a sulfate ion is (6.1)
    A. 1+   **B.** 2+   **C.** 1−   **D.** 2−   **E.** 3−

13. When the elements magnesium and sulfur react, (6.2)
    A. an ionic compound forms
    B. a molecular compound forms
    C. no reaction occurs
    D. the two repel each other and will not combine
    E. none of the above

14. An ionic bond typically occurs between (6.2)
    A. two different nonmetals   **B.** two of the same type of nonmetals
    C. two noble gases   **D.** two different metals
    E. a metal and a nonmetal

15. The formula for a compound between sodium and sulfur is (6.2)

    A. SoS   **B.** NaS   **C.** Na_2S **D.** NaS_2 **E.** Na_2SO_4

16. The formula for a compound between aluminum and oxygen is (6.2)

    A. AlO   **B.** Al_2O **C.** AlO_3 **D.** Al_2O_3 **E.** Al_3O_2

17. The formula for a compound between barium and sulfur is (6.2)

    A. BaS   **B.** Ba_2S **C.** BaS_2 **D.** Ba_2S_2 **E.** $BaSO_4$

18. The correct formula for iron(III) chloride, used to treat iron deficiency, is (6.2, 6.3)

    A. FeCl   **B.** $FeCl_2$ **C.** Fe_2Cl **D.** Fe_3Cl **E.** $FeCl_3$

19. The correct formula for ammonium sulfate is (6.2, 6.4)

    A. AmS   **B.** $AmSO_4$ **C.** $(NH_4)_2S$ **D.** NH_4SO_4 **E.** $(NH_4)_2SO_4$

20. The correct formula for copper(II) chloride is (6.2, 6.3)

    A. CoCl   **B.** CuCl   **C.** $CoCl_2$ **D.** $CuCl_2$ **E.** Cu_2Cl

21. The correct formula for lithium phosphate is (6.2, 6.4)

    A. $LiPO_4$ **B.** Li_2PO_4 **C.** Li_3PO_4 **D.** $Li_2(PO_4)_3$ **E.** $Li_3(PO_4)_2$

22. The correct formula for silver oxide is (6.2, 6.3)

    A. AgO   **B.** Ag_2O **C.** AgO_2 **D.** Ag_3O_2 **E.** Ag_3O

23. The correct formula for magnesium carbonate, used as a dietary magnesium supplement, is (6.2, 6.4)

    A. $MgCO_3$ **B.** Mg_2CO_3 **C.** $Mg(CO_3)_2$ **D.** MgCO   **E.** $Mg_2(CO_3)_3$

24. The correct formula for copper(I) sulfate, used as a fungicide, is (6.3, 6.4)

    A. $CuSO_3$ **B.** $CuSO_4$ **C.** Cu_2SO_3 **D.** $Cu(SO_4)_2$ **E.** Cu_2SO_4

25. The name of $Al_2(HPO_4)_3$ is (6.3, 6.4)

    A. aluminum hydrogen phosphite

    B. aluminum hydrogen phosphate

    C. aluminum hydrogen phosphorus

    D. aluminum hydrogen phosphorus oxide

    E. trialuminum dihydrogen phosphate

26. The name of CoS is (6.2, 6.3)

    A. copper sulfide   **B.** cobalt(II) sulfate   **C.** cobalt(I) sulfide

    D. cobalt sulfide   **E.** cobalt(II) sulfide

27. The name of $MnCl_2$, used as a supplement in intravenous solutions, is (6.2, 6.3)

    A. magnesium chloride   **B.** manganese(II) chlorine   **C.** manganese(II) chloride

    D. manganese chlorine   **E.** manganese(III) chloride

28. The name of $ZnCO_3$ is (6.3, 6.4)

    A. zinc(III) carbonate   **B.** zinc(II) carbonate   **C.** zinc bicarbonate

    D. zinc carbon trioxide   **E.** zinc carbonate

29. The name of Al_2O_3 is (6.2)

    A. aluminum oxide   **B.** aluminum(II) oxide   **C.** aluminum trioxide

    D. dialuminum trioxide   **E.** aluminum oxygenate

30. The name of $Cr_2(SO_3)_3$ is (6.3, 6.4)

    A. chromium sulfite   **B.** dichromium trisulfite   **C.** chromium(III) sulfite

    D. chromium(III) sulfate   **E.** chromium sulfate

31. The name of PH_3 is (6.5)

    A. potassium trihydrogen   **B.** phosphorus trihydride   **C.** phosphorus trihydrogen

    D. potassium trihydride   **E.** phosphorus trihydrogenide

32. The name of NCl_3 is (6.5)
   A. nitrogen chloride   **B.** nitrogen trichloride   **C.** trinitrogen chloride
   D. nitrogen chlorine three   **E.** nitrogen trichlorine

33. The name of CO is (6.5)
   A. carbon monoxide   **B.** carbonic oxide   **C.** carbon oxide
   D. carbonious oxide   **E.** carboxide

34. The formula for a compound between carbon and chlorine is (6.5)
   A. CCl **B.** CCl_2 **C.** C_4Cl **D.** CCl_4 **E.** C_4Cl_2

For questions 35 through 40, indicate the type of bonding expected between the following pairs of elements: (6.2, 6.5)
   A. ionic   **B.** nonpolar covalent   **C.** polar covalent   **D.** none

35. _____ silicon and oxygen

36. _____ chlorine and chlorine

37. _____ barium and chlorine

38. _____ sulfur and oxygen

39. _____ aluminum and fluorine

40. _____ neon and oxygen

For questions 41 through 46, determine the shape of each of the following molecules as: (6.8)
   A. linear   **B.** trigonal planar   **C.** tetrahedral
   D. trigonal pyramidal   **E.** bent (120°)   **F.** bent (109°)

41. _____ has a central atom with three electron groups and three bonded atoms

42. _____ has a central atom with two electron groups and two bonded atoms

43. _____ PCl_3

44. _____ has a central atom with three electron groups and two bonded atoms

45. _____ CCl_4

46. _____ H_2S

For questions 47 through 50, give the major type of attractive forces: (6.9)
   A. ionic bonds   **B.** dipole–dipole attractions   **C.** hydrogen bonds   **D.** dispersion forces

47. _____ NF_3 **48.** _____ HF

49. _____ LiCl   **50.** _____ N_2

Answers to the Practice Test

1. C	2. C	3. E	4. E	5. B
6. D	7. B	8. B	9. A	10. E
11. C	12. D	13. A	14. E	15. C
16. D	17. A	18. E	19. E	20. D
21. C	22. B	23. A	24. E	25. B
26. E	27. C	28. E	29. A	30. C
31. B	32. B	33. A	34. D	35. C
36. B	37. A	38. C	39. A	40. D
41. B	42. A	43. D	44. E	45. C
46. F	47. B	48. C	49. A	50. D

Ionic and Molecular Compounds

Learning Goals

- Write the symbols for the simple ions of the representative elements.
- Using charge balance, write the correct formula for an ionic compound.
- Given the formula of an ionic compound, write the correct name; given the name of an ionic compound, write the correct formula.
- Write the name and formula for an ionic compound containing a polyatomic ion.
- Given the formula of a molecular compound, write its correct name; given the name of a molecular compound, write its formula.
- Draw the Lewis structures for molecular compounds or polyatomic ions.
- Use electronegativity to determine the polarity of a bond.
- Predict the three-dimensional structure of a molecule, and classify it as polar or nonpolar.
- Describe the attractive forces between ions, polar covalent molecules, and nonpolar covalent molecules.

Chapter Outline

Chapter Opener: Pharmacy Technician

6.1   Ions: Transfer of Electrons

Chemistry Link to Health: Some Important Ions in the Body

6.2   Writing Formulas for Ionic Compounds

6.3   Naming and Writing Ionic Formulas

6.4   Polyatomic Ions

6.5   Molecular Compounds: Sharing Electrons

6.6   Lewis Structures for Molecules and Polyatomic Ions

6.7   Electronegativity and Bond Polarity

6.8   Shapes and Polarity of Molecules

6.9   Attractive Forces in Compounds

Chemistry Link to Health: Attractive Forces in Biological Compounds

Clinical Update: Compounds at the Pharmacy

✱ Core Chemistry Skills

- Writing Positive and Negative Ions (6.1)
- Writing Ionic Formulas (6.2)
- Naming Ionic Compounds (6.3)
- Writing the Names and Formulas for Molecular Compounds (6.5)
- Drawing Lewis Structures (6.6)
- Using Electronegativity (6.7)
- Predicting Shape (6.8)
- Identifying Polarity of Molecules (6.8)
- Identifying Attractive Forces (6.9)

Selected Answers and Solutions to Text Problems

6.1 Atoms with one, two, or three valence electrons will lose those electrons to acquire a noble gas electron configuration.
   a. Li loses $1\ e^-$.
   b. Ca loses $2\ e^-$.
   c. Ga loses $3\ e^-$.
   d. Cs loses $1\ e^-$.
   e. Ba loses $2\ e^-$.

6.3 Atoms form ions by losing or gaining valence electrons to achieve the same electron configuration as the nearest noble gas. Elements in Groups 1A (1), 2A (2), and 3A (13) lose valence electrons, whereas elements in Groups 5A (15), 6A (16), and 7A (17) gain valence electrons to complete octets.
   a. Sr loses $2\ e^-$.
   b. P gains $3\ e^-$.
   c. Elements in Group 7A (17) gain $1\ e^-$.
   d. Na loses $1\ e^-$.
   e. Br gains $1\ e^-$.

6.5 **a.** The element with 3 protons is lithium. In a lithium ion with 2 electrons, the ionic charge would be 1+, $(3+) + (2-) = 1+$. The lithium ion is written as Li^+.
   b. The element with 9 protons is fluorine. In a fluorine ion with 10 electrons, the ionic charge would be 1−, $(9+) + (10-) = 1-$. The fluoride ion is written as F^-.
   c. The element with 12 protons is magnesium. In a magnesium ion with 10 electrons, the ionic charge would be 2+, $(12+) + (10-) = 2+$. The magnesium ion is written as Mg^{2+}.
   d. The element with 26 protons is iron. In an iron ion with 23 electrons, the ionic charge would be 3+, $(26+) + (23-) = 3+$. This iron ion is written as Fe^{3+}.

6.7 **a.** Chlorine in Group 7A (17) gains one electron to form chloride ion, Cl^-.
   b. Cesium in Group 1A (1) loses one electron to form cesium ion, Cs^+.
   c. Nitrogen in Group 5A (15) gains three electrons to form nitride ion, N^{3-}.
   d. Radium in Group 2A (2) loses two electrons to form radium ion, Ra^{2+}.

6.9 **a.** There are 8 protons and 10 electrons in the O^{2-} ion; $(8+) + (10-) = 2-$.
   b. There are 19 protons and 18 electrons in the K^+ ion; $(19+) + (18-) = 1+$.
   c. There are 53 protons and 54 electrons in the I^- ion; $(53+) + (54-) = 1-$.
   d. There are 11 protons and 10 electrons in the Na^+ ion; $(11+) + (10-) = 1+$.

6.11 **a** (Li and Cl) and **c** (K and O) will form ionic compounds.

6.13 **a.** Na^+ and $O^{2-} \rightarrow Na_2O$
   b. Al^{3+} and $Br^- \rightarrow AlBr_3$
   c. Ba^{2+} and $N^{3-} \rightarrow Ba_3N_2$
   d. Mg^{2+} and $F^- \rightarrow MgF_2$
   e. Al^{3+} and $S^{2-} \rightarrow Al_2S_3$

6.15 **a.** Ions: K^+ and $S^{2-} \rightarrow K_2S$ Check: $2(1+) + 1(2-) = 0$
   b. Ions: Na^+ and $N^{3-} \rightarrow Na_3N$ Check: $3(1+) + 1(3-) = 0$
   c. Ions: Al^{3+} and $I^- \rightarrow AlI_3$ Check: $1(3+) + 3(1-) = 0$
   d. Ions: Ga^{3+} and $O^{2-} \rightarrow Ga_2O_3$ Check: $2(3+) + 3(2-) = 0$

6.17 **a.** aluminum oxide
   b. calcium chloride
   c. sodium oxide
   d. magnesium phosphide
   e. potassium iodide
   f. barium fluoride

6.19 **a.** iron(II)
   b. copper(II)
   c. zinc
   d. lead(IV)
   e. chromium(III)
   f. manganese(II)

6.21 **a.** Ions: Sn^{2+} and Cl^- → tin(II) chloride
b. Ions: Fe^{2+} and O^{2-} → iron(II) oxide
c. Ions: Cu^+ and S^{2-} → copper(I) sulfide
d. Ions: Cu^{2+} and S^{2-} → copper(II) sulfide
e. Ions: Cd^{2+} and Br^- → cadmium bromide
f. Ions: Hg^{2+} and Cl^- → mercury(II) chloride

6.23 **a.** Au^{3+} **b.** Fe^{3+}
c. Pb^{4+} **d.** Sn^{2+}

6.25 **a.** Ions: Mg^{2+} and Cl^- → $MgCl_2$ **b.** Ions: Na^+ and S^{2-} → Na_2S
c. Ions: Cu^+ and O^{2-} → Cu_2O **d.** Ions: Zn^{2+} and P^{3-} → Zn_3P_2
e. Ions: Au^{3+} and N^{3-} → AuN   **f.** Ions: Co^{3+} and F^- → CoF_3

6.27 **a.** Ions: Co^{3+} and Cl^- → $CoCl_3$ **b.** Ions: Pb^{4+} and O^{2-} → PbO_2
c. Ions: Ag^+ and I^- → AgI   **d.** Ions: Ca^{2+} and N^{3-} → Ca_3N_2
e. Ions: Cu^+ and P^{3-} → Cu_3P **f.** Ions: Cr^{2+} and Cl^- → $CrCl_2$

6.29 **a.** Ions: K^+ and P^{3-} → K_3P **b.** Ions: Cu^{2+} and Cl^- → $CuCl_2$
c. Ions: Fe^{3+} and Br^- → $FeBr_3$ **d.** Ions: Mg^{2+} and O^{2-} → MgO

6.31 **a.** HCO_3^- **b.** NH_4^+
c. PO_3^{3-} **d.** ClO_3^-

6.33 **a.** sulfate   **b.** carbonate
c. hydrogen sulfite (or bisulfite)   **d.** nitrate

6.35

	NO_2^-	CO_3^{2-}	HSO_4^-	PO_4^{3-}
Li^+	$LiNO_2$ Lithium nitrite	Li_2CO_3 Lithium carbonate	$LiHSO_4$ Lithium hydrogen sulfate	Li_3PO_4 Lithium phosphate
Cu^{2+}	$Cu(NO_2)_2$ Copper(II) nitrite	$CuCO_3$ Copper(II) carbonate	$Cu(HSO_4)_2$ Copper(II) hydrogen sulfate	$Cu_3(PO_4)_2$ Copper(II) phosphate
Ba^{2+}	$Ba(NO_2)_2$ Barium nitrite	$BaCO_3$ Barium carbonate	$Ba(HSO_4)_2$ Barium hydrogen sulfate	$Ba_3(PO_4)_2$ Barium phosphate

6.37 **a.** Ions: Ba^{2+} and OH^- → $Ba(OH)_2$ **b.** Ions: Na^+ and HSO_4^- → $NaHSO_4$
c. Ions: Fe^{2+} and NO_2^- → $Fe(NO_2)_2$ **d.** Ions: Zn^{2+} and PO_4^{3-} → $Zn_3(PO_4)_2$
e. Ions: Fe^{3+} and CO_3^{2-} → $Fe_2(CO_3)_3$

6.39 **a.** CO_3^{2-}, sodium carbonate   **b.** NH_4^+, ammonium sulfide
c. PO_4^{3-}, barium phosphate   **d.** NO_2^-, tin(II) nitrite

6.41 **a.** Ions: $Zn^{2+} + C_2H_3O_2^-$ → zinc acetate
b. Ions: Mg^{2+} and PO_4^{3-} → magnesium phosphate
c. Ions: $NH_4^+ + Cl^-$ → ammonium chloride
d. Ions: Na^+ and HCO_3^- → sodium bicarbonate or sodium hydrogen carbonate

6.43 When naming molecular compounds, prefixes are used to indicate the number of each atom as shown in the subscripts of the formula. The first nonmetal is named by its elemental name; the second nonmetal is named by using its elemental name with the ending changed to *ide*.
a. 1 P and 3 Br → phosphorus tribromide   **b.** 2 Cl and 1 O → dichlorine oxide
c. 1 C and 4 Br → carbon tetrabromide   **d.** 1 H and 1 F → hydrogen fluoride
e. 1 N and 3 F → nitrogen trifluoride

6.45 When naming molecular compounds, prefixes are used to indicate the number of each atom as shown in the subscripts of the formula. The first nonmetal is named by its elemental name; the second nonmetal is named by using its elemental name with the ending changed to *ide*.
 a. 2 N and 3 O → dinitrogen trioxide
 b. 2 Si and 6 Br → disilicon hexabromide
 c. 4 P and 3 S → tetraphosphorus trisulfide
 d. 1 P and 5 Cl → phosphorus pentachloride
 e. 1 Se and 6 F → selenium hexafluoride

6.47 **a.** 1 C and 4 Cl → CCl_4 **b.** 1 C and 1 O → CO
  c. 1 P and 3 Cl → PCl_3 **d.** 2 N and 4 O → N_2O_4

6.49 **a.** 1 O and 2 F → OF_2 **b.** 1 B and 3 Cl → BCl_3
  c. 2 N and 3 O → N_2O_3 **d.** 1 S and 6 F → SF_6

6.51 **a.** Ions: Al^{3+} and SO_4^{2-} → aluminum sulfate
  b. Ions: Ca^{2+} and CO_3^{2-} → calcium carbonate
  c. 2 N and 1 O → dinitrogen oxide
  d. Ions: Mg^{2+} + OH^- → magnesium hydroxide

6.53 **a.** $2 H(1 e^-) + 1 S(6 e^-) = 2 + 6 = 8$ valence electrons
  b. $2 I(7 e^-) = 14$ valence electrons
  c. $1 C(4 e^-) + 4 Cl(7 e^-) = 4 + 28 = 32$ valence electrons
  d. $1 O(6 e^-) + 1 H(1 e^-) + 1 e^-$ (negative charge) $= 6 + 1 + 1 = 8$ valence electrons

6.55 **a.** $1 H(1 e^-) + 1 F(7 e^-) = 1 + 7 = 8$ valence electrons

  H:F: or   H—F:

  b. $1 S(6 e^-) + 2 F(7 e^-) = 6 + 14 = 20$ valence electrons

  :F:S:F: or   :F—S—F:

  c. $1 N(5 e^-) + 3 Br(7 e^-) = 5 + 21 = 26$ valence electrons

  :Br:
  :Br:N:Br: or   :Br—N—Br:

  d. $1 B(3 e^-) + 4 H(1 e^-) + 1 e^-$ (negative charge) $= 3 + 4 + 1 = 8$ valence electrons

  [H H:B:H H]⁻   or   [H H—B—H H]⁻

6.57 If complete octets cannot be formed by using all the valence electrons, it is necessary to draw multiple bonds.

6.59 **a.** $1 C(4 e^-) + 1 O(6 e^-) = 4 + 6 = 10$ valence electrons

  :C::O: or   :C≡O:

  b. $1 N(5 e^-) + 3 O(6 e^-) + 1 e^-$ (negative charge) $= 5 + 18 + 1 = 24$ valence electrons

  [:O: :O:N:O:]⁻   or   [:O: :O—N—O:]⁻

c. $2\,H(1\,e^-) + 1\,C(4\,e^-) + 1\,O(6\,e^-) = 2 + 4 + 6 = 12$ valence electrons

$$
\begin{array}{ccc}
\text{:O:} & & \text{:O:} \\
\vdots & & \| \\
\text{H :C: H} & \text{or} & \text{H}\!-\!\text{C}\!-\!\text{H}
\end{array}
$$

6.61 **a.** The electronegativity values increase going from left to right across Period 2 from B to F.
   b. The electronegativity values decrease going down Group 2A (2) from Mg to Ba.
   c. The electronegativity values decrease going down Group 7A (17) from F to I.

6.63 **a.** Electronegativity increases going up a group: K, Na, Li.
   b. Electronegativity increases going left to right across a period: Na, P, Cl.
   c. Electronegativity increases going across a period and at the top of a group: Ca, Se, O.

6.65 **a.** Si — Br electronegativity difference: $2.8 - 1.8 = 1.0$, polar covalent
   b. Li — F electronegativity difference: $4.0 - 1.0 = 3.0$, ionic
   c. Br — F electronegativity difference: $4.0 - 2.8 = 1.2$, polar covalent
   d. I — I electronegativity difference: $2.5 - 2.5 = 0.0$, nonpolar covalent
   e. N — P electronegativity difference: $3.0 - 2.1 = 0.9$, polar covalent
   f. C — P electronegativity difference: $2.5 - 2.1 = 0.4$, nonpolar covalent

6.67 A dipole arrow points from the atom with the lower electronegativity value (more positive) to the atom in the bond that has the higher electronegativity value (more negative).

   a. $\overset{\delta^+\ \ \delta^-}{\text{N}\!-\!\text{F}}$ $\longrightarrow$ **b.** $\overset{\delta^+\ \ \delta^-}{\text{Si}\!-\!\text{Br}}$ $\longrightarrow$

   c. $\overset{\delta^+\ \ \delta^-}{\text{C}\!-\!\text{O}}$ $\longrightarrow$ **d.** $\overset{\delta^+\ \ \delta^-}{\text{P}\!-\!\text{Br}}$ $\longrightarrow$

   e. $\overset{\delta^-\ \ \delta^+}{\text{N}\!-\!\text{P}}$ $\longleftarrow$

6.69 **a.** 6. tetrahedral; Four electron groups around a central atom have a tetrahedral electron arrangement. With four bonded atoms, the shape of the molecule is tetrahedral.
   b. 5. trigonal pyramidal; Four electron groups around a central atom have a tetrahedral electron arrangement. With three bonded atoms (and one lone pair of electrons), the shape of the molecule is trigonal pyramidal.
   c. 3. trigonal planar; Three electron groups around a central atom have a trigonal planar electron arrangement. With three bonded atoms, the shape of the molecule is trigonal planar.

6.71 SeO_3 $1\,Se(6\,e^-) + 3\,O(6\,e^-) = 6 + 18 = 24$ valence electrons

$$
\begin{array}{c}
\text{:O:} \\
\| \\
\text{:O}\!-\!\text{Se}\!-\!\text{O:}
\end{array}
$$

   a. There are <u>three</u> electron groups around the central Se atom.
   b. The electron-group geometry is <u>trigonal planar</u>.
   c. The number of atoms attached to the central Se atom is <u>three</u>.
   d. The shape of the molecule is <u>trigonal planar</u>.

6.73 In PH_3 and NH_3, the four electron groups on the central P and N atoms have a tetrahedral arrangement, which have 109° bond angles. The shapes of the molecules are determined by the number of bonded atoms: since both PH_3 and NH_3 have three bonded atoms and one lone pair of electrons, the shapes of both are trigonal pyramidal.

6.75 **a.** The central Se atom has four electron groups with two bonded atoms and two lone pairs of electrons, which gives $SeBr_2$ a bent shape (109°).

$$\ddot{:}Br\ddot{:}$$
$$\ |\ $$
$$:\ddot{B}r—\overset{..}{\underset{..}{Se}}:$$

b. The central C atom has four electron groups bonded to four chlorine atoms; CCl_4 has a tetrahedral shape.

$$:\overset{..}{Cl}:$$
$$\ |\ $$
$$:\overset{..}{Cl}—C—\overset{..}{Cl}:$$
$$\ |\ $$
$$:\overset{..}{Cl}:$$

c. The central O atom has four electron groups, but only two are bonded to bromine atoms; the shape of OBr_2 is bent (109°).

$$:\overset{..}{Br}:$$
$$\ |\ $$
$$:\overset{..}{B}r—\overset{..}{\underset{..}{O}}:$$

6.77 Cl_2 is a nonpolar molecule because there is a nonpolar covalent bond between Cl atoms, which have identical electronegativity values. In HCl, the bond is a polar covalent bond, which makes HCl a polar molecule.

$$:\overset{..}{\underset{..}{Cl}}—\overset{..}{\underset{..}{Cl}}: \qquad H—\overset{..}{\underset{..}{Cl}}:$$
$$\text{nonpolar} \qquad\quad \overset{\longleftrightarrow}{}$$
$$ \text{polar}$$

6.79 **a.** The molecule HBr contains the polar covalent H—Br bond; this single dipole makes HBr a polar molecule.

$$H—Br$$
$$\overset{\longleftrightarrow}{}$$
$$\text{polar}$$

b. The molecule NF_3 contains three polar covalent N—F bonds and a lone pair of electrons on the central N atom. This asymmetric trigonal pyramidal shape makes NF_3 a polar molecule.

$$F\overset{\longleftarrow}{\cdots}\overset{..}{N}$$
$$F\overset{\nearrow}{}\overset{\searrow}{}F$$
$$\text{polar}$$

c. In the molecule CHF_3, there are three polar covalent C—F bonds and one nonpolar covalent C—H bond, which makes CHF_3 a polar molecule.

$$H$$
$$|$$
$$\overset{\longleftarrow}{}C\overset{\longrightarrow}{}$$
$$F\overset{\cdots}{\nwarrow}\ \big\downarrow\ F$$
$$F$$
$$\text{polar}$$

6.81 a. BrF is a polar molecule. An attraction between the positive end of one polar molecule and the negative end of another polar molecule is called a dipole–dipole attraction.

b. An ionic bond is an attraction between a positive and negative ion, as in KCl.

c. NF_3 is a polar molecule. An attraction between the positive end of one polar molecule and the negative end of another polar molecule is called a dipole–dipole attraction.

d. Cl_2 is a nonpolar molecule. The weak attractions that occur between temporary dipoles in nonpolar molecules are called dispersion forces.

6.83 a. Hydrogen bonds are strong dipole–dipole attractions that occur between a partially positive hydrogen atom of one molecule and one of the strongly electronegative atoms F, O, or N in another, as is seen with CH_3OH molecules.

b. CO is a polar molecule. Dipole–dipole attractions occur between dipoles in polar molecules.

c. Dispersion forces occur between temporary dipoles in nonpolar CF_4 molecules.

d. Dispersion forces occur between temporary dipoles in nonpolar CH_3—CH_3 molecules.

6.85 a. HF would have a higher boiling point than HBr; the hydrogen bonds in HF are stronger than the dipole–dipole attractions in HBr.

b. NaF would have a higher boiling point than HF; the ionic bonds in NaF are stronger than the hydrogen bonds in HF.

c. $MgBr_2$ would have a higher boiling point than PBr_3; the ionic bonds in $MgBr_2$ are stronger than the dipole–dipole attractions in PBr_3.

d. CH_3OH would have a higher boiling point than CH_4; the hydrogen bonds in CH_3OH are stronger than the dispersion forces in CH_4.

6.87 a. Ions: $Mg^{2+} + SO_4^{2-} \rightarrow MgSO_4$ **b.** Ions: $Ca^{2+} + CO_3^{2-} \rightarrow CaCO_3$

c. Ions: $Al^{3+} + OH^- \rightarrow Al(OH)_3$

6.89 a. ionic   **b.** ionic   **c.** ionic

6.91 a. C—C electronegativity difference $2.5 - 2.5 = 0.0$

b. C—H electronegativity difference $2.5 - 2.1 = 0.4$

c. C—O electronegativity difference $3.5 - 2.5 = 1.0$

6.93 a. nonpolar covalent   **b.** nonpolar covalent

c. polar covalent

6.95 a. By losing two valence electrons from the third energy level, magnesium achieves an octet in the second energy level.

b. The magnesium ion Mg^{2+} has the same electron configuration as the noble gas Ne $(1s^2 2s^2 2p^6)$.

c. Group 1A (1) and 2A (2) elements achieve octets by losing electrons when they form compounds. Group 8A (18) elements already have a stable octet of valence electrons (or two electrons for helium), so they are not normally found in compounds.

6.97 a. The element with 15 protons is phosphorus. In an ion of phosphorus with 18 electrons, the ionic charge would be 3−, $(15+) + (18-) = 3-$. The phosphide ion is written P^{3-}.

b. The element with 8 protons is oxygen. Since there are also 8 electrons, this is an oxygen (O) atom.

c. The element with 30 protons is zinc. In an ion of zinc with 28 electrons, the ionic charge would be 2+, $(30+) + (28-) = 2+$. The zinc ion is written Zn^{2+}.

d. The element with 26 protons is iron. In an ion of iron with 23 electrons, the ionic charge would be 3+, $(26+) + (23-) = 3+$. This iron ion is written Fe^{3+}.

6.99   **a.** X is in Group 1A (1); Y is in Group 6A (16).
   b. ionic
   c. X^+, Y^{2-}
   d. X_2Y
   e. X^+ and $S^{2-} \rightarrow X_2S$
   f. 1 Y and 2 Cl $\rightarrow YCl_2$
   g. molecular

6.101 **a.** 2; trigonal pyramidal shape, polar molecule
   b. 1; bent shape (109°), polar molecule
   c. 3; tetrahedral shape, nonpolar molecule

6.103

Electron Configurations		Cation	Anion	Formula of Compound	Name of Compound
$1s^22s^22p^63s^2$	$1s^22s^22p^3$	Mg^{2+}	N^{3-}	Mg_3N_2	Magnesium nitride
$1s^22s^22p^63s^23p^64s^1$	$1s^22s^22p^4$	K^+	O^{2-}	K_2O	Potassium oxide
$1s^22s^22p^63s^23p^1$	$1s^22s^22p^63s^23p^5$	Al^{3+}	Cl^-	$AlCl_3$	Aluminum chloride

6.105 **a.** 2 valence electrons, 1 bonding pair, no lone pairs
   b. 8 valence electrons, 1 bonding pair, 3 lone pairs
   c. 14 valence electrons, 1 bonding pair, 6 lone pairs

6.107 **a.** N^{3-} has an electron configuration of $1s^22s^22p^6$, which is the same as neon (Ne).
   b. Mg^{2+} has an electron configuration of $1s^22s^22p^6$, which is the same as neon (Ne).
   c. P^{3-} has an electron configuration of $1s^22s^22p^63s^23p^6$, which is the same as argon (Ar).
   d. Al^{3+} has an electron configuration of $1s^22s^22p^6$, which is the same as neon (Ne).
   e. Li^+ has an electron configuration of $1s^2$, which is the same as helium (He).

6.109 **a.** An element that forms an ion with a 2+ charge would be in Group 2A (2).
   b. The Lewis symbol for an element in Group 2A (2) is $\overset{\bullet}{X}\!\cdot$
   c. Mg is the Group 2A (2) element in Period 3.
   d. Ions: X^{2+} and $N^{3-} \rightarrow X_3N_2$

6.111 **a.** Tin(IV) is Sn^{4+}.
   b. The Sn^{4+} ion has 50 protons and $50 - 4 = 46$ electrons.
   c. Ions: Sn^{4+} and $O^{2-} \rightarrow SnO_2$
   d. Ions: Sn^{4+} and $PO_4^{3-} \rightarrow Sn_3(PO_4)_4$

6.113 **a.** Ions: Sn^{2+} and $S^{2-} \rightarrow SnS$ **b.** Ions: Pb^{4+} and $O^{2-} \rightarrow PbO_2$
   c. Ions: Ag^+ and $Cl^- \rightarrow AgCl$ **d.** Ions: Ca^{2+} and $N^{3-} \rightarrow Ca_3N_2$
   e. Ions: Cu^+ and $P^{3-} \rightarrow Cu_3P$ **f.** Ions: Cr^{2+} and $Br^- \rightarrow CrBr_2$

6.115 **a.** 1 N and 3 Cl $\rightarrow$ nitrogen trichloride
   b. 2 N and 3 S $\rightarrow$ dinitrogen trisulfide
   c. 2 N and 1 O $\rightarrow$ dinitrogen oxide
   d. 1 I and 1 F $\rightarrow$ iodine fluoride
   e. 1 B and 3 F $\rightarrow$ boron trifluoride
   f. 2 P and 5 O $\rightarrow$ diphosphorus pentoxide

6.117 **a.** 1 C and 1 S $\rightarrow CS$ **b.** 2 P and 5 O $\rightarrow P_2O_5$
   c. 2 H and 1 S $\rightarrow H_2S$ **d.** 1 S and 2 Cl $\rightarrow SCl_2$

6.119 **a.** Ionic, ions are Fe^{3+} and Cl^- → iron(III) chloride
    b. Ionic, ions are Na^+ and SO_4^{2-} → sodium sulfate
    c. Molecular, 1 N and 2 O → nitrogen dioxide
    d. Molecular, diatomic element → nitrogen
    e. Molecular, 1 P and 5 F → phosphorus pentafluoride
    f. Molecular, 1 C and 4 F → carbon tetrafluoride

6.121 **a.** Ions: Sn^{2+} and CO_3^{2-} → $SnCO_3$ **b.** Ions: Li^+ and P^{3-} → Li_3P
    c. Covalent, 1 Si and 4 Cl → $SiCl_4$ **d.** Ions: Mn^{3+} and O^{2-} → Mn_2O_3
    e. Covalent, diatomic element → Br_2 **f.** Ions: Ca^{2+} and Br^- → $CaBr_2$

6.123 **a.** $1\,B(3\,e^-) + 4\,F(7\,e^-) + 1\,e^-\text{(negative charge)} = 3 + 28 + 1 = 32$ valence electrons

    b. $2\,Cl(7\,e^-) + 1\,O(6\,e^-) = 14 + 6 = 20$ valence electrons

    c. $1\,N(5\,e^-) + 3\,H(1\,e^-) + 1\,O(6\,e^-) = 5 + 3 + 6 = 14$ valence electrons

    d. $2\,C(4\,e^-) + 2\,H(1\,e^-) + 2\,Cl(7\,e^-) = 8 + 2 + 14 = 24$ valence electrons

6.125 **a.** $3\,N(5\,e^-) + 1\,e^-\text{(negative charge)} = 15 + 1 = 16$ valence electrons

    b. $1\,N(5\,e^-) + 2\,O(6\,e^-) - 1\,e^-\text{(positive charge)} = 5 + 12 - 1 = 16$ valence electrons

    c. $1\,C(4\,e^-) + 1\,N(5\,e^-) + 1\,S(6\,e^-) + 1\,e^-\text{(negative charge)}$
       $= 4 + 5 + 6 + 1 = 16$ valence electrons

6.127 **a.** C—O $(3.5 - 2.5 = 1.0)$ is more polar than C—N $(3.5 - 3.0 = 0.5)$.
    b. N—F $(4.0 - 3.0 = 1.0)$ is more polar than N—Br $(3.0 - 2.8 = 0.2)$.
    c. S—Cl $(3.0 - 2.5 = 0.5)$ is more polar than Br—Cl $(3.0 - 2.8 = 0.2)$.
    d. Br—I $(2.8 - 2.5 = 0.3)$ is more polar than Br—Cl $(3.0 - 2.8 = 0.2)$.
    e. N—F $(4.0 - 3.0 = 1.0)$ is more polar than N—O $(3.5 - 3.0 = 0.5)$.

6.129 a. Si — Cl electronegativity difference 3.0 − 1.8 = 1.2, polar covalent
b. C — C electronegativity difference 2.5 − 2.5 = 0.0, nonpolar covalent
c. Na — Cl electronegativity difference 3.0 − 0.9 = 2.1, ionic
d. C — H electronegativity difference 2.5 − 2.1 = 0.4, nonpolar covalent
e. F — F electronegativity difference 4.0 − 4.0 = 0.0, nonpolar covalent

6.131 a. A molecule that has a central atom with three bonded atoms and one lone pair will have a trigonal pyramidal shape. This asymmetric shape means the dipoles do not cancel, and the molecule will be polar.
b. A molecule that has a central atom with two bonded atoms and two lone pairs will have a bent shape (109°). This asymmetric shape means the dipoles do not cancel, and the molecule will be polar.

6.133 a. NH_3 is a polar molecule. The dipoles from the three polar covalent N — H bonds do not cancel because of the asymmetric trigonal pyramidal shape of the molecule.

$$\text{H} \cdots \overset{\cdot\cdot}{\text{N}}$$
$$\text{H} \diagup \qquad \diagdown \text{H}$$

b. The molecule CH_3Cl has a tetrahedral shape but the atoms bonded to the central atom, C, are not identical. The three C — H bonds are nonpolar, but the C — Cl bond is polar. The nonpolar C — H bonds do not cancel the dipole from the polar C — Cl bond, making it a polar molecule.

$$\text{Cl}$$
$$|$$
$$\text{C}$$
$$\text{H} \cdots \quad \diagdown \text{H}$$
$$\text{H}$$

c. The molecule SiF_4 consists of a central atom, Si, with four polar covalent Si — F bonds. Because it has a tetrahedral shape, the four dipoles cancel, which makes SiF_4 a nonpolar molecule.

$$\text{F}$$
$$|$$
$$\text{Si}$$
$$\text{F} \cdots \quad \diagdown \text{F}$$
$$\text{F}$$

6.135 a. The molecule SI_2 contains two nonpolar covalent bonds (EN 2.5 − 2.5 = 0) and two lone pairs of electrons on the central S atom. The molecule has a bent shape (109°), but since there are no dipoles from the S — I bonds, SI_2 is a nonpolar molecule.

$$\cdot\overset{\cdot\cdot}{\text{S}}\cdot$$
$$\text{I} \diagup \qquad \diagdown \text{I}$$

b. The molecule PF_3 contains three polar covalent P — F bonds (EN 4.0 − 2.1 = 1.9) and a lone pair of electrons on the central P atom. This asymmetric trigonal pyramidal shape makes PF_3 a polar molecule.

$$\text{F} \cdots \overset{\cdot\cdot}{\text{P}}$$
$$\text{F} \diagup \qquad \diagdown \text{F}$$

6.137 a. Hydrogen bonding (3) involves strong dipole–dipole attractions that occur between a partially positive hydrogen atom of one polar molecule and one of the strongly electronegative atoms F, O, or N in another, as is seen with NH_3 molecules.
b. HI is a polar molecule. Dipole–dipole attractions (2) occur between dipoles in polar molecules.
c. Dispersion forces (4) occur between temporary dipoles in nonpolar I_2 molecules.
d. Ionic bonds (1) are strong attractions between positive and negative ions, as in Cs_2O.

6.139

Atom or Ion	Number of Protons	Number of Electrons	Electrons Lost / Gained
K^+	$19\ p^+$	$18\ e^-$	$1\ e^-$ lost
Mg^{2+}	$12\ p^+$	$10\ e^-$	$2\ e^-$ lost
O^{2-}	$8\ p^+$	$10\ e^-$	$2\ e^-$ gained
Al^{3+}	$13\ p^+$	$10\ e^-$	$3\ e^-$ lost

6.141 a. X as a X^{3+} ion would be in Group 3A (13).
   b. X as a X^{2-} ion would be in Group 6A (16).
   c. X as a X^{2+} ion would be in Group 2A (2).

6.143 Compounds with a metal and nonmetal are classified as ionic; compounds with two nonmetals are molecular.
   a. Ionic, ions are Li^+ and $HPO_4^{2-} \rightarrow$ lithium hydrogen phosphate
   b. Ionic, ions are Cr^{2+} and $NO_2^- \rightarrow$ chromium(II) nitrite
   c. Ionic, ions are Mg^{2+} and $ClO_2^- \rightarrow$ magnesium chlorite
   d. Molecular, 1 N and 3 F $\rightarrow$ nitrogen trifluoride
   e. Ionic, ions are Ca^{2+} and $HSO_4^- \rightarrow$ calcium bisulfate or calcium hydrogen sulfate
   f. Ionic, ions are K^+ and $ClO_4^- \rightarrow$ potassium perchlorate
   g. Ionic, ions are Au^{3+} and $SO_3^{2-} \rightarrow$ gold(III) sulfite
   h. Molecular, iodine (diatomic element)

Selected Answers to Combining Ideas from Chapters 4 to 6

CI.7 a. Y has the higher electronegativity, since it is a nonmetal in Group 7A (17).

b. X^{2+}, Y^-

c. X has an electron configuration of $1s^2 2s^2 2p^6 3s^2$. Y has an electron configuration of $1s^2 2s^2 2p^6 3s^2 3p^5$.

d. X^{2+} has an electron configuration of $1s^2 2s^2 2p^6$. Y^- has an electron configuration of $1s^2 2s^2 2p^6 3s^2 3p^6$.

e. X^{2+} has the same electron configuration as the noble gas neon (Ne). Y^- has the same electron configuration as the noble gas argon (Ar).

f. $MgCl_2$, magnesium chloride

CI.9 a.

Isotope	Number of Protons	Number of Neutrons	Number of Electrons
$^{27}_{14}Si$	14	13	14
$^{28}_{14}Si$	14	14	14
$^{29}_{14}Si$	14	15	14
$^{30}_{14}Si$	14	16	14
$^{31}_{14}Si$	14	17	14

b. Electron configuration of Si: $1s^2 2s^2 2p^6 3s^2 3p^2$

c. $^{28}_{14}Si \quad 27.977 \times \dfrac{92.23}{100} = 25.80 \text{ amu}$

$^{29}_{14}Si \quad 28.976 \times \dfrac{4.683}{100} = 1.357 \text{ amu}$

$^{30}_{14}Si \quad 29.974 \times \dfrac{3.087}{100} = 0.9253 \text{ amu}$

Atomic mass of Si = 28.08 amu

d. $^{27}_{14}Si \longrightarrow {}^{27}_{13}Al + {}^{0}_{+1}e$

$^{31}_{14}Si \longrightarrow {}^{31}_{15}P + {}^{0}_{-1}e$

e.

$$:\ddot{C}l - \underset{\underset{:\ddot{C}l:}{|}}{\overset{\overset{:\ddot{C}l:}{|}}{Si}} - \ddot{C}l:$$

The central atom Si has four electron groups bonded to four chlorine atoms; $SiCl_4$ has a tetrahedral shape.

f. Half of a radioactive sample decays with each half-life:

16 μCi of $^{31}_{14}Si \xrightarrow{\text{1 half-life}}$ 8.0 μCi of $^{31}_{14}Si \xrightarrow{\text{2 half-lives}}$ 4.0 μCi of $^{31}_{14}Si \xrightarrow{\text{3 half-lives}}$ 2.0 μCi of $^{31}_{14}Si$

Therefore, 3 half-lives have passed.

3 half-lives $\times \dfrac{2.6 \text{ h}}{1 \text{ half-life}} = 7.8 \text{ h}$ (2 SFs)

CI.11 a. $^{40}_{19}\text{K} \longrightarrow {}^{40}_{20}\text{Ca} + {}^{0}_{-1}e$, beta particle   and $^{40}_{19}\text{K} \longrightarrow {}^{40}_{18}\text{Ar} + {}^{0}_{+1}e$, positron

b. $1.6 \text{ oz K} \times \dfrac{1 \text{ lb K}}{16 \text{ oz K}} \times \dfrac{454 \text{ g K}}{1 \text{ lb K}} \times \dfrac{0.012 \text{ g } {}^{40}_{19}\text{K}}{100 \text{ g K}} \times \dfrac{7.0 \text{ } \mu\text{Ci}}{1 \text{ g } {}^{40}_{19}\text{K}} \times \dfrac{1 \text{ mCi}}{1000 \text{ } \mu\text{Ci}}$

$= 3.8 \times 10^{-5} \text{ mCi } (2 \text{ SFs})$

$1.6 \text{ oz K} \times \dfrac{1 \text{ lb K}}{16 \text{ oz K}} \times \dfrac{454 \text{ g K}}{1 \text{ lb K}} \times \dfrac{0.012 \text{ g } {}^{40}_{19}\text{K}}{100 \text{ g K}} \times \dfrac{7.0 \text{ } \mu\text{Ci}}{1 \text{ g } {}^{40}_{19}\text{K}} \times \dfrac{1 \text{ Ci}}{10^{6} \text{ } \mu\text{Ci}} \times \dfrac{3.7 \times 10^{10} \text{ Bq}}{1 \text{ Ci}}$

$= 1400 \text{ Bq } (2 \text{ SFs})$

7

Chemical Reactions and Quantities

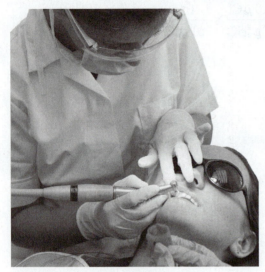

Jane is delighted with the teeth-whitening process and how her teeth look. The hydrogen peroxide gel caused a chemical reaction in the enamel coating of her teeth, which oxidized the brown and yellow stains she had on her teeth. Jane now avoids food or drinks such as dark tea and coffee that can stain her teeth. She now uses a teeth-whitening toothpaste once a week and will return to her dental hygienist in a year for a touch-up treatment. If hydrogen peroxide forms oxygen gas and water when it reacts, what is the balanced equation?

Credit: Craig Holmes Premium/Alamy

CHAPTER READINESS*

📟 Key Math Skills

- Calculating Percentages (1.4C)
- Solving Equations (1.4D)
- Writing Numbers in Scientific Notation (1.4F)

⚛ Core Chemistry Skills

- Counting Significant Figures (2.2)
- Using Significant Figures in Calculations (2.3)
- Writing Conversion Factors from Equalities (2.5)

- Using Conversion Factors (2.6)
- Using Energy Units (3.4)
- Writing Ionic Formulas (6.2)
- Naming Ionic Compounds (6.3)
- Writing the Names and Formulas for Molecular Compounds (6.5)

*These Key Math Skills and Core Chemistry Skills from previous chapters are listed here for your review as you proceed to the new material in this chapter.

7.1 Equations for Chemical Reactions

Learning Goal: Write a balanced chemical equation from the formulas of the reactants and products for a reaction; determine the number of atoms in the reactants and products.

- When new substances form, a chemical reaction has taken place.
- Chemical change may be indicated by a formation of a gas (bubbles), change in color, formation of a solid, and/or heat produced or heat absorbed.
- A chemical equation shows the formulas of the reactants on the left side of the arrow and the formulas of the products on the right side.
- In a balanced chemical equation, numbers called *coefficients*, which appear in front of the symbols or formulas, provide the same number of atoms for each kind of element on the reactant and product sides. When a coefficient is 1, it does not appear in the balanced equation.

- Each formula in an equation is followed by an abbreviation, in parentheses, that gives the physical state of the substance: solid (s), liquid (l), or gas (g), or aqueous solution (aq).
- The Greek letter delta (Δ) over the arrow in an equation indicates that the reaction requires heat.

♦ **Learning Exercise 7.1A**

Indicate the number of atoms of each element on the reactant side and on the product side for each of the following balanced equations:

a. $CaCO_3(s) \longrightarrow CaO(s) + CO_2(g)$

Element	Atoms on Reactant Side	Atoms on Product Side
Ca		
C		
O		

$2H_2(g) + O_2(g) \longrightarrow 2H_2O(g)$

H   O   H   O

Reactant atoms = Product atoms

When there are the same numbers of each type of atom in the reactants as in the products, the equation is balanced.

b. $2Na(s) + H_2O(l) \longrightarrow Na_2O(s) + H_2(g)$

Element	Atoms on Reactant Side	Atoms on Product Side
Na		
H		
O		

c. $C_5H_{12}(g) + 8O_2(g) \longrightarrow 5CO_2(g) + 6H_2O(g)$

Element	Atoms on Reactant Side	Atoms on Product Side
C		
H		
O		

d. $2AgNO_3(aq) + K_2S(aq) \longrightarrow Ag_2S(s) + 2KNO_3(aq)$

Element	Atoms on Reactant Side	Atoms on Product Side
Ag		
N		
O		
K		
S		

e. $2Al(OH)_3(s) + 3H_2SO_4(aq) \longrightarrow Al_2(SO_4)_3(aq) + 6H_2O(l)$

Element	Atoms on Reactant Side	Atoms on Product Side
Al		
O		
H		
S		

Answers

a. $CaCO_3(s) \longrightarrow CaO(s) + CO_2(g)$

Element	Atoms on Reactant Side	Atoms on Product Side
Ca	1	1
C	1	1
O	3	3

b. $2Na(s) + H_2O(l) \longrightarrow Na_2O(s) + H_2(g)$

Element	Atoms on Reactant Side	Atoms on Product Side
Na	2	2
H	2	2
O	1	1

c. $C_5H_{12}(g) + 8O_2(g) \longrightarrow 5CO_2(g) + 6H_2O(g)$

Element	Atoms on Reactant Side	Atoms on Product Side
C	5	5
H	12	12
O	16	16

d. $2AgNO_3(aq) + K_2S(aq) \longrightarrow Ag_2S(s) + 2KNO_3(aq)$

Element	Atoms on Reactant Side	Atoms on Product Side
Ag	2	2
N	2	2
O	6	6
K	2	2
S	1	1

e. $2Al(OH)_3(s) + 3H_2SO_4(aq) \longrightarrow Al_2(SO_4)_3(aq) + 6H_2O(l)$

Element	Atoms on Reactant Side	Atoms on Product Side
Al	2	2
O	18	18
H	12	12
S	3	3

Guide to Balancing a Chemical Equation	
STEP 1	Write an equation using the correct formulas for the reactants and products.
STEP 2	Count the atoms of each element in the reactants and products.
STEP 3	Use coefficients to balance each element.
STEP 4	Check the final equation to confirm it is balanced.

Example: Balance the following equation:

$$N_2(g) + H_2(g) \longrightarrow NH_3(g)$$

1. Write an equation using the correct formulas for the reactants and products.

$$N_2(g) + H_2(g) \longrightarrow NH_3(g)$$

2. Count the atoms of each element in the reactants and products.

$$N_2(g) + H_2(g) \longrightarrow NH_3(g)$$

2N   2H   1N, 3H

3. Use coefficients to balance each element. Balance the N atoms by placing a coefficient of 2 in front of NH_3. (This increases the number of H atoms, too.) Recheck the number of N atoms and the number of H atoms.

$$N_2(g) + H_2(g) \longrightarrow 2NH_3(g)$$

2N   2H   2N, 6H

Balance the H atoms by placing a coefficient of 3 in front of H_2.

$$N_2(g) + 3H_2(g) \longrightarrow 2NH_3(g)$$

4. Check the final equation to confirm it is balanced.

$$N_2(g) + 3H_2(g) \longrightarrow 2NH_3(g)$$

2N   6H   2N, 6H   *The equation is balanced.*

♦ **Learning Exercise 7.1B**

Balance each of the following equations by placing coefficients in front of the formulas as needed:

a. ___ $MgO(s) \longrightarrow$ ___ $Mg(s) +$ ___ $O_2(g)$

b. ___ $Zn(s) +$ ___ $HCl(aq) \longrightarrow$ ___ $ZnCl_2(aq) +$ ___ $H_2(g)$

c. ___ $Al(s) +$ ___ $CuSO_4(aq) \longrightarrow$ ___ $Cu(s) +$ ___ $Al_2(SO_4)_3(aq)$

d. ___ $Al_2S_3(s) +$ ___ $H_2O(l) \longrightarrow$ ___ $Al(OH)_3(s) +$ ___ $H_2S(g)$

e. ___ $BaCl_2(aq) +$ ___ $Na_2SO_4(aq) \longrightarrow$ ___ $BaSO_4(s) +$ ___ $NaCl(aq)$

f. ___ $CO(g) +$ ___ $Fe_2O_3(s) \longrightarrow$ ___ $Fe(s) +$ ___ $CO_2(g)$

g. ___ $K(s) +$ ___ $H_2O(l) \longrightarrow$ ___ $K_2O(s) +$ ___ $H_2(g)$

h. ___ $Fe(OH)_3(s) \longrightarrow$ ___ $Fe_2O_3(s) +$ ___ $H_2O(l)$

i. Galactose, $C_6H_{12}O_6(aq)$, is found in milk. In the body, galactose reacts with O_2 gas to form CO_2 gas and liquid water. Write a balanced chemical equation for the reaction.

j. Maltose, $C_{12}H_{22}O_{11}(aq)$, is found in corn syrup. In the body, maltose reacts with O_2 gas to form CO_2 gas and liquid water. Write a balanced chemical equation for the reaction.

Answers

a. $2MgO(s) \longrightarrow 2Mg(s) + O_2(g)$

b. $Zn(s) + 2HCl(aq) \longrightarrow ZnCl_2(aq) + H_2(g)$

c. $2Al(s) + 3CuSO_4(aq) \longrightarrow 3Cu(s) + Al_2(SO_4)_3(aq)$

d. $Al_2S_3(s) + 6H_2O(l) \longrightarrow 2Al(OH)_3(s) + 3H_2S(g)$

e. $BaCl_2(aq) + Na_2SO_4(aq) \longrightarrow BaSO_4(s) + 2NaCl(aq)$

f. $3CO(g) + Fe_2O_3(s) \longrightarrow 2Fe(s) + 3CO_2(g)$

g. $2K(s) + H_2O(l) \longrightarrow K_2O(s) + H_2(g)$

h. $2Fe(OH)_3(s) \longrightarrow Fe_2O_3(s) + 3H_2O(l)$

i. $C_6H_{12}O_6(aq) + 6O_2(g) \longrightarrow 6CO_2(g) + 6H_2O(l)$

j. $C_{12}H_{22}O_{11}(aq) + 12O_2(g) \longrightarrow 12CO_2(g) + 11H_2O(l)$

7.2   Types of Reactions

Learning Goal: Identify a chemical reaction as a combination, decomposition, single replacement, double replacement, or combustion.

- Reactions are classified as combination, decomposition, single replacement, double replacement, or combustion.

- In a *combination* reaction, two or more reactants form one product:

    $A + B \longrightarrow AB$

- In a *decomposition* reaction, a reactant splits into two or more simpler products:

    $AB \longrightarrow A + B$

- In a *single replacement* reaction, an uncombined element takes the place of an element in a compound:

    $A + BC \longrightarrow AC + B$

- In a *double replacement* reaction, the positive ions in the reactants switch places:

    $AB + CD \longrightarrow AD + CB$

- In a *combustion* reaction, a compound of carbon and hydrogen reacts with oxygen to form CO_2, H_2O, and energy.

    $$C_XH_Y(g) + ZO_2(g) \xrightarrow{\Delta} XCO_2(g) + \frac{Y}{2}H_2O(g) + \text{energy}$$

Key Terms for Sections 7.1–7.2

Match each of the following terms with the correct description below:

    a. combustion reaction   **b.** chemical equation   **c.** combination reaction

    d. decomposition reaction   **e.** single replacement reaction

1. ____ a reaction in which a single reactant splits into two or more simpler substances

2. ____ a reaction in which one element replaces a different element in a compound

3. ____ a reaction in which a carbon-containing compound burns in oxygen from the air to produce carbon dioxide, water, and energy

4. ____ a reaction in which reactants combine to form a single product

5. ____ a shorthand method of writing a chemical reaction with the formulas of the reactants written on the left side of an arrow and the formulas of the products written on the right side

Answers   **1.** d   **2.** e   **3.** a   **4.** c   **5.** b

---

♦ **Learning Exercise 7.2A**

Match each of the following reactions with the type of reaction:

    a. combination   **b.** decomposition

    c. single replacement   **d.** double replacement   **e.** combustion

⚛ **CORE CHEMISTRY SKILL**

Classifying Types of Chemical Reactions

1. ____ $N_2(g) + 3H_2(g) \longrightarrow 2NH_3(g)$

2. ____ $BaCl_2(aq) + K_2CO_3(aq) \longrightarrow BaCO_3(s) + 2KCl(aq)$

3. ____ $2H_2O_2(aq) \longrightarrow 2H_2O(l) + O_2(g)$

4. ____ $CuO(s) + H_2(g) \longrightarrow Cu(s) + H_2O(l)$

5. ____ $N_2(g) + 2O_2(g) \longrightarrow 2NO_2(g)$

6. ____ $C_2H_4(g) + 3O_2(g) \longrightarrow 2CO_2(g) + 2H_2O(g) + energy$

7. ____ $PbCO_3(s) \longrightarrow PbO(s) + CO_2(g)$

8. ____ $2Al(s) + Fe_2O_3(s) \longrightarrow 2Fe(s) + Al_2O_3(s)$

Answers   **1.** a   **2.** d   **3.** b   **4.** c

                  5. a   **6.** e   **7.** b   **8.** c

In a combustion reaction, a candle burns using the oxygen in the air.

Credit: Sergiy Zavgorodny / Shutterstock

♦ **Learning Exercise 7.2B**

1. One way to remove tarnish from silver is to place the silver object on a piece of aluminum foil and add boiling water and some baking soda. The unbalanced equation is the following:

    $Al(s) + Ag_2S(s) \longrightarrow Ag(s) + Al_2S_3(s)$

    a. Write the balanced equation for the reaction.

    b. What type of reaction takes place?

2. Octane, C_8H_{18}, a compound in gasoline, burns in oxygen (O_2) to produce carbon dioxide, water, and energy.

   a. Write the balanced equation for the reaction.

   b. What type of reaction takes place?

Answers   **1a.** $2Al(s) + 3Ag_2S(s) \longrightarrow 6Ag(s) + Al_2S_3(s)$ **1b.** single replacement

   2a. $2C_8H_{18}(l) + 25O_2(g) \longrightarrow 16CO_2(g) + 18H_2O(g)$ **2b.** combustion

7.3   Oxidation–Reduction Reactions

Learning Goal: Define the terms oxidation and reduction; identify the reactants oxidized and reduced.

* In an oxidation–reduction reaction, there is a loss and gain of electrons. In an oxidation, electrons are lost. In a reduction, electrons are gained.
* An oxidation must always be accompanied by a reduction. The number of electrons lost in the oxidation reaction is equal to the number of electrons gained in the reduction reaction.
* In biological systems, the term *oxidation* describes the gain of oxygen or the loss of hydrogen. The term *reduction* is used to describe a loss of oxygen or a gain of hydrogen.

◆ **Learning Exercise 7.3**

For each of the following reactions, indicate whether the underlined element is *oxidized or reduced*. Explain your answer.

⚛ **CORE CHEMISTRY SKILL**

Identifying Oxidized and Reduced Substances

   a. $4\underline{Al}(s) + 3O_2(g) \longrightarrow 2Al_2O_3(s)$ Al is   _____

   b. $\underline{Fe}^{3+}(aq) + e^- \longrightarrow Fe^{2+}(aq)$ Fe^{3+} is   _____

   c. $\underline{Cu}O(s) + H_2(g) \longrightarrow Cu(s) + H_2O(l)$ Cu^{2+} is   _____

   d. $2\underline{Cl}^-(aq) \longrightarrow Cl_2(g) + 2\,e^-$ Cl^- is   _____

   e. $\underline{Cu}Cl_2(aq) + Zn(s) \longrightarrow ZnCl_2(aq) + Cu(s)$ Cu^{2+} is   _____

Answers

   a. Al is oxidized to Al^{3+}; loss of electrons   **b.** Fe^{3+} is reduced to Fe^{2+}; gain of electrons

   c. Cu^{2+} is reduced to Cu; gain of electrons   **d.** Cl^- is oxidized to Cl_2; loss of electrons

   e. Cu^{2+} is reduced to Cu; gain of electrons

7.4 The Mole

Learning Goal: *Use Avogadro's number to determine the number of particles in a given number of moles.*

- A mole of any element contains Avogadro's number, 6.02×10^{23}, of atoms; a mole of any compound contains 6.02×10^{23} molecules or formula units.

- Avogadro's number provides a conversion factor between moles and number of particles:

$$\frac{1 \text{ mole}}{6.02 \times 10^{23} \text{ particles}} \quad \text{and} \quad \frac{6.02 \times 10^{23} \text{ particles}}{1 \text{ mole}}$$

- The subscripts in a formula indicate the number of moles of each element in 1 mole of the compound.

Guide to Calculating the Atoms or Molecules of a Substance	
STEP 1	State the given and needed quantities.
STEP 2	Write a plan to convert moles to atoms or molecules.
STEP 3	Use Avogadro's number to write conversion factors.
STEP 4	Set up the problem to calculate the number of particles.

♦ **Learning Exercise 7.4A**

CORE CHEMISTRY SKILL

Converting Particles to Moles

Use Avogadro's number to calculate each of the following:

a. number of P atoms in 1.50 moles of P

b. number of H_2S molecules in 0.0750 mole of H_2S

c. number of moles of Ag in 5.4×10^{24} atoms of Ag

d. number of moles of C_3H_8 in 8.25×10^{24} molecules of C_3H_8

e. number of O_2 molecules if the lungs contain 0.040 mole of O_2

Answers   **a.** 9.03×10^{23} P atoms   **b.** 4.52×10^{22} H_2S molecules   **c.** 9.0 moles of Ag
d. 13.7 moles of C_3H_8 **e.** 2.4×10^{22} O_2 molecules

Study Note

The subscripts in the formula of a compound indicate the number of moles of each element in exactly 1 mole of that compound. For example, consider the formula Mg_3N_2:

$$1 \text{ mole of } Mg_3N_2 = 3 \text{ moles of Mg atoms and 2 moles of N atoms}$$

Some conversion factors for the moles of elements can be written as follows:

$$\frac{3 \text{ moles Mg atoms}}{1 \text{ mole } Mg_3N_2} \quad \text{and} \quad \frac{1 \text{ mole } Mg_3N_2}{3 \text{ moles Mg atoms}} \qquad \frac{2 \text{ moles N atoms}}{1 \text{ mole } Mg_3N_2} \quad \text{and} \quad \frac{1 \text{ mole } Mg_3N_2}{2 \text{ moles N atoms}}$$

Guide to Calculating the Moles of an Element in a Compound	
STEP 1	State the given and needed quantities.
STEP 2	Write a plan to convert moles of compound to moles of an element.
STEP 3	Write equalities and conversion factors using subscripts.
STEP 4	Set up the problem to calculate the moles of an element.

♦ Learning Exercise 7.4B

Vitamin C (ascorbic acid) has the formula $C_6H_8O_6$.

a. How many moles of carbon are in 2.0 moles of vitamin C?

b. How many moles of hydrogen are in 5.0 moles of vitamin C?

c. How many moles of oxygen are in 1.5 moles of vitamin C?

Answers   **a.** 12 moles of carbon (C)   **b.** 40. moles of hydrogen (H)   **c.** 9.0 moles of oxygen (O)

♦ Learning Exercise 7.4C

For the compound ibuprofen ($C_{13}H_{18}O_2$) used in Advil and Motrin, determine each of the following:

a. moles of carbon in 2.20 moles of ibuprofen

b. moles of hydrogen in 0.575 mole of ibuprofen

c. moles of oxygen in 0.750 mole of ibuprofen

Ibuprofen is an anti-inflammatory.

Credit: Pearson Education / Pearson Science

d. molecules of ibuprofen that contain 8.42 moles of carbon

Answers **a.** 28.6 moles of C   **b.** 10.4 moles of H

      c. 1.50 moles of O   **d.** 3.90×10^{23} molecules of ibuprofen

7.5 Molar Mass and Calculations

Learning Goal: Calculate the molar mass for a substance given its chemical formula; use molar mass to convert between grams and moles.

- The molar mass (g/mole) of an element is numerically equal to its atomic mass in grams.

- The molar mass (g/mole) of a compound is the sum of the mass (grams) for each element in the formula.

- The molar mass (g/mole) is useful as a conversion factor to change a given quantity in moles to grams or grams to moles.

- The two conversion factors for the molar mass of NaOH (40.00 g/mole) are:

$$\frac{40.00 \text{ g NaOH}}{1 \text{ mole NaOH}} \text{ and } \frac{1 \text{ mole NaOH}}{40.00 \text{ g NaOH}}$$

Guide to Calculating Molar Mass	
STEP 1	Obtain the molar mass of each element.
STEP 2	Multiply each molar mass by the number of moles (subscript) in the formula.
STEP 3	Calculate the molar mass by adding the masses of the elements.

Example: What is the molar mass of silver nitrate, $AgNO_3$?

Solution: **STEP 1 Obtain the molar mass of each element.**

$$\frac{107.9 \text{ g Ag}}{1 \text{ mole Ag}} \quad \frac{14.01 \text{ g N}}{1 \text{ mole N}} \quad \frac{16.00 \text{ g O}}{1 \text{ mole O}}$$

STEP 2 Multiply each molar mass by the number of moles (subscript) in the formula.

$$1 \text{ mole Ag} \times \frac{107.9 \text{ g Ag}}{1 \text{ mole Ag}} = 107.9 \text{ g of Ag}$$

$$1 \text{ mole N} \times \frac{14.01 \text{ g N}}{1 \text{ mole N}} = 14.01 \text{ g of N}$$

$$3 \text{ moles O} \times \frac{16.00 \text{ g O}}{1 \text{ mole O}} = 48.00 \text{ g of O}$$

STEP 3 Calculate the molar mass by adding the masses of the elements.

$$\text{Molar mass of AgNO}_3 = (107.9 \text{ g} + 14.01 \text{ g} + 48.00 \text{ g}) = 169.9 \text{ g}$$

Key Terms for Sections 7.3–7.5

Match each of the following terms with the correct description below:

    a. Avogadro's number   **b.** oxidation   **c.** reduction   **d.** mole   **e.** molar mass

1. ____ the amount of a substance that contains 6.02×10^{23} particles

2. ____ the loss of electrons by a substance

3. ____ the mass, in grams, of an element or compound that is numerically equal to its atomic mass or the sum of atomic masses

4. ____ the gain of electrons by a substance

5. ____ the number of items in a mole, equal to 6.02×10^{23}

Answers   **1.** d   **2.** b   **3.** e   **4.** c   **5.** a

♦ **Learning Exercise 7.5A**

🕸 CORE CHEMISTRY SKILL

Determine the molar mass for each of the following:

Calculating Molar Mass

    a. K_2O **b.** $AlCl_3$

    c. $C_{12}H_{22}O_{11}$ (sucrose; table sugar)   **d.** C_4H_{10}

    e. $Ca(NO_3)_2$ **f.** Mg_3N_2

    g. $FeCO_3$ **h.** $(NH_4)_3PO_4$

$C_{12}H_{22}O_{11}$
1 mole of sucrose contains 342.3 g of sucrose (table sugar).
Credit: Pearson Education / Pearson Science

Answers   **a.** 94.20 g   **b.** 133.33 g   **c.** 342.3 g   **d.** 58.12 g
                e. 164.10 g   **f.** 100.95 g   **g.** 115.86 g   **h.** 149.10 g

Guide to Calculating the Moles (or Grams) of a Substance from Grams (or Moles)	
STEP 1	State the given and needed quantities.
STEP 2	Write a plan to convert moles to grams (grams to moles).
STEP 3	Determine the molar mass and write conversion factors.
STEP 4	Set up the problem to convert moles to grams (or grams to moles).

Example: What is the mass in grams of 0.254 mole of Na_2CO_3?

Solution: **STEP 1 State the given and needed quantities.**

Analyze the Problem	Given	Need
	0.254 mole of Na_2CO_3	grams of Na_2CO_3

      STEP 2 Write a plan to convert moles to grams.

$$\text{moles} \xrightarrow{\text{Molar mass}} \text{grams}$$

STEP 3 Determine the molar mass and write conversion factors.

$$1 \text{ mole of } Na_2CO_3 = 105.99 \text{ g of } Na_2CO_3$$

$$\frac{105.99 \text{ g } Na_2CO_3}{1 \text{ mole } Na_2CO_3} \quad \text{and} \quad \frac{1 \text{ mole } Na_2CO_3}{105.99 \text{ g } Na_2CO_3}$$

STEP 4 Set up the problem to convert moles to grams.

$$0.254 \text{ mole } Na_2CO_3 \times \frac{105.99 \text{ g } Na_2CO_3}{1 \text{ mole } Na_2CO_3} = 26.9 \text{ g of } Na_2CO_3$$

Molar mass factor (*cancels mole* Na_2CO_3)

♦ **Learning Exercise 7.5B**

Calculate the number of grams in each of the following quantities:

⚛ **CORE CHEMISTRY SKILL**

Using Molar Mass as a Conversion Factor

a. 0.75 mole of S

b. 3.18 moles of K_2SO_4

c. 2.50 moles of NH_4Cl

d. 4.08 moles of $FeCl_3$

e. 2.28 moles of PCl_3

f. 0.815 mole of $Mg(NO_3)_2$

Answers **a.** 24 g **b.** 554 g **c.** 134 g **d.** 662 g **e.** 313 g **f.** 121 g

---

Study Note

When the grams of a substance are given, the molar mass is used to calculate the number of moles of substance present.

$$\text{grams of substance} \times \frac{1 \text{ mole of substance}}{\text{grams of substance}} = \text{moles of substance}$$

Example: How many moles of NaOH are in 4.00 g of NaOH?

$$4.00 \text{ g } NaOH \times \frac{1 \text{ mole } NaOH}{40.00 \text{ g } NaOH} = 0.100 \text{ mole of } NaOH$$

Molar mass (*inverted, cancels g NaOH*)

♦ **Learning Exercise 7.5C**

Calculate the number of moles in each of the following quantities:

a. 108 g of CH_4

b. 6.12 g of CO_2

c. 38.7 g of $CaBr_2$

d. 236 g of Cl_2

e. 128 g of $Mg(OH)_2$

f. 172 g of Al_2O_3

g. The methane used to heat a home has a formula of CH_4. If 725 g of methane are used in one month, how many moles of methane were used during this time?

h. A vitamin tablet contains 18 mg of iron. If there are 100 tablets in a bottle, how many moles of iron are contained in the vitamins in the bottle?

Answers **a.** 6.73 moles **b.** 0.139 mole **c.** 0.194 mole **d.** 3.33 moles
e. 2.19 moles **f.** 1.69 moles **g.** 45.2 moles **h.** 0.032 mole

♦ **Learning Exercise 7.5D**

Valine, $C_5H_{11}NO_2$, is an essential amino acid.

a. What is the molar mass of valine?

b. How many moles of valine are in 25.0 g of valine?

c. How many grams of valine are in 0.888 mole of valine?

Sodium monofluorophosphate, Na_2PO_3F, is used to add fluoride to toothpaste.

d. What is the molar mass of sodium monofluorophosphate?

e. How many moles are in 16.7 g of sodium monofluorophosphate?

f. How many grams are in 0.345 mole of sodium monofluorophosphate?

Answers **a.** 117.15 g/mole **b.** 0.213 mole **c.** 104 g
d. 144.0 g/mole **e.** 0.116 mole **f.** 49.7 g

7.6   Mole Relationships in Chemical Equations

Learning Goal: Given a quantity in moles of reactant or product, use a mole–mole factor from the balanced chemical equation to calculate the number of moles of another substance in the reaction.

- The law of conservation of mass states that mass is not lost or gained during a chemical reaction.
- The coefficients in a balanced chemical equation indicate the number of moles of reactants and products in the reactions.
- Using the coefficients, mole–mole factors are written for any two substances in the equation.

- For the reaction of oxygen forming ozone, $3O_2(g) \longrightarrow 2O_3(g)$, the mole–mole factors are the following:

$$\frac{3 \text{ moles } O_2}{2 \text{ moles } O_3} \quad \text{and} \quad \frac{2 \text{ moles } O_3}{3 \text{ moles } O_2}$$

♦ **Learning Exercise 7.6A**

Write all of the possible mole–mole factors for the following equation:

$$N_2(g) + O_2(g) \longrightarrow 2NO(g)$$

Answers

For N_2 and O_2:

$$\frac{1 \text{ mole } N_2}{1 \text{ mole } O_2} \quad \text{and} \quad \frac{1 \text{ mole } O_2}{1 \text{ mole } N_2}$$

For N_2 and NO:

$$\frac{1 \text{ mole } N_2}{2 \text{ moles NO}} \quad \text{and} \quad \frac{2 \text{ moles NO}}{1 \text{ mole } N_2}$$

For NO and O_2:

$$\frac{1 \text{ mole } O_2}{2 \text{ moles NO}} \quad \text{and} \quad \frac{2 \text{ moles NO}}{1 \text{ mole } O_2}$$

Guide to Calculating the Quantities of Reactants and Products in a Chemical Reaction	
STEP 1	State the given and needed quantities (moles or grams).
STEP 2	Write a plan to convert the given to the needed quantity (moles or grams).
STEP 3	Use coefficients to write mole–mole factors; write molar mass factors if needed.
STEP 4	Set up the problem to give the needed quantity (moles or grams).

Study Note

The appropriate mole–mole factor is used to change the number of given moles to the number of needed moles.

Example: For the equation $N_2(g) + O_2(g) \longrightarrow 2NO(g)$, calculate the number of moles of NO produced from 3.0 moles of N_2.

Solution: **STEP 1** **State the given and needed quantities (moles).**

Given 3.0 moles of N_2 **Need** moles of NO

STEP 2 **Write a plan to convert the given to the needed moles.**

moles of $N_2 \rightarrow$ moles of NO

STEP 3 **Use coefficients to write mole–mole factors; write molar mass factors if needed.**

Mole–mole factors $\dfrac{2 \text{ moles NO}}{1 \text{ mole } N_2}$ and $\dfrac{1 \text{ mole } N_2}{2 \text{ moles NO}}$

STEP 4 **Set up the problem to give the needed quantity (moles).**

$$3.0 \text{ moles } N_2 \times \frac{2 \text{ moles NO}}{1 \text{ mole } N_2} = 6.0 \text{ moles of NO}$$

♦ **Learning Exercise 7.6B**

⚛ **CORE CHEMISTRY SKILL**

Using Mole–Mole Factors

Use the equation to answer the following questions:

$$C_3H_8(g) + 5O_2(g) \longrightarrow 3CO_2(g) + 4H_2O(g)$$

a. How many moles of O_2 are needed to react with 2.00 moles of C_3H_8?

b. How many moles of CO_2 are produced when 4.00 moles of O_2 react?

c. How many moles of C_3H_8 react with 3.00 moles of O_2?

d. How many moles of H_2O are produced from 0.500 mole of C_3H_8?

Answers   **a.** 10.0 moles of O_2 **b.** 2.40 moles of CO_2 **c.** 0.600 mole of C_3H_8
d. 2.00 moles of H_2O

7.7   Mass Calculations for Reactions

Learning Goal: Given the mass in grams of a substance in a reaction, calculate the mass in grams of another substance in the reaction.

*   The grams of a substance in an equation are converted to grams of another substance using their molar masses and mole–mole factors.

Substance A   **Substance B**

grams of A ⟩ Molar mass factor A ⟩ moles of A ⟩ Mole–mole factor B/A ⟩ moles of B ⟩ Molar mass factor B ⟩ grams of B

♦ **Learning Exercise 7.7**

⚛ **CORE CHEMISTRY SKILL**

Converting Grams to Grams

Use the following equation for the questions stated below:

$$2C_2H_6(g) + 7O_2(g) \longrightarrow 4CO_2(g) + 6H_2O(g)$$

a. How many grams of oxygen (O_2) are needed to react with 120. g of C_2H_6?

b. How many grams of C_2H_6 are needed to react with 115 g of O_2?

c. How many grams of C_2H_6 react if 2.00 g of CO_2 is produced?

d. How many grams of CO_2 are produced when 60.0 g of C_2H_6 react with sufficient oxygen?

e. How many grams of H_2O are produced when 82.5 g of O_2 react with sufficient C_2H_6?

Answers   **a.** 447 g of O_2 **b.** 30.9 g of C_2H_6 **c.** 0.683 g of C_2H_6
                   d. 176 g of CO_2 **e.** 39.8 g of H_2O

7.8   Limiting Reactants and Percent Yield

Learning Goal: Identify a limiting reactant and calculate the amount of product formed from that limiting reactant. Given the actual quantity of product, determine the percent yield for a reaction.

- In a limiting reactant problem, the availability of one of the reactants limits the amount of product.
- The reactant that is used up is the limiting reactant; the reactant that remains is the excess reactant.
- The limiting reactant produces the smaller number of moles of product.
- Theoretical yield is the maximum amount of product calculated for a given amount of a reactant.
- Percent yield is the ratio of the actual amount (yield) of product obtained to the theoretical yield.

Guide to Calculating the Grams of Product from a Limiting Reactant	
STEP 1	State the given and needed quantities.
STEP 2	Write a plan to convert the grams of each reactant to grams of product.
STEP 3	Write the molar mass factors and the mole–mole factors from the equation.
STEP 4	Calculate the number of grams of product from each reactant and select the smaller number of grams as the amount of product from the limiting reactant.

Example: The amount of product possible from a mixture of two reactants is determined by calculating the grams of product each will produce. The limiting reactant produces the smaller amount of product. In the reaction $S(l) + 3F_2(g) \longrightarrow SF_6(g)$, how many grams of SF_6 are possible when 16.1 g of S is mixed with 45.6 g of F_2?

Solution:

STEP 1   **State the given and needed quantities.**

Analyze the Problem	**Given**	**Need**
	16.1 g of S, 45.6 g of F_2	grams of SF_6

STEP 2   **Write a plan to convert the grams of each reactant to grams of product.**

grams of S $\rightarrow$ moles of S $\rightarrow$ moles of SF_6 $\rightarrow$ grams of SF_6
grams of F_2 $\rightarrow$ moles of F_2 $\rightarrow$ moles of SF_6 $\rightarrow$ grams of SF_6

STEP 3   **Write the molar mass factors and mole–mole factors from the equation.**

1 mole of S $=$ 1 mole of SF_6 3 moles of F_2 $=$ 1 mole of SF_6 1 mole of SF_6 $=$ 146.1 g of SF_6

$$\frac{1 \text{ mole S}}{1 \text{ mole } SF_6} \text{ and } \frac{1 \text{ mole } SF_6}{1 \text{ mole S}} \qquad \frac{3 \text{ moles } F_2}{1 \text{ mole } SF_6} \text{ and } \frac{1 \text{ mole } SF_6}{3 \text{ moles } F_2} \qquad \frac{146.1 \text{ g } SF_6}{1 \text{ mole } SF_6} \text{ and } \frac{1 \text{ mole } SF_6}{146.1 \text{ g } SF_6}$$

STEP 4 **Calculate the number of grams of product from each reactant and select the smaller number of grams as the amount of product from the limiting reactant.**

$$16.1 \text{ g S} \times \frac{1 \text{ mole S}}{32.07 \text{ g S}} \times \frac{1 \text{ mole SF}_6}{1 \text{ mole S}} \times \frac{146.1 \text{ g SF}_6}{1 \text{ mole SF}_6} = 73.3 \text{ g of SF}_6$$

$$45.6 \text{ g F}_2 \times \frac{1 \text{ mole F}_2}{38.00 \text{ g F}_2} \times \frac{1 \text{ mole SF}_6}{3 \text{ moles F}_2} \times \frac{146.1 \text{ g SF}_6}{1 \text{ mole SF}_6} = 58.4 \text{ g of SF}_6 \text{ from the limiting reactant F}_2$$
$$(\text{smaller amount of product})$$

♦ **Learning Exercise 7.8A**

⚛ **CORE CHEMISTRY SKILL**

Calculating Quantity of Product from a Limiting Reactant

    a. How many grams of Co_2S_3 can be produced from the reaction of 250. g of Co and 250. g of S?

$$2Co(s) + 3S(s) \longrightarrow Co_2S_3(s)$$

    b. How many grams of NO_2 can be produced from the reaction of 32.0 g of NO and 24.0 g of O_2?

$$2NO(g) + O_2(g) \longrightarrow 2NO_2(g)$$

Answers   **a.** 454 g   **b.** 49.1 g

Study Note

The percent yield is the ratio of the actual yield obtained to the theoretical yield, which is calculated for a given amount of starting reactant. If we calculate that a reaction can theoretically produce 43.1 g of NH_3, but the actual yield is 26.0 g of NH_3, the percent yield is:

$$\frac{26.0 \text{ g NH}_3 \,(\text{actual mass produced})}{43.1 \text{ g NH}_3 \,(\text{theoretical mass})} \times 100\% = 60.3\%$$

Guide to Calculations for Percent Yield

STEP 1	State the given and needed quantities.
STEP 2	Write a plan to calculate the theoretical yield and the percent yield.
STEP 3	Write the molar mass factors and the mole–mole factor from the balanced equation.
STEP 4	Calculate the percent yield by dividing the actual yield (given) by the theoretical yield and multiplying the result by 100%. $\text{Percent yield} \,(\%) = \dfrac{\text{actual yield of LiHCO}_3}{\text{theoretical yield of LiHCO}_3} \times 100\%$

♦ **Learning Exercise 7.8B**

⚛ **CORE CHEMISTRY SKILL**

Calculating Percent Yield

Consider the following reaction:

$$2H_2S(g) + 3O_2(g) \longrightarrow 2SO_2(g) + 2H_2O(g)$$

a. If 60.0 g of H_2S reacts with sufficient oxygen and produces 45.5 g of SO_2, what is the percent yield for SO_2?

b. If 25.0 g of O_2 reacting with H_2S produces 18.6 g of SO_2, what is the percent yield for SO_2?

Consider the following reaction:

$$2C_2H_6(g) + 7O_2(g) \longrightarrow 4CO_2(g) + 6H_2O(g)$$
Ethane

c. If 125 g of C_2H_6 reacting with sufficient oxygen produces 175 g of CO_2, what is the percent yield for CO_2?

d. When 35.0 g of O_2 reacts with sufficient ethane to produce 12.5 g of H_2O, what is the percent yield for water?

Answers **a.** 40.3% **b.** 55.7% **c.** 47.8% **d.** 74.0%

♦ **Learning Exercise 7.8C**

Valine, $C_5H_{11}NO_2$, an amino acid, reacts in the body according to the following reaction:

$$2C_5H_{11}NO_2(aq) + 12O_2(g) \longrightarrow 9CO_2(g) + 9H_2O(l) + CH_4N_2O(aq)$$
Valine   Urea

a. How many grams of O_2 will react with 15.0 g of valine?

b. How many grams of CO_2 are formed when 100. g of valine and 200. g of O_2 react?

c. If 45.0 g of valine reacts to give 6.75 g of urea, what is the percent yield of urea?

Galactose, $C_6H_{12}O_6(aq)$, found in milk products, reacts in the body by the following reaction:

$$C_6H_{12}O_6(aq) + 6O_2(g) \longrightarrow 6CO_2(g) + 6H_2O(l)$$

d. How many grams of O_2 will react with 46.4 g of galactose?

e. How many grams of CO_2 are formed when 77.0 g of galactose and 100. g of O_2 react?

f. If 23.3 g of galactose reacts to give 26.3 g of CO_2, what is the percent yield of CO_2?

Answers   **a.** 24.6 g   **b.** 169 g   **c.** 58.7%
             d. 49.4 g   **e.** 113 g   **f.** 77.1%

7.9   Energy in Chemical Reactions

Learning Goal: Given the heat of reaction, calculate the loss or gain of heat for an exothermic or endothermic reaction.

- The heat of reaction is the energy released or absorbed when the reaction occurs.

- The heat of reaction is the energy difference between the reactants and the products.

$$H_2(g) + Cl_2(g) \longrightarrow 2HCl(g) + energy$$

An exothermic reaction releases energy.

- In exothermic reactions, the energy of the reactants is greater than that of the products, which means that energy is released. The heat of reaction for an exothermic reaction is designated by writing the heat of reaction as a product.

- In endothermic reactions, the energy of the reactants is less than that of the products, which means that energy is absorbed. The heat of reaction for an endothermic reaction is designated by writing the heat of reaction as a reactant.

Key Terms for Sections 7.6–7.9

Match each of the following terms with the correct description below:

  a. actual yield   **b.** exothermic reaction   **c.** endothermic reaction
  d. theoretical yield   **e.** mole–mole factor

1. _____ a reaction in which the energy of the reactants is less than that of the products

2. _____ the maximum amount of product that a reaction can produce from a given amount of reactants

3. _____ a reaction in which the energy of the reactants is greater than that of the products

4. _____ a conversion factor that relates the number of moles of two compounds derived from the coefficients in a balanced equation

5. _____ the actual amount of product produced by a reaction

Answers   **1.** c   **2.** d   **3.** b   **4.** e   **5.** a

	Guide to Calculations Using Heat of Reaction
STEP 1	State the given and needed quantities.
STEP 2	Write a plan using the heat of reaction and any molar mass needed.
STEP 3	Write the conversion factors including heat of reaction.
STEP 4	Set up the problem to calculate the heat.

♦ **Learning Exercise 7.9A**

Indicate whether each of the following is an endothermic or exothermic reaction:

1. $2H_2(g) + O_2(g) \longrightarrow 2H_2O(g) + 582$ kJ   _____

2. $C_2H_4(g) + 176$ kJ $\longrightarrow H_2(g) + C_2H_2(g)$ _____

3. $2C(s) + O_2(g) \longrightarrow 2CO(g) + 220$ kJ   _____

4. $C_6H_{12}O_6(s) + 6O_2(g) \longrightarrow 6CO_2(g) + 6H_2O(l) + 670.$ kcal _____
   Glucose

5. $C_2H_5OH(l) + 21$ kcal $\longrightarrow C_2H_4(g) + H_2O(g)$ _____

Answers   1. exothermic   2. endothermic   3. exothermic   4. exothermic   5. endothermic

♦ **Learning Exercise 7.9B**

Consider the following reaction:

$$C_6H_{12}O_6(s) + 6O_2(g) \longrightarrow 6CO_2(g) + 6H_2O(l) + 670. \text{ kcal}$$

How much heat, in kilocalories and kilojoules, is produced when 50.0 g of CO_2 is formed?

Answers   127 kcal; 531 kJ

♦ **Learning Exercise 7.9C**   ⚛ **CORE CHEMISTRY SKILL**

Consider each of the following reactions, and calculate the number   Using the Heat of Reaction
of kilojoules absorbed or released for each:

1. $C_2H_4(g) + 176$ kJ $\longrightarrow H_2(g) + C_2H_2(g)$

   a. 3.50 moles of C_2H_2 is produced.   **b.** 75.0 g of C_2H_4 reacts.

2. $2H_2(g) + O_2(g) \longrightarrow 2H_2O(g) + 582$ kJ

   a. 0.820 mole of H_2 reacts.   **b.** 2.25 g of H_2O is produced.

Answers   **1a.** 616 kJ absorbed   **b.** 471 kJ absorbed   **2a.** 239 kJ released   **b.** 36.4 kJ released

Checklist for Chapter 7

You are ready to take the Practice Test for Chapter 7. Be sure that you have accomplished the following learning goals for this chapter. If not, review the section listed at the end of each goal. Then apply your new skills and understanding to the Practice Test.

After studying Chapter 7, I can successfully:

_____ State a chemical equation in words, and calculate the total number of atoms of each element in the reactants and products. (7.1)

_____ Write a balanced equation for a chemical reaction from the formulas of the reactants and products. (7.1)

_____ Identify a reaction as a combination, decomposition, single replacement, double replacement, or combustion reaction. (7.2)

_____ Identify an oxidation and reduction reaction. (7.3)

_____ Calculate the number of particles in a mole of a substance. (7.4)

_____ Calculate the molar mass when given the formula of a substance. (7.5)

_____ Convert the grams of a substance to moles; convert the moles of a substance to grams. (7.5)

_____ Use mole–mole factors for the mole relationships in an equation to calculate the moles of another substance in an equation for a chemical reaction. (7.6)

_____ Calculate the mass of a substance in an equation using mole–mole factors and molar masses. (7.7)

_____ Given the masses of reactants, find the limiting reactant and calculate the amount of product formed. (7.8)

_____ Calculate the percent yield, given the actual yield of a product. (7.8)

_____ Given the heat of reaction, describe a reaction as exothermic or endothermic. (7.9)

_____ Calculate the heat, in kilocalories or kilojoules, released or absorbed by a chemical reaction. (7.9)

Practice Test for Chapter 7

*For each of the unbalanced equations in questions 1 through 5, balance the equation and indicate the correct coefficient for the component in the equation written in **boldface type**.* (7.1)

    A. 1   **B.** 2   **C.** 3   **D.** 4   **E.** 5

1. _____ $Sn(s) + \mathbf{Cl_2}(g) \longrightarrow SnCl_4(s)$

2. _____ $Al(s) + H_2O(l) \longrightarrow Al_2O_3(s) + \mathbf{H_2}(g)$

3. _____ $\mathbf{C_3H_8}(g) + \mathbf{O_2}(g) \longrightarrow CO_2(g) + H_2O(g)$

4. _____ $\mathbf{NH_3}(g) + O_2(g) \longrightarrow N_2(g) + H_2O(g)$

5. _____ $N_2O(g) \longrightarrow N_2(g) + \mathbf{O_2}(g)$

For questions 6 through 10, classify each reaction as one of the following: (7.2)

    A. combination   **B.** decomposition   **C.** single replacement
    D. double replacement   **E.** combustion

6. _____ $S(s) + O_2(g) \longrightarrow SO_2(g)$

7. _____ $C_3H_8(g) + 5O_2(g) \longrightarrow 3CO_2(g) + 4H_2O(g)$

8. _____ $CaCO_3(s) \longrightarrow CaO(s) + CO_2(g)$

9. _____ $Mg(s) + 2AgNO_3(aq) \longrightarrow Mg(NO_3)_2(aq) + 2Ag(s)$

10. _____ $Na_2S(aq) + Pb(NO_3)_2(aq) \longrightarrow PbS(s) + 2NaNO_3(aq)$

For questions 11 through 15, identify each reaction as an (O) oxidation or a (R) reduction. (7.3)

11. $Ca \longrightarrow Ca^{2+} + 2\,e^-$ _____

12. $Fe^{3+} + 3\,e^- \longrightarrow Fe$ _____

13. $Al^{3+} + 3\,e^- \longrightarrow Al$ _____

14. $Br_2 + 2\,e^- \longrightarrow 2Br^-$ _____

15. $Sn^{2+} \longrightarrow Sn^{4+} + 2\,e^-$ _____

16. The number of moles of oxygen (O) in 2.0 moles of $Al(OH)_3$ is (7.4)
  A. 1.0 **B.** 2.0 **C.** 3.0 **D.** 4.0 **E.** 6.0

17. The number of atoms of Na in 0.0500 mole of Na is (7.4)
  A. 0.500 atom **B.** 6.02×10^{23} atoms **C.** 3.01×10^{23} atoms
  D. 3.01×10^{22} atoms **E.** 3.01×10^{25} atoms

For questions 18 through 21, calculate the moles of each of the elements in the formula: (7.4)
Tagamet has the formula $C_{10}H_{16}N_6S$. Tagamet is used to inhibit the production of acid in the stomach. Select the correct answer for the number of moles of each of the following in 0.25 mole of Tagamet.

Answers **A.** 0.25 **B.** 0.50 **C.** 1.5 **D.** 2.5 **E.** 4.0

18. moles of C **19.** moles of H **20.** moles of N **21.** moles of S

22. What is the molar mass of Li_2SO_4? (7.5)
  A. 55.01 g **B.** 62.10 g **C.** 103.01 g **D.** 109.95 g **E.** 103.11 g

23. What is the molar mass of $NaNO_3$? (7.5)
  A. 34.00 g **B.** 37.00 g **C.** 53.00 g **D.** 75.00 g **E.** 85.00 g

24. The number of grams in 0.600 mole of Cl_2 is (7.5)
  A. 71.0 g **B.** 21.3 g **C.** 42.5 g **D.** 84.5 g **E.** 4.30 g

25. How many grams are in 4.00 moles of NH_3? (7.5)
  A. 4.00 g **B.** 17.0 g **C.** 34.0 g **D.** 68.1 g **E.** 0.240 g

26. The number of moles of water in 3.60 g of H_2O is (7.5)
  A. 0.0500 mole **B.** 0.100 mole **C.** 0.200 mole
  D. 0.300 mole **E.** 0.400 mole

27. 0.200 g of H_2 = _____ mole of H_2 (7.5)
  A. 0.100 mole **B.** 0.200 mole **C.** 0.400 mole
  D. 0.500 mole **E.** 0.0100 mole

For questions 28 through 32, use the reaction: $(7.6, 7.7)$

$$C_2H_5OH(l) + 3O_2(g) \longrightarrow 2CO_2(g) + 3H_2O(l)$$
Ethanol

28. How many moles of oxygen (O_2) are needed to react with 1.00 mole of ethanol?
  A. 1.00 mole **B.** 2.00 moles **C.** 3.00 moles **D.** 4.00 moles **E.** 5.00 moles

29. How many moles of water are produced when 12.0 moles of oxygen (O_2) react?
  A. 3.00 moles **B.** 6.00 moles **C.** 8.00 moles **D.** 12.0 moles **E.** 36.0 moles

30. How many grams of carbon dioxide are produced when 92.0 g of ethanol react?
  A. 22.0 g **B.** 44.0 g **C.** 88.0 g **D.** 92.0 g **E.** 176 g

31. How many moles of oxygen (O_2) would be needed to produce 1.00 mole of CO_2?
    A. 0.670 mole   **B.** 1.00 mole   **C.** 1.50 moles   **D.** 2.00 moles   **E.** 3.00 moles

32. How many grams of water will be produced if 23.0 g of ethanol reacts?
    A. 54.0 g   **B.** 27.0 g   **C.** 18.0 g   **D.** 9.00 g   **E.** 6.00 g

For questions 33 and 34, use the reaction: $C_3H_8(g) + 5O_2(g) \longrightarrow 3CO_2(g) + 4H_2O(g)$

33. If 50.0 g of C_3H_8 and 150. g of O_2 react, the limiting reactant is (7.8)
    A. C_3H_8 **B.** O_2 **C.** both   **D.** neither   **E.** CO_2

34. If 50.0 g of C_3H_8 and 150. g of O_2 react, the mass of CO_2 formed is (7.8)
    A. 150. g   **B.** 206 g   **C.** 200. g   **D.** 124 g   **E.** 132 g

35. In the reaction $N_2(g) + 3H_2(g) \longrightarrow 2NH_3(g)$, a 25.0 g sample of N_2 is reacted. If the actual yield of NH_3 is 20.8 g, the percent yield of NH_3 is (7.8)
    A. 68.4%   **B.** 20.8%   **C.** 25.0%   **D.** 82.5%   **E.** 100.%

Consider the following equation and heat of reaction for questions 36 through 39: (7.9)

$$C_2H_6O(l) + 3O_2(g) \longrightarrow 2CO_2(g) + 3H_2O(l) + 1420 \text{ kJ}$$

36. The reaction is
    A. thermic   **B.** endothermic   **C.** exothermic   **D.** nonthermic   **E.** subthermic

37. How much heat, in kilojoules, is released when 0.500 mole of C_2H_6O reacts?
    A. 710. kJ   **B.** 1420 kJ   **C.** 2130 kJ   **D.** 2840 kJ   **E.** 4260 kJ

38. How many grams of CO_2 are produced if 355 kJ of heat are released?
    A. 11.0 g   **B.** 22.0 g   **C.** 33.0 g   **D.** 44.0 g   **E.** 88.0 g

39. How much heat, in kilojoules, is released when 16.0 g of O_2 reacts?
    A. 4260 kJ   **B.** 1420 kJ   **C.** 710. kJ   **D.** 237 kJ   **E.** 118 kJ

For questions 40 through 42, indicate if the reactions are exothermic (EX) or endothermic (EN): (8.9)

40. $N_2(g) + 3H_2(g) \longrightarrow 2NH_3(g) + 84 \text{ kJ}$ _____

41. $2HCl(g) + 44 \text{ kcal} \longrightarrow H_2(g) + Cl_2(g)$ _____

42. $C_3H_8(g) + 5O_2(g) \longrightarrow 3CO_2(g) + 4H_2O(g) + 531 \text{ kcal}$ _____

Answers to the Practice Test

1. B	2. C	3. E	4. D	5. A
6. A	7. E	8. B	9. C	10. D
11. O	12. R	13. R	14. R	15. O
16. E	17. D	18. D	19. E	20. C
21. A	22. D	23. E	24. C	25. D
26. C	27. A	28. C	29. D	30. E
31. C	32. B	33. B	34. D	35. A
36. C	37. A	38. B	39. D	40. EX
41. EN	42. EX			

Chemical Reactions and Quantities

Learning Goals

- Write a balanced chemical equation from the formulas of the reactants and products for a reaction; determine the number of atoms in the reactants and products.
- Identify a reaction as a combination, decomposition, single replacement, double replacement, or combustion.
- Define the terms oxidation and reduction; identify the reactants oxidized and reduced.
- Use Avogadro's number to determine the number of particles in a given number of moles.
- Calculate the molar mass for a substance given its chemical formula; use molar mass to convert between grams and moles.
- Given a quantity in moles of reactant or product, use a mole–mole factor from the balanced chemical equation to calculate the number of moles of another substance in the reaction.
- Given the mass in grams of a substance in a reaction, calculate the mass in grams of another substance in the reaction.
- Identify a limiting reactant and calculate the amount of product formed from the limiting reactant. Given the actual quantity of product, determine the percent yield for a reaction.
- Given the heat of reaction, calculate the loss or gain of heat for an exothermic or endothermic reaction.

Chapter Outline

Chapter Opener: Dental Hygienist

7.1 Equations for Chemical Reactions

7.2 Types of Reactions

Chemistry Link to Health: Incomplete Combustion: Toxicity of Carbon Monoxide

7.3 Oxidation–Reduction Reactions

Explore Your World: Oxidation of Fruits and Vegetables

7.4 The Mole

7.5 Molar Mass and Calculations

Explore Your World: Calculating Moles in the Kitchen

7.6 Mole Relationships in Chemical Equations

7.7 Mass Calculations for Reactions

7.8 Limiting Reactants and Percent Yield

7.9 Energy in Chemical Reactions

Chemistry Link to Health: Cold Packs and Hot Packs

Clinical Update: Whitening of Tooth Enamel

⚛ Core Chemistry Skills

- Balancing a Chemical Equation (7.1)
- Classifying Types of Chemical Reactions (7.2)
- Identifying Oxidized and Reduced Substances (7.3)

- Converting Particles to Moles (7.4)
- Calculating Molar Mass (7.5)
- Using Molar Mass as a Conversion Factor (7.5)
- Using Mole–Mole Factors (7.6)
- Converting Grams to Grams (7.7)
- Calculating Quantity of Product from a Limiting Reactant (7.8)
- Calculating Percent Yield (7.8)
- Using the Heat of Reaction (7.9)

Selected Answers and Solutions to Text Problems

7.1 Place coefficients in front of formulas until you make the atoms of each element equal on each side of the equation.
   a. $N_2(g) + O_2(g) \longrightarrow 2NO(g)$ **b.** $2HgO(s) \longrightarrow 2Hg(l) + O_2(g)$
   c. $4Fe(s) + 3O_2(g) \longrightarrow 2Fe_2O_3(s)$ **d.** $2Na(s) + Cl_2(g) \longrightarrow 2NaCl(s)$
   e. $2Cu_2O(s) + O_2(g) \longrightarrow 4CuO(s)$

7.3 **a.** $Mg(s) + 2AgNO_3(aq) \longrightarrow Mg(NO_3)_2(aq) + 2Ag(s)$
   b. $CuCO_3(s) \longrightarrow CuO(s) + CO_2(g)$
   c. $2Al(s) + 3CuSO_4(aq) \longrightarrow 3Cu(s) + Al_2(SO_4)_3(aq)$
   d. $Pb(NO_3)_2(aq) + 2NaCl(aq) \longrightarrow PbCl_2(s) + 2NaNO_3(aq)$
   e. $2Al(s) + 6HCl(aq) \longrightarrow 2AlCl_3(aq) + 3H_2(g)$

7.5 **a.** $Fe_2O_3(s) + 3CO(g) \longrightarrow 2Fe(s) + 3CO_2(g)$
   b. $2Li_3N(s) \longrightarrow 6Li(s) + N_2(g)$
   c. $2Al(s) + 6HBr(aq) \longrightarrow 2AlBr_3(aq) + 3H_2(g)$
   d. $3Ba(OH)_2(aq) + 2Na_3PO_4(aq) \longrightarrow Ba_3(PO_4)_2(s) + 6NaOH(aq)$
   e. $As_4S_6(s) + 9O_2(g) \longrightarrow As_4O_6(s) + 6SO_2(g)$

7.7 **a.** $2Li(s) + 2H_2O(l) \longrightarrow H_2(g) + 2LiOH(aq)$
   b. $2P(s) + 5Cl_2(g) \longrightarrow 2PCl_5(s)$
   c. $FeO(s) + CO(g) \longrightarrow Fe(s) + CO_2(g)$
   d. $2C_5H_{10}(l) + 15O_2(g) \overset{\Delta}{\longrightarrow} 10CO_2(g) + 10H_2O(g)$
   e. $3H_2S(g) + 2FeCl_3(s) \longrightarrow Fe_2S_3(s) + 6HCl(g)$

7.9 $NH_4NO_3(s) \overset{\Delta}{\longrightarrow} 2H_2O(g) + N_2O(g)$

7.11 $2C_3H_7NO_2(aq) + 7O_2(g) \longrightarrow 5CO_2(g) + 5H_2O(l) + CH_4N_2O(aq)$

7.13 **a.** This is a decomposition reaction because a single reactant splits into two simpler substances.
   b. This is a single replacement reaction because one element in the reacting compound (I in BaI_2) is replaced by the other reactant (Br in Br_2).
   c. This is a combustion reaction because a carbon-containing fuel burns in oxygen to produce carbon dioxide and water.
   d. This is a double replacement reaction because the positive ions in the two reactants exchange places to form two products.
   e. This is a combination reaction because atoms of two different elements bond to form one product.

7.15 **a.** combination   **b.** single replacement   **c.** decomposition
      d. double replacement   **e.** combustion

7.17 **a.** Since this is a combination reaction, the product is a single compound.
      $Mg(s) + Cl_2(g) \longrightarrow MgCl_2(s)$

b. Since this is a decomposition reaction, the single reactant breaks down into more than one simpler substance.

$$2HBr(g) \longrightarrow H_2(g) + Br_2(g)$$

c. Since this is a single replacement reaction, the uncombined metal element takes the place of the metal element in the compound.

$$Mg(s) + Zn(NO_3)_2(aq) \longrightarrow Zn(s) + Mg(NO_3)_2(aq)$$

d. Since this is a double replacement reaction, the positive ions in the reacting compounds switch places.

$$K_2S(aq) + Pb(NO_3)_2(aq) \longrightarrow 2KNO_3(aq) + PbS(s)$$

e. Since this is a combustion reaction, a fuel burns in oxygen to produce carbon dioxide and water.

$$2C_2H_6(g) + 7O_2(g) \xrightarrow{\Delta} 4CO_2(g) + 6H_2O(g)$$

7.19 Oxidation is the loss of electrons; reduction is the gain of electrons.

a. Na^+ gains an electron to form Na; this is a reduction.

b. Ni loses electrons to form Ni^{2+}; this is an oxidation.

c. Cr^{3+} gains electrons to form Cr; this is a reduction.

d. $2H^+$ gain electrons to form H_2; this is a reduction.

7.21 An oxidized substance has lost electrons; a reduced substance has gained electrons.

a. Zn loses electrons and is oxidized. Cl_2 gains electrons and is reduced.

b. Br^- (in NaBr) loses electrons and is oxidized. Cl_2 gains electrons and is reduced.

c. O^{2-} (in PbO) loses electrons and is oxidized. Pb^{2+} (in PbO) gains electrons and is reduced.

d. Sn^{2+} loses electrons and is oxidized. Fe^{3+} gains electrons and is reduced.

7.23 **a.** Fe^{3+} gains an electron to form Fe^{2+}; this is a reduction.

b. Fe^{2+} loses an electron to form Fe^{3+}; this is an oxidation.

7.25 Linoleic acid gains hydrogen atoms and is reduced.

7.27 One mole contains 6.02×10^{23} atoms of an element, molecules of a molecular substance, or formula units of an ionic substance.

7.29 **a.** $0.500 \text{ mole C} \times \dfrac{6.02 \times 10^{23} \text{ atoms C}}{1 \text{ mole C}} = 3.01 \times 10^{23}$ atoms of C (3 SFs)

b. $1.28 \text{ moles SO}_2 \times \dfrac{6.02 \times 10^{23} \text{ molecules SO}_2}{1 \text{ mole SO}_2} = 7.71 \times 10^{23}$ molecules of SO_2 (3 SFs)

c. $5.22 \times 10^{22} \text{ atoms Fe} \times \dfrac{1 \text{ mole Fe}}{6.02 \times 10^{23} \text{ atoms Fe}} = 0.0867$ mole of Fe (3 SFs)

d. $8.50 \times 10^{24} \text{ atoms C}_2H_6O \times \dfrac{1 \text{ mole C}_2H_6O}{6.02 \times 10^{23} \text{ atoms C}_2H_6O} = 14.1$ moles of C_2H_6O (3 SFs)

7.31 1 mole of H_3PO_4 contains 3 moles of H atoms, 1 mole of P atoms, and 4 moles of O atoms.

a. $2.00 \text{ moles H}_3PO_4 \times \dfrac{3 \text{ moles H}}{1 \text{ mole H}_3PO_4} = 6.00$ moles of H (3 SFs)

b. $2.00 \text{ moles H}_3PO_4 \times \dfrac{4 \text{ moles O}}{1 \text{ mole H}_3PO_4} = 8.00$ moles of O (3 SFs)

c. $2.00 \text{ moles H}_3PO_4 \times \dfrac{1 \text{ mole P}}{1 \text{ mole H}_3PO_4} \times \dfrac{6.02 \times 10^{23} \text{ atoms P}}{1 \text{ mole P}} = 1.20 \times 10^{24}$ atoms of P

(3 SFs)

d. $2.00 \text{ moles H}_3PO_4 \times \dfrac{4 \text{ moles O}}{1 \text{ mole H}_3PO_4} \times \dfrac{6.02 \times 10^{23} \text{ atoms O}}{1 \text{ mole O}} = 4.82 \times 10^{24}$ atoms of O

(3 SFs)

7.33 The subscripts indicate the moles of each element in one mole of that compound.

    a. $1.0 \text{ mole quinine} \times \dfrac{24 \text{ moles H}}{1 \text{ mole quinine}} = 24 \text{ moles of H (2 SFs)}$

    b. $5.0 \text{ moles quinine} \times \dfrac{20 \text{ moles C}}{1 \text{ mole quinine}} = 1.0 \times 10^2 \text{ moles of C (2 SFs)}$

    c. $0.020 \text{ mole quinine} \times \dfrac{2 \text{ moles N}}{1 \text{ mole quinine}} = 0.040 \text{ mole of N (2 SFs)}$

7.35 **a.** $2.30 \text{ moles naproxen} \times \dfrac{14 \text{ moles C}}{1 \text{ mole naproxen}} = 32.2 \text{ moles of C (3 SFs)}$

    b. $0.444 \text{ mole naproxen} \times \dfrac{14 \text{ moles H}}{1 \text{ mole naproxen}} = 6.22 \text{ moles of H (3 SFs)}$

    c. $0.0765 \text{ mole naproxen} \times \dfrac{3 \text{ moles O}}{1 \text{ mole naproxen}} = 0.230 \text{ mole of O (3 SFs)}$

7.37 **a.** $1 \text{ mole K} \times \dfrac{39.10 \text{ g K}}{1 \text{ mole K}} = 39.10 \text{ g of K}$

    $4 \text{ moles C} \times \dfrac{12.01 \text{ g C}}{1 \text{ mole C}} = 48.04 \text{ g of C}$

    $5 \text{ moles H} \times \dfrac{1.008 \text{ g H}}{1 \text{ mole H}} = 5.040 \text{ g of H}$

    $6 \text{ moles O} \times \dfrac{16.00 \text{ g O}}{1 \text{ mole O}} = 96.00 \text{ g of O}$

    $\begin{aligned}
1 \text{ mole of K} &= 39.10 \text{ g of K} \\
4 \text{ moles of C} &= 48.04 \text{ g of C} \\
5 \text{ moles of H} &= 5.040 \text{ g of H} \\
6 \text{ moles of O} &= 96.00 \text{ g of O} \\
\hline
\therefore \text{ Molar mass of } KC_4H_5O_6 &= 188.18 \text{ g}
\end{aligned}$

    b. $2 \text{ moles Fe} \times \dfrac{55.85 \text{ g Fe}}{1 \text{ mole Fe}} = 111.7 \text{ g of Fe}$

    $3 \text{ moles O} \times \dfrac{16.00 \text{ g O}}{1 \text{ mole O}} = 48.00 \text{ g of O}$

    $\begin{aligned}
2 \text{ moles of Fe} &= 111.7 \text{ g of Fe} \\
3 \text{ moles of O} &= 48.00 \text{ g of O} \\
\hline
\therefore \text{ Molar mass of } Fe_2O_3 &= 159.7 \text{ g}
\end{aligned}$

    c. $2 \text{ moles Al} \times \dfrac{26.98 \text{ g Al}}{1 \text{ mole Al}} = 53.96 \text{ g of Al}$

    $3 \text{ moles S} \times \dfrac{32.07 \text{ g S}}{1 \text{ mole S}} = 96.21 \text{ g of S}$

    $12 \text{ moles O} \times \dfrac{16.00 \text{ g O}}{1 \text{ mole O}} = 192.0 \text{ g of O}$

    $\begin{aligned}
2 \text{ moles of Al} &= 53.96 \text{ g of Al} \\
3 \text{ moles of S} &= 96.21 \text{ g of S} \\
12 \text{ moles of O} &= 192.0 \text{ g of O} \\
\hline
\therefore \text{ Molar mass of } Al_2(SO_4)_3 &= 342.2 \text{ g}
\end{aligned}$

    d. $1 \text{ mole Mg} \times \dfrac{24.31 \text{ g Mg}}{1 \text{ mole Mg}} = 24.31 \text{ g of Mg}$

$$2 \text{ moles O} \times \frac{16.00 \text{ g O}}{1 \text{ mole O}} = 32.00 \text{ g of O}$$

$$2 \text{ moles H} \times \frac{1.008 \text{ g H}}{1 \text{ mole H}} = 2.016 \text{ g of H}$$

$$
\begin{aligned}
1 \text{ mole of Mg} &= 24.31 \text{ g of Mg} \\
2 \text{ moles of O} &= 32.00 \text{ g of O} \\
2 \text{ moles of H} &= \underline{2.016 \text{ g of H}} \\
\therefore \text{ Molar mass of Mg(OH)}_2 &= 58.33 \text{ g}
\end{aligned}
$$

7.39 **a.** $2 \text{ moles Cl} \times \dfrac{35.45 \text{ g Cl}}{1 \text{ mole Cl}} = 70.90 \text{ g of Cl}$

$\therefore$ Molar mass of $Cl_2 = 70.90 \text{ g}$

b. $3 \text{ moles C} \times \dfrac{12.01 \text{ g C}}{1 \text{ mole C}} = 36.03 \text{ g of C}$

$6 \text{ moles H} \times \dfrac{1.008 \text{ g H}}{1 \text{ mole H}} = 6.048 \text{ g of H}$

$3 \text{ moles O} \times \dfrac{16.00 \text{ g O}}{1 \text{ mole O}} = 48.00 \text{ g of O}$

$$
\begin{aligned}
3 \text{ moles of C} &= 36.03 \text{ g of C} \\
6 \text{ moles of H} &= 6.048 \text{ g of H} \\
3 \text{ moles of O} &= \underline{48.00 \text{ g of O}} \\
\therefore \text{ Molar mass of C}_3\text{H}_6\text{O}_3 &= 90.08 \text{ g}
\end{aligned}
$$

c. $3 \text{ moles Mg} \times \dfrac{24.31 \text{ g Mg}}{1 \text{ mole Mg}} = 72.93 \text{ g of Mg}$

$2 \text{ moles P} \times \dfrac{30.97 \text{ g P}}{1 \text{ mole P}} = 61.94 \text{ g of P}$

$8 \text{ moles O} \times \dfrac{16.00 \text{ g O}}{1 \text{ mole O}} = 128.0 \text{ g of O}$

$$
\begin{aligned}
3 \text{ moles of Mg} &= 72.93 \text{ g of Mg} \\
2 \text{ moles of P} &= 61.94 \text{ g of P} \\
8 \text{ moles of O} &= \underline{128.0 \text{ g of O}} \\
\therefore \text{ Molar mass of Mg}_3(\text{PO}_4)_2 &= 262.9 \text{ g}
\end{aligned}
$$

d. $1 \text{ mole Al} \times \dfrac{26.98 \text{ g Al}}{1 \text{ mole Al}} = 26.98 \text{ g of Al}$

$3 \text{ moles F} \times \dfrac{19.00 \text{ g F}}{1 \text{ mole F}} = 57.00 \text{ g of F}$

$$
\begin{aligned}
1 \text{ mole of Al} &= 26.98 \text{ g of Al} \\
3 \text{ moles of F} &= \underline{57.00 \text{ g of F}} \\
\therefore \text{ Molar mass of AlF}_3 &= 83.98 \text{ g}
\end{aligned}
$$

7.41 **a.** $2.00 \text{ moles Na} \times \dfrac{22.99 \text{ g Na}}{1 \text{ mole Na}} = 46.0 \text{ g of Na (3 SFs)}$

b. $2.80 \text{ moles Ca} \times \dfrac{40.08 \text{ g Ca}}{1 \text{ mole Ca}} = 112 \text{ g of Ca (3 SFs)}$

c. $0.125 \text{ mole Sn} \times \dfrac{118.7 \text{ g Sn}}{1 \text{ mole Sn}} = 14.8 \text{ g of Sn (3 SFs)}$

d. $1.76 \text{ moles Cu} \times \dfrac{63.55 \text{ g Cu}}{1 \text{ mole Cu}} = 112 \text{ g of Cu (3 SFs)}$

7.43 **a.** Molar mass of NaCl

= 1 mole of Na + 1 mole of Cl = 22.99 g + 35.45 g = 58.44 g (4 SFs)

$$0.500 \text{ mole NaCl} \times \frac{58.44 \text{ g NaCl}}{1 \text{ mole NaCl}} = 29.2 \text{ g of NaCl (3 SFs)}$$

b. Molar mass of Na_2O

= 2 moles of Na + 1 mole of O = 2(22.99 g) + 16.00 g = 61.98 g (4 SFs)

$$1.75 \text{ moles Na}_2\text{O} \times \frac{61.98 \text{ g Na}_2\text{O}}{1 \text{ mole Na}_2\text{O}} = 108 \text{ g of Na}_2\text{O (3 SFs)}$$

c. Molar mass of H_2O

= 2 moles of H + 1 mole of O = 2(1.008 g) + 16.00 g = 18.02 g (4 SFs)

$$0.225 \text{ mole H}_2\text{O} \times \frac{18.02 \text{ g H}_2\text{O}}{1 \text{ mole H}_2\text{O}} = 4.05 \text{ g of H}_2\text{O (3 SFs)}$$

d. Molar mass of CO_2

= 1 mole of C + 2 moles of O = 12.01 g + 2(16.00 g) = 44.01 g (4 SFs)

$$4.42 \text{ moles CO}_2 \times \frac{44.01 \text{ g CO}_2}{1 \text{ mole CO}_2} = 195 \text{ g of CO}_2 \text{ (3 SFs)}$$

7.45 **a.** $50.0 \text{ g Ag} \times \dfrac{1 \text{ mole Ag}}{107.9 \text{ g Ag}} = 0.463 \text{ mole of Ag (3 SFs)}$

b. $0.200 \text{ g C} \times \dfrac{1 \text{ mole C}}{12.01 \text{ g C}} = 0.0167 \text{ mole of C (3 SFs)}$

c. Molar mass of NH_3

= 1 mole of N + 3 moles of H = 14.01 g + 3(1.008 g) = 17.03 g (4 SFs)

$$15.0 \text{ g NH}_3 \times \frac{1 \text{ mole NH}_3}{17.03 \text{ g NH}_3} = 0.881 \text{ mole of NH}_3 \text{ (3 SFs)}$$

d. Molar mass of SO_2

= 1 mole of S + 2 moles of O = 32.07 g + 2(16.00 g) = 64.07 g (4 SFs)

$$75.0 \text{ g SO}_2 \times \frac{1 \text{ mole SO}_2}{64.07 \text{ g SO}_2} = 1.17 \text{ moles of SO}_2 \text{ (3 SFs)}$$

7.47 **a.** $25.0 \text{ g Ne} \times \dfrac{1 \text{ mole Ne}}{20.18 \text{ g Ne}} = 1.24 \text{ moles of Ne (3 SFs)}$

b. Molar mass of O_2 = 2 moles of O = 2(16.00 g) = 32.00 g (4 SFs)

$$25.0 \text{ g O}_2 \times \frac{1 \text{ mole O}_2}{32.00 \text{ g O}_2} = 0.781 \text{ mole of O}_2 \text{ (3 SFs)}$$

c. Molar mass of $Al(OH)_3$

= 1 mole of Al + 3 moles of O + 3 moles of H = 26.98 g + 3(16.00 g) + 3(1.008 g)

= 78.00 g (4 SFs)

$$25.0 \text{ g Al(OH)}_3 \times \frac{1 \text{ mole Al(OH)}_3}{78.00 \text{ g Al(OH)}_3} = 0.321 \text{ mole of Al(OH)}_3 \text{ (3 SFs)}$$

d. Molar mass of Ga_2S_3

= 2 moles of Ga + 3 moles of S = 2(69.72 g) + 3(32.07 g) = 235.7 g (4 SFs)

$$25.0 \text{ g Ga}_2\text{S}_3 \times \frac{1 \text{ mole Ga}_2\text{S}_3}{235.7 \text{ g Ga}_2\text{S}_3} = 0.106 \text{ mole of Ga}_2\text{S}_3 \text{ (3 SFs)}$$

7.49 **a.** $25 \text{ g S} \times \dfrac{1 \text{ mole S}}{32.07 \text{ g S}} = 0.78 \text{ mole of S (2 SFs)}$

b. Molar mass of SO_2

= 1 mole of S + 2 moles of O = 32.07 g + 2(16.00 g) = 64.07 g (4 SFs)

$$125 \text{ g SO}_2 \times \frac{1 \text{ mole SO}_2}{64.07 \text{ g SO}_2} \times \frac{1 \text{ mole S}}{1 \text{ mole SO}_2} = 1.95 \text{ moles of S (3 SFs)}$$

c. $2.0 \text{ moles Al}_2\text{S}_3 \times \dfrac{3 \text{ moles S}}{1 \text{ mole Al}_2\text{S}_3} = 6.0 \text{ moles of S (2 SFs)}$

7.51 a. Molar mass of $MgSO_4$

$= 1 \text{ mole of Mg} + 1 \text{ mole of S} + 4 \text{ moles of O} = 24.31 \text{ g} + 32.07 \text{ g} + 4(16.00 \text{ g})$

$= 120.38 \text{ g (5 SFs)}$

$5.00 \text{ moles MgSO}_4 \times \dfrac{120.38 \text{ g MgSO}_4}{1 \text{ mole MgSO}_4} = 602 \text{ g of MgSO}_4 \text{ (3 SFs)}$

b. Molar mass of KI

$= 1 \text{ mole of K} + 1 \text{ mole of I} = 39.10 \text{ g} + 126.9 \text{ g} = 166.0 \text{ g (4 SFs)}$

$0.450 \text{ mole KI} \times \dfrac{166.0 \text{ g KI}}{1 \text{ mole KI}} = 74.7 \text{ g of KI (3 SFs)}$

7.53 a. Molar mass of N_2O

$= 2 \text{ moles of N} + 1 \text{ mole of O} = 2(14.01 \text{ g}) + 16.00 \text{ g} = 44.02 \text{ g (4 SFs)}$

$1.50 \text{ moles N}_2\text{O} \times \dfrac{44.02 \text{ g N}_2\text{O}}{1 \text{ mole N}_2\text{O}} = 66.0 \text{ g of N}_2\text{O (3 SFs)}$

b. $34.0 \text{ g N}_2\text{O} \times \dfrac{1 \text{ mole N}_2\text{O}}{44.02 \text{ g N}_2\text{O}} = 0.772 \text{ mole of N}_2\text{O (3 SFs)}$

c. $34.0 \text{ g N}_2\text{O} \times \dfrac{1 \text{ mole N}_2\text{O}}{44.02 \text{ g N}_2\text{O}} \times \dfrac{2 \text{ moles N}}{1 \text{ mole N}_2\text{O}} \times \dfrac{14.01 \text{ g N}}{1 \text{ mole N}} = 21.6 \text{ g of N (3 SFs)}$

7.55 a. $19 \text{ moles C} \times \dfrac{12.01 \text{ g C}}{1 \text{ mole C}} = 228.2 \text{ g of C}$

$20 \text{ moles H} \times \dfrac{1.008 \text{ g H}}{1 \text{ mole H}} = 20.16 \text{ g of H}$

$1 \text{ mole F} \times \dfrac{19.00 \text{ g F}}{1 \text{ mole F}} = 19.00 \text{ g of F}$

$1 \text{ mole N} \times \dfrac{14.01 \text{ g N}}{1 \text{ mole N}} = 14.01 \text{ g of N}$

$3 \text{ moles O} \times \dfrac{16.00 \text{ g O}}{1 \text{ mole O}} = 48.00 \text{ g of O}$

19 moles of C	=	228.2 g of C
20 moles of H	=	20.16 g of H
1 mole of F	=	19.00 g of F
1 mole of N	=	14.01 g of N
3 moles of O	=	48.00 g of O
$\therefore$ Molar mass of $C_{19}H_{20}FNO_3$	=	329.4 g

b. $3 \text{ moles Ca} \times \dfrac{40.08 \text{ g Ca}}{1 \text{ mole Ca}} = 120.2 \text{ g of Ca}$

$12 \text{ moles C} \times \dfrac{12.01 \text{ g C}}{1 \text{ mole C}} = 144.1 \text{ g of C}$

$10 \text{ moles H} \times \dfrac{1.008 \text{ g H}}{1 \text{ mole H}} = 10.08 \text{ g of H}$

$14 \text{ moles O} \times \dfrac{16.00 \text{ g O}}{1 \text{ mole O}} = 224.0 \text{ g of O}$

3 moles of Ca $\qquad$ = 120.2 g of Ca
12 moles of C $\qquad$ = 144.1 g of C
10 moles of H $\qquad$ = 10.08 g of H
14 moles of O $\qquad$ = 224.0 g of O
∴ Molar mass of $Ca_3C_{12}H_{10}O_{14}$ = 498.4 g

c. $3 \text{ moles C} \times \dfrac{12.01 \text{ g C}}{1 \text{ mole C}} = 36.03 \text{ g of C}$

$8 \text{ moles H} \times \dfrac{1.008 \text{ g H}}{1 \text{ mole H}} = 8.064 \text{ g of H}$

$1 \text{ mole O} \times \dfrac{16.00 \text{ g O}}{1 \text{ mole O}} = 16.00 \text{ g of O}$

3 moles of C $\qquad$ = 36.03 g of C
8 moles of H $\qquad$ = 8.064 g of H
1 mole of O $\qquad$ = 16.00 g of O
∴ Molar mass of C_3H_8O = 60.09 g

d. $17 \text{ moles C} \times \dfrac{12.01 \text{ g C}}{1 \text{ mole C}} = 204.2 \text{ g of C}$

$18 \text{ moles H} \times \dfrac{1.008 \text{ g H}}{1 \text{ mole H}} = 18.14 \text{ g of H}$

$1 \text{ mole F} \times \dfrac{19.00 \text{ g F}}{1 \text{ mole F}} = 19.00 \text{ g of F}$

$3 \text{ moles N} \times \dfrac{14.01 \text{ g N}}{1 \text{ mole N}} = 42.03 \text{ g of N}$

$3 \text{ moles O} \times \dfrac{16.00 \text{ g O}}{1 \text{ mole O}} = 48.00 \text{ g of O}$

17 moles of C $\qquad$ = 204.2 g of C
18 moles of H $\qquad$ = 18.14 g of H
1 mole of F $\qquad$ = 19.00 g of F
3 moles of N $\qquad$ = 42.03 g of N
3 moles of O $\qquad$ = 48.00 g of O
∴ Molar mass of $C_{17}H_{18}FN_3O_3$ = 331.4 g

7.57 a. $\dfrac{2 \text{ moles } SO_2}{1 \text{ mole } O_2}$ and $\dfrac{1 \text{ mole } O_2}{2 \text{ moles } SO_2}$; $\dfrac{2 \text{ moles } SO_2}{2 \text{ moles } SO_3}$ and $\dfrac{2 \text{ moles } SO_3}{2 \text{ moles } SO_2}$; $\dfrac{1 \text{ mole } O_2}{2 \text{ moles } SO_3}$ and $\dfrac{2 \text{ moles } SO_3}{1 \text{ mole } O_2}$

b. $\dfrac{4 \text{ moles P}}{5 \text{ moles } O_2}$ and $\dfrac{5 \text{ moles } O_2}{4 \text{ moles P}}$; $\dfrac{4 \text{ moles P}}{2 \text{ moles } P_2O_5}$ and $\dfrac{2 \text{ moles } P_2O_5}{4 \text{ moles P}}$; $\dfrac{5 \text{ moles } O_2}{2 \text{ moles } P_2O_5}$ and $\dfrac{2 \text{ moles } P_2O_5}{5 \text{ moles } O_2}$

7.59 a. $2.0 \text{ moles } H_2 \times \dfrac{1 \text{ mole } O_2}{2 \text{ moles } H_2} = 1.0 \text{ mole of } O_2 \text{ (2 SFs)}$

b. $5.0 \text{ moles } O_2 \times \dfrac{2 \text{ moles } H_2}{1 \text{ mole } O_2} = 10. \text{ moles of } H_2 \text{ (2 SFs)}$

c. $2.5 \text{ moles } O_2 \times \dfrac{2 \text{ moles } H_2O}{1 \text{ mole } O_2} = 5.0 \text{ moles of } H_2O \text{ (2 SFs)}$

7.61 a. $0.500 \text{ mole } SO_2 \times \dfrac{5 \text{ moles C}}{2 \text{ moles } SO_2} = 1.25 \text{ moles of C (3 SFs)}$

b. $1.2 \text{ moles C} \times \dfrac{4 \text{ moles CO}}{5 \text{ moles C}} = 0.96 \text{ mole of CO (2 SFs)}$

c. $0.50 \text{ mole CS}_2 \times \dfrac{2 \text{ moles SO}_2}{1 \text{ mole CS}_2} = 1.0 \text{ mole of SO}_2 \ (2 \text{ SFs})$

d. $2.5 \text{ moles C} \times \dfrac{1 \text{ mole CS}_2}{5 \text{ moles C}} = 0.50 \text{ mole of CS}_2 \ (2 \text{ SFs})$

7.63 **a.** $57.5 \text{ g Na} \times \dfrac{1 \text{ mole Na}}{22.99 \text{ g Na}} \times \dfrac{2 \text{ moles Na}_2\text{O}}{4 \text{ moles Na}} \times \dfrac{61.98 \text{ g Na}_2\text{O}}{1 \text{ mole Na}_2\text{O}} = 77.5 \text{ g of Na}_2\text{O} \ (3 \text{ SFs})$

b. $18.0 \text{ g Na} \times \dfrac{1 \text{ mole Na}}{22.99 \text{ g Na}} \times \dfrac{1 \text{ mole O}_2}{4 \text{ moles Na}} \times \dfrac{32.00 \text{ g O}_2}{1 \text{ mole O}_2} = 6.26 \text{ g of O}_2 \ (3 \text{ SFs})$

c. $75.0 \text{ g Na}_2\text{O} \times \dfrac{1 \text{ mole Na}_2\text{O}}{61.98 \text{ g Na}_2\text{O}} \times \dfrac{1 \text{ mole O}_2}{2 \text{ moles Na}_2\text{O}} \times \dfrac{32.00 \text{ g O}_2}{1 \text{ mole O}_2} = 19.4 \text{ g of O}_2 \ (3 \text{ SFs})$

7.65 **a.** $13.6 \text{ g NH}_3 \times \dfrac{1 \text{ mole NH}_3}{17.03 \text{ g NH}_3} \times \dfrac{3 \text{ moles O}_2}{4 \text{ moles NH}_3} \times \dfrac{32.00 \text{ g O}_2}{1 \text{ mole O}_2} = 19.2 \text{ g of O}_2 \ (3 \text{ SFs})$

b. $6.50 \text{ g O}_2 \times \dfrac{1 \text{ mole O}_2}{32.00 \text{ g O}_2} \times \dfrac{2 \text{ moles N}_2}{3 \text{ moles O}_2} \times \dfrac{28.02 \text{ g N}_2}{1 \text{ mole N}_2} = 3.79 \text{ g of N}_2 \ (3 \text{ SFs})$

c. $34.0 \text{ g NH}_3 \times \dfrac{1 \text{ mole NH}_3}{17.03 \text{ g NH}_3} \times \dfrac{6 \text{ moles H}_2\text{O}}{4 \text{ moles NH}_3} \times \dfrac{18.02 \text{ g H}_2\text{O}}{1 \text{ mole H}_2\text{O}} = 54.0 \text{ g of H}_2\text{O} \ (3 \text{ SFs})$

7.67 **a.** $28.0 \text{ g NO}_2 \times \dfrac{1 \text{ mole NO}_2}{46.01 \text{ g NO}_2} \times \dfrac{1 \text{ mole H}_2\text{O}}{3 \text{ moles NO}_2} \times \dfrac{18.02 \text{ g H}_2\text{O}}{1 \text{ mole H}_2\text{O}} = 3.66 \text{ g of H}_2\text{O} \ (3 \text{ SFs})$

b. $15.8 \text{ g NO}_2 \times \dfrac{1 \text{ mole NO}_2}{46.01 \text{ g NO}_2} \times \dfrac{1 \text{ mole NO}}{3 \text{ moles NO}_2} \times \dfrac{30.01 \text{ g NO}}{1 \text{ mole NO}} = 3.44 \text{ g of NO} \ (3 \text{ SFs})$

c. $8.25 \text{ g NO}_2 \times \dfrac{1 \text{ mole NO}_2}{46.01 \text{ g NO}_2} \times \dfrac{2 \text{ moles HNO}_3}{3 \text{ moles NO}_2} \times \dfrac{63.02 \text{ g HNO}_3}{1 \text{ mole HNO}_3} = 7.53 \text{ g of HNO}_3 \ (3 \text{ SFs})$

7.69 **a.** $2\text{PbS}(s) + 3\text{O}_2(g) \xrightarrow{\Delta} 2\text{PbO}(s) + 2\text{SO}_2(g)$

b. $30.0 \text{ g PbS} \times \dfrac{1 \text{ mole PbS}}{239.3 \text{ g PbS}} \times \dfrac{3 \text{ moles O}_2}{2 \text{ moles PbS}} \times \dfrac{32.00 \text{ g O}_2}{1 \text{ mole O}_2} = 6.02 \text{ g of O}_2 \ (3 \text{ SFs})$

c. $65.0 \text{ g PbS} \times \dfrac{1 \text{ mole PbS}}{239.3 \text{ g PbS}} \times \dfrac{2 \text{ moles SO}_2}{2 \text{ moles PbS}} \times \dfrac{64.07 \text{ g SO}_2}{1 \text{ mole SO}_2} = 17.4 \text{ g of SO}_2 \ (3 \text{ SFs})$

d. $128 \text{ g PbO} \times \dfrac{1 \text{ mole PbO}}{223.2 \text{ g PbO}} \times \dfrac{2 \text{ moles PbS}}{2 \text{ moles PbO}} \times \dfrac{239.3 \text{ g PbS}}{1 \text{ mole PbS}} = 137 \text{ g of PbS} \ (3 \text{ SFs})$

7.71 **a.** $15.0 \text{ g glycine} \times \dfrac{1 \text{ mole glycine}}{75.07 \text{ g glycine}} \times \dfrac{3 \text{ moles O}_2}{2 \text{ moles glycine}} \times \dfrac{32.00 \text{ g O}_2}{1 \text{ mole O}_2} = 9.59 \text{ g of O}_2 \ (3 \text{ SFs})$

b. $15.0 \text{ g glycine} \times \dfrac{1 \text{ mole glycine}}{75.07 \text{ g glycine}} \times \dfrac{1 \text{ mole urea}}{2 \text{ moles glycine}} \times \dfrac{60.06 \text{ g urea}}{1 \text{ mole urea}} = 6.00 \text{ g of urea} \ (3 \text{ SFs})$

c. $15.0 \text{ g glycine} \times \dfrac{1 \text{ mole glycine}}{75.07 \text{ g glycine}} \times \dfrac{3 \text{ moles CO}_2}{2 \text{ moles glycine}} \times \dfrac{44.01 \text{ g CO}_2}{1 \text{ mole CO}_2} = 13.2 \text{ g of CO}_2 \ (3 \text{ SFs})$

7.73 **a.** The limiting factor is the number of drivers: with only eight drivers available, only eight taxis can be used to pick up passengers.

b. The limiting factor is the number of taxis: only seven taxis are in working condition to be driven.

7.75 **a.** $3.0 \text{ moles N}_2 \times \dfrac{2 \text{ moles NH}_3}{1 \text{ mole N}_2} = 6.0 \text{ moles of NH}_3$

$5.0 \text{ moles H}_2 \times \dfrac{2 \text{ moles NH}_3}{3 \text{ moles H}_2} = 3.3 \text{ moles of NH}_3 \text{ (smaller amount of product)}$

The limiting reactant is 5.0 moles of H_2. (2 SFs)

b. $8.0 \text{ moles N}_2 \times \dfrac{2 \text{ moles NH}_3}{1 \text{ mole N}_2} = 16 \text{ moles of NH}_3$

$4.0 \text{ moles H}_2 \times \dfrac{2 \text{ moles NH}_3}{3 \text{ moles H}_2} = 2.7 \text{ moles of NH}_3 \text{ (smaller amount of product)}$

The limiting reactant is 4.0 moles of H_2. (2 SFs)

c. $3.0 \text{ moles N}_2 \times \dfrac{2 \text{ moles NH}_3}{1 \text{ mole N}_2} = 6.0 \text{ moles of NH}_3 \text{ (smaller amount of product)}$

$12.0 \text{ moles H}_2 \times \dfrac{2 \text{ moles NH}_3}{3 \text{ moles H}_2} = 8.0 \text{ moles of NH}_3$

The limiting reactant is 3.0 moles of N_2. (2 SFs)

7.77 **a.** $20.0 \text{ g Al} \times \dfrac{1 \text{ mole Al}}{26.98 \text{ g Al}} \times \dfrac{2 \text{ moles AlCl}_3}{2 \text{ moles Al}} \times \dfrac{133.33 \text{ g AlCl}_3}{1 \text{ mole AlCl}_3} = 98.8 \text{ g of AlCl}_3$

$20.0 \text{ g Cl}_2 \times \dfrac{1 \text{ mole Cl}_2}{70.90 \text{ g Cl}_2} \times \dfrac{2 \text{ moles AlCl}_3}{3 \text{ moles Cl}_2} \times \dfrac{133.33 \text{ g AlCl}_3}{1 \text{ mole AlCl}_3} = 25.1 \text{ g of AlCl}_3$
(smaller amount of product)

$\therefore$ Cl_2 is the limiting reactant, and 25.1 g of $AlCl_3$ (3 SFs) can be produced.

b. $20.0 \text{ g NH}_3 \times \dfrac{1 \text{ mole NH}_3}{17.03 \text{ g NH}_3} \times \dfrac{6 \text{ moles H}_2\text{O}}{4 \text{ moles NH}_3} \times \dfrac{18.02 \text{ g H}_2\text{O}}{1 \text{ mole H}_2\text{O}} = 31.7 \text{ g of H}_2\text{O}$

$20.0 \text{ g O}_2 \times \dfrac{1 \text{ mole O}_2}{32.00 \text{ g O}_2} \times \dfrac{6 \text{ moles H}_2\text{O}}{5 \text{ moles O}_2} \times \dfrac{18.02 \text{ g H}_2\text{O}}{1 \text{ mole H}_2\text{O}} = 13.5 \text{ g of H}_2\text{O}$
(smaller amount of product)

$\therefore$ O_2 is the limiting reactant, and 13.5 g of H_2O (3 SFs) can be produced.

c. $20.0 \text{ g CS}_2 \times \dfrac{1 \text{ mole CS}_2}{76.15 \text{ g CS}_2} \times \dfrac{2 \text{ moles SO}_2}{1 \text{ mole CS}_2} \times \dfrac{64.07 \text{ g SO}_2}{1 \text{ mole SO}_2} = 33.7 \text{ g of SO}_2$

$20.0 \text{ g O}_2 \times \dfrac{1 \text{ mole O}_2}{32.00 \text{ g O}_2} \times \dfrac{2 \text{ moles SO}_2}{3 \text{ moles O}_2} \times \dfrac{64.07 \text{ g SO}_2}{1 \text{ mole SO}_2} = 26.7 \text{ g of SO}_2$
(smaller amount of product)

$\therefore$ O_2 is the limiting reactant, and 26.7 g of SO_2 (3 SFs) can be produced.

7.79 **a.** $25.0 \text{ g SO}_2 \times \dfrac{1 \text{ mole SO}_2}{64.07 \text{ g SO}_2} \times \dfrac{2 \text{ moles SO}_3}{2 \text{ moles SO}_2} \times \dfrac{80.07 \text{ g SO}_3}{1 \text{ mole SO}_3} = 31.2 \text{ g of SO}_3$
(smaller amount of product)

$40.0 \text{ g O}_2 \times \dfrac{1 \text{ mole O}_2}{32.00 \text{ g O}_2} \times \dfrac{2 \text{ moles SO}_3}{1 \text{ mole O}_2} \times \dfrac{80.07 \text{ g SO}_3}{1 \text{ mole SO}_3} = 200. \text{ g of SO}_3$

$\therefore$ SO_2 is the limiting reactant, and 31.2 g of SO_3 (3 SFs) can be produced.

b. $25.0 \text{ g Fe} \times \dfrac{1 \text{ mole Fe}}{55.85 \text{ g Fe}} \times \dfrac{1 \text{ mole Fe}_3\text{O}_4}{3 \text{ moles Fe}} \times \dfrac{231.6 \text{ g Fe}_3\text{O}_4}{1 \text{ mole Fe}_3\text{O}_4} = 34.6 \text{ g of Fe}_3\text{O}_4$
(smaller amount of product)

$40.0 \text{ g H}_2\text{O} \times \dfrac{1 \text{ mole H}_2\text{O}}{18.02 \text{ g H}_2\text{O}} \times \dfrac{1 \text{ mole Fe}_3\text{O}_4}{4 \text{ moles H}_2\text{O}} \times \dfrac{231.6 \text{ g Fe}_3\text{O}_4}{1 \text{ mole Fe}_3\text{O}_4} = 129 \text{ g of Fe}_3\text{O}_4$

$\therefore$ Fe is the limiting reactant, and 34.6 g of Fe_3O_4 (3 SFs) can be produced.

c. $25.0 \text{ g C}_7\text{H}_{16} \times \dfrac{1 \text{ mole C}_7\text{H}_{16}}{100.20 \text{ g C}_7\text{H}_{16}} \times \dfrac{7 \text{ moles CO}_2}{1 \text{ mole C}_7\text{H}_{16}} \times \dfrac{44.01 \text{ g CO}_2}{1 \text{ mole CO}_2} = 76.9 \text{ g of CO}_2$

$40.0 \text{ g O}_2 \times \dfrac{1 \text{ mole O}_2}{32.00 \text{ g O}_2} \times \dfrac{7 \text{ moles CO}_2}{11 \text{ moles O}_2} \times \dfrac{44.01 \text{ g CO}_2}{1 \text{ mole CO}_2} = 35.0 \text{ g of CO}_2$

(smaller amount of product)

$\therefore$ O$_2$ is the limiting reactant, and 35.0 g of CO$_2$ (3 SFs) can be produced.

7.81 **a.** Theoretical yield of CS$_2$:

$40.0 \text{ g C} \times \dfrac{1 \text{ mole C}}{12.01 \text{ g C}} \times \dfrac{1 \text{ mole CS}_2}{5 \text{ moles C}} \times \dfrac{76.15 \text{ g CS}_2}{1 \text{ mole CS}_2} = 50.7 \text{ g of CS}_2$

Percent yield: $\dfrac{36.0 \text{ g CS}_2 \text{ (actual)}}{50.7 \text{ g CS}_2 \text{ (theoretical)}} \times 100\% = 71.0\%$ (3 SFs)

b. Theoretical yield of CS$_2$:

$32.0 \text{ g SO}_2 \times \dfrac{1 \text{ mole SO}_2}{64.07 \text{ g SO}_2} \times \dfrac{1 \text{ mole CS}_2}{2 \text{ moles SO}_2} \times \dfrac{76.15 \text{ g CS}_2}{1 \text{ mole CS}_2} = 19.0 \text{ g of CS}_2$

Percent yield: $\dfrac{12.0 \text{ g CS}_2 \text{ (actual)}}{19.0 \text{ g CS}_2 \text{ (theoretical)}} \times 100\% = 63.2\%$ (3 SFs)

7.83 Theoretical yield of Al$_2$O$_3$:

$50.0 \text{ g Al} \times \dfrac{1 \text{ mole Al}}{26.98 \text{ g Al}} \times \dfrac{2 \text{ moles Al}_2\text{O}_3}{4 \text{ moles Al}} \times \dfrac{101.96 \text{ g Al}_2\text{O}_3}{1 \text{ mole Al}_2\text{O}_3} = 94.5 \text{ g of Al}_2\text{O}_3$

Use the percent yield to convert theoretical to actual:

$94.5 \text{ g Al}_2\text{O}_3 \times \dfrac{75.0 \text{ g Al}_2\text{O}_3}{100 \text{ g Al}_2\text{O}_3} = 70.9 \text{ g of Al}_2\text{O}_3 \text{ (actual)}$ (3 SFs)

7.85 Theoretical yield of CO$_2$:

$30.0 \text{ g C} \times \dfrac{1 \text{ mole C}}{12.01 \text{ g C}} \times \dfrac{2 \text{ moles CO}}{3 \text{ moles C}} \times \dfrac{28.01 \text{ g CO}}{1 \text{ mole CO}} = 46.6 \text{ g of CO}$

Percent yield: $\dfrac{28.2 \text{ g CO (actual)}}{46.6 \text{ g CO (theoretical)}} \times 100\% = 60.5\%$ (3 SFs)

7.87 In exothermic reactions, the energy of the products is lower than that of the reactants.

7.89 **a.** An exothermic reaction releases energy.
  b. An endothermic reaction has a higher energy level for the products than the reactants.
  c. Metabolism is an exothermic reaction, providing energy for the body.

7.91 **a.** Heat is released, which makes the reaction exothermic with $\Delta H = -802$ kJ.
  b. Heat is absorbed, which makes the reaction endothermic with $\Delta H = +65.3$ kJ.
  c. Heat is released, which makes the reaction exothermic with $\Delta H = -850$ kJ.

7.93 **a.** $125 \text{ g Cl}_2 \times \dfrac{1 \text{ mole Cl}_2}{70.90 \text{ g Cl}_2} \times \dfrac{-657 \text{ kJ}}{2 \text{ moles Cl}_2} = -579 \text{ kJ}$ (3 SFs)

$\therefore$ 579 kJ are released.

b. $278 \text{ g PCl}_5 \times \dfrac{1 \text{ mole PCl}_5}{208.2 \text{ g PCl}_5} \times \dfrac{+67 \text{ kJ}}{1 \text{ mole PCl}_5} = +89 \text{ kJ}$ (2 SFs)

$\therefore$ 89 kJ are absorbed.

7.95 **a.** Since heat is absorbed, the reaction is endothermic.

b. $18.0 \text{ g CO}_2 \times \dfrac{1 \text{ mole CO}_2}{44.01 \text{ g CO}_2} \times \dfrac{1 \text{ mole glucose}}{6 \text{ moles CO}_2} \times \dfrac{180.2 \text{ g glucose}}{1 \text{ mole glucose}} = 12.3 \text{ g of glucose}$ (3 SFs)

c. $25.0 \text{ g glucose} \times \dfrac{1 \text{ mole glucose}}{180.2 \text{ g glucose}} \times \dfrac{680 \text{ kcal}}{1 \text{ mole glucose}} \times \dfrac{1000 \text{ cal}}{1 \text{ kcal}} \times \dfrac{4.184 \text{ J}}{1 \text{ cal}} \times \dfrac{1 \text{ kJ}}{1000 \text{ J}}$

$= 390 \text{ kJ (2 SFs)}$

7.97 a. $0.0500 \text{ mole Ca}_5(\text{PO}_4)_3\text{OH} \times \dfrac{3 \text{ moles P}}{1 \text{ mole Ca}_5(\text{PO}_4)_3\text{OH}} = 0.150 \text{ mole of P (3 SFs)}$

b. $0.250 \text{ mole Ca}_5(\text{PO}_4)_3\text{OH} \times \dfrac{5 \text{ moles Ca}^{2+}}{1 \text{ mole Ca}_5(\text{PO}_4)_3\text{OH}} \times \dfrac{6.02 \times 10^{23} \text{ Ca}^{2+} \text{ ions}}{1 \text{ mole Ca}^{2+}}$

$= 7.53 \times 10^{23} \text{ Ca}^{2+} \text{ ions (3 SFs)}$

c. $8.5 \times 10^{23} \text{ H atoms} \times \dfrac{1 \text{ mole H atoms}}{6.02 \times 10^{23} \text{ H atoms}} \times \dfrac{1 \text{ mole Ca}_5(\text{PO}_4)_3\text{OH}}{1 \text{ mole H atoms}}$

$= 1.41 \text{ moles of Ca}_5(\text{PO}_4)_3\text{OH (3 SFs)}$

d. Molar mass of hydroxyapatite $(\text{Ca}_5(\text{PO}_4)_3\text{OH})$

$= 5(40.08 \text{ g}) + 3(30.97 \text{ g}) + 13(16.00 \text{ g}) + 1.008 \text{ g} = 502.3 \text{ g (4 SFs)}$

7.99 a. $2\text{H}_2\text{O}_2(aq) \longrightarrow 2\text{H}_2\text{O}(l) + \text{O}_2(g)$

b. decomposition

c. $1.65 \text{ moles H}_2\text{O}_2 \times \dfrac{1 \text{ mole O}_2}{2 \text{ moles H}_2\text{O}_2} = 0.825 \text{ mole of O}_2 \text{ (3 SFs)}$

d. $4.28 \text{ g O}_2 \times \dfrac{1 \text{ mole O}_2}{32.00 \text{ g O}_2} \times \dfrac{2 \text{ moles H}_2\text{O}_2}{1 \text{ mole O}_2} \times \dfrac{34.02 \text{ g H}_2\text{O}_2}{1 \text{ mole H}_2\text{O}_2} = 9.10 \text{ g of H}_2\text{O}_2 \text{ (3 SFs)}$

e. $3.0 \text{ g gel} \times \dfrac{25 \text{ g H}_2\text{O}_2}{100 \text{ g gel}} \times \dfrac{1 \text{ mole H}_2\text{O}_2}{34.02 \text{ g H}_2\text{O}_2} \times \dfrac{1 \text{ mole O}_2}{2 \text{ moles H}_2\text{O}_2} \times \dfrac{32.00 \text{ g O}_2}{1 \text{ mole O}_2}$

$= 0.35 \text{ g of O}_2 \text{ (2 SFs)}$

f. theoretical yield of O_2:

$8.00 \text{ g H}_2\text{O}_2 \times \dfrac{1 \text{ mole H}_2\text{O}_2}{34.02 \text{ g H}_2\text{O}_2} \times \dfrac{1 \text{ mole O}_2}{2 \text{ moles H}_2\text{O}_2} \times \dfrac{32.00 \text{ g O}_2}{1 \text{ mole O}_2} = 3.76 \text{ g of O}_2$

percent yield: $\dfrac{2.33 \text{ g O}_2 \text{ (actual)}}{3.76 \text{ g O}_2 \text{ (theoretical)}} \times 100\% = 62.0\% \text{ (3 SFs)}$

7.101 a. 1, 1, 2 combination

b. 2, 2, 1 decomposition

7.103 a. reactants NO and O_2; product NO_2

b. $2\text{NO}(g) + \text{O}_2(g) \longrightarrow 2\text{NO}_2(g)$

c. combination

7.105 a. reactant NI_3; products N_2 and I_2

b. $2\text{NI}_3(g) \longrightarrow \text{N}_2(g) + 3\text{I}_2(g)$

c. decomposition

7.107 a. reactants Cl_2 and O_2; product OCl_2

b. $2\text{Cl}_2(g) + \text{O}_2(g) \longrightarrow 2\text{OCl}_2(g)$

c. combination

7.109 1. a. S_2Cl_2

b. Molar mass of $\text{S}_2\text{Cl}_2 = 2(32.07 \text{ g}) + 2(35.45 \text{ g}) = 135.04 \text{ g (5 SFs)}$

c. $10.0 \text{ g S}_2\text{Cl}_2 \times \dfrac{1 \text{ mole S}_2\text{Cl}_2}{135.04 \text{ g S}_2\text{Cl}_2} = 0.0741 \text{ mole of S}_2\text{Cl}_2 \text{ (3 SFs)}$

2. a. C_6H_6

b. Molar mass of $\text{C}_6\text{H}_6 = 6(12.01 \text{ g}) + 6(1.008 \text{ g}) = 78.11 \text{ g (4 SFs)}$

c. $10.0 \text{ g } C_6H_6 \times \dfrac{1 \text{ mole } C_6H_6}{78.11 \text{ g } C_6H_6} = 0.128 \text{ mole of } C_6H_6 \text{ (3 SFs)}$

7.111 a. Molar mass of dipyrithione $(C_{10}H_8N_2O_2S_2)$
$= 10(12.01 \text{ g}) + 8(1.008 \text{ g}) + 2(14.01 \text{ g}) + 2(16.00 \text{ g}) + 2(32.07 \text{ g}) = 252.3 \text{ g (4 SFs)}$

b. $25.0 \text{ g } C_{10}H_8N_2O_2S_2 \times \dfrac{1 \text{ mole } C_{10}H_8N_2O_2S_2}{252.3 \text{ g } C_{10}H_8N_2O_2S_2} = 0.0991 \text{ mole of } C_{10}H_8N_2O_2S_2 \text{ (3 SFs)}$

c. $25.0 \text{ g } C_{10}H_8N_2O_2S_2 \times \dfrac{1 \text{ mole } C_{10}H_8N_2O_2S_2}{252.3 \text{ g } C_{10}H_8N_2O_2S_2} \times \dfrac{10 \text{ moles C}}{1 \text{ mole } C_{10}H_8N_2O_2S_2}$
$= 0.991 \text{ mole of C (3 SFs)}$

d. $8.2 \times 10^{24} \text{ N atoms} \times \dfrac{1 \text{ mole N}}{6.02 \times 10^{23} \text{ N atoms}} \times \dfrac{1 \text{ mole } C_{10}H_8O_2N_2S_2}{2 \text{ moles N}}$
$= 6.8 \text{ moles of } C_{10}H_8O_2N_2S_2 \text{ (2 SFs)}$

7.113 a. $2NO + O_2 \longrightarrow 2NO_2$
b. NO is the limiting reactant.

7.115 a. $N_2 + 3H_2 \longrightarrow 2NH_3$
b. diagram A; N_2 is the excess reactant.

7.117 a. $2NI_3 \longrightarrow N_2 + 3I_2$
b. Theoretical yield: from the $6NI_3$ we could obtain

$6NI_3 \times \dfrac{1N_2}{2NI_3} = 3N_2 \qquad 6NI_3 \times \dfrac{3I_2}{2NI_3} = 9I_2$

Actual yield: in the actual products, we obtain $2N_2$ and $6I_2$.

Percent yield: $\dfrac{2N_2 \text{ and } 6I_2 \text{ (actual)}}{3N_2 \text{ and } 9I_2 \text{ (theoretical)}} \times 100\%$

$= \dfrac{2 (N_2 \text{ and } 3I_2) \text{ (actual)}}{3 (N_2 \text{ and } 3I_2) \text{ (theoretical)}} \times 100\% = 67\%$

7.119 a. Atoms of a metal and a nonmetal forming an ionic compound is a combination reaction.
b. When a compound of hydrogen and carbon reacts with oxygen, it is a combustion reaction.
c. When calcium carbonate is heated to produce calcium oxide and carbon dioxide, it is a decomposition reaction.
d. Zinc replacing copper in $Cu(NO_3)_2$ is a single replacement reaction.

7.121 a. $NH_3(g) + HCl(g) \longrightarrow NH_4Cl(s)$ combination
b. $C_4H_8(g) + 6O_2(g) \xrightarrow{\Delta} 4CO_2(g) + 4H_2O(g)$ combustion
c. $2Sb(s) + 3Cl_2(g) \longrightarrow 2SbCl_3(s)$ combination
d. $2NI_3(s) \longrightarrow N_2(g) + 3I_2(g)$ decomposition
e. $2KBr(aq) + Cl_2(aq) \longrightarrow 2KCl(aq) + Br_2(l)$ single replacement
f. $2Fe(s) + 3H_2SO_4(aq) \longrightarrow Fe_2(SO_4)_3(aq) + 3H_2(g)$ single replacement
g. $Al_2(SO_4)_3(aq) + 6NaOH(aq) \longrightarrow 3Na_2SO_4(aq)$ double replacement
$\qquad\qquad\qquad\qquad\qquad + 2Al(OH)_3(s)$

7.123 a. Since this is a single replacement reaction, the uncombined metal element takes the place of the metal element in the compound.
$Zn(s) + 2HCl(aq) \longrightarrow ZnCl_2(aq) + H_2(g)$
b. Since this is a decomposition reaction, the single reactant breaks down into more than one simpler substance.
$BaCO_3(s) \xrightarrow{\Delta} BaO(s) + CO_2(g)$

c. Since this is a double replacement reaction, the positive ions in the reacting compounds switch places.

$$NaOH(aq) + HCl(aq) \longrightarrow NaCl(aq) + H_2O(l)$$

d. Since this is a combination reaction, the product is a single compound.

$$2Al(s) + 3F_2(g) \longrightarrow 2AlF_3(s)$$

7.125 a. $1 \text{ mole Zn} \times \dfrac{65.41 \text{ g Zn}}{1 \text{ mole Zn}} = 65.41 \text{ g of Zn}$

$1 \text{ mole S} \times \dfrac{32.07 \text{ g S}}{1 \text{ mole S}} = 32.07 \text{ g of S}$

$4 \text{ moles O} \times \dfrac{16.00 \text{ g O}}{1 \text{ mole O}} = 64.00 \text{ g of O}$

1 mole of Zn	=	65.41 g of Zn
1 mole of S	=	32.07 g of S
4 moles of O	=	64.00 g of O
∴ Molar mass of $ZnSO_4$	=	161.48 g

b. $1 \text{ mole Ca} \times \dfrac{40.08 \text{ g Ca}}{1 \text{ mole Ca}} = 40.08 \text{ g of Ca}$

$2 \text{ moles I} \times \dfrac{126.9 \text{ g I}}{1 \text{ mole I}} = 253.8 \text{ g of I}$

$6 \text{ moles O} \times \dfrac{16.00 \text{ g O}}{1 \text{ mole O}} = 96.00 \text{ g of O}$

1 mole of Ca	=	40.08 g of Ca
2 moles of I	=	253.8 g of I
6 moles of O	=	96.00 g of O
∴ Molar mass of $Ca(IO_3)_2$	=	389.9 g

c. $5 \text{ moles C} \times \dfrac{12.01 \text{ g C}}{1 \text{ mole C}} = 60.05 \text{ g of C}$

$8 \text{ moles H} \times \dfrac{1.008 \text{ g H}}{1 \text{ mole H}} = 8.064 \text{ g of H}$

$1 \text{ mole N} \times \dfrac{14.01 \text{ g N}}{1 \text{ mole N}} = 14.01 \text{ g of N}$

$1 \text{ mole Na} \times \dfrac{22.99 \text{ g Na}}{1 \text{ mole Na}} = 22.99 \text{ g of Na}$

$4 \text{ moles O} \times \dfrac{16.00 \text{ g O}}{1 \text{ mole O}} = 64.00 \text{ g of O}$

5 moles of C	=	60.05 g of C
8 moles of H	=	8.064 g of H
1 mole of N	=	14.01 g of N
1 mole of Na	=	22.99 g of Na
4 moles of O	=	64.00 g of O
∴ Molar mass of $C_5H_8NNaO_4$	=	169.11 g

d. $6 \text{ moles C} \times \dfrac{12.01 \text{ g C}}{1 \text{ mole C}} = 72.06 \text{ g of C}$

$12 \text{ moles H} \times \dfrac{1.008 \text{ g H}}{1 \text{ mole H}} = 12.10 \text{ g of H}$

$2 \text{ moles O} \times \dfrac{16.00 \text{ g O}}{1 \text{ mole O}} = 32.00 \text{ g of O}$

$$6 \text{ moles of C} = 72.06 \text{ g of C}$$
$$12 \text{ moles of H} = 12.10 \text{ g of H}$$
$$2 \text{ moles of O} = 32.00 \text{ g of O}$$
$$\therefore \text{ Molar mass of } C_6H_{12}O_2 = \overline{116.16 \text{ g}}$$

7.127 a. $0.150 \text{ mole K} \times \dfrac{39.10 \text{ g K}}{1 \text{ mole K}} = 5.87 \text{ g of K (3 SFs)}$

b. $0.150 \text{ mole Cl}_2 \times \dfrac{70.90 \text{ g Cl}_2}{1 \text{ mole Cl}_2} = 10.6 \text{ g of Cl}_2 \text{ (3 SFs)}$

c. $0.150 \text{ mole Na}_2CO_3 \times \dfrac{105.99 \text{ g Na}_2CO_3}{1 \text{ mole Na}_2CO_3} = 15.9 \text{ g of Na}_2CO_3 \text{ (3 SFs)}$

7.129 a. $25.0 \text{ g CO}_2 \times \dfrac{1 \text{ mole CO}_2}{44.01 \text{ g CO}_2} = 0.568 \text{ mole of CO}_2 \text{ (3 SFs)}$

b. $25.0 \text{ g Al}_2O_3 \times \dfrac{1 \text{ mole Al}_2O_3}{101.96 \text{ g Al}_2O_3} = 0.245 \text{ mole of Al}_2O_3 \text{ (3 SFs)}$

c. $25.0 \text{ g MgCl}_2 \times \dfrac{1 \text{ mole MgCl}_2}{95.21 \text{ g MgCl}_2} = 0.263 \text{ mole of MgCl}_2 \text{ (3 SFs)}$

7.131 a. $2NH_3(g) + 5F_2(g) \longrightarrow N_2F_4(g) + 6HF(g)$

b. $4.00 \text{ moles HF} \times \dfrac{2 \text{ moles NH}_3}{6 \text{ moles HF}} = 1.33 \text{ moles of NH}_3 \text{ (3 SFs)}$

$4.00 \text{ moles HF} \times \dfrac{5 \text{ moles F}_2}{6 \text{ moles HF}} = 3.33 \text{ moles of F}_2 \text{ (3 SFs)}$

c. $25.5 \text{ g NH}_3 \times \dfrac{1 \text{ mole NH}_3}{17.03 \text{ g NH}_3} \times \dfrac{5 \text{ moles F}_2}{2 \text{ moles NH}_3} \times \dfrac{38.00 \text{ g F}_2}{1 \text{ mole F}_2} = 142 \text{ g of F}_2 \text{ (3 SFs)}$

d. $3.40 \text{ g NH}_3 \times \dfrac{1 \text{ mole NH}_3}{17.03 \text{ g NH}_3} \times \dfrac{1 \text{ mole N}_2F_4}{2 \text{ moles NH}_3} \times \dfrac{104.02 \text{ g N}_2F_4}{1 \text{ mole N}_2F_4} = 10.4 \text{ g of N}_2F_4 \text{ (3 SFs)}$

7.133 a. $3.00 \text{ moles H}_2O \times \dfrac{2 \text{ moles H}_2O_2}{2 \text{ moles H}_2O} = 3.00 \text{ moles of H}_2O_2 \text{ (3 SFs)}$

b. $36.5 \text{ g O}_2 \times \dfrac{1 \text{ mole O}_2}{32.00 \text{ g O}_2} \times \dfrac{2 \text{ moles H}_2O_2}{1 \text{ mole O}_2} \times \dfrac{34.02 \text{ g H}_2O_2}{1 \text{ mole H}_2O_2} = 77.6 \text{ g of H}_2O_2 \text{ (3 SFs)}$

c. $12.2 \text{ g H}_2O_2 \times \dfrac{1 \text{ mole H}_2O_2}{34.02 \text{ g H}_2O_2} \times \dfrac{2 \text{ moles H}_2O}{2 \text{ moles H}_2O_2} \times \dfrac{18.02 \text{ g H}_2O}{1 \text{ mole H}_2O} = 6.46 \text{ g of H}_2O \text{ (3 SFs)}$

7.135 $12.8 \text{ g Na} \times \dfrac{1 \text{ mole Na}}{22.99 \text{ g Na}} \times \dfrac{2 \text{ moles NaCl}}{2 \text{ moles Na}} \times \dfrac{58.44 \text{ g NaCl}}{1 \text{ mole NaCl}} = 32.5 \text{ g of NaCl}$

$10.2 \text{ g Cl}_2 \times \dfrac{1 \text{ mole Cl}_2}{70.90 \text{ g Cl}_2} \times \dfrac{2 \text{ moles NaCl}}{1 \text{ mole Cl}_2} \times \dfrac{58.44 \text{ g NaCl}}{1 \text{ mole NaCl}} = 16.8 \text{ g of NaCl}$ (smaller amount of product)

$\therefore$ Cl_2 is the limiting reactant, and 16.8 g of NaCl (3 SFs) can be produced.

7.137 a. $4.00 \text{ moles H}_2O \times \dfrac{1 \text{ mole C}_5H_{12}}{6 \text{ moles H}_2O} = 0.667 \text{ mole of C}_5H_{12} \text{ (3 SFs)}$

b. $32.0 \text{ g O}_2 \times \dfrac{1 \text{ mole O}_2}{32.00 \text{ g O}_2} \times \dfrac{5 \text{ moles CO}_2}{8 \text{ moles O}_2} \times \dfrac{44.01 \text{ g CO}_2}{1 \text{ mole CO}_2} = 27.5 \text{ g of CO}_2 \text{ (3 SFs)}$

c. $44.5 \text{ g C}_5H_{12} \times \dfrac{1 \text{ mole C}_5H_{12}}{72.15 \text{ g C}_5H_{12}} \times \dfrac{5 \text{ moles CO}_2}{1 \text{ mole C}_5H_{12}} \times \dfrac{44.01 \text{ g CO}_2}{1 \text{ mole CO}_2} = 136 \text{ g of CO}_2$

$$108 \text{ g } O_2 \times \frac{1 \text{ mole } O_2}{32.00 \text{ g } O_2} \times \frac{5 \text{ moles } CO_2}{8 \text{ moles } O_2} \times \frac{44.01 \text{ g } CO_2}{1 \text{ mole } CO_2} = 92.8 \text{ g of } CO_2$$
(smaller amount of product)

$\therefore O_2$ is the limiting reactant, and 92.8 g of CO_2 (3 SFs) can be produced.

7.139 a. Theoretical yield of CO_2:

$$22.0 \text{ g } C_2H_2 \times \frac{1 \text{ mole } C_2H_2}{26.04 \text{ g } C_2H_2} \times \frac{4 \text{ moles } CO_2}{2 \text{ moles } C_2H_2} \times \frac{44.01 \text{ g } CO_2}{1 \text{ mole } CO_2} = 74.4 \text{ g of } CO_2 \text{ (3 SFs)}$$

b. Percent yield: $\dfrac{64.0 \text{ g } CO_2 \text{ (actual)}}{74.4 \text{ g } CO_2 \text{ (theoretical)}} \times 100\% = 86.0\% \text{ (3 SFs)}$

7.141 Theoretical yield of C_2H_6:

$$28.0 \text{ g } C_2H_2 \times \frac{1 \text{ mole } C_2H_2}{26.04 \text{ g } C_2H_2} \times \frac{1 \text{ mole } C_2H_6}{1 \text{ mole } C_2H_2} \times \frac{30.07 \text{ g } C_2H_6}{1 \text{ mole } C_2H_6} = 32.3 \text{ g of } C_2H_6$$

Percent yield: $\dfrac{24.5 \text{ g } C_2H_6 \text{ (actual)}}{32.3 \text{ g } C_2H_6 \text{ (theoretical)}} \times 100\% = 75.9\% \text{ (3 SFs)}$

7.143 a. $3.00 \text{ g } NO \times \dfrac{1 \text{ mole } NO}{30.01 \text{ g } NO} \times \dfrac{+90.2 \text{ kJ}}{2 \text{ moles } NO} = +4.51 \text{ kJ (3 SFs)}$

$\therefore$ 4.51 kJ are required.

b. The equation for the decomposition of NO will be the reverse of the equation for the formation of NO.

$$2NO(g) \longrightarrow N_2(g) + O_2(g) + 90.2 \text{ kJ}$$

c. $5.00 \text{ g } NO \times \dfrac{1 \text{ mole } NO}{30.01 \text{ g } NO} \times \dfrac{-90.2 \text{ kJ}}{2 \text{ moles } NO} = -7.51 \text{ kJ (3 SFs)}$

$\therefore$ 7.51 kJ are released.

7.145 a. Heat is released, which makes the reaction exothermic.
   b. Heat is absorbed, which makes the reaction endothermic.

7.147 a. $124 \text{ g } C_2H_6O \times \dfrac{1 \text{ mole } C_2H_6O}{46.07 \text{ g } C_2H_6O} \times \dfrac{1 \text{ mole } C_6H_{12}O_6}{2 \text{ moles } C_2H_6O} \times \dfrac{180.16 \text{ g } C_6H_{12}O_6}{1 \text{ mole } C_6H_{12}O_6}$
$= 242 \text{ g of } C_6H_{12}O_6 \text{ (3 SFs)}$

b. $0.240 \text{ kg } C_6H_{12}O_6 \times \dfrac{1000 \text{ g}}{1 \text{ kg}} \times \dfrac{1 \text{ mole } C_6H_{12}O_6}{180.16 \text{ g } C_6H_{12}O_6} \times \dfrac{2 \text{ moles } C_2H_6O}{1 \text{ mole } C_6H_{12}O_6} \times \dfrac{46.07 \text{ g } C_2H_6O}{1 \text{ mole } C_2H_6O}$
$= 123 \text{ g of } C_2H_6O \text{ (3 SFs)}$

7.149 a. $4Al(s) + 3O_2(g) \longrightarrow 2Al_2O_3(s)$
   b. This is a combination reaction.

c. $4.50 \text{ moles } Al \times \dfrac{3 \text{ moles } O_2}{4 \text{ moles } Al} = 3.38 \text{ moles of } O_2 \text{ (3 SFs)}$

d. $50.2 \text{ g } Al \times \dfrac{1 \text{ mole } Al}{26.98 \text{ g } Al} \times \dfrac{2 \text{ moles } Al_2O_3}{4 \text{ moles } Al} \times \dfrac{101.96 \text{ g } Al_2O_3}{1 \text{ mole } Al_2O_3} = 94.9 \text{ g of } Al_2O_3 \text{ (3 SFs)}$

e. $8.00 \text{ g } O_2 \times \dfrac{1 \text{ mole } O_2}{32.00 \text{ g } O_2} \times \dfrac{2 \text{ moles } Al_2O_3}{3 \text{ moles } O_2} \times \dfrac{101.96 \text{ g } Al_2O_3}{1 \text{ mole } Al_2O_3} = 17.0 \text{ g of } Al_2O_3 \text{ (3 SFs)}$

7.151 a. $4.50 \text{ moles } Cr \times \dfrac{3 \text{ moles } O_2}{4 \text{ moles } Cr} = 3.38 \text{ moles of } O_2 \text{ (3 SFs)}$

b. $24.8 \text{ g } Cr \times \dfrac{1 \text{ mole } Cr}{52.00 \text{ g } Cr} \times \dfrac{2 \text{ moles } Cr_2O_3}{4 \text{ moles } Cr} \times \dfrac{152.0 \text{ g } Cr_2O_3}{1 \text{ mole } Cr_2O_3} = 36.2 \text{ g of } Cr_2O_3 \text{ (3 SFs)}$

c. $26.0 \text{ g Cr} \times \dfrac{1 \text{ mole Cr}}{52.00 \text{ g Cr}} \times \dfrac{2 \text{ moles Cr}_2\text{O}_3}{4 \text{ moles Cr}} \times \dfrac{152.0 \text{ g Cr}_2\text{O}_3}{1 \text{ mole Cr}_2\text{O}_3} = 38.0 \text{ g of Cr}_2\text{O}_3$

$8.00 \text{ g O}_2 \times \dfrac{1 \text{ mole O}_2}{32.00 \text{ g O}_2} \times \dfrac{2 \text{ moles Cr}_2\text{O}_3}{3 \text{ moles O}_2} \times \dfrac{152.0 \text{ g Cr}_2\text{O}_3}{1 \text{ mole Cr}_2\text{O}_3} = 25.3 \text{ g of Cr}_2\text{O}_3$
(smaller amount of product)

$\therefore$ O_2 is the limiting reactant, and 25.3 g of Cr_2O_3 (3 SFs) can be produced.

d. $74.0 \text{ g Cr} \times \dfrac{1 \text{ mole Cr}}{52.00 \text{ g Cr}} \times \dfrac{2 \text{ moles Cr}_2\text{O}_3}{4 \text{ moles Cr}} \times \dfrac{152.0 \text{ g Cr}_2\text{O}_3}{1 \text{ mole Cr}_2\text{O}_3} = 108 \text{ g of Cr}_2\text{O}_3$
(smaller amount of product)

$62.0 \text{ g O}_2 \times \dfrac{1 \text{ mole O}_2}{32.00 \text{ g O}_2} \times \dfrac{2 \text{ moles Cr}_2\text{O}_3}{3 \text{ moles O}_2} \times \dfrac{152.0 \text{ g Cr}_2\text{O}_3}{1 \text{ mole Cr}_2\text{O}_3} = 196 \text{ g of Cr}_2\text{O}_3$

$\therefore$ Cr is the limiting reactant, and 108 g of Cr_2O_3 (3 SFs) can be produced (theoretical yield).

Percent yield: $\dfrac{87.3 \text{ g Cr}_2\text{O}_3 \text{ (actual)}}{108 \text{ g Cr}_2\text{O}_3 \text{ (theoretical)}} \times 100\% = 80.8\%$ (3 SFs)

7.153 a. $0.225 \text{ mole C}_3\text{H}_4 \times \dfrac{4 \text{ moles O}_2}{1 \text{ mole C}_3\text{H}_4} = 0.900 \text{ mole of O}_2$ (3 SFs)

b. $64.0 \text{ g O}_2 \times \dfrac{1 \text{ mole O}_2}{32.00 \text{ g O}_2} \times \dfrac{2 \text{ moles H}_2\text{O}}{4 \text{ moles O}_2} \times \dfrac{18.02 \text{ g H}_2\text{O}}{1 \text{ mole H}_2\text{O}} = 18.0 \text{ g of H}_2\text{O}$ (3 SFs)

c. $78.0 \text{ g C}_3\text{H}_4 \times \dfrac{1 \text{ mole C}_3\text{H}_4}{40.06 \text{ g C}_3\text{H}_4} \times \dfrac{3 \text{ moles CO}_2}{1 \text{ mole C}_3\text{H}_4} \times \dfrac{44.01 \text{ g CO}_2}{1 \text{ mole CO}_2} = 257 \text{ g of CO}_2$ (3 SFs)

d. Percent yield: $\dfrac{186 \text{ g CO}_2 \text{ (actual)}}{257 \text{ g CO}_2 \text{ (theoretical)}} \times 100\% = 72.4\%$ (3 SFs)

7.155 a. The heat of reaction (ΔH) is positive, so the reaction is endothermic.

b. $1.5 \text{ moles SO}_3 \times \dfrac{+790 \text{ kJ}}{2 \text{ moles SO}_3} = +590 \text{ kJ}$ (2 SFs)

$\therefore$ 590 kJ are required.

c. $150 \text{ g O}_2 \times \dfrac{1 \text{ mole O}_2}{32.00 \text{ g O}_2} \times \dfrac{+790 \text{ kJ}}{3 \text{ moles O}_2} = +1200 \text{ kJ}$ (2 SFs)

$\therefore$ 1200 kJ are required.

8

Gases

After Whitney's asthma attack, she and her parents learned to identify and treat her asthma. Because her asthma is mild and intermittent, they follow a management plan to control the symptoms. Whitney participates in physical activity and exercise to maintain lung function and to prevent recurrent attacks. If her symptoms worsen, she uses a bronchodilator to help her breathing. If a child has a lung capacity of 2.0 L, a body temperature of 37 °C, and a lung pressure of 756 mmHg, what would the volume be at STP?

Credit: Adam Gault / Alamy

CHAPTER READINESS*

 Key Math Skills

• Solving Equations (1.4D)

 Core Chemistry Skills

• Using Significant Figures in Calculations (2.3)

• Writing Conversion Factors from Equalities (2.5)
• Using Conversion Factors (2.6)
• Using Molar Mass as a Conversion Factor (7.5)
• Using Mole–Mole Factors (7.6)

*These Key Math Skills and Core Chemistry Skills from previous chapters are listed here for your review as you proceed to the new material in this chapter.

8.1 Properties of Gases

Learning Goal: Describe the kinetic molecular theory of gases and the units of measurement used for gases.

• In a gas, small particles (atoms or molecules) are far apart and moving randomly with high velocities.
• The attractive forces between the particles of a gas are usually very small.
• The actual volume occupied by gas molecules is extremely small compared with the volume that the gas occupies.
• Gas particles are in constant motion, moving rapidly in straight paths.
• The average kinetic energy of gas molecules is proportional to the Kelvin temperature.
• A gas is described by the physical properties of pressure (P), volume (V), temperature (T), and amount (n).
• A gas exerts pressure, which is the force that gas particles exert on the walls of a container.
• Units of gas pressure include Torr, millimeters of mercury (mmHg), pascal (Pa), kilopascal (kPa), lb/in.² (psi), and atmosphere (atm).

♦ **Learning Exercise 8.1A**

Answer *true* (T) or *false* (F) for each of the following:

a. _____ Gases are composed of small particles.

b. _____ Gas molecules are usually close together.

c. _____ Gas molecules move rapidly because they are strongly attracted.

d. _____ Distances between gas molecules are large.

e. _____ Gas molecules travel in straight lines until they collide.

f. _____ Pressure is the force of gas particles striking the walls of a container.

g. _____ Kinetic energy decreases with increasing temperature.

Answers   a. T   b. F   c. F   d. T
              e. T   f. T   g. F

Units for Measuring Pressure

Unit	Abbreviation	Unit Equivalent to 1 atm
atmosphere	atm	1 atm (exact)
millimeters of Hg	mmHg	760 mmHg (exact)
torr	Torr	760 Torr (exact)
inches of Hg	inHg	29.9 inHg
pounds per square inch	$lb/in.^2$ (psi)	$14.7\ lb/in.^2$
pascal	Pa	101 325 Pa
kilopascal	kPa	101.325 kPa

♦ **Learning Exercise 8.1B**

Complete the following:

a. 1.50 atm = _____ mmHg

b. 550 mmHg = _____ atm

c. 0.725 atm = _____ kPa

d. 1520 mmHg = _____ atm

e. 30.5 psi = _____ mmHg

f. During the weather report on TV, the pressure is given as 29.4 in. (of mercury). What is this pressure in millimeters of mercury and in atmospheres?

Answers   a. 1140 mmHg   b. 0.72 atm   c. 73.5 kPa
              d. 2.00 atm   e. 1580 mmHg   f. 747 mmHg, 0.983 atm

8.2   Pressure and Volume (Boyle's Law)

Learning Goal: Use the pressure–volume relationship (Boyle's law) to determine the final pressure or volume when the temperature and amount of gas are constant.

- According to Boyle's law, pressure increases if volume decreases and pressure decreases if volume increases.
- If two properties change in opposite directions, the properties have an inverse relationship.
- The volume (V) of a gas changes inversely with the pressure (P) of the gas when T and n are held constant: $P_1 V_1 = P_2 V_2$. The subscripts 1 and 2 represent initial and final conditions.

Piston

$V = 4\,L$ $V = 2\,L$
$P = 1\,atm$ $P = 2\,atm$

Boyle's law: As volume decreases, gas molecules become more crowded, causing the pressure to increase. Pressure and volume are inversely related.

Guide to Using the Gas Laws	
STEP 1	Organize the data in a table of initial and final conditions.
STEP 2	Rearrange the gas law equation to solve for the unknown quantity.
STEP 3	Substitute values into the gas law equation and calculate.

Key Terms for Sections 8.1–8.2

Match the following terms with the correct description below:

  a. kinetic molecular theory   **b.** inverse relationship   **c.** Boyle's law
  d. pressure   **e.** atmospheric pressure

1. _____ the pressure exerted by the atmosphere

2. _____ a force exerted by gas particles when they collide with the sides of a container

3. _____ a relationship in which two properties change in opposite directions

4. _____ the volume of a gas varies inversely with the pressure of a gas (when T and n are constant)

5. _____ the model that explains the behavior of gas particles

Answers   **1.** e   **2.** d   **3.** b   **4.** c   **5.** a

♦ **Learning Exercise 8.2**

Calculate the unknown quantity in each of the following gas problems using Boyle's law:

⚛ CORE CHEMISTRY SKILL

Using the Gas Laws

  a. A sample of 4.0 L of He has a pressure of 800. mmHg. What is the new pressure, in millimeters of mercury, when the volume is reduced to 1.0 L (T and n constant)?

b. The maximum volume of air that can fill a person's lungs is 6250 mL at a pressure of 728 mmHg. Inhalation occurs as the pressure in the lungs drops to 721 mmHg with no change in temperature and amount of gas. To what volume, in milliliters, did the lungs expand?

c. A sample of O_2 at a pressure of 5.00 atm has a volume of 3.00 L. If the gas pressure is changed to 760. mmHg, what volume, in liters, will the O_2 occupy (T and n constant)?

d. A sample of 250. mL of N_2 is initially at a pressure of 2.50 atm. If the pressure changes to 825 mmHg, what is the new volume, in milliliters (T and n constant)?

Answers   **a.** 3200 mmHg   **b.** 6310 mL   **c.** 15.0 L   **d.** 576 mL

8.3 Temperature and Volume (Charles's Law)

Learning Goal: Use the temperature–volume relationship (Charles's law) to determine the final temperature or volume when the pressure and amount of gas are constant.

- According to Charles's law, at constant pressure and quantity, the volume of a gas increases when the temperature of the gas increases, and the volume decreases when the temperature decreases.
- In a direct relationship, two properties increase or decrease together.
- The volume (V) of a gas is directly related to its Kelvin temperature (T) when there is no change in the pressure or moles of the gas:

$$\frac{V_1}{T_1} = \frac{V_2}{T_2}$$ The subscripts 1 and 2 represent initial and final conditions.

♦ **Learning Exercise 8.3**

Solve each of the following problems using Charles's law:

a. A balloon has a volume of 2.5 L at a temperature of 0 °C. What is the new volume, in liters, of the balloon when the temperature rises to 120 °C, if there is no change in pressure and amount of gas?

b. A balloon is filled with He to a volume of 6600 L at a temperature of 223 °C. To what temperature, in degrees Celsius, must the gas be cooled to decrease the volume to 4800 L (P and n constant)?

c. A sample of 750. mL of Ne is heated from 120. °C to 350. °C. What is the new volume, in milliliters, if there is no change in pressure and amount of gas?

d. What is the final temperature, in degrees Celsius, of 350. mL of O_2 at 22 °C when its volume increases to 0.800 L, if there is no change in pressure and amount of gas?

Answers   **a.** 3.6 L   **b.** 88 °C   **c.** 1190 mL   **d.** 401 °C

8.4   Temperature and Pressure (Gay-Lussac's Law)

Learning Goal: Use the temperature–pressure relationship (Gay-Lussac's law) to determine the final temperature or pressure when the volume and amount of gas are constant.

- According to Gay-Lussac's law, at constant volume and amount, the gas pressure increases when the temperature of the gas increases, and the pressure decreases when the temperature decreases.
- The pressure (P) of a gas is directly related to its Kelvin temperature (T), when n and V are constant:

$$\frac{P_1}{T_1} = \frac{P_2}{T_2}$$ The subscripts 1 and 2 represent initial and final conditions.

♦ **Learning Exercise 8.4**
Solve the following problems using Gay-Lussac's law:

a. A sample of He has a pressure of 860. mmHg at a temperature of 225 K. What is the new pressure, in millimeters of mercury, when the He reaches a temperature of 675 K, if V and n do not change?

b. A balloon contains a gas with a pressure of 580. mmHg and a temperature of 227 °C. What is the new pressure, in millimeters of mercury, of the gas when the temperature drops to 27 °C, if V and n do not change?

c. A spray can contains a gas with a pressure of 3.0 atm at a temperature of 17 °C. What is the pressure, in atmospheres, inside the container if the temperature rises to 110 °C, if V and n do not change?

d. A gas has a pressure of 1200. mmHg at 300. °C. What will the temperature, in degrees Celsius, be when the pressure falls to 1.10 atm, if V and n do not change?

Answers   **a.** 2580 mmHg   **b.** 348 mmHg   **c.** 4.0 atm   **d.** 126 °C

8.5   The Combined Gas Law

Learning Goal: Use the combined gas law to calculate the final pressure, volume, or temperature of a gas when changes in two of these properties are given and the amount of gas is constant.

- When the amount of a gas is constant, the gas laws can be combined into a relationship of pressure (P), volume (V), and temperature (T):

$$\frac{P_1 V_1}{T_1} = \frac{P_2 V_2}{T_2}$$ The subscripts 1 and 2 represent initial and final conditions.

Key Terms for Sections 8.3–8.5

Match the following terms with the correct description below:

    a. vapor pressure   **b.** direct relationship   **c.** Charles's law
    d. combined gas law   **e.** Gay-Lussac's law

1. _____ a gas law that states that the volume of a gas changes directly with a change in Kelvin temperature when pressure and amount (moles) of the gas do not change

2. _____ the pressure exerted by the particles of vapor above a liquid

3. _____ a relationship in which two properties change in the same direction

4. _____ a gas law stating that the pressure of a gas changes directly with a change in Kelvin temperature when the number of moles of a gas and its volume remain constant

5. _____ a relationship that combines several gas laws relating pressure, volume, and temperature when the amount of gas remains constant

Answers   **1.** c   **2.** a   **3.** b   **4.** e   **5.** d

♦ **Learning Exercise 8.5**

Solve each of the following using the combined gas law:

a. A 4.0-L sample of N_2 has a pressure of 1200 mmHg at 220 K. What is the pressure, in millimeters of mercury, of the sample when the volume increases to 20. L at 440 K, if the amount of gas does not change?

b. A 25.0-mL bubble forms at the ocean depths when the pressure is 10.0 atm and the temperature is 5.0 °C. What is the volume, in milliliters, of that bubble at the ocean surface when the pressure is 760. mmHg and the temperature is 25 °C, if the amount of gas does not change?

c. A 35.0-mL sample of Ar has a pressure of 1.0 atm and a temperature of 15 °C. What is the final volume, in milliliters, if the pressure goes to 2.0 atm and the temperature to 45 °C, if the amount of gas does not change?

d. A weather balloon is launched from the Earth's surface with a volume of 315 L, a temperature is 12 °C, and pressure is 0.930 atm. What is the volume, in liters, of the balloon in the upper atmosphere when the pressure is 116 mmHg and the temperature is −35 °C, if the amount of gas does not change?

e. A 10.0-L sample of gas is emitted from a volcano with a pressure of 1.20 atm and a temperature of 150.0 °C. What is the volume, in liters, of the gas when its pressure is 0.900 atm and the temperature is −40.0 °C, if the amount of gas does not change?

Answers   **a.** 480 mmHg   **b.** 268 mL   **c.** 19 mL   **d.** 1.60×10^3 L   **e.** 7.34 L

8.6   Volume and Moles (Avogadro's Law)

Learning Goal: Use Avogadro's law to calculate the amount or volume of a gas when the pressure and temperature are constant.

- If the number of moles of gas increases, the volume increases; if the number of moles of gas decreases, the volume decreases.
- Avogadro's law states that equal volumes of gases at the same temperature and pressure contain the same number of moles. The volume (V) of a gas is directly related to the number of moles of the gas when the pressure and temperature of the gas do not change:

$$\frac{V_1}{n_1} = \frac{V_2}{n_2}$$ The subscripts 1 and 2 represent initial and final conditions.

- At STP conditions, standard temperature (0 °C) and pressure (1 atm), 1.00 mole of a gas occupies a volume of 22.4 L, the *molar volume*.

	Guide to Using Molar Volume
STEP 1	State the given and needed quantities.
STEP 2	Write a plan to calculate the needed quantity.
STEP 3	Write the equalities and conversion factors including 22.4 L/mole at STP.
STEP 4	Set up the problem with factors to cancel units.

Example: How many liters would 2.00 moles of N_2 occupy at STP?

Solution:

STEP 1: State the given and needed quantities.

Analyze the Problem	Given	Need
	2.00 moles of N_2 at STP	liters of N_2 at STP

STEP 2: Write a plan to calculate the needed quantity.

moles of N_2 $\xrightarrow{\text{Molar volume}}$ liters of N_2 (STP)

STEP 3: **Write the equalities and conversion factors including 22.4 L/mole at STP.**

$$1 \text{ mole of } N_2 = 22.4 \text{L of } N_2 \text{ (STP)}$$

$$\frac{22.4 \text{ L } N_2 \text{ (STP)}}{1 \text{ mole } N_2} \quad \text{and} \quad \frac{1 \text{ mole } N_2}{22.4 \text{ L } N_2 \text{ (STP)}}$$

STEP 4: **Set up the problem with factors to cancel units.**

$$2.00 \text{ moles } N_2 \times \frac{22.4 \text{ L } N_2 \text{ (STP)}}{1 \text{ mole } N_2} = 44.8 \text{ L of } N_2 \text{ (STP)}$$

♦ **Learning Exercise 8.6**

Use Avogadro's law to solve the following gas problems:

a. A gas containing 0.50 mole of He has a volume of 4.0 L. What is the new volume, in liters, when 1.0 mole of N_2 is added to the container, at constant pressure and temperature?

b. A balloon containing 1.0 mole of O_2 has a volume of 15 L. What is the new volume, in liters, of the balloon when 2.0 moles of He is added, at constant pressure and temperature?

c. What is the volume, in liters, occupied by 28.0 g of N_2 at STP?

d. What is the mass, in grams, of 4.48 L of O_2 at STP?

Answers   **a.** 12 L   **b.** 45 L   **c.** 22.4 L   **d.** 6.40 g

8.7 The Ideal Gas Law

Learning Goal: Use the ideal gas law equation to solve for P, V, T, or n of a gas when given three of the four values in the ideal gas law equation. Calculate the mass or volume of a gas in a chemical reaction.

- The ideal gas law $PV = nRT$ gives the relationship between the four properties: pressure, volume, moles, and temperature. When any three properties are given, the fourth can be calculated.
- R is the universal gas constant: 0.0821 L·atm/mole·K or 62.4 L·mmHg/mole·K.
- The ideal gas law can be used to determine the mass or volume of a gas in a chemical reaction.

	$\dfrac{0.0821 \text{ L·atm}}{\text{mole·K}}$	$\dfrac{62.4 \text{ L·mmHg}}{\text{mole·K}}$
Ideal gas constant (R)		
Pressure (P)	atm	mmHg
Volume (V)	L	L
Amount (n)	mole	mole
Temperature (T)	K	K

Guide to Using the Ideal Gas Law	
STEP 1	State the given and needed quantities.
STEP 2	Rearrange the ideal gas law equation to solve for the needed quantity.
STEP 3	Substitute the gas data into the equation and calculate the needed quantity.

Study Note

Identify the three known properties for the ideal gas law, and arrange the equation to solve for the unknown.
Example: Solve the ideal gas law for *P*.

Solution: $PV = nRT \quad \dfrac{P\cancel{V}}{\cancel{V}} = \dfrac{nRT}{V} \quad P = \dfrac{nRT}{V}$

♦ **Learning Exercise 8.7A**

Use the ideal gas law to solve for the unknown variable in each of the following:

CORE CHEMISTRY SKILL

Using the Ideal Gas Law

a. What volume, in liters, is occupied by 0.250 mole of N_2 at 0 °C and 1.50 atm?

b. What is the temperature, in degrees Celsius, of 0.500 mole of He that occupies a volume of 15.0 L at a pressure of 1210 mmHg?

c. What is the pressure, in atmospheres, of 1.50 moles of Ne in a 5.00-L steel container at a temperature of 125 °C?

d. What is the pressure, in atmospheres, of 8.0 g of O_2 that has a volume of 245 mL at a temperature of 22 °C?

e. A single-patient hyperbaric chamber has a volume of 650. L. At a temperature of 22 °C, how many grams of O_2 are needed to give a pressure of 1.80 atm?

Answers   **a.** 3.74 L   **b.** 309 °C   **c.** 9.80 atm   **d.** 25 atm   **e.** 1550 g of O_2

Guide to Using the Ideal Gas Law for Reactions	
STEP 1	State the given and needed quantities.
STEP 2	Write a plan to convert the given quantity to the needed moles.
STEP 3	Write the equalities and conversion factors for molar mass and mole–mole factors.
STEP 4	Set up the problem to calculate moles of needed quantity.
STEP 5	Convert the moles of needed quantity to mass or volume using the molar mass or the ideal gas law equation.

♦ **Learning Exercise 8.7B**

Use the ideal gas law equation to determine the quantity of a reactant or product in each of the following:

⚛ CORE CHEMISTRY SKILL

Calculating Mass or Volume of a Gas in a Chemical Reaction

    a. How many grams of KNO_3 must decompose to produce 35.8 L of O_2 at 28 °C and 745 mmHg?

$$2KNO_3(s) \longrightarrow 2KNO_2(s) + O_2(g)$$

    b. At a temperature of 325 °C and a pressure of 1.20 atm, how many liters of CO_2 can be produced when 50.0 g of propane (C_3H_8) reacts with O_2?

$$C_3H_8(g) + 5O_2(g) \longrightarrow 3CO_2(g) + 4H_2O(g)$$
Propane

Answers   **a.** 287 g of KNO_3 **b.** 139 L of CO_2

8.8   Partial Pressures (Dalton's Law)

Learning Goal: Use Dalton's law of partial pressures to calculate the total pressure of a mixture of gases.

•   In a mixture of two or more gases, the total pressure is the sum of the partial pressures (subscripts 1, 2, 3 . . . represent the partial pressures of the individual gases).

$$P_{total} = P_1 + P_2 + P_3 + \cdots$$

•   The partial pressure of a gas in a mixture is the pressure it would exert if it were the only gas in the container.

Key Terms for Sections 8.6–8.8

Match the following terms with the correct description below:

    a. molar volume   **b.** STP   **c.** Dalton's law
    d. partial pressure   **e.** Avogadro's law   **f.** ideal gas law

1. _____ the gas law stating that the total pressure exerted by a mixture of gases in a container is the sum of the pressures that each gas would exert alone

2. _____ the pressure exerted by a single gas in a gas mixture

3. _____ the volume occupied by 1 mole of a gas at STP

4. _____ the law that combines the four measured properties of a gas in the equation $PV = nRT$

5. _____ the gas law stating that the volume of a gas is directly related to the number of moles of gas when pressure and temperature do not change

6. _____ the standard conditions of 0 °C (273 K) and 1 atm, used for the comparison of gases

Oxygen therapy increases the amount of oxygen available to the tissues of the body.

Credit: Levent Konuk / Shutterstock

Answers   **1.** c   **2.** d   **3.** a   **4.** f   **5.** e   **6.** b

Guide to Calculating Partial Pressure	
STEP 1	Write the equation for the sum of the partial pressures.
STEP 2	Rearrange the equation to solve for the unknown pressure.
STEP 3	Substitute known pressures into the equation and calculate the unknown partial pressure.

♦ **Learning Exercise 8.8A**

Use Dalton's law to solve the following problems about gas mixtures:

CORE CHEMISTRY SKILL

Calculating Partial Pressure

    a. What is the total pressure, in millimeters of mercury, of a gas sample that contains O_2 at 0.500 atm, N_2 at 132 Torr, and He at 224 mmHg?

    b. What is the total pressure, in atmospheres, of a gas sample that contains He at 285 mmHg and O_2 at 1.20 atm?

c. A gas sample containing N_2 and O_2 has a pressure of 1500. mmHg. If the partial pressure of the N_2 is 0.900 atm, what is the partial pressure, in millimeters of mercury, of the O_2 in the mixture?

Answers   **a.** 736 mmHg   **b.** 1.58 atm   **c.** 816 mmHg

♦ **Learning Exercise 8.8B**

Fill in the blanks by writing I (*increases*) or D (*decreases*) for a gas in a closed container:

	Pressure	Volume	Moles	Temperature
a.	_____	Increases	Constant	Constant
b.	Increases	Constant	_____	Constant
c.	Constant	Decreases	_____	Constant
d.	Increases	Constant	Constant	_____
e.	Constant	_____	Constant	Decreases
f.	_____	Constant	Increases	Constant

Answers   **a.** D   **b.** I   **c.** D   **d.** I   **e.** D   **f.** I

♦ **Learning Exercise 8.8C**

Complete the following table for typical blood gas values for partial pressures:

Gas	Alveoli	Oxygenated blood	Deoxygenated blood	Tissues
O_2	_____	_____	_____	_____
CO_2	_____	_____	_____	_____

Answers

Gas	Alveoli	Oxygenated blood	Deoxygenated blood	Tissues
O_2	100 mmHg	100 mmHg	40 mmHg or less	30 mmHg or less
CO_2	40 mmHg	40 mmHg	46 mmHg	50 mmHg or greater

Checklist for Chapter 8

You are ready to take the Practice Test for Chapter 8. Be sure you have accomplished the following learning goals for this chapter. If not, review the section listed at the end of the goal. Then apply your new skills and understanding to the Practice Test.

After studying Chapter 8, I can successfully:

_____ Describe the kinetic molecular theory of gases. (8.1)

_____ Change the units of pressure from one to another. (8.1)

_____ Use the pressure–volume relationship (Boyle's law) to determine the new pressure or volume of a fixed amount of gas at constant temperature. (8.2)

_____ Use the temperature–volume relationship (Charles's law) to determine the new temperature or volume of a fixed amount of gas at a constant pressure. (8.3)

_____ Use the temperature–pressure relationship (Gay-Lussac's law) to determine the new temperature or pressure of a fixed amount of gas at a constant volume. (8.4)

_____ Use the combined gas law to find the new pressure, or volume, of a fixed amount of gas when changes in two of these properties are given. (8.5)

_____ Describe the relationship between the amount of a gas and its volume (Avogadro's law) at constant P and T, and use this relationship in calculations. (8.6)

_____ Use the ideal gas law to solve for pressure, volume, temperature, or amount of a gas. (8.7)

_____ Calculate the total pressure of a gas mixture from the partial pressures. (8.8)

Practice Test for Chapter 8

For questions 1 through 5, use the kinetic molecular theory of gases to answer true (T) or false (F): (8.1)

1. _____ A gas does not have its own volume or shape.

2. _____ The molecules of a gas are moving extremely fast.

3. _____ The collisions of gas molecules with the walls of their container create pressure.

4. _____ Gas molecules are close together and move in straight lines.

5. _____ Gas molecules have no attractions between them.

6. When a gas is heated in a closed metal container, the (8.3, 8.4)
   A. pressure increases
   B. pressure decreases
   C. volume increases
   D. volume decreases
   E. number of molecules increases

7. The pressure of a gas will increase when (8.2)
   A. the volume increases
   B. the temperature decreases
   C. more molecules of gas are added
   D. molecules of gas are removed
   E. none of these

8. If the temperature of a gas in a flexible container is increased (8.3, 8.4)
   A. the pressure will decrease
   B. the volume will increase
   C. the volume will decrease
   D. the number of molecules will increase
   E. none of these

9. The relationship that the volume of a gas is inversely related to its pressure at constant temperature is known as (8.2)
   A. Boyle's law   **B.** Charles's law   **C.** Gay-Lussac's law
   D. Dalton's law   **E.** Avogadro's law

10. What is the pressure, in atmospheres, of a gas with a pressure of 1200 mmHg? (8.1)
   A. 0.63 atm   **B.** 0.79 atm   **C.** 1.2 atm
   D. 1.6 atm   **E.** 2.0 atm

11. A 6.00-L sample of O_2 has a pressure of 660. mmHg. When the volume is reduced to 2.00 L at constant temperature and moles, it will have a new pressure of (8.2)
   A. 1980 mmHg   **B.** 1320 mmHg   **C.** 330. mmHg
   D. 220. mmHg   **E.** 110. mmHg

12. A sample of N_2 at 110 K has a pressure of 1.0 atm. When the temperature is increased to 360 K at constant moles and volume, the new pressure will be (8.4)
   A. 0.50 atm   **B.** 1.0 atm   **C.** 1.5 atm
   D. 3.3 atm   **E.** 4.0 atm

13. If two gases have the same volume, temperature, and pressure, they also have the same (8.5)
   A. density   **B.** number of particles   **C.** molar mass
   D. speed   **E.** size molecules

14. A gas sample with a volume of 4.0 L has a pressure of 750 mmHg and a temperature of 77 °C. What is its new volume at 277 °C and 250 mmHg (*n* constant)? (8.5)
   A. 7.6 L   **B.** 19 L   **C.** 2.1 L
   D. 0.00056 L   **E.** 3.3 L

15. If the temperature and amount of a gas does not change, but its volume doubles, its pressure will (8.2)
   A. double
   B. triple
   C. decrease to one-half the original pressure
   D. decrease to one-fourth the original pressure
   E. not change

16. A tank of O_2 used at home for a patient with pulmonary disease has a pressure of 220 mmHg, 2.0 moles of gas, and a volume of 4.0 L. What will the new pressure be when the volume expands to 5.0 L and 3.0 moles of O_2 is added, if temperature is constant? (8.6)
   A. 110 mmHg   **B.** 220 mmHg   **C.** 440 mmHg
   D. 550 mmHg   **E.** 700. mmHg

17. A sample of 2.00 moles of gas initially at STP is converted to a volume of 5.0 L and a temperature of 27 °C. What is its new pressure in atmospheres? (8.5, 8.6)
   A. 0.12 atm   **B.** 5.5 atm   **C.** 7.5 atm
   D. 9.8 atm   **E.** 10. atm

18. The conditions for standard temperature and pressure (STP) are (8.6)
   A. 0 K, 1 atm   **B.** 0 °C, 10 atm   **C.** 25 °C, 1 atm
   D. 273 K, 1 atm   **E.** 273 K, 0.5 atm

19. The volume occupied by 1.50 moles of CH_4 at STP is (8.6)
   A. 44.10 L   **B.** 33.6 L   **C.** 22.4 L
   D. 11.2 L   **E.** 5.60 L

20. How many grams of O_2 are present in 44.1 L of O_2 at STP? (8.6)
   A. 10.0 g   **B.** 16.0 g   **C.** 32.0 g
   D. 410.0 g   **E.** 63.0 g

21. What is the volume, in liters, of 0.50 mole of N_2 at 25 °C and 2.0 atm? (8.7)
   A. 0.51 L   **B.** 1.0 L   **C.** 4.2 L
   D. 6.1 L   **E.** 24 L

22. 2.50 g of $KClO_3$ decomposes by the equation: $2KClO_3(s) \longrightarrow 2KCl(s) + 3O_2(g)$. What volume, in milliliters, of O_2 is produced at 25 °C and a pressure of 750. mmHg? (8.7)
   - **A.** 9.98 mL
   - **B.** 759 mL
   - **C.** 63.6 mL
   - **D.** 506 mL
   - **E.** 1320 mL

23. A gas mixture contains He with a partial pressure of 0.100 atm, O_2 with a partial pressure of 445 mmHg, and N_2 with a partial pressure of 235 mmHg. What is the total pressure, in atmospheres, for the gas mixture? (8.8)
   - **A.** 0.995 atm
   - **B.** 1.39 atm
   - **C.** 1.69 atm
   - **D.** 2.00 atm
   - **E.** 10.0 atm

24. A mixture of O_2 and N_2 has a total pressure of 1040 mmHg. If O_2 has a partial pressure of 510 mmHg, what is the partial pressure, in milliliters of mercury, of N_2? (8.8)
   - **A.** 240 mmHg
   - **B.** 530 mmHg
   - **C.** 770 mmHg
   - **D.** 1040 mmHg
   - **E.** 1350 mmHg

25. 3.00 moles of He in a steel container has a pressure of 12.0 atm. What is the new pressure, in atmospheres, after 4.00 moles of He is added (T is constant) (8.8)
   - **A.** 5.14 atm
   - **B.** 16.0 atm
   - **C.** 28.0 atm
   - **D.** 32.0 atm
   - **E.** 45.0 atm

26. The exchange of gases between the alveoli, blood, and tissues of the body is a result of (8.8)
   - **A.** pressure gradients
   - **B.** different molecular masses
   - **C.** shapes of molecules
   - **D.** altitude
   - **E.** all of these

27. Oxygen moves into the tissues from the blood because its partial pressure (8.8)
   - **A.** in arterial blood is higher than in the tissues
   - **B.** in venous blood is higher than in the tissues
   - **C.** in arterial blood is lower than in the tissues
   - **D.** in venous blood is lower than in the tissues
   - **E.** is equal in the blood and in the tissues

Answers to the Practice Test

1. T	**2.** T	**3.** T	**4.** F	**5.** T
6. A	**7.** C	**8.** B	**9.** A	**10.** D
11. A	**12.** D	**13.** B	**14.** B	**15.** C
16. C	**17.** D	**18.** D	**19.** B	**20.** E
21. D	**22.** B	**23.** A	**24.** B	**25.** C
26. A	**27.** A			

8
Gases

Learning Goals

- Describe the kinetic molecular theory of gases and the units of measurement used for gases.
- Use the pressure–volume relationship (Boyle's law) to determine the final pressure or volume when the temperature and amount of gas are constant.
- Use the temperature–volume relationship (Charles's law) to determine the final temperature or volume when the pressure and amount of gas are constant.
- Use the temperature–pressure relationship (Gay-Lussac's law) to determine the final temperature or pressure when the volume and amount of gas are constant.
- Use the combined gas law to calculate the final pressure, volume, or temperature of a gas when changes in two of these properties are given and the amount of gas is constant.
- Use Avogadro's law to calculate the amount or volume of a gas when the pressure and temperature are constant.
- Use the ideal gas law equation to solve for P, V, T, or n of a gas when given three of the four values in the ideal gas law equation. Calculate mass or value of a gas in a chemical reaction.
- Use Dalton's law of partial pressures to calculate the total pressure of a mixture of gases.

Chapter Outline

Chapter Opener: Respiratory Therapist

8.1   Properties of Gases

Explore Your World: Forming a Gas

Chemistry Link to Health: Measuring Blood Pressure

8.2   Pressure and Volume (Boyle's Law)

Chemistry Link to Health: Pressure–Volume Relationship in Breathing

8.3   Temperature and Volume (Charles's Law)

8.4   Temperature and Pressure (Gay-Lussac's Law)

8.5   The Combined Gas Law

8.6   Volume and Moles (Avogadro's Law)

8.7   The Ideal Gas Law

Chemistry Link to Health: Hyperbaric Chambers

8.8   Partial Pressures (Dalton's Law)

Chemistry Link to Health: Blood Gases

Clinical Update: Exercise-Induced Asthma

⚛ Core Chemistry Skills

- Using the Gas Laws (8.2, 8.3, 8.4, 8.5, 8.6)
- Using the Ideal Gas Law (8.7)
- Calculating Mass or Volume of a Gas in a Chemical Reaction (8.7)
- Calculating Partial Pressure (8.8)

Selected Answers and Solutions to Text Problems

8.1 **a.** At a higher temperature, gas particles have greater kinetic energy, which makes them move faster.
  b. Because there are great distances between the particles of a gas, they can be pushed closer together and still remain a gas.
  c. Gas particles are very far apart, meaning that the mass of a gas in a certain volume is very small, resulting in a low density.

8.3 **a.** The temperature of a gas can be expressed in kelvins.
  b. The volume of a gas can be expressed in milliliters.
  c. The amount of a gas can be expressed in grams.
  d. Pressure can be expressed in millimeters of mercury (mmHg).

8.5 Statements **a**, **d**, and **e** describe the pressure of a gas.

8.7 **a.** $2.00 \text{ atm} \times \dfrac{760 \text{ Torr}}{1 \text{ atm}} = 1520 \text{ Torr (3 SFs)}$

  b. $2.00 \text{ atm} \times \dfrac{760 \text{ mmHg}}{1 \text{ atm}} = 1520 \text{ mmHg (3 SFs)}$

8.9 As the scuba diver ascends to the surface, external pressure decreases. If the air in the lungs, which is at a higher pressure, were not exhaled, its volume would expand and severely damage the lungs. The pressure of the gas in the lungs must adjust to changes in the external pressure.

8.11 **a.** The pressure is greater in cylinder A. According to Boyle's law, a decrease in volume pushes the gas particles closer together, which will cause an increase in the pressure.
  b.

Property	Conditions 1	Conditions 2	Know	Predict
Pressure (P)	$P_1 = 650 \text{ mmHg}$	$P_2 = 1.2 \text{ atm}$	P increases	
Volume (V)	$V_1 = 220 \text{ mL}$	$V_2 = ? \text{ mL}$		V decreases

According to Boyle's law, $P_1 V_1 = P_2 V_2$, then

$$V_2 = V_1 \times \frac{P_1}{P_2} = 220 \text{ mL} \times \frac{650 \text{ mmHg}}{1.2 \text{ atm}} \times \frac{1 \text{ atm}}{760 \text{ mmHg}} = 160 \text{ mL (2 SFs)}$$

8.13 **a.** The pressure of the gas *increases* to two times the original pressure when the volume is halved.
  b. The pressure *decreases* to one-third the original pressure when the volume expands to three times its initial value.
  c. The pressure *increases* to 10 times the original pressure when the volume decreases to one-tenth of the initial volume.

8.15 From Boyle's law, we know that pressure is inversely related to volume (for example, pressure increases when volume decreases).
  a. Volume increases; pressure must decrease.

$$P_2 = P_1 \times \frac{V_1}{V_2} = 655 \text{ mmHg} \times \frac{10.0 \text{ L}}{20.0 \text{ L}} = 328 \text{ mmHg (3 SFs)}$$

  b. Volume decreases; pressure must increase.

$$P_2 = P_1 \times \frac{V_1}{V_2} = 655 \text{ mmHg} \times \frac{10.0 \text{ L}}{2.50 \text{ L}} = 2620 \text{ mmHg (3 SFs)}$$

  c. The mL units must be converted to L for unit cancellation in the calculation, and because the volume increases, pressure must decrease.

$$P_2 = P_1 \times \frac{V_1}{V_2} = 655 \text{ mmHg} \times \frac{10.0 \text{ L}}{13\ 800 \text{ mL}} \times \frac{1000 \text{ mL}}{1 \text{ L}} = 475 \text{ mmHg} \ (3 \text{ SFs})$$

d. The mL units must be converted to L for unit cancellation in the calculation, and because the volume decreases, pressure must increase.

$$P_2 = P_1 \times \frac{V_1}{V_2} = 655 \text{ mmHg} \times \frac{10.0 \text{ L}}{1250 \text{ mL}} \times \frac{1000 \text{ mL}}{1 \text{ L}} = 5240 \text{ mmHg} \ (3 \text{ SFs})$$

8.17 From Boyle's law, we know that pressure is inversely related to volume.
a. Pressure decreases; volume must increase.

$$V_2 = V_1 \times \frac{P_1}{P_2} = 50.0 \text{ L} \times \frac{760. \text{ mmHg}}{725 \text{ mmHg}} = 52.4 \text{ L} \ (3 \text{ SFs})$$

b. The mmHg units must be converted to atm for unit cancellation in the calculation, and because the pressure increases, volume must decrease.

$$P_1 = 760. \text{ mmHg} \times \frac{1 \text{ atm}}{760 \text{ mmHg}} = 1.00 \text{ atm}$$

$$V_2 = V_1 \times \frac{P_1}{P_2} = 50.0 \text{ L} \times \frac{1.00 \text{ atm}}{2.0 \text{ atm}} = 25 \text{ L} \ (2 \text{ SFs})$$

c. The mmHg units must be converted to atm for unit cancellation in the calculation, and because the pressure decreases, volume must increase.

$$P_1 = 760. \text{ mmHg} \times \frac{1 \text{ atm}}{760 \text{ mmHg}} = 1.00 \text{ atm}$$

$$V_2 = V_1 \times \frac{P_1}{P_2} = 50.0 \text{ L} \times \frac{1.00 \text{ atm}}{0.500 \text{ atm}} = 100. \text{ L} \ (3 \text{ SFs})$$

d. The mmHg units must be converted to torr for unit cancellation in the calculation, and because the pressure increases, volume must decrease.

$$P_1 = 760. \text{ mmHg} \times \frac{760 \text{ Torr}}{760 \text{ mmHg}} = 760. \text{ Torr}$$

$$V_2 = V_1 \times \frac{P_1}{P_2} = 50.0 \text{ L} \times \frac{760. \text{ Torr}}{850 \text{ Torr}} = 45 \text{ L} \ (2 \text{ SFs})$$

8.19 Pressure decreases; volume must increase.

$$V_2 = V_1 \times \frac{P_1}{P_2} = 5.0 \text{ L} \times \frac{5.0 \text{ atm}}{1.0 \text{ atm}} = 25 \text{ L} \ (2 \text{ SFs})$$

8.21 **a.** *Inspiration* begins when the diaphragm flattens, causing the lungs to expand. The increased volume of the thoracic cavity reduces the pressure in the lungs such that air flows into the lungs.
b. *Expiration* occurs as the diaphragm relaxes, causing a decrease in the volume of the lungs. The pressure of the air in the lungs increases, and air flows out of the lungs.
c. *Inspiration* occurs when the pressure within the lungs is less than that of the atmosphere.

8.23 According to Charles's law, there is a direct relationship between Kelvin temperature and volume (for example, volume increases when temperature increases, if the pressure and amount of gas remain constant).
a. Diagram C shows an increased volume corresponding to an increase in temperature.
b. Diagram A shows a decreased volume corresponding to a decrease in temperature.
c. Diagram B shows no change in volume, which corresponds to no net change in temperature.

8.25 According to Charles's law, the volume of a gas is directly related to the Kelvin temperature. In all gas law computations, temperatures must be in kelvins. (Temperatures in °C are converted to K by the addition of 273.) The initial temperature for all cases here is $T_1 = 15\,°C + 273 = 288\,K$.

a. Volume increases; temperature must have increased.

$$T_2 = T_1 \times \frac{V_2}{V_1} = 288\,K \times \frac{5.00\,L}{2.50\,L} = 576\,K \quad 576\,K - 273 = 303\,°C\ (3\ SFs)$$

b. Volume decreases; temperature must have decreased.

$$T_2 = T_1 \times \frac{V_2}{V_1} = 288\,K \times \frac{1250\,mL}{2.50\,L} \times \frac{1\,L}{1000\,mL} = 144\,K \quad 144\,K - 273 = -129\,°C\ (3\ SFs)$$

c. Volume increases; temperature must have increased.

$$T_2 = T_1 \times \frac{V_2}{V_1} = 288\,K \times \frac{7.50\,L}{2.50\,L} = 864\,K \quad 864\,K - 273 = 591\,°C\ (3\ SFs)$$

d. Volume increases; temperature must have increased.

$$T_2 = T_1 \times \frac{V_2}{V_1} = 288\,K \times \frac{3550\,mL}{2.50\,L} \times \frac{1\,L}{1000\,mL} = 409\,K \quad 409\,K - 273 = 136\,°C\ (3\ SFs)$$

8.27 According to Charles's law, the volume of a gas is directly related to the Kelvin temperature. In all gas law computations, temperatures must be in kelvins. (Temperatures in °C are converted to K by the addition of 273.) The initial temperature for all cases here is $T_1 = 75\,°C + 273 = 348\,K$.

a. When temperature decreases, volume must also decrease.

$T_2 = 55\,°C + 273 = 328\,K$

$$V_2 = V_1 \times \frac{T_2}{T_1} = 2500\,mL \times \frac{328\,K}{348\,K} = 2400\,mL\ (2\ SFs)$$

b. When temperature increases, volume must also increase.

$$V_2 = V_1 \times \frac{T_2}{T_1} = 2500\,mL \times \frac{680.\,K}{348\,K} = 4900\,mL\ (2\ SFs)$$

c. When temperature decreases, volume must also decrease.

$T_2 = -25\,°C + 273 = 248\,K$

$$V_2 = V_1 \times \frac{T_2}{T_1} = 2500\,mL \times \frac{248\,K}{348\,K} = 1800\,mL\ (2\ SFs)$$

d. When temperature decreases, volume must also decrease.

$$V_2 = V_1 \times \frac{T_2}{T_1} = 2500\,mL \times \frac{240.\,K}{348\,K} = 1700\,mL\ (2\ SFs)$$

8.29 According to Gay-Lussac's law, temperature is directly related to pressure. In all gas law computations, temperatures must be in kelvins. (Temperatures in °C are converted to K by the addition of 273.)

a. When temperature decreases, pressure must also decrease.

$T_1 = 155\,°C + 273 = 428\,K \qquad T_2 = 0\,°C + 273 = 273\,K$

$$P_2 = P_1 \times \frac{T_2}{T_1} = 1200\,Torr \times \frac{1\,mmHg}{1\,Torr} \times \frac{273\,K}{428\,K} = 770\,mmHg\ (2\ SFs)$$

b. When temperature increases, pressure must also increase.

$T_1 = 12\,°C + 273 = 285\,K \qquad T_2 = 35\,°C + 273 = 308\,K$

$$P_2 = P_1 \times \frac{T_2}{T_1} = 1.40 \text{ atm} \times \frac{760 \text{ mmHg}}{1 \text{ atm}} \times \frac{308 \text{ K}}{285 \text{ K}} = 1150 \text{ mmHg (3 SFs)}$$

8.31 According to Gay-Lussac's law, temperature is directly related to pressure. For example, temperature increases when the pressure increases. In all gas law computations, temperatures must be in kelvins. (Temperatures in °C are converted to K by the addition of 273.)

   a. Pressure decreases; temperature must have decreased.

   $T_1 = 25\,°\text{C} + 273 = 298 \text{ K}$

   $$T_2 = T_1 \times \frac{P_2}{P_1} = 298 \text{ K} \times \frac{620.\ \text{mmHg}}{740.\ \text{mmHg}} = 250.\ \text{K} \quad 250.\ \text{K} - 273 = -23\,°\text{C (2 SFs)}$$

   b. Pressure increases; temperature must have increased.

   $T_1 = -18\,°\text{C} + 273 = 255 \text{ K}$

   $$T_2 = T_1 \times \frac{P_2}{P_1} = 255 \text{ K} \times \frac{1250 \text{ Torr}}{0.950 \text{ atm}} \times \frac{1 \text{ atm}}{760 \text{ Torr}} = 441 \text{ K} \quad 441 \text{ K} - 273 = 168\,°\text{C (3 SFs)}$$

8.33 According to Gay-Lussac's law, pressure is directly related to temperature. In all gas law computations, temperatures must be in kelvins. (Temperatures in °C are converted to K by the addition of 273.)

   When temperature increases, pressure must also increase.

   $T_1 = 5\,°\text{C} + 273 = 278 \text{ K} \quad T_2 = 22\,°\text{C} + 273 = 295 \text{ K}$

   $$P_2 = P_1 \times \frac{T_2}{T_1} = 1.8 \text{ atm} \times \frac{295 \text{ K}}{278 \text{ K}} = 1.9 \text{ atm (2 SFs)}$$

8.35 $T_1 = 25\,°\text{C} + 273 = 298 \text{ K}; \quad V_1 = 6.50 \text{ L}; \quad P_1 = 845 \text{ mmHg}$

   a. $T_2 = 325 \text{ K}; \quad V_2 = 1850 \text{ mL} = 1.85 \text{ L}; \quad P_2 = ?\text{ atm}$

   $$P_2 = P_1 \times \frac{V_1}{V_2} \times \frac{T_2}{T_1} = 845 \text{ mmHg} \times \frac{6.50 \text{ L}}{1.85 \text{ L}} \times \frac{325 \text{ K}}{298 \text{ K}} \times \frac{1 \text{ atm}}{760 \text{ mmHg}} = 4.26 \text{ atm (3 SFs)}$$

   b. $T_2 = 12\,°\text{C} + 273 = 285 \text{ K}; \quad V_2 = 2.25 \text{ L}; \quad P_2 = ?\text{ atm}$

   $$P_2 = P_1 \times \frac{V_1}{V_2} \times \frac{T_2}{T_1} = 845 \text{ mmHg} \times \frac{6.50 \text{ L}}{2.25 \text{ L}} \times \frac{285 \text{ K}}{298 \text{ K}} \times \frac{1 \text{ atm}}{760 \text{ mmHg}} = 3.07 \text{ atm (3 SFs)}$$

   c. $T_2 = 47\,°\text{C} + 273 = 320.\ \text{K}; \quad V_2 = 12.8 \text{ L}; \quad P_2 = ?\text{ atm}$

   $$P_2 = P_1 \times \frac{V_1}{V_2} \times \frac{T_2}{T_1} = 845 \text{ mmHg} \times \frac{6.50 \text{ L}}{12.8 \text{ L}} \times \frac{320.\ \text{K}}{298 \text{ K}} \times \frac{1 \text{ atm}}{760 \text{ mmHg}} = 0.606 \text{ atm (3 SFs)}$$

8.37 $T_1 = 212\,°\text{C} + 273 = 485 \text{ K}; \quad V_1 = 124 \text{ mL}; \quad P_1 = 1.80 \text{ atm}$
   $T_2 = ?\,°\text{C}; \quad V_2 = 138 \text{ mL}; \quad P_2 = 0.800 \text{ atm}$

   $$T_2 = T_1 \times \frac{P_2}{P_1} \times \frac{V_2}{V_1} = 485 \text{ K} \times \frac{0.800 \text{ atm}}{1.80 \text{ atm}} \times \frac{138 \text{ mL}}{124 \text{ mL}} = 240.\ \text{K}$$

   $240.\ \text{K} - 273 = -33\,°\text{C (2 SFs)}$

8.39 The volume increases because the number of gas particles in the tire or basketball is increased.

8.41 According to Avogadro's law, the volume of a gas is directly related to the number of moles of gas.

   $n_1 = 1.50 \text{ moles Ne}; \quad V_1 = 8.00 \text{ L}$

   a. $V_2 = V_1 \times \dfrac{n_2}{n_1} = 8.00 \text{ L} \times \dfrac{\frac{1}{2}(1.50) \text{ moles Ne}}{1.50 \text{ moles Ne}} = 4.00 \text{ L (3 SFs)}$

b. $n_2 = 1.50$ moles Ne $+ 3.50$ moles Ne $= 5.00$ moles of Ne

$$V_2 = V_1 \times \frac{n_2}{n_1} = 8.00 \text{ L} \times \frac{5.00 \text{ moles Ne}}{1.50 \text{ moles Ne}} = 26.7 \text{ L (3 SFs)}$$

c. $25.0 \text{ g Ne} \times \dfrac{1 \text{ mole Ne}}{20.18 \text{ g Ne}} = 1.24$ moles of Ne added

$n_2 = 1.50$ moles Ne $+ 1.24$ moles Ne $= 2.74$ moles of Ne

$$V_2 = V_1 \times \frac{n_2}{n_1} = 8.00 \text{ L} \times \frac{2.74 \text{ moles Ne}}{1.50 \text{ moles Ne}} = 14.6 \text{ L (3 SFs)}$$

8.43 At STP, 1 mole of any gas occupies a volume of 22.4 L.

a. $44.8 \text{ L } O_2 \text{ (STP)} \times \dfrac{1 \text{ mole } O_2}{22.4 \text{ L } O_2 \text{ (STP)}} = 2.00$ moles of O_2 (3 SFs)

b. $0.420 \text{ mole He} \times \dfrac{22.4 \text{ L He (STP)}}{1 \text{ mole He}} = 9.41$ L at STP (3 SFs)

8.45 a. $6.40 \text{ g } O_2 \times \dfrac{1 \text{ mole } O_2}{32.00 \text{ g } O_2} \times \dfrac{22.4 \text{ L } O_2 \text{ (STP)}}{1 \text{ mole } O_2} = 4.48$ L at STP (3 SFs)

b. $1620 \text{ mL } H_2 \text{ (STP)} \times \dfrac{1 \text{ L } H_2}{1000 \text{ mL } H_2} \times \dfrac{1 \text{ mole } H_2}{22.4 \text{ L } H_2 \text{ (STP)}} \times \dfrac{2.016 \text{ g } H_2}{1 \text{ mole } H_2}$

$= 0.146$ g of H_2 (3 SFs)

8.47 Analyze the Problem: Using the Ideal Gas Law to Calculate Pressure

Property	P	V	n	R	T
Given		10.0 L	2.00 moles	$\dfrac{0.0821 \text{ L} \cdot \text{atm}}{\text{mole} \cdot \text{K}}$	27 °C 27 °C + 273 = 300. K
Need	? atm				

$$P = \frac{nRT}{V} = \frac{(2.00 \text{ moles})\left(\dfrac{0.0821 \text{ L} \cdot \text{atm}}{\text{mole} \cdot \text{K}}\right)(300. \text{ K})}{(10.0 \text{ L})} = 4.93 \text{ atm (3 SFs)}$$

8.49 Analyze the Problem: Using the Ideal Gas Law to Calculate Moles

Property	P	V	n	R	T
Given	845 mmHg	20.0 L		$\dfrac{62.4 \text{ L} \cdot \text{mmHg}}{\text{mole} \cdot \text{K}}$	22 °C 22 °C + 273 = 295 K
Need			? moles (? g)		

$$n = \frac{PV}{RT} = \frac{(845 \text{ mmHg})(20.0 \text{ L})}{\left(\dfrac{62.4 \text{ L} \cdot \text{mmHg}}{\text{mole} \cdot \text{K}}\right)(295 \text{ K})} = 0.918 \text{ mole of } O_2$$

$$0.918 \text{ mole } O_2 \times \frac{32.00 \text{ g } O_2}{1 \text{ mole } O_2} = 29.4 \text{ g of } O_2 \text{ (3 SFs)}$$

8.51 $n = 25.0 \text{ g N}_2 \times \dfrac{1 \text{ mole N}_2}{28.02 \text{ g N}_2} = 0.892 \text{ mole of N}_2$

Analyze the Problem: Using the Ideal Gas Law to Calculate Temperature

Property	P	V	n	R	T
Given	630. mmHg	50.0 L	25.0 g (0.892 mole)	$\dfrac{62.4 \text{ L} \cdot \text{mmHg}}{\text{mole} \cdot \text{K}}$	
Need					? K (? °C)

$T = \dfrac{PV}{nR} = \dfrac{(630. \text{ mmHg})(50.0 \text{ L})}{(0.892 \text{ mole})\left(\dfrac{62.4 \text{ L} \cdot \text{mmHg}}{\text{mole} \cdot \text{K}}\right)} = 566 \text{ K} - 273 = 293 \,°\text{C} \ (3 \text{ SFs})$

8.53 a. $8.25 \text{ g Mg} \times \dfrac{1 \text{ mole Mg}}{24.31 \text{ g Mg}} \times \dfrac{1 \text{ mole H}_2}{1 \text{ mole Mg}} \times \dfrac{22.4 \text{ L (STP)}}{1 \text{ mole H}_2} = 7.60 \text{ L of H}_2$ released at STP (3 SFs)

b. Analyze the Problem: Using the Ideal Gas Law to Calculate Moles

Property	P	V	n	R	T
Given	735 mmHg	5.00 L		$\dfrac{62.4 \text{ L} \cdot \text{mmHg}}{\text{mole} \cdot \text{K}}$	18 °C 18 °C + 273 = 291 K
Need			? moles H$_2$		

$n = \dfrac{PV}{RT} = \dfrac{(735 \text{ mmHg})(5.00 \text{ L})}{\left(\dfrac{62.4 \text{ L} \cdot \text{mmHg}}{\text{mole} \cdot \text{K}}\right)(291 \text{ K})} = 0.202 \text{ mole of H}_2$

Analyze the Problem: Reactant and Product

	Reactant	Product
Mass	? g Mg	
Molar Mass	1 mole of Mg = 24.31 g of Mg	
Moles		0.202 mole H$_2$
Equation	$\text{Mg}(s) + 2\text{HCl}(aq) \longrightarrow \text{H}_2(g) + \text{MgCl}_2(aq)$	

$0.202 \text{ mole H}_2 \times \dfrac{1 \text{ mole Mg}}{1 \text{ mole H}_2} \times \dfrac{24.31 \text{ g Mg}}{1 \text{ mole Mg}} = 4.91 \text{ g of Mg} \ (3 \text{ SFs})$

8.55 Analyze the Problem: Reactant and Reactant

	Reactant 1	Reactant 2
Mass	55.2 g C$_4$H$_{10}$	
Molar Mass	1 mole of C$_4$H$_{10}$ = 58.12 g of C$_4$H$_{10}$	
Moles		? moles O$_2$
Equation	$2\text{C}_4\text{H}_{10}(g) + 13\text{O}_2(g) \xrightarrow{\Delta} 8\text{CO}_2(g) + 10\text{H}_2\text{O}(g)$	

$$55.2 \text{ g } C_4H_{10} \times \frac{1 \text{ mole } C_4H_{10}}{58.12 \text{ g } C_4H_{10}} \times \frac{13 \text{ moles } O_2}{2 \text{ moles } C_4H_{10}} = 6.17 \text{ moles of } O_2$$

Analyze the Problem: Using the Ideal Gas Law to Calculate Volume

Property	*P*	*V*	*n*	*R*	*T*
Given	0.850 atm		6.17 moles O_2	$\dfrac{0.0821 \text{ L} \cdot \text{atm}}{\text{mole} \cdot \text{K}}$	25 °C 25 °C + 273 = 298 K
Need		? L			

$$V = \frac{nRT}{P} = \frac{(6.17 \text{ moles})\left(\dfrac{0.0821 \text{ L} \cdot \text{atm}}{\text{mole} \cdot \text{K}}\right)(298 \text{ K})}{(0.850 \text{ atm})} = 178 \text{ L of } O_2 \text{ (3 SFs)}$$

8.57 Analyze the Problem: Reactant and Reactant

	Reactant 1	Reactant 2
Mass	5.4 g Al	
Molar Mass	1 mole of Al = 26.98 g of Al	
Moles		? moles O_2 (? L O_2)
Molar Volume		1 mole of O_2 = 22.4 L of O_2 (STP)
Equation	$4Al(s) + 3O_2(g) \xrightarrow{\Delta} 2Al_2O_3(s)$	

$$5.4 \text{ g Al} \times \frac{1 \text{ mole Al}}{26.98 \text{ g Al}} \times \frac{3 \text{ moles } O_2}{4 \text{ moles Al}} \times \frac{22.4 \text{ L } O_2 \text{ (STP)}}{1 \text{ mole } O_2} = 3.4 \text{ L of } O_2 \text{ at STP (2 SFs)}$$

8.59 Analyze the Problem: Using the Ideal Gas Law to Calculate Moles

Property	*P*	*V*	*n*	*R*	*T*
Given	1.6 atm	640 L		$\dfrac{0.0821 \text{ L} \cdot \text{atm}}{\text{mole} \cdot \text{K}}$	24 °C 24 °C + 273 = 297 K
Need			? moles O_2		

$$n = \frac{PV}{RT} = \frac{(1.6 \text{ atm})(640 \text{ L})}{\left(\dfrac{0.0821 \text{ L} \cdot \text{atm}}{\text{mole} \cdot \text{K}}\right)(297 \text{ K})} = 42 \text{ moles of } O_2$$

$$42 \text{ moles } O_2 \times \frac{32.00 \text{ g } O_2}{1 \text{ mole } O_2} = 1300 \text{ g of } O_2 \text{ (2 SFs)}$$

8.61 To obtain the total pressure of a gas mixture, add up all of the partial pressures using the same pressure unit.

$$P_{\text{total}} = P_{\text{nitrogen}} + P_{\text{oxygen}} + P_{\text{helium}} = 425 \text{ Torr} + 115 \text{ Torr} + 225 \text{ Torr} = 765 \text{ Torr (3 SFs)}$$

8.63 Because the total pressure of a gas mixture is the sum of the partial pressures using the same pressure unit, addition and subtraction are used to obtain the "missing" partial pressure.

$$P_{\text{nitrogen}} = P_{\text{total}} - (P_{\text{oxygen}} + P_{\text{helium}}) = 925 \text{ Torr} - (425 \text{ Torr} + 75 \text{ Torr}) = 425 \text{ Torr (3 SFs)}$$

8.65 a. If oxygen cannot readily cross from the lungs into the bloodstream, then the partial pressure of oxygen will be lower in the blood of an emphysema patient.

b. Breathing a higher concentration of oxygen will help to increase the supply of oxygen in the lungs and blood and raise the partial pressure of oxygen in the blood.

8.67 $P_{total} = P_{oxygen} + P_{nitrogen} + P_{carbon\ dioxide} + P_{water\ vapor}$

$= 93\ mmHg + 565\ mmHg + 38\ mmHg + 47\ mmHg = 743\ mmHg$

$743\ \cancel{mmHg} \times \dfrac{1.00\ atm}{760\ \cancel{mmHg}} = 0.978\ atm\ (3\ SFs)$

8.69 **Analyze the Problem: Using the Ideal Gas Law to Calculate Moles**

Property	P	V	n	R	T
Given	745 mmHg	3.2 L		$\dfrac{62.4\ L \cdot mmHg}{mole \cdot K}$	$37\ °C$ $37\ °C + 273 = 310\ K$
Need			? moles air		

$n = \dfrac{PV}{RT} = \dfrac{(745\ \cancel{mmHg})(3.2\ \cancel{L})}{\left(\dfrac{62.4\ \cancel{L} \cdot \cancel{mmHg}}{mole \cdot \cancel{K}}\right)(310\ \cancel{K})} = 0.12\ mole\ of\ air$

and since air is 21% O_2,

$0.12\ \cancel{mole\ air} \times \dfrac{21\ moles\ O_2}{100\ \cancel{moles\ air}} = 0.025\ mole\ of\ O_2\ (2\ SFs)$

8.71 **a.** True. The flask containing helium has more moles of helium and thus more atoms of helium to collide with the walls of the container to give a higher pressure.
  b. True. The mass and volume of each are the same, meaning that the mass/volume ratio or density is the same in both flasks.

8.73 **a.** 2; The fewest number of gas particles will exert the lowest pressure.
  b. 1; The greatest number of gas particles will exert the highest pressure.

8.75 **a.** A; Volume decreases when temperature decreases (at constant P and n).
  b. C; Volume increases when pressure decreases (at constant n and T).
  c. A; Volume decreases when the number of moles of gas decreases (at constant T and P).
  d. B; Doubling the Kelvin temperature doubles the volume, but when half of the gas escapes, the volume decreases by half. These two opposing effects cancel each other, and there is no overall change in the volume (at constant P).
  e. C; Increasing the moles of gas causes an increase in the volume to keep T and P constant.

8.77 **a.** The volume of the chest and lungs will decrease when compressed during the Heimlich maneuver.
  b. A decrease in volume causes the pressure to increase. A piece of food would be dislodged with a sufficiently high pressure.

8.79 $T_1 = 127\ °C + 273 = 400.\ K;$ $\quad P_1 = 2.00\ atm$
  $T_2 = ?\ °C;$ $\quad\quad\quad\quad\quad\quad P_2 = 0.25\ atm$

$T_2 = T_1 \times \dfrac{P_2}{P_1} = 400.\ K \times \dfrac{0.25\ \cancel{atm}}{2.00\ \cancel{atm}} = 50.\ K \quad 50.\ K - 273 = -223\ °C$

8.81 $T_1 = 22\ °C + 273 = 295\ K;$ $\quad P_1 = 755\ mmHg;$ $\quad V_1 = 31\ 000\ L$
  $T_2 = -8\ °C + 273 = 265\ K;$ $\quad P_2 = 658\ mmHg;$ $\quad V_2 = ?\ L$

$V_2 = V_1 \times \dfrac{P_1}{P_2} \times \dfrac{T_2}{T_1} = 31\ 000\ L \times \dfrac{755\ \cancel{mmHg}}{658\ \cancel{mmHg}} \times \dfrac{265\ K}{295\ K} = 32\ 000\ L\ (2\ SFs)$

8.83   Analyze the Problem: Using the Ideal Gas Law to Calculate Moles

Property	P	V	n	R	T
Given	2500. mmHg	2.00 L		$\dfrac{62.4 \text{ L} \cdot \text{mmHg}}{\text{mole} \cdot \text{K}}$	18 °C 18 °C + 273 = 291 K
Need			? moles		

$$n = \frac{PV}{RT} = \frac{(2500. \text{ mmHg})(2.00 \text{ L})}{\left(\dfrac{62.4 \text{ L} \cdot \text{mmHg}}{\text{mole} \cdot \text{K}}\right)(291 \text{ K})} = 0.275 \text{ mole of CH}_4$$

$$0.275 \text{ mole CH}_4 \times \frac{16.04 \text{ g CH}_4}{1 \text{ mole CH}_4} = 4.41 \text{ g of CH}_4 \text{ (3 SFs)}$$

8.85   Analyze the Problem: Using the Ideal Gas Law to Calculate Moles

Property	P	V	n	R	T
Given	1.20 atm	35.0 L		$\dfrac{0.0821 \text{ L} \cdot \text{atm}}{\text{mole} \cdot \text{K}}$	5 °C 5 °C + 273 = 278 K
Need			? moles		

$$n = \frac{PV}{RT} = \frac{(1.20 \text{ atm})(35.0 \text{ L})}{\left(\dfrac{0.0821 \text{ L} \cdot \text{atm}}{\text{mole} \cdot \text{K}}\right)(278 \text{ K})} = 1.84 \text{ moles of CO}_2$$

$$1.84 \text{ moles CO}_2 \times \frac{44.01 \text{ g CO}_2}{1 \text{ mole CO}_2} = 81.0 \text{ g of CO}_2 \text{ (3 SFs)}$$

8.87 $25.0 \text{ g Zn} \times \dfrac{1 \text{ mole Zn}}{65.41 \text{ g Zn}} \times \dfrac{1 \text{ mole H}_2}{1 \text{ mole Zn}} \times \dfrac{22.4 \text{ L (STP)}}{1 \text{ mole H}_2} = 8.56 \text{ L of H}_2 \text{ released at STP (3 SFs)}$

8.89   Analyze the Problem: Using the Ideal Gas Law to Calculate Moles

Property	P	V	n	R	T
Given	725 mmHg	5.00 L		$\dfrac{62.4 \text{ L} \cdot \text{mmHg}}{\text{mole} \cdot \text{K}}$	375 °C 375 °C + 273 = 648 K
Need			? moles H$_2$O		

$$n = \frac{PV}{RT} = \frac{(725 \text{ mmHg})(5.00 \text{ L})}{\left(\dfrac{62.4 \text{ L} \cdot \text{mmHg}}{\text{mole} \cdot \text{K}}\right)(648 \text{ K})} = 0.0896 \text{ mole of H}_2\text{O}$$

Analyze the Problem: Reactant and Product

	Reactant	Product
Mass		? g NH$_3$
Molar Mass		1 mole of NH$_3$ = 17.03 g of NH$_3$
Moles	0.0896 mole H$_2$O	
Equation	$4NO_2(g) + 6H_2O(g) \longrightarrow 7O_2(g) + 4NH_3(g)$	

$$0.0896 \text{ mole H}_2\text{O} \times \frac{4 \text{ moles NH}_3}{6 \text{ moles H}_2\text{O}} \times \frac{17.03 \text{ g NH}_3}{1 \text{ mole NH}_3} = 1.02 \text{ g of NH}_3 \text{ (3 SFs)}$$

8.91 Because the partial pressure of nitrogen is to be reported in torr, the atm and mmHg units (for oxygen and argon, respectively) must be converted to torr, as follows:

$$P_{oxygen} = 0.60 \text{ atm} \times \frac{760 \text{ Torr}}{1 \text{ atm}} = 460 \text{ Torr} \quad \text{and}$$

$$P_{argon} = 425 \text{ mmHg} \times \frac{1 \text{ Torr}}{1 \text{ mmHg}} = 425 \text{ Torr}$$

$$\therefore P_{nitrogen} = P_{total} - (P_{oxygen} + P_{argon})$$
$$= 1250 \text{ Torr} - (460 \text{ Torr} + 425 \text{ Torr}) = 370 \text{ Torr (2 SFs)}$$

8.93 $T_1 = 24\,°C + 273 = 297 \text{ K};$ $\quad P_1 = 745 \text{ mmHg};$ $\quad V_1 = 425 \text{ mL}$

$T_2 = -95\,°C + 273 = 178 \text{ K};$ $\quad P_2 = 0.115 \text{ atm} \times \dfrac{760 \text{ mmHg}}{1 \text{ atm}} = 87.4 \text{ mmHg};$ $\quad V_2 = ? \text{ mL}$

$$V_2 = V_1 \times \frac{P_1}{P_2} \times \frac{T_2}{T_1} = 425 \text{ mL} \times \frac{745 \text{ mmHg}}{87.4 \text{ mmHg}} \times \frac{178 \text{ K}}{297 \text{ K}} = 2170 \text{ mL (3 SFs)}$$

8.95 $T_1 = 15\,°C + 273 = 288 \text{ K};$ $\quad P_1 = 745 \text{ mmHg};$ $\quad V_1 = 4250 \text{ mL}$

$T_2 = ?\,°C;$ $\quad P_2 = 1.20 \text{ atm} \times \dfrac{760 \text{ mmHg}}{1 \text{ atm}} = 912 \text{ mmHg};$

$$V_2 = 2.50 \text{ L} \times \frac{1000 \text{ mL}}{1 \text{ L}} = 2.50 \times 10^3 \text{ mL}$$

$$T_2 = T_1 \times \frac{V_2}{V_1} \times \frac{P_2}{P_1} = 288 \text{ K} \times \frac{2.50 \times 10^3 \text{ mL}}{4250 \text{ mL}} \times \frac{912 \text{ mmHg}}{745 \text{ mmHg}} = 207 \text{ K} - 273$$

$$= -66\,°C \text{ (2 SFs)}$$

8.97 Analyze the Problem: Reactant and Product

	Reactant	Product
Mass	881 g C_3H_8	
Molar Mass	1 mole of C_3H_8 = 44.09 g of C_3H_8	
Moles		? moles CO_2 (? L CO_2)
Molar Volume		1 mole of CO_2 = 22.4 L of CO_2 (STP)
Equation	$C_3H_8(g) + 5O_2(g) \xrightarrow{\Delta} 3CO_2(g) + 4H_2O(g)$	

$$881 \text{ g } C_3H_8 \times \frac{1 \text{ mole } C_3H_8}{44.09 \text{ g } C_3H_8} \times \frac{3 \text{ moles } CO_2}{1 \text{ mole } C_3H_8} \times \frac{22.4 \text{ L } CO_2 \text{ (STP)}}{1 \text{ mole } CO_2}$$
$$= 1340 \text{ L } CO_2 \text{ at STP (3 SFs)}$$

8.99 Analyze the Problem: Using the Ideal Gas Law to Calculate Moles

Property	P	V	n	R	T
Given	1.00 atm	7.50 L		$\dfrac{0.0821 \text{ L} \cdot \text{atm}}{\text{mole} \cdot \text{K}}$	37 °C 37 °C + 273 = 310 K
Need			? moles O_2		

$$n = \frac{PV}{RT} = \frac{(1.00 \text{ atm})(7.50 \text{ L})}{\left(\dfrac{0.0821 \text{ L} \cdot \text{atm}}{\text{mole} \cdot \text{K}}\right)(310 \text{ K})} = 0.295 \text{ mole of } O_2$$

$$0.295 \text{ mole } O_2 \times \frac{6 \text{ moles } H_2O}{6 \text{ moles } O_2} \times \frac{18.02 \text{ g } H_2O}{1 \text{ mole } H_2O} = 5.32 \text{ g of } H_2O \text{ (smaller amount of product)}$$

$$18.0 \text{ g } C_6H_{12}O_6 \times \frac{1 \text{ mole } C_6H_{12}O_6}{180.16 \text{ g } C_6H_{12}O_6} \times \frac{6 \text{ moles } H_2O}{1 \text{ mole } C_6H_{12}O_6} \times \frac{18.02 \text{ g } H_2O}{1 \text{ mole } H_2O} = 10.8 \text{ g of } H_2O$$

Thus, O_2 is the limiting reactant, and 5.32 g of H_2O (3 SFs) can be produced.

8.101 $2400 \text{ g } O_2 \times \dfrac{1 \text{ mole } O_2}{32.00 \text{ g } O_2} = 75 \text{ moles of } O_2$

Analyze the Problem: Using the Ideal Gas Law to Calculate Volume

Property	P	V	n	R	T
Given	3.0 atm		75 moles	$\dfrac{0.0821 \text{ L} \cdot \text{atm}}{\text{mole} \cdot \text{K}}$	28 °C 28 °C + 273 = 301 K
Need		? L			

$$V = \frac{nRT}{P} = \frac{(75 \text{ moles})\left(\dfrac{0.0821 \text{ L} \cdot \text{atm}}{\text{mole} \cdot \text{K}}\right)(301 \text{ K})}{(3.0 \text{ atm})} = 620 \text{ L (2 SFs)}$$

8.103 Analyze the Problem: Using the Ideal Gas Law to Calculate Moles

Property	P	V	n	R	T
Given	20. mmHg	4.00 L		$\dfrac{62.4 \text{ L} \cdot \text{mmHg}}{\text{mole} \cdot \text{K}}$	32 °C 32 °C + 273 = 305 K
Need			? moles		

$$n = \frac{PV}{RT} = \frac{(20. \text{ mmHg})(4.00 \text{ L})}{\left(\dfrac{62.4 \text{ L} \cdot \text{mmHg}}{\text{mole} \cdot \text{K}}\right)(305 \text{ K})} = 0.0042 \text{ mole of } CO_2$$

$$0.0042 \text{ mole } CO_2 \times \frac{44.01 \text{ g } CO_2}{1 \text{ mole } CO_2} = 0.18 \text{ g of } CO_2 \text{ (2 SFs)}$$

CI.13 a. Reactants: A and B_2; Products: AB_3

    b. $2A + 3B_2 \longrightarrow 2AB_3$

    c. combination

CI.15 a. The formula of shikimic acid is $C_7H_{10}O_5$.

    b. Molar mass of shikimic acid $(C_7H_{10}O_5)$
$$= 7(12.01 \text{ g}) + 10(1.008 \text{ g}) + 5(16.00 \text{ g}) = 174.15 \text{ g (5 SFs)}$$

    c. $130 \text{ g shikimic acid} \times \dfrac{1 \text{ mole shikimic acid}}{174.15 \text{ g shikimic acid}} = 0.75 \text{ mole of shikimic acid (2 SFs)}$

    d. $155 \text{ g star anise} \times \dfrac{0.13 \text{ g shikimic acid}}{2.6 \text{ g star anise}} \times \dfrac{1 \text{ capsule Tamiflu}}{0.13 \text{ g shikimic acid}}$
$$= 59 \text{ capsules of Tamiflu (2 SFs)}$$

    e. Molar mass of Tamiflu $(C_{16}H_{28}N_2O_4)$
$$= 16(12.01 \text{ g}) + 28(1.008 \text{ g}) + 2(14.01 \text{ g}) + 4(16.00 \text{ g}) = 312.4 \text{ g (4 SFs)}$$

    f. $500\,000 \text{ people} \times \dfrac{2 \text{ capsules}}{1 \text{ day 1 person}} \times 5 \text{ days} \times \dfrac{75 \text{ mg Tamiflu}}{1 \text{ capsule}} \times \dfrac{1 \text{ g Tamiflu}}{1000 \text{ mg Tamiflu}}$

    $\times \dfrac{1 \text{ kg Tamiflu}}{1000 \text{ g Tamiflu}} = 400 \text{ kg of Tamiflu (1 SF)}$

CI.17 a. CH_4 H:C:H   or   H—C—H (with H above and below, lone pairs shown)

    b. $7.0 \times 10^6 \text{ gal} \times \dfrac{4 \text{ qt}}{1 \text{ gal}} \times \dfrac{946 \text{ mL}}{1 \text{ qt}} \times \dfrac{0.45 \text{ g}}{1 \text{ mL}} \times \dfrac{1 \text{ kg}}{1000 \text{ g}}$
$$= 1.2 \times 10^7 \text{ kg of LNG (methane) (2 SFs)}$$

    c. Molar mass of methane $(CH_4) = 12.01 \text{ g} + 4(1.008 \text{ g}) = 16.04 \text{ g}$
$$7.0 \times 10^6 \text{ gal} \times \dfrac{4 \text{ qt}}{1 \text{ gal}} \times \dfrac{946 \text{ mL}}{1 \text{ qt}} \times \dfrac{0.45 \text{ g}}{1 \text{ mL}} \times \dfrac{1 \text{ mole CH}_4}{16.04 \text{ g}} \times \dfrac{22.4 \text{ L CH}_4 \text{ (STP)}}{1 \text{ mole CH}_4}$$
$$= 1.7 \times 10^{10} \text{ L of LNG (methane) at STP (2 SFs)}$$

    d. $CH_4(g) + 2O_2(g) \xrightarrow{\Delta} CO_2(g) + 2H_2O(g) + 883 \text{ kJ}$

    e. $7.0 \times 10^6 \text{ gal} \times \dfrac{4 \text{ qt}}{1 \text{ gal}} \times \dfrac{946 \text{ mL}}{1 \text{ qt}} \times \dfrac{0.45 \text{ g}}{1 \text{ mL}} \times \dfrac{1 \text{ mole CH}_4}{16.04 \text{ g}} \times \dfrac{2 \text{ moles O}_2}{1 \text{ mole CH}_4}$

    $\times \dfrac{32.00 \text{ g O}_2}{1 \text{ mole O}_2} \times \dfrac{1 \text{ kg O}_2}{1000 \text{ g O}_2}$
$$= 4.8 \times 10^7 \text{ kg of O}_2 \text{ (2 SFs)}$$

    f. $7.0 \times 10^6 \text{ gal} \times \dfrac{4 \text{ qt}}{1 \text{ gal}} \times \dfrac{946 \text{ mL}}{1 \text{ qt}} \times \dfrac{0.45 \text{ g}}{1 \text{ mL}} \times \dfrac{1 \text{ mole CH}_4}{16.04 \text{ g}} \times \dfrac{883 \text{ kJ}}{1 \text{ mole CH}_4}$
$$= 6.6 \times 10^{11} \text{ kJ (2 SFs)}$$

9
Solutions

Michelle has hemodialysis treatment three times a week for 4 h each visit. The treatment removes harmful waste products and extra salt and fluid. Her blood pressure is maintained because the electrolytes potassium and sodium are adjusted each time. Michelle measures the amount of fluid she takes in each day. Her diet is low in protein and includes fruits and vegetables that are low in potassium. She and her husband are now learning about performing hemodialysis at home. Soon she will have her own hemodialysis machine. If 65 mEq of potassium ion is removed using a dialysate with a low potassium concentration, how many moles of potassium ion are removed?

Credit: AJPhoto / Science Source

CHAPTER READINESS*

🧮 Key Math Skills

- Calculating a Percentage (1.4C)
- Solving Equations (1.4D)
- Interpreting a Graph (1.4E)

⚛ Core Chemistry Skills

- Writing Conversion Factors from Equalities (2.5)
- Using Conversion Factors (2.6)
- Identifying Attractive Forces (6.9)
- Using Mole–Mole Factors (7.6)

*These Key Math Skills and Core Chemistry Skills from previous chapters are listed here for your review as you proceed to the new material in this chapter.

9.1 Solutions

Learning Goal: Identify the solute and solvent in a solution; describe the formation of a solution.

- A solution is a homogeneous mixture that forms when a solute dissolves in a solvent. The solvent is the substance that is present in a greater amount.

- Solvents and solutes can be solids, liquids, or gases. The solution is the same physical state as the solvent.

- A polar solute is soluble in a polar solvent; a nonpolar solute is soluble in a nonpolar solvent.

- Water molecules form hydrogen bonds because the partial positive charge of the hydrogen in one water molecule is attracted to the partial negative charge of oxygen in another water molecule.

- An ionic solute dissolves in water, a polar solvent, because the polar water molecules attract and pull the positive and negative ions into solution. In solution, water molecules surround the ions in a process called *hydration*.

- Some ionic compounds are insoluble compounds, which contain cations and anions held together by stronger forces than those between the ions and water.

♦ **Learning Exercise 9.1A**

Water is polar, and hexane is nonpolar. In which solvent is each of the following solutes soluble?

a. bromine, Br_2, nonpolar _____   b. HCl, polar _____

c. cholesterol, nonpolar _____   d. vitamin D, nonpolar _____

e. vitamin C, polar _____

Answers   **a.** hexane   **b.** water   **c.** hexane
                d. hexane   **e.** water

Solute: The substance present in lesser amount

— Salt

— Water

Solvent: The substance present in greater amount

A solution consists of at least one solute dispersed in a solvent.
Credit: Pearson Education / Pearson Science

♦ **Learning Exercise 9.1B**

Indicate the solute and solvent in each of the following:

	Solute	Solvent
a. 10 g of KCl dissolved in 100 g of H_2O	_____	_____
b. soda water: $CO_2(g)$ dissolved in H_2O	_____	_____
c. an alloy composed of 80% Zn and 20% Cu	_____	_____
d. a mixture of O_2 (200 mmHg) and He (500 mmHg)	_____	_____
e. a solution of 40 mL of CCl_4 and 2 mL of Br_2	_____	_____

Answers   **a.** KCl; water   **b.** CO_2; water   **c.** Cu; Zn
                d. O_2; He   **e.** Br_2; CCl_4

9.2 Electrolytes and Nonelectrolytes

Learning Goal: Identify solutes as electrolytes or nonelectrolytes.

- Electrolytes conduct an electrical current because they produce ions in aqueous solutions.
- Strong electrolytes are completely dissociated into ions, whereas weak electrolytes are partially dissociated into ions.
- Nonelectrolytes do not form ions in solution but dissolve as molecules.
- An equivalent is the amount of an electrolyte that carries 1 mole of positive or negative charge.
- The number of equivalents per mole of a positive or negative ion is equal to the charge on the ion.

Key Terms for Sections 9.1–9.2

Match the following terms with the correct definition below:

    a. solution   **b.** nonelectrolyte   **c.** solvent
    d. solute   **e.** strong electrolyte   **f.** equivalent

1. _____ a substance that dissociates as molecules, not ions, when it dissolves in water

2. _____ the substance that comprises the lesser amount in a solution

3. _____ a solute that dissociates 100% into ions in solution

4. _____ the substance that comprises the greater amount in a solution

5. _____ the quantity of ion equal to 1 mole of positive or negative charge

6. _____ a mixture of at least two components called a solute and a solvent

Answers   **1.** b   **2.** d   **3.** e   **4.** c   **5.** f   **6.** a

♦ **Learning Exercise 9.2A**

Write an equation for the formation of an aqueous solution of each of the following strong electrolytes:

  a. LiCl

  b. $Ca(NO_3)_2$

  c. Na_3PO_4

  d. K_2SO_4

  e. $MgCl_2$

Answers

  a. $LiCl(s) \xrightarrow{H_2O} Li^+(aq) + Cl^-(aq)$
  b. $Ca(NO_3)_2(s) \xrightarrow{H_2O} Ca^{2+}(aq) + 2NO_3^-(aq)$
  c. $Na_3PO_4(s) \xrightarrow{H_2O} 3Na^+(aq) + PO_4^{3-}(aq)$
  d. $K_2SO_4(s) \xrightarrow{H_2O} 2K^+(aq) + SO_4^{2-}(aq)$
  e. $MgCl_2(s) \xrightarrow{H_2O} Mg^{2+}(aq) + 2Cl^-(aq)$

♦ **Learning Exercise 9.2B**

Indicate whether an aqueous solution of each of the following contains ions only, molecules only, or mostly molecules with some ions. Write an equation for the formation of the solution.

  a. glucose, $C_6H_{12}O_6$, a nonelectrolyte

  b. NaOH, a strong electrolyte

  c. KCl, a strong electrolyte

  d. HF, a weak electrolyte

Answers

a. $C_6H_{12}O_6(s) \xrightarrow{H_2O} C_6H_{12}O_6(aq)$ 　　　　　　molecules only

b. $NaOH(s) \xrightarrow{H_2O} Na^+(aq) + OH^-(aq)$ 　　　　ions only

c. $KCl(s) \xrightarrow{H_2O} K^+(aq) + Cl^-(aq)$ 　　　　　ions only

d. $HF(g) + H_2O(l) \rightleftharpoons H_3O^+(aq) + F^-(aq)$ 　　mostly molecules and a few ions

♦ **Learning Exercise 9.2C**

Calculate the following:

a. the number of equivalents in 1 mole of Mg^{2+}

b. the number of equivalents of Cl^- in 2.5 moles of Cl^-

c. the number of equivalents of Ca^{2+} in 2.0 moles of Ca^{2+}

Answers 　　　**a.** 2 Eq 　　　**b.** 2.5 Eq 　　　**c.** 4.0 Eq

♦ **Learning Exercise 9.2D**

A maintenance IV solution contains 40 mEq Na^+, 35 mEq K^+, 40 mEq Cl^-, 20 mEq lactate$^-$, and HPO_4^{2-}.

a. What is the total number of milliequivalents of cations?

b. What is the total number of milliequivalents of anions?

c. What is the number of milliequivalents of HPO_4^{2-}?

Answers 　　　**a.** 75 mEq 　　　**b.** 75 mEq 　　　**c.** 15 mEq

♦ **Learning Exercise 9.2E**

A replacement IV solution contains 140 mEq Na^+, 10 mEq K^+, 5 mEq Ca^{2+}, 3 mEq Mg^{2+}, 47 mEq acetate$^-$, 8 mEq citrate^{3-}, and Cl^-.

    a. What is the total number of milliequivalents of cations?

    b. What is the total number of milliequivalents of anions?

    c. What is the number of milliequivalents of Cl^-?

Answers   **a.** 158 mEq   **b.** 158 mEq   **c.** 103 mEq

9.3 Solubility

Learning Goal: Define solubility; distinguish between an unsaturated and a saturated solution. Identify an ionic compound as soluble or insoluble.

- The amount of solute that dissolves depends on the nature of the solute and solvent.
- Solubility describes the maximum amount of a solute that dissolves in exactly 100 g of solvent at a given temperature.
- A saturated solution contains the maximum amount of dissolved solute at a certain temperature, whereas an unsaturated solution contains less than this amount.
- An increase in temperature increases the solubility of most solids, but decreases the solubility of gases in water.
- Henry's law states that the solubility of gases in liquids is directly related to the partial pressure of that gas above the liquid.
- The solubility rules describe the kinds of ionic combinations that are soluble and insoluble in water.

Solubility Rules for Ionic Compounds in Water

An ionic compound is soluble in water if it contains one of the following:

Positive Ions:	Li^+, Na^+, K^+, Rb^+, Cs^+, NH_4^+
Negative Ions:	NO_3^-, $C_2H_3O_2^-$
	Cl^-, Br^-, I^- except when combined with Ag^+, Pb^{2+}, or Hg_2^{2+}
	SO_4^{2-} except when combined with Ba^{2+}, Pb^{2+}, Ca^{2+}, Sr^{2+}, or Hg_2^{2+}

Ionic compounds that do not contain at least one of these ions are usually insoluble.

CdS

FeS

If an ionic compound contains a combination of a cation and an anion such as Cd^{2+} and S^{2-} or Fe^{2+} and S^{2-}, that are not soluble, that ionic compound is insoluble.

Credit: Pearson Education / Pearson Science

♦ **Learning Exercise 9.3A**

Identify each of the following as a saturated solution (S) or an unsaturated solution (U):

1. A sugar cube completely dissolves when added to a cup of coffee. _____

2. A KCl crystal added to a KCl solution does not change in size. _____

3. A layer of sugar forms in the bottom of a glass of iced tea after stirring. _____

4. The rate of crystal formation is equal to the rate of dissolving. _____

5. Upon heating, all the sugar in a solution dissolves. _____

Answers   **1.** U   **2.** S   **3.** S   **4.** S   **5.** U

♦ **Learning Exercise 9.3B**

Use the solubility data for $NaNO_3$ listed here to answer each of the following problems:

Temperature (°C)	Solubility (g of $NaNO_3$/100 g of H_2O)
40	100. g
60	120. g
80	150. g
100	200. g

a. How many grams of $NaNO_3$ will dissolve in 100. g of water at 40 °C? _____

b. How many grams of $NaNO_3$ will dissolve in 300. g of water at 60 °C? _____

c. A solution is prepared using 200. g of water and 350. g of $NaNO_3$ at 80 °C. Will any solute remain undissolved? If so, how much? _____

d. Will 150. g of $NaNO_3$ all dissolve when added to 100. g of water at 100 °C? _____

Answers   **a.** 100. g   **b.** 360. g
     c. 300. g of $NaNO_3$ will dissolve, leaving 50. g of $NaNO_3$ that will not dissolve.
     d. Yes, all 150. g of $NaNO_3$ will dissolve.

♦ **Learning Exercise 9.3C**

Predict whether the following ionic compounds are soluble (S) or insoluble (I) in water:

⊛ CORE CHEMISTRY SKILL

Using Solubility Rules

1. _____ NaCl   2. _____ $AgNO_3$ 3. _____ $PbCl_2$

4. _____ Ag_2S 5. _____ $BaSO_4$ 6. _____ Na_2CO_3

7. _____ K_2S 8. _____ $MgCl_2$ 9. _____ BaS

Answers   **1.** S   **2.** S   **3.** I   **4.** I   **5.** I
     6. S   **7.** S   **8.** S   **9.** I

♦ **Learning Exercise 9.3D**

Will an insoluble compound form (Yes or No) when the following solutions are mixed? If an insoluble compound forms, write the formula.

1. $NaCl(aq)$ and $Pb(NO_3)_2(aq)$　　　　_____

2. $BaCl_2(aq)$ and $Na_2SO_4(aq)$　　　　_____

3. $K_3PO_4(aq)$ and $NaNO_3(aq)$　　　　_____

4. $Na_2S(aq)$ and $AgNO_3(aq)$　　　　_____

Answers　　　1. Yes; $PbCl_2$　　　2. Yes; $BaSO_4$　　　3. No　　　4. Yes; Ag_2S

Guide to Writing an Equation for the Formation of an Insoluble Ionic Compound	
STEP 1	Write the ions of the reactants.
STEP 2	Write the combinations of ions and determine if any are insoluble.
STEP 3	Write the ionic equation including any solid.
STEP 4	Write the net ionic equation.

♦ **Learning Exercise 9.3E**

For the mixtures that form ionic compounds in Learning Exercise 9.3D, write the ionic equation and the net ionic equation.

1.

2.

3.

4.

Answers

1. $2Na^+(aq) + 2Cl^-(aq) + Pb^{2+}(aq) + 2NO_3^-(aq) \longrightarrow 2Na^+(aq) + PbCl_2(s) + 2NO_3^-(aq)$

   $2Cl^-(aq) + Pb^{2+}(aq) \longrightarrow PbCl_2(s)$

2. $Ba^{2+}(aq) + 2Cl^-(aq) + 2Na^+(aq) + SO_4^{2-}(aq) \longrightarrow 2Na^+(aq) + BaSO_4(s) + 2Cl^-(aq)$

   $Ba^{2+}(aq) + SO_4^{2-}(aq) \longrightarrow BaSO_4(s)$

3. No insoluble ionic compound forms.

4. $2Na^+(aq) + S^{2-}(aq) + 2Ag^+(aq) + 2NO_3^-(aq) \longrightarrow 2Na^+(aq) + Ag_2S(s) + 2NO_3^-(aq)$

   $S^{2-}(aq) + 2Ag^+(aq) \longrightarrow Ag_2S(s)$

9.4 Solution Concentrations and Reactions

Learning Goal: Calculate the concentration of a solute in a solution; use concentration units to calculate the amount of solute or solution. Given the volume and concentration of a solution, calculate the amount of another reactant or product in a reaction.

- The concentration of a solution is the relationship between the amount of solute, in grams or milliliters, and the amount of solution, in grams, milliliters, or liters.

- A mass percent (m/m) expresses the ratio of the mass of solute to the mass of solution multiplied by 100. Mass units must be the same, such as grams of solute/grams of solution × 100%.

$$\text{Mass percent (m/m)} = \frac{\text{mass of solute}}{\text{mass of solution}} \times 100\%$$

- A volume percent (v/v) expresses the ratio of the volume of solute to volume of solution multiplied by 100. Volume units must be the same, such as milliliters of solute/milliliters of solution × 100%.

$$\text{Volume percent (v/v)} = \frac{\text{volume of solute}}{\text{volume of solution}} \times 100\%$$

- A mass/volume percent (m/v) expresses the ratio of the mass of solute to the volume of solution multiplied by 100. The unit of mass of the solute is grams and the unit of the solution volume is milliliters.

$$\text{Mass/volume percent (m/v)} = \frac{\text{grams of solute}}{\text{milliliters of solution}} \times 100\%$$

- Molarity is a concentration term that indicates the number of moles of solute dissolved in 1 L (1000 mL) of solution.

$$\text{Molarity (M)} = \frac{\text{moles of solute}}{\text{L solution}}$$

- Concentrations can be used as conversion factors to relate the amount of solute and the volume or mass of the solution.

$$\frac{\text{amount of solute}}{\text{amount of solution}} \quad \text{and} \quad \frac{\text{amount of solution}}{\text{amount of solute}}$$

Key Terms for Sections 9.3–9.4

Match the following terms with the correct definition below:

    a. mass percent (m/m)   **b.** concentration   **c.** solubility
    d. unsaturated   **e.** molarity

1. _____ the number of moles of solute in 1 L of solution

2. _____ the amount of solute dissolved in a certain amount of solution

3. _____ the maximum amount of solute that can dissolve in a solution at a certain temperature

4. _____ a solution with less than the maximum amount of solute that can dissolve

5. _____ the concentration of a solution in terms of mass, in grams, of solute in 100 g of solution

Answers   **1.** e   **2.** b   **3.** c   **4.** d   **5.** a

Guide to Calculating Solution Concentration	
STEP 1	State the given and needed quantities.
STEP 2	Write the concentration expression.
STEP 3	Substitute solute and solution quantities into the expression and calculate.

Example: What is the mass percent (m/m) when 2.4 g of $NaHCO_3$ dissolves in water to make 120.0 g of solution?

Solution:

STEP 1 State the given and needed quantities.

	Given	Need
Analyze the Problem	2.4 g of $NaHCO_3$ solute, 120.0 g of $NaHCO_3$ solution	mass percent (m/m) concentration

STEP 2 Write the concentration expression.

$$\text{mass percent } (m/m) = \frac{\text{mass of solute}}{\text{mass of solution}} \times 100\%$$

STEP 3 Substitute solute and solution quantities into the expression and calculate.

$$\text{mass percent } (m/m) = \frac{2.4 \text{ g NaHCO}_3}{120.0 \text{ g NaHCO}_3 \text{ solution}} \times 100\% = 2.0\% \ (m/m)$$

♦ **Learning Exercise 9.4A**

Calculate the percent concentration for each of the following solutions:

⚛ **CORE CHEMISTRY SKILL**

Calculating Concentration

a. mass percent (m/m) for 18.0 g of NaCl in 90.0 g of NaCl solution

b. mass/volume percent (m/v) for 4.0 g of KOH in 50.0 mL of KOH solution

c. mass/volume percent (m/v) for 5.0 g of KCl in 2.0 L of KCl solution

d. volume percent (v/v) for 18 mL of ethanol in 350 mL of ethanol solution

Answers   **a.** 20.0% (m/m) **b.** 8.0% (m/v) **c.** 0.25% (m/v) **d.** 5.1% (v/v)

♦ **Learning Exercise 9.4B**

Calculate the molarity (M) of the following solutions:

    a. 1.45 moles of HCl in 0.250 L of HCl solution

    b. 10.0 moles of glucose $(C_6H_{12}O_6)$ in 2.50 L of glucose solution

    c. 80.0 g of NaOH in 1.60 L of NaOH solution

    d. 38.8 g of NaBr in 175 mL of NaBr solution

Answers   **a.** 5.80 M HCl solution   **b.** 4.00 M glucose solution
                 c. 1.25 M NaOH solution   **d.** 2.15 M NaBr solution

Guide to Using Concentration to Calculate Mass or Volume	
STEP 1	State the given and needed quantities.
STEP 2	Write a plan to calculate the mass or volume.
STEP 3	Write equalities and conversion factors.
STEP 4	Set up the problem to calculate the mass or volume.

Example: How many grams of KI are needed to prepare 225 g of a 4.0% (m/m) KI solution?

Solution:

    STEP 1 State the given and needed quantities.

Analyze the Problem	Given	Need
	225 g of 4.0% (m/m) KI solution	grams of KI

    STEP 2 Write a plan to calculate the mass or volume.

        grams of KI solution ⟶ grams of KI

    STEP 3 Write equalities and conversion factors.

        100 g of KI solution = 4.0 g of KI

$$\frac{4.0 \text{ g KI}}{100 \text{ g KI solution}} \quad \text{and} \quad \frac{100 \text{ g KI solution}}{4.0 \text{ g KI}}$$

    STEP 4 Set up the problem to calculate the mass or volume.

$$225 \text{ g solution} \times \frac{4.0 \text{ g KI}}{100 \text{ g solution}} = 9.0 \text{ g of KI}$$

◆ **Learning Exercise 9.4C**

⚛ **CORE CHEMISTRY SKILL**

Using Concentration as a
Conversion Factor

Calculate the number of grams of solute needed to prepare each
of the following solutions:

a. How many grams of glucose ($C_6H_{12}O_6$) are needed to prepare 480. mL of a 5.0% (m/v)
intravenous (IV) glucose solution?

b. How many grams of lidocaine, a local anesthetic, are needed to prepare 50.0 g of a 2.0%
(m/m) lidocaine solution?

c. How many grams of KCl are needed to prepare 1.2 L of a 4.0% (m/v) KCl solution?

d. How many grams of NaCl are needed to prepare 1.50 L of a 2.00% (m/v) NaCl solution?

Answers　　**a.** 24 g of glucose　　　**b.** 1.0 g of lidocaine
　　　　　　c. 48 g of KCl　　　　　**d.** 30.0 g of NaCl

◆ **Learning Exercise 9.4D**

Use percent concentration factors to calculate the quantity of each solution that contains the amount
of solute stated in each problem:

a. How many milliliters of a 1.00% (m/v) NaCl solution contain 2.00 g of NaCl?

b. How many milliliters of a 5.0% (m/v) glucose ($C_6H_{12}O_6$) solution contain 24 g of glucose?

c. How many milliliters of a 2.5% (v/v) methanol (CH_3OH) solution contain 7.0 mL of
methanol?

d. How many grams of a 15% (m/m) NaOH solution contain 7.5 g of NaOH?

Answers　　**a.** 200. mL　　**b.** 480 mL　　**c.** 280 mL　　**d.** 50. g

　　　　Copyright © 2015 Pearson Education, Inc.

Study Note

Molarity is used as a conversion factor to convert between the amount of solute and the volume of solution.

Example: How many grams of NaOH are in 0.250 L of a 5.00 M NaOH solution?

Solution:

STEP 1 State the given and needed quantities.

Analyze the Problem	Given	Need
	0.250 L of a 5.00 M NaOH solution	grams of NaOH

STEP 2 Write a plan to calculate the mass or volume.

liters of solution $\longrightarrow$ moles of solute $\longrightarrow$ grams of solute

STEP 3 Write equalities and conversion factors. The concentration 5.00 M can be expressed as two conversion factors.

1 L of NaOH solution = 5.00 moles of NaOH

$$\frac{5.00 \text{ moles NaOH}}{1 \text{ L NaOH solution}} \quad \text{and} \quad \frac{1 \text{ L NaOH solution}}{5.00 \text{ moles NaOH}}$$

STEP 4 Set up the problem to calculate the mass or volume.

$$0.250 \text{ L solution} \times \frac{5.00 \text{ moles NaOH}}{1 \text{ L solution}} \times \frac{40.00 \text{ g NaOH}}{1 \text{ mole NaOH}} = 50.0 \text{ g of NaOH}$$

♦ **Learning Exercise 9.4E**

Calculate the quantity of solute in each of the following solutions:

    a. How many moles of HCl are in 1.50 L of a 6.00 M HCl solution?

    b. How many moles of KOH are in 0.750 L of a 10.0 M KOH solution?

    c. How many grams of NaOH are needed to prepare 0.500 L of a 4.40 M NaOH solution?

    d. How many grams of NaCl are in 285 mL of a 1.75 M NaCl solution?

Answers   **a.** 9.00 moles of HCl   **b.** 7.50 moles of KOH
                c. 88.0 g of NaOH   **d.** 29.1 g of NaCl

♦ **Learning Exercise 9.4F**

Calculate the volume, in milliliters, of each solution needed to obtain the given quantity of solute:

    a. 1.50 moles of $Mg(OH)_2$ from a 2.00 M $Mg(OH)_2$ solution

    b. 0.150 mole of glucose from a 2.20 M glucose solution

    c. 18.5 g of KI from a 3.00 M KI solution

    d. 18.0 g of NaOH from a 6.00 M NaOH solution

Answers   **a.** 750. mL   **b.** 68.2 mL   **c.** 37.1 mL   **d.** 75.0 mL

♦ **Learning Exercise 9.4G**

1. A patient receives 150 mL of a 10.% (m/v) dextrose solution each hour.

    a. How many grams of dextrose are given in 1 h?

    b. How many grams of dextrose are given in 8 h?

2. A patient receives 125 mL of half-normal saline, which is a 0.45% (m/v) NaCl solution, each hour.

    a. How many grams of NaCl are given in 1 h?

    b. How many grams of NaCl are given in 12 h?

Answers   **1a.** 15 g   **1b.** 120 g   **2a.** 0.56 g   **2b.** 6.8 g

Guide to Calculations Involving Solutions in Chemical Reactions	
STEP 1	State the given and needed quantities.
STEP 2	Write a plan to calculate the needed quantity or concentration.
STEP 3	Write equalities and conversion factors including mole–mole and concentration factors.
STEP 4	Set up the problem to calculate the needed quantity or concentration.

⚛ CORE CHEMISTRY SKILL

Calculating the Quantity of a Reactant or Product for a Chemical Reaction in Solution

♦ **Learning Exercise 9.4H**

For the following reaction:

$$2AgNO_3(aq) + H_2SO_4(aq) \longrightarrow Ag_2SO_4(s) + 2H_2O(l)$$

    a. How many milliliters of a 1.5 M $AgNO_3$ solution will react with 40.0 mL of a 1.0 M H_2SO_4 solution?

    b. How many grams of Ag_2SO_4 will be produced?

Answers   **a.** 53 mL   **b.** 12 g of Ag_2SO_4

♦ **Learning Exercise 9.4I**

Calculate the milliliters of a 1.80 M KOH solution that react with 18.5 mL of a 2.20 M HCl solution.

$$HCl(aq) + KOH(aq) \longrightarrow KCl(aq) + H_2O(l)$$

Answer   22.6 mL of KOH solution

9.5   Dilution of Solutions

Learning Goal: Describe the dilution of a solution; calculate the unknown concentration or volume when a solution is diluted.

- Dilution is the process of mixing a solution with solvent to obtain a solution with a lower concentration.
- For dilutions, use the expression $C_1V_1 = C_2V_2$ and solve for the unknown value.

Guide to Calculating Dilution Quantities	
STEP 1	Prepare a table of the concentrations and volumes of the solutions.
STEP 2	Rearrange the dilution expression to solve for the unknown quantity.
STEP 3	Substitute the known quantities into the dilution expression and calculate.

Example: What is the final molarity after 150. mL of a 2.00 M NaCl solution is diluted to a volume of 400. mL?

Solution:

STEP 1 **Prepare a table of the concentrations and volumes of the solutions.**

Analyze the Problem	Concentrated Solution	Diluted Solution	Know	Predict
	C_1 = 2.00 M NaCl	C_2 = ? M NaCl		C decreases
	V_1 = 150. mL	V_2 = 400. mL	V increases	

STEP 2 **Rearrange the dilution expression to solve for the unknown quantity.**

$$C_1 V_1 = C_2 V_2 \qquad C_2 = C_1 \times \frac{V_1}{V_2}$$

STEP 3 **Substitute the known quantities into the dilution expression and calculate.**

$$C_2 = 2.00 \text{ M} \times \frac{150. \cancel{\text{ mL}}}{400. \cancel{\text{ mL}}} = 0.750 \text{ M}$$

♦ **Learning Exercise 9.5A**

Solve each of the following dilution problems:

a. What is the molarity after 100. mL of a 5.0 M KCl solution is diluted to a total volume of 200. mL?

b. What is the molarity of the diluted solution when 5.0 mL of a 1.5 M KCl solution is diluted to a total volume of 25 mL?

c. What is the molarity after 250 mL of an 8.0 M NaOH solution is diluted with 750 mL of water? (Assume that the volumes are additive.)

d. 160. mL of water is added to 40. mL of a 1.0 M NaCl solution. What is the molarity of the diluted solution? (Assume that the volumes are additive.)

e. What volume of a 6.0 M HCl solution is needed to prepare 300. mL of a 1.0 M HCl solution? How much water, in milliliters, must be added? (Assume that the volumes are additive.)

Answers   **a.** 2.5 M   **b.** 0.30 M   **c.** 2.0 M   **d.** 0.20 M
                      e. V_1 = 50. mL; add 250. mL of water

9.6 Properties of Solutions

Learning Goal: Identify a mixture as a solution, a colloid, or a suspension. Describe how the number of particles in a solution affects the freezing point, the boiling point, and the osmotic pressure of a solution.

- Colloids contain particles that do not settle out; colloid particles pass through filters but not through semipermeable membranes.

- Suspensions are composed of large particles that settle out of solution.

- In the process of osmosis, water (solvent) moves through a semipermeable membrane from the solution that has a lower solute concentration to a solution where the solute concentration is higher.

- Osmotic pressure is the pressure that prevents the flow of water into a more concentrated solution.

- Isotonic solutions have osmotic pressures equal to that of body fluids. A hypotonic solution has a lower osmotic pressure than body fluids; a hypertonic solution has a higher osmotic pressure.

- A red blood cell maintains its volume in an isotonic solution, but it swells (hemolysis) in a hypotonic solution and shrinks (crenation) in a hypertonic solution.

- In dialysis, water and small solute particles can pass through a dialyzing membrane, while larger particles, such as blood cells, cannot.

- A solute added to water decreases the vapor pressure, increases the boiling point, decreases the freezing point, and increases osmolarity.

Key Terms for Sections 9.5–9.6

Match the following terms with the correct definition below:

    a. hypertonic solution   **b.** dilution   **c.** hemolysis
    d. osmosis   **e.** semipermeable membrane   **f.** colloid

1. _____ the particles that pass through filters but are too large to pass through semipermeable membranes

2. _____ the swelling and bursting of red blood cells when placed in a hypotonic solution

3. _____ a solution that has a higher osmotic pressure than the red blood cells of the body

4. _____ a process by which water is added to a solution and decreases its concentration

5. _____ a membrane that permits the passage of small particles while blocking larger particles

6. _____ the flow of solvent through a semipermeable membrane into a solution of higher solute concentration

Answers   **1.** f   **2.** c   **3.** a   **4.** b   **5.** e   **6.** d

♦ **Learning Exercise 9.6A**

Identify each of the following as a solution, colloid, or suspension:

1. _____ the solute consists of single atoms, ions, or small molecules

2. _____ settles out with gravity

3. _____ retained by filters

4. _____ cannot diffuse through a cellular membrane

5. _____ contains large particles that are visible

Answers   1. solution   2. suspension   3. suspension
             4. colloid, suspension   5. suspension

♦ **Learning Exercise 9.6B**

Fill in the blanks:

In osmosis, the direction of solvent flow is from the (1) [higher/lower] solute concentration to the
(2) [higher/lower] solute concentration. A semipermeable membrane separates 5% (m/v) and 10%
(m/v) sucrose solutions. The (3) _____ % (m/v) solution has the greater osmotic pressure.
Water will move from the (4) _____ % (m/v) solution into the (5) _____ % (m/v)
solution. The compartment that contains the (6) _____ % (m/v) solution increases in volume.

Answers   1. lower   2. higher   3. 10   4. 5   5. 10   6. 10

♦ **Learning Exercise 9.6C**

A semipermeable membrane separates a 2% starch solution from a 10% starch solution. Complete
each of the following with 2% or 10%:

a. Water will flow from the _____ starch solution to the _____ starch solution.

b. The volume of the _____ starch solution will increase and the volume of the _____
   starch solution will decrease.

Answers   **a.** 2%, 10%   **b.** 10%, 2%

Calculating Freezing Point Lowering / Boiling Point Elevation	
STEP 1	State the given and needed quantities.
STEP 2	Determine the number of moles of solute particles.
STEP 3	Determine the temperature change using the moles of solute particles and the degrees Celsius change per mole of particles.
STEP 4	Subtract the temperature change from the freezing point or add the temperature change to the boiling point.

♦ **Learning Exercise 9.6D**

For the following solutes, each in 1000 g of water, calculate:

(1) the number of moles of particles present in the solution

(2) the freezing point change and freezing point of the solution

(3) the boiling point change and boiling point of the solution

Solute	Moles of Solute Particles	Freezing Point	Boiling Point
a. 1.00 mole of fructose (nonelectrolyte)			
b. 1.50 moles of KCl (strong electrolyte)			
c. 1.25 moles of $Ca(NO_3)_2$ (strong electrolyte)			

Answers

Solute	Moles of Solute Particles	Freezing Point	Boiling Point
a. 1.00 mole of fructose (nonelectrolyte)	1.00 mole	$-1.86\,°C$	$100.52\,°C$
b. 1.50 moles of KCl (strong electrolyte)	3.00 moles	$-5.58\,°C$	$101.56\,°C$
c. 1.25 moles of $Ca(NO_3)_2$ (strong electrolyte)	3.75 moles	$-6.98\,°C$	$101.95\,°C$

Guide to Calculating Osmolarity	
STEP 1	State the given and needed quantities.
STEP 2	Determine the number of osmoles in one mole of solute.
STEP 3	Calculate the osmolarity (Osm).

♦ **Learning Exercise 9.6E**

Calculate the osmolarity of each of the following solutions:

a. 0.25 M $CaCl_2$

b. 8.4% (m/v) $NaHCO_3$

    c. 10% (m/v) glucose ($C_6H_{12}O_6$, nonelectrolyte)

Answers   **a.** 0.75 Osm   **b.** 2.0 Osm   **c.** 0.56 Osm

♦ **Learning Exercise 9.6F**

Fill in the blanks:

A (1) _____ % (m/v) NaCl solution and a (2) _____ % (m/v) glucose solution are isotonic to the body fluids. A red blood cell placed in these solutions does not change in volume because these solutions are (3) _____ tonic. When a red blood cell is placed in water, it undergoes (4) _____ because water is (5) _____ tonic. A 20% (m/v) glucose solution will cause a red blood cell to undergo (6) _____ because the 20% (m/v) glucose solution is (7) _____ tonic.

Answers   **1.** 0.9   **2.** 5   **3.** iso   **4.** hemolysis
               5. hypo   **6.** crenation   **7.** hyper

♦ **Learning Exercise 9.6G**

Indicate whether the following are

    a. hypotonic   **b.** hypertonic   **c.** isotonic

1. ____ 5% (m/v) glucose   **2.** ____ 3% (m/v) NaCl   **3.** ____ 2% (m/v) glucose

4. ____ water   **5.** ____ 0.9% (m/v) NaCl   **6.** ____ 10% (m/v) glucose

Answers   **1.** c   **2.** b   **3.** a   **4.** a   **5.** c   **6.** b

♦ **Learning Exercise 9.6H**

Indicate whether the following will cause a red blood cell to undergo

    a. crenation   **b.** hemolysis   **c.** no change (stays the same)

1. ____ 10% (m/v) NaCl   **2.** ____ 1% (m/v) glucose   **3.** ____ 5% (m/v) glucose

4. ____ 0.5% (m/v) NaCl   **5.** ____ 10% (m/v) glucose   **6.** ____ water

Answers   **1.** a   **2.** b   **3.** c   **4.** b   **5.** a   **6.** b

♦ **Learning Exercise 9.6I**

A dialysis bag contains starch, glucose, NaCl, protein, and urea.

    a. When the dialysis bag is placed in water, what components would you expect to dialyze through the bag? Why?

    b. Which components will stay inside the dialysis bag? Why?

Answers
a. Glucose, NaCl, and urea are solution particles. Solution particles will pass through semipermeable membranes.
b. Starch and protein are colloidal particles; because of their size, colloidal particles are retained by semipermeable membranes.

Checklist for Chapter 9

You are ready to take the Practice Test for Chapter 9. Be sure you have accomplished the following learning goals for this chapter. If not, review the section listed at the end of the goal. Then apply your new skills and understanding to the Practice Test.

After studying Chapter 9, I can successfully:

_____ Identify the solute and solvent in a solution and describe the process of dissolving an ionic solute in water. (9.1)

_____ Identify the solute in a solution of an electrolyte or a nonelectrolyte. (9.2)

_____ Identify a saturated and an unsaturated solution. (9.3)

_____ Identify an ionic compound as soluble or insoluble. (9.3)

_____ Describe the effects of temperature and nature of a solute on its solubility in a solvent. (9.3)

_____ Determine the solubility of an ionic compound in water. (9.3)

_____ Determine if an insoluble compound forms after two aqueous solutions of ionic compounds are mixed. (9.3)

_____ Write an ionic and a net ionic equation for the formation of an insoluble compound. (9.3)

_____ Calculate the percent concentration, m/m, v/v, and m/v, of a solute in a solution. (9.4)

_____ Use percent concentration to calculate the amount of solute or solution. (9.4)

_____ Calculate the molarity of a solution. (9.4)

_____ Use molarity as a conversion factor to calculate the moles (or grams) of a solute or the volume of the solution. (9.4)

_____ Use the molarity of a solution in a chemical reaction to calculate the volume or quantity of a reactant or product. (9.4)

_____ Calculate the new concentration or new volume when a solution is diluted. (9.5)

_____ Identify a mixture as a solution, a colloid, or a suspension. (9.6)

_____ Identify a solution as isotonic, hypotonic, or hypertonic. (9.6)

_____ Explain the processes of osmosis and dialysis. (9.6)

_____ Use the concentration of particles in a solution to calculate the freezing point or boiling point of the solution. (9.6)

_____ Calculate the osmolarity of a solution.

Practice Test for Chapter 9

For questions 1 through 4, indicate if each of the following is more soluble in (W) water, a polar solvent, or (B) benzene, a nonpolar solvent: (9.1)

1. $I_2(s)$, nonpolar

2. $NaBr(s)$, polar

3. $KI(s)$, polar

4. C_6H_{12}, nonpolar

5. When dissolved in water, $Ca(NO_3)_2(s)$ dissociates into (9.2)
   A. $Ca^{2+}(aq) + (NO_3)_2^{2-}(aq)$
   B. $Ca^+(aq) + NO_3^-(aq)$
   C. $Ca^{2+}(aq) + 2NO_3^-(aq)$
   D. $Ca^{2+}(aq) + 2N^{5+}(aq) + 2O_3^{6-}(aq)$
   E. $CaNO_3^+(aq) + NO_3^-(aq)$

6. What is the number of equivalents in 2 moles of Mg^{2+}? (9.2)
   A. 0.50 Eq   B. 1 Eq   C. 1.5 Eq   D. 2 Eq   E. 4 Eq

7. The solubility of NH_4Cl is 46 g in 100. g of water at 40 °C. How many grams of NH_4Cl can dissolve in 500. g of water at 40 °C? (9.3)
   A. 9.2 g   B. 46 g   C. 100 g   D. 184 g   E. 230 g

For questions 8 through 11, indicate if each of the following is soluble (S) or insoluble (I) in water: (9.3)

8. NaCl   9. AgCl   10. $BaSO_4$ 11. FeO

12. A solution containing 1.20 g of sucrose in 50.0 g of solution has a percent (m/m) concentration of (9.4)
    A. 0.600%   B. 1.20%   C. 2.40%   D. 30.0%   E. 41.6%

13. The amount of lactose in 250 g of a 3.0% (m/m) lactose solution for infant formula is (9.4)
    A. 0.15 g   B. 1.2 g   C. 6.0 g   D. 7.5 g   E. 30 g

14. The mass of solution needed to obtain 0.40 g of glucose from a 5.0% (m/m) glucose solution is (9.4)
    A. 1.0 g   B. 2.0 g   C. 4.0 g   D. 5.0 g   E. 8.0 g

15. The amount of NaCl needed to prepare 50.0 g of a 4.00% (m/m) NaCl solution is (9.4)
    A. 20.0 g   B. 15.0 g   C. 10.0 g   D. 4.00 g   E. 2.00 g

16. A solution containing 6.0 g of NaCl in 1500 g of solution has a mass percent concentration of (9.4)
    A. 0.40% (m/m)   B. 0.25% (m/m)   C. 4.0% (m/m)   D. 0.90% (m/m)   E. 2.5% (m/m)

17. The number of moles of KOH needed to prepare 2400 mL of a 2.0 M KOH solution is (9.4)
    A. 1.2 moles   B. 2.4 moles   C. 4.8 moles   D. 12 moles   E. 48 moles

18. The number of grams of NaOH needed to prepare 7.5 mL of a 5.0 M NaOH solution is (9.4)
    A. 1.5 g   B. 3.8 g   C. 6.7 g   D. 15 g   E. 38 g

For questions 19 through 21, consider a 20.0-g sample of a solution that contains 2.0 g of NaOH: (9.4)

19. The percent (m/m) concentration of the solution is
    A. 1.0%   B. 4.0%   C. 5.0%   D. 10.%   E. 20.%

20. The number of moles of NaOH in the sample is
    A. 0.050 mole   B. 0.40 mole   C. 1.0 mole   D. 2.5 moles   E. 4.0 moles

21. If the solution has a volume of 0.025 L, what is the molarity of the solution?
    A. 0.10 M   B. 0.5 M   C. 1.0 M   D. 1.5 M   E. 2.0 M

22. Which of the following ionic compounds is soluble in water? (9.3)
    A. AgCl   B. $BaCO_3$ C. K_2SO_4 D. PbS   E. MgO

23. The insoluble ionic compound that forms when a solution of NaCl mixes with a $Pb(NO_3)_2$ solution is (9.3)
    A. Na_2Pb B. $ClNO_3$ C. $NaNO_3$ D. $PbCl_2$ E. no insoluble ionic compound forms

24. Which of the following ionic compounds is insoluble in water? (9.3)

    A. $CuCl_2$ **B.** $Pb(NO_3)_2$ **C.** K_2CO_3 **D.** $(NH_4)_2SO_4$ **E.** $CaCO_3$

25. What mass of Ag_2SO_4 forms when 25.0 mL of a 0.111 M $AgNO_3$ solution reacts? (9.4)

    $2AgNO_3(aq) + H_2SO_4(aq) \longrightarrow Ag_2SO_4(s) + 2H_2O(l)$

    A. 0.866 g   **B.** 1.74 g   **C.** 866 g   **D.** 0.433 g   **E.** 2.78 g

26. A 20.-mL sample of a 5.0 M HCl solution is diluted with water to give 100. mL of solution. The final concentration of the HCl solution is (9.5)

    A. 10 M   **B.** 5.0 M   **C.** 2.0 M   **D.** 1.0 M   **E.** 0.50 M

27. Water is added to 200. mL of a 4.00 M KNO_3 solution to give 400. mL of solution. The final concentration of the KNO_3 solution is (9.5)

    A. 1.00 M   **B.** 2.00 M   **C.** 4.00 M   **D.** 0.500 M   **E.** 0.100 M

28. 5.0 mL of a 2.0 M KOH solution is diluted with water to give 50.0 mL of solution. The final concentration of the KOH solution is (9.5)

    A. 1.5 M   **B.** 1.0 M   **C.** 20 M   **D.** 0.20 M   **E.** 0.50 M

For questions 29 through 31, indicate whether each statement describes a (9.6)

    A. solution   **B.** colloid   **C.** suspension

29. _____ settles out upon standing

30. _____ passes through a filter but not through a semipermeable membrane

31. _____ passes through semipermeable membranes

32. A solution contains 0.50 mole of $CaCl_2$ in 1000 g of water. The freezing point of the solution is _____ the freezing point of water. (9.6)

    A. higher than   **B.** lower than   **C.** the same as

33. If a solution contains 0.50 mole of $CaCl_2$ in 1000 g of water, what is the freezing point of the solution? (9.6)

    A. $0\,°C$ **B.** $2.8\,°C$ **C.** $-2.8\,°C$ **D.** $0.93\,°C$ **E.** $-0.93\,°C$

34. In osmosis, the net flow of water is (9.6)

    A. between solutions of equal concentrations

    B. from higher solute concentration to lower solute concentration

    C. from lower solute concentration to higher solute concentration

    D. from a colloid to a solution of equal concentration

    E. from lower solvent concentration to higher solvent concentration

35. A red blood cell undergoes hemolysis when placed in a solution that is (9.6)

    A. isotonic   **B.** hypotonic   **C.** hypertonic   **D.** colloidal   **E.** semitonic

36. A solution that has the same osmotic pressure as body fluids is (9.6)

    A. 0.1% (m/v) NaCl   **B.** 0.9% (m/v) NaCl   **C.** 5% (m/v) NaCl

    D. 10% (m/v) glucose   **E.** 15% (m/v) glucose

For questions 37 through 41, select the correct term from the following: (9.6)

    A. isotonic   **B.** hypertonic   **C.** hypotonic   **D.** osmosis   **E.** dialysis

37. a solution with a higher osmotic pressure than the blood

38. a solution of 10% (m/v) NaCl surrounding a red blood cell

39. a 1% (m/v) glucose solution

40. the cleansing process of the artificial kidney

41. the flow of water up the stem of a plant

42. The osmolarity (Osm) of an 8.0% (m/v) KCl solution is
    A. 0.55 Osm   **B.** 1.1 Osm   **C.** 1.6 Osm   **D.** 2.2 Osm   **E.** 16 Osm

Answers to the Practice Test

1. B	**2.** W	**3.** W	**4.** B	**5.** C
6. E	**7.** E	**8.** S	**9.** I	**10.** I
11. I	**12.** C	**13.** D	**14.** E	**15.** E
16. A	**17.** C	**18.** A	**19.** D	**20.** A
21. E	**22.** C	**23.** D	**24.** E	**25.** D
26. D	**27.** B	**28.** D	**29.** C	**30.** B
31. A	**32.** B	**33.** C	**34.** C	**35.** B
36. B	**37.** B	**38.** B	**39.** C	**40.** E
41. D	**42.** D			

Learning Goals

- Identify the solute and solvent in a solution; describe the formation of a solution.
- Identify solutes as electrolytes or nonelectrolytes.
- Define solubility; distinguish between an unsaturated and a saturated solution. Identify an ionic compound as soluble or insoluble.
- Calculate the concentration of a solute in a solution; use concentration units to calculate the amount of solute or solution.
- Given the volume and concentration of a solution, calculate the amount of another reactant or product in a reaction.
- Describe the dilution of a solution; calculate the unknown concentration or volume when a solution is diluted.
- Identify a mixture as a solution, a colloid, or a suspension. Describe how the number of particles in a solution affects the freezing point, the boiling point, and the osmotic pressure of a solution.

Chapter Outline

Chapter Opener: Dialysis Nurse

9.1   Solutions

Chemistry Link to Health: Water in the Body

Explore Your World: Like Dissolves Like

9.2   Electrolytes and Nonelectrolytes

Chemistry Link to Health: Electrolytes in Body Fluids

9.3   Solubility

Chemistry Link to Health: Gout and Kidney Stones: A Problem of Saturation in Body Fluids

Explore Your World: Preparing Rock Candy

Explore Your World: Preparing Solutions

9.4   Solution Concentrations and Reactions

9.5   Dilution of Solutions

9.6   Properties of Solutions

Chemistry Link to Health: Colloids and Solutions in the Body

Explore Your World: Everyday Osmosis

Chemistry Link to Health: Dialysis by the Kidneys and the Artificial Kidney

Clinical Update: Using Dialysis for Renal Failure

❈ Core Chemistry Skills

- Using Solubility Rules (9.3)
- Calculating Concentration (9.4)
- Using Concentration as a Conversion Factor (9.4)

- Calculating the Quantity of a Reactant or Product for a Chemical Reaction in Solution (9.4)
- Calculating the Boiling Point/Freezing Point of a Solution (9.6)

Selected Answers and Solutions to Text Problems

9.1 The component present in the smaller amount is the solute; the component present in the larger amount is the solvent.

    a. NaCl, solute; water, solvent

    b. water, solute; ethanol, solvent

    c. oxygen, solute; nitrogen, solvent

9.3 The K^+ and I^- ions at the surface of the solid are pulled into solution by the polar water molecules, where the hydration process surrounds separate ions with water molecules.

9.5   **a.** $CaCO_3$ (an ionic solute) would be soluble in water (a polar solvent).

    b. Retinol (a nonpolar solute) would be soluble in CCl_4 (a nonpolar solvent).

    c. Sucrose (a polar solute) would be soluble in water (a polar solvent).

    d. Cholesterol (a nonpolar solute) would be soluble in CCl_4 (a nonpolar solvent).

9.7 The strong electrolyte KF completely dissociates into K^+ and F^- ions when it dissolves in water. When the weak electrolyte HF dissolves in water, there are a few ions of H^+ and F^- present, but mostly dissolved HF molecules.

9.9 Strong electrolytes dissociate completely into ions.

    a. $KCl(s) \xrightarrow{H_2O} K^+(aq) + Cl^-(aq)$

    b. $CaCl_2(s) \xrightarrow{H_2O} Ca^{2+}(aq) + 2Cl^-(aq)$

    c. $K_3PO_4(s) \xrightarrow{H_2O} 3K^+(aq) + PO_4{}^{3-}(aq)$

    d. $Fe(NO_3)_3(s) \xrightarrow{H_2O} Fe^{3+}(aq) + 3NO_3{}^-(aq)$

9.11   **a.** $HC_2H_3O_2(l) \underset{\longleftarrow}{\overset{H_2O}{\longrightarrow}} H^+(aq) + C_2H_3O_2{}^-(aq)$ mostly molecules, a few ions

    An aqueous solution of a weak electrolyte like acetic acid will contain mostly $HC_2H_3O_2$ molecules, with a few H^+ ions and a few $C_2H_3O_2{}^-$ ions.

    b. $NaBr(s) \xrightarrow{H_2O} Na^+(aq) + Br^-(aq)$ ions only

    An aqueous solution of a strong electrolyte like NaBr will contain only the ions Na^+ and Br^-.

    c. $C_6H_{12}O_6(s) \xrightarrow{H_2O} C_6H_{12}O_6(aq)$ molecules only

    An aqueous solution of a nonelectrolyte like fructose will contain only $C_6H_{12}O_6$ molecules.

9.13   **a.** K_2SO_4 is a strong electrolyte because only ions are present in the K_2SO_4 solution.

    b. NH_3 is a weak electrolyte because only a few $NH_4{}^+$ and OH^- ions are present in the solution.

    c. $C_6H_{12}O_6$ is a nonelectrolyte because only $C_6H_{12}O_6$ molecules are present in the solution.

9.15   **a.** $1 \; \text{mole } K^+ \times \dfrac{1 \; \text{Eq } K^+}{1 \; \text{mole } K^+} = 1 \; \text{Eq of } K^+$

    b. $2 \; \text{moles } OH^- \times \dfrac{1 \; \text{Eq } OH^-}{1 \; \text{mole } OH^-} = 2 \; \text{Eq of } OH^-$

    c. $1 \; \text{mole } Ca^{2+} \times \dfrac{2 \; \text{Eq } Ca^{2+}}{1 \; \text{mole } Ca^{2+}} = 2 \; \text{Eq of } Ca^{2+}$

    d. $3 \; \text{moles } CO_3{}^{2-} \times \dfrac{2 \; \text{Eq } CO_3{}^{2-}}{1 \; \text{mole } CO_3{}^{2-}} = 6 \; \text{Eq of } CO_3{}^{2-}$

9.17 $1.00 \, \cancel{L} \times \dfrac{154 \, \cancel{\text{mEq Na}^+}}{1 \, \cancel{L}} \times \dfrac{1 \, \cancel{\text{Eq Na}^+}}{1000 \, \cancel{\text{mEq Na}^+}} \times \dfrac{1 \, \text{mole Na}^+}{1 \, \cancel{\text{Eq Na}^+}} = 0.154 \, \text{mole of Na}^+ \, (3 \, \text{SFs})$

$1.00 \, \cancel{L} \times \dfrac{154 \, \cancel{\text{mEq Cl}^-}}{1 \, \cancel{L}} \times \dfrac{1 \, \cancel{\text{Eq Cl}^-}}{1000 \, \cancel{\text{mEq Cl}^-}} \times \dfrac{1 \, \text{mole Cl}^-}{1 \, \cancel{\text{Eq Cl}^-}} = 0.154 \, \text{mole of Cl}^- \, (3 \, \text{SFs})$

9.19 In any solution, the total equivalents of anions must be equal to the equivalents of cations. mEq of anions = 40. mEq/L Cl$^-$ + 15 mEq/L HPO$_4^{2-}$ = 55 mEq/L of anions
mEq of Na$^+$ = mEq of anions = 55 mEq/L of Na$^+$

9.21 a. Given 0.45 g/dL Cl$^-$ **Need** mEq/L

  Plan g $\rightarrow$ mole $\rightarrow$ Eq $\rightarrow$ mEq; dL $\rightarrow$ L $\dfrac{1 \, \text{mole Cl}^-}{35.45 \, \text{g Cl}^-}$ $\dfrac{1 \, \text{Eq}}{1 \, \text{mole Cl}^-}$ $\dfrac{1000 \, \text{mEq}}{1 \, \text{Eq}}$ $\dfrac{10 \, \text{dL}}{1 \, \text{L}}$

  Set-up $\dfrac{0.45 \, \cancel{\text{g Cl}^-}}{1 \, \cancel{\text{dL}}} \times \dfrac{1 \, \cancel{\text{mole Cl}^-}}{35.45 \, \cancel{\text{g Cl}^-}} \times \dfrac{1 \, \cancel{\text{Eq}}}{1 \, \cancel{\text{mole Cl}^-}} \times \dfrac{1000 \, \text{mEq}}{1 \, \cancel{\text{Eq}}} \times \dfrac{10 \, \cancel{\text{dL}}}{1 \, \text{L}}$

  $= 130 \, \text{mEq/L} \, (2 \, \text{SFs})$

  b. The normal range for Cl$^-$ is 95 to 105 mEq/L of blood plasma, so a concentration of 130 mEq/L is above the normal range.

9.23 a. At 20 °C, KCl has a solubility of 34 g of KCl in 100 g of H$_2$O. Because 25 g of KCl is less than the maximum amount that can dissolve in 100 g of H$_2$O at 20 °C, the KCl solution is unsaturated.

  b. At 20 °C, NaNO$_3$ has a solubility of 88 g of NaNO$_3$ in 100 g of H$_2$O. Using the solubility as a conversion factor, we can calculate the maximum amount of NaNO$_3$ that can dissolve in 25 g of H$_2$O:

  $25 \, \cancel{\text{g H}_2\text{O}} \times \dfrac{88 \, \text{g NaNO}_3}{100 \, \cancel{\text{g H}_2\text{O}}} = 22 \, \text{g of NaNO}_3 \, (2 \, \text{SFs})$

  Because 11 g of NaNO$_3$ is less than the maximum amount that can dissolve in 25 g of H$_2$O at 20 °C, the NaNO$_3$ solution is unsaturated.

  c. At 20 °C, sugar has a solubility of 204 g of C$_{12}$H$_{22}$O$_{11}$ in 100 g of H$_2$O. Using the solubility as a conversion factor, we can calculate the maximum amount of sugar that can dissolve in 125 g of H$_2$O:

  $125 \, \cancel{\text{g H}_2\text{O}} \times \dfrac{204 \, \text{g sugar}}{100 \, \cancel{\text{g H}_2\text{O}}} = 255 \, \text{g of sugar} \, (3 \, \text{SFs})$

  Because 400. g of C$_{12}$H$_{22}$O$_{11}$ exceeds the maximum amount that can dissolve in 125 g of H$_2$O at 20 °C, the sugar solution is saturated, and excess undissolved sugar will be present on the bottom of the container.

9.25 a. At 20 °C, KCl has a solubility of 34 g of KCl in 100 g of H$_2$O.
  ∴ 200. g of H$_2$O will dissolve:

  $200. \, \cancel{\text{g H}_2\text{O}} \times \dfrac{34 \, \text{g KCl}}{100 \, \cancel{\text{g H}_2\text{O}}} = 68 \, \text{g of KCl} \, (2 \, \text{SFs})$

  At 20 °C, 68 g of KCl will remain in solution.

  b. Since 80. g of KCl dissolves at 50 °C and 68 g remains in solution at 20 °C, the mass of solid KCl that crystallizes after cooling is (80. g KCl − 68 g KCl) = 12 g of KCl. (2 SFs)

9.27 a. In general, the solubility of solid solutes (like sugar) increases as temperature is increased.

  b. The solubility of a gaseous solute (CO$_2$) is less at a higher temperature.

   c. The solubility of a gaseous solute is less at a higher temperature, and the CO_2 pressure in the can is increased. When the can of warm soda is opened, more CO_2 is released, producing more spray.

9.29   **a.** Salts containing Li^+ ions are soluble.
     b. The Cl^- salt containing Ag^+ is insoluble.
     c. Salts containing CO_3^{2-} ions are usually insoluble.
     d. Salts containing K^+ ions are soluble.
     e. Salts containing NO_3^- ions are soluble.

9.31   **a.** No solid forms; salts containing K^+ and Na^+ are soluble.
     b. Solid silver sulfide (Ag_2S) forms:

$$2AgNO_3(aq) + K_2S(aq) \longrightarrow Ag_2S(s) + 2KNO_3(aq)$$
$$2Ag^+(aq) + 2\cancel{NO_3^-(aq)} + 2\cancel{K^+(aq)} + S^{2-}(aq) \longrightarrow Ag_2S(s) + 2\cancel{K^+(aq)} + 2\cancel{NO_3^-(aq)}$$
$$2Ag^+(aq) + S^{2-}(aq) \longrightarrow Ag_2S(s) \quad \text{Net ionic equation}$$

     c. Solid calcium sulfate ($CaSO_4$) forms:

$$CaCl_2(aq) + Na_2SO_4(aq) \longrightarrow CaSO_4(s) + 2NaCl(aq)$$
$$Ca^{2+}(aq) + 2\cancel{Cl^-(aq)} + 2\cancel{Na^+(aq)} + SO_4^{2-}(aq) \longrightarrow CaSO_4(s) + 2\cancel{Na^+(aq)} + 2\cancel{Cl^-(aq)}$$
$$Ca^{2+}(aq) + SO_4^{2-}(aq) \longrightarrow CaSO_4(s) \quad \text{Net ionic equation}$$

     d. Solid copper phosphate ($Cu_3(PO_4)_2$) forms:

$$3CuCl_2(aq) + 2Li_3PO_4(aq) \longrightarrow Cu_3(PO_4)_2(s) + 6LiCl(aq)$$
$$3Cu^{2+}(aq) + 6\cancel{Cl^-(aq)} + 6\cancel{Li^+(aq)} + 2PO_4^{2-}(aq) \longrightarrow Cu_3(PO_4)_2(s) + 6\cancel{Li^+(aq)} + 6\cancel{Cl^-(aq)}$$
$$3Cu^{2+}(aq) + 2PO_4^{2-}(aq) \longrightarrow Cu_3(PO_4)_2(s) \quad \text{Net ionic equation}$$

9.33   mass percent (m/m) $= \dfrac{\text{mass of solute (g)}}{\text{mass of solution (g)}} \times 100\%$

     a. mass of solution = 25 g KCl + 125 g H_2O = 150. g of solution

$$\frac{25 \text{ g KCl}}{150. \text{ g solution}} \times 100\% = 17\% \text{ (m/m) KCl solution (2 SFs)}$$

     b. $\dfrac{12 \text{ g sucrose}}{225 \text{ g solution}} \times 100\% = 5.3\% \text{ (m/m) sucrose solution (2 SFs)}$

     c. $\dfrac{8.0 \text{ g } CaCl_2}{80.0 \text{ g solution}} \times 100\% = 10.\% \text{ (m/m) } CaCl_2 \text{ solution (2 SFs)}$

9.35   mass/volume percent (m/v) $= \dfrac{\text{mass of solute (g)}}{\text{volume of solution (mL)}} \times 100\%$

     a. $\dfrac{75 \text{ g } Na_2SO_4}{250 \text{ mL solution}} \times 100\% = 30.\% \text{ (m/v) } Na_2SO_4 \text{ solution (2 SFs)}$

     b. $\dfrac{39 \text{ g sucrose}}{355 \text{ mL solution}} \times 100\% = 11\% \text{ (m/v) sucrose solution (2 SFs)}$

9.37   **a.** $50.0 \text{ g solution} \times \dfrac{5.0 \text{ g KCl}}{100 \text{ g solution}} = 2.5 \text{ g of KCl (2 SFs)}$

     b. $1250 \text{ mL solution} \times \dfrac{4.0 \text{ g } NH_4Cl}{100 \text{ mL solution}} = 50. \text{ g of } NH_4Cl \text{ (2 SFs)}$

     c. $250. \text{ mL solution} \times \dfrac{10.0 \text{ mL acetic acid}}{100 \text{ mL solution}} = 25.0 \text{ mL of acetic acid (3 SFs)}$

9.39 $355 \; \text{mL solution} \times \dfrac{22.5 \; \text{mL alcohol}}{100 \; \text{mL solution}} = 79.9 \; \text{mL of alcohol} \; (3 \; \text{SFs})$

9.41 **a.** $5.0 \; \text{g LiNO}_3 \times \dfrac{100 \; \text{g solution}}{25 \; \text{g LiNO}_3} = 20. \; \text{g of LiNO}_3 \; \text{solution} \; (2 \; \text{SFs})$

b. $40.0 \; \text{g KOH} \times \dfrac{100 \; \text{mL solution}}{10.0 \; \text{g KOH}} = 400. \; \text{mL of KOH solution} \; (3 \; \text{SFs})$

c. $2.0 \; \text{mL formic acid} \times \dfrac{100 \; \text{mL solution}}{10.0 \; \text{mL formic acid}} = 20. \; \text{mL of formic acid solution} \; (2 \; \text{SFs})$

9.43 $\text{molarity} \; (M) = \dfrac{\text{moles of solute}}{\text{liters of solution}}$

a. $\dfrac{2.00 \; \text{moles glucose}}{4.00 \; \text{L solution}} = 0.500 \; \text{M glucose solution} \; (3 \; \text{SFs})$

b. $\dfrac{4.00 \; \text{g KOH}}{2.00 \; \text{L solution}} \times \dfrac{1 \; \text{mole KOH}}{56.11 \; \text{g KOH}} = 0.0356 \; \text{M KOH solution} \; (3 \; \text{SFs})$

c. $\dfrac{5.85 \; \text{g NaCl}}{400. \; \text{mL solution}} \times \dfrac{1 \; \text{mole NaCl}}{58.44 \; \text{g NaCl}} \times \dfrac{1000 \; \text{mL solution}}{1 \; \text{L solution}} = 0.250 \; \text{M NaCl solution} \; (3 \; \text{SFs})$

9.45 **a.** $2.00 \; \text{L solution} \times \dfrac{1.50 \; \text{moles NaOH}}{1 \; \text{L solution}} \times \dfrac{40.00 \; \text{g NaOH}}{1 \; \text{mole NaOH}} = 120. \; \text{g of NaOH} \; (3 \; \text{SFs})$

b. $4.00 \; \text{L solution} \times \dfrac{0.200 \; \text{mole KCl}}{1 \; \text{L solution}} \times \dfrac{74.55 \; \text{g KCl}}{1 \; \text{mole KCl}} = 59.6 \; \text{g of KCl} \; (3 \; \text{SFs})$

c. $25.0 \; \text{mL solution} \times \dfrac{1 \; \text{L solution}}{1000 \; \text{mL solution}} \times \dfrac{6.00 \; \text{moles HCl}}{1 \; \text{L solution}} \times \dfrac{36.46 \; \text{g HCl}}{1 \; \text{mole HCl}}$

$= 5.47 \; \text{g of HCl} \; (3 \; \text{SFs})$

9.47 **a.** $3.00 \; \text{moles KBr} \times \dfrac{1 \; \text{L solution}}{2.00 \; \text{moles KBr}} = 1.50 \; \text{L of KBr solution} \; (3 \; \text{SFs})$

b. $15.0 \; \text{moles NaCl} \times \dfrac{1 \; \text{L solution}}{1.50 \; \text{moles NaCl}} = 10.0 \; \text{L of NaCl solution} \; (3 \; \text{SFs})$

c. $0.0500 \; \text{mole Ca(NO}_3)_2 \times \dfrac{1 \; \text{L solution}}{0.800 \; \text{mole Ca(NO}_3)_2} \times \dfrac{1000 \; \text{mL solution}}{1 \; \text{L solution}}$

$= 62.5 \; \text{mL of Ca(NO}_3)_2 \; \text{solution} \; (3 \; \text{SFs})$

9.49 **a.** $50.0 \; \text{mL solution} \times \dfrac{1 \; \text{L solution}}{1000 \; \text{mL solution}} \times \dfrac{1.50 \; \text{moles KCl}}{1 \; \text{L solution}} = 0.0750 \; \text{mole of KCl}$

$0.0750 \; \text{mole KCl} \times \dfrac{1 \; \text{mole PbCl}_2}{2 \; \text{moles KCl}} \times \dfrac{278.1 \; \text{g PbCl}_2}{1 \; \text{mole PbCl}_2} = 10.4 \; \text{g of PbCl}_2 \; (3 \; \text{SFs})$

b. $50.0 \; \text{mL solution} \times \dfrac{1 \; \text{L solution}}{1000 \; \text{mL solution}} \times \dfrac{1.50 \; \text{moles KCl}}{1 \; \text{L solution}} = 0.0750 \; \text{mole of KCl}$

$0.0750 \; \text{mole KCl} \times \dfrac{1 \; \text{mole Pb(NO}_3)_2}{2 \; \text{moles KCl}} \times \dfrac{1 \; \text{L solution}}{2.00 \; \text{moles Pb(NO}_3)_2} \times \dfrac{1000 \; \text{mL solution}}{1 \; \text{L solution}}$

$= 18.8 \; \text{mL of Pb(NO}_3)_2 \; \text{solution} \; (3 \; \text{SFs})$

c. $30.0 \; \text{mL solution} \times \dfrac{1 \; \text{L solution}}{1000 \; \text{mL solution}} \times \dfrac{0.400 \; \text{mole Pb(NO}_3)_2}{1 \; \text{L solution}} \times \dfrac{2 \; \text{moles KCl}}{1 \; \text{mole Pb(NO}_3)_2}$

$= 0.0240 \; \text{mole of KCl}$

$$20.0 \text{ mL solution} \times \frac{1 \text{ L solution}}{1000 \text{ mL solution}} = 0.0200 \text{ L of solution}$$

$$\text{molarity (M)} = \frac{\text{moles of solute}}{\text{liters of solution}} = \frac{0.0240 \text{ mole KCl}}{0.0200 \text{ L solution}} = 1.20 \text{ M KCl solution (3 SFs)}$$

9.51 a. $15.0 \text{ g Mg} \times \dfrac{1 \text{ mole Mg}}{24.31 \text{ g Mg}} \times \dfrac{2 \text{ moles HCl}}{1 \text{ mole Mg}} \times \dfrac{1 \text{ L solution}}{6.00 \text{ moles HCl}} \times \dfrac{1000 \text{ mL solution}}{1 \text{ L solution}}$

$= 206 \text{ mL of HCl solution (3 SFs)}$

b. $0.500 \text{ L solution} \times \dfrac{2.00 \text{ moles HCl}}{1 \text{ L solution}} \times \dfrac{1 \text{ mole H}_2}{2 \text{ moles HCl}} \times \dfrac{22.4 \text{ L H}_2 \text{ (STP)}}{1 \text{ mole H}_2}$

$= 11.2 \text{ L of H}_2 \text{ at STP (3 SFs)}$

c. $n = \dfrac{PV}{RT} = \dfrac{(735 \text{ mmHg})(5.20 \text{ L})}{\left(\dfrac{62.4 \text{ L} \cdot \text{mmHg}}{\text{mole} \cdot \text{K}}\right)(298 \text{ K})} = 0.206 \text{ mole of H}_2 \text{ gas}$

$$0.206 \text{ mole H}_2 \times \frac{2 \text{ moles HCl}}{1 \text{ mole H}_2} = 0.412 \text{ mole of HCl}$$

$$45.2 \text{ mL solution} \times \frac{1 \text{ L solution}}{1000 \text{ mL solution}} = 0.0452 \text{ L of solution}$$

$$\text{molarity (M)} = \frac{\text{moles of solute}}{\text{liters of solution}} = \frac{0.412 \text{ mole HCl}}{0.0452 \text{ L solution}} = 9.12 \text{ M HCl solution (3 SFs)}$$

9.53 a. $1 \text{ L} \times \dfrac{100 \text{ mL solution}}{1 \text{ L}} \times \dfrac{20. \text{ g mannitol}}{100. \text{ mL solution}} = 20. \text{ g of mannitol (2 SFs)}$

b. $12 \text{ L} \times \dfrac{100 \text{ mL solution}}{1 \text{ L}} \times \dfrac{20. \text{ g mannitol}}{100. \text{ mL solution}} = 240 \text{ g of mannitol (2 SFs)}$

9.55 $100. \text{ g glucose} \times \dfrac{100 \text{ mL solution}}{5 \text{ g glucose}} \times \dfrac{1 \text{ L}}{1000 \text{ mL}} = 2 \text{ L of glucose solution (1 SF)}$

9.57 $0.075 \text{ g chlorpromazine} \times \dfrac{100 \text{ mL solution}}{2.5 \text{ g chlorpromazine}} = 3.0 \text{ mL of chlorpromazine solution (2 SFs)}$

9.59 $5.0 \text{ mL solution} \times \dfrac{10. \text{ g CaCl}_2}{100 \text{ mL solution}} = 0.50 \text{ g of CaCl}_2 \text{ (2 SFs)}$

9.61 Adding water (solvent) to the soup increases the volume and dilutes the tomato soup concentration.

9.63 $C_1 V_1 = C_2 V_2$

a. $C_2 = C_1 \times \dfrac{V_1}{V_2} = 6.0 \text{ M} \times \dfrac{2.0 \text{ L}}{6.0 \text{ L}} = 2.0 \text{ M HCl solution (2 SFs)}$

b. $C_2 = C_1 \times \dfrac{V_1}{V_2} = 12 \text{ M} \times \dfrac{0.50 \text{ L}}{3.0 \text{ L}} = 2.0 \text{ M NaOH solution (2 SFs)}$

c. $C_2 = C_1 \times \dfrac{V_1}{V_2} = 25\% \times \dfrac{10.0 \text{ mL}}{100.0 \text{ mL}} = 2.5\% \text{ (m/v) KOH solution (2 SFs)}$

d. $C_2 = C_1 \times \dfrac{V_1}{V_2} = 15\% \times \dfrac{50.0 \text{ mL}}{250 \text{ mL}} = 3.0\% \text{ (m/v) H}_2\text{SO}_4 \text{ solution (2 SFs)}$

9.65 $C_1 V_1 = C_2 V_2$

    a. $V_2 = V_1 \times \dfrac{C_1}{C_2} = 20.0 \text{ mL} \times \dfrac{6.0 \text{ M}}{1.5 \text{ M}} = 80. \text{ mL of diluted HCl solution (2 SFs)}$

    b. $V_2 = V_1 \times \dfrac{C_1}{C_2} = 50.0 \text{ mL} \times \dfrac{10.0 \text{ %}}{2.0 \text{ %}} = 250 \text{ mL of diluted LiCl solution (2 SFs)}$

    c. $V_2 = V_1 \times \dfrac{C_1}{C_2} = 50.0 \text{ mL} \times \dfrac{6.00 \text{ M}}{0.500 \text{ M}} = 600. \text{ mL of diluted H}_3\text{PO}_4 \text{ solution (3 SFs)}$

    d. $V_2 = V_1 \times \dfrac{C_1}{C_2} = 75 \text{ mL} \times \dfrac{12 \text{ %}}{5.0 \text{ %}} = 180 \text{ mL of diluted glucose solution (2 SFs)}$

9.67 $C_1 V_1 = C_2 V_2$

    a. $V_1 = V_2 \times \dfrac{C_2}{C_1} = 255 \text{ mL} \times \dfrac{0.200 \text{ M}}{4.00 \text{ M}} = 12.8 \text{ mL of the HNO}_3 \text{ solution (3 SFs)}$

    b. $V_1 = V_2 \times \dfrac{C_2}{C_1} = 715 \text{ mL} \times \dfrac{0.100 \text{ M}}{6.00 \text{ M}} = 11.9 \text{ mL of the MgCl}_2 \text{ solution (3 SFs)}$

    c. $V_2 = 0.100 \text{ L} \times \dfrac{1000 \text{ mL}}{1 \text{ L}} = 100. \text{ mL}$

        $V_1 = V_2 \times \dfrac{C_2}{C_1} = 100. \text{ mL} \times \dfrac{0.150 \text{ M}}{8.00 \text{ M}} = 1.88 \text{ mL of the KCl solution (3 SFs)}$

9.69 $C_1 V_1 = C_2 V_2$

    $V_1 = V_2 \times \dfrac{C_2}{C_1} = 500. \text{ mL} \times \dfrac{5.0\%}{25\%} = 1.0 \times 10^2 \text{ mL of the glucose solution (2 SFs)}$

9.71   **a.** A solution cannot be separated by a semipermeable membrane.

    b. A suspension settles out upon standing.

9.73   **a.** When 1.0 mole of glycerol (a nonelectrolyte) dissolves in water, it does not dissociate into ions and so will only produce 1.0 mole of particles. Similarly, 2.0 moles of ethylene glycol (also a nonelectrolyte) dissolves as molecules to produce only 2.0 moles of particles in water. The ethylene glycol solution has more particles in 1.0 L of water and will thus have a lower freezing point.

    b. When 0.50 mole of the strong electrolyte KCl dissolves in water, it will produce 1.0 mole of particles because each formula unit of KCl dissociates to give two particles, K^+ and Cl^-. When 0.50 mole of the strong electrolyte $MgCl_2$ dissolves in water, it will produce 1.5 moles of particles because each formula unit of $MgCl_2$ dissociates to give three particles, Mg^{2+} and $2Cl^-$. Thus, a solution of 0.50 mole of $MgCl_2$ in 2.0 L of water will have the lower freezing point.

9.75   **a.** A solution of 1.36 moles of the nonelectrolyte CH_3OH in 1.00 kg of water contains 1.36 moles of particles in 1.00 kg of water and has a freezing point change of

    $1.36 \text{ moles particles} \times \dfrac{1.86 \,°C}{1 \text{ mole particles}} = 2.53 \,°C$

    The freezing point would be $0.00 \,°C - 2.53 \,°C = -2.53 \,°C$

    b. $640. \text{ g } C_3H_8O_2 \times \dfrac{1 \text{ mole } C_3H_8O_2}{76.09 \text{ g } C_3H_8O_2} = 8.41 \text{ moles of } C_3H_8O_2 \text{ (3 SFs)}$

    A solution of 8.41 moles of the nonelectrolyte $C_3H_8O_2$ in 1.00 kg of water contains 8.41 moles of particles in 1.00 kg of water and has a freezing point change of

    $8.41 \text{ moles particles} \times \dfrac{1.86 \,°C}{1 \text{ mole particles}} = 15.6 \,°C$

    The freezing point would be $0.00 \,°C - 15.6 \,°C = -15.6 \,°C$

   c. $111 \text{ g KCl} \times \dfrac{1 \text{ mole KCl}}{74.55 \text{ g KCl}} = 1.49 \text{ moles of KCl (3 SFs)}$

   A solution of 1.49 moles of the strong electrolyte KCl in 1.00 kg of water contains 2.98 moles of particles (1.49 moles of K^+ and 1.49 moles of Cl^-) in 1.00 kg of water and has a freezing point change of

$$2.98 \text{ moles particles} \times \dfrac{1.86\,°C}{1 \text{ mole particles}} = 5.54\,°C$$

   The freezing point would be $0.00\,°C - 5.54\,°C = -5.54\,°C$

9.77 **a.** The 10% (m/v) starch solution has the higher solute concentration, more solute particles, and therefore the higher osmotic pressure.

     b. Initially, water will flow out of the 1% (m/v) starch solution into the more concentrated 10% (m/v) starch solution.

     c. The volume of the 10% (m/v) starch solution will increase due to inflow of water.

9.79 Water will flow from a region of higher solvent concentration (which corresponds to a lower solute concentration) to a region of lower solvent concentration (which corresponds to a higher solute concentration).

     a. B; The volume level will rise as water flows into compartment B, which contains the 10% (m/v) sucrose solution.

     b. A; The volume level will rise as water flows into compartment A, which contains the 8% (m/v) albumin solution.

     c. B; The volume level will rise as water flows into compartment B, which contains the 10% (m/v) starch solution.

9.81 **a.** 1 mole $NaCl(s) \longrightarrow$ 1 mole $Na^+(aq)$ + 1 mole $Cl^-(aq)$ = 2 moles of particles = 2 osmoles

$$\dfrac{3.0 \text{ g NaCl}}{100 \text{ mL solution}} \times \dfrac{1 \text{ mole NaCl}}{58.44 \text{ g NaCl}} \times \dfrac{2 \text{ osmoles}}{1 \text{ mole NaCl}} \times \dfrac{1000 \text{ mL solution}}{1 \text{ L solution}} = 1.0 \text{ Osm (2 SFs)}$$

     b. 1 mole $C_6H_{12}O_6(s) \longrightarrow$ 1 mole $C_6H_{12}O_6(aq)$ = 1 mole of particles = 1 osmole

$$\dfrac{50. \text{ g } C_6H_{12}O_6}{100 \text{ mL solution}} \times \dfrac{1 \text{ mole } C_6H_{12}O_6}{180.16 \text{ g } C_6H_{12}O_6} \times \dfrac{1 \text{ osmole}}{1 \text{ mole } C_6H_{12}O_6} \times \dfrac{1000 \text{ mL solution}}{1 \text{ L solution}}$$
$$= 2.8 \text{ Osm (2 SFs)}$$

9.83 A red blood cell has the same osmotic pressure as a 5% (m/v) glucose solution or a 0.9% (m/v) NaCl solution. In a hypotonic solution (lower osmotic pressure), solvent flows from the hypotonic solution into the red blood cell. When a red blood cell is placed into a hypertonic solution (higher osmotic pressure), solvent (water) flows from the red blood cell to the hypertonic solution. Isotonic solutions have the same osmotic pressure, and a red blood cell in an isotonic solution will not change volume because the flow of solvent into and out of the cell is equal.

     a. Distilled water is a hypotonic solution when compared with a red blood cell's contents.

     b. A 1% (m/v) glucose solution is a hypotonic solution.

     c. A 0.9% (m/v) NaCl solution is isotonic with a red blood cell's contents.

     d. A 15% (m/v) glucose solution is a hypertonic solution.

9.85 Colloids cannot pass through the semipermeable dialysis membrane; water and solutions freely pass through semipermeable membranes.

     a. Sodium and chloride ions will both pass through the membrane into the distilled water.

     b. The amino acid alanine can pass through a dialysis membrane; the colloid starch will not.

    c. Sodium and chloride ions will both be present in the water surrounding the dialysis bag; the colloid starch will not.

    d. Urea will diffuse through the dialysis bag into the surrounding water.

9.87 **a.** In her pre-dialysis blood test, Michelle has higher than normal serum values of K^+, Na^+, and Cl^-.

    b. In her pre-dialysis blood test, Michelle has lower than normal serum values of Ca^{2+} and Mg^{2+}.

    c. The levels of Ca^{2+} and Mg^{2+} in Michelle's blood serum need to be increased by dialysis.

    d. The levels of K^+, Na^+, and Cl^- in Michelle's blood serum need to be decreased by dialysis.

9.89 **a.** 1; A solution will form because both the solute and the solvent are polar.

    b. 2; Two layers will form because one component is nonpolar and the other is polar.

    c. 1; A solution will form because both the solute and the solvent are nonpolar.

9.91 **a.** 3; A nonelectrolyte will show no dissociation.

    b. 1; A weak electrolyte will show some dissociation, producing a few ions, but mostly remaining as molecules.

    c. 2; A strong electrolyte will be completely dissociated into ions.

9.93 **a.** Beaker 3; Solid silver chloride (AgCl) will precipitate when the two solutions are mixed.

    b. $NaCl(aq) + AgNO_3(aq) \longrightarrow AgCl(s) + NaNO_3(aq)$

    $Na^+\cancel{(aq)} + Cl^-(aq) + Ag^+(aq) + \cancel{NO_3^-(aq)} \longrightarrow AgCl(s) + Na^+\cancel{(aq)} + \cancel{NO_3^-(aq)}$

    c. $Ag^+(aq) + Cl^-(aq) \longrightarrow AgCl(s)$ Net ionic equation

9.95 A "brine" saltwater solution has a high concentration of Na^+ and Cl^- ions, which is hypertonic to the cucumber. The skin of the cucumber acts like a semipermeable membrane; therefore, water flows from the more dilute solution inside the cucumber into the more concentrated brine solution that surrounds it. The loss of water causes the cucumber to become a wrinkled pickle.

9.97 **a.** 2; Water will flow into the B (8% starch solution) side.

    b. 1; Water will continue to flow equally in both directions; no change in volumes.

    c. 3; Water will flow into the A (5% sucrose solution) side.

    d. 2; Water will flow into the B (1% sucrose solution) side.

9.99 Because iodine is a nonpolar molecule, it will dissolve in hexane, a nonpolar solvent. Iodine does not dissolve in water because water is a polar solvent.

9.101 At 20 °C, KNO_3 has a solubility of 32 g of KNO_3 in 100 g of H_2O.

    a. 200. g of H_2O will dissolve:

$$200. \text{ g } \cancel{H_2O} \times \frac{32 \text{ g } KNO_3}{100 \text{ g } \cancel{H_2O}} = 64 \text{ g of } KNO_3 \text{ (2 SFs)}$$

    Because 32 g of KNO_3 is less than the maximum amount that can dissolve in 200. g of H_2O at 20 °C, the KNO_3 solution is unsaturated.

    b. 50. g of H_2O will dissolve:

$$50. \text{ g } \cancel{H_2O} \times \frac{32 \text{ g } KNO_3}{100 \text{ g } \cancel{H_2O}} = 16 \text{ g of } KNO_3 \text{ (2 SFs)}$$

    Because 19 g of KNO_3 exceeds the maximum amount that can dissolve in 50. g of H_2O at 20 °C, the KNO_3 solution is saturated, and excess undissolved KNO_3 will be present on the bottom of the container.

    c. 150. g of H_2O will dissolve:

$$150. \text{ g } \cancel{H_2O} \times \frac{32 \text{ g } KNO_3}{100 \text{ g } \cancel{H_2O}} = 48 \text{ g of } KNO_3 \text{ (2 SFs)}$$

Because 68 g of KNO_3 exceeds the maximum amount that can dissolve in 150. g of H_2O at 20 °C, the KNO_3 solution is saturated, and excess undissolved KNO_3 will be present on the bottom of the container.

9.103 a. K^+ salts are soluble.
   b. The SO_4^{2-} salt of Mg^{2+} is soluble.
   c. The salt containing S^{2-} and Cu^{2+} is insoluble.
   d. Salts containing NO_3^- ions are soluble.
   e. The salt containing OH^- and Ca^{2+} is insoluble.

9.105 a. Solid silver chloride (AgCl) forms:

$$AgNO_3(aq) + LiCl(aq) \longrightarrow AgCl(s) + LiNO_3(aq)$$
$$Ag^+(aq) + \cancel{NO_3^-(aq)} + \cancel{Li^+(aq)} + Cl^-(aq) \longrightarrow AgCl(s) + \cancel{Li^+(aq)} + \cancel{NO_3^-(aq)}$$
$$Ag^+(aq) + Cl^-(aq) \longrightarrow AgCl(s) \quad \text{Net ionic equation}$$

   b. none; no solid forms; salts containing K^+ and Na^+ are soluble.

   c. Solid barium sulfate ($BaSO_4$) forms:

$$Na_2SO_4(aq) + BaCl_2(aq) \longrightarrow BaSO_4(s) + 2NaCl(aq)$$
$$2\cancel{Na^+(aq)} + SO_4^{2-}(aq) + Ba^{2+}(aq) + 2\cancel{Cl^-(aq)} \longrightarrow BaSO_4(s) + 2\cancel{Na^+(aq)} + 2\cancel{Cl^-(aq)}$$
$$Ba^{2+}(aq) + SO_4^{2-}(aq) \longrightarrow BaSO_4(s) \quad \text{Net ionic equation}$$

9.107 mass of solution = 15.5 g Na_2SO_4 + 75.5 g H_2O = 91.0 g of solution

$$\frac{15.5 \text{ g } Na_2SO_4}{91.0 \text{ g solution}} \times 100\% = 17.0\% \text{ (m/m) } Na_2SO_4 \text{ solution (3 SFs)}$$

9.109 $4.5 \text{ mL } \cancel{\text{propyl alcohol}} \times \dfrac{100 \text{ mL solution}}{12 \text{ mL } \cancel{\text{propyl alcohol}}} = 38$ mL of propyl alcohol solution (2 SFs)

9.111 $86.0 \text{ g } \cancel{\text{KOH}} \times \dfrac{100 \text{ mL } \cancel{\text{solution}}}{12 \text{ g } \cancel{\text{KOH}}} \times \dfrac{1 \text{ L solution}}{1000 \text{ mL } \cancel{\text{solution}}} = 0.72$ L of KOH solution (2 SFs)

9.113 $\dfrac{8.0 \text{ g } \cancel{\text{NaOH}}}{400. \text{ mL } \cancel{\text{solution}}} \times \dfrac{1 \text{ mole NaOH}}{40.00 \text{ g } \cancel{\text{NaOH}}} \times \dfrac{1000 \text{ mL } \cancel{\text{solution}}}{1 \text{ L solution}} = 0.50$ M NaOH solution (2 SFs)

9.115 a. $2.5 \text{ L } \cancel{\text{solution}} \times \dfrac{3.0 \text{ moles } \cancel{Al(NO_3)_3}}{1 \text{ L } \cancel{\text{solution}}} \times \dfrac{213.0 \text{ g } Al(NO_3)_3}{1 \text{ mole } \cancel{Al(NO_3)_3}}$
     = 1600 g of $Al(NO_3)_3$ (2 SFs)

   b. $75 \text{ mL } \cancel{\text{solution}} \times \dfrac{1 \text{ L } \cancel{\text{solution}}}{1000 \text{ mL } \cancel{\text{solution}}} \times \dfrac{0.50 \text{ mole } \cancel{C_6H_{12}O_6}}{1 \text{ L } \cancel{\text{solution}}} \times \dfrac{180.16 \text{ g } C_6H_{12}O_6}{1 \text{ mole } \cancel{C_6H_{12}O_6}}$
     = 6.8 g of $C_6H_{12}O_6$ (2 SFs)

   c. $235 \text{ mL } \cancel{\text{solution}} \times \dfrac{1 \text{ L } \cancel{\text{solution}}}{1000 \text{ mL } \cancel{\text{solution}}} \times \dfrac{1.80 \text{ moles } \cancel{\text{LiCl}}}{1 \text{ L } \cancel{\text{solution}}} \times \dfrac{42.39 \text{ g LiCl}}{1 \text{ mole } \cancel{\text{LiCl}}}$
     = 17.9 g of LiCl (3 SFs)

9.117 $C_1V_1 = C_2V_2$

   a. $C_2 = C_1 \times \dfrac{V_1}{V_2} = 0.200 \text{ M} \times \dfrac{25.0 \text{ } \cancel{\text{mL}}}{50.0 \text{ } \cancel{\text{mL}}} = 0.100$ M NaBr solution (3 SFs)

   b. $C_2 = C_1 \times \dfrac{V_1}{V_2} = 12.0\% \times \dfrac{15.0 \text{ } \cancel{\text{mL}}}{40.0 \text{ } \cancel{\text{mL}}} = 4.50\%$ (m/v) K_2SO_4 solution (3 SFs)

   c. $C_2 = C_1 \times \dfrac{V_1}{V_2} = 6.00 \text{ M} \times \dfrac{75.0 \text{ } \cancel{\text{mL}}}{255 \text{ } \cancel{\text{mL}}} = 1.76$ M NaOH solution (3 SFs)

9.119 $C_1 V_1 = C_2 V_2$

    a. $V_1 = V_2 \times \dfrac{C_2}{C_1} = 250 \text{ mL} \times \dfrac{3.0 \, \%}{10.0 \, \%} = 75 \text{ mL of the HCl solution (2 SFs)}$

    b. $V_1 = V_2 \times \dfrac{C_2}{C_1} = 500. \text{ mL} \times \dfrac{0.90 \, \%}{5.0 \, \%} = 90. \text{ mL of the NaCl solution (2 SFs)}$

    c. $V_1 = V_2 \times \dfrac{C_2}{C_1} = 350. \text{ mL} \times \dfrac{2.00 \text{ M}}{6.00 \text{ M}} = 117 \text{ mL of the NaOH solution (3 SFs)}$

9.121 a. A solution of 0.580 mole of the nonelectrolyte lactose in 1.00 kg of water contains 0.580 mole of particles in 1.00 kg of water and has a freezing point change of

$$0.580 \text{ mole particles} \times \frac{1.86 \,°C}{1 \text{ mole particles}} = 1.08 \,°C$$

The freezing point would be $0.00 \,°C - 1.08 \,°C = -1.08 \,°C$

    b. $45.0 \text{ g KCl} \times \dfrac{1 \text{ mole KCl}}{74.55 \text{ g KCl}} = 0.604 \text{ mole of KCl (3 SFs)}$

A solution of 0.604 mole of the strong electrolyte KCl in 1.00 kg of water contains 1.21 moles of particles $(0.604$ mole of K^+ and 0.604 mole of $Cl^-)$ in 1.00 kg of water and has a freezing point change of

$$1.21 \text{ moles particles} \times \frac{1.86 \,°C}{1 \text{ mole particles}} = 2.25 \,°C$$

The freezing point would be $0.00 \,°C - 2.25 \,°C = -2.25 \,°C$

    c. A solution of 1.5 moles of the strong electrolyte K_3PO_4 in 1.00 kg of water contains 6.0 moles of particles $(4.5$ moles of K^+ and 1.5 moles of $PO_4^{3-})$ in 1.00 kg of water and has a freezing point change of

$$6.0 \text{ moles particles} \times \frac{1.86 \,°C}{1 \text{ mole particles}} = 11 \,°C$$

The freezing point would be $0.00 \,°C - 11 \,°C = -11 \,°C$

9.123 $450 \text{ mg Al(OH)}_3 \times \dfrac{1 \text{ g Al(OH)}_3}{1000 \text{ mg Al(OH)}_3} \times \dfrac{1 \text{ mole Al(OH)}_3}{78.00 \text{ g Al(OH)}_3} \times \dfrac{3 \text{ moles HCl}}{1 \text{ mole Al(OH)}_3}$

    $\times \dfrac{1 \text{ L solution}}{0.20 \text{ mole HCl}} \times \dfrac{1000 \text{ mL solution}}{1 \text{ L solution}} = 87 \text{ mL of the HCl solution (2 SFs)}$

9.125 $1 \text{ mole NaCl}(s) \longrightarrow 1 \text{ mole Na}^+(aq) + 1 \text{ mole Cl}^-(aq) = 2 \text{ moles of particles} = 2 \text{ osmoles}$

$$\frac{0.45 \text{ g NaCl}}{100 \text{ mL solution}} \times \frac{1 \text{ mole NaCl}}{58.44 \text{ g NaCl}} \times \frac{2 \text{ osmoles}}{1 \text{ mole NaCl}} \times \frac{1000 \text{ mL solution}}{1 \text{ L solution}} = 0.15 \text{ Osm (2 SFs)}$$

9.127 A dialysis solution contains no sodium or urea so that these substances will flow out of the blood into the dialyzing solution. High levels of potassium are maintained in the dialyzing solution so that the potassium will dialyze into the blood to increase the K^+ level in the bloodstream back to a more normal range.

9.129 a. mass of NaCl = 25.50 g − 24.10 g = 1.40 g of NaCl

    mass of solution = 36.15 g − 24.10 g = 12.05 g of solution

$$\text{mass percent (m/m)} = \frac{1.40 \text{ g NaCl}}{12.05 \text{ g solution}} \times 100\% = 11.6\% \text{ (m/m) NaCl solution (3 SFs)}$$

b. molarity (M) $= \dfrac{1.40 \text{ g NaCl}}{10.0 \text{ mL solution}} \times \dfrac{1 \text{ mole NaCl}}{58.44 \text{ g NaCl}} \times \dfrac{1000 \text{ mL solution}}{1 \text{ L solution}}$

$= 2.40 \text{ M NaCl solution (3 SFs)}$

c. $C_1 V_1 = C_2 V_2 \quad C_2 = C_1 \times \dfrac{V_1}{V_2} = 2.40 \text{ M} \times \dfrac{10.0 \text{ mL}}{60.0 \text{ mL}} = 0.400 \text{ M NaCl solution (3 SFs)}$

9.131 At 18 °C, KF has a solubility of 92 g of KF in 100 g of H_2O.

a. 25 g of H_2O will dissolve:

$25 \text{ g } H_2O \times \dfrac{92 \text{ g KF}}{100 \text{ g } H_2O} = 23 \text{ g of KF (2 SFs)}$

Because 35 g of KF exceeds the maximum amount that can dissolve in 25 g of H_2O at 18 °C, the KF solution is saturated, and excess undissolved KF will be present on the bottom of the container.

b. 50. g of H_2O will dissolve:

$50. \text{ g } H_2O \times \dfrac{92 \text{ g KF}}{100 \text{ g } H_2O} = 46 \text{ g of KF (2 SFs)}$

Because 42 g of KF is less than the maximum amount that can dissolve in 50. g of H_2O at 18 °C, the solution is unsaturated.

c. 150. g of H_2O will dissolve:

$150. \text{ g } H_2O \times \dfrac{92 \text{ g KF}}{100 \text{ g } H_2O} = 140 \text{ g of KF (2 SFs)}$

Because 145 g of KF exceeds the maximum amount that can dissolve in 150. g of H_2O at 18 °C, the KF solution is saturated, and excess undissolved KF will be present on the bottom of the container.

9.133 mass of solution: 70.0 g HNO_3 + 130.0 g H_2O = 200.0 g of solution

a. $\dfrac{70.0 \text{ g } HNO_3}{200.0 \text{ g solution}} \times 100\% = 35.0\% \text{ (m/m) } HNO_3 \text{ solution (3 SFs)}$

b. $200.0 \text{ g solution} \times \dfrac{1 \text{ mL solution}}{1.21 \text{ g solution}} = 165 \text{ mL of solution (3 SFs)}$

c. $\dfrac{70.0 \text{ g } HNO_3}{165 \text{ mL solution}} \times 100\% = 42.4\% \text{ (m/v) } HNO_3 \text{ solution (3 SFs)}$

d. $\dfrac{70.0 \text{ g } HNO_3}{165 \text{ mL solution}} \times \dfrac{1 \text{ mole } HNO_3}{63.02 \text{ g } HNO_3} \times \dfrac{1000 \text{ mL solution}}{1 \text{ L solution}}$

$= 6.73 \text{ M } HNO_3 \text{ solution (3 SFs)}$

9.135 a. total positive charge $= \dfrac{45 \text{ mEq Na}^+}{1 \text{ L solution}} + \dfrac{20. \text{ mEq K}^+}{1 \text{ L solution}}$

$= \dfrac{65 \text{ mEq positive charge}}{1 \text{ L solution}} \text{ (2 SFs)}$

b. total negative charge $= \dfrac{35 \text{ mEq Cl}^-}{1 \text{ L solution}} + \dfrac{30. \text{ mEq citrate}^{3-}}{1 \text{ L solution}}$

$= \dfrac{65 \text{ mEq negative charge}}{1 \text{ L solution}} \text{ (2 SFs)}$

c. Na^+: $\dfrac{45 \text{ mEq}}{1 \text{ L solution}} \times \dfrac{1 \text{ Eq}}{1000 \text{ mEq}} \times \dfrac{1 \text{ mole Na}^+}{1 \text{ Eq}} \times \dfrac{1 \text{ osmole Na}^+}{1 \text{ mole Na}^+} = 0.045 \text{ Osm Na}^+$

K^+: $\dfrac{20. \text{ mEq}}{1 \text{ L solution}} \times \dfrac{1 \text{ Eq}}{1000 \text{ mEq}} \times \dfrac{1 \text{ mole K}^+}{1 \text{ Eq}} \times \dfrac{1 \text{ osmole K}^+}{1 \text{ mole K}^+} = 0.020 \text{ Osm K}^+$

Cl^-: $\dfrac{35 \text{ mEq}}{1 \text{ L solution}} \times \dfrac{1 \text{ Eq}}{1000 \text{ mEq}} \times \dfrac{1 \text{ mole Cl}^-}{1 \text{ Eq}} \times \dfrac{1 \text{ osmole Cl}^-}{1 \text{ mole Cl}^-} = 0.035 \text{ Osm Cl}^-$

$citrate^{3-}$: $\dfrac{30. \text{ mEq}}{1 \text{ L solution}} \times \dfrac{1 \text{ Eq}}{1000 \text{ mEq}} \times \dfrac{1 \text{ mole citrate}^{3-}}{3 \text{ Eq}} \times \dfrac{1 \text{ osmole citrate}^{3-}}{1 \text{ mole citrate}^{3-}}$

$\qquad = 0.010 \text{ Osm citrate}^{3-}$

glucose: $\dfrac{25 \text{ g glucose}}{1 \text{ L solution}} \times \dfrac{1 \text{ mole glucose}}{180.16 \text{ g glucose}} \times \dfrac{1 \text{ osmole glucose}}{1 \text{ mole glucose}} = 0.14 \text{ Osm glucose}$

$\therefore$ total osmolarity of solution $= 0.045 \text{ Osm Na}^+ + 0.020 \text{ Osm K}^+ + 0.035 \text{ Osm Cl}^-$
$\qquad + 0.010 \text{ Osm citrate}^{3-} + 0.14 \text{ Osm glucose}$

$\qquad = 0.25 \text{ Osm } (2 \text{ SFs})$

10
Reaction Rates and Chemical Equilibrium

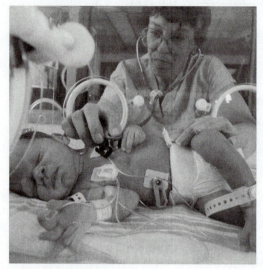

Credit: Fuse/Getty Images

Andrew was born 12 weeks early with infant respiratory distress syndrome (IRDS). After treatment with surfactants and an air–oxygen mixture for several days, he could breathe on his own. As a two-year-old, blood tests showed that his red-blood cell count and blood oxygen levels were below normal, and he was diagnosed with children's iron-deficiency anemia. The hemoglobin (Hb) in red blood cells contains iron, which carries oxygen from the lungs to the muscles and tissues of the body. There is an equilibrium between the gain of oxygen by the hemoglobin in the alveoli and the loss of oxygen at the tissues.

$$Hb(aq) + O_2(aq) \rightleftharpoons HbO_2(aq)$$

In the lungs where the O_2 is high, the forward reaction between Hb and O_2 is faster, which forms more of the product HbO_2. In the tissues where the O_2 concentration is low, the reverse reaction is faster, which forms more reactant Hb and releases oxygen.

Treatment for Andrew's anemia includes a diet that includes foods with high levels of iron such as chicken, fish, spinach, iron-fortified cereal, eggs, peas, beans, peanut butter, and whole-grain bread. After eight months, his hemoglobin increased to the normal range. In anemia, how does the low concentration of hemoglobin affect the concentration of O_2 transported to the tissues?

CHAPTER READINESS*

 Key Math Skills

- Solving Equations (1.4D)
- Writing Numbers in Scientific Notation (1.4F)

Core Chemistry Skills

- Using Significant Figures in Calculations (2.3)
- Balancing a Chemical Equation (7.1)
- Calculating Concentration (9.4)

* These Key Math Skills and Core Chemistry Skills from previous chapters are listed here for your review as you proceed to the new material in this chapter.

10.1 Rates of Reactions

Learning Goal: Describe how temperature, concentration, and catalysts affect the rate of a reaction.

- The rate of a reaction is the speed at which reactants are consumed or products are formed.
- At higher temperatures, reaction rates increase because reactants move faster, collide more often, and produce more collisions, which have the required energy of activation.
- Increasing the concentrations of reactants or lowering the energy of activation by adding a catalyst increases the rate of a reaction.
- The reaction rate slows when the temperature or the concentration of a reactant is decreased.

♦ **Learning Exercise 10.1A**

Indicate the effect of each of the following on the rate of a chemical reaction as:

> increase (I) decrease (D) no effect (N)

1. _____ adding a catalyst

2. _____ running the reaction at a lower temperature

3. _____ doubling the concentrations of the reactants

4. _____ removing a catalyst

5. _____ running the experiment under the same conditions in a different laboratory

6. _____ increasing the temperature

7. _____ using lower concentrations of reactants

When a catalyst lowers the activation energy, the reaction occurs at a faster rate.

Answers   1. I   2. D   3. I   4. D
             5. N   6. I   7. D

♦ **Learning Exercise 10.1B**

For the following reaction, $NO_2(g) + CO(g) \longrightarrow NO(g) + CO_2(g)$, indicate the effect of each of the following on the reaction rate as:

> increase (I) decrease (D) no effect (N)

1. _____ adding CO

2. _____ running the experiment under the same conditions two days later

3. _____ removing NO_2

4. _____ adding a catalyst

5. _____ adding NO_2

Answers   1. I   2. N   3. D   4. I   5. I

10.2 Chemical Equilibrium

Learning Goal: Use the concept of reversible reactions to explain chemical equilibrium.

- A reversible reaction proceeds in both the forward and reverse directions.
- Chemical equilibrium is achieved when the rate of the forward reaction becomes equal to the rate of the reverse reaction.
- In a system at equilibrium, there is no change in the concentrations of reactants and products.
- At equilibrium, the concentrations of reactants are typically different from the concentrations of products.

♦ Learning Exercise 10.2

Indicate whether each of the following indicates a system at equilibrium (E) or not (NE):

[Reactants] decrease

Equilibrium reached

[Products] increase

Progress of Reaction

1. _____ The rate of the forward reaction is faster than the rate of the reverse reaction.

2. _____ There is no change in the concentrations of reactants and products.

3. _____ The rate of the forward reaction is equal to the rate of the reverse reaction.

4. _____ The concentrations of reactants are decreasing.

5. _____ The concentrations of products are increasing.

Equilibrium is reached when there are no further changes in the concentrations of reactants and products.

Answers   **1.** NE   **2.** E   **3.** E   **4.** NE   **5.** NE

10.3   Equilibrium Constants

Learning Goal: Calculate the equilibrium constant for a reversible reaction given the concentrations of reactants and products at equilibrium.

- The equilibrium constant expression for a system at equilibrium is the ratio of the concentrations of the products to the concentrations of the reactants with the concentration of each substance raised to an exponent that is equal to its coefficient in the balanced chemical equation.

- For the general equation, $aA + bB \rightleftharpoons cC + dD$, the equilibrium constant expression is written as:

$$K_c = \frac{[C]^c[D]^d}{[A]^a[B]^b}$$

- The square brackets around each substance indicate that the concentrations are given in moles/L (M).

Guide to Writing the Equilibrium Constant Expression	
STEP 1	Write the balanced chemical equation.
STEP 2	Write the concentrations of the products as the numerator and the reactants as the denominator.
STEP 3	Write any coefficient in the equation as an exponent.

♦ Learning Exercise 10.3A

Write the equilibrium constant expression (K_c) for each of the following reactions:

⊗ CORE CHEMISTRY SKILL

Writing the Equilibrium Constant Expression

a. $2SO_3(g) \rightleftharpoons 2SO_2(g) + O_2(g)$

b. $2NO(g) + Br_2(g) \rightleftharpoons 2NOBr(g)$

c. $N_2(g) + 3H_2(g) \rightleftharpoons 2NH_3(g)$

d. $2NO_2(g) \rightleftharpoons N_2O_4(g)$

Answers

a. $K_c = \dfrac{[SO_2]^2[O_2]}{[SO_3]^2}$

b. $K_c = \dfrac{[NOBr]^2}{[NO]^2[Br_2]}$

c. $K_c = \dfrac{[NH_3]^2}{[N_2][H_2]^3}$

d. $K_c = \dfrac{[N_2O_4]}{[NO_2]^2}$

Guide to Calculating the K_c Value	
STEP 1	State the given and needed quantities.
STEP 2	Write the K_c expression for the equilibrium.
STEP 3	Substitute equilibrium (molar) concentrations and calculate K_c.

♦ **Learning Exercise 10.3B**

⚛ CORE CHEMISTRY SKILL

Calculate the K_c value using the following equilibrium concentrations: Calculating an Equilibrium Constant

a. $H_2(g) + I_2(g) \rightleftharpoons 2HI(g)$ $[H_2] = 0.28$ M $[I_2] = 0.28$ M $[HI] = 2.0$ M

b. $2NO_2(g) \rightleftharpoons N_2(g) + 2O_2(g)$ $[NO_2] = 0.60$ M $[N_2] = 0.010$ M $[O_2] = 0.020$ M

c. $N_2(g) + 3H_2(g) \rightleftharpoons 2NH_3(g)$ $[N_2] = 0.50$ M $[H_2] = 0.20$ M $[NH_3] = 0.80$ M

Answers

a. $K_c = \dfrac{[HI]^2}{[H_2][I_2]} = \dfrac{[2.0]^2}{[0.28][0.28]} = 51$

b. $K_c = \dfrac{[N_2][O_2]^2}{[NO_2]^2} = \dfrac{[0.010][0.020]^2}{[0.60]^2} = 1.1 \times 10^{-5}$

c. $K_c = \dfrac{[NH_3]^2}{[N_2][H_2]^3} = \dfrac{[0.80]^2}{[0.50][0.20]^3} = 1.6 \times 10^2$

10.4   Using Equilibrium Constants

Learning Goal: Use an equilibrium constant to predict the extent of reaction and to calculate equilibrium concentrations.

- A large K_c indicates that a reaction at equilibrium has more product(s) than reactant(s); a small K_c indicates that a reaction at equilibrium has more reactant(s) than product(s).
- The concentration of a component in an equilibrium mixture is calculated from the K_c and the concentrations of all the other components.

At equilibrium, a reaction with a large K_c contains mostly products, whereas a reaction with a small K_c contains mostly reactants.

♦ Learning Exercise 10.4A

Consider the reaction $2NOBr(g) \rightleftharpoons 2NO(g) + Br_2(g)$

   a. Write the equilibrium constant expression (K_c) for the reaction.

   b. If the equilibrium constant for the reaction is 2×10^3, does the equilibrium mixture contain mostly reactants, mostly products, or both reactants and products? Explain.

Answers

   a. $K_c = \dfrac{[NO]^2[Br_2]}{[NOBr]^2}$

   b. A large K_c (>1) means that the equilibrium mixture contains mostly products.

♦ Learning Exercise 10.4B

Consider the reaction $2HI(g) \rightleftharpoons H_2(g) + I_2(g)$

   a. Write the equilibrium constant expression (K_c) for the reaction.

   b. If the equilibrium constant for the reaction is 1.6×10^{-2}, does the equilibrium mixture contain mostly reactants, mostly products, or both reactants and products? Explain.

Answers

   a. $K_c = \dfrac{[H_2][I_2]}{[HI]^2}$

   b. A small K_c (<1) means that the equilibrium mixture contains mostly reactants.

Guide to Using the Equilibrium Constant	
STEP 1	State the given and needed quantities.
STEP 2	Write the K_c expression for the equilibrium and solve for the needed concentration.
STEP 3	Substitute the equilibrium (molar) concentrations and calculate the needed concentration.

♦ **Learning Exercise 10.4C**

Calculate the concentration of the indicated component for each of the following equilibrium systems:

⚛ CORE CHEMISTRY SKILL

Calculating Equilibrium
Concentrations

    a. $PCl_5(g) \rightleftharpoons PCl_3(g) + Cl_2(g)$ $K_c = 1.2 \times 10^{-2}$

       $[PCl_5] = 2.50\ M$ $[PCl_3] = 0.50\ M$ $[Cl_2] = ?$

    b. $CO(g) + H_2O(g) \rightleftharpoons CO_2(g) + H_2(g)$ $K_c = 1.6$

       $[CO] = 1.0\ M$ $[H_2O] = 0.80\ M$ $[CO_2] = ?$ $[H_2] = 1.2\ M$

Answers

    a. $K_c = \dfrac{[PCl_3][Cl_2]}{[PCl_5]}$ $[Cl_2] = \dfrac{K_c\,[PCl_5]}{[PCl_3]} = \dfrac{1.2 \times 10^{-2}\,[2.50]}{[0.50]} = 6.0 \times 10^{-2}\ M$

    b. $K_c = \dfrac{[CO_2][H_2]}{[CO][H_2O]}$ $[CO_2] = \dfrac{K_c\,[CO][H_2O]}{[H_2]} = \dfrac{1.6\,[1.0][0.80]}{[1.2]} = 1.1\ M$

10.5 Changing Equilibrium Conditions: Le Châtelier's Principle

Learning Goal: Use Le Châtelier's principle to describe the changes made in equilibrium concentrations when reaction conditions change.

⚛ CORE CHEMISTRY SKILL

Using Le Châtelier's Principle

- Le Châtelier's principle states that a change in the concentration of a reactant or product, the temperature, or the volume of gases will cause the reaction to shift in the direction that relieves the stress.

- The addition of a catalyst does not affect the equilibrium position of a reaction.

Key Terms for Sections 10.1–10.5

Match the following terms with the correct definition below:

    a. activation energy   **b.** equilibrium   **c.** catalyst
    d. equilibrium constant expression   **e.** Le Châtelier's principle   **f.** reversible reaction

1. _____ a substance that lowers the activation energy and increases the rate of reaction

2. _____ the ratio of the concentrations of products to those of the reactants raised to exponents equal to their coefficients

3. _____ the energy required to convert reactants to products in a chemical reaction

4. _____ states that a stress placed on a reaction at equilibrium causes the equilibrium to shift in the direction that relieves the stress

5. _____ a system in which the rate of the forward reaction is equal to the rate of the reverse reaction

6. _____ occurs when a reaction consists of both a forward reaction and a reverse reaction

Answers   **1.** c   **2.** d   **3.** a   **4.** e   **5.** b   **6.** f

♦ **Learning Exercise 10.5A**

Identify the effect (**A**, **B**, or **C**) of each of the following changes on the reaction equilibrium:

$$N_2(g) + O_2(g) + 180 \text{ kJ} \rightleftharpoons 2NO(g)$$

    A. shifts in the direction of the products
    B. shifts in the direction of the reactants
    C. no change

1. _____ adding more $O_2(g)$ **2.** _____ removing some $N_2(g)$

3. _____ removing some $NO(g)$ **4.** _____ increasing the temperature

5. _____ reducing the volume of the container   **6.** _____ increasing the volume of the container

Answers   **1.** A   **2.** B   **3.** A   **4.** A   **5.** C   **6.** C

♦ **Learning Exercise 10.5B**

Identify the effect (**A**, **B**, or **C**) of each of the following changes on the reaction equilibrium:

$$2NOBr(g) \rightleftharpoons 2NO(g) + Br_2(g) + 340 \text{ kJ}$$

    A. shifts in the direction of the products
    B. shifts in the direction of the reactants
    C. no change

1. _____ adding more $NO(g)$ **2.** _____ removing some $Br_2(g)$

3. _____ removing some $NOBr(g)$ **4.** _____ adding heat

5. _____ decreasing the temperature   **6.** _____ increasing the volume of the container

Answers   **1.** B   **2.** A   **3.** B   **4.** B   **5.** A   **6.** A

♦ **Learning Exercise 10.5C**

Use the following diagram of a reaction at equilibrium (the white atoms are nitrogen atoms and the black atoms are oxygen atoms) to answer questions **a** to **f**:

a. Write the balanced chemical equation for the reaction.

b. Write the equilibrium constant expression for the reaction.

Answer **c** to **f** with shifts in the direction of the products, shifts in the direction of the reactants, or no change.

c. What is the effect on the equilibrium when more NO_3 is added? _____

d. What is the effect on the equilibrium when more NO_2 is added? _____

e. What is the effect on the equilibrium when some NO is removed? _____

f. What is the effect on the equilibrium when the volume is decreased? _____

Answers

 a. $2NO_2(g) \rightleftharpoons NO_3(g) + NO(g)$

 b. $K_c = \dfrac{[NO_3][NO]}{[NO_2]^2}$

 c. shifts in the direction of the reactants
 d. shifts in the direction of the products
 e. shifts in the direction of the products
 f. no change

Checklist for Chapter 10

You are ready to take the Practice Test for Chapter 10. Be sure that you have accomplished the following learning goals for this chapter. If not, review the section listed at the end of the goal. Then apply your new skills and understanding to the Practice Test.

After studying Chapter 10, I can successfully:

_____ Describe the factors that increase or decrease the rate of a reaction. (10.1)

_____ Write the equations for the forward and reverse reactions of a reversible reaction. (10.2)

_____ Explain how equilibrium occurs when the rate of a forward reaction is equal to the rate of a reverse reaction. (10.2)

_____ Write the equilibrium constant expression for a reaction system at equilibrium. (10.3)

_____ Calculate the equilibrium constant from the equilibrium concentrations. (10.3)

_____ Use the equilibrium constant to determine whether a reaction favors the reactants or products. (10.4)

_____ Use the equilibrium constant to determine the equilibrium concentration of a component in the reaction. (10.4)

_____ Use Le Châtelier's principle to describe the shift in a system at equilibrium when stress is applied to the system. (10.5)

Practice Test for Chapter 10

1. The number of molecular collisions increases when (10.1)
   A. more reactants are added
   B. products are removed
   C. the energy of collision is below the energy of activation
   D. the reaction temperature is lowered
   E. the reacting molecules have an incorrect orientation upon impact

2. The energy of activation is lowered when (10.1)
   A. more reactants are added
   B. products are removed
   C. a catalyst is used
   D. the reaction temperature is lowered
   E. the reaction temperature is raised

3. Food deteriorates more slowly in a refrigerator because (10.1)
   A. more reactants are added
   B. products are removed
   C. the energy of activation is higher
   D. fewer collisions have the energy of activation
   E. collisions have the wrong orientation upon impact

4. A reaction reaches equilibrium when (10.2)
   A. the rate of the forward reaction is faster than the rate of the reverse reaction
   B. the rate of the reverse reaction is faster than the rate of the forward reaction
   C. the concentrations of reactants and products are changing
   D. fewer collisions have the energy of activation
   E. the rate of the forward reaction is equal to the rate of the reverse reaction

5. The equilibrium constant expression for the following reaction is (10.3)
   $$2NOCl(g) \rightleftharpoons 2NO(g) + Cl_2(g)$$

   A. $\dfrac{[NO][Cl_2]}{[NOCl]}$
   B. $\dfrac{[NOCl_2]^2}{[NO]^2[Cl_2]}$
   C. $\dfrac{[NOCl_2]}{[NO][Cl_2]}$

   D. $\dfrac{[NO]^2[Cl_2]}{[NOCl]}$
   E. $\dfrac{[NO]^2[Cl_2]}{[NOCl]^2}$

6. The equilibrium constant expression for the following reaction is (10.3)
   $$CO(g) + 2H_2(g) \rightleftharpoons CH_3OH(g)$$

   A. $[CO][2H_2]$
   B. $\dfrac{[CO][H_2]}{[CH_3OH]}$
   C. $\dfrac{[CH_3OH]}{[CO][H_2]^2}$

   D. $\dfrac{1}{[CH_3OH]}$
   E. $\dfrac{[CO][H_2]^2}{[CH_3OH]}$

7. The equilibrium constant expression for the following reaction is (10.3)

$$C_3H_8(g) + 5O_2(g) \rightleftharpoons 3CO_2(g) + 4H_2O(g)$$

A. $\dfrac{[CO_2][H_2O]}{[C_3H_8][O_2]}$

B. $\dfrac{[C_3H_8][O_2]^5}{[CO_2]^3[H_2O]^4}$

C. $\dfrac{[CO_2]^3[H_2O]^4}{[C_3H_8][O_2]^5}$

D. $[CO_2]^3[H_2O]^4$

E. $\dfrac{[CO_2]^3}{[C_3H_8][O_2]^5}$

8. The equilibrium equation that has the equilibrium constant expression $\dfrac{[H_2S]^2}{[H_2]^2[S_2]}$ is (10.3)

A. $H_2S(g) \rightleftharpoons H_2(g) + S_2(g)$
B. $2H_2S(g) \rightleftharpoons H_2(g) + S_2(g)$
C. $2H_2(g) + S_2(g) \rightleftharpoons 2H_2S(g)$
D. $2H_2S(g) \rightleftharpoons 2H_2(g)$
E. $2H_2(g) \rightleftharpoons 2H_2S(g)$

9. The value of the equilibrium constant for the following equation and concentrations is (10.3)

$$COBr_2(g) \rightleftharpoons CO(g) + Br_2(g)$$

$[COBr_2] = 0.93$ M $[CO] = [Br_2] = 0.42$ M

A. 0.19   B. 0.39   C. 0.42
D. 2.2   E. 5.3

10. The value of the equilibrium constant for the following equation and concentrations is (10.3)

$$2NO(g) + O_2(g) \rightleftharpoons 2NO_2(g)$$

$[NO] = 2.7$ M $[O_2] = 1.0$ M $[NO_2] = 3.0$ M

A. 0.81   B. 1.1   C. 1.2
D. 8.1   E. 9.0

11. Calculate the $[PCl_5]$ for the decomposition of PCl_5 that has a $K_c = 0.050$. (10.4)

$$PCl_5(g) \rightleftharpoons PCl_3(g) + Cl_2(g)$$

$[PCl_3] = [Cl_2] = 0.20$ M

A. 0.01 M   B. 0.050 M   C. 0.20 M
D. 0.40 M   E. 0.80 M

12. The reaction that has mostly products at equilibrium has a K_c value of (10.4)

A. 1.6×10^{-15} B. 2×10^{-11} C. 1.2×10^{-5}
D. 3×10^{-3} E. 1.4×10^5

13. The reaction that has mostly reactants at equilibrium has a K_c value of (10.4)

A. 1.1×10^{-4} B. 2×10^{-1} C. 1.2×10^2
D. 2×10^4 E. 1.3×10^{12}

14. The reaction that has about the same concentration of reactants and products at equilibrium has a K_c value of (10.4)

A. 1.4×10^{-12} B. 2×10^{-8} C. 1.2
D. 3×10^2 E. 1.3×10^7

For questions 15 through 19, answer A, B, or C for the correct change in equilibrium caused by each of the following: (10.5)

$$PCl_5(g) + heat \rightleftharpoons PCl_3(g) + Cl_2(g)$$

A. shifts in the direction of the products **B.** shifts in the direction of the reactants
C. no change

15. _____ adding more Cl_2 **16.** _____ increasing the temperature of the reaction

17. _____ removing some PCl_3 **18.** _____ decreasing the volume **19.** _____ removing some PCl_5

For questions 20 through 24, answer A, B, or C for the correct change in equilibrium caused by each of the following: (10.5)

A. shifts in the direction of the products **B.** shifts in the direction of the reactants
C. no change

$$2NO(g) + O_2(g) \rightleftharpoons 2NO_2(g) + heat$$

20. _____ adding more NO **21.** _____ increasing the temperature of the reaction

22. _____ adding a catalyst **23.** _____ decreasing the volume

24. _____ removing some NO_2

Answers to the Practice Test

1. A	**2.** C	**3.** D	**4.** E	**5.** E
6. C	**7.** C	**8.** C	**9.** A	**10.** C
11. E	**12.** E	**13.** A	**14.** C	**15.** B
16. B	**17.** A	**18.** A	**19.** B	**20.** A
21. B	**22.** C	**23.** A	**24.** A	

Reaction Rates and Chemical Equilibrium

Learning Goals

- Describe how temperature, concentration, and catalysts affect the rate of a reaction.
- Use the concept of reversible reactions to explain chemical equilibrium.
- Calculate the equilibrium constant for a reversible reaction given the concentrations of reactants and products at equilibrium.
- Use an equilibrium constant to predict the extent of reaction and to calculate equilibrium concentrations.
- Use Le Châtelier's principle to describe the changes made in equilibrium concentrations when reaction conditions change.

Chapter Outline

Chapter Opener: Neonatal Nurse

10.1 Rates of Reactions

Chemistry Link to the Environment: Catalytic Converters

10.2 Chemical Equilibrium

10.3 Equilibrium Constants

10.4 Using Equilibrium Constants

10.5 Changing Equilibrium Conditions: Le Châtelier's Principle

Chemistry Link to Health: Oxygen–Hemoglobin Equilibrium and Hypoxia

Chemistry Link to Health: Homeostasis: Regulation of Body Temperature

Clinical Update: An Iron-Rich Diet for Children's Anemia

⚛ Core Chemistry Skills

- Writing the Equilibrium Constant Expression (10.3)
- Calculating an Equilibrium Constant (10.3)
- Calculating Equilibrium Concentrations (10.4)
- Using Le Châtelier's Principle (10.5)

Selected Answers and Solutions to Text Problems

10.1 **a.** The rate of a reaction indicates how fast the products form or how fast the reactants are used up.

　　　b. At room temperature, more of the reactants will have the energy necessary to proceed to products (the activation energy) than at the lower temperature of the refrigerator, so the rate of formation of bread mold will be faster.

10.3 Adding $Br_2(g)$ molecules increases the concentration of reactants, which increases the number of collisions that take place between the reactants.

10.5 a. Adding more reactant increases the number of collisions that take place between the reactants, which increases the reaction rate.

b. Increasing the temperature increases the kinetic energy of the reactant molecules, which increases the number of collisions and makes more collisions effective. The rate of reaction will be increased.

c. Adding a catalyst lowers the energy of activation, which increases the reaction rate.

d. Removing a reactant decreases the number of collisions that take place between the reactants, which decreases the reaction rate.

10.7 A reversible reaction is one in which a forward reaction converts reactants to products, while a reverse reaction converts products to reactants.

10.9 a. When the rate of the forward reaction is faster than the rate of the reverse reaction, the process is not at equilibrium.

b. When the concentrations of the reactants and the products do not change, the process is at equilibrium.

c. When the rate of either the forward or reverse reaction does not change, the process is at equilibrium.

10.11 The reaction has reached equilibrium because the number of reactants and products does not change; the concentrations of A and B have not changed between 3 h and 4 h.

10.13 In the expression for K_c, the products are divided by the reactants, with each concentration raised to a power equal to its coefficient in the balanced chemical equation:

a. $K_c = \dfrac{[CS_2][H_2]^4}{[CH_4][H_2S]^2}$

b. $K_c = \dfrac{[N_2][O_2]}{[NO]^2}$

c. $K_c = \dfrac{[CS_2][O_2]^4}{[SO_3]^2[CO_2]}$

d. $K_c = \dfrac{[H_2]^3[CO]}{[CH_4][H_2O]}$

10.15 $K_c = \dfrac{[XY]^2}{[X_2][Y_2]} = \dfrac{[6]^2}{[1][1]} = 36$

10.17 $K_c = \dfrac{[NO_2]^2}{[N_2O_4]} = \dfrac{[0.21]^2}{[0.030]} = 1.5 \text{ (2 SFs)}$

10.19 $K_c = \dfrac{[CH_4][H_2O]}{[CO][H_2]^3} = \dfrac{[1.8][2.0]}{[0.51][0.30]^3} = 260 \text{ (2 SFs)}$

10.21 Calculate the value of K_c for each diagram and compare to the given value ($K_c = 4$).

for **A**: $K_c = \dfrac{[XY]^2}{[X_2][Y_2]} = \dfrac{[6]^2}{[1][1]} = 36$

for **B**: $K_c = \dfrac{[XY]^2}{[X_2][Y_2]} = \dfrac{[4]^2}{[2][2]} = 4$

for **C**: $K_c = \dfrac{[XY]^2}{[X_2][Y_2]} = \dfrac{[2]^2}{[3][3]} = 0.44$

Therefore, diagram **B** represents the equilibrium mixture.

10.23 a. A large K_c value indicates that the equilibrium mixture contains mostly products.

b. A large K_c value indicates that the equilibrium mixture contains mostly products.

c. A small K_c value indicates that the equilibrium mixture contains mostly reactants.

10.25 $K_c = \dfrac{[HI]^2}{[H_2][I_2]} = 54$

Rearrange the K_c expression to solve for $[H_2]$ and substitute in known values.

$$[H_2] = \dfrac{[HI]^2}{K_c[I_2]} = \dfrac{[0.030]^2}{54[0.015]} = 1.1 \times 10^{-3}\,M\ (2\ SFs)$$

10.27 $K_c = \dfrac{[NO]^2[Br_2]}{[NOBr]^2} = 2.0$

Rearrange the K_c expression to solve for $[NOBr]$ and substitute in known values.

$$[NOBr]^2 = \dfrac{[NO]^2[Br_2]}{K_c} = \dfrac{[2.0]^2[1.0]}{2.0} = 2.0$$

Take the square root of both sides of the equation.

$$[NOBr] = \sqrt{2.0} = 1.4\,M\ (2\ SFs)$$

10.29 a. Adding more reactant shifts equilibrium in the direction of the product.
   b. Adding more product shifts equilibrium in the direction of the reactants.
   c. Increasing the temperature of an endothermic reaction shifts equilibrium in the direction of the product.
   d. Increasing the volume of the container shifts the equilibrium in the direction of the reactants, which has more moles of gas.
   e. No shift in equilibrium occurs when a catalyst is added.

10.31 a. Adding more reactant shifts equilibrium in the direction of the product.
   b. Increasing the temperature of an endothermic reaction shifts equilibrium in the direction of the product to remove heat.
   c. Removing product shifts equilibrium in the direction of the product.
   d. No shift in equilibrium occurs when a catalyst is added.
   e. Removing reactant shifts equilibrium in the direction of the reactants.

10.33 a. When an athlete first arrives at high altitude, the oxygen concentration is decreased.
   b. Removing reactant shifts equilibrium in the direction of the reactants.

10.35 a. Adding more reactant shifts equilibrium in the direction of the products.
   b. Adding more product shifts equilibrium in the direction of the reactants.
   c. Removing reactant shifts equilibrium in the direction of the reactants.

10.37 Without enough iron, Andrew will not have sufficient hemoglobin. When Hb is decreased, the equilibrium shifts in the direction of the reactants, Hb and O_2.

10.39 a. $K_c = \dfrac{[CO_2][H_2O]^2}{[CH_4][O_2]^2}$

   b. $K_c = \dfrac{[N_2]^2[H_2O]^6}{[NH_3]^4[O_2]^3}$

   c. $K_c = \dfrac{[CH_4]}{[H_2]^2}$

10.41 At equilibrium, the diagram shows mostly products and a few reactants, so the equilibrium constant K_c for the reaction would have a large value.

10.43 T_2 is lower than T_1. This would cause the exothermic reaction shown to shift in the direction of the products to add heat; more product is seen in the T_2 diagram.

10.45 **a.** Increasing the temperature of an exothermic reaction shifts equilibrium in the direction of the reactants.
b. Decreasing volume favors the side of the reaction with fewer moles of gas, so there is a shift in the direction of the products.
c. Adding a catalyst does not shift equilibrium.
d. Adding more reactant shifts equilibrium in the direction of the products.

10.47 **a.** A large K_c value indicates that the equilibrium mixture contains mostly products.
b. A K_c value close to 1 indicates that the equilibrium mixture contains both reactants and products.
c. A small K_c value indicates that the equilibrium mixture contains mostly reactants.
d. A K_c value close to 1 indicates that the equilibrium mixture contains both reactants and products.

10.49 **a.** $K_c = \dfrac{[N_2][H_2]^3}{[NH_3]^2}$

b. $K_c = \dfrac{[3.0][0.50]^3}{[0.20]^2} = 9.4 \ (2 \text{ SFs})$

10.51 $K_c = \dfrac{[N_2O_4]}{[NO_2]^2} = 5.0$

Rearrange the K_c expression to solve for $[N_2O_4]$ and substitute in known values.

$[N_2O_4] = K_c[NO_2]^2 = 5.0[0.50]^2 = 1.3 \text{ M } (2 \text{ SFs})$

10.53 **a.** When the reactant $[O_2]$ increases, the rate of the forward reaction increases to shift the equilibrium in the direction of the products.
b. When the product $[O_2]$ increases, the rate of the reverse reaction increases to shift the equilibrium in the direction of the reactants.
c. When the reactant $[O_2]$ increases, the rate of the forward reaction increases to shift the equilibrium in the direction of the products.
d. When the product $[O_2]$ increases, the rate of the reverse reaction increases to shift the equilibrium in the direction of the reactants.

10.55 Decreasing the volume of an equilibrium mixture shifts the equilibrium in the direction of the side of the reaction that has the fewer number of moles of gas. No shift occurs when there are an equal number of moles of gas on both sides of the equation.
a. With 3 moles of gas on the reactant side and 2 moles of gas on the product side, decreasing the volume will shift equilibrium in the direction of the products.
b. With 2 moles of gas on the reactant side and 3 moles of gas on the product side, decreasing the volume will shift equilibrium in the direction of the reactants.
c. With 6 moles of gas on reactant side and 0 mole of gas on the product side, decreasing the volume will shift equilibrium in the direction of the products.
d. With 4 moles of gas on the reactant side and 5 moles of gas on the product side, decreasing the volume will shift equilibrium in the direction of the reactants.

10.57 **a.** A small K_c value indicates that the equilibrium mixture contains mostly reactants.
b. A large K_c value indicates that the equilibrium mixture contains mostly products.

10.59 a. $K_c = \dfrac{[\text{NO}]^2[\text{Br}_2]}{[\text{NOBr}]^2}$

    b. When the concentrations are substituted into the expression, the result is 1.0, which is not equal to K_c (2.0). Therefore, the system is not at equilibrium.

$$K_c = \dfrac{[\text{NO}]^2[\text{Br}_2]}{[\text{NOBr}]^2} = \dfrac{[1.0]^2[1.0]}{[1.0]^2} = 1.0 \ (2 \text{ SFs})$$

    c. Since the calculated value in part **b** is less than K_c, the rate of the forward reaction will initially increase.

    d. When the system has reestablished equilibrium, the $[\text{NO}]$ and $[\text{Br}_2]$ will have increased, and the $[\text{NOBr}]$ will have decreased.

10.61 a. When more product molecules are added to an equilibrium mixture, the system shifts in the direction of the reactants. This will cause an increase in the equilibrium concentration of the reactant NH_3.

    b. When the temperature is increased for an endothermic reaction, the system shifts in the direction of the products to remove heat. This will cause a decrease in the equilibrium concentration of the reactant NH_3.

    c. Increasing the volume of the reaction container favors the side of the reaction with the greater number of moles of gas, so this system shifts in the direction of the products. This will cause a decrease in the equilibrium concentration of the reactant NH_3.

    d. Decreasing the volume of the reaction container favors the side of the reaction with the fewer moles of gas, so this system shifts in the direction of the reactants. This will cause an increase in the equilibrium concentration of the reactant NH_3.

    e. When a catalyst is added, the rates of both forward and reverse reactions increase; the equilibrium position does not change. No change will be observed in the equilibrium concentration of the reactant NH_3.

10.63 Increasing the volume of an equilibrium mixture shifts the system toward the side of the reaction that has the greater number of moles of gas; decreasing the volume shifts the equilibrium toward the side of the reaction that has the fewer moles of gas.

    a. Since the product side has the fewer number of moles of gas, decreasing the volume of the container will increase the yield of products.

    b. Since the product side has the greater number of moles of gas, increasing the volume of the container will increase the yield of products.

    c. Since the product side has the fewer moles of gas, decreasing the volume of the container will increase the yield of products.

11

Acids and Bases

Credit: Lisa S./Shutterstock

When Larry was in the emergency room after an automobile accident, a blood sample was analyzed by Brianna, a clinical laboratory technician. The results showed that Larry's blood pH was 7.30 and the partial pressure of CO_2 gas was above the desired level. Blood pH is typically in the range of 7.35 to 7.45, and a value less than 7.35 indicates a state of acidosis. Larry had respiratory acidosis because an increase in the partial pressure of CO_2 gas in the bloodstream decreases the pH. In the emergency room, Larry was given an IV containing bicarbonate to increase his blood pH.

$$HCO_3^- + H^+ \rightleftharpoons H_2CO_3 \rightleftharpoons CO_2 + H_2O$$

Soon Larry's blood pH and partial pressure of CO_2 gas returned to normal.

What is the pH of a sample of blood that has $[H_3O^+] = 3.5 \times 10^{-8}$ M?

CHAPTER READINESS*

🖩 Key Math Skills

- Solving Equations (1.4D)
- Writing Numbers in Scientific Notation (1.4F)

⚛ Core Chemistry Skills

- Writing Ionic Formulas (6.2)
- Balancing a Chemical Equation (7.1)

- Using Concentration as a Conversion Factor (9.4)
- Writing the Equilibrium Constant Expression (10.3)
- Calculating Equilibrium Concentrations (10.4)
- Using Le Châtelier's Principle (10.5)

* These Key Math Skills and Core Chemistry Skills from previous chapters are listed here for your review as you proceed to the new material in this chapter.

11.1 Acids and Bases

Learning Goal: Describe and name acids and bases.

- In water, an Arrhenius acid produces hydrogen ions, H^+, and an Arrhenius base produces hydroxide ions, OH^-.
- An acid with a simple nonmetal anion is named with the prefix *hydro* in front the name of the anion, and its *ide* ending changed to *ic* acid.
- An acid with a polyatomic anion is named as an *ic acid* when its anion ends in *ate* and as an *ous acid* when its anion ends in *ite*.
- Arrhenius bases are named as metal or ammonium hydroxides.

♦ Learning Exercise 11.1A

Indicate if each of the following characteristics describes an (A) acid or a (B) base:

1. _____ turns blue litmus red

2. _____ tastes sour

3. _____ contains more OH^- than H_3O^+

4. _____ neutralizes bases

5. _____ tastes bitter   **6.** _____ turns red litmus blue

7. _____ contains more H_3O^+ than OH^- **8.** _____ neutralizes acids

Answers   **1.** A   **2.** A   **3.** B   **4.** A   **5.** B   **6.** B   **7.** A   **8.** B

♦ **Learning Exercise 11.1B**

Fill in the blanks with the formula or name of an acid or base.

1. HCl _____   **2.** _____ sodium hydroxide

3. _____ sulfurous acid   **4.** _____ nitric acid

5. $Ca(OH)_2$ _____   **6.** H_2CO_3 _____

7. $Al(OH)_3$ _____   **8.** _____ potassium hydroxide

9. $HClO_4$ _____   **10.** H_3PO_3 _____

Answers   **1.** hydrochloric acid   **2.** NaOH   **3.** H_2SO_3
           4. HNO_3 **5.** calcium hydroxide   **6.** carbonic acid
           7. aluminum hydroxide   **8.** KOH   **9.** perchloric acid
           10. phosphorous acid

11.2 Brønsted–Lowry Acids and Bases

Learning Goal: Identify conjugate acid–base pairs for Brønsted–Lowry acids and bases.

- According to the Brønsted–Lowry theory, acids are hydrogen ion, H^+, donors, and bases are hydrogen ion, H^+, acceptors.
- In water, hydrogen ions, H^+, from acids bond to polar water molecules in solution to form hydronium ions, H_3O^+.
- Conjugate acid–base pairs are molecules or ions linked by the loss and gain of one hydrogen ion, H^+.
- Every hydrogen ion transfer reaction involves two acid–base conjugate pairs.

Guide to Writing Conjugate Acid–Base Pairs	
STEP 1	Identify the reactant that loses H^+ as the acid.
STEP 2	Identify the reactant that gains H^+ as the base.
STEP 3	Write the conjugate acid–base pairs.

♦ **Learning Exercise 11.2A**

Complete the following conjugate acid–base pairs:

Conjugate Acid	**Conjugate Base**
1. H_2O	_____
2. HSO_4^-	_____
3. _____	F^-
4. _____	CO_3^{2-}
5. HNO_3	_____

Conjugate acid–base pair

Donates H^+ HF → F^-

Conjugate acid–base pair

Accepts H^+ H_2O → H_3O^+

6. NH_4^+ _____

7. _____ HS^-

8. _____ $H_2PO_4^-$

Answers   **1.** OH^- **2.** SO_4^{2-} **3.** HF **4.** HCO_3^-
            5. NO_3^- **6.** NH_3 **7.** H_2S **8.** H_3PO_4

♦ Learning Exercise 11.2B

Identify the conjugate acid–base pairs in each of the following reactions:

1. $NH_3(aq) + H_2O(l) \rightleftharpoons NH_4^+(aq) + OH^-(aq)$

2. $NH_4^+(aq) + SO_4^{2-}(aq) \rightleftharpoons NH_3(aq) + HSO_4^-(aq)$

3. $HF(aq) + H_2O(l) \rightleftharpoons F^-(aq) + H_3O^+(aq)$

4. $HNO_3(aq) + OH^-(aq) \rightleftharpoons NO_3^-(aq) + H_2O(l)$

⚛ CORE CHEMISTRY SKILL

Identifying Conjugate Acid–Base Pairs

HF, an acid, loses one H^+ to form its conjugate base F^-. Water acts as a base by gaining one H^+ to form its conjugate acid H_3O^+.

Answers   **1.** H_2O/OH^- and NH_4^+/NH_3 **2.** NH_4^+/NH_3 and HSO_4^-/SO_4^{2-}
          3. HF/F^- and H_3O^+/H_2O **4.** HNO_3/NO_3^- and H_2O/OH^-

♦ Learning Exercise 11.2C

Write the equilibrium equation with conjugate acid–base pairs starting with each of the following pairs of reactants:

1. HBr (acid) and CO_3^{2-} (base)

2. HSO_4^- (acid) and OH^- (base)

3. NH_4^+ (acid) and H_2O (base)

4. HCl (acid) and SO_4^{2-} (base)

Answers   **1.** $HBr(aq) + CO_3^{2-}(aq) \rightleftharpoons Br^-(aq) + HCO_3^-(aq)$

          2. $HSO_4^-(aq) + OH^-(aq) \rightleftharpoons SO_4^{2-}(aq) + H_2O(l)$

          3. $NH_4^+(aq) + H_2O(l) \rightleftharpoons NH_3(aq) + H_3O^+(aq)$

          4. $HCl(aq) + SO_4^{2-}(aq) \rightleftharpoons Cl^-(aq) + HSO_4^-(aq)$

11.3 Strengths of Acids and Bases

Learning Goal: Write equations for the dissociation of strong and weak acids; identify the direction of reaction.

- In aqueous solution, a strong acid donates all its hydrogen ions to water, whereas a weak acid donates only a small percentage of hydrogen ions to water.
- All hydroxides of Group 1A (1) and most hydroxides of Group 2A (2) are strong bases, which dissociate completely in water.
- In an aqueous ammonia solution, a weak base, NH_3, accepts only a small percentage of hydrogen ions to form the conjugate acid, NH_4^+.
- As the strength of an acid decreases, the strength of the conjugate base increases. By comparing relative strengths, the direction of an acid–base reaction can be predicted.

Study Note

Only six common acids are strong acids; other acids are weak acids.

HCl	HNO_3
HBr	H_2SO_4 (first H)
HI	$HClO_4$

Example: Is H_2S a strong or a weak acid?

Solution: H_2S is a weak acid because it is not one of the six strong acids.

◆ Learning Exercise 11.3A

Identify each of the following as a strong or weak acid or base:

1. HNO_3 _____   2. H_2CO_3 _____

3. $H_2PO_4^-$ _____   4. NH_3 _____

5. LiOH _____   6. H_3BO_3 _____

7. $Ca(OH)_2$ _____   8. H_2SO_4 _____

Answers   1. strong acid   2. weak acid   3. weak acid
4. weak base   5. strong base   6. weak acid
7. strong base   8. strong acid (first H^+)

◆ Learning Exercise 11.3B

Using Table 11.3 (in textbook), identify the stronger acid in each of the following pairs of acids:

1. HCl or H_2CO_3 _____   2. HNO_2 or HCN _____

3. H_2S or HBr _____   4. H_2SO_4 or HSO_4^- _____

5. HF or H_3PO_4 _____

Answers   **1.** HCl   **2.** HNO_2 **3.** HBr   **4.** H_2SO_4 **5.** H_3PO_4

Acetic acid ($HC_2H_3O_2$) is a weak acid because it dissociates slightly in water, producing only a small percentage of H_3O^+.

Credit: Pearson Education / Pearson Science

> **Study Note**
>
> In an acid–base reaction, the relative strengths of the two acids or two bases indicate whether the equilibrium mixture contains mostly reactants or products:
>
> *Example:* Does the following equilibrium mixture contain mostly reactants or products?
>
> $$NO_3^-(aq) + H_2O(l) \rightleftharpoons HNO_3(aq) + OH^-(aq)$$
>
> *Solution:* The reactants contain the weaker base and acid (NO_3^- and H_2O), which means the equilibrium mixture contains mostly reactants.

♦ **Learning Exercise 11.3C**

Using Table 11.3 in the text, indicate whether each of the following equilibrium mixtures contains mostly reactants or products:

1. $H_2SO_4(aq) + H_2O(l) \rightleftharpoons H_3O^+(aq) + HSO_4^-(aq)$ _____

2. $I^-(aq) + H_3O^+(aq) \rightleftharpoons H_2O(l) + HI(aq)$ _____

3. $NH_3(aq) + H_2O(l) \rightleftharpoons NH_4^+(aq) + OH^-(aq)$ _____

4. $HCl(aq) + CO_3^{2-}(aq) \rightleftharpoons Cl^-(aq) + HCO_3^-(aq)$ _____

Answers   1. products   2. reactants   3. reactants   4. products

11.4 Dissociation Constants for Acids and Bases

Learning Goal: Write the expression for the dissociation constant of a weak acid or weak base.

- An acid or base dissociation constant expression is the equilibrium constant when the concentration of water is considered a constant.

- For an acid dissociation constant expression, as with other equilibrium expressions, the molar concentrations of the products are divided by the molar concentrations of the reactants.

$$HA(aq) + H_2O(l) \rightleftharpoons H_3O^+(aq) + A^-(aq)$$

$$K_a = K_c[H_2O] = \frac{[H_3O^+][A^-]}{[HA]}$$

- The numerical value of the acid dissociation constant expression is the acid dissociation constant, K_a.

- An acid or a base with a large dissociation constant is more dissociated than an acid or base with a small dissociation constant.

- Equilibrium mixtures of acids or bases with dissociation constants greater than one ($K > 1$) contain mostly products, whereas constants smaller than one ($K < 1$) contain mostly reactants.

♦ **Learning Exercise 11.4A**

Write the equation for the dissociation and the acid dissociation constant expression for the dissociation of the following weak acids:

1. HCN

2. HNO_2

3. H_2CO_3 (first dissociation only)

4. H_2S (first dissociation only)

Answers

1. $HCN(aq) + H_2O(l) \rightleftharpoons H_3O^+(aq) + CN^-(aq)$ $K_a = \dfrac{[H_3O^+][CN^-]}{[HCN]}$

2. $HNO_2(aq) + H_2O(l) \rightleftharpoons H_3O^+(aq) + NO_2^-(aq)$ $K_a = \dfrac{[H_3O^+][NO_2^-]}{[HNO_2]}$

3. $H_2CO_3(aq) + H_2O(l) \rightleftharpoons H_3O^+(aq) + HCO_3^-(aq)$ $K_a = \dfrac{[H_3O^+][HCO_3^-]}{[H_2CO_3]}$

4. $H_2S(aq) + H_2O(l) \rightleftharpoons H_3O^+(aq) + HS^-(aq)$ $K_a = \dfrac{[H_3O^+][HS^-]}{[H_2S]}$

♦ **Learning Exercise 11.4B**

For each of the following pairs of acid dissociation constants, indicate the dissociation constant of the weaker acid:

1. 5.2×10^{-5} or 3.8×10^{-3} _____   **2.** 3.0×10^{-8} or 1.6×10^{-10} _____

3. 4.5×10^{-2} or 7.2×10^{-6} _____

Answers   **1.** 5.2×10^{-5} **2.** 1.6×10^{-10} **3.** 7.2×10^{-6}

♦ **Learning Exercise 11.4C**

Indicate whether the equilibrium mixture contains mostly reactants or products for each of the following acid dissociation constants:

1. 5.2×10^{-5} _____   **2.** 3.0×10^{8} _____

3. 4.5×10^{-3} _____   **4.** 7.2×10^{15} _____

Answers   **1.** reactants   **2.** products   **3.** reactants   **4.** products

11.5 Dissociation of Water

Learning Goal: Use the water dissociation constant expression to calculate the $[H_3O^+]$ ***and*** $[OH^-]$ ***in an aqueous solution.***

- In pure water, a few water molecules transfer hydrogen ions to other water molecules, producing small, but equal, amounts of each ion such that $[H_3O^+]$ and $[OH^-]$ each $= 1.0 \times 10^{-7}$ M.

$$H_2O(l) + H_2O(l) \rightleftharpoons H_3O^+(aq) + OH^-(aq)$$

- K_w, the water dissociation constant expression $[H_3O^+][OH^-] = [1.0 \times 10^{-7}][1.0 \times 10^{-7}] = 1.0 \times 10^{-14}$, applies to all aqueous solutions.
- In acidic solutions, the $[H_3O^+]$ is greater than the $[OH^-]$. In basic solutions, the $[OH^-]$ is greater than the $[H_3O^+]$.

	Guide to Calculating $[H_3O^+]$ and $[OH^-]$ in Aqueous Solutions	
STEP 1	State the given and needed quantities.	
STEP 2	Write the K_w for water and solve for the unknown $[H_3O^+]$ or $[OH^-]$.	
STEP 3	Substitute the known $[H_3O^+]$ or $[OH^-]$ into the equation and calculate.	

Example: What is the $[H_3O^+]$ in an urine sample that has $[OH^-] = 2.0 \times 10^{-9}$ M?

Solution: **STEP 1 State the given and needed quantities.**

Analyze the Problem	**Given**	**Need**
	$[OH^-] = 2.0 \times 10^{-9}$ M	$[H_3O^+]$

STEP 2 Write the K_w for water and solve for the unknown $[H_3O^+]$.

$$[H_3O^+][OH^-] = 1.0 \times 10^{-14}$$

$$[H_3O^+] = \frac{1.0 \times 10^{-14}}{[OH^-]}$$

A dipstick is used to measure the pH of a urine sample.

Credit: Alexander Gospodinov / Fotolia

STEP 3 Substitute the known [OH⁻] into the equation and calculate.

$$[H_3O^+] = \frac{1.0 \times 10^{-14}}{2.0 \times 10^{-9}} = 5.0 \times 10^{-6} \text{ M}$$

♦ **Learning Exercise 11.5A**

Use the K_w to calculate the $[H_3O^+]$ when the $[OH^-]$ has each of the following values:

⚛ CORE CHEMISTRY SKILL

Calculating $[H_3O^+]$ and $[OH^-]$ in Solutions

    a. $[OH^-] = 1.0 \times 10^{-10}$ M $[H_3O^+] = $ _____

    b. $[OH^-] = 2.0 \times 10^{-5}$ M $[H_3O^+] = $ _____

    c. $[OH^-] = 4.5 \times 10^{-7}$ M $[H_3O^+] = $ _____

    d. $[OH^-] = 8.0 \times 10^{-4}$ M $[H_3O^+] = $ _____

    e. $[OH^-] = 5.5 \times 10^{-8}$ M $[H_3O^+] = $ _____

Answers   **a.** 1.0×10^{-4} M   **b.** 5.0×10^{-10} M   **c.** 2.2×10^{-8} M
                        d. 1.3×10^{-11} M   **e.** 1.8×10^{-7} M

♦ **Learning Exercise 11.5B**

Use the K_w to calculate the $[OH^-]$ when the $[H_3O^+]$ has each of the following values:

    a. $[H_3O^+] = 1.0 \times 10^{-3}$ M $[OH^-] = $ _____

    b. $[H_3O^+] = 3.0 \times 10^{-10}$ M $[OH^-] = $ _____

    c. $[H_3O^+] = 4.0 \times 10^{-6}$ M $[OH^-] = $ _____

    d. $[H_3O^+] = 2.8 \times 10^{-13}$ M $[OH^-] = $ _____

    e. $[H_3O^+] = 8.6 \times 10^{-7}$ M $[OH^-] = $ _____

Answers   **a.** 1.0×10^{-11} M   **b.** 3.3×10^{-5} M   **c.** 2.5×10^{-9} M
                        d. 3.6×10^{-2} M   **e.** 1.2×10^{-8} M

11.6 The pH Scale

Learning Goal: Calculate pH from $[H_3O^+]$; given the pH, calculate the $[H_3O^+]$ and $[OH^-]$ of a solution.

- The pH scale is a range of numbers from 0 to 14 related to the $[H_3O^+]$ of the solution.
- A neutral solution has a pH of 7.0. In acidic solutions, the pH is below 7.0, and in basic solutions, the pH is above 7.0.
- Mathematically, pH is the negative logarithm of the hydronium ion concentration: $pH = -\log[H_3O^+]$.

♦ **Learning Exercise 11.6A**

Indicate whether each of the following solutions is acidic, basic, or neutral:

    a. $[H_3O^+] = 2.5 \times 10^{-9}$ M _____   **b.** $[OH^-] = 1.6 \times 10^{-2}$ M _____

    c. $[H_3O^+] = 7.9 \times 10^{-3}$ M _____   **d.** $[OH^-] = 2.9 \times 10^{-12}$ M _____

Answers   **a.** basic   **b.** basic   **c.** acidic   **d.** acidic

♦ **Learning Exercise 11.6B**

State whether the following pH values are acidic, basic, or neutral:

1. ____ blood plasma, pH = 7.4   **2.** ____ soft drink, pH = 2.8

3. ____ maple syrup, pH = 6.8   **4.** ____ beans, pH = 5.0

5. ____ tomatoes, pH = 4.2   **6.** ____ lemon juice, pH = 2.2

7. ____ saliva, pH = 7.0   **8.** ____ egg white, pH = 7.8

9. ____ lye, pH = 12.4   **10.** ____ strawberries, pH = 3.0

Answers   **1.** basic   **2.** acidic   **3.** acidic   **4.** acidic   **5.** acidic
               6. acidic   **7.** neutral   **8.** basic   **9.** basic   **10.** acidic

Guide to Calculating pH of an Aqueous Solution	
STEP 1	State the given and needed quantities.
STEP 2	Enter the $[H_3O^+]$ into the pH equation and calculate.
STEP 3	Adjust the number of SFs on the *right* of the decimal point.

♦ **Learning Exercise 11.6C**

     KEY MATH SKILL

Calculate the pH of each of the following solutions: Calculating pH from $[H_3O^+]$

    a. $[H_3O^+] = 1.0 \times 10^{-8}$ M _____   **b.** $[OH^-] = 1 \times 10^{-12}$ M _____

    c. $[H_3O^+] = 1 \times 10^{-3}$ M _____   **d.** $[OH^-] = 1 \times 10^{-10}$ M _____

    e. $[H_3O^+] = 3.4 \times 10^{-8}$ M _____   **f.** $[OH^-] = 7.8 \times 10^{-2}$ M _____

Answers   **a.** 8.00   **b.** 2.0   **c.** 3.0   **d.** 4.0   **e.** 7.47   **f.** 12.89

♦ **Learning Exercise 11.6D**

Calculate the pH of each of the following solutions:

    a. $[H_3O^+] = 5.0 \times 10^{-3}$ M   **b.** $[OH^-] = 4.0 \times 10^{-6}$ M

    c. $[H_3O^+] = 7.5 \times 10^{-8}$ M   **d.** $[OH^-] = 2.5 \times 10^{-10}$ M

Answers   **a.** 2.30   **b.** 8.60   **c.** 7.12   **d.** 4.40

Guide to Calculating $[H_3O^+]$ from pH	
STEP 1	State the given and needed quantities.
STEP 2	Enter the pH value into the inverse log equation and calculate.
STEP 3	Adjust the SFs for the coefficient.

♦ **Learning Exercise 11.6E**

Complete the following table:

KEY MATH SKILL

Calculating $[H_3O^+]$ from pH

	$[H_3O^+]$	$[OH^-]$	pH
a.	_____	1×10^{-12} M	_____
b.	_____	_____	8.0
c.	5.0×10^{-11} M	_____	_____
d.	_____	_____	7.80
e.	_____	_____	4.25
f.	2.0×10^{-10} M	_____	_____

Answers	$[H_3O^+]$	$[OH^-]$	pH
a.	1×10^{-2} M	1×10^{-12} M	2.0
b.	1×10^{-8} M	1×10^{-6} M	8.0
c.	5.0×10^{-11} M	2.0×10^{-4} M	10.30
d.	1.6×10^{-8} M	6.3×10^{-7} M	7.80
e.	5.6×10^{-5} M	1.8×10^{-10} M	4.25
f.	2.0×10^{-10} M	5.0×10^{-5} M	9.70

11.7 Reactions of Acids and Bases

Learning Goal: Write balanced equations for reactions of acids with metals, carbonates or bicarbonates, and bases.

- Acids react with many metals to yield hydrogen gas, H_2, and the salt of the metal.
- Acids react with carbonates and bicarbonates to yield CO_2, H_2O, and the salt of the metal.
- Acids neutralize bases in a reaction that produces water and a salt.

- The net ionic equation for any strong acid–strong base neutralization is
  $H^+(aq) + OH^-(aq) \longrightarrow H_2O(l)$.
- In a balanced neutralization equation, an equal number of moles of H^+ and OH^- must react.
- A titration is used to determine the volume or concentration of an acid or a base from the laboratory data.

◆ **Learning Exercise 11.7A**

⚛ **CORE CHEMISTRY SKILL**

Complete and balance each of the following reactions of acids:

Writing Equations for Reactions of Acids and Bases

1. ____ $Zn(s)$ + ____ $HCl(aq)$ $\longrightarrow$ ____ + ____ $ZnCl_2(aq)$

2. ____ $HCl(aq)$ + ____ $Li_2CO_3(aq)$ $\longrightarrow$ ____ + ____ + ____

3. ____ $HCl(aq)$ + ____ $NaHCO_3(aq)$ $\longrightarrow$ ____ $CO_2(g)$ + ____ $H_2O(l)$ + ____

4. ____ $Al(s)$ + ____ $H_2SO_4(aq)$ $\longrightarrow$ ____ + ____ $Al_2(SO_4)_3(aq)$

Answers
1. $Zn(s) + 2HCl(aq) \longrightarrow H_2(g) + ZnCl_2(aq)$
2. $2HCl(aq) + Li_2CO_3(aq) \longrightarrow CO_2(g) + H_2O(l) + 2LiCl(aq)$
3. $HCl(aq) + NaHCO_3(aq) \longrightarrow CO_2(g) + H_2O(l) + NaCl(aq)$
4. $2Al(s) + 3H_2SO_4(aq) \longrightarrow 3H_2(g) + Al_2(SO_4)_3(aq)$

Guide to Balancing an Equation for Neutralization	
STEP 1	Write the reactants and products.
STEP 2	Balance the H^+ in the acid with the OH^- in the base.
STEP 3	Balance the H_2O with the H^+ and the OH^-.
STEP 4	Write the salt from the remaining ions.

◆ **Learning Exercise 11.7B**

Complete and balance each of the following neutralization reactions:

1. ____ $NaOH(aq)$ + ____ $H_2SO_4(aq)$ $\longrightarrow$ _____ + _____

2. ____ $Mg(OH)_2(s)$ + ____ $HCl(aq)$ $\longrightarrow$ _____ + _____

3. ____ $Al(OH)_3(s)$ + ____ $HNO_3(aq)$ $\longrightarrow$ _____ + _____

4. ____ $Ca(OH)_2(s)$ + ____ $H_3PO_4(aq)$ $\longrightarrow$ _____ + _____

Answers
1. $2NaOH(aq) + H_2SO_4(aq) \longrightarrow 2H_2O(l) + Na_2SO_4(aq)$
2. $Mg(OH)_2(s) + 2HCl(aq) \longrightarrow 2H_2O(l) + MgCl_2(aq)$
3. $Al(OH)_3(s) + 3HNO_3(aq) \longrightarrow 3H_2O(l) + Al(NO_3)_3(aq)$
4. $3Ca(OH)_2(s) + 2H_3PO_4(aq) \longrightarrow 6H_2O(l) + Ca_3(PO_4)_2(s)$

♦ **Learning Exercise 11.7C**

Complete and balance each of the following neutralization reactions:

a. _____ KOH(*aq*) + _____ H$_3$PO$_4$(*aq*) ⟶ _____ H$_2$O(*l*) + _____

b. _____ NaOH(*aq*) + _____ ⟶ _____ + _____ Na$_2$SO$_4$(*aq*)

c. _____ + _____ ⟶ _____ + _____ AlCl$_3$(*aq*)

d. _____ + _____ ⟶ _____ + _____ Fe$_2$(SO$_4$)$_3$(*aq*)

Answers

      a. 3KOH(*aq*) + H$_3$PO$_4$(*aq*) ⟶ 3H$_2$O(*l*) + K$_3$PO$_4$(*aq*)

      b. 2NaOH(*aq*) + H$_2$SO$_4$(*aq*) ⟶ 2H$_2$O(*l*) + Na$_2$SO$_4$(*aq*)

      c. Al(OH)$_3$(*s*) + 3HCl(*aq*) ⟶ 3H$_2$O(*l*) + AlCl$_3$(*aq*)

      d. 2Fe(OH)$_3$(*s*) + 3H$_2$SO$_4$(*aq*) ⟶ 6H$_2$O(*l*) + Fe$_2$(SO$_4$)$_3$(*aq*)

11.8 Acid–Base Titration

Learning Goal: Calculate the molarity or volume of an acid or base solution from titration information.

- In a laboratory procedure called a titration, an acid or base sample is neutralized.
- A titration is used to determine the volume or concentration of an acid or a base from the laboratory data.

	Guide to Calculations for an Acid–Base Titration
STEP 1	State the given and needed quantities and concentrations.
STEP 2	Write a plan to calculate the molarity or volume.
STEP 3	State equalities and conversion factors, including concentrations.
STEP 4	Set up the problem to calculate the needed quantity.

♦ **Learning Exercise 11.8**

Solve the following problems using the titration data given:

CORE CHEMISTRY SKILL

Calculating Molarity or Volume of an Acid or Base in a Titration

  a. A 5.00-mL sample of HCl solution is placed in a flask. In the titration, 15.0 mL of a 0.200 M NaOH solution is required for neutralization. What is the molarity of the HCl solution?

      HCl(*aq*) + NaOH(*aq*) ⟶ H$_2$O(*l*) + NaCl(*aq*)

  b. How many milliliters of a 0.200 M NaOH solution are required to neutralize completely 8.50 mL of a 0.500 M H$_2$SO$_4$ solution?

      H$_2$SO$_4$(*aq*) + 2NaOH(*aq*) ⟶ 2H$_2$O(*l*) + Na$_2$SO$_4$(*aq*)

c. A 10.0-mL sample of H_3PO_4 solution is placed in a flask. If titration requires 42.0 mL of a 0.100 M NaOH solution for complete neutralization, what is the molarity of the H_3PO_4 solution?

$$H_3PO_4(aq) + 3NaOH(aq) \longrightarrow 3H_2O(l) + Na_3PO_4(aq)$$

d. A 24.6-mL sample of HCl solution reacts completely with 33.0 mL of a 0.222 M NaOH solution. What is the molarity of the HCl solution (see reaction in part **a**)?

e. A 15.7-mL sample of a 0.165 M H_2SO_4 solution reacts completely with 0.187 M NaOH solution. How many milliliters of the NaOH solution are needed (see reaction in part **b**)?

Answers   **a.** 0.600 M HCl solution   **b.** 42.5 mL   **c.** 0.140 M H_3PO_4 solution
              d. 0.298 M HCl solution   **e.** 27.7 mL

11.9   Buffers

Learning Goal: Describe the role of buffers in maintaining the pH of a solution; calculate the pH of a buffer.

- A buffer solution resists a change in pH when small amounts of acid or base are added.
- A buffer contains either (1) a weak acid and its salt or (2) a weak base and its salt.
- The weak acid reacts with added OH^-, and the anion of the salt reacts with added H_3O^+, which maintains the pH of the solution.
- The weak base reacts with added H_3O^+, and the cation of the salt reacts with added OH^-, which maintains the pH of the solution.

Key Terms for Sections 11.1–11.9

Match each of the following key terms with the correct definition:

a. acid   **b.** base   **c.** pH   **d.** neutralization
e. buffer   **f.** K_a **g.** dissociation

1. _____ a substance that forms OH^- in water and/or accepts H^+

2. _____ a reaction between an acid and a base to form a salt and water

3. _____ a substance that forms H^+ in water

4. _____ a mixture of a weak acid (or base) and its salt that maintains the pH of a solution

5. _____ a measure of the acidity of a solution

6. _____ the separation of a substance into ions in water

7. _____ the product of the molar concentrations of the ions from a weak acid divided by the molar concentration of the weak acid

Answers   **1.** b   **2.** d   **3.** a   **4.** e
               5. c   **6.** g   **7.** f

♦ **Learning Exercise 11.9A**

State whether each of the following represents a buffer system and explain why:

    a. HCl + NaCl

                                                                     b. K_2SO_4

    c. H_2CO_3

                                                                         d. H_2CO_3 + $NaHCO_3$

Answers   **a.** No. A strong acid and its salt do not make a buffer.
                      b. No. A salt alone cannot act as a buffer.
                      c. No. A weak acid alone cannot act as a buffer.
                      d. Yes. A weak acid and its salt act as a buffer system.

♦ **Learning Exercise 11.9B**

A buffer system contains dihydrogen phosphate $H_2PO_4^-$ and its conjugate base, hydrogen phosphate HPO_4^{2-}.

$$H_2PO_4^-(aq) + H_2O(l) \rightleftharpoons H_3O^+(aq) + HPO_4^{2-}(aq)$$

    a. The purpose of this buffer system is to _____
        1. maintain $H_2PO_4^-$ **2.** maintain HPO_4^{2-} **3.** maintain pH

    b. The weak acid is needed to _____
        1. provide the conjugate base   **2.** neutralize added OH^- **3.** provide the conjugate acid

    c. If H_3O^+ is added, it is neutralized by _____
        1. HPO_4^{2-} **2.** H_2O **3.** OH^-

    d. When OH^- is added, the equilibrium shifts in the direction of _____
        1. the reactants   **2.** the products   **3.** does not change

Answers   **a.** 3   **b.** 2   **c.** 1   **d.** 2

Guide to Calculating pH of a Buffer	
STEP 1	State the given and needed quantities.
STEP 2	Write the K_a expression and rearrange for $[H_3O^+]$.
STEP 3	Substitute $[HA]$ and $[A^-]$ into the K_a expression.
STEP 4	Use $[H_3O^+]$ to calculate pH.

♦ **Learning Exercise 11.9C**   🔬 **CORE CHEMISTRY SKILL**

The K_a for acetic acid, $HC_2H_3O_2$, is 1.8×10^{-5}.   Calculating the pH of a Buffer

    a. What is the pH of a buffer that contains 1.0 M $HC_2H_3O_2$ and 1.0 M $NaC_2H_3O_2$?

    b. What is the pH of a buffer that contains 1.0 M $HC_2H_3O_2$ and 0.10 M $NaC_2H_3O_2$?

    c. What is the pH of a buffer that contains 0.10 M $HC_2H_3O_2$ and 1.0 M $NaC_2H_3O_2$?

Answers

    a. $[H_3O^+] = 1.8 \times 10^{-5} \times \dfrac{[1.0]}{[1.0]} = 1.8 \times 10^{-5}$ M $pH = -\log[1.8 \times 10^{-5}] = 4.74$

    b. $[H_3O^+] = 1.8 \times 10^{-5} \times \dfrac{[1.0]}{[0.1]} = 1.8 \times 10^{-4}$ M $pH = -\log[1.8 \times 10^{-4}] = 3.74$

    c. $[H_3O^+] = 1.8 \times 10^{-5} \times \dfrac{[0.1]}{[1.0]} = 1.8 \times 10^{-6}$ M $pH = -\log[1.8 \times 10^{-6}] = 5.74$

Checklist for Chapter 11

You are ready to take the Practice Test for Chapter 11. Be sure you have accomplished the following learning goals for this chapter. If not, review the section listed at the end of the goal. Then apply your new skills and understanding to the Practice Test.

After studying Chapter 11, I can successfully:

_____ Describe the properties of Arrhenius acids and bases and write their names. (11.1)

_____ Describe the Brønsted–Lowry concept of acids and bases. (11.2)

_____ Write conjugate acid–base pairs for an acid–base reaction. (11.2)

_____ Write equations for the dissociation of strong and weak acids and bases. (11.3)

_____ Write the expression for the dissociation constant for a weak acid or base. (11.4)

_____ Use K_a values to compare the strengths of acids. (11.4)

_____ Use the water dissociation constant expression of water to calculate $[H_3O^+]$ and $[OH^-]$. (11.5)

_____ Calculate pH from the $[H_3O^+]$ or $[OH^-]$ of a solution. (11.6)

_____ Write a balanced equation for the reactions of acids with metals, carbonates or bicarbonates, and bases. (11.7)

_____ Calculate the molarity or volume of an acid or base from titration information. (11.8)

_____ Describe the role of buffers in maintaining the pH of a solution. (11.9)

_____ Calculate the pH of a buffer solution. (11.9)

Practice Test for Chapter 11

1. An acid is a compound that when placed in water yields this characteristic ion. (11.1)
   A. H_3O^+ **B.** OH^- **C.** Na^+ **D.** Cl^- **E.** CO_3^{2-}

2. $MgCl_2$ would be classified as a(an) (11.1)
   A. acid   **B.** base   **C.** salt   **D.** buffer   **E.** nonelectrolyte

3. $Mg(OH)_2$ would be classified as a (11.1)
   A. weak acid   **B.** strong base   **C.** salt   **D.** buffer   **E.** nonelectrolyte

4. Which of the following would turn litmus blue? (11.1)
   A. HCl   **B.** NH_4Cl **C.** Na_2SO_4 **D.** KOH   **E.** $NaNO_3$

5. What is the name of $HClO_3$? (11.1)
   A. hypochlorous acid   **B.** chloric acid   **C.** chlorous acid
   D. chloric trioxide acid   **E.** perchloric acid

6. What is the name of NH_4OH? (11.1)
   A. ammonium oxide
   B. nitrogen tetrahydride hydroxide
   C. ammonium hydroxide
   D. perammonium hydroxide
   E. amine oxide hydride

7. Which of the following pairs is a conjugate acid–base pair? (11.2)
   A. HCl/HNO_3 **B.** HNO_2/NO_2^- **C.** $NaOH/KOH$ **D.** HSO_4^-/HCO_3^- **E.** Cl^-/F^-

8. The conjugate base of HSO_4^- is (11.2)
   A. SO_4^{2-} **B.** H_2SO_4 **C.** HS^- **D.** H_2S **E.** SO_3^{2-}

9. In which of the following reactions does H_2O act as an acid? (11.2)
   A. $H_3PO_4(aq) + H_2O(l) \longrightarrow H_3O^+(aq) + H_2PO_4^-(aq)$
   B. $H_2SO_4(aq) + H_2O(l) \longrightarrow H_3O^+(aq) + HSO_4^-(aq)$
   C. $H_2O(l) + HS^-(aq) \longrightarrow H_3O^+(aq) + S^{2-}(aq)$
   D. $NaOH(aq) + HCl(aq) \longrightarrow NaCl(aq) + H_2O(l)$
   E. $NH_3(g) + H_2O(l) \longrightarrow NH_4^+(aq) + OH^-(aq)$

10. Which of the following acids has the smallest K_a value? (11.3)
    A. HNO_3 **B.** H_2SO_4 **C.** HCl   **D.** H_2CO_3 **E.** HBr

11. Using the following K_a values, identify the strongest acid in the group: (11.3)
    A. 7.5×10^{-3} **B.** 1.8×10^{-5} **C.** 4.5×10^8 **D.** 4.9×10^{-10} **E.** 3.2×10^4

12. Acetic acid is a weak acid because (11.3)
    A. it forms a dilute acid solution   **B.** it is isotonic
    C. it is slightly dissociated in water   **D.** it is a nonpolar molecule
    E. it can form a buffer

13. A weak base when added to water (11.3)
    A. makes the solution slightly basic   **B.** does not affect the pH
    C. dissociates completely   **D.** does not dissociate
    E. makes the solution slightly acidic

14. The weak acid formic acid dissociates in water.
    $$HCHO_2(aq) + H_2O(l) \rightleftharpoons H_3O^+(aq) + CHO_2^-(aq)$$

    The correctly written acid dissociation constant expression is: (11.4)

A. $K_a = \dfrac{[HCHO_2]}{[H_3O^+][CHO_2^-]}$ **B.** $K_a = \dfrac{[HCHO_2]}{[CHO_2^-]}$

C. $K_a = \dfrac{[H_3O^+][CHO_2^-]}{[HCHO_2][H_2O]}$ **D.** $K_a = \dfrac{[H_3O^+][CHO_2^-]}{[HCHO_2]}$

E. $K_a = \dfrac{[HCHO_2][H_2O]}{[H_3O^+][CHO_2^-]}$

15. In the K_w expression for pure H_2O, the $[H_3O^+]$ has the value (11.5)
  A. 1.0×10^{-7} M **B.** 1.0×10^{-1} M **C.** 1.0×10^{-14} M
  D. 1.0×10^{-6} M **E.** 1.0×10^{12} M

For questions 16 and 17, consider a solution with $[H_3O^+] = 1 \times 10^{-11}$ M. (11.5)

16. The hydroxide ion concentration is
  A. 1×10^{-1} M **B.** 1×10^{-3} M **C.** 1×10^{-4} M **D.** 1×10^{-7} M **E.** 1×10^{-11} M

17. The solution is
  A. acidic **B.** basic **C.** neutral **D.** a buffer **E.** neutralized

For questions 18 and 19, consider a solution with $[OH^-] = 1 \times 10^{-5}$ M. (11.5)

18. The hydrogen ion concentration of the solution is
  A. 1×10^{-5} M **B.** 1×10^{-7} M **C.** 1×10^{-9} M **D.** 1×10^{-10} M **E.** 1×10^{-14} M

19. The solution is
  A. acidic **B.** basic **C.** neutral **D.** a buffer **E.** neutralized

20. What is the $[H_3O^+]$ of a solution that has a pH = 8.7? (11.6)
  A. 7×10^{-8} **B.** 2×10^{-9} **C.** 2×10^9 **D.** 8×10^{-7} **E.** 2×10^{-8}

21. Of the following pH values, which is the most acidic? (11.6)
  A. 8.0 **B.** 5.5 **C.** 1.5 **D.** 3.2 **E.** 9.0

22. Of the following pH values, which is the most basic? (11.6)
  A. 10.0 **B.** 4.0 **C.** 2.2 **D.** 11.5 **E.** 9.0

23. Which is an equation for neutralization of an acid and a base? (11.7)
  A. $CaCO_3(s) \longrightarrow CaO(s) + CO_2(g)$
  B. $Na_2SO_4(s) \longrightarrow 2Na^+(aq) + SO_4^{2-}(aq)$
  C. $H_2SO_4(aq) + 2NaOH(aq) \longrightarrow 2H_2O(l) + Na_2SO_4(aq)$
  D. $Na_2O(s) + SO_3(g) \longrightarrow Na_2SO_4(aq)$
  E. $H_2CO_3(aq) \longrightarrow CO_2(g) + H_2O(l)$

24. What is the molarity of a 10.0-mL sample of HCl solution that is neutralized by 15.0 mL of a 2.0 M NaOH solution? (11.8)
  A. 0.50 M HCl **B.** 1.0 M HCl **C.** 1.5 M HCl **D.** 2.0 M HCl **E.** 3.0 M HCl

25. In a titration, 6.0 moles of NaOH will completely neutralize _____ moles of H_2SO_4. (11.8)
  A. 1.0 **B.** 2.0 **C.** 3.0 **D.** 6.0 **E.** 11

26. What is the name given to components in the body that keep blood pH within its normal 7.35 to 7.45 range? (11.9)
  A. nutrients **B.** buffers **C.** metabolites **D.** regufluids **E.** neutralizers

27. A buffer system (11.9)
  A. maintains a pH of 7.0
  B. contains only a weak base
  C. contains only a salt
  D. contains a strong acid and its salt
  E. maintains the pH of a solution

28. Which of the following would act as a buffer system? (11.9)
  A. HCl
  B. Na_2CO_3
  C. $NaOH + NaNO_3$
  D. NH_4OH
  E. $NaHCO_3 + H_2CO_3$

Answers to the Practice Test

1. A	**2.** C	**3.** B	**4.** D	**5.** B
6. C	**7.** B	**8.** A	**9.** E	**10.** D
11. C	**12.** C	**13.** A	**14.** D	**15.** A
16. B	**17.** B	**18.** C	**19.** B	**20.** B
21. C	**22.** D	**23.** C	**24.** E	**25.** C
26. B	**27.** E	**28.** E		

11

Acids and Bases

Learning Goals

- Describe and name acids and bases.
- Identify conjugate acid–base pairs for Brønsted–Lowry acids and bases.
- Write equations for the dissociation of strong and weak acids; identify the direction of reaction.
- Write the expression for the dissociation constant of a weak acid or weak base.
- Use the water dissociation constant expression to calculate the $[H_3O^+]$ and $[OH^-]$ in an aqueous solution.
- Calculate pH from $[H_3O^+]$; given the pH, calculate $[H_3O^+]$ and $[OH^-]$ of a solution.
- Write balanced equations for reactions of acids with metals, carbonates or bicarbonates, and bases.
- Calculate the molarity or volume of an acid or base solution from titration information.
- Describe the role of buffers in maintaining the pH of a solution; calculate the pH of a buffer.

Chapter Outline

Chapter Opener: Clinical Laboratory Technician

11.1 **Acids and Bases**

11.2 **Brønsted–Lowry Acids and Bases**

11.3 **Strengths of Acids and Bases**

11.4 **Dissociation Constants for Acids and Bases**

11.5 **Dissociation of Water**

11.6 **The pH Scale**

Chemistry Link to Health: Stomach Acid, HCl

11.7 **Reactions of Acids and Bases**

Chemistry Link to Health: Antacids

11.8 **Acid–Base Titration**

11.9 **Buffers**

Chemistry Link to Health: Buffers in the Blood Plasma

Clinical Update: Acid Reflux Disease

▣ Key Math Skills

- Calculating pH from $[H_3O^+]$ (11.6)
- Calculating $[H_3O^+]$ from pH (11.6)

⚛ Core Chemistry Skills

- Identifying Conjugate Acid–Base Pairs (11.2)
- Calculating $[H_3O^+]$ and $[OH^-]$ in Solutions (11.5)
- Writing Equations for Reactions of Acids and Bases (11.7)
- Calculating Molarity or Volume of an Acid or Base in a Titration (11.8)
- Calculating the pH of a Buffer (11.9)

Selected Answers and Solutions to Text Problems

11.1 **a.** Acids taste sour.
    b. Acids neutralize bases.
    c. Acids produce H^+ ions in water.
    d. Barium hydroxide is the name of a base.
    e. Both acids and bases are electrolytes.

11.3 Acids containing a simple nonmetal anion use the prefix *hydro*, followed by the name of the anion with its *ide* ending changed to *ic acid*. When the anion is an oxygen-containing polyatomic ion, the *ate* ending of the polyatomic anion is replaced with *ic acid*. Acids with one oxygen less than the common *ic acid* name are named as *ous acids*. Bases are named as ionic compounds containing hydroxide anions.
    a. hydrochloric acid   **b.** calcium hydroxide   **c.** perchloric acid
    d. nitric acid   **e.** sulfurous acid   **f.** bromous acid

11.5 **a.** RbOH   **b.** HF   **c.** H_3PO_4
    d. LiOH   **e.** NH_4OH **f.** HIO_4

11.7 A Brønsted–Lowry acid donates a hydrogen ion (H^+), whereas a Brønsted–Lowry base accepts a hydrogen ion.
    a. HI is the acid $(H^+$ donor$)$; H_2O is the base $(H^+$ acceptor$)$.
    b. H_2O is the acid $(H^+$ donor$)$; F^- is the base $(H^+$ acceptor$)$.
    c. H_2S is the acid $(H^+$ donor$)$; $CH_3-CH_2-NH_2$ is the base $(H^+$ acceptor$)$.

11.9 To form the conjugate base, remove a hydrogen ion (H^+) from the acid.
    a. F^- **b.** OH^- **c.** $HPO_3{}^{2-}$
    d. $SO_4{}^{2-}$ **e.** $ClO_2{}^-$

11.11 To form the conjugate acid, add a hydrogen ion (H^+) to the base.
    a. $HCO_3{}^-$ **b.** H_3O^+ **c.** H_3PO_4
    d. HBr   **e.** $HClO_4$

11.13 The conjugate acid is an H^+ donor, and the conjugate base is an H^+ acceptor.
    a. In the reaction, the acid H_2CO_3 donates an H^+ to the base H_2O. The conjugate acid–base pairs are $H_2CO_3/HCO_3{}^-$ and H_3O^+/H_2O.
    b. In the reaction, the acid $NH_4{}^+$ donates an H^+ to the base H_2O. The conjugate acid–base pairs are $NH_4{}^+/NH_3$ and H_3O^+/H_2O.
    c. In the reaction, the acid HCN donates an H^+ to the base $NO_2{}^-$. The conjugate acid–base pairs are HCN/CN^- and $HNO_2/NO_2{}^-$.
    d. In the reaction, the acid HF donates an H^+ to the base $CHO_2{}^-$. The conjugate acid–base pairs are HF/F^- and $HCHO_2/CHO_2{}^-$.

11.15 $NH_4{}^+(aq) + H_2O(l) \rightleftharpoons NH_3(aq) + H_3O^+(aq)$

11.17 A strong acid is a good H^+ donor, whereas its conjugate base is a poor H^+ acceptor.

11.19 Use Table 11.3 to answer (the stronger acid will be closer to the top of the table).

    a. HBr is the stronger acid.

    b. HSO_4^- is the stronger acid.

    c. H_2CO_3 is the stronger acid.

11.21 Use Table 11.3 to answer (the weaker acid will be closer to the bottom of the table).

    a. HSO_4^- is the weaker acid.

    b. HF is the weaker acid.

    c. HCO_3^- is the weaker acid.

11.23 a. From Table 11.3, we see that H_2CO_3 is a weaker acid than H_3O^+ and that H_2O is a weaker base than HCO_3^-. Thus, the solution will contain mostly reactants at equilibrium.

    b. From Table 11.3, we see that NH_4^+ is a weaker acid than H_3O^+ and that H_2O is a weaker base than NH_3. Thus, the solution will contain mostly reactants at equilibrium.

    c. From Table 11.3, we see that NH_4^+ is a weaker acid than HNO_2 and that NO_2^- is a weaker base than NH_3. Thus, the solution will contain mostly products at equilibrium.

11.25 $NH_4^+(aq) + SO_4^{2-}(aq) \rightleftharpoons NH_3(aq) + HSO_4^-(aq)$

This equilibrium contains mostly reactants because NH_4^+ is a weaker acid than HSO_4^-, and SO_4^{2-} is a weaker base than NH_3.

11.27 a. True

    b. False; a strong acid has a large value of K_a.

    c. False; a strong acid has a weak conjugate base.

    d. True

    e. False; a strong acid is completely dissociated in aqueous solution.

11.29 The smaller the K_a value, the weaker the acid. The weaker acid has the stronger conjugate base.

    a. H_2SO_3, which has a larger K_a value than HS^-, is the stronger acid.

    b. The conjugate base HSO_3^- is formed by removing an H^+ from the acid H_2SO_3.

    c. The stronger acid, H_2SO_3, has the weaker conjugate base, HSO_3^-.

    d. The weaker acid, HS^-, has the stronger conjugate base, S^{2-}.

    e. The stronger acid, H_2SO_3, dissociates more and produces more ions.

11.31 $H_3PO_4(aq) + H_2O(l) \rightleftharpoons H_3O^+(aq) + H_2PO_4^-(aq)$

The K_a expression is the ratio of the [products] divided by the [reactants] with [H_2O] considered constant and part of the K_a:

$$K_a = \frac{[H_3O^+][H_2PO_4^-]}{[H_3PO_4]} = 7.5 \times 10^{-3}$$

11.33 In pure water, a small fraction of the water molecules break apart to form H^+ and OH^-. The H^+ combines with H_2O to form H_3O^+. Every time an H^+ is formed, an OH^- is also formed. Therefore, the concentration of the two must be equal in pure water.

11.35 In an acidic solution, the [H_3O^+] is greater than the [OH^-], which means that at 25 °C, the [H_3O^+] is greater than 1.0×10^{-7} M and the [OH^-] is less than 1.0×10^{-7} M.

11.37 The value of $K_w = [H_3O^+][OH^-] = 1.0 \times 10^{-14}$ at 25 °C.

If [H_3O^+] needs to be calculated from [OH^-], then rearranging the K_w for [H_3O^+] gives

$$[H_3O^+] = \frac{1.0 \times 10^{-14}}{[OH^-]}.$$

If $[OH^-]$ needs to be calculated from $[H_3O^+]$, then rearranging the K_w for $[OH^-]$ gives

$$[OH^-] = \frac{1.0 \times 10^{-14}}{[H_3O^+]}.$$

A neutral solution has $[OH^-] = [H_3O^+]$. If the $[OH^-] > [H_3O^+]$, the solution is basic; if the $[H_3O^+] > [OH^-]$, the solution is acidic.

a. $[OH^-] = \dfrac{1.0 \times 10^{-14}}{[H_3O^+]} = \dfrac{1.0 \times 10^{-14}}{[2.0 \times 10^{-5}]} = 5.0 \times 10^{-10}$ M; since $[H_3O^+] > [OH^-]$,

the solution is acidic.

b. $[OH^-] = \dfrac{1.0 \times 10^{-14}}{[H_3O^+]} = \dfrac{1.0 \times 10^{-14}}{[1.4 \times 10^{-9}]} = 7.1 \times 10^{-6}$ M; since $[OH^-] > [H_3O^+]$,

the solution is basic.

c. $[H_3O^+] = \dfrac{1.0 \times 10^{-14}}{[OH^-]} = \dfrac{1.0 \times 10^{-14}}{[8.0 \times 10^{-3}]} = 1.3 \times 10^{-12}$ M; since $[OH^-] > [H_3O^+]$,

the solution is basic.

d. $[H_3O^+] = \dfrac{1.0 \times 10^{-14}}{[OH^-]} = \dfrac{1.0 \times 10^{-14}}{[3.5 \times 10^{-10}]} = 2.9 \times 10^{-5}$ M; since $[H_3O^+] > [OH^-]$,

the solution is acidic.

11.39 The value of $K_w = [H_3O^+][OH^-] = 1.0 \times 10^{-14}$ at 25 °C.

When $[OH^-]$ is known, the $[H_3O^+]$ can be calculated by rearranging the K_w for $[H_3O^+]$:

$$[H_3O^+] = \frac{1.0 \times 10^{-14}}{[OH^-]}$$

a. $[H_3O^+] = \dfrac{1.0 \times 10^{-14}}{[OH^-]} = \dfrac{1.0 \times 10^{-14}}{[1.0 \times 10^{-9}]} = 1.0 \times 10^{-5}$ M (2 SFs)

b. $[H_3O^+] = \dfrac{1.0 \times 10^{-14}}{[OH^-]} = \dfrac{1.0 \times 10^{-14}}{[1.0 \times 10^{-6}]} = 1.0 \times 10^{-8}$ M (2 SFs)

c. $[H_3O^+] = \dfrac{1.0 \times 10^{-14}}{[OH^-]} = \dfrac{1.0 \times 10^{-14}}{[2.0 \times 10^{-5}]} = 5.0 \times 10^{-10}$ M (2 SFs)

d. $[H_3O^+] = \dfrac{1.0 \times 10^{-14}}{[OH^-]} = \dfrac{1.0 \times 10^{-14}}{[4.0 \times 10^{-13}]} = 2.5 \times 10^{-2}$ M (2 SFs)

11.41 The value of $K_w = [H_3O^+][OH^-] = 1.0 \times 10^{-14}$ at 25 °C.

When $[H_3O^+]$ is known, the $[OH^-]$ can be calculated by rearranging the K_w for $[OH^-]$:

$$[OH^-] = \frac{1.0 \times 10^{-14}}{[H_3O^+]}$$

a. $[OH^-] = \dfrac{1.0 \times 10^{-14}}{[H_3O^+]} = \dfrac{1.0 \times 10^{-14}}{[4.0 \times 10^{-2}]} = 2.5 \times 10^{-13}$ M (2 SFs)

b. $[OH^-] = \dfrac{1.0 \times 10^{-14}}{[H_3O^+]} = \dfrac{1.0 \times 10^{-14}}{[5.0 \times 10^{-6}]} = 2.0 \times 10^{-9}$ M (2 SFs)

c. $[OH^-] = \dfrac{1.0 \times 10^{-14}}{[H_3O^+]} = \dfrac{1.0 \times 10^{-14}}{[2.0 \times 10^{-4}]} = 5.0 \times 10^{-11}$ M (2 SFs)

d. $[OH^-] = \dfrac{1.0 \times 10^{-14}}{[H_3O^+]} = \dfrac{1.0 \times 10^{-14}}{[7.9 \times 10^{-9}]} = 1.3 \times 10^{-6}$ M (2 SFs)

11.43 In a neutral solution, the $[H_3O^+] = 1.0 \times 10^{-7}$ M at 25 °C.

$pH = -\log[H_3O^+] = -\log[1.0 \times 10^{-7}] = 7.00$. The pH value contains two *decimal places*, which represent the two significant figures in the coefficient 1.0.

11.45 An acidic solution has a pH less than 7.0. A basic solution has a pH greater than 7.0. A neutral solution has a pH equal to 7.0.
  a. basic (pH 7.38 > 7.0)   **b.** acidic (pH 2.8 < 7.0)
  c. acidic (pH 5.52 < 7.0)   **d.** acidic (pH 4.2 < 7.0)
  e. basic (pH 7.6 > 7.0)

11.47 Since pH is a logarithmic scale, an increase or decrease of 1 pH unit changes the $[H_3O^+]$ by a factor of 10. Thus, a pH of 3 ($[H_3O^+] = 10^{-3}$ M, or 0.001 M) is 10 times more acidic than a pH of 4 ($[H_3O^+] = 10^{-4}$ M, or 0.0001 M).

11.49 $pH = -\log[H_3O^+]$

Since the value of $K_w = [H_3O^+][OH^-] = 1.0 \times 10^{-14}$ at 25 °C, if $[H_3O^+]$ needs to be calculated from $[OH^-]$, rearranging the K_w for $[H_3O^+]$ gives $[H_3O^+] = \dfrac{1.0 \times 10^{-14}}{[OH^-]}$.

  a. $pH = -\log[H_3O^+] = -\log[1 \times 10^{-4}] = 4.0$ (1 SF on the right of the decimal point)
  b. $pH = -\log[H_3O^+] = -\log[3 \times 10^{-9}] = 8.5$ (1 SF on the right of the decimal point)
  c. $[H_3O^+] = \dfrac{1.0 \times 10^{-14}}{[1 \times 10^{-5}]} = 1 \times 10^{-9}$ M

    $pH = -\log[1 \times 10^{-9}] = 9.0$ (1 SF on the right of the decimal point)

  d. $[H_3O^+] = \dfrac{1.0 \times 10^{-14}}{[2.5 \times 10^{-11}]} = 4.0 \times 10^{-4}$ M

    $pH = -\log[4.0 \times 10^{-4}] = 3.40$ (2 SFs on the right of the decimal point)
  e. $pH = -\log[H_3O^+] = -\log[6.7 \times 10^{-8}] = 7.17$ (2 SFs on the right of the decimal point)

  f. $[H_3O^+] = \dfrac{1.0 \times 10^{-14}}{[8.2 \times 10^{-4}]} = 1.2 \times 10^{-11}$ M

    $pH = -\log[1.2 \times 10^{-11}] = 10.92$ (2 SFs on the right of the decimal point)

11.51 On a calculator, pH is calculated by entering $-\log$, followed by the coefficient *EE* (*EXP*) key and the power of 10 followed by the change sign $(+/-)$ key. On some calculators, the concentration is entered first (coefficient *EXP* –power) followed by *log* and $+/-$ key.

$$[H_3O^+] = \dfrac{1.0 \times 10^{-14}}{[OH^-]}; \quad [OH^-] = \dfrac{1.0 \times 10^{-14}}{[H_3O^+]}; pH = -\log[H_3O^+]; [H_3O^+] = 10^{-pH}$$

Food	$[H_3O^+]$	$[OH^-]$	pH	Acidic, Basic, or Neutral?
Rye bread	1.6×10^{-9} M	6.3×10^{-6} M	8.80	Basic
Tomatoes	2.3×10^{-5} M	4.3×10^{-10} M	4.64	Acidic
Peas	6.2×10^{-7} M	1.6×10^{-8} M	6.21	Acidic

$[H_3O^+]$ and $[OH^-]$ all have 2 SFs here, so all pH values have 2 decimal places on the right of the decimal point.

11.53 $[H_3O^+] = 10^{-pH} = 10^{-6.92} = 1.2 \times 10^{-7}$ M (2 SFs)

11.55 Acids react with active metals to form $H_2(g)$ and a salt of the metal. The reaction of acids with carbonates or bicarbonates yields CO_2, H_2O, and a salt. In a neutralization reaction, an acid and a base react to form H_2O and a salt.
  a. $ZnCO_3(s) + 2HBr(aq) \longrightarrow CO_2(g) + H_2O(l) + ZnBr_2(aq)$
  b. $Zn(s) + 2HCl(aq) \longrightarrow H_2(g) + ZnCl_2(aq)$
  c. $HCl(aq) + NaHCO_3(s) \longrightarrow CO_2(g) + H_2O(l) + NaCl(aq)$
  d. $H_2SO_4(aq) + Mg(OH)_2(s) \longrightarrow 2H_2O(l) + MgSO_4(aq)$

11.57 In balancing a neutralization equation, the number of H^+ and OH^- must be equalized by placing coefficients in front of the formulas for the acid and base.
  a. $2HCl(aq) + Mg(OH)_2(s) \longrightarrow 2H_2O(l) + MgCl_2(aq)$
  b. $H_3PO_4(aq) + 3LiOH(aq) \longrightarrow 3H_2O(l) + Li_3PO_4(aq)$

11.59 The products of a neutralization are water and a salt. In balancing a neutralization equation, the number of H^+ and OH^- must be equalized by placing coefficients in front of the formulas for the acid and base.
  a. $H_2SO_4(aq) + 2NaOH(aq) \longrightarrow 2H_2O(l) + Na_2SO_4(aq)$
  b. $3HCl(aq) + Fe(OH)_3(s) \longrightarrow 3H_2O(l) + FeCl_3(aq)$
  c. $H_2CO_3(aq) + Mg(OH)_2(s) \longrightarrow 2H_2O(l) + MgCO_3(s)$

11.61 In the titration equation, 1 mole of HCl reacts with 1 mole of NaOH.

$$28.6 \text{ mL NaOH solution} \times \frac{1 \text{ L solution}}{1000 \text{ mL solution}} \times \frac{0.145 \text{ mole NaOH}}{1 \text{ L solution}} \times \frac{1 \text{ mole HCl}}{1 \text{ mole NaOH}}$$

$$= 0.004\ 15 \text{ mole of HCl}$$

$$5.00 \text{ mL HCl solution} \times \frac{1 \text{ L solution}}{1000 \text{ mL solution}} = 0.005\ 00 \text{ L of HCl solution}$$

$$\text{molarity (M) of HCl} = \frac{\text{moles of solute}}{\text{liters of solution}} = \frac{0.004\ 15 \text{ mole HCl}}{0.005\ 00 \text{ L solution}}$$

$$= 0.830 \text{ M HCl solution (3 SFs)}$$

11.63 In the titration equation, 1 mole of H_2SO_4 reacts with 2 moles of KOH.

$$38.2 \text{ mL KOH solution} \times \frac{1 \text{ L solution}}{1000 \text{ mL solution}} \times \frac{0.163 \text{ mole KOH}}{1 \text{ L solution}} \times \frac{1 \text{ mole H}_2\text{SO}_4}{2 \text{ moles KOH}}$$

$$= 0.003\ 11 \text{ mole of H}_2\text{SO}_4$$

$$25.0 \text{ mL H}_2\text{SO}_4 \text{ solution} \times \frac{1 \text{ L solution}}{1000 \text{ mL solution}} = 0.0250 \text{ L of H}_2\text{SO}_4 \text{ solution}$$

$$\text{molarity (M) of H}_2\text{SO}_4 = \frac{\text{moles of solute}}{\text{liters of solution}} = \frac{0.003\ 11 \text{ mole H}_2\text{SO}_4}{0.0250 \text{ L solution}}$$

$$= 0.124 \text{ M H}_2\text{SO}_4 \text{ solution (3 SFs)}$$

11.65 In the titration equation, 1 mole of H_3PO_4 reacts with 3 moles of NaOH.

$$50.0 \text{ mL H}_3\text{PO}_4 \text{ solution} \times \frac{1 \text{ L H}_3\text{PO}_4 \text{ solution}}{1000 \text{ mL H}_3\text{PO}_4 \text{ solution}} \times \frac{0.0224 \text{ mole H}_3\text{PO}_4}{1 \text{ L H}_3\text{PO}_4 \text{ solution}} \times \frac{3 \text{ moles NaOH}}{1 \text{ mole H}_3\text{PO}_4}$$

$$\times \frac{1 \text{ L NaOH solution}}{0.204 \text{ mole NaOH}} \times \frac{1000 \text{ mL NaOH solution}}{1 \text{ L NaOH solution}} = 16.5 \text{ mL of NaOH solution (3 SFs)}$$

11.67 A buffer system contains a weak acid and a salt containing its conjugate base (or a weak base and a salt containing its conjugate acid).
  a. This is not a buffer system because it only contains the strong base NaOH and the neutral salt NaCl.
  b. This is a buffer system; it contains the weak acid H_2CO_3 and a salt containing its conjugate base HCO_3^-.
  c. This is a buffer system; it contains the weak acid HF and a salt containing its conjugate base F^-.
  d. This is not a buffer system because it only contains the neutral salts KCl and NaCl.

11.69 a. The purpose of this buffer system is to (3) maintain pH.
  b. The salt of the weak acid is needed to (1) provide the conjugate base and (2) neutralize added H_3O^+.
  c. If OH^- is added, it is neutralized by (3) H_3O^+.
  d. When H_3O^+ is added, the equilibrium shifts in the direction of the (1) reactants.

11.71 $HNO_2(aq) + H_2O(l) \rightleftharpoons NO_2^-(aq) + H_3O^+(aq)$

Rearrange the K_a for $[H_3O^+]$ and use it to calculate the pH.

$$[H_3O^+] = K_a \times \frac{[HNO_2]}{[NO_2^-]} = 4.5 \times 10^{-4} \times \frac{[0.10\ M]}{[0.10\ M]} = 4.5 \times 10^{-4}\ M$$

$$pH = -\log[H_3O^+] = -\log[4.5 \times 10^{-4}] = 3.35 \text{ (2 SFs on the right of the decimal point)}$$

11.73 $HF(aq) + H_2O(l) \rightleftharpoons F^-(aq) + H_3O^+(aq)$

Rearrange the K_a for $[H_3O^+]$ and use it to calculate the pH.

$$[H_3O^+] = K_a \times \frac{[HF]}{[F^-]} = 3.5 \times 10^{-4} \times \frac{[0.10\ M]}{[0.10\ M]} = 3.5 \times 10^{-4}\ M$$

$$pH = -\log[3.5 \times 10^{-4}] = 3.46 \text{ (2 SFs on the right of the decimal point)}$$

$$[H_3O^+] = K_a \times \frac{[HF]}{[F^-]} = 3.5 \times 10^{-4} \times \frac{[0.060\ M]}{[0.120\ M]} = 1.75 \times 10^{-4}\ M$$

$$pH = -\log[1.75 \times 10^{-4}] = 3.76 \text{ (2 SFs on the right of the decimal point)}$$

∴ The solution with 0.10 M HF/0.10 M NaF is more acidic.

11.75 If you breathe fast, CO_2 is expelled and the equilibrium shifts to lower $[H_3O^+]$, which raises the pH.

11.77 If large amounts of HCO_3^- are lost, the equilibrium shifts to higher $[H_3O^+]$, which lowers the pH.

11.79 $pH = -\log[H_3O^+] = -\log[2.0 \times 10^{-4}] = 3.70$ (2 SFs on the right of the decimal point)

11.81 $[H_3O^+] = 10^{-pH} = 10^{-3.60} = 2.5 \times 10^{-4}\ M$ (2 SFs)

11.83 $CaCO_3(s) + 2HCl(aq) \longrightarrow CO_2(g) + H_2O(l) + CaCl_2(aq)$

11.85 From the neutralization equation in problem 11.83, 1 mole of $CaCO_3$ reacts with 2 moles of HCl.

$$100.\ \text{mL HCl solution} \times \frac{1\ \text{L HCl solution}}{1000\ \text{mL HCl solution}} \times \frac{0.0400\ \text{mole HCl}}{1\ \text{L HCl solution}} \times \frac{1\ \text{mole CaCO}_3}{2\ \text{moles HCl}}$$
$$\times \frac{100.09\ \text{g CaCO}_3}{1\ \text{mole CaCO}_3} = 0.200\ \text{g of CaCO}_3 \text{ (3 SFs)}$$

11.87 a. This diagram represents a weak acid; only a few HX molecules dissociate into H_3O^+ and X^- ions.
b. This diagram represents a strong acid; all of the HX molecules dissociate into H_3O^+ and X^- ions.

11.89 a. H_2SO_4 is an acid.
b. RbOH is a base.
c. $Ca(OH)_2$ is a base.
d. HI is an acid.

11.91

Acid	Conjugate Base
H_2O	OH^-
HCN	CN^-
HNO_2	NO_2^-
H_3PO_4	$H_2PO_4^-$

11.93 a. Hyperventilation will lower the CO_2 concentration in the blood, which lowers the $[H_2CO_3]$, which decreases the $[H_3O^+]$ and increases the blood pH.
b. Breathing into a paper bag will increase the CO_2 concentration in the blood, increase the $[H_2CO_3]$, increase $[H_3O^+]$, and lower the blood pH back toward the normal range.

11.95 An acidic solution has a pH less than 7.0. A neutral solution has a pH equal to 7.0. A basic solution has a pH greater than 7.0.
a. acidic (pH 5.2 < 7.0)
b. basic (pH 7.5 > 7.0)
c. basic (pH 8.1 > 7.0)
d. acidic (pH 2.5 < 7.0)

11.97 a. acid; bromous acid
b. base; cesium hydroxide
c. salt; magnesium nitrate
d. acid; perchloric acid

11.99

Acid	Conjugate Base
HI	I^-
HCl	Cl^-
NH_4^+	NH_3
H_2S	HS^-

11.101 Use Table 11.3 to answer (the stronger acid will be closer to the top of the table).
a. HF is the stronger acid.
b. H_3O^+ is the stronger acid.
c. HNO_2 is the stronger acid.
d. HCO_3^- is the stronger acid.

11.103 $[H_3O^+] = \dfrac{1.0 \times 10^{-14}}{[OH^-]}$; $pH = -\log[H_3O^+]$

a. $pH = -\log[H_3O^+] = -\log[2.0 \times 10^{-8}] = 7.70$ (2 SFs on the right of the decimal point)
b. $pH = -\log[5.0 \times 10^{-2}] = 1.30$ (2 SFs on the right of the decimal point)

c. $[H_3O^+] = \dfrac{1.0 \times 10^{-14}}{[3.5 \times 10^{-4}]} = 2.9 \times 10^{-11}$ M

$pH = -\log[2.9 \times 10^{-11}] = 10.54$ (2 SFs on the right of the decimal point)

d. $[H_3O^+] = \dfrac{1.0 \times 10^{-14}}{[0.0054]} = 1.9 \times 10^{-12}$ M

$pH = -\log[1.9 \times 10^{-12}] = 11.73$ (2 SFs on the right of the decimal point)

11.105 a. basic (pH > 7.0)
    b. acidic (pH < 7.0)
    c. basic (pH > 7.0)
    d. basic (pH > 7.0)

11.107 If the pH is given, the $[H_3O^+]$ can be found by using the relationship $[H_3O^+] = 10^{-pH}$.

The $[OH^-]$ can be found by rearranging $K_w = [H_3O^+][OH^-] = 1 \times 10^{-14}$.

    a. pH = 3.00; $[H_3O^+] = 10^{-pH} = 10^{-3.00} = 1.0 \times 10^{-3}$ M (2 SFs)

$$[OH^-] = \frac{1.0 \times 10^{-14}}{[H_3O^+]} = \frac{1.0 \times 10^{-14}}{[1.0 \times 10^{-3}]} = 1.0 \times 10^{-11} \text{ M (2 SFs)}$$

    b. pH = 6.2; $[H_3O^+] = 10^{-pH} = 10^{-6.2} = 6 \times 10^{-7}$ M (1 SF)

$$[OH^-] = \frac{1.0 \times 10^{-14}}{[H_3O^+]} = \frac{1.0 \times 10^{-14}}{[6.3 \times 10^{-7}]} = 2 \times 10^{-8} \text{ M (1 SF)}$$

    c. pH = 8.85; $[H_3O^+] = 10^{-pH} = 10^{-8.85} = 1.4 \times 10^{-9}$ M (2 SFs)

$$[OH^-] = \frac{1.0 \times 10^{-14}}{[H_3O^+]} = \frac{1.0 \times 10^{-14}}{[1.4 \times 10^{-9}]} = 7.1 \times 10^{-6} \text{ M (2 SFs)}$$

    d. pH = 11.00; $[H_3O^+] = 10^{-pH} = 10^{-11.00} = 1.0 \times 10^{-11}$ M (2 SFs)

$$[OH^-] = \frac{1.0 \times 10^{-14}}{[H_3O^+]} = \frac{1.0 \times 10^{-14}}{[1.0 \times 10^{-11}]} = 1.0 \times 10^{-3} \text{ M (2 SFs)}$$

11.109 a. Solution A, with a pH of 4.5, is more acidic.
    b. In solution A, the $[H_3O^+] = 10^{-pH} = 10^{-4.5} = 3 \times 10^{-5}$ M (1 SF)

    In solution B, the $[H_3O^+] = 10^{-pH} = 10^{-6.7} = 2 \times 10^{-7}$ M (1 SF)

    c. In solution A, the $[OH^-] = \dfrac{1.0 \times 10^{-14}}{[H_3O^+]} = \dfrac{1.0 \times 10^{-14}}{[3 \times 10^{-5}]} = 3 \times 10^{-10}$ M (1 SF)

    In solution B, the $[OH^-] = \dfrac{1.0 \times 10^{-14}}{[H_3O^+]} = \dfrac{1.0 \times 10^{-14}}{[2 \times 10^{-7}]} = 5 \times 10^{-8}$ M (1 SF)

11.111 The $[OH^-]$ can be calculated from the moles of NaOH (each NaOH produces 1 OH^-) and the volume of the solution (in L).

$$0.225 \text{ g NaOH} \times \frac{1 \text{ mole NaOH}}{40.00 \text{ g NaOH}} \times \frac{1 \text{ mole } OH^-}{1 \text{ mole NaOH}} = 0.005\,63 \text{ mole of } OH^-$$

$$[OH^-] = \frac{0.005\,63 \text{ mole } OH^-}{0.250 \text{ L solution}} = 0.0225 \text{ M (3 SFs)}$$

11.113 $2.5 \text{ g HCl} \times \dfrac{1 \text{ mole HCl}}{36.46 \text{ g HCl}} \times \dfrac{1 \text{ mole } H_3O^+}{1 \text{ mole HCl}} = 0.069 \text{ mole of } H_3O^+$ (2 SFs)

$$[H_3O^+] = \frac{0.069 \text{ mole } H_3O^+}{0.425 \text{ L solution}} = 0.16 \text{ M (2 SFs)}$$

$$pH = -\log[H_3O^+] = -\log[0.16] = 0.80 \text{ (2 SFs on the right of the decimal point)}$$

11.115 a. To form the conjugate base, remove a hydrogen ion (H^+) from the acid.
1. HS^- **2.** $H_2PO_4^-$

b. 1. $\dfrac{[H_3O^+][HS^-]}{[H_2S]}$ **2.** $\dfrac{[H_3O^+][H_2PO_4^-]}{[H_3PO_4]}$

c. H_2S (see Table 11.3; the weaker acid will be closer to the bottom of the table)

11.117 a. NH_4^+/NH_3 and HNO_3/NO_3^-
From Table 11.3, we see that NH_4^+ is a weaker acid than HNO_3 and that NO_3^- is a weaker base than NH_3. Thus, the equilibrium mixture will contain mostly products.

b. H_3O^+/H_2O and HBr/Br^-
From Table 11.3, we see that H_3O^+ is a weaker acid than HBr and that Br^- is a weaker base than H_2O. Thus, the equilibrium mixture will contain mostly products.

11.119 a. $ZnCO_3(s) + H_2SO_4(aq) \longrightarrow CO_2(g) + H_2O(l) + ZnSO_4(aq)$
b. $2Al(s) + 6HNO_3(aq) \longrightarrow 3H_2(g) + 2Al(NO_3)_3(aq)$

11.121 KOH (strong base) $\longrightarrow K^+(aq) + OH^-(aq)$ (100% dissociation)
$[OH^-] = 0.050\ M = 5.0 \times 10^{-2}\ M$

a. $[H_3O^+] = \dfrac{1.0 \times 10^{-14}}{[OH^-]} = \dfrac{1.0 \times 10^{-14}}{[5.0 \times 10^{-2}]} = 2.0 \times 10^{-13}\ M$ (2 SFs)

b. $pH = -\log[H_3O^+] = -\log[2.0 \times 10^{-13}] = 12.70$ (2 SFs on the right of the decimal point)

c. $H_2SO_4(aq) + 2KOH(aq) \longrightarrow 2H_2O(l) + K_2SO_4(aq)$

d. In the titration equation, 1 mole of H_2SO_4 reacts with 2 moles of KOH.

$$40.0\ \text{mL H}_2\text{SO}_4\ \text{solution} \times \frac{1\ \text{L H}_2\text{SO}_4\ \text{solution}}{1000\ \text{mL H}_2\text{SO}_4\ \text{solution}} \times \frac{0.035\ \text{mole H}_2\text{SO}_4}{1\ \text{L H}_2\text{SO}_4\ \text{solution}} \times \frac{2\ \text{moles KOH}}{1\ \text{mole H}_2\text{SO}_4}$$

$$\times \frac{1\ \text{L KOH solution}}{0.050\ \text{mole KOH}} \times \frac{1000\ \text{mL KOH solution}}{1\ \text{L KOH solution}} = 56\ \text{mL of KOH solution (2 SFs)}$$

11.123 a. The $[H_3O^+]$ can be found by using the relationship $[H_3O^+] = 10^{-pH}$.

$[H_3O^+] = 10^{-pH} = 10^{-4.2} = 6 \times 10^{-5}\ M$ (1 SF)

$[OH^-] = \dfrac{1.0 \times 10^{-14}}{[H_3O^+]} = \dfrac{1.0 \times 10^{-14}}{[6 \times 10^{-5}]} = 2 \times 10^{-10}\ M$ (1 SF)

b. $[H_3O^+] = 10^{-pH} = 10^{-6.5} = 3 \times 10^{-7}\ M$ (1 SF)

$[OH^-] = \dfrac{1.0 \times 10^{-14}}{[H_3O^+]} = \dfrac{1.0 \times 10^{-14}}{[3 \times 10^{-7}]} = 3 \times 10^{-8}\ M$ (1 SF)

c. In the titration equation, 1 mole of $CaCO_3$ reacts with 1 mole of H_2SO_4.

$$1.0\ \text{kL solution} \times \frac{1000\ \text{L solution}}{1\ \text{kL solution}} \times \frac{6 \times 10^{-5}\ \text{mole H}_3\text{O}^+}{1\ \text{L solution}}$$

$$\times \frac{1\ \text{mole H}_2\text{SO}_4}{2\ \text{moles H}_3\text{O}^+} \times \frac{1\ \text{mole CaCO}_3}{1\ \text{mole H}_2\text{SO}_4} \times \frac{100.09\ \text{g CaCO}_3}{1\ \text{mole CaCO}_3} = 3\ \text{g of CaCO}_3\ (1\ \text{SF})$$

11.125 a. In the titration equation, 1 mole of HCl reacts with 1 mole of NaOH.

$$HCl(aq) + NaOH(aq) \longrightarrow H_2O(l) + NaCl(aq)$$

$$25.0 \text{ mL HCl solution} \times \frac{1 \text{ L HCl solution}}{1000 \text{ mL HCl solution}} \times \frac{0.288 \text{ mole HCl}}{1 \text{ L HCl solution}} \times \frac{1 \text{ mole NaOH}}{1 \text{ mole HCl}}$$

$$\times \frac{1 \text{ L NaOH solution}}{0.150 \text{ mole NaOH}} \times \frac{1000 \text{ mL NaOH solution}}{1 \text{ L NaOH solution}} = 48.0 \text{ mL of NaOH solution (3 SFs)}$$

b. In the titration equation, 1 mole of H_2SO_4 reacts with 2 moles of NaOH.

$$H_2SO_4(aq) + 2NaOH(aq) \longrightarrow 2H_2O(l) + Na_2SO_4(aq)$$

$$10.0 \text{ mL H}_2\text{SO}_4 \text{ solution} \times \frac{1 \text{ L H}_2\text{SO}_4 \text{ solution}}{1000 \text{ mL H}_2\text{SO}_4 \text{ solution}} \times \frac{0.560 \text{ mole H}_2\text{SO}_4}{1 \text{ L H}_2\text{SO}_4 \text{ solution}} \times \frac{2 \text{ moles NaOH}}{1 \text{ mole H}_2\text{SO}_4}$$

$$\times \frac{1 \text{ L NaOH solution}}{0.150 \text{ mole NaOH}} \times \frac{1000 \text{ mL NaOH solution}}{1 \text{ L NaOH solution}} = 74.7 \text{ mL of NaOH solution (3 SFs)}$$

11.127 In the titration equation, 1 mole of H_2SO_4 reacts with 2 moles of NaOH.

$$45.6 \text{ mL NaOH solution} \times \frac{1 \text{ L solution}}{1000 \text{ mL solution}} \times \frac{0.205 \text{ mole NaOH}}{1 \text{ L solution}} \times \frac{1 \text{ mole H}_2\text{SO}_4}{2 \text{ moles NaOH}}$$

$$= 0.004\ 67 \text{ mole of H}_2\text{SO}_4$$

$$20.0 \text{ mL H}_2\text{SO}_4 \text{ solution} \times \frac{1 \text{ L solution}}{1000 \text{ mL solution}} = 0.0200 \text{ L of H}_2\text{SO}_4 \text{ solution}$$

$$\text{molarity (M) of H}_2\text{SO}_4 = \frac{\text{moles of solute}}{\text{liters of solution}} = \frac{0.004\ 67 \text{ mole H}_2\text{SO}_4}{0.0200 \text{ L solution}}$$

$$= 0.234 \text{ M H}_2\text{SO}_4 \text{ solution (3 SFs)}$$

11.129 This buffer solution is made from the weak acid H_3PO_4 and a salt containing its conjugate base $H_2PO_4^-$.
a. Add acid: $H_2PO_4^-(aq) + H_3O^+(aq) \longrightarrow H_3PO_4(aq) + H_2O(l)$
b. Add base: $H_3PO_4(aq) + OH^-(aq) \longrightarrow H_2PO_4^-(aq) + H_2O(l)$

c. $[H_3O^+] = K_a \times \dfrac{[H_3PO_4]}{[H_2PO_4^-]} = 7.5 \times 10^{-3} \times \dfrac{[0.50 \text{ M}]}{[0.20 \text{ M}]} = 1.9 \times 10^{-2} \text{ M}$

$\text{pH} = -\log[1.9 \times 10^{-2}] = 1.72 \text{ (2 SFs on the right of the decimal point)}$

CI.19 a. $[H_2] = \dfrac{2.02 \text{ g } H_2}{10.0 \text{ L}} \times \dfrac{1 \text{ mole } H_2}{2.016 \text{ g } H_2} = 0.100 \text{ M}$

$[S_2] = \dfrac{10.3 \text{ g } S_2}{10.0 \text{ L}} \times \dfrac{1 \text{ mole } S_2}{64.14 \text{ g } S_2} = 0.0161 \text{ M}$

$[H_2S] = \dfrac{68.2 \text{ g } H_2S}{10.0 \text{ L}} \times \dfrac{1 \text{ mole } H_2S}{34.09 \text{ g } H_2S} = 0.200 \text{ M}$

$K_c = \dfrac{[H_2S]^2}{[H_2]^2[S_2]} = \dfrac{[0.200]^2}{[0.100]^2[0.0161]} = 248 \ (3 \text{ SFs})$

b. If more H_2 (a reactant) is added, the equilibrium will shift in the direction of the products.

c. If the volume decreases from 10.0 L to 5.00 L (at constant temperature), the equilibrium will shift in the direction of the products (fewer moles of gas).

d. $[H_2] = \dfrac{0.300 \text{ mole } H_2}{5.00 \text{ L}} = 0.0600 \text{ M}$

$[H_2S] = \dfrac{2.50 \text{ moles } H_2S}{5.00 \text{ L}} = 0.500 \text{ M}$

$K_c = \dfrac{[H_2S]^2}{[H_2]^2[S_2]} = 248$

Rearrange the expression to solve for $[S_2]$ and substitute in known values.

$[S_2] = \dfrac{[H_2S]^2}{[H_2]^2 K_c} = \dfrac{[0.500]^2}{[0.0600]^2(248)} = 0.280 \text{ M} \ (3 \text{ SFs})$

CI.21 a. $2M(s) + 6HCl(aq) \longrightarrow 3H_2(g) + 2MCl_3(aq)$

b. $34.8 \text{ mL solution} \times \dfrac{1 \text{ L solution}}{1000 \text{ mL solution}} \times \dfrac{0.520 \text{ mole HCl}}{1 \text{ L solution}} \times \dfrac{3 \text{ moles } H_2}{6 \text{ moles HCl}}$

$= 0.00905 \text{ mole of } H_2 \ (3 \text{ SFs})$

$T = 24\,°C + 273 = 297 \text{ K}$

Rearrange the ideal gas law $PV = nRT$ to solve for V,

$V = \dfrac{nRT}{P} = \dfrac{(0.00905 \text{ mole})\left(\dfrac{62.4 \text{ L} \cdot \text{mmHg}}{\text{mole} \cdot \text{K}}\right)(297 \text{ K})}{(720. \text{ mmHg})} \times \dfrac{1000 \text{ mL}}{1 \text{ L}} = 233 \text{ mL of } H_2 \ (3 \text{ SFs})$

c. $34.8 \text{ mL solution} \times \dfrac{1 \text{ L solution}}{1000 \text{ mL solution}} \times \dfrac{0.520 \text{ mole HCl}}{1 \text{ L solution}} \times \dfrac{2 \text{ moles M}}{6 \text{ moles HCl}}$

$= 6.03 \times 10^{-3} \text{ mole of M} \ (3 \text{ SFs})$

d. $\dfrac{0.420 \text{ g M}}{6.03 \times 10^{-3} \text{ mole M}} = 69.7 \text{ g/mole of M} \ (3 \text{ SFs}); \therefore \text{ metal M is gallium}$

e. $2Ga(s) + 6HCl(aq) \longrightarrow 3H_2(g) + 2GaCl_3(aq)$

CI.23 a. $\dfrac{8.57 \text{ g KOH}}{850. \text{ mL solution}} \times \dfrac{1 \text{ mole KOH}}{56.11 \text{ g KOH}} \times \dfrac{1000 \text{ mL solution}}{1 \text{ L solution}} = 0.180 \text{ M KOH solution (3 SFs)}$

b. $[\text{H}_3\text{O}^+] = \dfrac{K_w}{[\text{OH}^-]} = \dfrac{1.0 \times 10^{-14}}{[0.180]} = 5.56 \times 10^{-14} \text{ M}$

$\text{pH} = -\log[\text{H}_3\text{O}^+] = -\log[5.56 \times 10^{-14}] = 13.255 \text{ (3 SFs on the right of the decimal point)}$

c. $2\text{KOH}(aq) + \text{H}_2\text{SO}_4(aq) \longrightarrow 2\text{H}_2\text{O}(l) + \text{K}_2\text{SO}_4(aq)$

d. $10.0 \text{ mL KOH solution} \times \dfrac{1 \text{ L KOH solution}}{1000 \text{ mL KOH solution}} \times \dfrac{0.180 \text{ mole KOH}}{1 \text{ L KOH solution}} \times \dfrac{1 \text{ mole H}_2\text{SO}_4}{2 \text{ moles KOH}}$

$\times \dfrac{1 \text{ L H}_2\text{SO}_4 \text{ solution}}{0.250 \text{ mole H}_2\text{SO}_4} \times \dfrac{1000 \text{ mL H}_2\text{SO}_4 \text{ solution}}{1 \text{ L H}_2\text{SO}_4 \text{ solution}}$

$= 3.60 \text{ mL of H}_2\text{SO}_4 \text{ solution (3 SFs)}$

CI.25 a. $[\text{H}_2\text{CO}_3] = \dfrac{0.0149 \text{ g H}_2\text{CO}_3}{200.0 \text{ mL solution}} \times \dfrac{1 \text{ mole H}_2\text{CO}_3}{62.03 \text{ g H}_2\text{CO}_3} \times \dfrac{1000 \text{ mL solution}}{1 \text{ L solution}}$

$= 0.00120 \text{ M (3 SFs)}$

b. $[\text{HCO}_3^-] = \dfrac{0.403 \text{ g NaHCO}_3}{200.0 \text{ mL solution}} \times \dfrac{1 \text{ mole NaHCO}_3}{84.01 \text{ g NaHCO}_3} \times \dfrac{1 \text{ mole HCO}_3^-}{1 \text{ mole NaHCO}_3} \times \dfrac{1000 \text{ mL solution}}{1 \text{ L solution}}$

$= 0.0240 \text{ M (3 SFs)}$

c. $[\text{H}_3\text{O}^+] = K_a \times \dfrac{[\text{H}_2\text{CO}_3]}{[\text{HCO}_3^-]} = 7.9 \times 10^{-7} \times \dfrac{[0.00120]}{[0.0240]} = 4.0 \times 10^{-8} \text{ M (2 SFs)}$

d. $\text{pH} = -\log[4.0 \times 10^{-8}] = 7.40 \text{ (2 SFs on the right of the decimal point)}$

e. $\text{HCO}_3^-(aq) + \text{H}_3\text{O}^+(aq) \longrightarrow \text{H}_2\text{CO}_3(aq) + \text{H}_2\text{O}(l)$

f. $\text{H}_2\text{CO}_3(aq) + \text{OH}^-(aq) \longrightarrow \text{HCO}_3^-(aq) + \text{H}_2\text{O}(l)$

12

Introduction to Organic Chemistry: Hydrocarbons

Credit: Andrew Poertner | AP Images

For three months after her house fire, Diane remained in the hospital's burn unit, where she continued to have treatment for burns, including removing damaged tissue, skin grafts, and preventing infection. For some of the large burn areas, some of Diane's own skin cells were removed and grown for three weeks to give a layer of skin that covered the burn areas. By covering the burn areas, the incidence of dehydration and infection were decreased. After three months, she was discharged.

The arson investigators determined that gasoline was the primary accelerant used to start the fire at Diane's house. However, they later determined there was also kerosene and some diesel fuel. About 70% of kerosene consists of alkanes and cycloalkanes; about 30% of kerosene is aromatic hydrocarbons. Write a balanced chemical equation for the combustion of $C_{11}H_{24}$, which is a compound in kerosene.

CHAPTER READINESS*

⚛ Core Chemistry Skills

- Drawing Lewis Structures (6.6)
- Predicting Shape (6.8)
- Balancing a Chemical Equation (7.1)

* These Core Chemistry Skills from previous chapters are listed here for your review as you proceed to the new material in this chapter.

12.1 Organic Compounds

Learning Goal: Identify properties characteristic of organic or inorganic compounds.

- Organic compounds are compounds of carbon and hydrogen that have covalent bonds, have low melting and boiling points, burn vigorously, are mostly nonpolar molecules, and are usually more soluble in nonpolar solvents than in water.
- Alkanes are hydrocarbons that have only single bonds, C—C and C—H.
- Each carbon in an alkane has four bonds arranged so that the bonded atoms are in the corners of a tetrahedron.

◆ **Learning Exercise 12.1A**

Identify each of the following as characteristic of organic (O) or inorganic (I) compounds:

1. _____ have covalent bonds   2. _____ have low boiling points

3. _____ burn in air   4. _____ are soluble in water

5. _____ have high melting points   6. _____ are soluble in nonpolar solvents

7. _____ have ionic bonds   8. _____ form long carbon chains

9. _____ contain carbon and hydrogen   10. _____ do not burn in air

Vegetable oil, an organic compound, is not soluble in water.

Credit: Pearson Education / Pearson Science

Answers	**1.** O	**2.** O	**3.** O	**4.** I	**5.** I
	6. O	**7.** I	**8.** O	**9.** O	**10.** I

◆ **Learning Exercise 12.1B**

1. What is the name of the three-dimensional shape of methane shown here?

2. Draw the expanded structural formula for methane.

Answers   **1.** tetrahedron

2. $H—\underset{\displaystyle H}{\overset{\displaystyle H}{C}}—H$

12.2 Alkanes

Learning Goal: Write the IUPAC names and draw the condensed or line-angle structural formulas for alkanes and cycloalkanes.

- An expanded structural formula shows all of the atoms and the bonds connected to each atom.
- A condensed structural formula depicts each carbon atom and its attached hydrogen atoms as a group.
- A line-angle structural formula shows the carbon atoms as the corners or ends of a zigzag line.
- A molecular formula gives the total number of each kind of atom.

Expanded Structural Formula	Condensed Structural Formula	Line-Angle Structural Formula	Molecular Formula
$H—\overset{\displaystyle H}{\underset{\displaystyle H}{C}}—\overset{\displaystyle H}{\underset{\displaystyle H}{C}}—\overset{\displaystyle H}{\underset{\displaystyle H}{C}}—H$	$CH_3—CH_2—CH_3$	⋀	C_3H_8

• In an IUPAC (International Union of Pure and Applied Chemistry) name, the prefix indicates the number of carbon atoms, and the suffix describes the family of the compound. For example, in the name *propane*, the prefix *prop* indicates a chain of three carbon atoms and the ending *ane* indicates single bonds (alkane). The names of the first six alkanes follow:

Name	Number of Carbon Atoms	Condensed Structural Formula	Line-Angle Structural Formula
Methane	1	CH_4	
Ethane	2	CH_3-CH_3	
Propane	3	$CH_3-CH_2-CH_3$	
Butane	4	$CH_3-CH_2-CH_2-CH_3$	
Pentane	5	$CH_3-CH_2-CH_2-CH_2-CH_3$	
Hexane	6	$CH_3-CH_2-CH_2-CH_2-CH_2-CH_3$	

Guide to Drawing Structural Formulas for Alkanes	
STEP 1	Draw the carbon chain.
STEP 2	Draw the expanded structural formula by adding the hydrogen atoms using single bonds to each of the carbon atoms.
STEP 3	Draw the condensed structural formula by combining the H atoms with each C atom.
STEP 4	Draw the line-angle structural formula as a zigzag line in which the ends and corners represent C atoms.

♦ **Learning Exercise 12.2A**

⚛ CORE CHEMISTRY SKILL

Naming and Drawing Alkanes

Indicate if each of the following is an expanded structural formula (E), a condensed structural formula (C), a line-angle structural formula (L), or a molecular formula (M):

1. _____ CH_3-CH_3 2. _____ C_5H_{12} 3. _____ $CH_3-CH_2-CH_3$

4. _____
```
    H   H   H
    |   |   |
H — C — C — C — H
    |   |   |
    H   H   H
```

5. _____ (line-angle zigzag structure)

Answers   **1.** C   **2.** M   **3.** C   **4.** E   **5.** L

♦ **Learning Exercise 12.2B**

Draw the condensed structural formula for each of the following expanded or line-angle structural formulas:

1.
```
    H   H
    |   |
H — C — C — H
    |   |
    H   H
```

2.
```
    H   H   H
    |   |   |
H — C — C — C — H
    |   |   |
    H   H   H
```

3.
```
    H   H   H   H
    |   |   |   |
H — C — C — C — C — H
    |   |   |   |
    H   H   H   H
```

4. (line-angle zigzag structure)

Answers   **1.** $CH_3—CH_3$ **2.** $CH_3—CH_2—CH_3$
          3. $CH_3—CH_2—CH_2—CH_3$ **4.** $CH_3—CH_2—CH_2—CH_2—CH_3$

♦ **Learning Exercise 12.2C**

Draw the condensed structural formula and give the name for the continuous-chain alkane with each of the following molecular formulas:

1. C_2H_6 _____

2. C_3H_8 _____

3. C_4H_{10} _____

4. C_5H_{12} _____

5. C_6H_{14} _____

Answers   **1.** $CH_3—CH_3$, ethane

          2. $CH_3—CH_2—CH_3$, propane

          3. $CH_3—CH_2—CH_2—CH_3$, butane

          4. $CH_3—CH_2—CH_2—CH_2—CH_3$, pentane

          5. $CH_3—CH_2—CH_2—CH_2—CH_2—CH_3$, hexane

Study Note

A cycloalkane is named by adding the prefix *cyclo* to the name of the corresponding alkane. For example, the name *cyclopropane* indicates a cyclic structure of three carbon atoms, usually represented by the geometric shape of a triangle.

♦ **Learning Exercise 12.2D**

Give the IUPAC name for each of the following cycloalkanes:

1.   **2.** ▢   **3.** ⬠   **4.** △

Answers   **1.** cyclohexane   **2.** cyclobutane   **3.** cyclopentane   **4.** cyclopropane

♦ **Learning Exercise 12.2E**

Draw the line-angle structural formula for each of the following:

1. butane   _____

2. pentane   _____

3. hexane   _____

4. octane   _____

5. cyclohexane   _____

Answers   1.   2. /\/\/\   3. /\/\/\/

4. /\/\/\/\/   5. (hexagon)

12.3 Alkanes with Substituents

Learning Goal: Write the IUPAC names for alkanes with substituents and draw their condensed and line-angle structural formulas.

- In the IUPAC system each substituent is numbered and listed alphabetically in front of the name of the longest chain.

- Carbon groups that are substituents are named as alkyl groups or alkyl substituents. An alkyl group is named by replacing the *ane* of the alkane name with *yl*. For example, CH_3— is methyl (from CH_4 methane), and CH_3—CH_2— is ethyl (from CH_3—CH_3 ethane).

- In a haloalkane, a halogen atom, —F, —Cl, —Br, or —I replaces a hydrogen atom in an alkane.

- A halogen atom is named as a substituent (*fluoro, chloro, bromo, iodo*) attached to the alkane chain.

Guide to Naming Alkanes with Substituents	
STEP 1	Write the alkane name for the longest chain of carbon atoms.
STEP 2	Number the carbon atoms starting from the end nearer a substituent.
STEP 3	Give the location and name for each substituent (alphabetical order) as a prefix to the name of the main chain.

Study Note

Example:

Write the IUPAC name for the following compound:

$$CH_3—CH_2—\overset{\overset{\displaystyle CH_3}{|}}{CH}—CH_3$$

Solution:

STEP 1 Write the alkane name for the longest chain of carbon atoms. In this compound, the longest chain has four carbon atoms, which is named butane.

STEP 2 Number the carbon atoms starting from the end nearer a substituent. In this compound, the methyl group (substituent) is on carbon 2.

STEP 3 Give the location and name for each substituent (alphabetical order) as a prefix to the name of the main chain. The compound with a methyl group on carbon 2 of a four-carbon chain butane is named 2-methylbutane.

When there are two or more of the same substituent, a prefix (*di, tri, tetra*) is used in front of the name. Commas are used to separate the numbers for the location of the substituents.

$$CH_3—CH_2—\overset{\overset{\displaystyle CH_3}{|}}{CH}—\overset{\overset{\displaystyle CH_3}{|}}{CH}—CH_3$$

2,3-Dimethylpentane

◆ **Learning Exercise 12.3A**

Give the IUPAC name for each of the following compounds:

$$\begin{array}{c} CH_3 \\ | \\ 1. \ \ CH_3{-}CH{-}CH_3 \end{array}$$ _____

$$\begin{array}{c} CH_3 \quad\quad CH_3 \\ | \quad\quad\quad | \\ 2. \ \ CH_3{-}CH{-}CH_2{-}CH{-}CH_2{-}CH_3 \end{array}$$ _____

3. _____

$$\begin{array}{c} CH_3 \\ | \\ 4. \ \ CH_3{-}C{-}CH_2{-}CH_3 \\ | \\ CH_3 \end{array}$$ _____

Answers   **1.** 2-methylpropane   **2.** 2,4-dimethylhexane   **3.** 2,5-dimethylheptane
4. 2,2-dimethylbutane

Guide to Drawing Structural Formulas for Alkanes with Substituents	
STEP 1	Draw the main chain of carbon atoms.
STEP 2	Number the chain and place the substituents on the carbons indicated by the numbers.
STEP 3	For the condensed structural formula, add the correct number of hydrogen atoms to give four bonds to each C atom.

◆ **Learning Exercise 12.3B**

Draw the condensed structural formulas for **1**, **2**, and **3** and the line-angle structural formulas for **4**, **5**, and **6**.

1. 2-methylbutane

2. 2-methylpentane

3. 4-ethyl-2-methylhexane

4. 2,2,4-trimethylhexane

5. 3-ethylpentane

6. methylcyclohexane

Answers

1. $CH_3-\overset{\displaystyle CH_3}{\underset{\displaystyle |}{CH}}-CH_2-CH_3$

2. $CH_3-\overset{\displaystyle CH_3}{\underset{\displaystyle |}{CH}}-CH_2-CH_2-CH_3$

3. $CH_3-\overset{\displaystyle CH_3}{\underset{\displaystyle |}{CH}}-CH_2-\overset{\displaystyle CH_2-CH_3}{\underset{\displaystyle |}{CH}}-CH_2-CH_3$

4.

5.

6.

♦ **Learning Exercise 12.3C**

Give the IUPAC name for each of the following:

1. CH_3-CH_2-Br

2. $CH_3-CH_2-\overset{\displaystyle Cl}{\underset{\displaystyle \underset{\displaystyle Cl}{|}}{\overset{\displaystyle |}{C}}}-CH_2-CH_3$

3.

4. $CH_3-CH_2-CH_2-\overset{\displaystyle F}{\underset{\displaystyle |}{CH}}-Cl$

5.

Answers
1. bromoethane
3. 2-bromo-4-chlorohexane
5. bromocyclopropane

2. 3,3-dichloropentane
4. 1-chloro-1-fluorobutane

♦ **Learning Exercise 12.3D**

Draw the condensed structural formulas for **1**, **2**, and **3** and the line-angle structural formulas for **4**, **5**, and **6**.

1. ethyl chloride

2. bromomethane

3. 3-bromo-1-chloropentane

4. 1,1-dichlorohexane

5. 2,2,3-trichlorobutane

6. 2,4-dibromo-2,4-dichloropentane

Answers
1. CH_3-CH_2-Cl

2. CH_3-Br

3. $Cl-CH_2-CH_2-\overset{\overset{\displaystyle Br}{|}}{CH}-CH_2-CH_3$

4.

5.

6.

12.4 Properties of Alkanes

Learning Goal: Identify the properties of alkanes and write a balanced chemical equation for combustion.

- Alkanes are less dense than water, and mostly unreactive, except that they burn vigorously.
- Alkanes are found in natural gas, gasoline, and diesel fuels.
- Alkanes are nonpolar and insoluble in water, and they have low boiling points.
- In combustion, an alkane reacts rapidly with oxygen at a high temperature to produce carbon dioxide, water, and a great amount of heat.

Key Terms for Sections 12.1–12.4

Match the statements below with the following key terms:

   a. line-angle structural formula   **b.** isomers   **c.** alkane
   d. condensed structural formula   **e.** combustion   **f.** cycloalkane
   g. substituent

1. _____ groups of atoms such as an alkyl group or a halogen bonded to a carbon chain

2. _____ a type of formula for carbon compounds that indicates the carbon atoms as corners or ends of a zigzag line

3. _____ compounds having the same molecular formula but a different arrangement of atoms

4. _____ a straight-chain hydrocarbon that contains only carbon–carbon and carbon–hydrogen single bonds

5. _____ an alkane that exists as a cyclic structure

6. _____ the chemical reaction of an alkane and oxygen that yields CO_2, H_2O, and heat

7. _____ the type of formula that shows the arrangement of the carbon atoms grouped with their attached H atoms

Answers   **1.** g   **2.** a   **3.** b   **4.** c   **5.** f   **6.** e   **7.** d

---

Study Note

Example: Write the balanced chemical equation for the combustion of methane.

Solution: Write the molecular formulas for the reactants: methane (CH_4) and oxygen (O_2) Write the products CO_2 and H_2O and balance the equation.

$$CH_4(g) + O_2(g) \xrightarrow{\Delta} CO_2(g) + H_2O(g) + \text{heat}$$

$$CH_4(g) + 2O_2(g) \xrightarrow{\Delta} CO_2(g) + 2H_2O(g) + \text{heat} \quad \textit{balanced}$$

♦ **Learning Exercise 12.4A**

Write a balanced chemical equation for the complete combustion of each of the following:

1. propane _____

2. hexane _____

3. pentane _____

4. cyclobutane _____

Answers

1. $C_3H_8(g) + 5O_2(g) \xrightarrow{\Delta} 3CO_2(g) + 4H_2O(g) + \text{heat}$

2. $2C_6H_{14}(g) + 19O_2(g) \xrightarrow{\Delta} 12CO_2(g) + 14H_2O(g) + \text{heat}$

3. $C_5H_{12}(g) + 8O_2(g) \xrightarrow{\Delta} 5CO_2(g) + 6H_2O(g) + \text{heat}$

4. $C_4H_8(g) + 6O_2(g) \xrightarrow{\Delta} 4CO_2(g) + 4H_2O(g) + \text{heat}$

♦ **Learning Exercise 12.4B**

Indicate which property in each of the following pairs is more likely to be a property of hexane:

a. density is 0.66 g/mL or 1.66 g/mL _____

b. solid or liquid at room temperature _____

c. soluble or insoluble in water _____

d. flammable or nonflammable _____

e. melting point 95 °C or −95 °C _____

Answers   **a.** 0.66 g/mL   **b.** liquid   **c.** insoluble
              d. flammable   **e.** −95 °C

12.5 Alkenes and Alkynes

Learning Goal: Identify structural formulas as alkenes, cycloalkenes, and alkynes, and write their IUPAC names.

- Alkenes are unsaturated hydrocarbons that contain one or more carbon–carbon double bonds.
- In alkenes, each carbon in the double bond is connected to two other groups in addition to the other carbon of the double bond, all being in the same plane and having bond angles of 120°.
- Alkynes are unsaturated hydrocarbons that contain at least one carbon–carbon triple bond.
- The IUPAC names of alkenes are derived by changing the *ane* ending of the parent alkane to *ene*. For example, the IUPAC name of $H_2C{=}CH_2$ is ethene. It has a common name of ethylene. In alkenes, the longest carbon chain containing the double bond is numbered from the end nearer the

double bond. In cycloalkenes with substituents, the double-bond carbons are given positions of 1 and 2, and the ring is numbered to give the next lower numbers to the substituents.

$$CH_3-CH=CH_2 \qquad H_2C=CH-CH_2-CH_3 \qquad CH_3-CH=CH-CH_3$$

Propene (propylene)   1-Butene   2-Butene

- The IUPAC names of alkynes are derived by changing the *ane* ending of the parent alkane to *yne*. In alkynes, the longest carbon chain containing the triple bond is numbered from the end nearer the triple bond.

$$HC\equiv CH \qquad CH_3-C\equiv CH \qquad CH_3-CH_2-C\equiv CH$$

Ethyne   Propyne   1-Butyne

H — C ≡ C — H

Ethyne

Ball-and-stick models show the double bond of an alkene and the triple bond of an alkyne.

♦ **Learning Exercise 12.5A**

Classify each of the following as alkane, alkene, cycloalkene, or alkyne:

1. _____ $CH_3-CH_2-CH_3$ 2. _____

3. _____ $CH_3-C\equiv C-CH_3$

4. _____ $CH_3-CH_2-CH=\overset{\displaystyle CH_3}{\overset{\displaystyle |}{C}}-CH_2-CH_3$

Answers   **1.** alkane   **2.** alkene   **3.** alkyne   **4.** alkene

Guide to Naming Alkenes and Alkynes	
STEP 1	Name the longest carbon chain that contains the double or triple bond.
STEP 2	Number the carbon chain starting from the end nearer the double or triple bond.
STEP 3	Give the location and name for each substituent (alphabetical order) as a prefix to the alkene or alkyne name.

♦ **Learning Exercise 12.5B**

Write the IUPAC name for each of the following alkenes:

1. $CH_3-CH=CH_2$

_____

2. $CH_3-\overset{\displaystyle CH_3}{\overset{\displaystyle |}{C}}=CH-CH_3$

_____

3. ⬡

_____

4. $H_2C=CH-\overset{\displaystyle Cl}{\overset{\displaystyle |}{C}}H-CH_2-\overset{\displaystyle CH_3}{\overset{\displaystyle |}{C}}H-CH_3$

_____

5. $CH_3-CH=\overset{\displaystyle CH_2-CH_3}{\overset{\displaystyle |}{C}}-CH_2-CH_3$

6.

Answers **1.** propene **2.** 2-methyl-2-butene **3.** cyclohexene
4. 3-chloro-5-methyl-1-hexene **5.** 3-ethyl-2-pentene **6.** 1-butene

♦ **Learning Exercise 12.5C**

Write the IUPAC name for each of the following alkynes:

1. HC≡CH

_____

2. CH₃—C≡CH

_____

3. CH₃—CH₂—C≡CH

_____

4.
$$CH_3—\overset{\displaystyle CH_3}{\overset{|}{CH}}—C≡C—CH_3$$

_____

Answers **1.** ethyne **2.** propyne
3. 1-butyne **4.** 4-methyl-2-pentyne

♦ **Learning Exercise 12.5D**

Draw the condensed structural formulas for **1** and **2** and the line-angle structural formulas for **3** and **4**.

1. 2-pentyne

2. 2-chloro-2-butene

3. 3-bromo-2-methyl-2-pentene

4. 3-methylcyclohexene

Answers

1. CH₃—C≡C—CH₂—CH₃

2.
$$CH_3—\overset{\displaystyle Cl}{\overset{|}{C}}=CH—CH_3$$

3.

4.

12.6 Cis–Trans Isomers

Learning Goal: Draw the condensed and line-angle structural formulas and give the names for the cis–trans isomers of alkenes.

• Cis–trans isomers are possible for alkenes because there is no rotation around the rigid double bond.
• In the cis isomer, carbon groups or halogen atoms are attached on the same side of the double bond, whereas in the trans isomer, they are attached on the opposite sides of the double bond.

◆ **Learning Exercise 12.6A**

Draw the condensed structural formulas for the cis and trans isomers of 1,2-dibromoethene.

cis-2-Butene

Answers   In the cis isomer, the bromine (halogen) atoms are attached on the same side of the double bond; in the trans isomer, they are on opposite sides.

H   H   H   Br
 \   /   \   /
  C=C   C=C
 /   \   /   \
Br   Br   Br   H

cis-1,2-Dibromoethene   *trans*-1,2-Dibromoethene

trans-2-Butene

Ball-and-stick models show the cis and trans isomers of 2-butene.

◆ **Learning Exercise 12.6B**

Name the following alkenes using the cis–trans prefix where isomers are possible:

1. Br   Cl
     \   /
      C=C
     /   \
    H   H

_____

2. H   CH₃
     \   /
      C=C
     /   \
   CH₃   H

_____

3. H   H
     \   /
      C=C
     /   \
   CH₃   H

_____

4. H   CH₂—CH₃
     \   /
      C=C
     /   \
   CH₃   H

_____

Answers   1. *cis*-1-bromo-2-chloroethene   2. *trans*-2-butene
            3. propene (not a cis–trans isomer)   4. *trans*-2-pentene

12.7   Addition Reactions for Alkenes

Learning Goal: Draw the condensed or line-angle structural formulas and give the names for the organic products of addition reactions of alkenes. Draw a condensed structural formula for a section of a polymer.

- The addition of small molecules to the double bond is a characteristic reaction of alkenes.
- Hydrogenation adds hydrogen atoms to the double bond of an alkene to yield an alkane.

$$H_2C=CH_2 + H_2 \xrightarrow{\text{Pt}} CH_3-CH_3$$

Table 12.1 Summary of Addition Reactions

Name of Addition Reaction	Reactants	Conditions/ Catalysts	Product
Hydrogenation	Alkene + H_2	Pt, Ni, or Pd	Alkane
Hydration	Alkene + H_2O	H^+ (strong acid)	Alcohol
Polymerization	Alkene monomers	High temperature, high pressure	Polymer

- Hydration, in the presence of a strong acid, adds water to a double bond. According to Markovnikov's rule, the H— from the reactant H—OH bonds to the carbon in the double bond that has the greater number of hydrogen atoms.

$$CH_3-CH{=}CH_2 + H_2O \xrightarrow{H^+} CH_3-\underset{\underset{\displaystyle OH}{|}}{CH}-CH_3$$

- Polymers are large molecules prepared from the bonding of many small units called *monomers*.
- Many synthetic polymers used in medicine are made from small alkene monomers.

Hydrogenation is used to convert unsaturated fats in vegetable oils to saturated fats that make a more solid product.
Credit: Pearson Education / Pearson Science

⚛ CORE CHEMISTRY SKILL

Writing Equations for Hydrogenation, Hydration, and Polymerization

♦ **Learning Exercise 12.7A**

Draw the condensed or line-angle structural formulas for the products of the following reactions:

1. $CH_3-CH_2-CH{=}CH_2 + H_2 \xrightarrow{Pt}$

2. ⬠ + H_2 $\xrightarrow{Pt}$

3. $CH_3-CH{=}CH_2 + H_2 \xrightarrow{Pt}$

4. ⌇ + H_2 $\xrightarrow{Ni}$

5. $CH_3-CH_2-CH{=}CH_2 + H_2O \xrightarrow{H^+}$

6. ⬠ + H_2O $\xrightarrow{H^+}$

Answers   1. $CH_3-CH_2-CH_2-CH_3$ 2. ⬠

3. $CH_3-CH_2-CH_3$ 4. ⌇

5. $CH_3-CH_2-\underset{\underset{\displaystyle OH}{|}}{CH}-CH_3$ 6. (cyclopentane with OH)

♦ **Learning Exercise 12.7B**

Draw the condensed structural formula for the starting monomer for each of the following polymers:

1.

$$-\overset{\displaystyle H}{\underset{\displaystyle H}{C}}-\overset{\displaystyle H}{\underset{\displaystyle H}{C}}-\overset{\displaystyle H}{\underset{\displaystyle H}{C}}-\overset{\displaystyle H}{\underset{\displaystyle H}{C}}-\overset{\displaystyle H}{\underset{\displaystyle H}{C}}-\overset{\displaystyle H}{\underset{\displaystyle H}{C}}-$$

2.

$$-\overset{\displaystyle H}{\underset{\displaystyle H}{C}}-\overset{\displaystyle CH_3}{\underset{\displaystyle H}{C}}-\overset{\displaystyle H}{\underset{\displaystyle H}{C}}-\overset{\displaystyle CH_3}{\underset{\displaystyle H}{C}}-\overset{\displaystyle H}{\underset{\displaystyle H}{C}}-\overset{\displaystyle CH_3}{\underset{\displaystyle H}{C}}-$$

3.

$$-\overset{\displaystyle F}{\underset{\displaystyle F}{C}}-\overset{\displaystyle F}{\underset{\displaystyle F}{C}}-\overset{\displaystyle F}{\underset{\displaystyle F}{C}}-\overset{\displaystyle F}{\underset{\displaystyle F}{C}}-\overset{\displaystyle F}{\underset{\displaystyle F}{C}}-\overset{\displaystyle F}{\underset{\displaystyle F}{C}}-$$

Answers   **1.** $H_2C=CH_2$ **2.** $H_2C=\overset{\displaystyle CH_3}{\overset{|}{CH}}$ **3.** $F_2C=CF_2$

♦ **Learning Exercise 12.7C**

Draw the structure of the polymer formed from the addition of three monomers of 1,1-difluoroethene.

Answer

$$-\overset{\displaystyle F}{\underset{\displaystyle F}{C}}-\overset{\displaystyle H}{\underset{\displaystyle H}{C}}-\overset{\displaystyle F}{\underset{\displaystyle F}{C}}-\overset{\displaystyle H}{\underset{\displaystyle H}{C}}-\overset{\displaystyle F}{\underset{\displaystyle F}{C}}-\overset{\displaystyle H}{\underset{\displaystyle H}{C}}-$$

Synthetic polymers are used to replace diseased veins and arteries.

12.8 Aromatic Compounds

Learning Goal: Describe the bonding in benzene; name aromatic compounds, and draw their line-angle structural formulas.

- Most aromatic compounds contain benzene, a cyclic structure containing six CH units. The structure of benzene can be represented as a hexagon with alternating single and double bonds or with a circle in the center.

Equivalent structures for benzene

Structural formulas for benzene

Toluene
(methylbenzene)

Aniline
(aminobenzene)

Phenol
(hydroxybenzene)

- When benzene has only one substituent, the ring is not numbered. The names of many aromatic compounds use the parent name benzene, although many common names were retained as IUPAC names, such as toluene, phenol, and aniline. The position of two substituents on the ring is often shown by *o*, *m*, and *p*, representing the prefixes *ortho* (1,2-), *meta* (1,3-), and *para* (1,4-).

Key Terms for Sections 12.5–12.8

Match the statements below with the following key terms:

    a. alkene   **b.** hydrogenation   **c.** alkyne
    d. hydration   **e.** aromatic

1. _____ contains a cyclic structure with six CH units

2. _____ the addition of H_2 to a carbon–carbon double bond

3. _____ a compound that contains a carbon–carbon double bond

4. _____ the addition of H_2O to a carbon–carbon double bond

5. _____ a compound that contains a carbon–carbon triple bond

Answers   **1.** e   **2.** b   **3.** a   **4.** d   **5.** c

♦ **Learning Exercise 12.8**

Write the IUPAC and any common name for each of the following:

Answers   **1.** benzene   **2.** methylbenzene, toluene
           3. 1,3-dichlorobenzene (*m*-dichlorobenzene)   **4.** 4-bromotoluene (*p*-bromotoluene)

Checklist for Chapter 12

You are ready to take the Practice Test for Chapter 12. Be sure that you have accomplished the following learning goals for this chapter. If not, review the section listed at the end of the goal. Then apply your new skills and understanding to the Practice Test.

After studying Chapter 12, I can successfully:

_____ Identify properties as characteristic of organic or inorganic compounds. (12.1)

_____ Identify the number of bonds to carbon. (12.1)

_____ Describe the shape around carbon in organic compounds. (12.1)

_____ Draw the expanded, condensed, and line-angle structural formulas for an alkane. (12.2)

_____ Use the IUPAC system to write the names for alkanes and cycloalkanes. (12.2)

_____ Draw the condensed structural formulas for alkanes. (12.2)

_____ Use the IUPAC system to write the names for alkanes with substituents. (12.3)

_____ Draw the condensed and line-angle structural formulas for alkanes with substituents. (12.3)

_____ Describe some physical properties of alkanes. (12.4)

_____ Write and balance equations for the combustion of alkanes. (12.4)

_____ Identify the structural features of alkenes and alkynes. (12.5)

_____ Name alkenes and alkynes using IUPAC rules and draw their condensed and line-angle structural formulas. (12.5)

_____ Identify alkenes that exist as cis–trans isomers; draw their condensed and line-angle structural formulas and give their names. (12.6)

_____ Draw the condensed and line-angle structural formulas for the products of the addition of hydrogen and water to alkenes. (12.7)

_____ Draw a condensed structural formula for a section of a polymer. (12.7)

_____ Give the names and draw the line-angle structural formulas for compounds that contain a benzene ring. (12.8)

Practice Test for Chapter 12

For questions 1 through 8, indicate whether the following characteristics are typical of organic (O) or inorganic (I) compounds: (12.1)

1. _____ high melting points

2. _____ fewer compounds

3. _____ covalent bonds

4. _____ soluble in water

5. _____ ionic bonds

6. _____ flammable

7. _____ low boiling points

8. _____ soluble in nonpolar solvents

For questions 9 through 13, match the formula with the correct name: (12.2)

A. methane   **B.** ethane   **C.** propane   **D.** pentane   **E.** heptane

9. _____ $CH_3—CH_2—CH_3$

10. _____ $CH_3—CH_2—CH_2—CH_2—CH_2—CH_2—CH_3$

11. _____ CH_4

12. _____ ⟋\⟋\

13. _____ $CH_3—CH_3$

For questions 14 through 17, match the compounds with one of the following families: (12.2, 12.5)

A. alkane   **B.** alkene   **C.** alkyne   **D.** cycloalkene

14. $CH_3—CH=CH_2$

15. ⬡

16. $CH_3—CH_2—\overset{\displaystyle CH_3}{\overset{|}{CH}}—CH_2—CH_3$

17. $CH_3—CH_2—C\equiv CH$

For questions 18 through 21, match the formula with the correct name: (12.2, 12.3)

A. butane
D. 3,5-dimethylhexane

B. 1,1-dichlorobutane
E. 2,4-dimethylhexane

C. 1,2-dichloropropane
F. 1,2-dichlorobutane

18. $CH_3—CH_2—CH_2—CH_3$

19. $CH_3—\overset{\displaystyle CH_3}{\overset{|}{CH}}—CH_2—\overset{\displaystyle CH_3}{\overset{|}{CH}}—CH_2—CH_3$

20.

21. Cl⟍⟋\ with Cl on second carbon

For questions 22 through 24, match the formula with the correct name: (12.2, 12.3)

A. methylcyclopentane
C. cyclohexane

B. cyclobutane
D. ethylcyclopentane

22. _____ ⬡

23. _____ ⬠ with methyl

24. _____ ⬠ with ethyl

For questions 25 through 27, match the formula with the correct name: (12.3)

    A. 2,4-dichloropentane   **B.** chlorocyclopentane

    C. 1,2-dichloropentane   **D.** 4,5-dichloropentane

25. ____ $CH_3-CH_2-CH_2-\overset{\displaystyle Cl}{\overset{|}{CH}}-CH_2-Cl$ **26.** ____

27. ____ $CH_3-\overset{\displaystyle Cl}{\overset{|}{CH}}-CH_2-\overset{\displaystyle Cl}{\overset{|}{CH}}-CH_3$

For questions 28 through 30, refer to the following compounds (A) *and* (B): (12.2, 12.5)

$H_2C=CH-CH_3$ $\overset{\displaystyle CH_2}{H_2C-CH_2}$

    (A)   (B)

28. Compound (A) is a(an)

    A. alkane   **B.** alkene   **C.** cycloalkane   **D.** alkyne   **E.** aromatic

29. Compound (B) is named

    A. propane   **B.** propylene   **C.** cyclobutane   **D.** cyclopropane   **E.** cyclopropene

30. Compound (A) is named

    A. propane   **B.** propene   **C.** 2-propene   **D.** propyne   **E.** 1-butene

31. The correctly balanced equation for the complete combustion of ethane is (12.4)

    A. $C_2H_6(g) + O_2(g) \overset{\Delta}{\longrightarrow} 2CO(g) + 3H_2O(g) +$ heat

    B. $C_2H_6(g) + O_2(g) \overset{\Delta}{\longrightarrow} CO_2(g) + H_2O(g) +$ heat

    C. $C_2H_6(g) + 2O_2(g) \overset{\Delta}{\longrightarrow} 2CO_2(g) + 3H_2O(g) +$ heat

    D. $2C_2H_6(g) + 7O_2(g) \overset{\Delta}{\longrightarrow} 4CO_2(g) + 6H_2O(g) +$ heat

    E. $2C_2H_6(g) + 4O_2(g) \overset{\Delta}{\longrightarrow} 4CO_2(g) + 6H_2O(g) +$ heat

In questions 32 through 35, match each formula with its name: (12.5)

    A. cyclopentene   **B.** methylpropene   **C.** cyclohexene

    D. ethene   **E.** 3-methylcyclopentene

32. $H_2C=CH_2$

33. $CH_3-\overset{\displaystyle CH_3}{\overset{|}{C}}=CH_2$

34.

35.

36. What is the IUPAC name of $CH_3-CH_2-C\equiv CH$? (12.5)

    A. methylacetylene   **B.** propyne   **C.** propylene

    D. 4-butyne   **E.** 1-butyne

37. The cis isomer of 2-butene is (12.6)

    A. $H_2C=CH-CH_2-CH_3$ **B.** $CH_3-CH=CH-CH_3$

    C.
$$\underset{H}{\overset{CH_3}{C}}=\underset{CH_3}{\overset{H}{C}}$$

    D.
$$\underset{H}{\overset{CH_3}{C}}=\underset{H}{\overset{CH_3}{C}}$$

    E. $\underset{CH=CH}{\overset{CH_3 \quad CH_3}{\big|\qquad\big|}}$

38. The name of this compound is (12.6)

$$\underset{H}{\overset{Cl}{C}}=\underset{Cl}{\overset{H}{C}}$$

    A. dichloroethene   **B.** *cis*-1,2-dichloroethene

    C. *trans*-1,2-dichloroethene   **D.** *cis*-chloroethene

    E. *trans*-chloroethene

39. Hydrogenation of $CH_3-CH=CH_2$ gives (12.7)

    A. $3CO_2 + 6H_2$ **B.** $CH_3-CH_2-CH_3$

    C. $H_2C=CH-CH_3$ **D.** no reaction

    E. $CH_3-CH_2-CH_2-CH_3$

40. Choose the product of the following reaction: $CH_3-CH=CH_2 + H_2O \xrightarrow{H^+}$ (12.7)

    A. $CH_3-CH_2-CH_2-OH$ **B.** no reaction   **C.** $CH_3-CH_2-CH_3$

    D. $CH_3-\overset{\overset{\displaystyle OH}{|}}{C}H-CH_2-OH$ **E.** $CH_3-\overset{\overset{\displaystyle OH}{|}}{C}H-CH_3$

41. Hydration of 2-butene gives (12.7)

    A. $CH_3-CH_2-CH_2-CH_3$ **B.** $CH_3-CH_2-CH_2-CH_2-OH$

    C. $CH_3-\overset{\overset{\displaystyle OH}{|}}{C}H-CH_2-CH_3$

    D. ▢   **E.** ▢–OH

42. The following reaction is called: (12.7)

$$CH_3-CH=CH_2 + H_2O \xrightarrow{H^+} CH_3-\overset{\overset{\displaystyle OH}{|}}{C}H-CH_3$$

    A. hydrogenation   **B.** decomposition   **C.** reduction

    D. hydration   **E.** combustion

43. What is the common name of methylbenzene? (12.8)

    A. aniline   **B.** phenol   **C.** toluene

    D. xylene   **E.** toluidine

For questions 44 through 48, match the name of each of the following aromatic compounds with the correct structure: (12.8)

A.

B. [benzene ring with CH₃]

C. [benzene ring with two CH₃ groups]

D. [benzene ring with Cl]

E. [benzene ring with CH₃ and Cl]

44. _____ chlorobenzene

45. _____ benzene

46. _____ toluene

47. _____ 4-chlorotoluene

48. _____ 1,3-dimethylbenzene

Answers to the Practice Test

1. I	2. I	3. O	4. I	5. I
6. O	7. O	8. O	9. C	10. E
11. A	12. D	13. B	14. B	15. D
16. A	17. C	18. A	19. E	20. B
21. F	22. C	23. A	24. D	25. C
26. B	27. A	28. B	29. D	30. B
31. D	32. D	33. B	34. E	35. C
36. E	37. D	38. C	39. B	40. E
41. C	42. D	43. C	44. D	45. A
46. B	47. E	48. C		

12

Introduction to Organic Chemistry: Hydrocarbons

Learning Goals

- Identify properties characteristic of organic or inorganic compounds.
- Write the IUPAC names and draw the condensed or line-angle structural formulas for alkanes and cycloalkanes.
- Write the IUPAC names for alkanes with substituents and draw their condensed and line-angle structural formulas.
- Identify the properties of alkanes and write a balanced chemical equation for combustion.
- Identify structural formulas as alkenes, cycloalkenes, and alkynes, and write their IUPAC names.
- Draw the condensed and line-angle structural formulas and give the names for the cis–trans isomers of alkenes.
- Draw the condensed or line-angle structural formulas and give the names for the organic products of addition reactions of alkenes. Draw a condensed structural formula for a section of a polymer.
- Describe the bonding in benzene; name aromatic compounds, and draw their line-angle structural formulas.

Chapter Outline

Chapter Opener: Firefighter / Emergency Medical Technician

12.1 Organic Compounds

12.2 Alkanes

12.3 Alkanes with Substituents

12.4 Properties of Alkanes

12.5 Alkenes and Alkynes

Explore Your World: Ripening Fruit

Chemistry Link to the Environment: Fragrant Alkenes

12.6 Cis–Trans Isomers

Explore Your World: Modeling Cis–Trans Isomers

Chemistry Link to the Environment: Pheromones in Insect Communication

Chemistry Link to Health: Cis–Trans Isomers for Night Vision

12.7 Addition Reactions for Alkenes

Explore Your World: Unsaturation in Fats and Oils

Chemistry Link to Health: Hydrogenation of Unsaturated Fats

Explore Your World: Polymers and Recycling Plastics

12.8 Aromatic Compounds

Chemistry Link to Health: Some Common Aromatic Compounds in Nature and Medicine

Chemistry Link to Health: Polycyclic Aromatic Hydrocarbons (PAHs)

Clinical Update: Diane's Treatment in the Burn Unit

⚛ Core Chemistry Skills

- Naming and Drawing Alkanes (12.2)
- Writing Equations for Hydrogenation, Hydration, and Polymerization (12.7)

Selected Answers and Solutions to Text Problems

12.1 Organic compounds always contain C and H and sometimes O, S, N, P, or a halogen atom. Inorganic compounds usually contain elements other than C and H.
   a. KCl is inorganic.   **b.** C_4H_{10} is organic.   **c.** C_2H_6O is organic.
   d. H_2SO_4 is inorganic.   **e.** $CaCl_2$ is inorganic.   **f.** C_3H_7Cl is organic.

12.3 **a.** Inorganic compounds are usually soluble in water.
   b. Organic compounds have lower boiling points than most inorganic compounds.
   c. Organic compounds contain carbon and hydrogen.
   d. Inorganic compounds contain ionic bonds.

12.5 **a.** Ethane boils at $-89\,°C$.
   b. Ethane burns vigorously in air.
   c. NaBr is a solid at $250\,°C$.
   d. NaBr dissolves in water.

12.7 In methane, the covalent bonds from the carbon atom to each hydrogen atom are directed to the corners of a tetrahedron with bond angles of $109°$.

12.9 **a.** Pentane has a chain of five carbon atoms.
   b. Ethane has a chain of two carbon atoms.
   c. Hexane has a chain of six carbon atoms.
   d. Cycloheptane has a ring of seven carbon atoms.

12.11 a. CH_4
   b. CH_3-CH_3
   c. $CH_3-CH_2-CH_2-CH_2-CH_3$
   d. △

12.13 Two structures are isomers if they have the same molecular formula, but different arrangements of atoms.
   a. These condensed structural formulas represent the same molecule; the only difference is due to rotation of the structure. Each has a CH_3- group attached to the middle carbon in a three-carbon chain.
   b. The molecular formula of both these condensed structural formulas is C_5H_{12}. However, they represent isomers because the C atoms are bonded in a different order; they have different arrangements. In the first, there is a CH_3- group attached to carbon 2 of a four-carbon chain, and in the other, there is a five-carbon chain.
   c. The molecular formula of both these condensed structural formulas is C_6H_{14}. However, they represent isomers because the C atoms are bonded in a different order; they have different arrangements. In the first, there is a CH_3- group attached to carbon 3 of a five-carbon chain, and in the other, there is a CH_3- group on carbon 2 and carbon 3 of a four-carbon chain.

12.15 a. dimethylpropane   **b.** 2,3-dimethylpentane
   c. 4-*tert*-butyl-2,6-dimethylheptane   **d.** methylcyclobutane
   e. 1-bromo-3-chlorocyclohexane

12.17 Draw the main chain with the number of carbon atoms in the ending of the name. For example, butane has a main chain of four carbon atoms, and hexane has a main chain of six carbon atoms. Attach substituents on the carbon atoms indicated. For example, in 3-methylpentane, a CH_3- group is bonded to carbon 3 of a five-carbon chain.

a.
$$CH_3-CH_2-\overset{\overset{\displaystyle CH_3}{|}}{\underset{\underset{\displaystyle CH_3}{|}}{C}}-CH_2-CH_3$$

b.
$$CH_3-\overset{\overset{\displaystyle CH_3}{|}}{CH}-\overset{\overset{\displaystyle CH_3}{|}}{CH}-CH_2-\overset{\overset{\displaystyle CH_3}{|}}{CH}-CH_3$$

c.
$$CH_3-CH_2-\overset{\overset{\displaystyle CH_2-CH_3}{|}}{CH}-CH_2-\overset{\overset{\displaystyle CH}{\diagup \diagdown}}{\underset{CH_3 \ CH_3}{CH}}-CH_2-CH_2-CH_3$$

d. $Br-CH_2-CH_2-Cl$

12.19 a.

b.

c.

d.

12.21 a. $CH_3-CH_2-CH_2-CH_2-CH_2-CH_2-CH_3$
  b. Heptane is a liquid at room temperature since it has a boiling point of 98 °C.
  c. Heptane contains only nonpolar $C-H$ bonds, which makes it insoluble in water.
  d. Since the density of heptane (0.68 g/mL) is less than that of water, heptane will float on water.
  e. $C_7H_{16}(l) + 11O_2(g) \xrightarrow{\Delta} 7CO_2(g) + 8H_2O(g) + \text{energy}$

12.23 In combustion, a hydrocarbon reacts with oxygen to yield CO_2 and H_2O.
  a. $2C_2H_6(g) + 7O_2(g) \xrightarrow{\Delta} 4CO_2(g) + 6H_2O(g) + \text{energy}$
  b. $2C_3H_6(g) + 9O_2(g) \xrightarrow{\Delta} 6CO_2(g) + 6H_2O(g) + \text{energy}$
  c. $2C_8H_{18}(g) + 25O_2(g) \xrightarrow{\Delta} 16CO_2(g) + 18H_2O(g) + \text{energy}$

12.25 Longer carbon chains have higher boiling points. The boiling points of straight-chain alkanes are usually higher than their branched-chain isomers. Cycloalkanes have higher boiling points than their straight-chain counterparts.
  a. Heptane has a greater molar mass and so will have a higher boiling point than pentane.
  b. The cyclic alkane cyclopropane will have a higher boiling point than its straight-chain counterpart propane.
  c. The straight-chain alkane hexane will have a higher boiling point than its branched isomer 2-methylpentane.

12.27 a. A condensed structural formula with a carbon–carbon double bond is an alkene.
   b. A condensed structural formula with a carbon–carbon triple bond is an alkyne.
   c. A line-angle structural formula with a carbon–carbon double bond is an alkene.
   d. A line-angle structural formula with a carbon–carbon double bond in a ring is a cycloalkene.

12.29 a. This alkene has a three-carbon chain with the double bond between carbon 1 and carbon 2, and a one-carbon methyl group attached to carbon 2. The IUPAC name is 2-methylpropene.
   b. This alkyne has a five-carbon chain with the triple bond between carbon 2 and carbon 3, and a bromine atom attached to carbon 4. The IUPAC name is 4-bromo-2-pentyne.
   c. This is a five-carbon cyclic structure with a double bond (between carbon 1 and 2 of the ring), and a two-carbon ethyl group attached to carbon 4 of the ring. The IUPAC name is 4-ethylcyclopentene.
   d. This alkene has a six-carbon chain with the double bond between carbon 2 and carbon 3, and a two-carbon ethyl group attached to carbon 4. The IUPAC name is 4-ethyl-2-hexene.

12.31 a. 1-Pentene is the five-carbon compound with a double bond between carbon 1 and carbon 2.
   $H_2C{=}CH{-}CH_2{-}CH_2{-}CH_3$
   b. 2-Methyl-1-butene has a four-carbon chain with a double bond between carbon 1 and carbon 2 and a methyl group attached to carbon 2.

$$
\begin{array}{c}
CH_3 \\
| \\
H_2C{=}C{-}CH_2{-}CH_3
\end{array}
$$

   c. 3-Methylcyclohexene is a six-carbon cyclic compound with a double bond and a methyl group attached to carbon 3 of the ring.

   d. 1-Chloro-3-hexyne is a six-carbon compound with a triple bond between carbon 3 and carbon 4 and a chlorine atom bonded to carbon 1.

12.33 a. *cis*-2-Butene; this is a four-carbon compound with a double bond between carbon 2 and carbon 3. Both methyl groups are on the same side of the double bond; it is the cis isomer.
   b. *trans*-3-Octene; this compound has eight carbons with a double bond between carbon 3 and carbon 4. The alkyl groups are on the opposite sides of the double bond; it is the trans isomer.
   c. *cis*-3-Heptene; this is a seven-carbon compound with a double bond between carbon 3 and carbon 4. Both alkyl groups are on the same side of the double bond; it is the cis isomer.

12.35 a. *trans*-1-Bromo-2-chloroethene has a two-carbon chain with a double bond. The trans isomer has the attached groups on the opposite sides of the double bond.

   b. *cis*-2-Hexene has a six-carbon chain with a double bond between carbon 2 and carbon 3. The cis isomer has the alkyl groups on the same side of the double bond.

c. *trans*-3-Heptene has a seven-carbon chain with a double bond between carbon 3 and carbon 4. The trans isomer has the alkyl groups on the opposite sides of the double bond.

$$CH_3-CH_2 \diagdown \quad \diagup H$$
$$C=C$$
$$H \diagup \quad \diagdown CH_2-CH_2-CH_3$$

12.37 a. This compound cannot have cis–trans isomers since there are two identical hydrogen atoms attached to the first carbon of the double bond.

b. This compound can have cis–trans isomers since there are different groups attached to each carbon atom of the double bond.

c. This compound cannot have cis–trans isomers since there are two of the same groups attached to each carbon of the double bond.

12.39 a. Hydrogenation of an alkene gives the saturated compound, the alkane.

$$CH_3-CH_2-CH_2-CH_2-CH_3$$

b. In a hydration reaction, the H— and —OH from water (HOH) add to the carbon atoms in the double bond to form an alcohol. The H— adds to the carbon with more hydrogens, and the —OH bonds to the carbon with fewer hydrogen atoms.

$$\begin{array}{c} CH_3 \\ | \\ CH_3-C-CH_2-CH_3 \\ | \\ OH \end{array}$$

c. Hydrogenation of an alkene gives the saturated compound, the alkane.

d. The H— and —OH from water (HOH) add to the carbon atoms in the double bond to form an alcohol. The H— adds to the carbon with more hydrogens, and the —OH bonds to the carbon with fewer hydrogen atoms.

12.41 A polymer is a very large molecule composed of small units (monomers) that are repeated many times.

12.43 $3\ H_2C{=}CH$ (with CH_3) $\longrightarrow$

$$\begin{array}{c} H \quad CH_3\,H \quad CH_3\,H \quad CH_3 \\ | \quad\ \ | \quad\ | \quad\ \ | \quad\ | \quad\ \ | \\ -C-C-C-C-C-C- \\ | \quad\ \ | \quad\ | \quad\ \ | \quad\ | \quad\ \ | \\ H \quad H \quad H \quad H \quad H \quad H \end{array}$$

12.45

$$\begin{array}{c} F \quad H \quad F \quad H \quad F \quad H \\ | \quad | \quad | \quad | \quad | \quad | \\ -C-C-C-C-C-C- \\ | \quad | \quad | \quad | \quad | \quad | \\ F \quad H \quad F \quad H \quad F \quad H \end{array}$$

12.47 Aromatic compounds that contain a benzene ring with a single substituent are usually named as benzene derivatives. A benzene ring with a methyl substituent is named toluene. The methyl group is attached to carbon 1, and the ring is numbered to give the lower numbers to other substituents. If two groups are in the 1,2-position, this is *ortho-* (*o-*); 1,3- is *meta-* (*m-*); and 1,4- is *para-* (*p-*).

   a. 1-chloro-2-methylbenzene, *o*-chloromethylbenzene, 2-chlorotoluene, *o*-chlorotoluene
   b. ethylbenzene
   c. 1,3,5-trichlorobenzene
   d. 1,3-dimethylbenzene, *m*-xylene
   e. 3-bromo-5-chloro-1-methylbenzene, 3-bromo-5-chlorotoluene
   f. isopropylbenzene

12.49 a.   **b.**

c.   **d.**

12.51
$$
\begin{array}{cccccc}
\text{Cl} & \text{F} & \text{Cl} & \text{F} & \text{Cl} & \text{F} \\
| & | & | & | & | & | \\
-\text{C}- & \text{C}- & \text{C}- & \text{C}- & \text{C}- & \text{C}- \\
| & | & | & | & | & | \\
\text{F} & \text{F} & \text{F} & \text{F} & \text{F} & \text{F}
\end{array}
$$

12.53 a. $C_9H_{20}(l) + 14O_2(g) \xrightarrow{\Delta} 9CO_2(g) + 10H_2O(g) + \text{energy}$
   b. $C_5H_{12}(l) + 8O_2(g) \xrightarrow{\Delta} 5CO_2(g) + 6H_2O(g) + \text{energy}$
   c. $C_9H_{12}(l) + 12O_2(g) \xrightarrow{\Delta} 9CO_2(g) + 6H_2O(g) + \text{energy}$

12.55 a. Butane melts at $-138\,°C$.
   b. Butane burns vigorously in air.
   c. KCl melts at $770\,°C$.
   d. KCl contains ionic bonds.
   e. Butane is a gas at room temperature.

12.57 Two structures are isomers if they have the same molecular formula, but different arrangements of atoms.
   a. The molecular formula of both these line-angle structural formulas is C_6H_{12}. However, they represent structural isomers because the C atoms are bonded in a different order; they have different arrangements. In the first, there is a methyl group attached to a five-carbon ring, and in the other, there is a six-carbon ring.
   b. The molecular formula of the first line-angle structure is C_5H_{12}; the molecular formula of the second is C_6H_{14}. They are not structural isomers.

12.59 a.
$$
\begin{array}{ccc}
& \text{CH}_3 & \text{CH}_3 \\
& | & | \\
\text{CH}_3- & \text{CH}-\text{CH}_2- & \text{CH}-\text{CH}_3
\end{array} \quad \text{2,4-Dimethylpentane}
$$

   b.
$$
\begin{array}{cccc}
& \text{Cl} & \text{CH}_3 & \text{Br} \\
& | & | & | \\
\text{CH}_3- & \text{CH}- & \text{CH}- & \text{CH}-\text{CH}_2-\text{CH}_3
\end{array} \quad \text{4-Bromo-2-chloro-3-methylhexane}
$$

12.61
$$
\begin{array}{cccccc}
\text{F} & \text{F} & \text{F} & \text{F} & \text{F} & \text{F} \\
| & | & | & | & | & | \\
-\text{C}- & \text{C}- & \text{C}- & \text{C}- & \text{C}- & \text{C}- \\
| & | & | & | & | & | \\
\text{F} & \text{F} & \text{F} & \text{F} & \text{F} & \text{F}
\end{array}
$$

12.63 a. Propane has three carbon atoms and two carbon–carbon single bonds.

  b. Cyclopropane has three carbon atoms and three carbon–carbon single bonds in a ring.

  c. Propene has three carbon atoms, one carbon–carbon single bond, and one carbon–carbon double bond.

  d. Propyne has three carbon atoms, one carbon–carbon single bond, and one carbon–carbon triple bond.

12.65 a. 2,2-dimethylbutane   **b.** chloroethane

  c. 2-bromo-4-ethylhexane   **d.** methylcyclopentane

12.67 a.

  b. $CH_3-C{\equiv}C-CH_2-CH_2-CH_3$

  c.

12.69 a. This compound contains a five-carbon chain with a double bond between carbon 2 and carbon 3. The alkyl groups are on the opposite sides of the double bond. The IUPAC name is *trans*-2-pentene.

  b. This alkene has a six-carbon chain with the double bond between carbon 1 and carbon 2. The substituents are a bromine atom attached to carbon 4 and a methyl group on carbon 5. The IUPAC name is 4-bromo-5-methyl-1-hexene.

  c. This is a five-carbon cyclic structure with a double bond and a methyl group attached to carbon 1 of the ring. The name is 1-methylcyclopentene.

12.71 a. These structures represent a pair of structural isomers. Both have the molecular formula C_5H_7Cl. In one isomer, the chlorine is attached to one of the carbons in the double bond; in the other isomer, the carbon bonded to the chlorine is not part of the double bond.

  b. These structures are cis–trans isomers. In the cis isomer, the two methyl groups are on the same side of the double bond. In the trans isomer, the methyl groups are on opposite sides of the double bond.

12.73 a. *cis*-3-heptene

  b. *trans*-2-methyl-3-hexene

  c. *trans*-2-heptene

12.75 a.

cis-2-Pentene; both alkyl groups are on the same side of the double bond.

trans-2-Pentene; both alkyl groups are on the opposite sides of the double bond.

  b.

cis-3-Hexene; both alkyl groups are on the same side of the double bond.

trans-3-Hexene; both alkyl groups are on the opposite sides of the double bond.

12.77 a. $C_5H_{12}(g) + 8O_2(g) \xrightarrow{\Delta} 5CO_2(g) + 6H_2O(g) + \text{energy}$

b. $C_4H_8(g) + 6O_2(g) \xrightarrow{\Delta} 4CO_2(g) + 4H_2O(g) + \text{energy}$

c. $2C_7H_{14}(l) + 21O_2(g) \xrightarrow{\Delta} 14CO_2(g) + 14H_2O(g) + \text{energy}$

12.79 During hydrogenation, the multiple bonds are converted to single bonds and two H atoms are added for each bond converted.

a. 3-methylpentane   **b.** methylcyclohexane   **c.** butane

12.81 a. Hydrogenation of a cycloalkene gives the saturated compound, the cycloalkane.

b. The H— and —OH from water (HOH) add to the carbon atoms in the double bond to form an alcohol. The H— adds to the carbon with more hydrogens (carbon 1), and the —OH bonds to the carbon with fewer hydrogen atoms (carbon 2).

c. The H— and —OH from water (HOH) add to the carbon atoms in the double bond to form an alcohol. The H— adds to the carbon with more hydrogens (carbon 1), and the —OH bonds to the carbon with fewer hydrogen atoms (carbon 2).

$$CH_3-CH_2-\overset{\overset{\displaystyle OH}{|}}{\underset{\underset{\displaystyle CH_3}{|}}{C}}-CH_3$$

12.83 Styrene is $H_2C{=}CH$ and acrylonitrile is $H_2C{=}\overset{\overset{\displaystyle CN}{|}}{CH}$. A section of the copolymer of styrene and acrylonitrile would be

12.85 Aromatic compounds that contain a benzene ring with a single substituent are usually named as benzene derivatives. A benzene ring with a methyl or amino substituent is named toluene or aniline, respectively. The methyl or amino group is attached to carbon 1, and the ring is numbered to give the lower numbers to other substituents.

a. 4-methylaniline, *p*-methylaniline

b. 1-chloro-2-methylbenzene, 2-chlorotoluene, *o*-chlorotoluene

c. 1,2-difluorobenzene, *o*-difluorobenzene

12.87 a. The prefix *p*- means that the two groups are in the 1 and 4 positions on the ring.

b.

c.

12.89 Molar mass of bombykol $(C_{16}H_{30}O) = 16(12.01 \text{ g}) + 30(1.008 \text{ g}) + 16.00 \text{ g} = 238.4 \text{ g/mole}$
(4 SFs)

$$50 \text{ ng} \times \frac{1 \text{ g}}{10^9 \text{ ng}} \times \frac{1 \text{ mole}}{238.4 \text{ g}} \times \frac{6.02 \times 10^{23} \text{ molecules}}{1 \text{ mole}} = 1 \times 10^{14} \text{ molecules of bombykol}$$
(1 SF)

12.91 $H_2C{=}CH{-}CH_2{-}CH_2{-}CH_3$ 1-Pentene

     cis-2-Pentene

     trans-2-Pentene

12.93 a.

b.

13

Alcohols, Phenols, Thiols, and Ethers

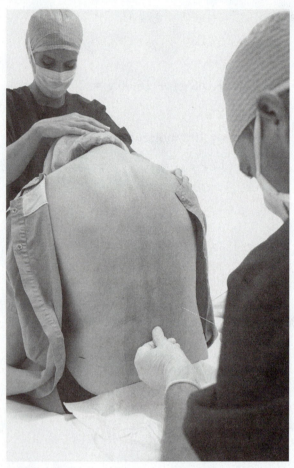

Anesthesia is a condition in which the sensation of pain is blocked by some type of drug. Anesthesia may be local, regional, or general. A local anesthetic might be used when only a small part of the body needs to be numbed such as when a tooth is extracted. A regional anesthetic blocks pain in a larger portion of the body such as an arm during wrist surgery or an epidural used during childbirth. The anesthetic is injected near the spinal cord and numbs the nerves in that area. A general anesthetic causes unconsciousness by blocking pain within the brain. One of the first local anesthetics was cocaine from which the local anesthetics procaine and lidocaine were derived.

Personnel involved in the administration of anesthesia include an anesthesiologist as well as a registered nurse anesthetist. An anesthetist may also specialize in the administration of anesthesia for a particular type of surgery such as obstetrical, cardiothoracic, or pediatric. What is the functional group in $CH_3-CH_2-O-CH_2-CH_3$, a compound previously used as a general anesthetic?

Credit: Picture Partners / Alamy

CHAPTER READINESS*

🏵 Core Chemistry Skill

• Naming and Drawing Alkanes (12.2)

*This Core Chemistry Skill from the previous chapter is listed here for your review as you proceed to the new material in this chapter.

13.1 Alcohols, Phenols, and Thiols

Learning Goal: Give the IUPAC and common names for alcohols, phenols, and thiols; draw their condensed and line-angle structural formulas.

🏵 **CORE CHEMISTRY SKILL**

Identifying Alcohols, Phenols, and Thiols

• An alcohol contains the hydroxyl group ($-OH$) attached to a carbon chain.

• In the IUPAC system, alcohols are named by replacing the *e* of the alkane name with *ol.* The location of the $-OH$ group is given by numbering the carbon chain.

- Simple alcohols are generally named by their common names with the alkyl name preceding the term *alcohol.* For example, CH_3—OH is methyl alcohol, and CH_3—CH_2—OH is ethyl alcohol.

CH_3—OH CH_3—CH_2—OH CH_3—CH_2—CH_2—OH

Methanol   Ethanol   1-Propanol

(methyl alcohol)   (ethyl alcohol)   (propyl alcohol)

- When a hydroxyl group is attached to a benzene ring, the compound is a phenol.
- Thiols are similar to alcohols, except they have an —SH group in place of the —OH group.

CH_3—OH CH_3—CH_2—SH

—OH

Methanol   Phenol   Ethanethiol

Guide to Naming Alcohols and Phenols	
STEP 1	Name the longest carbon chain attached to the —OH group by replacing the *e* in the corresponding alkane name with *ol*. Name an aromatic alcohol as a *phenol*.
STEP 2	Number the chain starting at the end nearer to the —OH group.
STEP 3	Give the location and name for each substituent relative to the —OH group.

♦ **Learning Exercise 13.1A**

Give the correct IUPAC and common name (if any) for each of the following compounds:

⚛ **CORE CHEMISTRY SKILL**

Naming Alcohols and Phenols

1. CH_3—CH_2—OH

2. CH_3—CH_2—CH_2—OH

3. CH_3—$\overset{\overset{\text{OH}}{|}}{CH}$—$CH_2$—$CH_2$—$CH_3$

4.

5.

6.

Answers   1. ethanol (ethyl alcohol)   2. 1-propanol (propyl alcohol)
            3. 2-pentanol   4. 4-methyl-2-heptanol
            5. cyclopentanol   6. phenol

♦ Learning Exercise 13.1B

Draw the correct condensed structural formula for **1**, **2**, and **3**, and draw the line-angle structural formula for **4**, **5**, and **6**.

1. 2-butanol

2. 2-chloro-1-propanol

3. 2,4-dimethyl-1-pentanol

4. 2-bromoethanol

5. cyclohexanol

6. 2-chlorophenol

Answers

13.2 Ethers

Learning Goal: Give the IUPAC and common names for ethers; draw their condensed or line-angle structural formulas.

- In ethers, an oxygen atom is connected by single bonds to alkyl or aromatic groups.
- In the IUPAC name, the smaller alkyl group and the oxygen are named as an *alkoxy group* attached to the longer alkane chain, which is numbered to give the location of the alkoxy group.
- In the common names of ethers, the alkyl groups are listed alphabetically followed by the name *ether*.

Guide to Writing IUPAC Names for Ethers	
STEP 1	Write the alkane name of the longer carbon chain.
STEP 2	Name the oxygen and smaller alkyl group as an alkoxy group.
STEP 3	Number the longer carbon chain from the end nearer the alkoxy group and give its location.

Example: Write the IUPAC and common names for $CH_3—CH_2—CH_2—O—CH_3$.

Solution:

Analyze the Problem	Given	Need
	ether	IUPAC and common name

STEP 1   **Write the alkane name of the longer carbon chain.**

$CH_3—CH_2—CH_2—O—CH_3$ propane

STEP 2   **Name the oxygen and smaller alkyl group as an alkoxy group.**

Methoxy

$CH_3—CH_2—CH_2—O—CH_3$ methoxypropane

STEP 3   **Number the longer carbon chain from the end nearer the alkoxy group and give its location.**

$\underset{3}{CH_3}—\underset{2}{CH_2}—\underset{1}{CH_2}—O—CH_3$ 1-methoxypropane

The common name lists the alkyl groups alphabetically before the name ether.

Propyl   *Methyl*

$CH_3—CH_2—CH_2—O—CH_3$ Methyl propyl ether

♦ **Learning Exercise 13.2A**

Write an IUPAC and common name for each of the following:

1. $CH_3—O—CH_3$

2.

3. $CH_3—CH_2—CH_2—CH_2—O—CH_3$

4. $CH_3—O—CH_2—CH_3$

5.

Answers
1. methoxymethane (dimethyl ether)
3. 1-methoxybutane (butyl methyl ether)
5. methoxybenzene (methyl phenyl ether)

2. ethoxyethane (diethyl ether)
4. methoxyethane (ethyl methyl ether)

♦ **Learning Exercise 13.2B**

Draw the condensed structural formulas for **1** and **2**, and the line-angle structural formulas for **3** and **4**.

1. ethyl propyl ether

2. 2-methoxypropane

3. dipropyl ether

4. 3-ethoxypentane

Answers   **1.** $CH_3-CH_2-O-CH_2-CH_2-CH_3$ **2.** $CH_3-\overset{\overset{\displaystyle O-CH_3}{|}}{CH}-CH_3$

3. (structure)

4. (structure)

♦ **Learning Exercise 13.2C**

Identify each of the following pairs of compounds as isomers or the same compound:

1. CH_3-O-CH_3 and CH_3-CH_2-OH _____

2. (structure) and (structure) _____

3. $CH_3-\overset{\overset{\displaystyle CH_3}{|}}{CH}-OH$ and $CH_3-\overset{\overset{\displaystyle OH}{|}}{CH}-CH_3$ _____

Answers   **1.** isomers   **2.** isomers   **3.** same compound

♦ **Learning Exercise 13.2D**

Identify the functional groups of alcohol, phenol, thiol, and/or ether in each of the following compounds:

A. _____

(structure)

an anesthetic

B. _____

$CH_3-\overset{\overset{\displaystyle CH_3}{|}}{CH}-CH_2-CH_2-SH$

a component of skunk odor

C. _____

$CH_3-O-CH_2-CH_2-OH$

a solvent

D. _____

$CH_3-O-CH_2-CH_2-O-CH_3$

used in lithium batteries

E. _____

(structure)

the odor of fennel

F. _____

(structure)

the odor of thyme

Answers   **A.** phenol   **B.** thiol   **C.** alcohol, ether
          D. ether   **E.** ether   **F.** phenol

13.3 Physical Properties of Alcohols, Phenols, and Ethers

Learning Goal: Describe the classification of alcohols; describe the boiling points and solubility of alcohols, phenols, and ethers.

* Alcohols are classified according to the number of alkyl groups attached to the carbon bonded to the —OH group.

* In a primary alcohol, there is one alkyl group attached to the carbon atom bonded to the —OH. In a secondary alcohol, there are two alkyl groups, and in a tertiary alcohol, there are three alkyl groups attached to the carbon atom with the —OH group.

$$CH_3-CH_2-OH \qquad CH_3-\overset{\displaystyle CH_3}{\underset{}{CH}}-OH \qquad CH_3-\overset{\displaystyle CH_3}{\underset{\displaystyle CH_3}{C}}-OH$$

   Primary (1°)   Secondary (2°)   Tertiary (3°)

* The polar —OH group gives alcohols higher boiling points than alkanes and ethers of similar mass.

* Alcohols with one to three carbons are completely soluble in water because the —OH group forms hydrogen bonds with water molecules.

* Although ethers can form hydrogen bonds with water, they do not form as many hydrogen bonds with water as do the alcohols. Ethers containing one to four carbon atoms are slightly soluble in water.

* Phenol is slightly soluble in water and acts as a weak acid.

♦ Learning Exercise 13.3A

Classify each of the following alcohols as primary (1°), secondary (2°), or tertiary (3°):

1. ____ CH_3-CH_2-OH

2. ____

3. ____ $CH_3-\overset{\displaystyle OH}{\underset{\displaystyle CH_3}{C}}-CH_2-CH_3$

4. ____

5. ____ $CH_3-\overset{\displaystyle CH_3}{\underset{\displaystyle CH_3}{C}}-CH_2-OH$

6. ____

Answers   **1.** primary (1°)   **2.** secondary (2°)   **3.** tertiary (3°)
          4. tertiary (3°)   **5.** primary (1°)   **6.** secondary (2°)

♦ **Learning Exercise 13.3B**

Select the compound in each pair with the higher boiling point.

1. $CH_3-CH_2-CH_3$ or CH_3-CH_2-OH

2. $CH_3-O-CH_2-CH_3$ or $CH_3-CH_2-CH_2-OH$

3. $CH_3-CH_2-CH_2-OH$ or $CH_3-CH_2-CH_2-CH_3$

Answers   **1.** CH_3-CH_2-OH **2.** $CH_3-CH_2-CH_2-OH$ **3.** $CH_3-CH_2-CH_2-OH$

♦ **Learning Exercise 13.3C**

Select the compound in each pair that is more soluble in water.

1. CH_3-CH_3 or CH_3-CH_2-OH

2. $CH_3-CH_2-CH_2-OH$ or $CH_3-CH_2-CH_2-CH_2-CH_2-OH$

3. ⌁ or ⌁OH

4. benzene or phenol

5. methoxymethane or methoxypentane

Answers   **1.** CH_3-CH_2-OH **2.** $CH_3-CH_2-CH_2-OH$

3. ⌁OH   **4.** phenol

5. methoxymethane

13.4   Reactions of Alcohols and Thiols

Learning Goal: Write equations for the combustion, dehydration, and oxidation of alcohols and thiols.

- At high temperatures, an alcohol dehydrates in the presence of an acid to yield an alkene and water.

$$CH_3-CH_2-OH \xrightarrow{H^+, \text{ heat}} H_2C=CH_2 + H_2O$$

- Using an oxidizing agent $[O]$, primary alcohols oxidize to aldehydes, which usually oxidize further to carboxylic acids. Secondary alcohols are oxidized to ketones, but tertiary alcohols do not oxidize.

$$CH_3-CH_2-OH \xrightarrow{[O]} CH_3-\overset{\overset{\textstyle O}{\|}}{C}-H + H_2O$$
1° Alcohol   Aldehyde

$$CH_3-\overset{\overset{\textstyle OH}{|}}{C}H-CH_3 \xrightarrow{[O]} CH_3-\overset{\overset{\textstyle O}{\|}}{C}-CH_3 + H_2O$$
2° Alcohol   Ketone

- Thiols undergo oxidation and lose hydrogen from the $-SH$ group to form disulfides, $-S-S-$.

Key Terms for Sections 13.1–13.4

Match the following terms with the correct description below:

a. primary alcohol   **b.** thiol   **c.** dehydration

d. phenol   **e.** tertiary alcohol   **f.** ether

1. _____ has one alkyl group bonded to the carbon with the —OH group

2. _____ contains an —SH group

3. _____ contains an oxygen atom attached to two carbon groups that are alkyl or aromatic

4. _____ has three alkyl groups bonded to the carbon with the —OH group

5. _____ contains a benzene ring bonded to a hydroxyl group

6. _____ a reaction that removes water from an alcohol in the presence of an acid to form an alkene

Answers   **1.** a   **2.** b   **3.** f   **4.** e   **5.** d   **6.** c

---

Study Note

When a secondary alcohol is dehydrated, two products may be formed. According to Saytzeff's rule, the major product will be the alkene formed by removing the hydrogen atom from the carbon with the smaller number of hydrogen atoms.

♦ **Learning Exercise 13.4A**

Draw the condensed or line-angle structural formulas for the products expected from dehydration of each of the following alcohols:

⚛ **CORE CHEMISTRY SKILL**

Writing Equations for the Dehydration of Alcohols

1. $CH_3-CH_2-CH_2-CH_2-OH \xrightarrow{\text{H}^+,\ \text{heat}}$

2. $\xrightarrow{\text{H}^+,\ \text{heat}}$

3. $\xrightarrow{\text{H}^+,\ \text{heat}}$

4. $CH_3-CH_2-\overset{\overset{\displaystyle OH}{|}}{CH}-CH_2-CH_3 \xrightarrow{\text{H}^+,\ \text{heat}}$

Answers   **1.** $CH_3-CH_2-CH=CH_2$ **2.**

3.   **4.** $CH_3-CH_2-CH=CH-CH_3$

♦ **Learning Exercise 13.4B**

Draw the condensed or line-angle structural formula for the major product expected from dehydration of each of the following:

1. [structure with OH] $\xrightarrow{H^+, \text{ heat}}$

2. $CH_3\!-\!CH_2\!-\!\underset{\underset{OH}{|}}{CH}\!-\!\underset{\underset{CH_3}{|}}{CH}\!-\!CH_3 \xrightarrow{H^+, \text{ heat}}$

3. [cyclopentane with OH and CH$_3$] $\xrightarrow{H^+, \text{ heat}}$

Answers   1. [line-angle alkene]   2. $CH_3\!-\!CH_2\!-\!CH\!=\!\underset{\underset{CH_3}{|}}{C}\!-\!CH_3$ 3. [methylcyclopentene]

♦ **Learning Exercise 13.4C**

Draw the condensed or line-angle structural formulas for the aldehyde or ketone expected in the oxidation of each of the following:

CORE CHEMISTRY SKILL

Writing Equations for the Oxidation of Alcohols

1. $CH_3\!-\!CH_2\!-\!CH_2\!-\!CH_2\!-\!OH \xrightarrow{[O]}$

2. [cyclohexane with OH] $\xrightarrow{[O]}$

3. [isopropanol structure with OH] $\xrightarrow{[O]}$

4. $CH_3\!-\!CH_2\!-\!\underset{\underset{OH}{|}}{CH}\!-\!CH_2\!-\!CH_3 \xrightarrow{[O]}$

Answers   1. $CH_3\!-\!CH_2\!-\!CH_2\!-\!\underset{\underset{O}{\|}}{C}\!-\!H$ 2. [cyclohexanone]

3. [acetone structure]   4. $CH_3\!-\!CH_2\!-\!\underset{\overset{O}{\|}}{C}\!-\!CH_2\!-\!CH_3$

Checklist for Chapter 13

You are ready to take the Practice Test for Chapter 13. Be sure you have accomplished the following learning goals for this chapter. If not, review the section listed at the end of the goal. Then apply your new skills and understanding to the Practice Test.

After studying Chapter 13, I can successfully:

_____ Give the IUPAC or common name for an alcohol, phenol, or thiol and draw the condensed or line-angle structural formula. (13.1)

_____ Give the IUPAC or common name for an ether and draw the condensed or line-angle structural formula. (13.2)

_____ Classify an alcohol as primary, secondary, or tertiary. (13.3)

_____ Describe the solubility of alcohols, phenols, and ethers in water and compare their boiling points. (13.3)

_____ Write the products of alcohols that undergo dehydration and oxidation. (13.4)

Practice Test for Chapter 13

For questions 1 through 5, match the names of the following compounds with their correct structure: (13.1, 13.2)

A. 1-propanol   **B.** cyclobutanol   **C.** 2-propanol
D. ethyl methyl ether   **E.** diethyl ether

1.
              2. $CH_3—CH_2—CH_2—OH$ **3.** $CH_3—O—CH_2—CH_3$

4.   **5.** $CH_3—CH_2—O—CH_2—CH_3$

6. The compound $CH_3—\overset{\overset{\textstyle O}{\|}}{C}—CH_3$ is formed by the oxidation of (13.4)
    A. 2-propanol   **B.** propane   **C.** 1-propanol
    D. dimethyl ether   **E.** ethyl methyl ketone

7. Why are short-chain alcohols water-soluble? (13.3)
    A. They are nonpolar.   **B.** They can hydrogen bond.   **C.** They are organic.
    D. They are bases.   **E.** They are acids.

8. Phenol is (13.1)
    A. the alcohol of benzene   **B.** the aldehyde of benzene   **C.** the phenyl group of benzene
    D. the ketone of benzene   **E.** another name for cyclohexanol

9. When (structure) undergoes oxidation, the product is (13.4)
    A. an alkane   **B.** an aldehyde   **C.** a ketone
    D. an ether   **E.** a phenol

10. The dehydration of cyclohexanol gives (13.4)
    A. cyclohexane   **B.** cyclohexene   **C.** cyclohexyne
    D. benzene   **E.** phenol

11. The condensed structural formula for ethanethiol is (13.1)
    A. $CH_3—SH$ **B.** $CH_3—CH_2—OH$ **C.** $CH_3—CH_2—SH$
    D. $CH_3—CH_2—S—CH_3$ **E.** $CH_3—S—OH$

For questions 12 through 16, classify each alcohol as (13.3)

    A. primary (1°)   **B.** secondary (2°)   **C.** tertiary (3°)

12. CH₃—CH₂—CH₂—OH

13.

14.

$$CH_3 \overset{\displaystyle OH}{\underset{\displaystyle \overset{|}{CH_3}}{\overset{|}{\underset{|}{C}}}} - CH_2 - CH_2 - CH_3$$

15. CH₃—C—CH₂—CH₂—CH₃ (with OH and CH₃ on central C)

16. CH₃—CH—CH₂—CH₂—CH₂—CH₃ (with OH on second C)

Complete questions 17 through 19 by indicating the product (A to E) formed in each of the following reactions: (13.4)

    A. primary alcohol   **B.** secondary alcohol   **C.** aldehyde   **D.** ketone   **E.** alkene

17. _____ oxidation of a primary alcohol

18. _____ oxidation of a secondary alcohol

19. _____ dehydration of 1-propanol

20. The major product from the dehydration of 2-methylcyclobutanol is: (13.4)

    A. cyclobutene   **B.** 1-methylcyclobutene   **C.** 2-methylcyclobutene
    D. 3-methylcyclobutene   **E.** 1-methylcyclobutane

Answers to the Practice Test

1. C	**2.** A	**3.** D	**4.** B	**5.** E
6. A	**7.** B	**8.** A	**9.** C	**10.** B
11. C	**12.** A	**13.** B	**14.** C	**15.** C
16. B	**17.** C	**18.** D	**19.** E	**20.** B

13

Alcohols, Phenols, Thiols, and Ethers

Learning Goals

- Give the IUPAC and common names for alcohols, phenols, and thiols; draw their condensed and line-angle structural formulas.
- Give the IUPAC and common names for ethers; draw their condensed or line-angle structural formulas.
- Describe the classification of alcohols; describe the boiling points and solubility of alcohols, phenols, and ethers.
- Write equations for the combustion, dehydration, and oxidation of alcohols and thiols.

Chapter Outline

Chapter Opener: Nurse Anesthetist

13.1 Alcohols, Phenols, and Thiols

Explore Your World: Alcohols in Household Products

Chemistry Link to Health: Some Important Alcohols and Phenols

13.2 Ethers

Chemistry Link to Health: Ethers as Anesthetics

13.3 Physical Properties of Alcohols, Phenols, and Ethers

Chemistry Link to Health: Hand Sanitizers and Ethanol

13.4 Reactions of Alcohols and Thiols

Chemistry Link to Health: Methanol Poisoning

Chemistry Link to Health: Oxidation of Alcohol in the Body

Clinical Update: Janet's New Diet Plan

⚛ Core Chemistry Skills

- Identifying Alcohols, Phenols, and Thiols (13.1)
- Naming Alcohols and Phenols (13.1)
- Writing Equations for the Dehydration of Alcohols (13.4)
- Writing Equations for the Oxidation of Alcohols (13.4)

Selected Answers and Solutions to Text Problems

13.1 **a.** This compound has a two-carbon chain. The final *e* from ethane is dropped, and *ol* is added to indicate an alcohol. The IUPAC name is ethanol. The common name is ethyl alcohol.

b. This compound has a four-carbon chain with a hydroxyl group attached to carbon 2. The IUPAC name is 2-butanol. The common name is *sec*-butyl alcohol.

c. This is the line-angle structural formula of a five-carbon chain with a hydroxyl group attached to carbon 2. The IUPAC name is 2-pentanol.

d. This compound has a six-carbon ring with a hydroxyl group attached to carbon 1, and a methyl group attached to carbon 4 of the ring. The IUPAC name is 4-methylcyclohexanol.

e. This compound is a phenol because the —OH group is attached to a benzene ring. For a phenol, the carbon atom attached to the —OH group is understood to be carbon 1; no number is needed to give the location of the —OH group. This compound also has a fluorine atom attached to carbon 3 of the ring; the IUPAC name is 3-fluorophenol. The common name is *m*-fluorophenol.

13.3 a. 1-Propanol has a three-carbon chain with a hydroxyl group attached to carbon 1.

$CH_3-CH_2-CH_2-OH$

b. 3-Pentanol has a five-carbon chain with a hydroxyl group attached to carbon 3.

$CH_3-CH_2-\overset{\overset{\displaystyle OH}{|}}{CH}-CH_2-CH_3$

c. 2-Methyl-2-butanol has a four-carbon chain with a methyl group and a hydroxyl group attached to carbon 2.

$CH_3-\overset{\overset{\displaystyle OH}{|}}{\underset{\underset{\displaystyle CH_3}{|}}{C}}-CH_2-CH_3$

d. *p*-Chlorophenol has an —OH group attached to carbon 1 of a benzene ring, and a chlorine attached to carbon 4 of the ring (*para*- position).

e. 2-Bromo-5-chlorophenol has an —OH group attached to carbon 1 of a benzene ring, a bromine atom attached to carbon 2, and a chlorine attached to carbon 5 of the ring.

13.5 a. The IUPAC name of the ether with a one-carbon alkyl group and a two-carbon alkyl group attached to an oxygen atom is methoxyethane. The common name is ethyl methyl ether.

b. The IUPAC name of the ether with a one-carbon alkyl group and a six-carbon cycloalkyl group attached to an oxygen atom is methoxycyclohexane. The common name is cyclohexyl methyl ether.

c. The IUPAC name of the ether with a two-carbon alkyl group and a four-carbon cycloalkyl group attached to an oxygen atom is ethoxycyclobutane. The common name is cyclobutyl ethyl ether.

d. The IUPAC name of the ether with a one-carbon alkyl group and a three-carbon alkyl group attached to an oxygen atom is 1-methoxypropane. The common name is methyl propyl ether.

13.7 a. Ethyl propyl ether has a two-carbon group and a three-carbon group attached to oxygen by single bonds.

$CH_3-CH_2-O-CH_2-CH_2-CH_3$

b. Cyclopropyl ethyl ether has a two-carbon group and a three-carbon cycloalkyl group attached to oxygen by single bonds.

c. Methoxycyclopentane has a one-carbon group and a five-carbon cycloalkyl group attached to oxygen by single bonds.

d. 1-Ethoxy-2-methylbutane has a four-carbon chain with a methyl group attached to carbon 2, and an ethoxy group attached to carbon 1.

$$CH_3-CH_2-O-CH_2-\underset{\underset{CH_3}{|}}{CH}-CH_2-CH_3$$

e. 2,3-Dimethoxypentane has a five-carbon chain with two methoxy groups attached, one to carbon 2 and the other to carbon 3.

$$CH_3-\underset{\underset{O-CH_3}{|}}{\overset{\overset{O-CH_3}{|}}{CH}}-CH-CH_2-CH_3$$

13.9 The carbon bonded to the hydroxyl group ($-OH$) is attached to one alkyl group in a primary ($1°$) alcohol, except for methanol; to two alkyl groups in a secondary ($2°$) alcohol; and to three alkyl groups in a tertiary ($3°$) alcohol.
   a. primary ($1°$) alcohol
   b. primary ($1°$) alcohol
   c. tertiary ($3°$) alcohol
   d. secondary ($2°$) alcohol

13.11 a. Methanol molecules can form hydrogen bonds and will have a higher boiling point than the alkane ethane.
   b. 1-Butanol molecules can form hydrogen bonds and will have a higher boiling point than diethyl ether, which cannot form hydrogen bonds with other ether molecules.
   c. 1-Butanol molecules can form hydrogen bonds and will have a higher boiling point than the alkane pentane.

13.13 a. Soluble; ethanol with a short carbon chain is soluble because the hydroxyl group forms hydrogen bonds with water.
   b. Slightly soluble; ethers with up to four carbon atoms are slightly soluble in water because they can form a few hydrogen bonds with water.
   c. Insoluble; an alcohol with a carbon chain of five or more carbon atoms is not soluble in water.

13.15 a. Methanol has a polar $-OH$ group that can form hydrogen bonds with water, but the alkane ethane does not.
   b. 2-Propanol is more soluble in water than 1-butanol because 2-propanol has a shorter carbon chain.
   c. 1-Propanol is more soluble because it can form more hydrogen bonds with water than the ether can.

13.17 a. CH₃—OH   Molecular formula of methanol = CH₄O

$$2CH_4O + 3O_2 \xrightarrow{\Delta} 2CO_2 + 4H_2O + \text{energy}$$

b.
$$\overset{\text{OH}}{\underset{|}{CH_3-CH-CH_2-CH_3}}$$ Molecular formula of 2-butanol = C₄H₁₀O

$$C_4H_{10}O + 6O_2 \xrightarrow{\Delta} 4CO_2 + 5H_2O + \text{energy}$$

13.19 Dehydration is the removal of an H— and an —OH from adjacent carbon atoms of an alcohol to form a water molecule and the corresponding alkene.

a.
$$\overset{\text{CH}_3}{\underset{|}{CH_3-CH-CH=CH_2}}$$

b.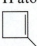

c. For the dehydration of an asymmetrical alcohol, we use Saytzeff's rule to remove —OH from carbon 1 of the ring and H— from carbon 2, which has the smaller number of H atoms.

d. For the dehydration of an asymmetrical alcohol, we use Saytzeff's rule to remove —OH from carbon 2 and H— from carbon 3, which has the smaller number of H atoms.

$$\overset{\text{CH}_3}{\underset{|}{CH_3-CH-CH_2-CH=CH-CH_3}}$$

13.21 Alcohols can produce alkenes and ethers by the loss of water (dehydration).

a. CH₃—CH₂—OH

b.

c.

13.23 A primary alcohol oxidizes to an aldehyde, and a secondary alcohol oxidizes to a ketone.

a.
$$CH_3-CH_2-CH_2-CH_2-\overset{\displaystyle O}{\overset{\displaystyle \|}{C}}-H$$

b.
$$CH_3-CH_2-\overset{\displaystyle O}{\overset{\displaystyle \|}{C}}-CH_3$$

c.

d.

e.

$$CH_3-\overset{\overset{\displaystyle CH_3}{|}}{CH}-CH_2-\overset{\overset{\displaystyle O}{\|}}{C}-H$$

13.25 a. An aldehyde is the product of the oxidation of a primary alcohol.

$$CH_3-OH$$

b. A ketone is the product of the oxidation of a secondary alcohol.

c. A ketone is the product of the oxidation of a secondary alcohol.

d. An aldehyde is the product of the oxidation of a primary alcohol.

e. A ketone is the product of the oxidation of a secondary alcohol.

13.27 a. Gingerol and capsaicin both have aromatic rings bonded to long hydrocarbon groups, with phenol and methoxy ether groups on the aromatic ring.
b. Resveratrol contains phenol and alkene functional groups.
c. 2-Propene-1-thiol contains alkene and thiol functional groups.

13.29 a. alcohol   **b.** ether
      c. thiol   **d.** alcohol

13.31 a. 2-chloro-4-methylcyclohexanol
b. methoxybenzene, methyl phenyl ether
c. 2-propanethiol
d. 2,4-dimethyl-2-pentanol

13.33 a. ether   **b.** thiol
      c. alcohol   **d.** phenol

13.35 a. 1-methoxypropane, methyl propyl ether
b. 2-butanethiol
c. 4-bromo-2-pentanol
d. 3-methylphenol, *m*-methylphenol, *m*-cresol

13.37 a.

b.

c. $CH_3-\overset{\displaystyle CH_3}{\underset{\displaystyle |}{CH}}-\overset{\displaystyle OH}{\underset{\displaystyle |}{CH}}-CH_2-CH_3$

d. (structure: benzene ring with $-O-$ ethyl group)

13.39 a. $CH_3-CH_2-\overset{\displaystyle SH}{\underset{\displaystyle |}{CH}}-CH_2-CH_3$

b. $CH_3-\overset{\displaystyle O-CH_3}{\underset{\displaystyle |}{CH}}-CH_2-CH_2-CH_3$

c. (structure: benzene ring with OH, and two Br substituents)

d. $CH_3-\overset{\displaystyle CH_3}{\underset{\displaystyle |}{C}}-\overset{\displaystyle CH_3}{\underset{\displaystyle |}{CH}}-CH_3$ with OH below the C

13.41 a. 2-methyl-2-propanol
b. 2,4-dimethyl-2-pentanol
c. 3-bromophenol
d. 2-ethoxypentane
e. methoxycyclopentane

13.43 Write the carbon chain first, and place the $-OH$ group on the carbon atoms in the chain to give different structural formulas. Shorten the chain by one carbon, and attach a methyl group and $-OH$ group to give different compounds.

$CH_3-CH_2-CH_2-CH_2-OH$

$CH_3-\overset{\displaystyle OH}{\underset{\displaystyle |}{CH}}-CH_2-CH_3$

$CH_3-\overset{\displaystyle CH_3}{\underset{\displaystyle |}{CH}}-CH_2-OH$

$CH_3-\overset{\displaystyle OH}{\underset{\displaystyle |}{\underset{\displaystyle |}{\underset{\displaystyle CH_3}{C}}}}-CH_3$

13.45 The carbon bonded to the hydroxyl group ($-OH$) is attached to one alkyl group in a primary (1°) alcohol, except for methanol; to two alkyl groups in a secondary (2°) alcohol; and to three alkyl groups in a tertiary (3°) alcohol.
a. secondary (2°) alcohol
b. primary (1°) alcohol
c. primary (1°) alcohol
d. secondary (2°) alcohol
e. primary (1°) alcohol
f. tertiary (3°) alcohol

13.47 a. 1-Propanol molecules can form hydrogen bonds and will have a higher boiling point than the alkane butane.
b. 1-Propanol molecules can form hydrogen bonds and will have a higher boiling point than ethyl methyl ether, which cannot form hydrogen bonds with other ether molecules.
c. 1-Butanol has a greater molar mass than ethanol and will have a higher boiling point.

13.49 a. Soluble; 2-propanol with a short carbon chain is soluble because the hydroxyl group forms hydrogen bonds with water.
b. Insoluble; the long carbon chain in dipropyl ether diminishes the effect of hydrogen bonding of water to the $-O-$ group.
c. Insoluble; the long carbon chain in 1-hexanol diminishes the effect of the polar $-OH$ group on hydrogen bonding with water.

13.51 a. 1-Propanol has a polar —OH group that can form hydrogen bonds with water, but the alkane butane does not.

b. 1-Propanol is more soluble because it can form more hydrogen bonds with water than the ether can.

c. Ethanol is more soluble in water than 1-hexanol because it has a shorter carbon chain.

13.53 a. Molecular formula of 1-butanol = $C_4H_{10}O$

$$C_4H_{10}O + 6O_2 \xrightarrow{\Delta} 4CO_2 + 5H_2O + \text{energy}$$

b. Molecular formula of ethoxypropane = $C_5H_{12}O$

$$2C_5H_{12}O + 15O_2 \xrightarrow{\Delta} 10CO_2 + 12H_2O + \text{energy}$$

c. Molecular formula of cyclopentanol = $C_5H_{10}O$

$$C_5H_{10}O + 7O_2 \xrightarrow{\Delta} 5CO_2 + 5H_2O + \text{energy}$$

13.55 a. 2,5-Dichlorophenol is a benzene ring with a hydroxyl group on carbon 1, and chlorine atoms on carbon 2 and carbon 5.

b. 3-Methyl-1-butanethiol is a four-carbon chain with a methyl group on carbon 3, and a thiol group on carbon 1.

$$
\begin{array}{c}
\quad\;\; CH_3 \\
\quad\;\; | \\
CH_3-CH-CH_2-CH_2-SH
\end{array}
$$

trans-2-Butene-1-thiol is similar in structure to 3-methyl-1-butanethiol except that there is a double bond between carbon 2 and carbon 3, and the carbon chains on the double bond are on opposite sides of the double bond.

$$
\begin{array}{cc}
CH_3 & \quad H \\
\diagdown & \diagup \\
C=C \\
\diagup & \diagdown \\
H & \quad CH_2-SH
\end{array}
$$

c. Pentachlorophenol is a benzene ring with one hydroxyl group and five chlorine atoms attached to the ring.

13.57 a. Dehydration of an alcohol produces an alkene.

$$CH_3-CH=CH_2$$

b. Oxidation of a primary alcohol produces an aldehyde.

$$
\begin{array}{c}
\quad\quad\quad O \\
\quad\quad\quad \| \\
CH_3-CH_2-C-H
\end{array}
$$

c. Dehydration of an alcohol produces an alkene.

d. Dehydration of an alcohol produces an alkene.

e. Oxidation of a secondary alcohol produces a ketone.

13.59 The name 4-hexyl-1,3-benzenediol tells us that there is a six-carbon alkyl group attached to carbon 4 of a benzene ring, and hydroxyl groups attached to carbon 1 and carbon 3 of the ring.

$$CH_2-CH_2-CH_2-CH_2-CH_2-CH_3$$

13.61 Since the compound is synthesized from a primary alcohol and oxidizes to give a carboxylic acid, it must be an aldehyde.

$$CH_3-\overset{CH_3}{\underset{}{CH}}-\overset{O}{\underset{}{C}}-H$$

13.63 A $CH_3-CH_2-CH_2-OH$ 1-Propanol

B $CH_3-CH=CH_2$ Propene

C $CH_3-CH_2-\overset{O}{\underset{}{C}}-H$ Propanal

13.65 a. $CH_3-\overset{OH}{\underset{CH_3}{C}}-CH_3 \xrightarrow{H^+, heat} CH_3-\overset{}{\underset{CH_3}{C}}=CH_2 + H_2 \xrightarrow{Pt} CH_3-\overset{}{\underset{CH_3}{CH}}-CH_3$

b. $CH_3-CH_2-CH_2-OH \xrightarrow{H^+, heat} CH_3-CH=CH_2 + H_2O \xrightarrow{H^+, heat} CH_3-\overset{OH}{\underset{}{CH}}-CH_3$

$\xrightarrow{[O]} CH_3-\overset{O}{\underset{}{C}}-CH_3$

14

Aldehydes, Ketones, and Chiral Molecules

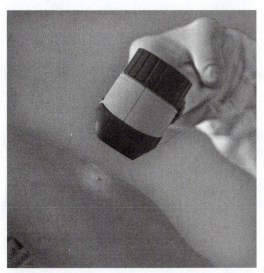

Credit: viappy / Fotolia

Recently, Diana noticed a change in color of a small patch of skin on her arm, which her dermatologist determined was basal cell carcinoma. Because the cancer was detected early, a skin biopsy was sufficient to remove it.

Skin cancer begins in the cells that make up the outer layer (epidermis) of your skin. Limiting exposure to UV (ultraviolet) radiation from the Sun or from tanning salons can help to reduce the risk of developing skin cancer. Sunscreen absorbs UV light radiation when the skin is exposed to sunlight and thus helps protect against sunburn. The sun protection factor (SPF) number gives the amount of time for protected skin to sunburn compared to the time for unprotected skin to sunburn. One of the principal ingredients in sunscreens is oxybenzone.

Treatment for skin cancer depends on the size, type, and location of the cancer. If a skin biopsy cannot completely remove the growth, additional treatment may include using liquid nitrogen to freeze the cancer and excising all the cancerous tissue along with a noncancerous margin of skin around the cancer. Identify the functional groups in oxybenzone.

Oxybenzone

CHAPTER READINESS*

🕸 Core Chemistry Skills

- Naming and Drawing Alkanes (12.2)
- Naming Alcohols and Phenols (13.1)
- Writing Equations for the Oxidation of Alcohols (13.4)

*These Core Chemistry Skills from previous chapters are listed here for your review as you proceed to the new material in this chapter.

14.1 Aldehydes and Ketones

Learning Goal: Identify compounds with carbonyl groups as aldehydes and ketones. Write the IUPAC and common names for aldehydes and ketones; draw their condensed or line-angle structural formulas.

Carbonyl group

Aldehyde   Ketone

The carbonyl group is found in aldehydes and ketones.

- The carbonyl group contains a carbon–oxygen double bond ($C=O$).
- In an aldehyde, the carbonyl group appears at the end of a carbon chain and is attached to at least one hydrogen atom.
- In a ketone, the carbonyl group is attached to two carbon groups.
- In the IUPAC system, aldehydes and ketones are named by replacing the *e* in the longest chain containing the carbonyl group with *al* for aldehydes and *one* for ketones. The location of the carbonyl group in a ketone is given if there are more than four carbon atoms in the chain.

$$CH_3-\overset{\overset{\displaystyle O}{\|}}{C}-H \qquad CH_3-\overset{\overset{\displaystyle O}{\|}}{C}-CH_3$$

Ethanal   Propanone
(acetaldehyde)   (dimethyl ketone)

♦ **Learning Exercise 14.1A**

Classify each of the compounds below as one of the following:
   A. alcohol   **B.** aldehyde   **C.** ketone   **D.** ether

1. _____ $CH_3-CH_2-CH_2-\overset{\overset{\displaystyle O}{\|}}{C}-H$

2. _____ ⌇⌇⌇OH

3. _____ (line-angle ketone structure)

4. _____ $CH_3-CH_2-O-CH_3$

5. _____ $CH_3-\overset{\overset{\displaystyle O}{\|}}{C}-CH_2-CH_3$

6. _____ $CH_3-\overset{\overset{\displaystyle O}{\|}}{C}-H$

7. _____ (cyclopentane ring with $\overset{\overset{\displaystyle O}{\|}}{C}-H$ group)

8. _____ $CH_3-CH_2-\overset{\overset{\displaystyle OH}{|}}{CH}-CH_3$

Answers   **1.** B   **2.** A   **3.** C   **4.** D
               5. C   **6.** B   **7.** B   **8.** A

♦ **Learning Exercise 14.1B**

Indicate whether the compounds in each of the following pairs are isomers (I) or the same compound (S):

1. CH₃—CH₂—C(=O)—H and CH₃—C(=O)—CH₃

2. and

3. and

Answers   **1.** I   **2.** S   **3.** I

Guide to Naming Aldehydes	
STEP 1	Name the longest carbon chain by replacing the *e* in the alkane name with *al*.
STEP 2	Name and number any substituents by counting the carbonyl group as carbon 1.

♦ **Learning Exercise 14.1C**

⚛ **CORE CHEMISTRY SKILL**

Write the IUPAC and common name, if any, for each of the following aldehydes:

Naming Aldehydes and Ketones

1. CH₃—C(=O)—H

2.

3. CH₃—CH₂—CH(CH₃)—CH₂—CH₂—C(=O)—H

4.

5. H—C(=O)—H

Answers   **1.** ethanal (acetaldehyde)   **2.** pentanal   **3.** 4-methylhexanal
4. butanal (butyraldehyde)   **5.** methanal (formaldehyde)

Guide to Naming Ketones	
STEP 1	Name the longest carbon chain by replacing the *e* in the alkane name with *one*.
STEP 2	Number the carbon chain starting from the end nearer the carbonyl group and indicate its location.
STEP 3	Name and number any substituents on the carbon chain.

♦ **Learning Exercise 14.1D**

Write the IUPAC name and common name, if any, for each of the following ketones:

1. CH₃—C(=O)—CH₃

2. (line-angle structure)

3. CH₃—CH₂—C(=O)—CH₂—CH₃

4. (cyclopentanone ring structure)

5. (line-angle structure with Cl)

Answers
1. propanone (dimethyl ketone, acetone)
2. 2-pentanone (methyl propyl ketone)
3. 3-pentanone (diethyl ketone)
4. cyclopentanone
5. 3-chloro-4-methyl-2-hexanone

♦ **Learning Exercise 14.1E**

Draw the condensed structural formulas for **1** to **4** and the line-angle structural formulas for **5** and **6**.

1. ethanal
2. 2-methylbutanal
3. 2-chloropropanal
4. ethyl methyl ketone
5. 3-pentanone
6. benzaldehyde

Answers
1. CH₃—C(=O)—H
2. CH₃—CH₂—CH(CH₃)—C(=O)—H
3. CH₃—CH(Cl)—C(=O)—H
4. CH₃—CH₂—C(=O)—CH₃
5. (line-angle structure)
6. (benzaldehyde structure)

♦ **Learning Exercise 14.1F**

Identify the functional groups of alcohol, phenol, ether, aldehyde, and/or ketone in each of the following compounds:

1. _____

designer drug, illegal
stimulant

2. _____

citrus odor

3. _____

sunless tanning compound

4. _____

vanilla flavor

5. _____

male sex hormone

6. _____

anti-inflammatory compound
from soybeans

Answers   **1.** ketone   **2.** aldehyde   **3.** alcohol, ketone
            4. phenol, ether, aldehyde   **5.** alcohol, ketone   **6.** phenol, ether, ketone

14.2   Physical Properties of Aldehydes and Ketones

*Learning Goal: Describe the boiling points and solubilities
of aldehydes and ketones.*

Hydrogen bonds

- The polarity of the carbonyl group provides aldehydes and ketones with dipole–dipole attractions that alkanes do not have. Thus, aldehydes and ketones have higher boiling points than alkanes. However, aldehydes and ketones cannot form hydrogen bonds with each other as do alcohols. Thus, alcohols have higher boiling points than aldehydes and ketones of similar molar mass.

The polar carbonyl group hydrogen bonds with water, which makes aldehydes and ketones with one to four carbons soluble in water.

- The polarity of the carbonyl group makes aldehydes and ketones with one to four carbon atoms soluble in water.

- For aldehydes and ketones, the boiling points increase as the number of carbon atoms in the chain increases. As the molecules become larger, there are more temporary dipoles (dispersion forces), which give higher boiling points.

♦ **Learning Exercise 14.2A**

Indicate the compound with the highest boiling point in each of the following groups of compounds:

1. $CH_3-CH_2-\overset{\overset{\displaystyle O}{\|}}{C}-H$, $CH_3-CH_2-CH_2-OH$ or $CH_3-\overset{\overset{\displaystyle O}{\|}}{C}-CH_3$

2. acetaldehyde or propionaldehyde

3. propanone or butanone

4. methylcyclohexane or cyclohexanone

Answers   **1.** $CH_3-CH_2-CH_2-OH$ **2.** propionaldehyde
              3. butanone   **4.** cyclohexanone

♦ **Learning Exercise 14.2B**

Indicate whether each of the following compounds is soluble (S) or not soluble (NS) in water:

1. _____ 3-hexanone   **2.** _____ propanal   **3.** _____ acetaldehyde

4. _____ butanal   **5.** _____ cyclohexanone

Answers   **1.** NS   **2.** S   **3.** S   **4.** S   **5.** NS

14.3 Oxidation and Reduction of Aldehydes and Ketones

Learning Goal: Draw the condensed or line-angle structural formulas for the reactants and products in the oxidation or reduction of aldehydes and ketones.

- Using an oxidizing agent, primary alcohols are oxidized to aldehydes, which usually oxidize further to carboxylic acids. Secondary alcohols are oxidized to ketones, but tertiary alcohols do not oxidize.

$$CH_3-CH_2-OH \xrightarrow{[O]} CH_3-\overset{\displaystyle O}{\overset{\displaystyle \|}{C}}-H + H_2O$$
Primary alcohol   Aldehyde

$$CH_3-\overset{\displaystyle OH}{\overset{\displaystyle |}{C}H}-CH_3 \xrightarrow{[O]} CH_3-\overset{\displaystyle O}{\overset{\displaystyle \|}{C}}-CH_3 + H_2O$$
Secondary alcohol   Ketone

- Aldehydes and ketones are reduced by hydrogen (H_2) or sodium borohydride ($NaBH_4$) to produce primary or secondary alcohols. A metal catalyst is needed in the addition of hydrogen.

$$CH_3-\overset{\displaystyle O}{\overset{\displaystyle \|}{C}}-H + H_2 \xrightarrow{Pt} CH_3-CH_2-OH$$
Aldehyde   Primary alcohol

$$CH_3-\overset{\displaystyle O}{\overset{\displaystyle \|}{C}}-CH_3 + H_2 \xrightarrow{Pt} CH_3-\overset{\displaystyle OH}{\overset{\displaystyle |}{C}H}-CH_3$$
Ketone   Secondary alcohol

- In the Tollens' test, an aldehyde is oxidized as Ag^+ is reduced to a silver mirror.
- In the Benedict's test, an aldehyde with an adjacent hydroxyl group is oxidized and Cu^{2+} is reduced to Cu_2O.

♦ **Learning Exercise 14.3A**

Draw the condensed or line-angle structural formula for the aldehyde or ketone expected in the oxidation of each of the following:

1. $CH_3-CH_2-CH_2-CH_2-OH \xrightarrow{[O]}$

2. cyclohexanol $\xrightarrow{[O]}$

3. $\xrightarrow{[O]}$

4. $CH_3-CH_2-\underset{\underset{OH}{|}}{CH}-CH_2-CH_3 \xrightarrow{[O]}$

Answers

1. $CH_3-CH_2-CH_2-\overset{\overset{\displaystyle O}{\|}}{C}-H$

2.

3.

4. $CH_3-CH_2-\overset{\overset{\displaystyle O}{\|}}{C}-CH_2-CH_3$

♦ **Learning Exercise 14.3B**

Draw the condensed structural formula for the alcohol that was oxidized to give each of the following compounds:

1. $CH_3-\overset{\overset{\displaystyle O}{\|}}{C}-CH_2-CH_3$

2.

3. $CH_3-CH_2-\overset{\overset{\displaystyle O}{\|}}{C}-H$

Answers

1. $CH_3-\underset{\underset{OH}{|}}{CH}-CH_2-CH_3$

2.

3. $CH_3-CH_2-CH_2-OH$

♦ **Learning Exercise 14.3C**

Draw the condensed or line-angle structural formula for the reduction product from each of the following:

1. $CH_3-\overset{\overset{\displaystyle O}{\|}}{C}-CH_2-CH_3 + H_2 \xrightarrow{Pt}$

2. $CH_3-CH_2-\overset{\overset{\displaystyle O}{\|}}{C}-H + H_2 \xrightarrow{Pt}$

3. $+ H_2 \xrightarrow{Pt}$

4. H + H$_2$ $\xrightarrow{\text{Pt}}$

Answers

1.
$$\overset{\overset{\displaystyle OH}{|}}{CH_3-CH-CH_2-CH_3}$$

2. $CH_3-CH_2-CH_2-OH$

3.

4.

14.4 Hemiacetals and Acetals

Learning Goal: Draw the condensed or line-angle structural formulas for the products of the addition of alcohols to aldehydes and ketones.

- Alcohols add to the carbonyl group of aldehydes and ketones.
- Hemiacetals form when one alcohol adds to aldehydes or ketones.
- Acetals form when a second alcohol molecule adds to hemiacetals.

The addition of an alcohol to an aldehyde or ketone produces a hemiacetal that can add a second alcohol to produce an acetal.

♦ Learning Exercise 14.4A

Match the descriptions shown below with the following types of compounds:

   A. hemiacetal   **B.** acetal

1. _____ the product from the addition of one alcohol to an aldehyde

2. _____ the product from the addition of one alcohol to a ketone

3. _____ a compound that contains two ether groups

4. _____ a compound that consists of one ether group, an alcohol group, and two alkyl groups

Answers   1. A   2. A   3. B   4. A

♦ Learning Exercise 14.4B

Identify each of the following condensed structural formulas as a hemiacetal, acetal, or neither:

1. CH_3-O-CH_2-OH

2.
$$\overset{\overset{\displaystyle OH}{|}}{\underset{\underset{\displaystyle O-CH_3}{|}}{CH_3-C-H}}$$

3. $CH_3 - \overset{\overset{\displaystyle O-CH_2-CH_3}{|}}{\underset{\underset{\displaystyle O-CH_2-CH_3}{|}}{C}} - CH_3$

4. $CH_3 - \overset{\overset{\displaystyle O-CH_3}{|}}{\underset{\underset{\displaystyle O-CH_3}{|}}{C}} - H$

Answers   **1.** hemiacetal   **2.** hemiacetal   **3.** acetal   **4.** acetal

♦ **Learning Exercise 14.4C**

Draw the condensed structural formula for the hemiacetal and acetal products when methanol adds to propanone.

Answers $CH_3 - \overset{\overset{\displaystyle OH}{|}}{\underset{\underset{\displaystyle CH_3}{|}}{C}} - O - CH_3$ $CH_3 - \overset{\overset{\displaystyle O-CH_3}{|}}{\underset{\underset{\displaystyle CH_3}{|}}{C}} - O - CH_3$

                     Hemiacetal   Acetal

14.5   Chiral Molecules

Learning Goal: Identify chiral and achiral carbon atoms in an organic molecule.

- Chiral molecules have mirror images that cannot be superimposed.
- When the mirror image of an object is identical and can be superimposed on the original, it is achiral.
- In a chiral molecule, one or more carbon atoms are attached to four different atoms or groups.
- The mirror images of a chiral molecule represent two different molecules called enantiomers.
- In a Fischer projection, the prefixes D and L are used to distinguish between the mirror images.
- In D-glyceraldehyde, the —OH group is on the right of the chiral carbon; it is on the left in L-glyceraldehyde.

L-Glyceraldehyde   D-Glyceraldehyde

- For compounds with two or more chiral carbons, the designation as a D or L stereoisomer is determined by the position of the —OH group attached to the chiral carbon *farthest from the carbonyl group*.

L-Erythrose   D-Erythrose

Key Terms for Sections 14.1–14.5

Match the following terms with the correct description shown below:

a. chiral carbon   **b.** hemiacetal   **c.** Fischer projection   **d.** aldehyde   **e.** ketone

1. _____ an organic compound with a carbonyl group attached to two carbon groups

2. _____ a carbon that is bonded to four different groups

3. _____ the product that forms when an alcohol adds to an aldehyde or a ketone

4. _____ a system for drawing chiral molecules that uses horizontal lines for bonds coming forward and vertical lines for bonds going back, with the chiral atom at the center

5. _____ an organic compound that contains a carbonyl group and a hydrogen atom at the end of the carbon chain

Answers   **1.** e   **2.** a   **3.** b   **4.** c   **5.** d

♦ Learning Exercise 14.5A

⚛ CORE CHEMISTRY SKILL

Identifying Chiral Molecules

Indicate whether each of the following objects would be chiral or achiral:

1. a piece of blank piece of computer paper   2. a glove

3. a plain baseball cap   4. a volleyball net

5. a left foot

Answers   **1.** achiral   **2.** chiral   **3.** achiral   **4.** achiral   **5.** chiral

♦ Learning Exercise 14.5B

State whether each of the following molecules is chiral or achiral:

1.
$$
\begin{array}{c}
\text{Cl} \\
| \\
\text{H}-\text{C}-\text{Cl} \underline{\hspace{2cm}} \\
| \\
\text{CH}_3
\end{array}
$$

2.
$$
\begin{array}{c}
\text{Cl} \\
| \\
\text{H}-\text{C}-\text{OH} \underline{\hspace{2cm}} \\
| \\
\text{CH}_3
\end{array}
$$

3.
$$
\begin{array}{c}
\text{H} \quad\quad \text{O} \\
\text{C} \\
| \\
\text{H}-\text{C}-\text{OH} \underline{\hspace{2cm}} \\
| \\
\text{CH}_3
\end{array}
$$

Answers   **1.** achiral   **2.** chiral   **3.** chiral

♦ Learning Exercise 14.5C

Identify each of the following features as characteristic of a chiral compound or a compound that is achiral:

1. central atom attached to two identical groups

2. contains a carbon attached to four different groups

3. has identical mirror images

Answers   **1.** achiral   **2.** chiral   **3.** achiral

♦ **Learning Exercise 14.5D**

Indicate whether each pair of Fischer projections represents enantiomers (E) or identical structures (I).

1. HO——H and H——OH

(top group: HO–C=O; bottom group: CH_2OH)

2. Cl——H and Cl——H

(top group: CH_2OH; bottom group: CH_3)

3. Cl——Br and Br——Cl

(top group: H–C=O; bottom group: CH_3)

4. H——OH and HO——H

(top group: CH_3; bottom group: CH_3)

Answers   **1.** E   **2.** I   **3.** E   **4.** I

♦ **Learning Exercise 14.5E**

Identify each of the following compounds as chiral or achiral:

1. _____

treat hyperactivity

2. _____

analgesic

3. _____

butter flavoring

4. _____

anti-inflammatory

Answers   **1.** chiral   **2.** achiral   **3.** achiral   **4.** chiral

♦ **Learning Exercise 14.5F**

Identify each of the following as the D or L stereoisomer:

🔬 **CORE CHEMISTRY SKILL**

Identifying D-and L-Fischer Projections

1. _____   **2.** _____   **3.** _____

Answers   **1.** D   **2.** L   **3.** L

Checklist for Chapter 14

You are ready to take the Practice Test for Chapter 14. Be sure you have accomplished the following learning goals for this chapter. If not, review the section listed at the end of the goal. Then apply your new skills and understanding to the Practice Test.

After studying Chapter 14, I can successfully:

_____ Identify the condensed or line-angle structural formulas as aldehydes or ketones. (14.1)

_____ Give the IUPAC and common names for an aldehyde or ketone; draw the condensed or line-angle structural formula from the name. (14.1)

_____ Compare the physical properties of aldehydes and ketones to those of alcohols and alkanes. (14.2)

_____ Draw the condensed or line-angle structural formulas for the reactants and products in the oxidation or reduction of aldehydes and ketones. (14.3)

_____ Draw the condensed or line-angle structural formulas for the hemiacetals and acetals that form when alcohols add to aldehydes or ketones. (14.4)

_____ Identify a molecule as chiral or achiral; draw the D- and L-Fischer projections. (14.5)

Practice Test for Chapter 14

For questions 1 through 5, match each of the following compounds with the names given: (14.1)

A. butanal   **B.** acetaldehyde   **C.** methanal   **D.** dimethyl ketone   **E.** propanal

1. ____ $H-\overset{\overset{\displaystyle O}{\|}}{C}-H$

2. ____ (line-angle structure ending in H with C=O)

3. ____ $CH_3-\overset{\overset{\displaystyle O}{\|}}{C}-CH_3$

4. ____ $CH_3-\overset{\overset{\displaystyle O}{\|}}{C}-H$

5. ____ $CH_3-CH_2-\overset{\overset{\displaystyle O}{\|}}{C}-H$

Copyright © 2015 Pearson Education, Inc.

6. The compound with the highest boiling point is (14.2)

    A. $CH_3-CH_2-CH_2-CH_3$ **B.** $CH_3-CH_2-CH_2-OH$

                           O O

                           $\parallel$ $\parallel$

    C. CH_3-C-CH_3 **D.** CH_3-CH_2-C-H

    E. $CH_3-CH_2-O-CH_3$

*For questions 7 through 11, indicate the product (**A** to **E**) formed in each of the following reactions:* (14.3)

    A. primary alcohol   **B.** secondary alcohol   **C.** aldehyde
    D. ketone   **E.** carboxylic acid

7. _____ oxidation of a primary alcohol   **8.** _____ oxidation of a secondary alcohol

9. _____ oxidation of an aldehyde   **10.** _____ reduction of a ketone

11. _____ reduction of an aldehyde

12. Benedict's reagent will oxidize (14.3)

                   O OH

                   $\parallel$ $\mid$

    A. CH_3-C-CH_3 **B.** $CH_3-CH-CH_2-OH$

                   O OH O

                   $\parallel$ $\mid$ $\parallel$

    C. CH_3-C-CH_2-OH **D.** $CH_3-CH-C-H$

                 OH O

                 $\mid$ $\parallel$

    E. $CH_3-CH-C-OH$

13. In the Tollens' test (14.3)

    A. an aldehyde is oxidized and Ag^+ is reduced

    B. an aldehyde is reduced and Ag^+ is oxidized

    C. a ketone is oxidized and Ag^+ is reduced

    D. a ketone is reduced and Ag^+ is oxidized

    E. all of these

For questions 14 through 17, match the name with one of the following condensed structural formulas: (14.4)

14. alcohol   **15.** ether   **16.** hemiacetal   **17.** acetal

                   OH OH

                   $\mid$ $\mid$

    A. $CH_3-CH_2-CH-CH_3$ **B.** CH_3-C-H

                                                               $\mid$

                                                               $O-CH_3$

                   $O-CH_2-CH_3$ $O-CH_3$

                   $\mid$ $\mid$

    C. CH_3-C-CH_3 **D.** CH_3-C-CH_3

                   $\mid$ $\mid$

                   $O-CH_2-CH_3$ CH_3

18. The line-angle structural formula for 4-bromo-3-methylcyclohexanone is (14.1)

A.

B.

C.

D.

E.

19. The name of the following compound is: (14.1)

$$CH_3-CH-CH_2-CH-CH_2-C-H$$

with CH_3 groups on the two CH carbons and =O on the final carbon.

A. 3,5-dimethyl-1-hexanal
B. 2,4-dimethyl-6-hexanal
C. 3,5-dimethylhexanal
D. 1-aldo-3,5-dimethylhexane
E. 2,4-dimethylhexanal

20. The reaction of an alcohol with an aldehyde is called a(n) (14.4)

A. elimination   **B.** addition   **C.** substitution   **D.** hydrolysis   **E.** oxidation

For questions 21 through 24, identify each of the following pairs of Fischer projections as enantiomers (E) or identical compounds (I): (14.5)

21. Cl—|—OH and HO—|—Cl (with CH_2OH top, CH_3 bottom)

22. Br—|—H and H—|—Br (with CHO top, CH_2OH bottom)

23. Cl—|—Cl and Cl—|—Cl (with CHO top, CH_3 bottom)

24. Br—|—H and H—|—Br (with CH_2OH top, CH_2OH bottom)

25. Identify the following as the D or L stereoisomer: (14.5)

$$CHO$$
HO—|—H
H—|—OH
$$CH_2OH$$

Answers to the Practice Test

1. C	**2.** A	**3.** D	**4.** B	**5.** E
6. B	**7.** C, E	**8.** D	**9.** E	**10.** B
11. A	**12.** D	**13.** A	**14.** A	**15.** D
16. B	**17.** C	**18.** B	**19.** C	**20.** B
21. E	**22.** E	**23.** I	**24.** I	**25.** D

14

Aldehydes, Ketones, and Chiral Molecules

Learning Goals

- Identify compounds with carbonyl groups as aldehydes and ketones.
- Write the IUPAC and common names for aldehydes and ketones; draw their condensed or line-angle structural formulas.
- Describe the boiling points and solubilities of aldehydes and ketones.
- Draw the condensed or line-angle structural formulas for the reactants and products in the oxidation or reduction of aldehydes and ketones.
- Draw the condensed or line-angle structural formulas for the products of the addition of alcohols to aldehydes and ketones.
- Identify chiral and achiral carbon atoms in an organic molecule.

Chapter Outline

Chapter Opener: Dermatology Nurse

14.1 Aldehydes and Ketones

Chemistry Link to Health: Some Important Aldehydes and Ketones

14.2 Physical Properties of Aldehydes and Ketones

14.3 Oxidation and Reduction of Aldehydes and Ketones

14.4 Hemiacetals and Acetals

14.5 Chiral Molecules

Explore Your World: Using Gumdrops and Toothpicks to Model Chiral Objects

Chemistry Link to Health: Enantiomers in Biological Systems

Clinical Update: Diana's Skin Protection Plan

❀ Core Chemistry Skills

- Naming Aldehydes and Ketones (14.1)
- Identifying Chiral Molecules (14.5)
- Identifying D- and L-Fischer Projections (14.5)

Selected Answers and Solutions to Text Problems

14.1 **a.** A carbonyl group ($C=O$) attached to two carbon atoms within the carbon chain makes this compound a ketone.

  b. A carbonyl group ($C=O$) attached to a hydrogen atom at the end of the carbon chain makes this compound an aldehyde.

  c. A carbonyl group ($C=O$) attached to two carbon atoms within the carbon chain makes this compound a ketone.

  d. A carbonyl group ($C=O$) attached to a hydrogen atom at the end of the carbon chain makes this compound an aldehyde.

14.3 a. These compounds are structural isomers of C_3H_6O: The first is a ketone, and the second is an aldehyde.

  b. These compounds are structural isomers of $C_5H_{10}O$: The first is a ketone with the carbonyl group on carbon 3, and the second is a ketone with the carbonyl group on carbon 2.

  c. These compounds are not structural isomers: The first has a molecular formula of C_4H_8O, and the second has a molecular formula of $C_5H_{10}O$.

14.5 a. 3-bromobutanal
  b. 4-hydroxy-2-pentanone
  c. 2-methylcyclopentanone
  d. 3-bromobenzaldehyde

14.7 a. acetaldehyde
  b. methyl propyl ketone
  c. formaldehyde

14.9 a.

  b.

  c.

  d.

14.11 The name 4-methoxybenzaldehyde tells us that there is a methyl ether at carbon 4 of the ring in benzaldehyde.

14.13 a. $CH_3-\overset{\overset{O}{\|}}{C}-H$ will have the higher boiling point since aldehydes have a polar carbonyl group and form dipole–dipole attractions that alkanes like propane do not.

  b. Pentanal has a longer carbon chain, more electrons, and more dispersion forces than propanal, which give pentanal a higher boiling point.

  c. 1-Butanol has a polar hydroxyl group and can form hydrogen bonds, which are stronger than the dipole–dipole attractions in butanal; 1-butanol will have the higher boiling point.

14.15 a. $CH_3-\overset{\overset{O}{\|}}{C}-\overset{\overset{O}{\|}}{C}-CH_2-CH_3$ is more soluble in water because it has two polar carbonyl groups and can form more hydrogen bonds with water.

  b. Propanal is more soluble in water because it has a shorter carbon chain than pentanal, in which the longer hydrocarbon chain diminishes the effect on solubility of the polar carbonyl group.

   c. Acetone is more soluble in water because it has a shorter carbon chain than 2-pentanone, in which the longer hydrocarbon chain diminishes the effect on solubility of the polar carbonyl group.

14.17 No. A hydrocarbon chain of eight carbon atoms reduces the effect on solubility of the polar carbonyl group.

14.19 a. An aldehyde can be oxidized to a carboxylic acid.

$$H-\overset{\overset{\displaystyle O}{\|}}{C}-OH$$

   b. None; a ketone cannot be further oxidized.
   c. An aldehyde can be oxidized to a carboxylic acid.

$$\overset{\overset{\displaystyle O}{\|}}{C}-OH$$

   d. None; a ketone cannot be further oxidized.

14.21 a. An aldehyde will react with Tollens' reagent.
   b. A ketone will react with neither Tollens' reagent nor Benedict's reagent.
   c. An aldehyde with an adjacent hydroxyl group will react with both Tollens' reagent and Benedict's reagent.

14.23 In reduction, an aldehyde will give a primary alcohol, and a ketone will give a secondary alcohol.
   a. Butyraldehyde is the four-carbon aldehyde; it will be reduced to a four-carbon primary alcohol.

$$CH_3-CH_2-CH_2-CH_2-OH$$

   b. Acetone is a three-carbon ketone; it will be reduced to a three-carbon secondary alcohol.

$$CH_3-\overset{\overset{\displaystyle OH}{|}}{CH}-CH_3$$

   c. 3-Bromohexanal is a six-carbon aldehyde with a bromine atom on carbon 3; it reduces to the corresponding six-carbon primary alcohol with a bromine atom on carbon 3.

$$CH_3-CH_2-CH_2-\overset{\overset{\displaystyle Br}{|}}{CH}-CH_2-CH_2-OH$$

   d. 2-Methyl-3-pentanone is a five-carbon ketone with a methyl group attached to carbon 2. It will be reduced to a five-carbon secondary alcohol with a methyl group attached to carbon 2.

$$CH_3-\overset{\overset{\displaystyle CH_3}{|}}{CH}-\overset{\overset{\displaystyle OH}{|}}{CH}-CH_2-CH_3$$

14.25 a. hemiacetal   **b.** hemiacetal
    c. acetal   **d.** hemiacetal
    e. acetal

14.27 A hemiacetal forms when an alcohol is added to the carbonyl of an aldehyde or ketone.

a.
$$CH_3-\underset{\underset{OH}{|}}{\overset{\overset{O-CH_3}{|}}{C}}-H$$

b.
$$CH_3-\underset{\underset{OH}{|}}{\overset{\overset{O-CH_3}{|}}{C}}-CH_3$$

c.
$$CH_3-CH_2-CH_2-\underset{\underset{OH}{|}}{\overset{\overset{O-CH_3}{|}}{C}}-H$$

14.29 An acetal forms when a second molecule of alcohol reacts with a hemiacetal.

a.
$$CH_3-\underset{\underset{O-CH_3}{|}}{\overset{\overset{O-CH_3}{|}}{C}}-H$$

b.
$$CH_3-\underset{\underset{O-CH_3}{|}}{\overset{\overset{O-CH_3}{|}}{C}}-CH_3$$

c.
$$CH_3-CH_2-CH_2-\underset{\underset{O-CH_3}{|}}{\overset{\overset{O-CH_3}{|}}{C}}-H$$

14.31 a. Achiral; there are no carbon atoms attached to four different groups.

b. Chiral;

Br *Chiral carbon*

c. Chiral;

Chiral carbon

$$CH_3-\underset{\overset{|}{Br}}{C}H-\overset{\overset{O}{\|}}{C}-H$$

d. Achiral; there are no carbon atoms attached to four different groups.

14.33 a.
$$H-\overset{\overset{O}{\nearrow}}{C}$$
$$HO-\!\!\!\!\!\underset{\underset{CH_3}{|}}{+}\!\!\!\!\!-Br$$

b.
$$H-\overset{\overset{O}{\nearrow}}{C}$$
$$Cl-\!\!\!\!\!\underset{\underset{OH}{|}}{+}\!\!\!\!\!-Br$$

c.
$$H-\overset{\overset{O}{\nearrow}}{C}$$
$$HO-\!\!\!\!\!\underset{\underset{CH_2CH_3}{|}}{+}\!\!\!\!\!-H$$

14.35 Enantiomers are nonsuperimposable mirror images.
    a. identical structures (no chiral carbons)   **b.** enantiomers
    c. enantiomers   **d.** enantiomers

14.37 a. When the —OH group is drawn to the right of the chiral carbon, it is the D stereoisomer.
    b. When the —OH group is drawn to the right of the chiral carbon, it is the D stereoisomer.
    c. When the —OH group is drawn to the left of the chiral carbon farthest from the top of the Fischer projection, it is the L stereoisomer.

14.39 a. CH₃—C(CH₃)=CH—CH₂—CH₂—CH(—)—CH₂—CH₂—OH   *Chiral carbon*

b. H₂N—CH(CH₃)—C(=O)—OH   *Chiral carbon*

14.41 a. Oxybenzone contains ether, phenol, ketone, and aromatic functional groups.

b. Molecular formula of oxybenzone = $C_{14}H_{12}O_3$
Molar mass of oxybenzone $(C_{14}H_{12}O_3)$
= 14(12.01 g) + 12(1.008) + 3(16.00) = 228.2 g/mole (4 SFs)

c. $178 \text{ mL sunscreen} \times \dfrac{6.0 \text{ g oxybenzone}}{100 \text{ mL sunscreen}} = 11 \text{ g of oxybenzone (2 SFs)}$

14.43 Cinnamaldehyde contains aromatic, alkene, and aldehyde functional groups.

14.45 a. CH₃—CH₂—CH₂ ...

b. CH₃—C(CH₃)=CH—CH₂—CH₂—CH(CH₃)—C(=O)—H

14.47 The C=O double bond has a dipole because the oxygen atom is highly electronegative compared to the carbon atom. In the C=C double bond, both atoms have the same electronegativity, and there is no dipole.

14.49 a. An aldehyde will react with Tollens' reagent and produce a silver mirror.

b. An aldehyde will react with Tollens' reagent and produce a silver mirror.

c. An ether will not react with Tollens' reagent.

14.51 a. 2-bromo-4-chlorocyclopentanone   **b.** 2,4-dibromobenzaldehyde
c. 3-chloropropanal   **d.** 2-chloro-3-pentanone
e. 5-chloro-3-hexanone

14.53 a.

b. CH₃—CH₂—CH₂—CH₂—C(=O)—H

c. CH₃—CH₂—C(=O)—CH₃

d. CH₃—CH₂—CH(CH₃)—CH₂—CH₂—C(=O)—H

e. CH₃—C(=O)—CH₂—CH₂—C(=O)—H

14.55 Compounds **a** and **b** are soluble in water because they have a polar group with an oxygen atom that hydrogen bonds with water and fewer than five carbon atoms.

14.57 a. $CH_3-CH_2-CH_2-OH$

b. $CH_3-CH_2-\overset{\overset{\displaystyle O}{\|}}{C}-H$

c. CH_3-CH_2-OH

14.59 Aldehydes oxidize to form carboxylic acids; ketones do not oxidize further.

a. $CH_3-CH_2-\overset{\overset{\displaystyle O}{\|}}{C}-OH$

b. $CH_3-CH_2-CH_2-\overset{\overset{\displaystyle O}{\|}}{C}-OH$

c. no reaction

14.61 In reduction, an aldehyde will give a primary alcohol, and a ketone will give a secondary alcohol.

a. $CH_3-\overset{\overset{\displaystyle OH}{|}}{CH}-CH_3$

b. ⬡$-CH_2-CH_2-OH$

c. $CH_3-\overset{\overset{\displaystyle CH_3}{|}}{CH}-CH_2-\overset{\overset{\displaystyle OH}{|}}{CH}-CH_3$

14.63 a. propanal
c. 2-butanol

b. 2-pentanone
d. cyclohexanone

14.65 a. acetal; propanal and methanol
c. acetal; cyclohexanone and ethanol

b. hemiacetal; butanone and ethanol

14.67 A chiral carbon is bonded to four different groups.

a. $H-\overset{\overset{\displaystyle Cl}{|}}{\underset{\underset{\displaystyle Cl}{|}}{C}}-\overset{\overset{\displaystyle Cl}{|}}{\underset{\underset{\displaystyle H}{|}}{\textcircled{C}}}-OH$

b. none

c. none

d. $CH_3-\overset{\overset{\displaystyle NH_2}{|}}{\textcircled{C}H}-\overset{\overset{\displaystyle O}{\|}}{C}-H$

e. $CH_3-CH_2-\overset{\overset{\displaystyle Br}{|}}{\textcircled{C}H}-CH_2-CH_2-CH_3$

f. none

14.69 Enantiomers are nonsuperimposable mirror images.
a. identical compounds (no chiral carbons)   **b.** enantiomers
c. enantiomers   **d.** identical compounds (no chiral carbons)

14.71 a. True; both **A** and **B** have the molecular formula $C_5H_{10}O$, but a different arrangement of atoms.
b. True; both **D** and **F** contain a carbonyl group attached to one hydrogen atom.
c. True; both **B** and **C** are 2-pentanone.
d. True; both **C** and **D** have the molecular formula $C_5H_{10}O$, but a different arrangement of atoms.

14.73 Since the compound is synthesized from a secondary alcohol and cannot be further oxidized, it must be a ketone.

$CH_3-\overset{\overset{\displaystyle O}{\|}}{C}-CH_2-CH_3$ Butanone

14.75 $CH_3-CH_2-CH_2-\overset{\overset{\displaystyle O}{\|}}{C}-H$ Butanal

$CH_3-\overset{\overset{\displaystyle CH_3}{|}}{CH}-\overset{\overset{\displaystyle O}{\|}}{C}-H$ 2-Methylpropanal

$CH_3-\overset{\overset{\displaystyle O}{\|}}{C}-CH_2-CH_3$ Butanone

14.77 A $CH_3-CH_2-CH_2-OH$ 1-Propanol

  B $CH_3-CH=CH_2$ Propene

  C $CH_3-CH_2-\overset{\overset{\displaystyle O}{\|}}{C}-H$ Propanal

CI.27 a.

b.

OH

4-Methylphenol   2-Methylpropene

c. Molecular formula = $C_{15}H_{24}O$
Molar mass of BHT $(C_{15}H_{24}O)$
= 15(12.01 g) + 24(1.008 g) + 16.00 g = 220.4 g/mole (4 SFs)

d. 50. ppm BHT = 50. mg BHT/kg cereal

$$15 \ \cancel{oz} \times \frac{1 \ \cancel{lb}}{16 \ \cancel{oz}} \times \frac{1 \ \cancel{kg \ cereal}}{2.20 \ \cancel{lb}} \times \frac{50. \ mg \ BHT}{1 \ \cancel{kg \ cereal}} = 21 \ mg \ of \ BHT \ (2 \ SFs)$$

CI.29 a. $CH_3-\overset{\overset{\displaystyle O}{\|}}{C}-CH_3$

b. Molecular formula = C_3H_6O
Molar mass of propanone (C_3H_6O)
= 3(12.01 g) + 6(1.008 g) + 16.00 g = 58.08 g/mole (4 SFs)

c. $CH_3-\overset{\overset{\displaystyle OH}{|}}{CH}-CH_3$

CI.31 a. $2C_8H_{18}(l) + 25O_2(g) \xrightarrow{\Delta} 16CO_2(g) + 18H_2O(g) + 11 \ 020 \ kJ$

b. The combustion of octane is an exothermic reaction.

c. Molar mass of octane (C_8H_{18}) = 8(12.01 g) + 18(1.008 g) = 114.22 g (5 SFs)
Given 1 tank of octane **Need** moles of octane
Plan gal → qt → mL → g of C_8H_{18} → moles of C_8H_{18}

Set-up $1 \ \cancel{tank} \times \dfrac{11.9 \ \cancel{gal}}{1 \ \cancel{tank}} \times \dfrac{4 \ \cancel{qt}}{1 \ \cancel{gal}} \times \dfrac{946 \ \cancel{mL}}{1 \ \cancel{qt}} \times \dfrac{0.803 \ \cancel{g \ C_8H_{18}}}{1 \ \cancel{mL \ C_8H_{18}}} \times \dfrac{1 \ mole \ C_8H_{18}}{114.22 \ \cancel{g \ C_8H_{18}}}$
= 317 moles of C_8H_{18} (3 SFs)

d. Given miles travelled **Need** kilograms of CO_2 produced
Plan mi → gal → qt → mL → g of C_8H_{18} → moles of C_8H_{18}
→ moles of CO_2 → g of CO_2 → kg of CO_2

Set-up $24 \ 500 \ \cancel{mi} \times \dfrac{1 \ \cancel{gal}}{45 \ \cancel{mi}} \times \dfrac{4 \ \cancel{qt}}{1 \ \cancel{gal}} \times \dfrac{946 \ \cancel{mL}}{1 \ \cancel{qt}} \times \dfrac{0.803 \ \cancel{g \ C_8H_{18}}}{1 \ \cancel{mL \ C_8H_{18}}}$

$\times \dfrac{1 \ \cancel{mole \ C_8H_{18}}}{114.22 \ \cancel{g \ C_8H_{18}}} \times \dfrac{16 \ \cancel{moles \ CO_2}}{2 \ \cancel{moles \ C_8H_{18}}} \times \dfrac{44.01 \ \cancel{g \ CO_2}}{1 \ \cancel{mole \ CO_2}} \times \dfrac{1 \ kg \ CO_2}{1000 \ \cancel{g \ CO_2}}$

= 5.10×10^3 kg of CO_2 (3 SFs)

CI.33 a. $CH_3-CH_2-CH_2-\overset{\displaystyle O}{\overset{\displaystyle \|}{C}}-H$

b.

c. The IUPAC name of butyraldehyde is butanal.

d. $CH_3-CH_2-CH_2-CH_2-OH$

Credit: Rolf Bruderer / Alamy

Kate completed her diabetes educational class taught by Paula, a diabetes nurse. Kate now follows a healthy meal plan, which includes 45 to 60 g of carbohydrates in the form of fruits and vegetables. She is walking 0.5 h three or four times a week and has lost 10 lb. Kate measures her blood glucose level before and after a meal using a blood glucose meter. She writes the results in her log, which helps determine if she is maintaining a consistent blood glucose level or if the level is too high or too low. Her blood glucose level should be 70 to 110 mg/dL before a meal, and less than 180 mg/dL 2 h after a meal. Draw the Fischer projection for D-glucose.

CHAPTER READINESS*

⚛ Core Chemistry Skills

- Naming Alcohols and Phenols (13.1)
- Writing Equations for the Oxidation of Alcohols (13.4)

- Naming Aldehydes and Ketones (14.1)

*These Core Chemistry Skills from previous chapters are listed here for your review as you proceed to the new material in this chapter.

15.1 Carbohydrates

Learning Goal: Classify a monosaccharide as an aldose or a ketose, and indicate the number of carbon atoms.

- Photosynthesis is the process of using water, carbon dioxide, and the energy from the Sun to form monosaccharides and oxygen.

- Carbohydrates are classified as monosaccharides (simple sugars), disaccharides (two monosaccharide units), and polysaccharides (many monosaccharide units).

- Monosaccharides are polyhydroxy aldehydes (aldoses) or ketones (ketoses).

- Monosaccharides are classified as *aldo* for an aldehyde or *keto* for a ketone and by the number of carbon atoms as *trioses*, *tetroses*, *pentoses*, or *hexoses*.

♦ **Learning Exercise 15.1A**

Complete and balance the equations for the photosynthesis of

1. Glucose: _____ + _____ $\longrightarrow$ $C_6H_{12}O_6$ + _____

2. Ribose: _____ + _____ $\longrightarrow$ $C_5H_{10}O_5$ + _____

Answers   1. $6CO_2 + 6H_2O \longrightarrow C_6H_{12}O_6 + 6O_2$ 2. $5CO_2 + 5H_2O \longrightarrow C_5H_{10}O_5 + 5O_2$

♦ **Learning Exercise 15.1B**

Indicate the number of monosaccharide units (one, two, or many) in each of the following carbohydrates:

1. sucrose, a disaccharide   _____   2. cellulose, a polysaccharide _____

3. glucose, a monosaccharide_____   4. amylose, a polysaccharide _____

5. maltose, a disaccharide   _____

Answers   1. two   2. many   3. one   4. many   5. two

♦ **Learning Exercise 15.1C**

Identify each of the following monosaccharides as an aldotriose, a ketotriose, an aldotetrose, a ketotetrose, an aldopentose, a ketopentose, an aldohexose, or a ketohexose:

1.
```
CH2OH
|
C=O
|
CH2OH
```
Dihydroxyacetone

2.
```
   H    O
    \  //
     C
     |
H—C—OH
     |
H—C—OH
     |
HO—C—H
     |
   CH2OH
```
Lyxose

3.
```
CH2OH
|
C=O
|
HO—C—H
|
HO—C—H
|
H—C—OH
|
CH2OH
```
Tagatose

4.
```
   H    O
    \  //
     C
     |
H—C—OH
     |
HO—C—H
     |
H—C—OH
     |
H—C—OH
     |
   CH2OH
```
Glucose

5.
```
   H    O
    \  //
     C
     |
H—C—OH
     |
H—C—OH
     |
   CH2OH
```
Erythrose

_____   _____   _____   _____   _____

Answers   1. ketotriose   2. aldopentose   3. ketohexose   4. aldohexose   5. aldotetrose

15.2   Fischer Projections of Monosaccharides

Learning Goal: Identify and draw the D and L configurations of the Fischer projections for common monosaccharides.

• In a Fischer projection, the carbon chain is written vertically, with the most oxidized carbon (usually an aldehyde or ketone) at the top.

- In the Fischer projection for a monosaccharide, the chiral —OH group *farthest* from the carbonyl group (C=O) is written on the left side in the L enantiomer and on the right side in the D enantiomer.
- Important monosaccharides are the aldopentose ribose, the aldohexoses glucose and galactose, and the ketohexose fructose.

♦ **Learning Exercise 15.2A**

Identify each of the following Fischer projections of sugars as the D or L enantiomer:

⚛ CORE CHEMISTRY SKILL

Identifying D- and L-Fischer Projections

1.
```
    CH2OH
     |
    C=O
HO——H
 H——OH
    CH2OH
```

2.
```
   H    O
    \  /
     C
 H——OH
 H——OH
HO——H
HO——H
    CH2OH
```

3.
```
   H    O
    \  /
     C
HO——H
 H——OH
    CH2OH
```

4.
```
    CH2OH
     |
    C=O
HO——H
HO——H
    CH2OH
```

_____ Xylulose   _____ Mannose   _____ Threose   _____ Ribulose

Answers   1. D-Xylulose   2. L-Mannose   3. D-Threose   4. L-Ribulose

♦ **Learning Exercise 15.2B**

Draw the mirror image of each of the sugars in Learning Exercise 15.2A and give the D or L name.

1.   **2.**   **3.**   **4.**

Answers

1.
```
    CH2OH
     |
    C=O
 H——OH
HO——H
    CH2OH
```
L-Xylulose

2.
```
   H    O
    \  /
     C
HO——H
HO——H
 H——OH
 H——OH
    CH2OH
```
D-Mannose

3.
```
  H    O
   \  /
    C
 H——OH
HO——H
    CH2OH
```
L-Threose

4.
```
    CH2OH
     |
    C=O
 H——OH
 H——OH
    CH2OH
```
D-Ribulose

♦ **Learning Exercise 15.2C**

Identify the monosaccharide (D-glucose, D-fructose, or D-galactose) that fits each of the following descriptions:

1. a building block in cellulose _____

2. also known as fruit sugar _____

3. accumulates in the disease known as *galactosemia* _____

4. the most common monosaccharide _____

5. the sweetest monosaccharide _____

Answers   **1.** D-glucose   **2.** D-fructose   **3.** D-galactose
            4. D-glucose   **5.** D-fructose

♦ **Learning Exercise 15.2D**

Draw the Fischer projection for each of the following monosaccharides:

D-Glucose   D-Galactose   D-Fructose

Answers

D-Glucose   D-Galactose   D-Fructose

15.3 Haworth Structures of Monosaccharides

Learning Goal: Draw and identify the Haworth structures for monosaccharides.

- The Haworth structure is a representation of the cyclic, stable form of monosaccharides, which are rings of five or six atoms.

- The Haworth structure forms by a reaction between the —OH group on carbon 5 of hexoses and the carbonyl group on carbon 1 or 2 of the same molecule.

- The formation of a new —OH group on carbon 1 (or 2 in fructose) gives α and β anomers of the cyclic monosaccharide. Because the molecule opens and closes continuously in solution, both α and β anomers are present.

	Guide to Drawing Haworth Structures
STEP 1	Turn the Fischer projection clockwise by 90°.
STEP 2	Fold the horizontal chain into a hexagon, rotate the groups on carbon 5, and bond the O on carbon 5 to carbon 1.
STEP 3	Draw the new —OH group on carbon 1 below the ring to give the α anomer or above the ring to give the β anomer.

◆ **Learning Exercise 15.3**

Draw the α anomer of the Haworth structure for each of the following:

CORE CHEMISTRY SKILL

Drawing Haworth Structures

1. D-Glucose

2. D-Galactose

3. D-Fructose

Answers

1. [Haworth structure of α-D-glucose with CH₂OH group]

2. [Haworth structure of α-D-galactose with CH₂OH group]

3. [Haworth structure of α-D-fructose with HOCH₂ and CH₂OH groups]

15.4 Chemical Properties of Monosaccharides

Learning Goal: Identify the products of oxidation or reduction of monosaccharides; determine whether a carbohydrate is a reducing sugar.

- Monosaccharides contain aldehyde or ketone groups that undergo oxidation or reduction.
- Monosaccharides are called *reducing sugars* because the aldehyde group (also available in ketoses) is oxidized by Cu^{2+} in Benedict's solution, which is reduced.
- Monosaccharides are also reduced to give sugar alcohols.

♦ **Learning Exercise 15.4A**

What changes occur when a reducing sugar reacts with Benedict's reagent?

Answer   The carbonyl group of the reducing sugar is oxidized to a carboxylic acid group; the Cu^{2+} ion in Benedict's reagent is reduced to Cu^+, which forms a brick-red solid of Cu_2O.

♦ **Learning Exercise 15.4B**

Draw the Fischer projection for D-lyxitol that is produced when D-lyxose is reduced. Lyxitol is a sugar substitute used in gum and mouthwashes to inhibit bacteria that cause cavities.

D-Lyxose

Answer

D-Lyxitol

Copyright © 2015 Pearson Education, Inc.

15.5 Disaccharides

Learning Goal: Describe the monosaccharide units and linkages in disaccharides.

- Disaccharides are two monosaccharide units joined together by a glycosidic bond.

  Monosaccharide (1) + monosaccharide (2) $\longrightarrow$ disaccharide + H_2O

- In the most common disaccharides, maltose, lactose, and sucrose, there is at least one glucose unit.
- In the disaccharide maltose, two glucose units are linked by an $\alpha(1 \rightarrow 4)$ glycosidic bond. The $\alpha(1 \rightarrow 4)$ indicates that the —OH group on carbon 1 of alpha-D-glucose is bonded to carbon 4 of the other glucose molecule.

  Glucose + glucose $\longrightarrow$ maltose + H_2O

  Glucose + galactose $\longrightarrow$ lactose + H_2O

  Glucose + fructose $\longrightarrow$ sucrose + H_2O

Lactose is a disaccharide found in milk and milk products.

♦ **Learning Exercise 15.5**

For the following disaccharides, state **(a)** the monosaccharide units, **(b)** the type of glycosidic bond, and **(c)** the name of the disaccharide:

1.

2.

3.

4.

	a. Monosaccharide(s)	b. Type of Glycosidic Bond	c. Name of Disaccharide
1.			
2.			
3.			
4.			

Answers

1. **a.** two glucose units   **b.** $\alpha(1 \rightarrow 4)$-glycosidic bond   **c.** β-maltose

2. **a.** galactose + glucose   **b.** $\beta(1 \rightarrow 4)$-glycosidic bond   **c.** α-lactose

3. **a.** fructose + glucose   **b.** $\alpha,\beta(1 \rightarrow 2)$-glycosidic bond   **c.** sucrose

4. **a.** two glucose units   **b.** $\alpha(1 \rightarrow 4)$-glycosidic bond   **c.** α-maltose

15.6 Polysaccharides

Learning Goal: Describe the structural features of amylose, amylopectin, glycogen, and cellulose.

- Polysaccharides are polymers of monosaccharide units.
- Starches consist of amylose, an unbranched chain of glucose, and amylopectin, a branched polymer of glucose. Glycogen, the storage form of glucose in animals, is similar to amylopectin, with more branching.
- Cellulose is also a polymer of glucose, but in cellulose the glycosidic bonds are β bonds rather than α bonds as in the starches. Humans can digest starches, but not cellulose, to obtain energy. However, cellulose is important as a source of fiber in our diets.

The polysaccharide cellulose is the structural material in plants such as cotton.
Credit: Danny E Hooks / Shutterstock

Key Terms for Sections 15.1–15.6

Match the following key terms with the correct description:

a. carbohydrate   **b.** glucose   **c.** disaccharide

d. Haworth structure   **e.** cellulose

1. ____ a simple or complex sugar composed of a carbon chain with an aldehyde or ketone group and several hydroxyl groups

2. ____ a cyclic structure that represents the closed-chain form of a monosaccharide

3. ____ an unbranched polysaccharide that cannot be digested by humans

4. ____ an aldohexose that is the most prevalent monosaccharide in the diet

5. ____ a carbohydrate that contains two monosaccharides linked by a glycosidic bond

Answers   **1.** a   **2.** d   **3.** e   **4.** b   **5.** c

♦ **Learning Exercise 15.6**

List the monosaccharides and describe the glycosidic bonds in each of the following carbohydrates:

	Monosaccharides	Type(s) of glycosidic bonds
a. amylose	_____	_____
b. amylopectin	_____	_____
c. glycogen	_____	_____
d. cellulose	_____	_____

Answers
a. glucose; $\alpha(1 \rightarrow 4)$-glycosidic bonds
b. glucose; $\alpha(1 \rightarrow 4)$- and $\alpha(1 \rightarrow 6)$-glycosidic bonds
c. glucose; $\alpha(1 \rightarrow 4)$- and $\alpha(1 \rightarrow 6)$-glycosidic bonds
d. glucose; $\beta(1 \rightarrow 4)$-glycosidic bonds

Checklist for Chapter 15

You are ready to take the Practice Test for Chapter 15. Be sure that you have accomplished the learning goals for each of the sections in this chapter. If not, review the section listed at the end of the goal. Then apply your new skills and understanding to the Practice Test.

After studying Chapter 15, I can successfully:

_____ Classify carbohydrates as monosaccharides, disaccharides, and polysaccharides. (15.1)

_____ Classify a monosaccharide as an aldose or a ketose, and indicate the number of carbon atoms. (15.1)

_____ Draw and identify D- and L-Fischer projections for carbohydrate molecules. (15.2)

_____ Draw the open-chain structures for D-glucose, D-galactose, and D-fructose. (15.2)

_____ Draw or identify the Haworth structures of monosaccharides. (15.3)

_____ Describe some chemical properties of carbohydrates. (15.4)

_____ Describe the monosaccharide units and linkages in disaccharides. (15.5)

_____ Describe the structural features of amylose, amylopectin, glycogen, and cellulose. (15.6)

Practice Test for Chapter 15

1. The requirements for photosynthesis are (15.1)
   A. sun
   B. sun and water
   C. water and carbon dioxide
   D. sun, water, and carbon dioxide
   E. carbon dioxide and sun

2. What are the products of photosynthesis? (15.1)
   A. carbohydrates
   B. carbohydrates and oxygen
   C. carbon dioxide and oxygen
   D. carbohydrates and carbon dioxide
   E. water and oxygen

3. The name "carbohydrate" came from the fact that (15.1)
   A. carbohydrates are hydrates of water
   B. carbohydrates contain hydrogen and oxygen in a 2:1 ratio
   C. carbohydrates contain a great quantity of water
   D. all plants produce carbohydrates
   E. carbon and hydrogen atoms are abundant in carbohydrates

4. What functional groups are in the open-chain forms of monosaccharides? (15.1)
   A. hydroxyl groups
   B. aldehyde groups
   C. ketone groups
   D. hydroxyl and aldehyde or ketone groups
   E. hydroxyl and ether groups

5. What is the classification of the following sugar? (15.1)

CH_2OH
|
$C=O$
|
CH_2OH

   A. aldotriose   B. ketotriose   C. aldotetrose   D. ketotetrose   E. ketopentose

For questions 6 through 10, refer to the following monosaccharide: (15.1, 15.3, 15.4, 15.6)

6. It is the Haworth structure of a(n)
   A. aldotriose   B. ketopentose   C. aldopentose   D. aldohexose   E. aldoheptose

7. It is the Haworth structure for
   A. fructose   B. glucose   C. ribose   D. glyceraldehyde   E. galactose

8. It is one of the products of the complete hydrolysis of
   A. maltose   B. sucrose   C. lactose   D. glycogen   E. all of these

9. A Benedict's test with this sugar would
   A. be positive   B. be negative
   C. produce a blue precipitate   D. give no color change
   E. produce a silver mirror

10. It is the monosaccharide unit used to build the following polymers:
    A. amylose   B. amylopectin   C. cellulose   D. glycogen   E. all of these

For questions 11 through 15, identify each carbohydrate described as one of the following: (15.5, 15.6)
    A. maltose   B. sucrose   C. cellulose   D. amylopectin   E. glycogen

11. _____ a disaccharide that is not a reducing sugar

12. _____ a disaccharide that occurs as a breakdown product of amylose

13. _____ a carbohydrate that is produced as a storage form of energy in plants

14. _____ the storage form of energy in humans

15. _____ a carbohydrate that is used for structural purposes by plants

For questions 16 through 20, identify each carbohydrate described as one of the following: (15.5, 15.6)
    A. amylose   **B.** cellulose   **C.** glycogen   **D.** lactose   **E.** sucrose

16. _____ a polysaccharide composed of many glucose units linked only by $\alpha(1 \rightarrow 4)$-glycosidic bonds

17. _____ a sugar containing both glucose and galactose

18. _____ a sugar composed of glucose units joined by both $\alpha(1 \rightarrow 4)$- and $\alpha(1 \rightarrow 6)$-glycosidic bonds

19. _____ a disaccharide that is a reducing sugar

20. _____ a carbohydrate composed of glucose units joined by $\beta(1 \rightarrow 4)$-glycosidic bonds

For questions 21 through 25, identify each carbohydrate described as one of the following: (15.4, 15.5)
    A. glucose   **B.** lactose   **C.** sucrose   **D.** maltose

21. _____ a sugar composed of glucose and fructose

22. _____ also called table sugar

23. _____ found in milk and milk products

24. _____ gives glucitol upon reduction

25. _____ gives galactose upon hydrolysis

Answers to the Practice Test

1. D	**2.** B	**3.** B	**4.** D	**5.** B
6. D	**7.** B	**8.** E	**9.** A	**10.** E
11. B	**12.** A	**13.** D	**14.** E	**15.** C
16. A	**17.** D	**18.** C	**19.** D	**20.** B
21. C	**22.** C	**23.** B	**24.** A	**25.** B

15

Carbohydrates

Learning Goals

- Classify a monosaccharide as an aldose or a ketose, and indicate the number of carbon atoms.
- Identify and draw the D and L configurations of the Fischer projections for common monosaccharides.
- Draw and identify the Haworth structures for monosaccharides.
- Identify the products of oxidation or reduction of monosaccharides; determine whether a carbohydrate is a reducing sugar.
- Describe the monosaccharide units and linkages in disaccharides.
- Describe the structural features of amylose, amylopectin, glycogen, and cellulose.

Chapter Outline

Chapter Opener: Diabetes Nurse

15.1 Carbohydrates

15.2 Fischer Projections of Monosaccharides

Chemistry Link to Health: Hyperglycemia and Hypoglycemia

15.3 Haworth Structures of Monosaccharides

15.4 Chemical Properties of Monosaccharides

Chemistry Link to Health: Testing for Glucose

15.5 Disaccharides

Explore Your World: Sugar and Sweeteners

Chemistry Link to Health: How Sweet Is My Sweetener?

Chemistry Link to Health: Blood Types and Carbohydrates

15.6 Polysaccharides

Explore Your World: Polysaccharides

Clinical Update: Kate's Program for Type 2 Diabetes

⚛ Core Chemistry Skills

- Identifying D- and L-Fischer Projections (15.2)
- Drawing Haworth Structures (15.3)

Selected Answers and Solutions to Text Problems

15.1 Photosynthesis requires CO_2, H_2O, and the energy from the Sun. Respiration requires O_2 from the air and glucose from our foods.

15.3 Monosaccharides are composed of a chain of three to eight carbon atoms—one in a carbonyl group as an aldehyde or ketone, and the rest attached to hydroxyl groups. A monosaccharide cannot be split or hydrolyzed into smaller carbohydrates. A disaccharide consists of two monosaccharide units joined together. A disaccharide can be hydrolyzed into two monosaccharide units.

15.5 Hydroxyl groups are found in all monosaccharides, along with a carbonyl on the first or second carbon that gives an aldehyde or ketone functional group.

15.7 A ketopentose contains hydroxyl and ketone functional groups and has five carbon atoms.

15.9 a. This six-carbon monosaccharide has a carbonyl group on carbon 2; it is a ketohexose.
 b. This five-carbon monosaccharide has a carbonyl group on carbon 1; it is an aldopentose.

15.11 a. This structure is the D enantiomer since the hydroxyl group on the chiral carbon farthest from the carbonyl group is on the right.
 b. This structure is the D enantiomer since the hydroxyl group on the chiral carbon farthest from the carbonyl group is on the right.
 c. This structure is the L enantiomer since the hydroxyl group on the chiral carbon farthest from the carbonyl group is on the left.
 d. This structure is the D enantiomer since the hydroxyl group on the chiral carbon farthest from the carbonyl group is on the right.

15.13

15.15 L-Glucose is the mirror image of D-glucose.

D-Glucose   L-Glucose

15.17 In D-galactose, the —OH group on carbon 4 extends to the left; in D-glucose, this —OH group goes to the right.

15.19 a. Glucose is also called blood sugar.
   b. Galactose is not metabolized in the condition called galactosemia.

15.21 In the cyclic structure of glucose, there are five carbon atoms and an oxygen atom.

15.23 In the α anomer, the —OH group on carbon 1 is drawn down; in the β anomer, the —OH group on carbon 1 is drawn up.

α-D-Glucose   β-D-Glucose

15.25 a. This is the α anomer because the —OH group on carbon 2 is down.
   b. This is the α anomer because the —OH group on carbon 1 is down.

15.27

CH$_2$OH
H——OH
HO——H
H——OH
CH$_2$OH

D-Xylitol

15.29 Oxidation product: Reduction product (sugar alcohol):

HO   C=O
HO——H
H——OH
H——OH
CH$_2$OH

D-Arabinonic acid

CH$_2$OH
HO——H
H——OH
H——OH
CH$_2$OH

D-Arabitol

15.31 a. When this disaccharide is hydrolyzed, galactose and glucose are produced. The glycosidic bond is a β(1→4) bond since the ether bond is drawn up from carbon 1 of the galactose unit, which is on the left in the drawing, to carbon 4 of the glucose on the right. β-Lactose is the name of this disaccharide since the —OH group on carbon 1 of the glucose unit is drawn up.
   b. When this disaccharide is hydrolyzed, two molecules of glucose are produced. The glycosidic bond is an α(1→4) bond since the ether bond is drawn down from carbon 1 of the glucose unit on the left to carbon 4 of the glucose on the right. α-Maltose is the name of this disaccharide since the —OH group on the rightmost glucose unit is drawn down.

15.33 a. β-Lactose is a reducing sugar; the ring on the right can open up to form an aldehyde that can undergo oxidation.
   b. α-Maltose is a reducing sugar; the ring on the right can open up to form an aldehyde that can undergo oxidation.

15.35 a. Another name for table sugar is sucrose.
  b. Lactose is the disaccharide found in milk and milk products.
  c. Maltose is also called malt sugar.
  d. When lactose is hydrolyzed, the products are the monosaccharides galactose and glucose.

15.37 a. Amylose is an unbranched polymer of glucose units joined by $\alpha(1 \rightarrow 4)$-glycosidic bonds. Amylopectin is a branched polymer of glucose units joined by $\alpha(1 \rightarrow 4)$- and $\alpha(1 \rightarrow 6)$-glycosidic bonds.
  b. Amylopectin, which is produced in plants, is a branched polymer of glucose units joined by $\alpha(1 \rightarrow 4)$- and $\alpha(1 \rightarrow 6)$-glycosidic bonds. The branches in amylopectin occur about every 25 glucose units. Glycogen, which is produced in animals, is a highly branched polymer of glucose units joined by $\alpha(1 \rightarrow 4)$- and $\alpha(1 \rightarrow 6)$-glycosidic bonds. The branches in glycogen occur about every 10 to 15 glucose units.

15.39 a. Cellulose is not digestible by humans.
  b. Amylose and amylopectin are the storage forms of carbohydrates in plants.
  c. Amylose is the polysaccharide that contains only $\alpha(1 \rightarrow 4)$-glycosidic bonds.
  d. Glycogen is the most highly branched polysaccharide.

15.41 $3.9 \text{ L blood} \times \dfrac{10 \text{ dL blood}}{1 \text{ L blood}} \times \dfrac{178 \text{ mg glucose}}{1 \text{ dL blood}} \times \dfrac{1 \text{ g glucose}}{1000 \text{ mg glucose}} = 6.9 \text{ g of glucose (2 SFs)}$

15.43 a. Total carbohydrate $= 23 \text{ g} + 24 \text{ g} + 26 \text{ g} + 0 \text{ g} = 73 \text{ g (2 SFs)}$

   Therefore, Kate has exceeded her limit of 45 to 60 g of carbohydrate.

  b. $73 \text{ g carbohydrate} \times \dfrac{4 \text{ kcal}}{1 \text{ g carbohydrate}} = 290 \text{ kcal (rounded off to the tens place)}$

15.45 a. Isomaltose is a disaccharide.
  b. Isomaltose consists of two α-D-glucose units.
  c. The glycosidic link in isomaltose is an $\alpha(1 \rightarrow 6)$-glycosidic bond.
  d. The structure shown is α-isomaltose.
  e. α-Isomaltose is a reducing sugar; the ring on the right can open up to form an aldehyde that can undergo oxidation.

15.47 a. Melezitose is a trisaccharide.
  b. Melezitose contains two units of the aldohexose α-D-glucose and one unit of the ketohexose β-D-fructose.
  c. Melezitose, like sucrose, is not a reducing sugar; the rings on the right cannot open up to form an aldehyde that can undergo oxidation.

15.49 D-Fructose is a ketohexose with the carbonyl group on carbon 2; D-galactose is an aldohexose where the carbonyl group is on carbon 1. In the Fischer projection of D-galactose, the —OH group on carbon 4 is drawn on the left; in fructose, the —OH group on carbon 4 is drawn on the right.

15.51 D-Galactose is the mirror image of L-galactose. In the Fischer projection of D-galactose, the —OH groups on carbon 2 and carbon 5 are drawn on the right side, but they are drawn on the left for carbon 3 and carbon 4. In L-galactose, the —OH groups are reversed: carbon 2 and carbon 5 have —OH groups drawn on the left, and carbon 3 and carbon 4 have —OH groups drawn on the right.

15.53 a.

H—C=O
HO—H
HO—H
H—OH
HO—H
CH₂OH

L-Gulose

b.

α-D-Gulose

β-D-Gulose

15.55 Since D-sorbitol can be oxidized to D-glucose, it must contain the same number of carbons with the same groups attached as glucose. The difference is that sorbitol has only hydroxyl groups, while glucose has an aldehyde group. In sorbitol, the aldehyde group is changed to a hydroxyl group.

CH₂OH ← This hydroxyl group is an aldehyde in glucose.
H—OH
HO—H
H—OH
H—OH
CH₂OH

15.57 When the α-galactose forms an open-chain structure in water, it can close to form either α- or β-galactose.

15.59

$\beta(1{\longrightarrow}4)$-Glycosidic bond

15.61 a.

$\beta(1{\longrightarrow}6)$-Glycosidic bond

b. Yes. Gentiobiose is a reducing sugar. The ring on the right can open up to form an aldehyde that can undergo oxidation.

Carboxylic Acids and Esters

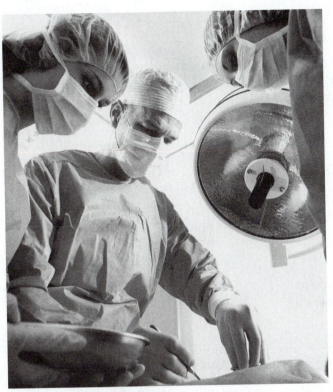

Robert has recuperated well from his heart surgery. After his operation, Maureen, a surgical technician, applied Indermil, a liquid adhesive, to close Robert's incision sites. The adhesive, which contains an ester, was applied to the edges of his skin. Once applied, it hardened quickly to close his incisions and keep the edges together. Within 8 to 10 days after his surgery, the clear, dry adhesive was peeled from the incision sites, leaving his skin with minimal scarring.

Indermil

The carboxylic acid 2-hydroxypropanoic acid is used in skin products; the common name is lactic acid. Draw the condensed structural formula for 2-hydroxypropanoic acid.

Credit: stefanolunardi / Shutterstock

CHAPTER READINESS*

⚛ **Core Chemistry Skills**

• Writing Equations for Reactions of Acids and Bases (11.7)

• Naming and Drawing Alkanes (12.2)

*These Core Chemistry Skills from previous chapters are listed here for your review as you proceed to the new material in this chapter.

16.1 Carboxylic Acids

Learning Goal: Write the IUPAC and common names for carboxylic acids and draw their condensed and line-angle structural formulas.

•   The IUPAC names of carboxylic acids replace the *e* of the corresponding alkane with *oic acid*. Simple acids usually are

The sour taste of vinegar is due to ethanoic acid (acetic acid).

Credit: Pearson Education / Pearson Science

named by the common system using the prefixes *form* (1C), *acet* (2C), *propion* (3C), or *butyr* (4C), followed by *ic acid*.

| Methanoic acid (formic acid) | Ethanoic acid (acetic acid) | Butanoic acid (butyric acid) | Pentanoic acid |

- The name of the carboxylic acid of benzene is benzoic acid. When substituents are bonded to benzoic acid, the ring is numbered from the carboxylic acid on carbon 1 in the direction that gives substituents the smallest possible numbers. For common names, the prefixes *ortho*, *meta*, and *para* are used to show the position of substituents.

Benzoic acid

4-Aminobenzoic acid
(*p*-aminobenzoic acid,
PABA)

3,4-Dichlorobenzoic acid

Guide to Naming Carboxylic Acids

| STEP 1 | Identify the longest carbon chain and replace the *e* in the corresponding alkane name with *oic acid*. |
| STEP 2 | Name and number any substituents by counting the carboxyl group as carbon 1. |

♦ **Learning Exercise 16.1A**

Give the IUPAC and common name, if any, for each of the following carboxylic acids:

🕸 **CORE CHEMISTRY SKILL**

Naming Carboxylic Acids

1. $CH_3-C(=O)-OH$

2. $CH_3-CH(OH)-C(=O)-OH$

3. [structure]

4. [structure with Cl]

Answers

1. ethanoic acid (acetic acid)
2. 2-hydroxypropanoic acid (α-hydroxypropionic acid)
3. 3-methylbutanoic acid (β-methylbutyric acid)
4. 4-chlorobenzoic acid (*p*-chlorobenzoic acid)

♦ **Learning Exercise 16.1B**

Draw the condensed structural formula for **1** to **3** and the line-angle formula for **4** to **6**.

1. acetic acid

2. 3-hydroxypropanoic acid

3. formic acid

4. *β*-bromobutyric acid

5. benzoic acid

6. 3-methylpentanoic acid

Answers

1. $CH_3-\overset{\displaystyle O}{\overset{\|}{C}}-OH$ **2.** $HO-CH_2-CH_2-\overset{\displaystyle O}{\overset{\|}{C}}-OH$ **3.** $H-\overset{\displaystyle O}{\overset{\|}{C}}-OH$

4. [line-angle structure with Br and OH]   **5.** [benzoic acid line-angle structure]   **6.** [3-methylpentanoic acid line-angle structure]

16.2 Properties of Carboxylic Acids

Learning Goal: Describe the boiling points, solubility, dissociation, and neutralization of carboxylic acids.

- Carboxylic acids have higher boiling points than other polar compounds such as alcohols.
- Because they have two polar groups, carboxylic acids form a dimer, which contains two sets of hydrogen bonds.
- Carboxylic acids with one to four carbon atoms are very soluble in water.
- As weak acids, carboxylic acids dissociate slightly in water to form acidic solutions of H_3O^+ and carboxylate ions.
- When bases neutralize carboxylic acids, the products are carboxylate salts and water.

♦ Learning Exercise 16.2A

Identify the compound in each pair that has the higher boiling point:

1. acetic acid or butyric acid

2. propanoic acid or 2-propanol

3. propanoic acid or propanone

4. acetic acid or acetaldehyde

Answers　　**1.** butyric acid　　**2.** propanoic acid　　**3.** propanoic acid　　**4.** acetic acid

♦ Learning Exercise 16.2B

Indicate whether each of the following carboxylic acids is soluble (S) or not soluble (NS) in water:

1. _____ hexanoic acid

2. _____ acetic acid

3. _____ propanoic acid

4. _____ benzoic acid

5. _____ formic acid

6. _____ octanoic acid

Answers　　**1.** no　　**2.** yes　　**3.** yes　　**4.** no　　**5.** yes　　**6.** no

♦ Learning Exercise 16.2C

Draw the condensed structural formulas for the products from the dissociation of each of the following carboxylic acids in water:

1.
$$CH_3-CH_2-\overset{\overset{\displaystyle O}{\|}}{C}-OH + H_2O \rightleftarrows$$

2.
$$OH + H_2O \rightleftarrows$$

Answers　　**1.** $CH_3-CH_2-\overset{\overset{\displaystyle O}{\|}}{C}-O^- + H_3O^+$

2.
$$O^- + H_3O^+$$

♦ Learning Exercise 16.2D

Draw the condensed structural formulas for the products and give the name of the carboxylate salt produced in each of the following reactions:

1.
$$CH_3-CH_2-\overset{\overset{\displaystyle O}{\|}}{C}-OH + NaOH \longrightarrow$$

2.
$$H-\overset{\overset{\displaystyle O}{\|}}{C}-OH + KOH \longrightarrow$$

Answers

1. $CH_3-CH_2-\overset{\displaystyle O}{\overset{\displaystyle \|}{C}}-O^-\ Na^+ + H_2O$

Sodium propanoate
(sodium propionate)

2. $H-\overset{\displaystyle O}{\overset{\displaystyle \|}{C}}-O^-\ K^+ + H_2O$

Potassium methanoate
(potassium formate)

16.3 Esters

Learning Goal: Write a balanced chemical equation for the formation of an ester.

- In the presence of a strong acid, a carboxylic acid reacts with an alcohol to produce an ester and water.

$$CH_3-\overset{\displaystyle O}{\overset{\displaystyle \|}{C}}-OH + HO-CH_2-CH_3 \underset{\longleftarrow}{\overset{H^+,\ heat}{\longrightarrow}} CH_3-\overset{\displaystyle O}{\overset{\displaystyle \|}{C}}-O-CH_2-CH_3 + H_2O$$

◆ Learning Exercise 16.3

Draw the condensed structural formulas of the products of each of the following esterification reactions:

1. $CH_3-\overset{\displaystyle O}{\overset{\displaystyle \|}{C}}-OH + HO-CH_3 \underset{\longleftarrow}{\overset{H^+,\ heat}{\longrightarrow}}$

2. $H-\overset{\displaystyle O}{\overset{\displaystyle \|}{C}}-OH + HO-CH_2-CH_3 \underset{\longleftarrow}{\overset{H^+,\ heat}{\longrightarrow}}$

3. (benzoic acid structure) $-\overset{\displaystyle O}{\overset{\displaystyle \|}{C}}-OH + HO-CH_3 \underset{\longleftarrow}{\overset{H^+,\ heat}{\longrightarrow}}$

4. propanoic acid and ethanol $\underset{\longleftarrow}{\overset{H^+,\ heat}{\longrightarrow}}$

Answers

1. $CH_3-\overset{\displaystyle O}{\overset{\displaystyle \|}{C}}-O-CH_3 + H_2O$

2. $H-\overset{\displaystyle O}{\overset{\displaystyle \|}{C}}-O-CH_2-CH_3 + H_2O$

3. (benzene ring)$-\overset{\displaystyle O}{\overset{\displaystyle \|}{C}}-O-CH_3$ $+ H_2O$

4. $CH_3-CH_2-\overset{\displaystyle O}{\overset{\displaystyle \|}{C}}-O-CH_2-CH_3 + H_2O$

16.4 Naming Esters

Learning Goal: Write the IUPAC and common names for esters; draw condensed and line-angle structural formulas.

- The name of an ester is derived from the alcohol, and the carboxylic acid used to form that ester in which the *ic acid* ending is replaced by *ate*.

Guide to Naming Esters	
STEP 1	Write the name for the carbon chain from the alcohol as an *alkyl* group.
STEP 2	Change the *ic acid* of the acid name to *ate*.

The odor of grapes is due to ethyl heptanoate.

Credit: Lynn Watson / Shutterstock

♦ **Learning Exercise 16.4A**

Give the IUPAC and common name, if any, for each of the following:

1. [structure: CH₃—C(=O)—O—CH₂CH₃]

2. $CH_3-CH_2-CH_2-\overset{O}{\underset{}{C}}-O-CH_3$

3. $CH_3-CH_2-\overset{O}{\underset{}{C}}-O-CH_2-CH_2-CH_3$

4. [structure: benzene ring—C(=O)—O—CH₃]

Answers   1. ethyl ethanoate (ethyl acetate)   2. methyl butanoate (methyl butyrate)
             3. propyl propanoate (propyl propionate)   4. methyl benzoate

♦ **Learning Exercise 16.4B**

For **1, 2,** and **3**, draw the condensed structural formula and for **4**, draw the line-angle formula.

1. propyl acetate   2. ethyl butyrate

3. ethyl benzoate   4. ethyl propanoate

Answers   1. $CH_3-\overset{O}{\underset{}{C}}-O-CH_2-CH_2-CH_3$ 2. $CH_3-CH_2-CH_2-\overset{O}{\underset{}{C}}-O-CH_2-CH_3$

             3. [structure: benzene ring—C(=O)—O—CH₂—CH₃]   4. [line-angle ester structure]

16.5 Properties of Esters

Learning Goal: Describe the boiling points and solubility of esters; draw the condensed structural formulas for the hydrolysis products.

- Esters have higher boiling points than alkanes but lower boiling points than alcohols and carboxylic acids of similar mass.
- In hydrolysis, esters are split apart by a reaction with water. When the catalyst is an acid, the products are a carboxylic acid and an alcohol.

$$CH_3-\overset{\overset{\displaystyle O}{\|}}{C}-O-CH_3 + H_2O \underset{}{\overset{H^+, \text{ heat}}{\rightleftharpoons}} CH_3-\overset{\overset{\displaystyle O}{\|}}{C}-OH + HO-CH_3$$

Methyl ethanoate   Ethanoic acid   Methanol
(methyl acetate)   (acetic acid)   (methyl alcohol)

- Saponification is the hydrolysis of an ester in the presence of a base, which produces a carboxylate salt and an alcohol.

$$CH_3-\overset{\overset{\displaystyle O}{\|}}{C}-O-CH_3 + NaOH \longrightarrow CH_3-\overset{\overset{\displaystyle O}{\|}}{C}-O^- \ Na^+ + HO-CH_3$$

Methyl ethanoate   Sodium ethanoate   Methanol
(methyl acetate)   (sodium acetate)   (methyl alcohol)

Key Terms for Sections 16.1–16.5

Match the following key terms with the correct description:

     a. carboxylic acid   **b.** saponification   **c.** esterification
     d. hydrolysis   **e.** ester

1. _____ an organic compound containing the carboxyl group ($-COOH$)

2. _____ a reaction of a carboxylic acid and an alcohol in the presence of an acid catalyst

3. _____ a type of organic compound that produces pleasant aromas in flowers and fruits

4. _____ the hydrolysis of an ester with a strong base, producing a salt of the carboxylic acid and an alcohol

5. _____ the splitting of a molecule such as an ester by the addition of water in the presence of an acid

Answers   **1.** a   **2.** c   **3.** e   **4.** b   **5.** d

♦ Learning Exercise 16.5A

Identify the compound with the higher boiling point in each of the following pairs of compounds:

1. CH_3-CH_2-OH or $H-\overset{\overset{\displaystyle O}{\|}}{C}-O-CH_3$

2. $CH_3-\overset{\overset{\displaystyle O}{\|}}{C}-O-CH_3$ or $CH_3-\overset{\overset{\displaystyle OH}{|}}{CH}-CH_2-CH_3$

3. $CH_3-\overset{\overset{\displaystyle O}{\|}}{C}-O-CH_3$ or $CH_3-CH_2-CH_2-CH_2-CH_3$

Answers

1. CH_3-CH_2-OH

2. $CH_3-\overset{\overset{\displaystyle OH}{|}}{CH}-CH_2-CH_3$

3. $CH_3-\overset{\overset{\displaystyle O}{\|}}{C}-O-CH_3$

♦ **Learning Exercise 16.5B**

⚛ **CORE CHEMISTRY SKILL**

Draw the condensed or line-angle structural formulas for the products Hydrolyzing Esters
of hydrolysis or saponification for each of the following esters:

1. $CH_3-CH_2-CH_2-\overset{\overset{\displaystyle O}{\|}}{C}-O-CH_3 + H_2O \underset{\longleftarrow}{\overset{H^+}{\longrightarrow}}$

2. $CH_3-\overset{\overset{\displaystyle O}{\|}}{C}-O-CH_3 + NaOH \longrightarrow$

3. [benzene ring with $-C(=O)-O-CH_2CH_3$] $+ KOH \longrightarrow$

4. [benzene ring with $-C(=O)-O-CH_2CH_2CH_3$] $+ H_2O \underset{\longleftarrow}{\overset{H^+}{\longrightarrow}}$

Answers

1. $CH_3-CH_2-CH_2-\overset{\overset{\displaystyle O}{\|}}{C}-OH + HO-CH_3$

2. $CH_3-\overset{\overset{\displaystyle O}{\|}}{C}-O^-\ Na^+ + HO-CH_3$

3. [benzene ring with $-C(=O)-O^-\ K^+$] $+ HO$ [ethyl]

4. [benzene ring with $-C(=O)-OH$] $+ HO$ [propyl]

Checklist for Chapter 16

You are ready to take the Practice Test for Chapter 16. Be sure that you have accomplished the following learning goals for this chapter. If not, review the section listed at the end of the goal. Then apply your new skills and understanding to the Practice Test.

After studying Chapter 16, I can successfully:

_____ Write the IUPAC and common names, and draw condensed and line-angle structural formulas for carboxylic acids. (16.1)

_____ Describe the boiling points, solubility, and dissociation of carboxylic acids. (16.2)

_____ Describe the behavior of carboxylic acids as weak acids and draw the condensed and line-angle structural formulas for the products of neutralization. (16.2)

_____ Write equations for the preparation of esters. (16.3)

_____ Write the IUPAC or common names and draw the condensed and line-angle structural formulas for esters. (16.4)

_____ Write equations for the hydrolysis and saponification of esters. (16.5)

Practice Test for Chapter 16

For questions 1 through 5, match each condensed or line-angle structural formula to its functional group: (16.1, 16.3)

A. alcohol   **B.** aldehyde   **C.** carboxylic acid   **D.** ester   **E.** ketone

1. _____ $CH_3-\overset{\overset{\textstyle CH_3}{|}}{CH}-CH_2-OH$ 2. _____ $CH_3-CH_2-\overset{\overset{\textstyle O}{||}}{C}-OH$

3. _____ $CH_3-CH_2-\overset{\overset{\textstyle O}{||}}{C}-H$ 4. _____ $CH_3-\overset{\overset{\textstyle O}{||}}{C}-O-CH_3$

5. _____

For questions 6 through 11, match the names of the compounds with their condensed or line-angle structural formulas: (16.1, 16.2, 16.4)

A. $CH_3-\overset{\overset{\textstyle O}{||}}{C}-O-CH_2-CH_3$ **B.** $CH_3-CH_2-CH_2-\overset{\overset{\textstyle O}{||}}{C}-O^-\ Na^+$

C. $CH_3-\overset{\overset{\textstyle O}{||}}{C}-O^-\ Na^+$ **D.**

E. $CH_3-CH_2-\overset{\overset{\textstyle O}{||}}{C}-O-CH_3$ **F.**

6. _____ α-methylbutyric acid   7. _____ methyl propanoate

8. _____ sodium butanoate   9. _____ ethyl acetate

10. _____ sodium acetate   11. _____ benzoic acid

12. What is the product when a carboxylic acid reacts with sodium hydroxide? (16.2)
    A. carboxylate salt   **B.** alcohol   **C.** ester
    D. aldehyde   **E.** no reaction

13. Carboxylic acids are water-soluble due to their (16.2)
    A. nonpolar nature   **B.** ionic bonds   **C.** ability to lower pH
    D. ability to hydrogen bond   **E.** high melting points

For questions 14 through 17, refer to the following reactions: (16.2, 16.3, 16.5)

A. $CH_3-\overset{\overset{\textstyle O}{||}}{C}-OH + HO-CH_3 \underset{}{\overset{H^+,\ heat}{\rightleftharpoons}} CH_3-\overset{\overset{\textstyle O}{||}}{C}-O-CH_3 + H_2O$

B. $CH_3-\overset{\displaystyle O}{\overset{\|}{C}}-OH + NaOH \longrightarrow CH_3-\overset{\displaystyle O}{\overset{\|}{C}}-O^- \ Na^+ + H_2O$

C. $CH_3-\overset{\displaystyle O}{\overset{\|}{C}}-O-CH_3 + H_2O \underset{}{\overset{H^+, \ heat}{\rightleftharpoons}} CH_3-\overset{\displaystyle O}{\overset{\|}{C}}-OH + HO-CH_3$

D. $CH_3-\overset{\displaystyle O}{\overset{\|}{C}}-O-CH_3 + NaOH \longrightarrow CH_3-\overset{\displaystyle O}{\overset{\|}{C}}-O^- \ Na^+ + HO-CH_3$

14. _____ is an ester hydrolysis

15. _____ is a neutralization

16. _____ is a saponification

17. _____ is an esterification

18. What is the name of the organic product in the following reaction? (16.4)

$CH_3-\overset{\displaystyle O}{\overset{\|}{C}}-OH + HO-CH_3 \underset{}{\overset{H^+, \ heat}{\rightleftharpoons}} CH_3-\overset{\displaystyle O}{\overset{\|}{C}}-O-CH_3 + H_2O$

    A. methyl acetate   **B.** acetic acid   **C.** methyl alcohol
    D. acetaldehyde   **E.** ethyl methanoate

19. The compound with the highest boiling point is (16.5)
    A. formic acid   **B.** acetic acid   **C.** propanol
    D. propanoic acid   **E.** ethyl acetate

20. The ester produced from the reaction of 1-butanol and propanoic acid is (16.3, 16.4)
    A. butyl propanoate   **B.** butyl propanone   **C.** propyl butyrate
    D. propyl butanone   **E.** heptanoate

21. The reaction of methyl acetate with NaOH produces (16.5)
    A. ethanol and formic acid
    B. ethanol and sodium formate
    C. ethanol and sodium ethanoate
    D. methanol and acetic acid
    E. methanol and sodium acetate

22. Identify the carboxylic acid and alcohol needed to produce the compound shown below (16.3)

$CH_3-CH_2-CH_2-\overset{\displaystyle O}{\overset{\|}{C}}-O-CH_2-CH_3$

    A. propanoic acid and ethanol   **B.** acetic acid and 1-pentanol
    C. acetic acid and 1-butanol   **D.** butanoic acid and ethanol
    E. hexanoic acid and methanol

23. The name of $CH_3-CH_2-\overset{\displaystyle O}{\overset{\|}{C}}-O-CH_2-CH_3$ is (16.4)

    A. ethyl acetate   **B.** ethyl ethanoate   **C.** ethyl propanoate
    D. propyl ethanoate   **E.** ethyl butyrate

24. In a hydrolysis reaction, (16.5)
- **A.** an acid reacts with an alcohol
- **B.** an ester reacts with NaOH
- **C.** an ester reacts with H_2O
- **D.** an acid neutralizes a base
- **E.** water is added to an alkene

25. Esters (16.3, 16.5)
- **A.** have pleasant odors
- **B.** can undergo hydrolysis
- **C.** are formed from alcohols and carboxylic acids
- **D.** have a lower boiling point than the corresponding acid
- **E.** all of the above

26. The products of the following reaction are: (16.2)

$$H-\overset{\overset{\displaystyle O}{\|}}{C}-OH + H_2O \rightleftharpoons$$

A. $H-\overset{\overset{\displaystyle O}{\|}}{C}-O^- + H_3O^+$

B. $H-\overset{\overset{\displaystyle O}{\|}}{C}-\overset{+}{O}H_2 + OH^-$

C. $H-\overset{\overset{\displaystyle O}{\|}}{C}-O-CH_3$

D. $CH_3-\overset{\overset{\displaystyle O}{\|}}{C}-OH$

E. $H-\overset{\overset{\displaystyle O}{\|}}{C}-O^- Na^+ + H_2O$

27. The name of the following compound is: (16.1)

- **A.** *p*-chlorobenzoic acid
- **B.** chlorobenzoic acid
- **C.** *m*-chlorobenzoic acid
- **D.** 4-chlorobenzoic acid
- **E.** benzoic acid chloride

28. The name of the following compound is: (16.2)

- **A.** benzene sodium
- **B.** sodium benzoate
- **C.** *o*-benzoic acid
- **D.** sodium benzene carboxylate
- **E.** benzoic acid

Answers to the Practice Test

1. A	**2.** C	**3.** B	**4.** D	**5.** E
6. D	**7.** E	**8.** B	**9.** A	**10.** C
11. F	**12.** A	**13.** D	**14.** C	**15.** B
16. D	**17.** A	**18.** A	**19.** D	**20.** A
21. E	**22.** D	**23.** C	**24.** C	**25.** E
26. A	**27.** C	**28.** B		

16

Carboxylic Acids and Esters

Learning Goals

- Write the IUPAC and common names for carboxylic acids and draw their condensed and line-angle structural formulas.
- Describe the boiling points, solubility, dissociation, and neutralization of carboxylic acids.
- Write a balanced chemical equation for the formation of an ester.
- Write the IUPAC and common names for esters; draw condensed and line-angle structural formulas.
- Describe the boiling points and solubility of esters; draw the condensed structural formulas for the hydrolysis products.

Chapter Outline

Chapter Opener: Surgical Technician

16.1 Carboxylic Acids

Chemistry Link to Health: Alpha Hydroxy Acids

16.2 Properties of Carboxylic Acids

Chemistry Link to Health: Carboxylic Acids in Metabolism

16.3 Esters

Chemistry Link to Health: Salicylic Acid from a Willow Tree

Chemistry Link to the Environment: Plastics

16.4 Naming Esters

16.5 Properties of Esters

Clinical Update: Liquid Bandages

⚛ Core Chemistry Skills

- Naming Carboxylic Acids (16.1)
- Hydrolyzing Esters (16.5)

Selected Answers and Solutions to Text Problems

16.1 Methanoic acid (formic acid) is the carboxylic acid that is responsible for the pain associated with ant stings.

16.3 a. $CH_3-CH_2-CH_2-CH_2-CH_2-\overset{\displaystyle O}{\overset{\displaystyle \|}{C}}-OH$ Hexanoic acid

    b. $CH_3-CH_2-\overset{\displaystyle CH_3-CH_2}{\overset{\displaystyle |}{CH}}-\overset{\displaystyle O}{\overset{\displaystyle \|}{C}}-OH$ 2-Ethylbutanoic acid

16.5 a. Ethanoic acid (acetic acid) is the carboxylic acid with two carbons.
  b. Butanoic acid (butyric acid) is the carboxylic acid with four carbons.
  c. 3-Methylhexanoic acid is a six-carbon carboxylic acid with a methyl group on carbon 3 of the chain.
  d. 3,4-Dibromobenzoic acid is an aromatic carboxylic acid with bromine atoms on carbon 3 and carbon 4 of the ring.

16.7 a. 2-Chloroethanoic acid is a carboxylic acid that has a two-carbon chain with a chlorine atom on carbon 2.

$$Cl-CH_2-\overset{\displaystyle O}{\overset{\|}{C}}-OH$$

  b. 3-Hydroxypropanoic acid is a carboxylic acid that has a three-carbon chain with a hydroxyl group on carbon 3.

$$HO-CH_2-CH_2-\overset{\displaystyle O}{\overset{\|}{C}}-OH$$

  c. α-Methylbutyric acid is a carboxylic acid that has a four-carbon chain with a methyl group on the carbon adjacent to the carboxyl group.

$$CH_3-CH_2-\overset{\displaystyle CH_3}{\overset{|}{C}}H-\overset{\displaystyle O}{\overset{\|}{C}}-OH$$

  d. 3,5-Dibromoheptanoic acid is a carboxylic acid that has a seven-carbon chain with bromine atoms attached to carbon 3 and carbon 5.

$$CH_3-CH_2-\overset{\displaystyle Br}{\overset{|}{C}}H-CH_2-\overset{\displaystyle Br}{\overset{|}{C}}H-CH_2-\overset{\displaystyle O}{\overset{\|}{C}}-OH$$

16.9 Aldehydes and primary alcohols oxidize to produce the corresponding carboxylic acid.

  a. $H-\overset{\displaystyle O}{\overset{\|}{C}}-OH$

  b. $CH_3-\overset{\displaystyle O}{\overset{\|}{C}}-OH$

  c.

  d.

16.11 a. Butanoic acid has a greater molar mass and would have a higher boiling point than ethanoic acid.
  b. Propanoic acid can form dimers, effectively doubling the molar mass, which gives propanoic acid a higher boiling point than 1-propanol.
  c. Butanoic acid can form dimers, effectively doubling the molar mass, which gives butanoic acid a higher boiling point than butanone.

16.13 a. Propanoic acid is the most soluble of the group because it has the fewest number of carbon atoms in its hydrocarbon chain. Solubility of carboxylic acids decreases as the number of carbon atoms in the hydrocarbon chain increases.

b. Propanoic acid is more soluble than 1-hexanol because it has fewer carbon atoms in its hydrocarbon chain. Propanoic acid is also more soluble because the carboxyl group forms more hydrogen bonds with water than does the hydroxyl group of an alcohol. An alkane is not soluble in water.

16.15 a. $$CH_3-CH_2-CH_2-\overset{\overset{O}{\|}}{C}-OH + H_2O \rightleftharpoons CH_3-CH_2-CH_2-\overset{\overset{O}{\|}}{C}-O^- + H_3O^+$$

b. $$CH_3-\overset{\overset{CH_3}{|}}{CH}-\overset{\overset{O}{\|}}{C}-OH + H_2O \rightleftharpoons CH_3-\overset{\overset{CH_3}{|}}{CH}-\overset{\overset{O}{\|}}{C}-O^- + H_3O^+$$

16.17 a.

$$CH_3-CH_2-CH_2-CH_2-\overset{\overset{O}{\|}}{C}-OH + NaOH \longrightarrow CH_3-CH_2-CH_2-CH_2-\overset{\overset{O}{\|}}{C}-O^-\ Na^+ + H_2O$$

b. $$CH_3-\overset{\overset{Cl}{|}}{CH}-\overset{\overset{O}{\|}}{C}-OH + NaOH \longrightarrow CH_3-\overset{\overset{Cl}{|}}{CH}-\overset{\overset{O}{\|}}{C}-O^-\ Na^+ + H_2O$$

c.

16.19 A carboxylic acid salt is named by replacing the *ic* ending of the acid name with *ate*.

a. sodium pentanoate

b. sodium 2-chloropropanoate (sodium α-chloropropionate)

c. sodium benzoate

16.21 a. This is an aldehyde since it has a carbonyl group bonded to a hydrogen atom.

b. This is an ester since it has a carboxyl group bonded to two carbon groups.

c. This is a ketone since it has a carbonyl group bonded to two carbon groups.

d. This is a carboxylic acid since it has a carboxyl group bonded to a hydrogen atom.

16.23 A carboxylic acid reacts with an alcohol to form an ester and water. In an ester, the —H of the carboxylic acid is replaced by an alkyl group.

a. $$CH_3-\overset{\overset{O}{\|}}{C}-O-CH_2-CH_3$$

b. $$CH_3-CH_2-CH_2-\overset{\overset{O}{\|}}{C}-O-CH_2-CH_3$$

c.

16.25 A carboxylic acid and an alcohol react to give an ester with the elimination of water.

a. (structure of an ester)

b. $CH_3—CH_2—CH_2—CH_2—\overset{\overset{\displaystyle O}{\|}}{C}—O—\overset{\overset{\displaystyle CH_3}{|}}{CH}—CH_3$

16.27 a. The carboxylic acid part of the ester is from methanoic acid (formic acid), and the alcohol part is from methanol (methyl alcohol).
   b. The carboxylic acid part of the ester is from butanoic acid (butyric acid), and the alcohol part is 1-propanol (propyl alcohol).
   c. The carboxylic acid part of the ester is from butanoic acid (butyric acid), and the alcohol part is from methanol (methyl alcohol).
   d. The carboxylic acid part of the ester is from 3-methylbutanoic acid (β-methylbutyric acid), and the alcohol part is from ethanol (ethyl alcohol).

16.29 a. The alcohol part of the ester is from methanol (methyl alcohol), and the carboxylic acid part is from methanoic acid (formic acid). The ester is named methyl methanoate (methyl formate).
   b. The alcohol part of the ester is from ethanol (ethyl alcohol), and the carboxylic acid part is from propanoic acid (propionic acid). The ester is named ethyl propanoate (ethyl propionate).
   c. The alcohol part of the ester is from methanol (methyl alcohol), and the carboxylic acid part is from butanoic acid (butyric acid). The ester is named methyl butanoate (methyl butyrate).
   d. The alcohol part of the ester is from 2-methyl-1-propanol, and the carboxylic acid part is from pentanoic acid. The ester is named 2-methylpropyl pentanoate.

16.31 a. The alkyl part of the ester comes from the one-carbon methanol, and the carboxylate part comes from the two-carbon acetic acid.

$CH_3—\overset{\overset{\displaystyle O}{\|}}{C}—O—CH_3$

   b. The alkyl part of the ester comes from the four-carbon 1-butanol, and the carboxylate part comes from the one-carbon formic acid.

$H—\overset{\overset{\displaystyle O}{\|}}{C}—O—CH_2—CH_2—CH_2—CH_3$

   c. The alkyl part of the ester comes from the two-carbon ethanol, and the carboxylate part comes from the five-carbon pentanoic acid.

$CH_3—CH_2—CH_2—CH_2—\overset{\overset{\displaystyle O}{\|}}{C}—O—CH_2—CH_3$

   d. The alkyl part of the ester comes from the three-carbon 1-propanol that has a bromine atom attached to carbon 2, and the carboxylate part comes from the three-carbon propanoic acid.

$CH_3—CH_2—\overset{\overset{\displaystyle O}{\|}}{C}—O—CH_2—\overset{\overset{\displaystyle Br}{|}}{CH}—CH_3$

16.33 a. The flavor and odor of bananas is due to pentyl ethanoate (pentyl acetate).
   b. The flavor and odor of oranges is due to octyl ethanoate (octyl acetate).
   c. The flavor and odor of apricots is due to pentyl butanoate (pentyl butyrate).

16.35 a. $CH_3-CH_2-\overset{\overset{O}{\|}}{C}-OH$

   b. $CH_3-CH_2-CH_2-CH_2-OH$

   c.

16.37 Acid hydrolysis of an ester gives the carboxylic acid and the alcohol that were combined to form the ester; base hydrolysis of an ester gives the salt of the carboxylic acid and the alcohol that were combined to form the ester.

   a. $CH_3-CH_2-\overset{\overset{O}{\|}}{C}-O^-\ Na^+ + HO-CH_3$

   b. $OH + HO$

   c. $CH_3-CH_2-CH_2-\overset{\overset{O}{\|}}{C}-OH + HO-CH_2-CH_3$

   d. $-\overset{\overset{O}{\|}}{C}-O^-\ Na^+ + HO-CH_2-CH_3$

   e. $OH + HO$

16.39 a. $H_2C=\overset{\overset{CN}{|}}{C}-\overset{\overset{O}{\|}}{C}-OH + HO-CH_2-CH_2-CH_2-CH_3 \underset{}{\overset{H^+,\ heat}{\rightleftharpoons}}$

   $H_2C=\overset{\overset{CN}{|}}{C}-\overset{\overset{O}{\|}}{C}-O-CH_2-CH_2-CH_2-CH_3 + H_2O$

   b. butyl 2-cyano-2-propenoate

16.41 $CH_3-CH_2-CH_2-\overset{\overset{O}{\|}}{C}-OH$ Butanoic acid

   $CH_3-\overset{\overset{CH_3}{|}}{CH}-\overset{\overset{O}{\|}}{C}-OH$ 2-Methylpropanoic acid

16.43 $CH_3-\overset{\overset{\displaystyle O}{\|}}{C}-O-CH_3$ Methyl ethanoate

$H-\overset{\overset{\displaystyle O}{\|}}{C}-O-CH_2-CH_3$ Ethyl methanoate

16.45 a. $CH_3-CH_2-CH_2-\overset{\overset{\displaystyle O}{\|}}{C}-O-CH_3$

b. butanoic acid and methanol

c. $CH_3-CH_2-CH_2-\overset{\overset{\displaystyle O}{\|}}{C}-O-CH_3 + H_2O \underset{}{\overset{H^+,\ heat}{\rightleftharpoons}}$

$CH_3-CH_2-CH_2-\overset{\overset{\displaystyle O}{\|}}{C}-OH + HO-CH_3$

d. $CH_3-CH_2-CH_2-\overset{\overset{\displaystyle O}{\|}}{C}-O-CH_3 + NaOH \overset{Heat}{\longrightarrow}$

$CH_3-CH_2-CH_2-\overset{\overset{\displaystyle O}{\|}}{C}-O^-\ Na^+ + HO-CH_3$

16.47 a. 3-methylbutanoic acid (β-methylbutyric acid)
b. ethyl benzoate
c. ethyl propanoate (ethyl propionate)
d. 2-chlorobenzoic acid (*o*-chlorobenzoic acid)
e. 4-hydroxypentanoic acid
f. 2-propyl ethanoate (isopropyl acetate)

16.49

16.51 a. $CH_3-CH_2-CH_2-CH_2-CH_2-\overset{\overset{\displaystyle O}{\|}}{C}-O-CH_3$

b.

c. $Cl-CH_2-CH_2-\overset{\overset{\displaystyle O}{\|}}{C}-OH$

d. $CH_3-CH_2-CH_2-\overset{\overset{\displaystyle O}{\|}}{C}-O-CH_2-CH_3$

e. $CH_3-CH_2-\overset{\overset{\displaystyle CH_3}{|}}{CH}-CH_2-\overset{\overset{\displaystyle O}{||}}{C}-OH$

f. $\overset{\overset{\displaystyle O}{||}}{C}-O-CH_2-CH_3$ (attached to benzene ring)

16.53 a. Ethanoic acid has a higher boiling point than 1-propanol because two molecules of ethanoic acid hydrogen bond to form a dimer, which effectively doubles the molar mass and requires a higher temperature to reach the boiling point.

b. Ethanoic acid has the higher boiling point because it forms hydrogen bonds, whereas butane does not.

16.55 Of the three compounds, methyl formate would have the lowest boiling point since it has only dipole–dipole attractions. Both acetic acid and 1-propanol can form hydrogen bonds, but because acetic acid can form dimers and double the effective molar mass, it has the highest boiling point. Methyl formate, 32 °C; 1-propanol, 97 °C; acetic acid, 118 °C.

16.57 a, **c**, and **d** are soluble in water.

16.59 a. $CH_3-CH_2-\overset{\overset{\displaystyle O}{||}}{C}-O^- + H_3O^+$

b. $CH_3-CH_2-\overset{\overset{\displaystyle O}{||}}{C}-O^-\ K^+ + H_2O$

c. (ester structure) $+ H_2O$

d. $\overset{\overset{\displaystyle O}{||}}{C}-O-CH_2-CH_3$ (attached to benzene ring) $+ H_2O$

16.61 a. 3-methylbutanoic acid and methanol
b. 3-chlorobenzoic acid and ethanol
c. hexanoic acid and ethanol

16.63 a. $CH_3-CH_2-\overset{\overset{\displaystyle O}{||}}{C}-OH\ +\ HO-\overset{\overset{\displaystyle CH_3}{|}}{CH}-CH_3$

b. $CH_3-\overset{\overset{\displaystyle CH_3}{|}}{CH}-\overset{\overset{\displaystyle O}{||}}{C}-O^-\ Na^+ + HO-CH_2-CH_2-CH_3$

16.65 a. $H_2C=CH_2 + H_2O \xrightarrow{H^+} CH_3-CH_2-OH \xrightarrow{[O]} CH_3-\overset{\displaystyle O}{\overset{\|}{C}}-OH$

b. $CH_3-CH_2-CH_2-CH_2-OH \xrightarrow{[O]} CH_3-CH_2-CH_2-\overset{\displaystyle O}{\overset{\|}{C}}-OH$

16.67 In basic solution, the ester undergoes saponification to form the carboxylate salt potassium benzoate and methanol, which are soluble in water. When HCl is added, the salt is converted to benzoic acid, which is insoluble.

$\langle\text{C}_6\text{H}_5\rangle-\overset{\displaystyle O}{\overset{\|}{C}}-O-CH_3 + KOH \xrightarrow{\text{Heat}} \langle\text{C}_6\text{H}_5\rangle-\overset{\displaystyle O}{\overset{\|}{C}}-O^- K^+ + HO-CH_3$

16.69 a. $CH_3-\overset{\displaystyle O}{\overset{\|}{C}}-O-CH_2-CH_2-CH_3$

b. $CH_3-\overset{\displaystyle O}{\overset{\|}{C}}-OH + HO-CH_2-CH_2-CH_3 \underset{}{\overset{H^+, \text{ heat}}{\rightleftarrows}} CH_3-\overset{\displaystyle O}{\overset{\|}{C}}-O-CH_2-CH_2-CH_3 + H_2O$

c. $CH_3-\overset{\displaystyle O}{\overset{\|}{C}}-O-CH_2-CH_2-CH_3 + H_2O \underset{}{\overset{H^+, \text{ heat}}{\rightleftarrows}} CH_3-\overset{\displaystyle O}{\overset{\|}{C}}-OH + HO-CH_2-CH_2-CH_3$

d.

$CH_3-\overset{\displaystyle O}{\overset{\|}{C}}-O-CH_2-CH_2-CH_3 + NaOH \xrightarrow{\text{Heat}} CH_3-\overset{\displaystyle O}{\overset{\|}{C}}-O^- Na^+ + HO-CH_2-CH_2-CH_3$

e. Molar mass of propyl acetate $(C_5H_{10}O_2)$
$= 5(12.01 \text{ g}) + 10(1.008 \text{ g}) + 2(16.00 \text{ g}) = 102.13 \text{ g/mole} (5 \text{ SFs})$

$$1.58 \text{ g } C_5H_{10}O_2 \times \frac{1 \text{ mole } C_5H_{10}O_2}{102.13 \text{ g } C_5H_{10}O_2} \times \frac{1 \text{ mole NaOH}}{1 \text{ mole } C_5H_{10}O_2} \times \frac{1000 \text{ mL solution}}{0.208 \text{ mole NaOH}}$$

$= 74.4 \text{ mL of a } 0.208 \text{ M NaOH solution} (3 \text{ SFs})$

17 Lipids

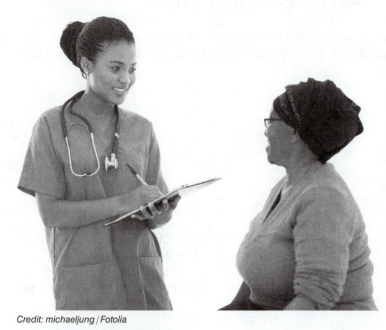

Rebecca changed her diet by decreasing the fat content and increasing the amount of vegetables for more dietary fiber. She also drinks six glasses of water every day and is on a regular exercise program and walks every day. Recently, Rebecca had a gallbladder attack. In the body, the gallbladder stores bile, which is used in the intestine for the digestion of fats. If the bile is not moving out of the gallbladder, it can form gallstones, which are mostly cholesterol. If a gallstone blocks the bile duct, gallbladder disease can occur. Rebecca's doctor prescribed a medication that dissolves gallstones and recommended a liver flush to remove small gallstones.

What is the line-angle structural formula of cholesterol?

Credit: michaeljung / Fotolia

CHAPTER READINESS*

✊ Core Chemistry Skills

- Writing Equations for Hydrogenation, Hydration, and Polymerization (12.7)

- Naming Alcohols and Phenols (13.1)
- Naming Carboxylic Acids (16.1)
- Hydrolyzing Esters (16.5)

*These Core Chemistry Skills from previous chapters are listed here for your review as you proceed to the new material in this chapter.

17.1 Lipids

Learning Goal: Describe the classes of lipids.

- Lipids are nonpolar compounds that are not soluble in water but are soluble in organic solvents.
- A wax is an ester of a long-chain alcohol and a long-chain saturated fatty acid.
- A triacylglycerol consists of three fatty acids bonded through ester bonds to glycerol.
- A sphingomyelin consists of sphingosine that forms an amide bond to a fatty acid and an ester bond to a phosphate group bonded to an amino alcohol.
- A glycerophospholipid contains glycerol attached to two fatty acids and a phosphate group connected to an amino alcohol.
- A steroid contains a multicyclic ring

♦ Learning Exercise 17.1
Match the correct class of lipids with the compositions below:

  a. wax   **b.** triacylglycerol   **c.** glycerophospholipid   **d.** steroid   **e.** sphingomyelin

1. _____ a fused structure of four cycloalkanes

2. _____ a long-chain alcohol and a long-chain saturated fatty acid

3. _____ glycerol and three fatty acids

4. _____ sphingosine, fatty acid, phosphate group, and an amino alcohol

5. _____ glycerol, two fatty acids, phosphate group, and choline

Answers **1.** d **2.** a **3.** b **4.** e **5.** c

17.2 Fatty Acids

Learning Goal: Draw the condensed or line-angle structural formula for a fatty acid and identify it as saturated or unsaturated.

- Fatty acids are unbranched carboxylic acids that typically contain an even number (12 to 20) of carbon atoms.
- Fatty acids may be saturated, monounsaturated with one double bond, or polyunsaturated with two or more carbon–carbon double bonds. The double bonds in naturally occurring unsaturated fatty acids are almost always cis.

♦ **Learning Exercise 17.2A**

Draw the condensed and line-angle structural formulas for each of the following fatty acids:

1. linoleic acid

2. stearic acid

3. palmitoleic acid

⚛ **CORE CHEMISTRY SKILL**

Identifying Fatty Acids

Answers

1. $CH_3-(CH_2)_4-CH=CH-CH_2-CH=CH-(CH_2)_7-\overset{\displaystyle O}{\overset{\|}{C}}-OH$

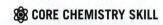

2. $CH_3-(CH_2)_{16}-\overset{\displaystyle O}{\overset{\|}{C}}-OH$

3. $CH_3-(CH_2)_5-CH=CH-(CH_2)_7-\overset{\displaystyle O}{\overset{\|}{C}}-OH$

♦ **Learning Exercise 17.2B**

For the fatty acids in Learning Exercise 17.2A, identify which

    a. _____ is the most saturated   **b.** _____ is the most unsaturated
    c. _____ has the lowest melting point   **d.** _____ has the highest melting point
    e. _____ is/are found in vegetables   **f.** _____ is/are from animal sources

Answers   **a.** 2   **b.** 1   **c.** 1   **d.** 2   **e.** 1, 3   **f.** 2

♦ **Learning Exercise 17.2C**

For the following questions, refer to the line-angle structural formula for a fatty acid:

1. What is the name of this fatty acid?   _____

2. Is it a saturated or an unsaturated compound? Why?   _____

3. Is the double bond cis or trans?   _____

4. Is it likely to be a solid or a liquid at room temperature?   _____

5. Why is it insoluble in water?   _____

Answers   **1.** oleic acid   **2.** unsaturated; double bond   **3.** cis
               4. liquid   **5.** It has a long hydrocarbon chain.

17.3 Waxes and Triacylglycerols

Learning Goal: Draw the condensed or line-angle structural formula for a wax or triacylglycerol produced by the reaction of a fatty acid and an alcohol or glycerol.

- A wax is an ester of a long-chain saturated fatty acid and a long-chain alcohol.
- The triacylglycerols in fats and oils are esters of glycerol with three long-chain fatty acids.
- Fats from animal sources contain more saturated fatty acids and have higher melting points than fats found in most vegetable oils.

♦ **Learning Exercise 17.3A**

Draw the condensed structural formula for the wax formed by the reaction of palmitic acid,

$$CH_3-(CH_2)_{14}-\overset{\overset{\displaystyle O}{\|}}{C}-OH$$, and cetyl alcohol, $CH_3-(CH_2)_{14}-CH_2-OH$.

Answer $$CH_3-(CH_2)_{14}-\overset{\overset{\displaystyle O}{\|}}{C}-O-CH_2-(CH_2)_{14}-CH_3$$

♦ **Learning Exercise 17.3B**

⚛ **CORE CHEMISTRY SKILL**

Drawing Structures for Triacylglycerols

Draw the condensed structural formula for the triacylglycerol from glycerol and three molecules of each of the following and give the name:

1. palmitic acid, $$CH_3-(CH_2)_{14}-\overset{\overset{\displaystyle O}{\|}}{C}-OH$$

2. myristic acid, $$CH_3-(CH_2)_{12}-\overset{\overset{\displaystyle O}{\|}}{C}-OH$$

Answers

1.
$$CH_2-O-\overset{\overset{\displaystyle O}{\|}}{C}-(CH_2)_{14}-CH_3$$
$$CH-O-\overset{\overset{\displaystyle O}{\|}}{C}-(CH_2)_{14}-CH_3$$
$$CH_2-O-\overset{\overset{\displaystyle O}{\|}}{C}-(CH_2)_{14}-CH_3$$
Glyceryl tripalmitate
(tripalmitin)

2.
$$CH_2-O-\overset{\overset{\displaystyle O}{\|}}{C}-(CH_2)_{12}-CH_3$$
$$CH-O-\overset{\overset{\displaystyle O}{\|}}{C}-(CH_2)_{12}-CH_3$$
$$CH_2-O-\overset{\overset{\displaystyle O}{\|}}{C}-(CH_2)_{12}-CH_3$$
Glyceryl trimyristate
(trimyristin)

♦ **Learning Exercise 17.3C**

Draw the condensed structural formulas for the following triacylglycerols:

1. glyceryl tristearate (tristearin)   **2.** glyceryl trioleate (triolein)

Answers

1. CH₂—O—C(=O)—(CH₂)₁₆—CH₃
CH—O—C(=O)—(CH₂)₁₆—CH₃
CH₂—O—C(=O)—(CH₂)₁₆—CH₃
Glyceryl tristearate
(tristearin)

2. CH₂—O—C(=O)—(CH₂)₇—CH=CH—(CH₂)₇—CH₃
CH—O—C(=O)—(CH₂)₇—CH=CH—(CH₂)₇—CH₃
CH₂—O—C(=O)—(CH₂)₇—CH=CH—(CH₂)₇—CH₃
Glyceryl trioleate
(triolein)

17.4 Chemical Properties of Triacylglycerols

Learning Goal: Draw the condensed or line-angle structural formula for the products of a triacylglycerol that undergoes hydrogenation, hydrolysis, or saponification.

- The hydrogenation of unsaturated fatty acids converts carbon–carbon double bonds to carbon–carbon single bonds.

- The hydrolysis of the ester bonds in fats or oils produces glycerol and fatty acids.

- In saponification, a fat heated with a strong base produces glycerol and the salts of the fatty acids (soaps).

Shortening (soft)

Vegetable oils (liquids) H_2 Tub (soft) margarine   Stick margarine (solid)

Many soft margarines, stick margarines, and solid shortenings are produced by the partial hydrogenation of vegetable oils.
Credit: Pearson Education / Pearson Science

♦ **Learning Exercise 17.4**

Write the equations for the following reactions of glyceryl trioleate (triolein):

⚛ CORE CHEMISTRY SKILL

Drawing the Products for the Hydrogenation, Hydrolysis, and Saponification of a Triacylglycerol

1. hydrogenation with a nickel catalyst

2. acid hydrolysis with HCl

3. saponification with NaOH

Answers

1.

$$CH_2-O-\overset{\displaystyle O}{\overset{\|}{C}}-(CH_2)_7-CH=CH-(CH_2)_7-CH_3$$
$$CH-O-\overset{\displaystyle O}{\overset{\|}{C}}-(CH_2)_7-CH=CH-(CH_2)_7-CH_3 + 3H_2 \xrightarrow{Ni}$$
$$CH_2-O-\overset{\displaystyle O}{\overset{\|}{C}}-(CH_2)_7-CH=CH-(CH_2)_7-CH_3$$

$$CH_2-O-\overset{\displaystyle O}{\overset{\|}{C}}-(CH_2)_{16}-CH_3$$
$$CH-O-\overset{\displaystyle O}{\overset{\|}{C}}-(CH_2)_{16}-CH_3$$
$$CH_2-O-\overset{\displaystyle O}{\overset{\|}{C}}-(CH_2)_{16}-CH_3$$

2.

$$CH_2-O-\overset{\displaystyle O}{\overset{\|}{C}}-(CH_2)_7-CH=CH-(CH_2)_7-CH_3$$
$$CH-O-\overset{\displaystyle O}{\overset{\|}{C}}-(CH_2)_7-CH=CH-(CH_2)_7-CH_3 + 3H_2O \xrightarrow{H^+}$$
$$CH_2-O-\overset{\displaystyle O}{\overset{\|}{C}}-(CH_2)_7-CH=CH-(CH_2)_7-CH_3$$

$$CH_2-OH$$
$$CH-OH$$
$$CH_2-OH$$

$$+ 3HO-\overset{\displaystyle O}{\overset{\|}{C}}-(CH_2)_7-CH=CH-(CH_2)_7-CH_3$$

3.

$$CH_2-O-\overset{\overset{O}{\|}}{C}-(CH_2)_7-CH=CH-(CH_2)_7-CH_3$$

$$CH-O-\overset{\overset{O}{\|}}{C}-(CH_2)_7-CH=CH-(CH_2)_7-CH_3 + 3NaOH \longrightarrow$$

$$CH_2-O-\overset{\overset{O}{\|}}{C}-(CH_2)_7-CH=CH-(CH_2)_7-CH_3$$

$$CH_2-OH$$
$$CH-OH$$
$$CH_2-OH$$

$$+ 3Na^+ \ ^-O-\overset{\overset{O}{\|}}{C}-(CH_2)_7-CH=CH-(CH_2)_7-CH_3$$

17.5 Phospholipids

Learning Goal: Describe the structure of a phospholipid containing glycerol or sphingosine.

- The phospholipids are a family of lipids similar in structure to triacylglycerols.
- Glycerophospholipids are esters of glycerol with two fatty acids and a phosphate group attached to an amino alcohol.

$$CH_2-O-\overset{\overset{O}{\|}}{C}-(CH_2)_{16}-CH_3$$
$$\text{Glycerol } CH-O-\overset{\overset{O}{\|}}{C}-(CH_2)_{16}-CH_3 \quad \Big\} \text{ Stearic acids}$$
$$CH_2-O-\overset{}{\underset{\underset{O^-}{|}}{P}}-O-CH_2-\overset{\overset{+}{NH_3}}{\underset{}{CH}}-\overset{\overset{O}{\|}}{C}-O^-$$
$$\text{Phosphate} \qquad \text{Serine}$$

- The fatty acids form a nonpolar region, whereas the phosphate group and the ionized amino alcohol make up a polar region.
- In sphingomyelins, the amine group in the long-chain alcohol sphingosine forms an amide bond with a fatty acid and the hydroxyl group forms a phosphoester bond with choline.

$$HO-CH-CH=CH-(CH_2)_{12}-CH_3$$
$$\text{Sphingosine } CH-\overset{}{\underset{H}{N}}-\overset{\overset{O}{\|}}{C}-(CH_2)_{16}-CH_3 \quad \text{Stearic acid}$$
$$CH_2-O-\overset{}{\underset{\underset{O^-}{|}}{P}}-O-CH_2-CH_2-\overset{+}{N}H_3$$
$$\qquad\qquad \text{Ethanolamine}$$

♦ **Learning Exercise 17.5A**

Draw the condensed structural formula for a glycerophospholipid that is formed from two molecules of palmitic acid and serine, an amino alcohol:

$$CH_3-(CH_2)_{14}-\overset{O}{\overset{\|}{C}}-OH$$
Palmitic acid

$$HO-CH_2-\overset{\overset{+}{NH_3}}{\underset{}{CH}}-\overset{O}{\overset{\|}{C}}-O^-$$
Serine

Answer

$$CH_2-O-\overset{O}{\overset{\|}{C}}-(CH_2)_{14}-CH_3$$
$$CH-O-\overset{O}{\overset{\|}{C}}-(CH_2)_{14}-CH_3$$
$$CH_2-O-\overset{O}{\underset{O^-}{\overset{\|}{P}}}-O-CH_2-\overset{\overset{+}{NH_3}}{CH}-\overset{O}{\overset{\|}{C}}-O^-$$

♦ **Learning Exercise 17.5B**

Use the following glycerophospholipid to answer parts **A** to **F** and **1** to **3**:

$$CH_2-O-\overset{O}{\overset{\|}{C}}-(CH_2)_{14}-CH_3$$
$$CH-O-\overset{O}{\overset{\|}{C}}-(CH_2)_{14}-CH_3$$
$$CH_2-O-\overset{O}{\underset{O^-}{\overset{\|}{P}}}-O-CH_2-CH_2-\overset{+}{NH_3}$$

On the above condensed structural formula, indicate the:

A. two fatty acids
B. part from the glycerol molecule
C. phosphate section
D. amino alcohol
E. nonpolar region
F. polar region

1. What is the name of the amino alcohol? _____

2. What type of glycerophospholipid is it? _____

3. Why is a glycerophospholipid more soluble in water than most lipids? _____

Answers

B Glycerol
$CH_2-O-\overset{\overset{\displaystyle O}{\|}}{C}-(CH_2)_{14}-CH_3$
$CH-O-\overset{\overset{\displaystyle O}{\|}}{C}-(CH_2)_{14}-CH_3$ **A** Fatty acids   **E** Nonpolar region
$CH_2-O-\overset{\overset{\displaystyle O}{\|}}{\underset{\underset{\displaystyle O^-}{|}}{P}}-O-CH_2-CH_2-\overset{+}{N}H_3$
C Phosphate group   **F** Polar region   **D** Amino alcohol

1. ethanolamine

2. cephalin (ethanolamine glycerophospholipid)

3. The polar portion of the glycerophospholipid is attracted to water, which makes it more soluble in water than other lipids.

♦ **Learning Exercise 17.5C**

Answer the following questions for the phospholipid shown below, which is needed for brain and nerve tissues:

$HO-CH-CH=CH\sim\sim\sim\sim\sim\sim\sim\sim$

$CH-\overset{\overset{\displaystyle H}{|}}{N}-\overset{\overset{\displaystyle O}{\|}}{C}\sim\sim\sim\sim\sim\sim\sim$

$CH_2-O-\overset{\overset{\displaystyle O}{\|}}{\underset{\underset{\displaystyle O^-}{|}}{P}}-O\sim\overset{+}{N}\overset{\overset{\displaystyle CH_3}{|}}{\underset{\underset{\displaystyle CH_3}{|}}{}}-CH_3$

a. Is the phospholipid formed from glycerol or sphingosine? _____

b. What is the fatty acid? _____

c. What type of bond connects the fatty acid? _____

d. What is the name of the ionized amino alcohol? _____

Answers
a. sphingosine   **b.** myristic acid   **c.** an amide bond   **d.** choline

17.6 Steroids: Cholesterol, Bile Salts, and Steroid Hormones

Learning Goal: Draw the structures of steroids.

- Steroids are lipids containing the steroid nucleus, which is a fused structure of three cyclohexane rings and one cyclopentane ring.
- Steroids include cholesterol, bile salts, and steroid hormones.
- The steroid hormones are closely related in structure to cholesterol and depend on cholesterol for their synthesis.
- The sex hormones such as estrogen and testosterone are responsible for sexual characteristics and reproduction.
- The adrenal corticosteroids include aldosterone, which regulates water balance, and cortisone, which regulates glucose levels in the blood.
- There are a variety of lipoproteins, which differ in density, lipid composition, and function. They include chylomicrons, very-low-density lipoproteins (VLDLs), low-density lipoproteins (LDLs), and high-density lipoproteins (HDLs).
- The LDLs carries cholesterol to the tissues where it can be used for the synthesis of cell membranes and steroid hormones.
- The HDLs picks up cholesterol from the tissues and carries it to the liver, where it can be converted to bile salts, which are eliminated from the body.

HO
Steroid nucleus
Cholesterol

⚛ **CORE CHEMISTRY SKILL**

Identifying the Steroid Nucleus

◆ **Learning Exercise 17.6A**

1. Draw the line-angle structure for the steroid nucleus.

2. Draw the line-angle structure for cholesterol.

Answers   1.   2.

HO

◆ **Learning Exercise 17.6B**

Match each of the following compounds with the correct phrase below:

    a. estrogen   **b.** testosterone   **c.** cortisone   **d.** aldosterone   **e.** bile salts

1. _____ increases the blood glucose level

2. _____ increases the reabsorption of Na^+ by the kidneys

3. _____ stimulates the development of secondary sex characteristics in females

4. _____ stimulates the retention of water by the kidneys

5. _____ stimulates the development of secondary sex characteristics in males

6. _____ secreted by the gallbladder into the small intestine to emulsify fats in the diet

Answers   **1.** c   **2.** d   **3.** a   **4.** d   **5.** b   **6.** e

17.7 Cell Membranes

Learning Goal: Describe the composition and function of the lipid bilayer in cell membranes.

- Cell membranes surround all of our cells and separate the cellular contents from the external aqueous environment.
- In the fluid mosaic model (lipid bilayer) of a cell membrane, two layers of phospholipids are arranged with their hydrophilic heads at the outer and inner surfaces of the membrane, and their hydrophobic tails in the center.
- Molecules of cholesterol, proteins, and carbohydrates are embedded in the lipid bilayer.
- Nutrients and waste products move through the cell membrane using diffusion (passive transport), facilitated transport, or active transport.

Key Terms for Sections 17.1–17.7

Match each of the following key terms with the correct description below:

    a. lipid   **b.** fatty acid   **c.** triacylglycerol   **d.** lipid bilayer
    e. saponification   **f.** glycerophospholipid   **g.** steroid

1. _____ a compound consisting of glycerol bonded to two fatty acids and a phosphate group that is attached to an amino alcohol

2. _____ a type of compound that is not soluble in water, but is soluble in nonpolar solvents

3. _____ the hydrolysis of a triacylglycerol with a strong base, producing salts called soaps and glycerol

4. _____ a compound consisting of glycerol bonded to three fatty acids

5. _____ a compound composed of a multicyclic ring system

6. _____ a model for cell membranes in which phospholipids are arranged in two rows

7. _____ a long-chain carboxylic acid found in triacylglycerols

Answers   **1.** f   **2.** a   **3.** e   **4.** c   **5.** g   **6.** d   **7.** b

◆ **Learning Exercise 17.7A**

    a. What is the function of the lipid bilayer in cell membranes?

    b. What type of lipid makes up the lipid bilayer?

    c. What is the general arrangement of the lipids in a lipid bilayer?

Answers

 a. The lipid bilayer separates the contents of a cell from the surrounding aqueous environment.
 b. The lipid bilayer is primarily composed of glycerophospholipids.
 c. The nonpolar hydrocarbon tails are in the center of the bilayer, whereas the polar sections are aligned along the outside of the bilayer.

◆ **Learning Exercise 17.7B**

Identify the type of transport described by each of the following:

 a. The K^+ ions move from low to high concentration in a cell. _____

 b. Water moves through a cell membrane. _____

 c. A molecule moves through a protein channel. _____

Answers **a.** active transport **b.** diffusion (passive transport) **c.** facilitated transport

Checklist for Chapter 17

You are ready to take the Practice Test for Chapter 17. Be sure that you have accomplished the learning goals for each of the sections in this chapter. If not, review the section listed at the end of the goal. Then apply your new skills and understanding to the Practice Test.

After studying Chapter 17, I can successfully:

_____ Describe the classes of lipids. (17.1)

_____ Identify a fatty acid as saturated or unsaturated. (17.2)

_____ Draw the condensed structural formula for a wax or triacylglycerol produced by the reaction of a fatty acid and an alcohol or glycerol. (17.3)

_____ Draw the condensed structural formula for the product from the reaction of a triacylglycerol with hydrogen, an acid, or a base. (17.4)

_____ Describe the components of glycerophospholipids and sphingomyelins. (17.5)

_____ Draw the structures of a steroid and cholesterol. (17.6)

_____ Describe the composition and function of the lipid bilayer in cell membranes. (17.7)

Practice Test for Chapter 17

 1. An ester of a fatty acid is called a(an) (17.1, 17.3)
  A. carbohydrate **B.** lipid **C.** protein **D.** oxyacid **E.** soap

 2. A fatty acid that is unsaturated is usually (17.2)
  A. from animal sources and liquid at room temperature
  B. from animal sources and solid at room temperature
  C. from vegetable sources and liquid at room temperature
  D. from vegetable sources and solid at room temperature
  E. from both vegetable and animal sources and solid at room temperature

3. The following condensed structural formula is a(an): (17.2)

$$CH_3-(CH_2)_{16}-\overset{\overset{O}{\|}}{C}-OH$$

   A. unsaturated fatty acid   **B.** saturated fatty acid   **C.** wax
   D. triacylglycerol   **E.** sphingolipid

For questions 4 through 7, consider the following compound:

$$CH_2-O-\overset{\overset{O}{\|}}{C}-(CH_2)_{16}-CH_3$$
$$CH-O-\overset{\overset{O}{\|}}{C}-(CH_2)_{16}-CH_3$$
$$CH_2-O-\overset{\overset{O}{\|}}{C}-(CH_2)_{16}-CH_3$$

4. This compound belongs to the family called (17.3)
   A. waxes   **B.** triacylglycerols   **C.** glycerophospholipids
   D. sphingolipids   **E.** steroids

5. The compound was formed by (17.3)
   A. esterification   **B.** hydrolysis (acid)   **C.** saponification
   D. emulsification   **E.** oxidation

6. If this compound reacts with a strong base such as NaOH, the products would be (17.4)
   A. glycerol and fatty acid
   B. glycerol and water
   C. glycerol and the sodium salt of the fatty acid
   D. an ester and the sodium salt of the fatty acid
   E. an ester and fatty acid

7. The compound would be expected to be (17.3)
   A. saturated and a solid at room temperature
   B. saturated and a liquid at room temperature
   C. unsaturated and a solid at room temperature
   D. unsaturated and a liquid at room temperature
   E. supersaturated and a liquid at room temperature

8. Which of these are found in glycerophospholipids? (17.5)
   A. fatty acids   **B.** glycerol   **C.** a nitrogen compound
   D. phosphate   **E.** all of these

For questions 9 and 10, consider the following reaction: (17.4)

Triacylglycerol + 3NaOH $\xrightarrow{\text{Heat}}$ glycerol + 3 sodium salts of fatty acids

9. The reaction of a triacylglycerol with a strong base such as NaOH is called
   A. esterification   **B.** lipogenesis   **C.** hydrolysis   **D.** saponification   **E.** β oxidation

10. What is another name for the sodium salts of the fatty acids?
   A. margarines   **B.** fat substitutes   **C.** soaps   **D.** perfumes   **E.** vitamins

For questions 11 through 16, consider the following phospholipid:

A
$$CH_2-O-\overset{\overset{O}{\|}}{C}-(CH_2)_{14}-CH_3$$
B
$$CH-O-\overset{\overset{O}{\|}}{C}-(CH_2)_{14}-CH_3$$
$$CH_2-O-\overset{\overset{O}{\|}}{\underset{\underset{O^-}{|}}{P}}-O-CH_2-CH_2-\overset{+}{N}H_3$$
C
D

Match the labels with the following: (17.5)

11. _____ the glycerol portion   **12.** _____ the phosphate portion

13. _____ the amino alcohol   **14.** _____ the polar region

15. _____ the nonpolar region

16. This phospholipid belongs to the family called (17.5)
- **A.** cholines
- **B.** cephalins
- **C.** sphingomyelins
- **D.** glycolipids
- **E.** cerebrosides

For questions 17 through 20, classify each lipid as a (17.1, 17.2, 17.3, 17.5, 17.6)
- **A.** wax
- **B.** triacylglycerol
- **C.** glycerophospholipid
- **D.** steroid
- **E.** fatty acid

17. _____ cholesterol

18. _____ $CH_3-(CH_2)_{14}-\overset{\overset{O}{\|}}{C}-OH$

19. _____ $CH_3-(CH_2)_{14}-\overset{\overset{O}{\|}}{C}-O-(CH_2)_{30}-CH_3$

20. _____ an ester of glycerol with three palmitic acid molecules

For questions 21 through 25, select answers from the following: (17.6)
- **A.** testosterone
- **B.** estrogen
- **C.** prednisone
- **D.** cortisone
- **E.** aldosterone

21. _____ stimulates development of the female sexual characteristics

22. _____ increases the retention of water by the kidneys

23. _____ stimulates development of the male sexual characteristics

24. _____ increases the blood glucose level

25. _____ used medically to reduce inflammation and treat asthma

26. The following compound is a (17.2)

- **A.** cholesterol
- **B.** sphingosine
- **C.** fatty acid
- **D.** glycerosphingolipid
- **E.** steroid

27. The lipid bilayer of a cell consists of (17.7)

   A. cholesterol   **B.** phospholipids   **C.** proteins

   D. carbohydrates   **E.** all of these

28. The type of transport that allows chloride ions to move through the integral proteins in the cell membrane is (17.7)

   A. passive transport   **B.** active transport   **C.** facilitated transport

   D. all of these   **E.** none of these

29. The movement of small molecules through a cell membrane from a higher concentration to a lower concentration is (17.7)

   A. passive transport   **B.** active transport   **C.** facilitated transport

   D. all of these   **E.** none of these

30. The type of lipoprotein that transports cholesterol to the liver for elimination is called a (17.6)

   A. chylomicron   **B.** high-density lipoprotein

   C. low-density lipoprotein   **D.** very-low-density lipoprotein

   E. all of these

Answers to the Practice Test

1. B	**2.** C	**3.** B	**4.** B	**5.** A
6. C	**7.** A	**8.** E	**9.** D	**10.** C
11. A	**12.** D	**13.** C	**14.** C, D	**15.** B
16. B	**17.** D	**18.** E	**19.** A	**20.** B
21. B	**22.** E	**23.** A	**24.** D	**25.** C
26. C	**27.** E	**28.** C	**29.** A	**30.** B

17
Lipids

Learning Goals

- Describe the classes of lipids.
- Draw the condensed or line-angle structural formula for a fatty acid and identify it as saturated or unsaturated.
- Draw the condensed or line-angle structural formula for a wax or triacylglycerol produced by the reaction of a fatty acid and an alcohol or glycerol.
- Draw the condensed or line-angle structural formula for the products of a triacylglycerol that undergoes hydrogenation, hydrolysis, or saponification.
- Describe the structure of a phospholipid containing glycerol or sphingosine.
- Describe the structures of steroids.
- Describe the composition and function of the lipid bilayer in cell membranes.

Chapter Outline

Chapter Opener: Clinical Lipid Specialist

17.1 Lipids

17.2 Fatty Acids

Explore Your World: Solubility of Fats and Oils

Chemistry Link to Health: Omega-3 Fatty Acids in Fish Oils

17.3 Waxes and Triacylglycerols

17.4 Chemical Properties of Triacylglycerols

Chemistry Link to Health: Converting Unsaturated Fats to Saturated Fats: Hydrogenation and Interesterification

Explore Your World: Types of Fats

Chemistry Link to the Environment: Biodiesel as an Alternative Fuel

17.5 Phospholipids

Chemistry Link to Health: Infant Respiratory Distress Syndrome (IRDS)

17.6 Steroids: Cholesterol, Bile Salts, and Steroid Hormones

Chemistry Link to Health: Anabolic Steroids

17.7 Cell Membranes

Clinical Update: Rebecca's Program to Lower Cholesterol in Familial Hypercholesterolemia (FH)

❀ Core Chemistry Skills

- Identifying Fatty Acids (17.2)
- Drawing Structures for Triacylglycerols (17.3)
- Drawing the Products for the Hydrogenation, Hydrolysis, and Saponification of a Triacylglycerol (17.4)
- Identifying the Steroid Nucleus (17.6)

Selected Answers and Solutions to Text Problems

17.1 Because lipids are not soluble in water, a polar solvent, they are nonpolar molecules.

17.3 Lipids provide energy, protection, and insulation for the organs in the body. Lipids are also an important component of cell membranes.

17.5 All fatty acids contain a long chain of carbon atoms with a carboxylic acid group. Saturated fatty acids contain only carbon–carbon single bonds; unsaturated fatty acids contain one or more double bonds.

17.7 **a.**

 b.

17.9 **a.** Lauric acid (12:0) has only carbon–carbon single bonds; it is saturated.
 b. Linolenic acid (18:3) has three carbon–carbon double bonds; it is polyunsaturated.
 c. Palmitoleic acid (16:1) has one carbon–carbon double bond; it is monounsaturated.
 d. Stearic acid (18:0) has only carbon–carbon single bonds; it is saturated.

17.11 In a cis fatty acid, the hydrogen atoms are on the same side of the double bond, which produces a kink in the carbon chain. In a trans fatty acid, the hydrogen atoms are on opposite sides of the double bond, which gives a carbon chain without any kink.

17.13 In an omega-3 fatty acid, there is a double bond beginning at carbon 3 counting from the methyl group. In an omega-6 fatty acid, there is a double bond beginning at carbon 6 counting from the methyl group.

17.15 Arachidonic acid and PGE_1 are both carboxylic acids with 20 carbon atoms. The differences are that arachidonic acid contains four cis double bonds and no other functional groups, whereas PGE_1 has one trans double bond, one ketone functional group, and two hydroxyl functional groups. In addition, a part of the PGE_1 chain forms a cyclopentane ring.

17.17 Prostaglandins raise or lower blood pressure, stimulate contraction and relaxation of smooth muscle, and may cause inflammation and pain.

17.19 Palmitic acid is the 16-carbon saturated fatty acid (16:0), and myricyl alcohol is a 30-carbon long-chain alcohol.

$$CH_3-(CH_2)_{14}-\overset{\overset{\displaystyle O}{\|}}{C}-O-(CH_2)_{29}-CH_3$$

17.21 Triacylglycerols are composed of fatty acids and glycerol. In this case, the fatty acid is stearic acid, an 18-carbon saturated fatty acid (18:0).

17.23 Glyceryl tricaprylate (tricaprylin) has three caprylic acids (an 8-carbon saturated fatty acid, 8:0) forming ester bonds with glycerol.

$$CH_2-O-\overset{\overset{\displaystyle O}{\|}}{C}-(CH_2)_6-CH_3$$

$$CH-O-\overset{\overset{\displaystyle O}{\|}}{C}-(CH_2)_6-CH_3$$

$$CH_2-O-\overset{\overset{\displaystyle O}{\|}}{C}-(CH_2)_6-CH_3$$

17.25 Safflower oil has a lower melting point because it contains mostly polyunsaturated fatty acids, whereas olive oil contains a large amount of monounsaturated oleic acid. A polyunsaturated fatty acid has two or more kinks in its carbon chain, which means it does not have as many dispersion forces compared to the hydrocarbon chains in olive oil.

17.27 Sunflower oil has about 24% monounsaturated fats, while safflower oil has about 18%. Sunflower oil has about 66% polyunsaturated fats, while safflower oil has about 73%.

17.29 a. The reaction of palm oil with KOH is saponification, and the products are glycerol and the potassium salts of the fatty acids, which are soaps.

   b. In acid hydrolysis, glyceryl trilinoleate reacts with water, which splits the ester bonds to produce glycerol and three molecules of linoleic acid.

17.31 Hydrogenation of an unsaturated triacylglycerol adds H_2 to each of the double bonds, producing a saturated triacylglycerol containing only carbon–carbon single bonds.

$$CH_2-O-\overset{\overset{\displaystyle O}{\|}}{C}-(CH_2)_7-CH{=}CH-(CH_2)_5-CH_3$$

$$CH-O-\overset{\overset{\displaystyle O}{\|}}{C}-(CH_2)_7-CH{=}CH-(CH_2)_5-CH_3 + 3H_2 \xrightarrow{Ni}$$

$$CH_2-O-\overset{\overset{\displaystyle O}{\|}}{C}-(CH_2)_7-CH{=}CH-(CH_2)_5-CH_3$$

$$CH_2-O-\overset{\overset{\displaystyle O}{\|}}{C}-(CH_2)_{14}-CH_3$$

$$CH-O-\overset{\overset{\displaystyle O}{\|}}{C}-(CH_2)_{14}-CH_3$$

$$CH_2-O-\overset{\overset{\displaystyle O}{\|}}{C}-(CH_2)_{14}-CH_3$$

17.33 Acid hydrolysis of a fat gives glycerol and the fatty acids.

$$CH_2-O-\overset{\overset{\displaystyle O}{\|}}{C}-(CH_2)_{12}-CH_3$$

$$CH-O-\overset{\overset{\displaystyle O}{\|}}{C}-(CH_2)_{12}-CH_3 + 3H_2O \xrightarrow{H^+, \text{ heat}}$$

$$CH_2-O-\overset{\overset{\displaystyle O}{\|}}{C}-(CH_2)_{12}-CH_3$$

$$CH_2-OH$$
$$CH-OH + 3HO-\overset{\overset{\displaystyle O}{\|}}{C}-(CH_2)_{12}-CH_3$$
$$CH_2-OH$$

17.35 Basic hydrolysis (saponification) of a fat gives glycerol and the salts of the fatty acids.

$$CH_2-O-\overset{\overset{\displaystyle O}{\|}}{C}-(CH_2)_{12}-CH_3$$

$$CH-O-\overset{\overset{\displaystyle O}{\|}}{C}-(CH_2)_{12}-CH_3 + 3NaOH \xrightarrow{\text{Heat}}$$

$$CH_2-O-\overset{\overset{\displaystyle O}{\|}}{C}-(CH_2)_{12}-CH_3$$

$$CH_2-OH$$
$$CH-OH + 3Na^+\ {}^-O-\overset{\overset{\displaystyle O}{\|}}{C}-(CH_2)_{12}-CH_3$$
$$CH_2-OH$$

17.37

$$CH_2-O-\overset{\overset{\displaystyle O}{\|}}{C}-(CH_2)_{16}-CH_3$$
$$CH-O-\overset{\overset{\displaystyle O}{\|}}{C}-(CH_2)_{16}-CH_3$$
$$CH_2-O-\overset{\overset{\displaystyle O}{\|}}{C}-(CH_2)_{16}-CH_3$$

17.39 A triacylglycerol consists of glycerol and three fatty acids. A glycerophospholipid also consists of glycerol, but has two fatty acids with the hydroxyl group on the third carbon attached by a phosphate bond to phosphoric acid, which forms another phosphoester bond to an ionized amino alcohol.

17.41

$$CH_2-O-\overset{\overset{\displaystyle O}{\|}}{C}-(CH_2)_{14}-CH_3$$
$$CH-O-\overset{\overset{\displaystyle O}{\|}}{C}-(CH_2)_{14}-CH_3$$
$$CH_2-O-\overset{\overset{\displaystyle O}{\|}}{\underset{\underset{\displaystyle O^-}{|}}{P}}-O-CH_2-CH_2-\overset{+}{N}H_3$$

17.43 This glycerophospholipid is a cephalin. It contains glycerol, oleic acid, stearic acid, a phosphate group, and ethanolamine.

17.45 a. This phospholipid is formed from sphingosine.
   b. The fatty acid is palmitic acid (16:0).
   c. An amide bond connects the fatty acid to sphingosine.
   d. The ionized amino alcohol is ethanolamine.

17.47

17.49 Bile salts act to emulsify fat globules, allowing the fat to be more easily digested by lipases.

17.51 Chylomicrons have a lower density than VLDL (very-low-density lipoprotein). They pick up triacylglycerols from the intestine, whereas VLDL transports triacylglycerols synthesized in the liver.

17.53 "Bad" cholesterol is the cholesterol carried by LDL that can form deposits in the arteries called plaque, which narrows the arteries.

17.55 Both estradiol and testosterone contain the steroid nucleus and a hydroxyl group. Testosterone has a ketone group, a double bond, and two methyl groups. Estradiol has an aromatic ring, a hydroxyl group in place of the ketone, and a methyl group.

17.57 Cortisol (b), estradiol (c), and testosterone (d) are steroid hormones.

17.59 The function of the lipid bilayer in the cell membrane is to keep the cell contents separated from the outside environment and to allow the cell to regulate the movement of substances into and out of the cell.

17.61 Because the molecules of cholesterol are large and rigid, they reduce the flexibility of the lipid bilayer and add strength to the cell membrane.

17.63 The peripheral proteins in the membrane emerge on the inner or outer surface only, whereas the integral proteins extend through the membrane to both surfaces.

17.65 a. A molecule moving through a protein channel is an example of facilitated transport.
  b. A molecule, like O_2, moving from higher concentration to lower concentration is an example of passive transport (diffusion).

17.67 The functional groups in Pravachol are ester, alcohol, alkene, and carboxylic acid.

17.69 a. $\dfrac{80.\ \text{mg Pravachol}}{1\ \text{day}} \times \dfrac{1\ \text{g Pravachol}}{1000\ \text{mg Pravachol}} \times \dfrac{7\ \text{days}}{1\ \text{week}} = 0.56\ \text{g of Pravachol/week (2 SFs)}$

  b. $\dfrac{18\ \text{mg cholesterol}}{5.0\ \text{mL blood}} \times \dfrac{100\ \text{mL blood}}{1\ \text{dL blood}} = 360\ \text{mg/dL (2 SFs)}$

17.71

$$CH_2\!-\!O\!-\!\overset{\displaystyle O}{\overset{\|}{C}}\!-\!(CH_2)_{14}\!-\!CH_3$$
$$CH\!-\!O\!-\!\overset{\displaystyle O}{\overset{\|}{C}}\!-\!(CH_2)_{14}\!-\!CH_3$$
$$CH_2\!-\!O\!-\!\overset{\displaystyle O}{\overset{\|}{C}}\!-\!(CH_2)_{14}\!-\!CH_3$$

17.73 a. monounsaturated fatty acid
  b. polyunsaturated omega-6 fatty acid
  c. polyunsaturated omega-3 fatty acid

17.75 a. Beeswax and carnauba are waxes. Vegetable oil and glyceryl tricaprate (tricaprin) are triacylglycerols.

  b.
$$CH_2\!-\!O\!-\!\overset{\displaystyle O}{\overset{\|}{C}}\!-\!(CH_2)_8\!-\!CH_3$$
$$CH\!-\!O\!-\!\overset{\displaystyle O}{\overset{\|}{C}}\!-\!(CH_2)_8\!-\!CH_3$$
$$CH_2\!-\!O\!-\!\overset{\displaystyle O}{\overset{\|}{C}}\!-\!(CH_2)_8\!-\!CH_3$$

17.77 a. A typical unsaturated fatty acid has a cis double bond.
  b. A cis unsaturated fatty acid contains hydrogen atoms on the same side of each double bond. A trans unsaturated fatty acid has hydrogen atoms on opposite sides of each double bond.

  c. $CH_3\!-\!(CH_2)_6\!-\!CH_2$
$$\underset{\displaystyle CH_3-(CH_2)_6-CH_2}{\overset{\displaystyle H}{}}\!\!\diagdown C\!=\!C\diagup\!\!\overset{\displaystyle CH_2-(CH_2)_6-\overset{O}{\overset{\|}{C}}-OH}{\underset{\displaystyle H}{}}$$

17.79 a. $46\ \text{g fat} \times \dfrac{9\ \text{kcal}}{1\ \text{g fat}} = 410\ \text{kcal from fat} \qquad \dfrac{410\ \text{kcal}}{830\ \text{kcal}} \times 100\% = 49\%\ \text{fat (2 SFs)}$

  b. $29\ \text{g fat} \times \dfrac{9\ \text{kcal}}{1\ \text{g fat}} = 260\ \text{kcal from fat} \qquad \dfrac{260\ \text{kcal}}{520\ \text{kcal}} \times 100\% = 50.\%\ \text{fat (2 SFs)}$

  c. $18\ \text{g fat} \times \dfrac{9\ \text{kcal}}{1\ \text{g fat}} = 160\ \text{kcal from fat} \qquad \dfrac{160\ \text{kcal}}{560\ \text{kcal}} \times 100\% = 29\%\ \text{fat (2 SFs)}$

The fats in these foods are from animal sources and would be mostly saturated fats.

17.81 a. Beeswax is a wax.
   b. Cholesterol is a steroid.
   c. Lecithin is a glycerophospholipid.
   d. Glyceryl tripalmitate (tripalmitin) is a triacylglycerol.
   e. Sodium stearate is a soap.
   f. Safflower oil is a triacylglycerol.

17.83 a. Estrogen contains the steroid nucleus (5).
   b. Cephalin contains glycerol (1), fatty acids (2), phosphate (3), and an amino alcohol (4).
   c. Waxes contain fatty acid (2).
   d. Triacylglycerols contain glycerol (1) and fatty acids (2).

17.85 Cholesterol (a) and carbohydrates (c) are found in cell membranes.

17.87
$$CH_2-O-\overset{\overset{\displaystyle O}{\|}}{C}-(CH_2)_{16}-CH_3$$
$$CH-O-\overset{\overset{\displaystyle O}{\|}}{C}-(CH_2)_{16}-CH_3$$
$$CH_2-O-\overset{\overset{\displaystyle O}{\|}}{\underset{\underset{\displaystyle O^-}{|}}{P}}-O-CH_2-CH_2-\overset{+}{N}H_3$$

17.89 a. HDL (4) is known as "good" cholesterol.
   b. LDL (3) transports most of the cholesterol to the cells.
   c. Chylomicrons (1) carry triacylglycerols from the intestine to the fat cells.
   d. HDL (4) transports cholesterol to the liver.

17.91 a. Adding NaOH will saponify lipids such as glyceryl tristearate (tristearin), forming glycerol and salts of the fatty acids that are soluble in water and would wash down the drain.

   b.
$$CH_2-O-\overset{\overset{\displaystyle O}{\|}}{C}-(CH_2)_{16}-CH_3$$
$$CH-O-\overset{\overset{\displaystyle O}{\|}}{C}-(CH_2)_{16}-CH_3 \ + 3NaOH \xrightarrow{\text{Heat}}$$
$$CH_2-O-\overset{\overset{\displaystyle O}{\|}}{C}-(CH_2)_{16}-CH_3$$

$$CH_2-OH$$
$$CH-OH \ + 3Na^+ \ ^-O-\overset{\overset{\displaystyle O}{\|}}{C}-(CH_2)_{16}-CH_3$$
$$CH_2-OH$$

   Glycerol   Salts of stearic acid

   c. Tristearin = $C_{57}H_{110}O_6$
   Molar mass of tristearin ($C_{57}H_{110}O_6$)
   = 57(12.01 g) + 110(1.008 g) + 6(16.00 g) = 891.5 g/mole

   $$10.0 \text{ g tristearin} \times \frac{1 \text{ mole tristearin}}{891.5 \text{ g tristearin}} \times \frac{3 \text{ moles NaOH}}{1 \text{ mole tristearin}} \times \frac{1000 \text{ mL solution}}{0.500 \text{ mole NaOH}}$$
   = 67.3 mL of NaOH solution (3 SFs)

Lance, an environmental health practitioner, has returned to a farm where he found small amounts of fenbendazole, a sheep dewormer, in the soil. When he is working on-site, he wears protective clothing while he obtains samples of soil and water. His recent tests indicate that the presence of fenbendazole is now within the acceptable range in both the soil and the water in the lake near the farm. Lance specializes in measuring levels of contaminants in soil and water caused by manufacturing processes or farming. In his work, Lance also acts as an advisor, consultant, and safety officer to ensure that soil and water on the farm are safe and to maintain protection of the environment.

Draw the line-angle structural formula for imidazole, a component of fenbendazole.

Credit: Bart Coenders/E+/Getty Images

CHAPTER READINESS*

⚛ Core Chemistry Skills

- Writing Equations for Reactions of Acids and Bases (10.6)

- Naming and Drawing Alkanes (11.2)

*These Core Chemistry Skills from previous chapters are listed here for your review as you proceed to the new material in this chapter.

18.1 Amines

Learning Goal: Name amines using IUPAC and common names; draw the condensed or line-angle structural formulas given the names. Classify amines as primary (1°), secondary (2°), and tertiary (3°).

- Amines are derivatives of ammonia (NH_3), in which alkyl or aromatic groups replace one or more hydrogen atoms.

- In the IUPAC system, the *e* in the corresponding alkane name of the longest chain bonded to the N atom is replaced by *amine*. Alkyl groups or aromatic groups attached to the N atom are named with the prefix *N-*.

- Amines may be named by their common names in which the names of the alkyl groups are listed alphabetically preceding the suffix *amine*.

Methylamine

Dimethylamine

CH_3-NH_2	$CH_3-\overset{\displaystyle CH_3}{\underset{\displaystyle \,}{N}}-H$	$CH_3-\overset{\displaystyle CH_3}{\underset{\displaystyle \,}{N}}-CH_3$
Methanamine (methylamine)	*N*-Methylmethanamine (dimethylamine)	*N, N*-Dimethylmethanamine (trimethylamine)

- The NH$_2$ group is named as an *amino* group in compounds that also contain the functional group carboxylic acid, ester, amide, aldehyde, ketone, or alcohol.

Trimethylamine

2-aminopropanoic acid

- The amine of benzene is named aniline.

NH$_2$

aniline

- Amines are classified as primary, secondary, or tertiary when the nitrogen atom is bonded to one, two, or three alkyl or aromatic groups.

CH$_3$—NH$_2$ CH$_3$—N—H   CH$_3$—N—CH$_3$

Primary (1°)   Secondary (2°)   Tertiary (3°)   Primary (1°)

- Many amines, which are prevalent in synthetic and naturally occurring compounds, have physiological activity.

	Guide to the IUPAC Naming of Amines
STEP 1	Name the longest carbon chain bonded to the N atom by replacing the *e* of its alkane name with *amine*.
STEP 2	Number the carbon chain to show the position of the amine group and other substituents.
STEP 3	Any alkyl group attached to the nitrogen atom is indicated by the prefix *N-* and the alkyl name, which is placed in front of the amine name.

	Guide to Naming Compounds with Two Functional Groups
STEP 1	Identify the functional group with the highest priority and use the longest carbon chain to give the compound name.
STEP 2	Number the carbon chain, and give the position and name of the main group and the substituent group on the carbon chain.

♦ **Learning Exercise 18.1A**

Give the IUPAC name and common name, if any, for each of the following:

1. $CH_3-\overset{\overset{H}{|}}{N}-CH_2-CH_3$

2. [line-angle structure of N-ethyl-1-butanamine]

3. [cyclohexane with NH_2]

4. [benzene ring with NH_2 and Br]

5. $CH_3-CH_2-\overset{\overset{CH_3}{|}}{N}-CH_3$

6. [line-angle structure with NH_2 and O / OH]

Answers

1. *N*-methylethanamine (ethylmethylamine)
2. *N*-ethyl-1-butanamine (butylethylamine)
3. cyclohexanamine (cyclohexylamine)
4. 3-bromoaniline (*m*-bromoaniline)
5. *N,N*-dimethylethanamine (ethyldimethylamine)
6. 3-aminobutanoic acid (β-aminobutyric acid)

♦ **Learning Exercise 18.1B**

Draw the condensed structural formulas for **1** and **2** and the line-angle structural formulas for **3** and **4**:

1. 2-propanamine

2. *N*-ethyl-*N*-methyl-1-butanamine

3. 4-bromoaniline

4. *N,N*-dimethyl-3-pentanamine

Answers

1. $CH_3-\overset{\overset{NH_2}{|}}{CH}-CH_3$

2. $CH_3-CH_2-\overset{\overset{CH_3}{|}}{N}-CH_2-CH_2-CH_2-CH_3$

3. [benzene ring with NH_2 and Br]

4. [line-angle structure with N]

♦ **Learning Exercise 18.1C**

Identify each of the following as a primary (1°), secondary (2°), or tertiary (3°) amine:

1. $CH_3-CH_2-CH_2-CH_2-\overset{\overset{CH_3}{|}}{N}-H$

2. $CH_3-CH_2-\overset{\overset{CH_3}{|}}{N}-CH_2-CH_2-CH_2-CH_3$

3.

NH_2

Cl

4.

Answers   **1.** secondary (2°)   **2.** tertiary (3°)   **3.** primary (1°)   **4.** tertiary (3°)

18.2   Properties of Amines

Learning Goal: Describe the boiling points and solubility of amines; write equations for the dissociation and neutralization of amines.

- The N—H bonds in primary and secondary amines form hydrogen bonds.
- Amines have higher boiling points than hydrocarbons but lower boiling points than alcohols of similar mass because the N atom is not as electronegative as the O atom in alcohols.
- Hydrogen bonding makes amines with one to six carbon atoms soluble in water.
- In water, amines act as weak bases by accepting protons from water to produce ammonium and hydroxide ions.

$$CH_3—NH_2 + H_2O \rightleftharpoons CH_3—\overset{+}{N}H_3 \quad + \quad OH^-$$

Methylamine   Methylammonium ion   Hydroxide ion

- Strong acids neutralize amines to yield ammonium salts.

$$CH_3—NH_2 + HCl \longrightarrow CH_3—\overset{+}{N}H_3\,Cl^-$$

Methylamine   Methylammonium chloride

- In a quaternary ammonium salt, a nitrogen atom is bonded to four carbon groups.

♦ Learning Exercise 18.2A

Indicate the compound in each pair that has the higher boiling point.

1. $CH_3—NH_2$ or $CH_3—OH$ _____

2. $CH_3—CH_2—CH_2$ or $CH_3—CH_2—NH_2$ _____

3. $CH_3—\overset{\overset{\displaystyle H}{|}}{N}—CH_3$ or $CH_3—CH_2—NH_2$ _____

Answers   **1.** $CH_3—OH$ **2.** $CH_3—CH_2—NH_2$ **3.** $CH_3—CH_2—NH_2$

♦ **Learning Exercise 18.2B**

Draw the condensed or line-angle structural formula for the product of each of the following reactions:

1. $CH_3-CH_2-NH_2 + H_2O \rightleftharpoons$

2. $CH_3-CH_2-CH_2-NH_2 + HCl \longrightarrow$

3. $CH_3-CH_2-NH-CH_3 + HCl \longrightarrow$

4. (cyclohexane with NH_2) $+ HBr \longrightarrow$

5. (cyclopentane with NH_2) $+ H_2O \rightleftharpoons$

6. $CH_3-CH_2-NH_3^+ Cl^- + NaOH \longrightarrow$

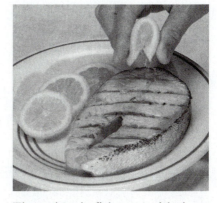

The amines in fish react with the acid in lemon to neutralize the "fishy" odor.

Credit: Pearson Education / Pearson Science

Answers

1. $CH_3-CH_2-NH_3^+ + OH^-$

2. $CH_3-CH_2-CH_2-NH_3^+ Cl^-$

3. $CH_3-CH_2-\overset{+}{N}H_2-CH_3Cl^-$

4. (cyclohexane with $\overset{+}{N}H_3\, Br^-$)

5. (cyclopentane with $\overset{+}{N}H_3 + OH^-$)

6. $CH_3-CH_2-NH_2 + NaCl + H_2O$

♦ **Learning Exercise 18.2C**

Indicate if each of the following is soluble in water. Explain.

a. $CH_3-CH_2-CH_2-\underset{\underset{CH_2-CH_3}{|}}{\overset{\overset{CH_2-CH_2-CH_3}{|}}{N}}$

b. $CH_3-CH_2-\underset{\underset{H}{}}{\overset{\overset{NH_2}{|}}{C}}H-CH_2-CH_3$

c. (line-angle structure with NH_2)

Answers

a. No, an amine with eight carbon atoms is mostly nonpolar and not soluble in water.
b. Yes, amines with five carbon atoms form hydrogen bonds, which makes them soluble in water.
c. Yes, amines with four carbon atoms form hydrogen bonds, which makes them soluble in water.

18.3 Heterocyclic Amines

Learning Goal: Identify heterocyclic amines; distinguish between the types of heterocyclic amines.

- A heterocyclic amine is a cyclic compound containing one or more nitrogen atoms in the ring.
- Most heterocyclic amines contain five or six atoms in the ring.
- An alkaloid is a physiologically active amine obtained from plants.

Pyrrolidine   Pyrrole   Imidazole   Piperidine   Pyridine   Pyrimidine

♦ **Learning Exercise 18.3**

Match each of the following heterocyclic structures with its correct name:

a.

b.

c.

d.

e.

f.

1. _____ pyrrolidine   2. _____ imidazole   3. _____ pyridine

4. _____ pyrrole   5. _____ pyrimidine   6. _____ piperidine

Answers   1. c   2. e   3. f   4. a   5. b   6. d

18.4 Neurotransmitters

Learning Goal: Describe the role of amines as neurotransmitters.

- Neurotransmitters are chemical compounds that transit impulses from a nerve cell (neuron) to a target cell in another nerve cell, a muscle cell, or a gland cell.
- A neuron consists of a cell body and filaments called axons and dendrites that form synapses.
- When an impulse arrives at the neuron, a neurotransmitter that is stored at the ends of the axon terminal is released into the synapse and diffuses to its receptor sites on the dendrites of adjacent nerve cells.
- Some examples of neurotransmitters are: acetylcholine, dopamine, epinephrine, norepinephrine, serotonin, and histamine.

♦ **Learning Exercise 18.4A**

Draw the condensed structural formulas for each of the following neurotransmitters:

1. histamine
2. epinephrine

3. gamma (γ)-aminobutyric acid (GABA)

Answers

1.

$$\text{imidazole ring}\!-\!CH_2\!-\!CH_2\!-\!\overset{+}{N}H_3$$

2.

$$HO,\ HO\!-\!\bigcirc\!-\!CH\!-\!CH_2\!-\!\overset{+}{N}H_2\!-\!CH_3$$
$$\qquad\qquad\qquad |$$
$$\qquad\qquad\qquad OH$$

3. $H_3\overset{+}{N}\!-\!CH_2\!-\!CH_2\!-\!CH_2\!-\!\overset{\displaystyle O}{\overset{\|}{C}}\!-\!O^-$

♦ **Learning Exercise 18.4B**

Match the physiological process affected by each of the following neurotransmitters (**a** to **e**) with the correct physiological function or effect (**1** to **5**).

a. _____ dopamine   **b.** _____ serotonin   **c.** _____ GABA

d. _____ epinephrine   **e.** _____ acetylcholine

1. excitatory function that stimulates muscle contraction and plays a role in memory and sleep

2. inhibitory function that blocks the firing by a neuron

3. inhibitory function that lowers anxiety

4. low levels can lead to depression, anxiety, and eating disorders

5. an excitatory function that increases heart rate and blood pressure

Answers   **a.** 1   **b.** 4   **c.** 3   **d.** 5   **e.** 2

♦ **Learning Exercise 18.4C**

Match the disorder (**1** to **4**) that may be caused by abnormal levels of each of the following neurotransmitters (**a** to **d**):

a. _____ dopamine   **b.** _____ norepinephrine

c. _____ histamine   **d.** _____ acetylcholine

Chapter 18

1. Low levels can cause Parkinson's disease.

2. Low levels can cause Alzheimer's disease.

3. Low levels can lead to attention deficit disorder.

4. High levels can cause allergic reactions.

Answers   **a.** 1   **b.** 3   **c.** 4   **d.** 2

18.5 Amides

Learning Goal: Draw the amide products from amidation, and give the IUPAC and common names.

- Amides are derivatives of carboxylic acids in which an amine group replaces the —OH group in the carboxylic acid.

- Amides are named by replacing the *ic acid* or *oic acid* ending by *amide*. When an alkyl group is attached to the N atom, it is listed as *N*-alkyl.

$$CH_3-\overset{\overset{\displaystyle O}{\|}}{C}-NH_2 \qquad \text{Ethanamide (acetamide)}$$

$$CH_3-\overset{\overset{\displaystyle O}{\|}}{C}-NH-CH_3 \qquad \textit{N}\text{-Methylethanamide; (}\textit{N}\text{-methylacetamide)}$$

- When a carboxylic acid reacts with ammonia or an amine, an amide is produced.

$$CH_3-\overset{\overset{\displaystyle O}{\|}}{C}-OH + NH_3 \xrightarrow{\text{Heat}} CH_3-\overset{\overset{\displaystyle O}{\|}}{C}-NH_2 + H_2O$$

$$CH_3-\overset{\overset{\displaystyle O}{\|}}{C}-OH + NH_2-CH_3 \xrightarrow{\text{Heat}} CH_3-\overset{\overset{\displaystyle O}{\|}}{C}-NH-CH_3 + H_2O$$

- Amides with one to five carbons are soluble in water.

Guide to Naming Amides	
STEP 1	Replace *oic acid* (IUPAC) or *ic acid* (common) in the carboxyl name with *amide*.
STEP 2	Name each substituent on the N atom using the prefix *N*- and the alkyl name.

♦ **Learning Exercise 18.5A**

Draw the condensed structural formulas of the amides formed in each of the following reactions:

CORE CHEMISTRY SKILL

Forming Amides

1. $CH_3-CH_2-\overset{\overset{\displaystyle O}{\|}}{C}-OH + NH_3 \xrightarrow{\text{Heat}}$

2. $\langle\bigcirc\rangle-\overset{\overset{\displaystyle O}{\|}}{C}-OH + CH_3-NH_2 \xrightarrow{\text{Heat}}$

438   Copyright © 2015 Pearson Education, Inc.

3. $CH_3-\overset{\overset{\displaystyle O}{\|}}{C}-OH + \overset{\overset{\displaystyle CH_3}{|}}{N}H-CH_3 \xrightarrow{\text{Heat}}$

Answers

1. $CH_3-CH_2-\overset{\overset{\displaystyle O}{\|}}{C}-NH_2$

2. benzamide structure with $\overset{\overset{\displaystyle O}{\|}}{C}$ and $NH-CH_3$

3. $CH_3-\overset{\overset{\displaystyle O}{\|}}{C}-\overset{\overset{\displaystyle CH_3}{|}}{N}-CH_3$

♦ Learning Exercise 18.5B

Name each of the following amides:

1. $CH_3-CH_2-\overset{\overset{\displaystyle O}{\|}}{C}-NH_2$ _____

2. benzamide structure with $\overset{\overset{\displaystyle O}{\|}}{C}$ and NH_2 _____

3. line-angle structure with NH_2 _____

4. $CH_3-\overset{\overset{\displaystyle O}{\|}}{C}-NH-CH_2-CH_3$ _____

5. benzamide ring structure with $\overset{\overset{\displaystyle O}{\|}}{C}$, N, H _____

Answers
1. propanamide (propionamide)   2. benzamide
3. pentanamide   4. *N*-ethylethanamide (*N*-ethylacetamide)
5. *N*-ethylbenzamide

♦ Learning Exercise 18.5C

Draw the condensed structural formulas for **1** and **2** and line-angle structural formulas for **3** and **4**.

1. butanamide

2. *N*-methylbutanamide

3. 3-chloropentanamide

4. benzamide

Answers

1. $CH_3-CH_2-CH_2-\overset{\overset{\displaystyle O}{\|}}{C}-NH_2$ 2. $CH_3-CH_2-CH_2-\overset{\overset{\displaystyle O}{\|}}{C}-NH-CH_3$

3. [structure: butanamide with Cl substituent and NH_2]

4. [structure: benzamide, benzene ring with $\overset{\overset{\displaystyle O}{\|}}{C}-NH_2$]

18.6 Hydrolysis of Amides

Learning Goal: Write balanced chemical equations for the hydrolysis of amides.

- Amides undergo acid and base hydrolysis to produce the carboxylic acid (or carboxylate salt) and the amine (or amine salt).

$$CH_3-\overset{\overset{\displaystyle O}{\|}}{C}-NH_2 + HCl + H_2O \xrightarrow{\text{Heat}} CH_3-\overset{\overset{\displaystyle O}{\|}}{C}-OH + NH_4^+ \, Cl^-$$

$$CH_3-\overset{\overset{\displaystyle O}{\|}}{C}-NH_2 + NaOH \xrightarrow{\text{Heat}} CH_3-\overset{\overset{\displaystyle O}{\|}}{C}-O^-Na^+ + NH_3$$

Key Terms for Sections 18.1–18.6

✴ CORE CHEMISTRY SKILL

Hydrolyzing Amides

Match the key term with the correct description below:

a. heterocyclic amine	**b.** amidation	**c.** amine
d. amide	**e.** alkaloid	**f.** neurotransmitter

1. _____ a compound that contains nitrogen and is active physiologically

2. _____ a cyclic organic compound that contains one or more nitrogen atoms

3. _____ the reaction of a carboxylic acid and an amine

4. _____ the hydrolysis of this compound produces a carboxylic acid and an amine

5. _____ an organic compound that contains an amino group

6. _____ a compound that transmits an impulse from a neuron to a target cell

Answers   1. e   2. a   3. b   4. d   5. c   6. f

♦ **Learning Exercise 18.6**

Draw the condensed structural formulas for the products formed by the hydrolysis of each of the following with HCl and with NaOH:

1. $CH_3-CH_2-\overset{\overset{\displaystyle O}{\|}}{C}-NH_2$

2. $CH_3-\overset{\overset{O}{\|}}{C}-\overset{\overset{H}{|}}{N}-CH_2-CH_3$

Answers

1. (HCl) $CH_3-CH_2-\overset{\overset{O}{\|}}{C}-OH + NH_4^+ Cl^-$ (NaOH) $CH_3-CH_2-\overset{\overset{O}{\|}}{C}-O^-Na^+ + NH_3$

2. (HCl) $CH_3-\overset{\overset{O}{\|}}{C}-OH + \overset{+}{N}H_3-CH_2-CH_3\ Cl^-$ (NaOH) $CH_3-\overset{\overset{O}{\|}}{C}-O^-Na^+ + NH_2-CH_2-CH_3$

Checklist for Chapter 18

You are ready to take the Practice Test for Chapter 18. Be sure that you have accomplished the following learning goals for this chapter. If not, review the section listed at the end of the goal. Then apply your new skills and understanding to the Practice Test.

After studying Chapter 18, I can successfully:

_____ Write the IUPAC and common names of amines. (18.1)

_____ Draw the condensed and line-angle structural formulas of amines. (18.1)

_____ Classify amines as primary, secondary, or tertiary. (18.1)

_____ Compare the boiling points and solubility of alkanes, alcohols, and amines of similar mass. (18.2)

_____ Write equations for the ionization and neutralization of amines. (18.2)

_____ Identify heterocyclic amines. (18.3)

_____ Describe the role of amines as neurotransmitters. (18.4)

_____ Draw the condensed structural formulas of neurotransmitters. (18.4)

_____ Write the IUPAC and common names of amides, and draw their condensed structural formulas. (18.5)

_____ Write equations for the acidic and basic hydrolysis of amides. (18.6)

Practice Test

Classify the amines in questions 1 through 6 as a: (18.1)

    A. primary amine   **B.** secondary amine   **C.** tertiary amine

1. _____ $CH_3-\overset{\overset{CH_3}{|}}{CH}-NH_2$ 2. _____ $CH_3-CH_2-\overset{\overset{CH_3}{|}}{N}-CH_3$

3. _____ $CH_3-CH_2-\overset{\overset{\displaystyle NH_2}{|}}{CH}-CH_2-CH_3$

4. _____ $CH_3-\overset{\overset{\displaystyle H}{|}}{N}-CH_2-CH_3$

5. _____ $CH_3-\overset{\overset{\displaystyle CH_3}{|}}{CH}-CH_2-\overset{\overset{\displaystyle H}{|}}{N}-\overset{\overset{\displaystyle CH_3}{|}}{CH}-CH_3$

6. _____ $CH_3-\overset{\overset{\displaystyle CH_3}{|}}{\underset{\underset{\displaystyle CH_3}{|}}{C}}-CH_2-NH_2$

Match the amines and amides in questions 7 through 11 with the following names: (18.1)

   A. ethyldimethylamine   **B.** butanamide   **C.** *N*-methylacetamide

   D. benzamide   **E.** *N*-ethylbutyramide

7. _____ $CH_3-CH_2-\overset{\overset{\displaystyle CH_3}{|}}{N}-CH_3$

8. _____ $CH_3-CH_2-CH_2-\overset{\overset{\displaystyle O}{||}}{C}-NH_2$

9. _____ benzamide structure with $\overset{\overset{\displaystyle O}{||}}{C}-NH_2$

10. _____ $CH_3-CH_2-CH_2-\overset{\overset{\displaystyle O}{||}}{C}-\overset{\overset{\displaystyle H}{|}}{N}-CH_2-CH_3$

11. _____ $CH_3-\overset{\overset{\displaystyle O}{||}}{C}-\overset{\overset{\displaystyle H}{|}}{N}-CH_3$

In questions 12 through 15, identify the compound with the higher boiling point: (18.2)

12. **A.** $CH_3-CH_2-NH_2$ or **B.** CH_3-CH_2-OH

13. **A.** $CH_3-NH-CH_3$ or **B.** $CH_3-CH_2-NH_2$

14. **A.** $CH_3-CH_2-CH_2-CH_3$ or **B.** $CH_3-CH_2-CH_2-NH_2$

15. **A.** $CH_3-CH_2-CH_2-OH$ or **B.** $CH_3-CH_2-CH_2-NH_2$

For questions 16 through 19, identify the product as A to D: (18.2, 18.5, 18.6)

   A. $CH_3-CH_2-\overset{\overset{\displaystyle O}{||}}{C}-OH + NH_4^+ Cl^-$ **B.** $CH_3-CH_2-\overset{+}{N}H_3\,Cl^-$

   C. $CH_3-CH_2-CH_2-\overset{+}{N}H_3 + OH^-$ **D.** $CH_3-\overset{\overset{\displaystyle O}{||}}{C}-NH_2$

16. _____ ionization of 1-propanamine in water

17. _____ acid hydrolysis of propanamide

18. _____ reaction of ethanamine and hydrochloric acid

19. _____ amidation of acetic acid

20. Amines used in drugs are converted to their amine salt because the salt is (18.2)

   A. a solid at room temperature   **B.** soluble in water   **C.** odorless

   D. soluble in body fluids   **E.** all of these

21. Piperidine is a heterocyclic amine that (18.3)

   A. has a ring of six atoms
   B. has a ring of five atoms
   C. contains two nitrogen atoms in a ring
   D. has one nitrogen atom in an aromatic ring system
   E. has two nitrogen atoms in an aromatic ring system

22. Alkaloids are (18.3)

   A. physiologically active nitrogen-containing compounds
   B. produced by plants
   C. used in anesthetics, in antidepressants, and as stimulants
   D. often habit-forming
   E. all of these

For questions 23 to 26, match the name of the alkaloid (A to D) with the correct description (18.3)

   A. caffeine   **B.** nicotine   **C.** morphine   **D.** quinine

23. _____ a painkiller from the opium poppy plant

24. _____ obtained from the bark of the cinchona tree and used in the treatment of malaria

25. _____ a stimulant obtained from the leaves of tobacco plants

26. _____ a stimulant obtained from coffee beans and tea leaves

For questions 27 to 30, match the name of the neurotransmitter (A to D) with its structure: (18.4)

   A. dopamine   **B.** glutamate   **C.** acetylcholine   **D.** serotonin

27. _____ $CH_3-\overset{O}{\underset{}{C}}-O-CH_2-CH_2-\overset{CH_3}{\underset{CH_3}{\overset{+}{N}}}-CH_3$

28. _____ [serotonin structure: HO on indole ring with $CH_2-CH_2-\overset{+}{N}H_3$]

29. _____ [dopamine structure: HO, HO on benzene ring with $-CH_2-CH_2-\overset{+}{N}H_3$]

30. _____ [glutamate structure: $\overset{O}{\underset{O^-}{C}}-\overset{}{\underset{\overset{+}{N}H_3... }{CH}}... H_3\overset{+}{N}-CH-CH_2-CH_2-\overset{O}{C}-O^-$]

Answers to the Practice Test

1. A	**2.** C	**3.** A	**4.** B	**5.** B
6. A	**7.** A	**8.** B	**9.** D	**10.** E
11. C	**12.** B	**13.** B	**14.** B	**15.** A
16. C	**17.** A	**18.** B	**19.** D	**20.** E
21. A	**22.** E	**23.** C	**24.** D	**25.** B
26. A	**27.** C	**28.** D	**29.** A	**30.** B

18

Amines and Amides

Learning Goals

- Name amines using IUPAC and common names; draw the condensed or line-angle structural formulas given the names.
- Classify amines as primary (1°), secondary (2°), or tertiary (3°).
- Describe the boiling points and solubility of amines; write equations for the dissociation and neutralization of amines.
- Identify heterocyclic amines; distinguish between the types of heterocyclic amines.
- Describe the role of amines as neurotransmitters.
- Draw the amide product from amidation, and give the IUPAC and common names.
- Write balanced chemical equations for the hydrolysis of amides.

Chapter Outline

Chapter Opener: Environmental Health Practitioner

18.1 Amines

18.2 Properties of Amines

18.3 Heterocyclic Amines

Chemistry Link to Health: Synthesizing Drugs

18.4 Neurotransmitters

18.5 Amides

Chemistry Link to Health: Amides in Health and Medicine

18.6 Hydrolysis of Amides

Clinical Update: Testing Soil and Water Samples for Chemicals

⚛ Core Chemistry Skills

- Forming Amides (18.5)
- Hydrolyzing Amides (18.6)

Selected Answers and Solutions to Text Problems

18.1 In a primary (1°) amine, there is one alkyl group (and two hydrogens) attached to a nitrogen atom.

18.3 **a.** This is a primary (1°) amine; there is only one alkyl group (and two hydrogens) attached to the nitrogen atom.
  b. This is a secondary (2°) amine; there are two alkyl groups (and one hydrogen) attached to the nitrogen atom.
  c. This is the line-angle structural formula of a primary (1°) amine; there is only one alkyl group (and two hydrogens) attached to the nitrogen atom.
  d. This is a tertiary (3°) amine; there are two alkyl groups and one aromatic group (and no hydrogens) attached to the nitrogen atom.

    e. This is a tertiary (3°) amine; there are three alkyl groups (and no hydrogens) attached to the nitrogen atom.

18.5 The common name of an amine consists of naming the alkyl groups bonding to the nitrogen atom in alphabetical order. In the IUPAC name, the *e* in the name of the corresponding alkane is replaced with *amine*.

    a. A two-carbon alkyl group attached to —NH_2 is ethylamine. In the IUPAC name, the *e* in ethane is replaced with *amine* to give ethanamine.

    b. A one-carbon and a three-carbon alkyl group attached to nitrogen form methylpropylamine. The IUPAC name is *N*-methyl-1-propanamine.

    c. A one-carbon and two two-carbon alkyl groups attached to nitrogen form diethylmethylamine. The IUPAC name is *N*-ethyl-*N*-methylethanamine.

    d. A three-carbon isopropyl group attached to nitrogen forms isopropylamine. The IUPAC name is 2-propanamine.

18.7   **a.** The carboxylic acid has priority over the amine in naming. The IUPAC name is 4-aminopentanoic acid.

    b. The amine has priority over the halogen atom in naming. The IUPAC name is 2-chloroaniline.

    c. The aldehyde has priority over the amine in naming. The IUPAC name is 3-aminopropanal.

    d. The alcohol has priority over the amine in naming. The IUPAC name is 5-amino-3-hexanol.

18.9   **a.** $Cl—CH_2—CH_2—NH_2$

    b.

    c. $CH_3—CH_2—CH_2—CH_2—\overset{\overset{\displaystyle H}{|}}{N}—CH_2—CH_2—CH_3$

    d. $CH_3—CH_2—\overset{\overset{\displaystyle NH_2}{|}}{C}H—\overset{\overset{\displaystyle O}{||}}{C}—H$

18.11 Amines have higher boiling points than hydrocarbons but lower boiling points than alcohols of similar mass. Boiling point increases with molecular mass.

    a. $CH_3—CH_2—OH$ has the higher boiling point because the —OH group forms stronger hydrogen bonds than the —NH_2 group.

    b. $CH_3—CH_2—CH_2—NH_2$ has the higher boiling point because it has a greater molar mass.

    c. $CH_3—CH_2—CH_2—NH_2$ has the higher boiling point because it is a primary amine that forms hydrogen bonds. A tertiary amine cannot form hydrogen bonds with other tertiary amines.

18.13 As a primary amine, propylamine can form two hydrogen bonds, which gives it the highest boiling point. Ethylmethylamine, a secondary amine, can form one hydrogen bond, and butane cannot form hydrogen bonds. Thus, butane has the lowest boiling point of the three compounds.

18.15 Amines with six or fewer carbon atoms are soluble in water. In larger amines, the nonpolar hydrocarbon groups diminish the effect of hydrogen bonding.

    a. Yes; amines with six or fewer carbon atoms hydrogen bond with water molecules and are soluble in water.

    b. Yes; amines with six or fewer carbon atoms hydrogen bond with water molecules and are soluble in water.

    c. No; an amine with nine carbon atoms has large hydrocarbon sections that make it insoluble in water.

    d. Yes; amines with six or fewer carbon atoms hydrogen bond with water molecules and are soluble in water.

18.17 Amines, which are weak bases, accept H^+ from water to give a hydroxide ion and the related ammonium ion.

    a. $CH_3-NH_2 + H_2O \rightleftharpoons CH_3-\overset{+}{N}H_3 + OH^-$

    b. $CH_3-\overset{\overset{\displaystyle H}{|}}{N}-CH_3 + H_2O \rightleftharpoons CH_3-\overset{\overset{\displaystyle H}{|+}}{\underset{\underset{\displaystyle H}{|}}{N}}-CH_3 + OH^-$

    c. $+ H_2O \rightleftharpoons$ $+ OH^-$

18.19 Amines, which are weak bases, combine with the H^+ from HCl to yield the ammonium chloride salt.

    a. $CH_3-\overset{+}{N}H_3\,Cl^-$

    b. $CH_3-\overset{+}{N}H_2-CH_3\,Cl^-$

    c.

18.21 a.

    b. The ammonium salt Novocain is more soluble in water and body fluids than the amine procaine.

18.23 Heterocyclic amines contain one or more nitrogen atoms in a ring.

    a. Piperidine is a six-atom ring with one nitrogen atom and no double bonds.

    b. Pyrimidine is a six-atom ring with two nitrogen atoms and three double bonds.

    c. Pyrrole is a five-atom ring with one nitrogen atom and two double bonds.

18.25 The six-atom ring with one nitrogen atom and no double bonds in Ritalin is piperidine.

18.27 The five-atom ring with one nitrogen atom and two double bonds in serotonin is pyrrole.

18.29 A neurotransmitter is a chemical compound that transmits an impulse from a nerve cell to a target cell.

18.31 When a nerve impulse reaches the axon terminal, it stimulates the release of neurotransmitters into the synapse.

18.33 A neurotransmitter must be removed from its receptor so that new signals can come from the nerve cells.

18.35 Acetylcholine is a neurotransmitter that communicates between the nervous system and muscle cells.

18.37 Dopamine is a neurotransmitter that controls muscle movement, regulates the sleep–wake cycle, and helps to improve cognition, attention, memory, and learning.

18.39 Serotonin is a neurotransmitter that helps to decrease anxiety and improve mood, learning, and memory; it also reduces appetite and induces sleep.

18.41 Histamine is a neurotransmitter that causes allergic reactions, which may include inflammation, watery eyes, itchy skin, and hay fever.

18.43 Excess glutamate in the synapse can lead to destruction of brain cells.

18.45 GABA is a neurotransmitter that regulates muscle tone, sleep, and anxiety.

18.47 Carboxylic acids react with amines to form amides with the elimination of water.

a. $CH_3-\overset{\overset{\displaystyle O}{\|}}{C}-NH_2$

b. $CH_3-\overset{\overset{\displaystyle O}{\|}}{C}-\overset{\overset{\displaystyle H}{|}}{N}-CH_2-CH_3$

c. $\langle\bigcirc\rangle-\overset{\overset{\displaystyle O}{\|}}{C}-\overset{\overset{\displaystyle H}{|}}{N}-CH_2-CH_2-CH_3$

18.49 a. *N*-methylethanamide (*N*-methylacetamide); the "*N*-methyl" means that there is a one-carbon alkyl group attached to the nitrogen. The "ethanamide" component tells us that the carbonyl portion has two carbon atoms.
   b. Butanamide (butyramide) has a four-carbon carbonyl portion bonded to an amino group.
   c. Methanamide (formamide) has only the carbonyl carbon bonded to the amino group.
   d. *N*-methylbenzamide; the "*N*-methyl" means that there is a one-carbon alkyl group attached to the nitrogen. The "benzamide" component tells us that this is the amide of benzoic acid.

18.51 a. This is an amide of propionic acid, which has three carbon atoms.

$CH_3-CH_2-\overset{\overset{\displaystyle O}{\|}}{C}-NH_2$

   b. This is an amide of pentanoic acid, which has five carbon atoms.

$CH_3-CH_2-CH_2-CH_2-\overset{\overset{\displaystyle O}{\|}}{C}-NH_2$

   c. The nitrogen atom in *N*-ethylbenzamide is bonded to a two-carbon ethyl group. The "benzamide" component tells us that this is the amide of benzoic acid.

$\langle\bigcirc\rangle-\overset{\overset{\displaystyle O}{\|}}{C}-\overset{\overset{\displaystyle H}{|}}{N}-CH_2-CH_3$

   d. This is an amide of butyric acid, which has four carbon atoms. The "*N*-ethyl" means that there is a two-carbon alkyl group attached to the nitrogen.

$CH_3-CH_2-CH_2-\overset{\overset{\displaystyle O}{\|}}{C}-\overset{\overset{\displaystyle H}{|}}{N}-CH_2-CH_3$

18.53 a. Ethanamide has the higher melting point because it can form more hydrogen bonds as a primary amide than can *N*-methylethanamide, which is a secondary amide.
   b. Propionamide has the higher melting point because it forms hydrogen bonds, but butane does not.

c. *N*-methylpropanamide, a secondary amide, has the higher melting point because it can form hydrogen bonds, whereas *N,N*-dimethylpropanamide, a tertiary amide, cannot form hydrogen bonds.

18.55 Acid hydrolysis of an amide gives the carboxylic acid and the ammonium salt.

a. $CH_3-\overset{\overset{\displaystyle O}{\|}}{C}-OH$ and $\overset{+}{N}H_4\,Cl^-$

b. $CH_3-CH_2-\overset{\overset{\displaystyle O}{\|}}{C}-OH$ and $\overset{+}{N}H_4\,Cl^-$

c. $CH_3-CH_2-CH_2-\overset{\overset{\displaystyle O}{\|}}{C}-OH$ and $CH_3-\overset{+}{N}H_3\,Cl^-$

d. $\langle\!\!\!\bigcirc\!\!\!\rangle-\overset{\overset{\displaystyle O}{\|}}{C}-OH$ and $\overset{+}{N}H_4\,Cl^-$

18.57 amine, heterocyclic amine (pyrimidine)

18.59 $70.\ \cancel{\text{kg body mass}} \times \dfrac{65\ \cancel{\text{mg dicyclanil}}}{1\ \cancel{\text{kg body mass}}} \times \dfrac{1\ \text{mL spray}}{50.\ \cancel{\text{mg dicyclanil}}} = 91\ \text{mL of dicyclanil spray (2 SFs)}$

18.61 amine, carboxylic acid, amide, aromatic, ester

18.63 phenol, alcohol, amine

18.65 Excitatory neurotransmitters, like glutamate, open ion channels and stimulate the receptors to send more signals.

18.67 Dopamine, norepinephrine, and epinephrine all have catechol (3,4-dihydroxyphenyl) and amine components.

18.69 a. tetraethylammonium bromide; quaternary (4°) ammonium salt
b. 1-pentanamine (pentylamine); primary (1°) amine
c. *N*-ethyl-1-propanamine (ethylpropylamine); secondary (2°) amine

18.71 a. An amino group is bonded to carbon 3 of a five-carbon alkane chain.

$$CH_3-CH_2-\overset{\overset{\displaystyle NH_2}{|}}{C}H-CH_2-CH_3$$

b. A six-carbon cycloalkyl group (and two hydrogens) are bonded to a nitrogen atom.

NH_2

c. This is an ammonium salt with two methyl groups bonded to the nitrogen atom.

$$CH_3-\overset{\overset{\displaystyle CH_3}{|}}{\overset{+}{N}}H_2\,Cl^-$$

d. Three two-carbon ethyl groups are bonded to a nitrogen atom.

$$CH_3-CH_2-\overset{\overset{\displaystyle CH_2-CH_3}{|}}{N}-CH_2-CH_3$$

18.73 a. An alcohol with an —OH group such as 1-butanol forms stronger hydrogen bonds than an amine and has a higher boiling point than an amine.

    b. Ethylamine, a primary amine, forms more hydrogen bonds and has a higher boiling point than dimethylamine, which forms fewer hydrogen bonds as a secondary amine.

18.75 a. Ethylamine is a small amine that is soluble because it forms hydrogen bonds with water. Dibutylamine has two large nonpolar alkyl groups that decrease its solubility in water.

    b. Trimethylamine is a small tertiary amine that is soluble because it hydrogen bonds with water. *N*-ethylcyclohexylamine has a large nonpolar cycloalkyl group that decreases its solubility in water.

18.77 a. *N*-ethylethanamide; the "*N*-ethyl" means that there is a two-carbon alkyl group attached to the nitrogen. The "ethanamide" component tells us that the carbonyl portion has two carbon atoms.

    b. Propanamide has a three-carbon carbonyl portion bonded to an amino group.

    c. 3-Methylbutanamide has a four-carbon chain with a methyl substituent on carbon 3 as its carbonyl portion bonded to an amino group.

18.79 a. An ammonium salt and a strong base produce the amine, a salt, and water.

$$CH_3-CH_2-\overset{\overset{\displaystyle H}{|}}{N}-CH_3 + NaCl + H_2O$$

    b. An amine in water accepts H^+ from water, which produces an ammonium ion and OH^-.

$$CH_3-CH_2-\overset{+}{N}H_2-CH_3 + OH^-$$

18.81 carboxylate salt, aromatic, amine

18.83 a. The alkaloid from the bark of the cinchona tree used in treating malaria is quinine.

    b. The alkaloid found in tobacco is nicotine.

    c. The alkaloid found in coffee and tea is caffeine.

    d. The alkaloids that are painkillers found in the opium poppy plant are morphine and codeine.

18.85 Tryptophan contains a carboxylic acid group that is not present in serotonin. Serotonin has a hydroxyl group (—OH) on the aromatic ring that is not present in tryptophan.

18.87 SSRI stands for selective serotonin reuptake inhibitor.

18.89 $CH_3-CH_2-CH_2-NH_2$ $CH_3-CH_2-\overset{\overset{\displaystyle H}{|}}{N}-CH_3$ $CH_3-\overset{\overset{\displaystyle CH_3}{|}}{N}-CH_3$

      Propylamine (1°)   Ethylmethylamine (2°)   Trimethylamine (3°)

$$CH_3-\overset{\overset{\displaystyle CH_3}{|}}{C}H-NH_2 \quad \text{Isopropylamine (1°)}$$

18.91 a. aromatic, amine, amide, carboxylic acid, cycloalkene

    b. aromatic, ether, alcohol, amine

    c. aromatic, carboxylic acid

    d. phenol, amine, carboxylic acid

    e. aromatic, ether, amine, alcohol, ketone

    f. aromatic, amine

18.93 Dopamine is needed in the brain, where it is important in controlling muscle movement. Since dopamine cannot cross the blood–brain barrier, persons with low levels of dopamine are given L-dopa, which can cross the blood–brain barrier, where it is converted to dopamine.

Selected Answers to Combining Ideas from Chapters 15 to 18

CI.35 a.

$$HO-\underset{\overset{\|}{O}}{C}-\text{⬡}-\underset{\overset{\|}{O}}{C}-O-CH_2-CH_2-OH$$

b.

$$HO-CH_2-CH_2-O-\underset{\overset{\|}{O}}{C}-\text{⬡}-\underset{\overset{\|}{O}}{C}-O-CH_2-CH_2-OH$$

c. $1.5 \times 10^9 \text{ lb PETE} \times \dfrac{1 \text{ kg PETE}}{2.20 \text{ lb PETE}} = 6.8 \times 10^8 \text{ kg of PETE (2 SFs)}$

d. $6.8 \times 10^8 \text{ kg PETE} \times \dfrac{1000 \text{ g PETE}}{1 \text{ kg PETE}} \times \dfrac{1 \text{ mL PETE}}{1.38 \text{ g PETE}} \times \dfrac{1 \text{ L PETE}}{1000 \text{ mL PETE}}$
$= 4.9 \times 10^8 \text{ L of PETE (2 SFs)}$

e. $4.9 \times 10^8 \text{ L PETE} \times \dfrac{1 \text{ landfill}}{2.7 \times 10^7 \text{ L PETE}} = 18 \text{ landfills (2 SFs)}$

CI.37 a.

$$\text{⬡}-\underset{\overset{\|}{O}}{C}-\underset{}{N}-CH_2-CH_3$$
with CH_2-CH_3 above N and CH_3 on the ring

b. The molecular formula of DEET is $C_{12}H_{17}NO$.

c. Molar mass of DEET $(C_{12}H_{17}NO)$
$= 12(12.01 \text{ g}) + 17(1.008 \text{ g}) + 14.01 \text{ g} + 16.00 \text{ g} = 191.3 \text{ g/mole (4 SFs)}$

d. $6.0 \text{ fl oz} \times \dfrac{1 \text{ qt}}{32 \text{ fl oz}} \times \dfrac{946 \text{ mL}}{1 \text{ qt}} \times \dfrac{25 \text{ g DEET}}{100 \text{ mL solution}} = 44 \text{ g of DEET (2 SFs)}$

e. $6.0 \text{ fl oz} \times \dfrac{1 \text{ qt}}{32 \text{ fl oz}} \times \dfrac{946 \text{ mL}}{1 \text{ qt}} \times \dfrac{25 \text{ g DEET}}{100 \text{ mL solution}} \times \dfrac{1 \text{ mole DEET}}{191.3 \text{ g DEET}}$

$\times \dfrac{6.02 \times 10^{23} \text{ molecules DEET}}{1 \text{ mole DEET}} = 1.4 \times 10^{23} \text{ molecules of DEET (2 SFs)}$

CI.39 a. **A**, **B**, and **C** are all glucose units.

b. An $\alpha(1 \rightarrow 6)$-glycosidic bond connects monosaccharides **A** and **B**.

c. An $\alpha(1 \rightarrow 4)$-glycosidic bond connects monosaccharides **B** and **C**.

d. The structure drawn is β-panose.

e. Panose is a reducing sugar because it has a free hydroxyl group on carbon 1 of structure **C**, which allows glucose (**C**) to form an aldehyde.

Credit: Tyler Olson / Shutterstock

Edith has become forgetful and unable to complete simple tasks. She does not recognize close friends at times. Since Edith's doctor suspects that she may be in the early stages of Alzheimer's disease, Edith is referred to a neurologist for testing. Patients with Alzheimer's have impaired brain function caused by the accumulation of beta-amyloid proteins that form plaques that block transmission in nerve cells. Proteins like beta-amyloid consist of chains of about 40 amino acids. Amino acids contain an ammonium group, a carboxylate group, and a unique side chain, or R group, which distinguishes one amino acid from another.

In preparation for a PET scan, Edith is given an injection of a radioactive fluorine compound called Vizamyl (flutemetamol F 18), which binds to the beta-amyloid proteins. The PET scan images show dark regions in the brain that indicate beta-amyloid plaque formation. Edith is diagnosed with early Alzheimer's. Her doctor prescribes an acetylcholinesterase inhibitor that can slow the progression of the disease by keeping levels of the neurotransmitter acetylcholine high. Edith's husband is relieved to have a diagnosis so that he can better assist Edith in the future. What structural level of proteins is represented by the sequence of amino acids in beta-amyloid proteins?

CHAPTER READINESS*

 Key Math Skill

• Calculating pH from $[H_3O^+]$ (11.6)

Core Chemistry Skills

• Writing Equations for Reactions of Acids and Bases (11.7)
• Naming Carboxylic Acids (16.1)
• Forming Amides (18.5)

*This Key Math Skill and Core Chemistry Skills from previous chapters are listed here for your review as you proceed to the new material in this chapter.

19.1 Proteins and Amino Acids

Learning Goal: Classify proteins by their functions. Give the name and abbreviations for an amino acid, and draw its zwitterion.

• Some proteins are enzymes or hormones, while others are important in structure, transport, protection, storage, and contraction of muscles.

• A group of 20 amino acids provides the molecular building blocks of proteins.

• In an amino acid, a central (alpha) carbon is attached to an ammonium group ($-NH_3^+$), a carboxylate group ($-COO^-$), a hydrogen atom ($-H$), and a side chain or R group, which is unique for each amino acid.

- Each specific R group determines whether an amino acid is nonpolar, polar neutral, acidic, or basic. Nonpolar amino acids contain hydrocarbon side chains, whereas polar amino acids contain electronegative atoms such as oxygen or sulfur. Acidic side chains contain a carboxylate group ($-COO^-$), and basic side chains contain an ammonium group ($-NH_3^+$).

- Certain combinations of vegetables are complementary when the protein from one provides the missing amino acid in the other. For example, garbanzo beans and rice have complementary proteins because tryptophan, which is low in garbanzo beans, is present in rice, and lysine, which is low in rice, is present in garbanzo beans.

♦ **Learning Exercise 19.1A**

Match one of the following functions with each protein below:

a. structural	**b.** contractile	**c.** storage	**d.** transport
e. hormone	**f.** enzyme	**g.** protection	

1. _____ hemoglobin, carries oxygen in blood

2. _____ amylase, hydrolyzes starch

3. _____ casein, a protein in milk

4. _____ vasopressin, regulates blood pressure

5. _____ collagen, makes up connective tissue

6. _____ immunoglobulin, an antibody

7. _____ keratin, a major protein of hair

8. _____ lipoprotein, carries lipids in blood

Answers **1.** d **2.** f **3.** c **4.** e
5. a **6.** g **7.** a **8.** d

♦ **Learning Exercise 19.1B**

Using the appropriate R group, complete the condensed structural formula of each of the following amino acids. Indicate whether the amino acid would be nonpolar, polar neutral, acidic, or basic, and give its three- and one-letter abbreviations:

⚛ CORE CHEMISTRY SKILL

Drawing the Zwitterion for an Amino Acid

1. $H_3\overset{+}{N}-C-C-O^-$ Glycine _____

2. $H_3\overset{+}{N}-C-C-O^-$ Alanine _____

3. $H_3\overset{+}{N}-C-C-O^-$ Serine _____

4. $H_3\overset{+}{N}-C-C-O^-$ Aspartate _____

Answers

1. $H_3\overset{+}{N}-\overset{\overset{\displaystyle H}{|}}{\underset{\underset{\displaystyle H}{|}}{C}}-\overset{\overset{\displaystyle O}{||}}{C}-O^-$

   Glycine, nonpolar, Gly, G

2. $H_3\overset{+}{N}-\overset{\overset{\displaystyle CH_3}{|}}{\underset{\underset{\displaystyle H}{|}}{C}}-\overset{\overset{\displaystyle O}{||}}{C}-O^-$

   Alanine, nonpolar, Ala, A

3. $H_3\overset{+}{N}-\overset{\overset{\displaystyle CH_2-OH}{|}}{\underset{\underset{\displaystyle H}{|}}{C}}-\overset{\overset{\displaystyle O}{||}}{C}-O^-$

   Serine, polar neutral, Ser, S

4. $H_3\overset{+}{N}-\overset{\overset{\displaystyle CH_2-\overset{\overset{\displaystyle O}{||}}{C}-O^-}{|}}{\underset{\underset{\displaystyle H}{|}}{C}}-\overset{\overset{\displaystyle O}{||}}{C}-O^-$

   Aspartate, acidic, Asp, D

♦ **Learning Exercise 19.1C**

Many seeds, vegetables, and legumes are low in one or more of the essential amino acids tryptophan, isoleucine, and lysine.

	Tryptophan	**Isoleucine**	**Lysine**
Sesame seeds	OK	low	low
Sunflower seeds	OK	OK	low
Garbanzo beans	low	OK	OK
Rice	OK	OK	low
Cornmeal	low	OK	low

Indicate whether the following protein combinations are complementary or not:

1. _____ sesame seeds and sunflower seeds

2. _____ sunflower seeds and garbanzo beans

3. _____ sesame seeds and rice

4. _____ sesame seeds and garbanzo beans

5. _____ garbanzo beans and rice

6. _____ cornmeal and garbanzo beans

Answers

1. not complementary; both are low in lysine
2. complementary
3. not complementary; both are low in lysine
4. complementary
5. complementary
6. not complementary; both are low in tryptophan

19.2 Amino Acids as Acids and Bases

Using the zwitterion for an amino acid at its isoelectric point, draw its ionized structures at pH values above or below its isoelectric point.

• An amino acid exists as an ion with an overall charge of zero at a pH called the isoelectric point (pI).

• An amino acid has an overall positive charge at pH levels below its pI and an overall negative charge at pH levels above its pI.

Study Note

Example: Glycine has an isoelectric point at a pH of 6.0. Draw the structural formula for glycine at its isoelectric point (pI) and at pH levels above and below its isoelectric point.

Solution: In an acidic solution that has a pH lower than the pI, glycine has an overall positive charge. In a basic solution that has a pH greater than the pI, glycine has an overall negative charge.

$$
\underset{below\ pI}{\overset{+}{H_3N}-\underset{H}{\overset{H}{C}}-\overset{O}{\overset{\|}{C}}-OH} \xleftarrow{H^+} \underset{at\ pI}{\overset{+}{H_3N}-\underset{H}{\overset{H}{C}}-\overset{O}{\overset{\|}{C}}-O^-} \xrightarrow{OH^-} \underset{above\ pI}{H_2N-\underset{H}{\overset{H}{C}}-\overset{O}{\overset{\|}{C}}-O^-}
$$

♦ **Learning Exercise 19.2A**

Draw the zwitterion for each of the following amino acids:

a. Val

b. C

c. threonine

d. F

Answers

a. $\underset{H}{\overset{CH_3\ CH_3}{\overset{CH}{\overset{+}{H_3N}-C-\overset{O}{\overset{\|}{C}}-O^-}}}$

b. $\underset{H}{\overset{SH}{\overset{CH_2}{\overset{+}{H_3N}-C-\overset{O}{\overset{\|}{C}}-O^-}}}$

c. $\underset{H}{\overset{CH_3}{\overset{HO-CH}{\overset{+}{H_3N}-C-\overset{O}{\overset{\|}{C}}-O^-}}}$

d. $\underset{H}{\overset{CH_2}{\overset{+}{H_3N}-C-\overset{O}{\overset{\|}{C}}-O^-}}$

♦ **Learning Exercise 19.2B**

Draw the ionized structural formulas for the amino acids under each of the given conditions:

Zwitterion (pI)	pH below pI	pH above pI
1a. Alanine	**1b.**	**1c.**
2a. Serine	**2b.**	**2c.**

Answers

Zwitterion (pI)	pH below pI	pH above pI
1a. Alanine CH_3 $H_3\overset{+}{N}—C—COO^-$ H	**1b.** CH_3 $H_3\overset{+}{N}—C—COOH$ H	**1c.** CH_3 $H_2N—C—COO^-$ H
2a. Serine $CH_2—OH$ $H_3\overset{+}{N}—C—COO^-$ H	**2b.** $CH_2—OH$ $H_3\overset{+}{N}—C—COOH$ H	**2c.** $CH_2—OH$ $H_2N—C—COO^-$ H

19.3 Formation of Peptides

Draw the structure for a peptide, give its three-letter and one-letter abbreviations, and name.

- A peptide bond is an amide bond between the carboxylate group ($—COO^-$) of one amino acid and the ammonium group ($—NH_3^+$) of another amino acid.

$$H_3\overset{+}{N}—\underset{}{CH}—\overset{O}{\underset{}{C}}—\overset{H}{N}—\underset{}{CH}—COO^-$$

Peptide bond

- Short chains of amino acids are called peptides. Long chains of amino acids are called proteins.

♦ **Learning Exercise 19.3**

Draw the ionized structural formulas for the following di- and tripeptides:

  1. serylglycine   **2.** CV

  3. Gly–Ser–Cys

Answers

1. H₃N⁺–CH(CH₂–OH)–C(O)–N(H)–CH₂–COO⁻

2. H₃N⁺–CH(CH₂–SH)–C(O)–N(H)–CH(CH(CH₃)₂)–COO⁻

3. H₃N⁺–CH₂–C(O)–N(H)–CH(CH₂–OH)–C(O)–N(H)–CH(CH₂–SH)–COO⁻

19.4 Protein Structure: Primary and Secondary Levels

Describe the primary and secondary structures of a protein.

- The primary structure of a protein is the sequence of amino acids connected by peptide bonds.
- In a secondary structure, hydrogen bonds between the amino acid residues of the peptide produce the characteristic shape of an α helix or a β-pleated sheet.
- Collagen, which contains a triple helix of peptide chains, makes up as much as one-third of all the protein in the body.

♦ **Learning Exercise 19.4A**

Identify the following descriptions of protein structure as primary or secondary:

  1. _____ hydrogen bonding forming an α helix

  2. _____ hydrogen bonding occurring between C=O and N—H within a peptide chain

  3. _____ the order of amino acids linked by peptide bonds

  4. _____ hydrogen bonds between protein chains forming a β-pleated sheet

Answers   **1.** secondary   **2.** secondary   **3.** primary   **4.** secondary

19.5   Protein Structure: Tertiary and Quaternary Levels

Describe the tertiary and quaternary structures of a protein.

- In a globular protein, the polypeptide chain, including its α helix and β-pleated sheet, folds upon itself to form a tertiary structure.

- In a tertiary structure, hydrophobic R groups are found on the inside and hydrophilic R groups are found on the surface. The tertiary structure is stabilized by interactions between R groups.

- In a quaternary structure, two or more subunits must combine for biological activity. They are held together by the same interactions found in tertiary structures.

♦ **Learning Exercise 19.5**

Identify the following descriptions of protein structure as tertiary, quaternary, or both:

⚛ CORE CHEMISTRY SKILL

Identifying the Primary, Secondary, Tertiary, and Quaternary Structures of Proteins

1. _____ a disulfide bond joining distant parts of a protein

2. _____ the combination of two or more protein subunits

3. _____ hydrophilic side groups seeking contact with water

4. _____ a salt bridge forming between two oppositely charged side chains

5. _____ hydrophobic side groups forming a nonpolar center

Answers
    1. tertiary   **2.** quaternary
    3. both tertiary and quaternary   **4.** both tertiary and quaternary
    5. both tertiary and quaternary

19.6   Protein Hydrolysis and Denaturation

Describe the hydrolysis and denaturation of proteins.

- Denaturation of a protein occurs when denaturing agents destroy the secondary, tertiary, and quaternary structures (but not the primary structure), which causes a loss of biological activity.

- Denaturing agents include heat, acids, bases, organic solvents, agitation, and heavy metal ions.

Key Terms for Sections 19.1–19.6

Match each of the following key terms with the correct description below:

    a. tertiary   **b.** peptide   **c.** alpha helix   **d.** zwitterion   **e.** denaturation

1. _____ the dipolar form of an amino acid at its isoelectric point

2. _____ the folding of a protein into a compact structure

3. _____ the loss of secondary, tertiary, and/or quaternary structure of a protein

4. _____ the combination of two or more amino acids

5. _____ a secondary level of protein structure

Answers   **1.** d   **2.** a   **3.** e   **4.** b   **5.** c

♦ **Learning Exercise 19.6**

Indicate the denaturing agent in the following examples:

    a. heat or UV light   **b.** pH change   **c.** organic solvent
    d. heavy metal ions   **e.** agitation

1. _____ placing surgical instruments in a 120 °C autoclave

2. _____ whipping cream to make a dessert topping

3. _____ applying tannic acid to a burn

4. _____ placing $AgNO_3$ drops in the eyes of newborns

5. _____ using alcohol to disinfect a wound

6. _____ using a *Lactobacillus* bacteria culture to produce acid that converts milk to yogurt

Answers   **1.** a   **2.** e   **3.** b   **4.** d   **5.** c   **6.** b

Checklist for Chapter 19

You are ready to take the Practice Test for Chapter 19. Be sure that you have accomplished the learning goals for each of the sections in this chapter. If not, review the section listed at the end of each goal. Then apply your new skills and understanding to the Practice Test.

After studying Chapter 19, I can successfully:

_____ Classify proteins by their functions in the body. (19.1)

_____ Draw the zwitterion for an amino acid. (19.1)

_____ Draw the ionized structural formulas for an amino acid at its isoelectric point (pI), as well as above and below its pI. (19.2)

_____ Describe a peptide bond; draw the ionized structural formulas for a peptide. (19.3)

_____ Distinguish between the primary and secondary structures of a protein. (19.4)

_____ Distinguish between the tertiary and quaternary structures of a protein. (19.5)

_____ Describe the ways that denaturation affects the structure of a protein. (19.6)

Practice Test for Chapter 19

1. Which amino acid is nonpolar? (19.1)
   A. serine   **B.** aspartate   **C.** valine   **D.** cysteine   **E.** lysine

2. Which amino acid will form disulfide bonds in a tertiary structure? (19.5)
   A. serine   **B.** aspartate   **C.** valine   **D.** cysteine   **E.** lysine

3. Which amino acid has a basic R group? (19.1)
   A. serine   **B.** aspartate   **C.** valine   **D.** cysteine   **E.** lysine

4. All amino acids (19.1, 19.2)
   A. have the same side chains   **B.** form zwitterions
   C. have the same isoelectric points   **D.** show hydrophobic tendencies
   E. are essential amino acids

5. Essential amino acids (19.1, 19.4)
   A. are the amino acids that must be supplied by the diet
   B. are not synthesized by the body
   C. are missing in incomplete proteins
   D. are present in proteins from animal sources
   E. all of the above

For questions 6 through 9, use the following condensed structural formulas for alanine: (19.2)

A. $H_3\overset{+}{N}-\underset{\underset{\displaystyle CH_3}{|}}{CH}-\overset{\overset{\displaystyle O}{\|}}{C}-O^-$ **B.** $H_2N-\underset{\underset{\displaystyle CH_3}{|}}{CH}-\overset{\overset{\displaystyle O}{\|}}{C}-O^-$ **C.** $H_3\overset{+}{N}-\underset{\underset{\displaystyle CH_3}{|}}{CH}-\overset{\overset{\displaystyle O}{\|}}{C}-OH$

6. _____ alanine as a zwitterion

7. _____ alanine at a low pH

8. _____ alanine at a high pH

9. _____ alanine at its isoelectric point

10. The sequence Tyr–Ala–Gly (19.3)
    A. is a tripeptide
    B. has two peptide bonds
    C. has tyrosine as the N-terminus
    D. has glycine as the N-terminus
    E. all of these

11. The type of bonding expected between lysine and aspartate is a (19.5)
    A. salt bridge   **B.** hydrogen bond   **C.** disulfide bond
    D. hydrophobic interaction   **E.** hydrophilic attraction

12. What type of bond is used to form the α-helix structure of a protein? (19.4)
    A. peptide bond   **B.** hydrogen bond   **C.** salt bridge
    D. disulfide bond   **E.** hydrophobic attraction

13. What type of bond places portions of the protein chain in the center of a tertiary structure? (19.5)
    A. peptide bond   **B.** salt bridge   **C.** disulfide bond
    D. hydrophobic interaction   **E.** hydrophilic attraction

For questions 14 through 18, identify the protein structural level that each of the phrases below describes: (19.4, 19.5)
    A. primary   **B.** secondary   **C.** tertiary   **D.** quaternary   **E.** pentenary

14. peptide bonds   **15.** a β-pleated sheet

16. two or more protein subunits   **17.** an α helix

18. disulfide bonds

For questions 19 through 22, match the function to the correct protein (**A** to **D**): (19.1)
    A. myoglobin in muscle   **B.** α-keratin in skin   **C.** peptidase for protein hydrolysis   **D.** casein in milk

19. enzyme   **20.** structural

21. transport   **22.** storage

23. Denaturation of a protein (19.6)
    A. occurs at a pH of 7   **B.** causes a change in protein structure
    C. hydrolyzes a protein   **D.** oxidizes the protein
    E. adds amino acids to a protein

24. Which of the following will not cause denaturation? (19.6)
    A. 0 °C   **B.** $AgNO_3$ **C.** 80 °C   **D.** ethanol   **E.** pH 1

Answers to the Practice Test

1. C	**2.** D	**3.** E	**4.** B	**5.** E
6. A	**7.** C	**8.** B	**9.** A	**10.** E
11. A	**12.** B	**13.** D	**14.** A	**15.** B
16. D	**17.** B	**18.** C, D	**19.** C	**20.** B
21. A	**22.** D	**23.** B	**24.** A	

19

Amino Acids and Proteins

Learning Goals

- Classify proteins by their functions. Give the name and abbreviations for an amino acid, and draw its zwitterion.
- Using the zwitterion for an amino acid at its isoelectric point, draw its ionized structures at pH values above or below its isoelectric point.
- Draw the structure for a peptide, give its three-letter and one-letter abbreviations, and name.
- Describe the primary and secondary structures of a protein.
- Describe the tertiary and quaternary structures of a protein.
- Describe the hydrolysis and denaturation of proteins.

Chapter Outline

Chapter Opener: Radiology Technician

19.1 Proteins and Amino Acids

Chemistry Link to Health: Essential Amino Acids

19.2 Amino Acids as Acids and Bases

19.3 Formation of Peptides

Chemistry Link to Health: Polypeptides in the Body

19.4 Protein Structure: Primary and Secondary Levels

Chemistry Link to Health: Protein Sequencing

Chemistry Link to Health: Protein Secondary Structures and Alzheimer's Disease

19.5 Protein Structure: Tertiary and Quaternary Levels

Chemistry Link to Health: Sickle Cell Anemia

19.6 Protein Hydrolysis and Denaturation

Explore Your World: Denaturation of Milk Protein

Clinical Update: Alzheimer's Diagnosis

⚛ Core Chemistry Skills

- Drawing the Zwitterion for an Amino Acid (19.1)
- Identifying the Primary, Secondary, Tertiary, and Quaternary Structures of Proteins (19.4, 19.5)

Selected Answers and Solutions to Text Problems

19.1 **a.** Hemoglobin, which carries oxygen in the blood, is a transport protein.
  b. Collagen, which is a major component of tendons and cartilage, is a structural protein.
  c. Keratin, which is found in hair, is a structural protein.
  d. Amylases, which catalyze the breakdown of starch, are enzymes.

19.3 a.

$$CH_3$$
$$|$$
$$CH_2$$
$$CH_3-CH \quad O$$
$$\qquad\quad | \qquad \parallel$$
$$\overset{+}{H_3N}-\overset{|}{\underset{|}{C}}-C-O^-$$
$$\qquad\quad H$$

Ile, I

b.

$$O=\overset{\displaystyle NH_2}{\underset{\displaystyle C}{}}$$
$$|$$
$$CH_2$$
$$|$$
$$CH_2 \quad O$$
$$\qquad\quad | \qquad \parallel$$
$$\overset{+}{H_3N}-\overset{|}{\underset{|}{C}}-C-O^-$$
$$\qquad\quad H$$

Gln, Q

c.

$$O=\overset{\displaystyle O^-}{\underset{\displaystyle C}{}}$$
$$|$$
$$CH_2$$
$$|$$
$$CH_2 \quad O$$
$$\qquad\quad | \qquad \parallel$$
$$\overset{+}{H_3N}-\overset{|}{\underset{|}{C}}-C-O^-$$
$$\qquad\quad H$$

Glu, E

d.

$$CH_2$$
$$H_2C \qquad CH_2 \quad O$$
$$\qquad\quad | \qquad\quad \parallel$$
$$\overset{+}{H_2N}-\overset{|}{\underset{|}{C}}-C-O^-$$
$$\qquad\qquad H$$

Pro, P

19.5 a. Isoleucine has an alkyl (hydrocarbon) R group making it a nonpolar amino acid, which would be hydrophobic.

b. Glutamine has an R group that contains the polar amide group making glutamine a polar neutral amino acid, which would be hydrophilic.

c. Glutamate has an R group containing a polar carboxylic acid group. Glutamate is a polar acidic amino acid, which would be hydrophilic.

d. Proline has an alkyl (hydrocarbon) R group making it a nonpolar amino acid, which would be hydrophobic.

19.7 Amino acids have both three-letter and one-letter abbreviations.

a. His is the three-letter abbreviation for the amino acid histidine.

b. V is the one-letter abbreviation for the amino acid valine.

c. K is the one-letter abbreviation for the amino acid lysine.

d. Ile is the three-letter abbreviation for the amino acid isoleucine.

19.9 In the L enantiomer, the $-NH_3^+$ group is on the left side of the horizontal line of the Fischer projection; in the D enantiomer, the $-NH_3^+$ group is on the right.

a.

$$O=\overset{\displaystyle O^-}{\underset{\displaystyle C}{}}$$
$$|$$
$$\overset{+}{H_3N}-\!\!-\!\!-H$$
$$|$$
$$CH_2$$
$$|$$
$$OH$$

b.

$$O=\overset{\displaystyle O^-}{\underset{\displaystyle C}{}}$$
$$|$$
$$\overset{+}{H_3N}-\!\!-\!\!-H$$
$$|$$
$$CH_2$$
$$|$$
$$CH$$
$$H_3C \qquad CH_3$$

19.11 a. Lysine and tryptophan are lacking in corn but supplied by peas; methionine is lacking in peas but supplied by corn.

b. Lysine is lacking in rice but supplied by soy; methionine is lacking in soy but supplied by rice.

19.13 A zwitterion is a molecule with both positive and negative charges. In the case of an amino acid, the zwitterion form has a positively charged ammonium group and a negatively charged carboxylate group on the α-carbon.

a. (amino acid structure with CH₃, CH₃, CH, O, H₃N⁺—C—C—O⁻, H)

b. (amino acid structure with SH, CH₂, O, H₃N⁺—C—C—O⁻, H)

c. (amino acid structure with CH₃, HO—CH, O, H₃N⁺—C—C—O⁻, H)

d. (amino acid structure with CH₃, O, H₃N⁺—C—C—O⁻, H)

19.15 At low pH (highly acidic), the —COO⁻ group of the zwitterion accepts H⁺ to become —COOH and the amino acid has a positive charge overall.

a. (structure: CH₃, CH₃, CH, O, H₃N⁺—C—C—OH, H)

b. (structure: SH, CH₂, O, H₃N⁺—C—C—OH, H)

c. (structure: CH₃, HO—CH, O, H₃N⁺—C—C—OH, H)

d. (structure: CH₃, O, H₃N⁺—C—C—OH, H)

19.17 a. When valine is in a solution with a <u>pH above its pI</u>, the —NH₃⁺ group loses H⁺ to form an uncharged amino group (—NH₂). The negative charge on the ionized carboxylate group (—COO⁻) gives valine an overall negative charge (1−).

b. When valine is in a solution with a <u>pH below its pI</u>, the —COO⁻ group gains H⁺ to form an uncharged carboxylic acid group (—COOH). The positive charge on the ionized ammonium group (—NH₃⁺) gives valine an overall positive charge (1+).

c. In a solution with a <u>pH equal to its pI</u> (6.0), valine is in its zwitterion form, containing both a carboxylate anion (—COO⁻) and an ammonium cation (—NH₃⁺), which give an overall charge of zero (0).

19.19 In a peptide, the amino acids are joined by peptide bonds (amide bonds). At physiological pH (7.4), the first amino acid has a free —NH₃⁺ group, and the last one has a free —COO⁻ group.

a. (dipeptide structure: CH₃, O, H, SH, CH₂, O, H₃N⁺—C—C—N—C—C—O⁻, H, H)

Ala–Cys, AC

b. (dipeptide structure: OH, benzene ring, CH₂, O, H, CH₂, O, H₃N⁺—C—C—N—C—C—O⁻, H, H)

Ser–Phe, SF

c. (structure) Gly–Ala–Val, GAV

d. (structure) Val–Ile–Trp, VIW

19.21 a. Methionine (Met) is the C-terminus of met-enkephalin.
   b. Tyrosine (Tyr) is the N-terminus of met-enkephalin.
   c. YGGFM

19.23 a. (structure) RIY

   b. (structure) VWIS

19.25 The primary structure of a protein is the order of amino acids; the bonds that hold the amino acids together in a protein are amide or peptide bonds.

19.27 The possible primary structures of a tripeptide of one valine and two methionines are Val–Met–Met (VMM), Met–Val–Met (MVM), and Met–Met–Val (MMV).

19.29 The primary structure remains unchanged and intact as hydrogen bonds form between carbonyl oxygen atoms and amino hydrogen atoms of peptide bonds in the polypeptide chain.

19.31 In the α helix, hydrogen bonds form between the carbonyl oxygen atom and the amino hydrogen atom of a peptide bond in the next turn of the helical chain. In the β-pleated sheet, hydrogen bonds occur between parallel peptides or across sections of a long polypeptide chain.

19.33 Asp–Arg–Val–Tyr–Ile–His–Pro–Phe

19.35 a. The two cysteines have —SH groups, which react to form a disulfide bond.
  b. Glutamate is acidic and lysine is basic; an ionic bond, or salt bridge, is formed between the —COO⁻ in the R group of Glu and the —NH₃⁺ in the R group of Lys.
  c. Serine has a polar —OH group that can form a hydrogen bond with the carboxyl group of aspartate.
  d. Two leucines have R groups that are hydrocarbons and nonpolar. They would have a hydrophobic interaction.

19.37 a. The R group of cysteine contains a —SH group that can form a disulfide bond with another cysteine.
  b. Leucine and valine will be found on the inside of the protein structure since they have nonpolar R groups that are hydrophobic.
  c. Cysteine and aspartate would be on the outside of the protein since they have R groups that are polar.
  d. The order of the amino acids (the primary structure) provides the R groups whose interactions determine the tertiary structure of the protein.

19.39 a. Disulfide bonds and ionic bonds join different sections of the protein chain to give a three-dimensional shape. Disulfide bonds and ionic bonds are important in the tertiary and quaternary structures.
  b. Peptide bonds join the amino acid building blocks in the primary structure of a polypeptide.
  c. Hydrogen bonds that hold adjacent polypeptide chains together are found in the secondary structures of β-pleated sheets.
  d. In the secondary structure of α helices, hydrogen bonding occurs between amino acid residues in the same polypeptide to give a coiled shape to the protein.

19.41 The products of complete hydrolysis would be the amino acids glycine, alanine, and serine.

19.43 The dipeptides that could be produced by partial hydrolysis of this tetrapeptide are His–Met (HM), Met–Gly (MG), and Gly–Val (GV).

19.45 Hydrolysis splits the amide linkages in the primary structure.

19.47 a. Placing an egg in boiling water coagulates the proteins of the egg by disrupting hydrogen bonds and hydrophobic interactions.
  b. The alcohol on the swab coagulates the proteins of any bacteria present on the surface of the skin by forming hydrogen bonds and disrupting hydrophobic interactions.
  c. The heat from an autoclave will coagulate the proteins of any bacteria on the surgical instruments by disrupting hydrogen bonds and hydrophobic interactions.
  d. Heat will coagulate the surrounding proteins to close the wound by disrupting hydrogen bonds and hydrophobic interactions.

19.49 Because 5.5 hours have passed, some of the fluorine-18 will have decayed. To determine the amount of remaining radioisotope, we must determine the number of half-lives that have elapsed:

$$5.5 \text{ h} \times \frac{60 \text{ min}}{1 \text{ h}} \times \frac{1 \text{ half-life}}{110 \text{ min}} = 3.0 \text{ half-lives}$$

$$4.0 \text{ mCi of } {}^{18}_{9}\text{F} \xrightarrow{\text{1 half-life}} 2.0 \text{ mCi of } {}^{18}_{9}\text{F} \xrightarrow{\text{2 half-lives}} 1.0 \text{ mCi of } {}^{18}_{9}\text{F} \xrightarrow{\text{3 half-lives}} 0.50 \text{ mCi of } {}^{18}_{9}\text{F}$$

(2 SFs)

19.51 The secondary structure of beta-amyloid protein in the brain of a normal person is alpha-helical, whereas the secondary structure in the brain of a person with Alzheimer's disease changes to beta-pleated sheet.

19.53 Glu–Phe–Arg–His–Asp–Ser–Gly–Tyr–Glu–Val

19.55 **a.** Yes, a combination of rice and garbanzo beans provides all the essential amino acids; garbanzo beans contain the lysine missing in rice.
    b. No, a combination of lima beans and cornmeal does not provide all the essential amino acids; both are deficient in the amino acid tryptophan.
    c. No, a combination of garbanzo beans and lima beans does not provide all the essential amino acids; both are deficient in the amino acid tryptophan.

19.57 **a.** Because a pH of 10.5 is more basic and above the pI of cysteine, the $-NH_3^+$ group loses H^+ to form an uncharged amino group ($-NH_2$). The negative charge on the ionized carboxylate group ($-COO^-$) gives cysteine an overall negative charge ($1-$), as in diagram 1.
    b. Since the pI of cysteine is 5.1, at that pH cysteine exists as a zwitterion with an overall charge of zero (0) as in diagram 3.
    c. Because a pH of 1.8 is more acidic and below the pI of cysteine, the $-COO^-$ group gains H^+ to form an uncharged carboxylic acid group ($-COOH$). The positive charge on the ionized ammonium group ($-NH_3^+$) gives cysteine an overall positive charge ($1+$), as in diagram 2.

19.59 The possible primary structures of a tripeptide of one valine and two serines are Val–Ser–Ser (VSS), Ser–Val–Ser (SVS), and Ser–Ser–Val (SSV).

19.61 **a.** Asparagine and serine are both polar neutral amino acids; their R groups can interact by hydrogen bonding.
    b. The polar neutral amino acid cysteine contains the $-SH$ group; two cysteines can form a disulfide bond.
    c. Leucine and alanine are both nonpolar amino acids; their R groups have a hydrophobic interaction.

19.63 At low pH (highly acidic), the $-COO^-$ group of the zwitterion accepts H^+ and the polar neutral amino acids will have an overall charge of $1+$. Polar basic amino acids will have a charge of $2+$.

19.65 a.

$$H_3\overset{+}{N}-\underset{\underset{H}{|}}{\overset{\overset{OH}{|}}{\overset{CH_2}{\underset{|}{C}}}}-\underset{}{\overset{O}{\overset{||}{C}}}-\underset{H}{\overset{|}{N}}-\underset{\underset{H}{|}}{\overset{\overset{\overset{\overset{\overset{\overset{+}{NH_3}}{|}}{CH_2}}{|}}{\overset{CH_2}{|}}}{\overset{CH_2}{\underset{|}{C}}}}-\overset{O}{\overset{||}{C}}-\underset{H}{\overset{|}{N}}-\underset{\underset{H}{|}}{\overset{\overset{\overset{O\diagdown\diagup O^-}{C}}{|}}{\overset{CH_2}{\underset{|}{C}}}}-\overset{O}{\overset{||}{C}}-O^-$$

b. This segment contains polar R groups, which would be found on the surface of a globular protein where they can hydrogen bond with water.

19.67 a. Collagen is found in connective tissue, blood vessels, skin, tendons, ligaments, the cornea of the eye, and cartilage.
   b. Collagen consists of three helical polypeptides woven together like a braid, called a triple helix.

19.69 A polypeptide with a high content of amino acids with large R groups, like His, Met, and Leu, would be expected to have more α-helical than β-pleated sheet sections. In an α helix, these large R groups could extend toward the outside of the helix, away from the central corkscrew shape.

19.71 Serine is a polar amino acid, whereas valine is nonpolar. Serine would move to the outside surface of the protein where it can form hydrogen bonds with water. However, valine, which is nonpolar, would be pushed to the center of the tertiary structure where it is stabilized by forming hydrophobic interactions.

19.73 a. Because it has a nonpolar R group, proline will be found in hydrophobic regions.
   b. Because they have polar R groups, lysine and glutamate will be found in hydrophilic regions.
   c. The basic R group of lysine and the acidic R group of glutamate can form a salt bridge.

19.75 The acid from the lemon juice and the mechanical whipping (agitation) of the egg white denature the proteins, which turn into solids as meringue.

19.77 a. The amino acids in aspartame are aspartate and phenylalanine.
   b. The dipeptide in aspartame would be named aspartylphenylalanine.
   c. The abbreviated form of the name for the dipeptide in aspartame would be named Asp–Phe or DF.

19.79 a. Since the pI of serine is 5.7, at that pH serine exists as a zwitterion with an overall charge of zero (0).
   b. Because a pH of 2.0 is more acidic and below the pI of threonine (5.6), the $-COO^-$ group gains H^+ to form an uncharged carboxylic acid group ($-COOH$). The positive charge on the ionized ammonium group ($-NH_3^+$) gives threonine an overall positive charge (1+).
   c. Because a pH of 3.0 is more acidic and below the pI of isoleucine (6.0), the $-COO^-$ group gains H^+ to form an uncharged carboxylic acid group ($-COOH$). The positive charge on the ionized ammonium group ($-NH_3^+$) gives isoleucine an overall positive charge (1+).
   d. Because a pH of 9.0 is more basic and above the pI of leucine (6.0), the $-NH_3^+$ group loses H^+ to form an uncharged amino group ($-NH_2$). The negative charge on the ionized carboxylate group ($-COO^-$) gives leucine an overall negative charge (1−).

19.81 a. The secondary structure of a protein depends on hydrogen bonds between atoms involved in the peptide bonds to form a helix or a pleated sheet; the tertiary structure is determined by the interactions of R groups such as disulfide bonds and salt bridges, and determines the three-dimensional shape of the protein.

b. Nonessential amino acids can be synthesized by the body, but essential amino acids must be supplied by the diet.

c. Polar amino acids have hydrophilic R groups, whereas nonpolar amino acids have hydrophobic R groups.

d. Dipeptides contain two amino acids, whereas tripeptides contain three amino acids.

20
Enzymes and Vitamins

Credit: *Diedra Laird/The Charlotte Observer/MCT/Newscom*

Two months ago, Noah's mother learned that Noah was lactose intolerant, which means that he lacks the lactase enzyme needed to completely digest lactose in milk and milk-based products. Under the guidance of Noah's physician assistant, Emma, Noah's mother now limits the amount of dairy products in Noah's diet by using lactose-free milk and milk products or soy milk. Because calcium is usually provided by milk, Noah's mother has added nonmilk products high in calcium such as rhubarb and spinach to his diet. She gives him lactase if he consumes a milk-based product. Noah no longer suffers from abdominal pain, gas, or diarrhea. What is the substrate for the enzyme lactase?

CHAPTER READINESS*

✿ Core Chemistry Skills

- Interpreting Graphs (1.4E)

- Identifying the Primary, Secondary, Tertiary, and Quaternary Structures of Proteins (19.4, 19.5)

*These Core Chemistry Skills from previous chapters are listed here for your review as you proceed to the new material in this chapter.

20.1 Enzymes and Enzyme Action

Learning Goal: Describe enzymes and their role in enzyme-catalyzed reactions.

- Enzymes are proteins that act as biological catalysts.
- Enzymes accelerate the rate of biological reactions by lowering the activation energy of a reaction.
- Within the structure of an enzyme, there is a small pocket called the active site, which has a specific shape that fits a specific substrate.
- In the induced-fit model, a substrate and a flexible active site adjust their shapes to form an enzyme–substrate complex in which the reaction of the substrate is catalyzed to give product(s).

♦ **Learning Exercise 20.1A**

Indicate whether each of the following is a characteristic of an enzyme: yes (Y) or no (N)

1. _____ is a biological catalyst

2. _____ does not change the equilibrium position of a reaction

✿ CORE CHEMISTRY SKILL

Describing Enzyme Action

3. _____ greatly increases the rate of a cellular reaction

4. _____ is needed for every reaction that takes place in the cell

5. _____ catalyzes at a faster rate at lower temperatures

6. _____ lowers the activation energy of a biological reaction

7. _____ increases the rate of the forward, but not the reverse, reaction

Answers   **1.** Y   **2.** Y   **3.** Y   **4.** Y   **5.** N   **6.** Y   **7.** N

♦ **Learning Exercise 20.1B**

Match the terms (**a** to **e**) with the following descriptions:

    a. active site   **b.** substrate   **c.** enzyme–substrate complex
    d. lock-and-key   **e.** induced-fit

1. _____ the combination of an enzyme with a substrate

2. _____ a model of enzyme action in which the rigid shape of the active site exactly fits the shape of the substrate

3. _____ has a tertiary structure that fits the structure of the active site

4. _____ a model of enzyme action in which the shape of the active site adjusts to fit the shape of a substrate

5. _____ the portion of an enzyme that binds to the substrate and catalyzes the reaction

Answers   **1.** c   **2.** d   **3.** b   **4.** e   **5.** a

♦ **Learning Exercise 20.1C**

Write a series of equations that represents the formation of a product (P) from an enzyme (E) and substrate (S).

Answers $E + S \rightleftharpoons ES \longrightarrow EP \longrightarrow E + P$

20.2 Classification of Enzymes

Learning Goal: Classify enzymes and give their names.

- The names of many enzymes describe the compound or the reaction that is catalyzed and end with *ase*.

- Enzymes are classified by the type of reaction they catalyze: oxidation–reduction, transfer of groups, hydrolysis, the addition or removal of a group, isomerization, or the joining of two smaller molecules.

♦ **Learning Exercise 20.2**

Match the classification for enzymes with each of the following types of reactions:

a. oxidoreductase **b.** transferase **c.** hydrolase **d.** lyase **e.** isomerase **f.** ligase

1. _____ combines small molecules using energy from ATP

2. _____ transfers phosphate groups

3. _____ hydrolyzes a disaccharide into two glucose units

4. _____ converts a substrate to an isomer of the substrate

5. _____ adds hydrogen to a substrate

6. _____ removes H_2O from a substrate

7. _____ adds oxygen to a substrate

8. _____ converts a cis structure to a trans structure

⚛ **CORE CHEMISTRY SKILL**

Classifying Enzymes

Answers **1.** f **2.** b **3.** c **4.** e **5.** a **6.** d **7.** a **8.** e

20.3 Factors Affecting Enzyme Activity

Learning Goal: Describe the effect of changes of temperature, pH, concentration of enzyme, and concentration of substrate on enzyme activity.

- Enzymes are most effective at their optimum temperature and pH. The rate of an enzyme-catalyzed reaction decreases at temperatures and pH above or below the optimum.

- An enzyme can be made inactive by changes in pH or temperature or by chemical compounds called inhibitors.

- An increase in substrate concentration increases the reaction rate of an enzyme-catalyzed reaction until all of the enzyme molecules combine with substrate.

♦ **Learning Exercise 20.3A**

An enzyme has an optimum pH of 7 and an optimum temperature of 37 °C.

⚛ **CORE CHEMISTRY SKILL**

Identifying Factors Affecting Enzyme Activity

a. Draw a graph to represent the activity of the enzyme at the pH values shown. Indicate the optimum pH.

b. Draw a graph to represent the activity of the enzyme at the temperatures shown. Indicate the optimum temperature.

Copyright © 2015 Pearson Education, Inc.

Answers

a.

b.

♦ **Learning Exercise 20.3B**

Urease has an optimum pH of 7.0. Indicate the effect of each of the following on the reaction rate of a urease-catalyzed reaction:

    a. increases   **b.** decreases   **c.** doesn't change

1. _____ adding more substrate when an excess of enzyme is present

2. _____ running the reaction at pH 9.0

3. _____ lowering the temperature to 0 °C

4. _____ running the reaction at 85 °C

5. _____ increasing the concentration of substrate when all of the enzyme molecules are bonded to substrate

6. _____ adjusting pH to its optimum

Answers   **1.** a   **2.** b   **3.** b   **4.** b   **5.** c   **6.** a

20.4 Regulation of Enzyme Activity

Learning Goal: Describe the role of allosteric enzymes, feedback control, and covalent modification in regulating enzyme activity.

- When allosteric enzymes bind regulator molecules on a different part of the enzyme, there is a change in the shape of the enzyme and the active site. A positive regulator speeds up a reaction, and a negative regulator slows down a reaction.

- In feedback control, the end product of an enzyme-catalyzed sequence acts as a negative regulator and binds to the first enzyme in the sequence, which slows the rate of catalytic activity.

- Covalent modification occurs when covalent bonds to a group on the polypeptide chain are formed or broken. As a regulatory mechanism, covalent modification is reversible. The formation of zymogens and phosphorylation are types of covalent modification.

- Many digestive enzymes are produced and stored as inactive forms called *zymogens*, which are activated at a later time.

♦ **Learning Exercise 20.4**

Match the following terms with the correct phrase:

    a. zymogen   **b.** allosteric enzyme   **c.** covalent modification

    d. negative regulator   **e.** feedback control   **f.** positive regulator

1. _____ an enzyme that binds molecules at a site that is not the active site to increase the rate of enzyme activity

2. _____ the binding of the end product of a reaction sequence to the first enzyme in the pathway

3. _____ a molecule that slows down a reaction by preventing proper binding to the substrate

4. _____ an inactive form of an enzyme that is activated by removing a peptide section

5. _____ a molecule that binds at a site different than the active site to speed up the reaction

6. _____ the addition or removal of a phosphate group that changes catalytic activity

Answers   **1.** b   **2.** e   **3.** d   **4.** a   **5.** f   **6.** c

20.5 Enzyme Inhibition

Learning Goal: Describe competitive and noncompetitive inhibition, and reversible and irreversible inhibition.

- A competitive inhibitor has a structure similar to the substrate and competes for the active site. When the active site is occupied by a competitive inhibitor, the enzyme cannot catalyze the reaction of the substrate.

- A noncompetitive inhibitor attaches elsewhere on the enzyme, changing the shape of both the enzyme and the active site. As long as the noncompetitive inhibitor is attached to the enzyme, the altered active site cannot bind or catalyze substrate.

- A reversible inhibitor causes a loss of enzymatic activity that can be reversed.

- An irreversible inhibitor forms a permanent covalent bond with an amino acid side group in the active site of the enzyme, which prevents enzymatic activity.

Guide to Determining Type of Enzyme Inhibition	
STEP 1	Compare the structure of the inhibitor to that of the substrate.
STEP 2	Describe the characteristics of the inhibitor.
STEP 3	Assign the type of inhibition based on the characteristics.

♦ **Learning Exercise 20.5**

Identify each of the following as characteristic of competitive inhibition (C), noncompetitive inhibition (N), or irreversible inhibition (I):

1. _____ An inhibitor binds to the surface of the enzyme away from the active site.

2. _____ An inhibitor resembling the substrate molecule blocks the active site on the enzyme.

3. _____ An inhibitor causes permanent damage to the enzyme with a total loss of biological activity.

4. _____ The action of this inhibitor can be reversed by adding more substrate.

5. _____ The action of this inhibitor is not reversed by adding more substrate, but can be reversed when chemical reagents remove the inhibitor.

6. _____ Sulfanilamide stops bacterial infections because its structure is similar to PABA (*p*-aminobenzoic acid), which is essential for bacterial growth.

Answers   **1.** N   **2.** C   **3.** I   **4.** C   **5.** N   **6.** C

20.6   Enzyme Cofactors and Vitamins

Learning Goal: Describe the types of cofactors found in enzymes.

- Simple enzymes are biologically active as a protein only, whereas other enzymes require a cofactor.
- A cofactor may be a metal ion, such as Cu^{2+} or Fe^{2+}, or an organic compound called a coenzyme, usually a vitamin.
- Vitamins are organic molecules that are essential for proper health.
- Vitamins must be obtained from the diet because they are not synthesized in the body.
- Vitamins B and C are water-soluble vitamins; vitamins A, D, E, and K are fat-soluble vitamins.
- Many water-soluble vitamins function as coenzymes or precursors of enzymes.

Key Terms for Sections 20.1–20.6

Match the following key terms with the correct description shown below:

a. lock-and-key model   **b.** vitamin   **c.** inhibitor   **d.** enzyme   **e.** active site

1. _____ the portion of an enzyme structure where a substrate undergoes reaction

2. _____ a protein that catalyzes a biological reaction in the cells

3. _____ a model of enzyme action in which the substrate exactly fits the shape of the active site of an enzyme

4. _____ a substance that makes an enzyme inactive by interfering with its ability to react with a substrate

5. _____ an organic compound essential for normal health and growth that must be obtained from the diet

Answers   **1.** e   **2.** d   **3.** a   **4.** c   **5.** b

♦ **Learning Exercise 20.6A**   ⚛ **CORE CHEMISTRY SKILL**

Indicate whether each enzyme described below does or does not require a cofactor:

Describing the Role of Cofactors

1. _____ an enzyme consisting only of protein

2. _____ an enzyme requiring magnesium ion for activity

3. _____ an enzyme containing a sugar group

4. _____ an enzyme that gives only amino acids upon hydrolysis

5. _____ an enzyme that requires zinc ions for activity

Answers   **1.** does not require a cofactor   **2.** requires a cofactor   **3.** requires a cofactor
              4. does not require a cofactor   **5.** requires a cofactor

♦ **Learning Exercise 20.6B**

Identify the water-soluble vitamin (**a** to **d**) associated with each of the following:

    a. pantothenic acid (B_5)   **b.** riboflavin (B_2)   **c.** niacin (B_3)   **d.** ascorbic acid (C)

1. _____ collagen formation   **2.** _____ FAD and FMN

3. _____ NAD^+ **4.** _____ coenzyme A

Answers   **1.** d   **2.** b   **3.** c   **4.** a

♦ **Learning Exercise 20.6C**

Identify the fat-soluble vitamin (**a** to **d**) associated with each of the following:

    a. vitamin A   **b.** vitamin D   **c.** vitamin E   **d.** vitamin K

1. _____ blood clotting   **2.** _____ vision

3. _____ antioxidant   **4.** _____ absorption of calcium

Answers   **1.** d   **2.** a   **3.** c   **4.** b

Checklist for Chapter 20

You are ready to take the Practice Test for Chapter 20. Be sure that you have accomplished the learning goals for each of the sections in this chapter. If not, review the section listed at the end of each goal. Then apply your new skills and understanding to the Practice Test.

After studying Chapter 20, I can successfully:

_____ Describe the lock-and-key and induced-fit models of enzyme action. (20.1)

_____ Classify enzymes according to the type of reaction they catalyze. (20.2)

_____ Discuss the effect of changes in temperature, pH, concentration of enzyme, and concentration of substrate on enzyme action. (20.3)

_____ Describe the reversible and irreversible inhibition of enzymes. (20.4)

_____ Discuss allosteric enzymes, feedback control, and covalent modification in the regulation of enzyme activity. (20.5)

_____ Identify the types of cofactors that are necessary for enzyme activity. (20.6)

_____ Describe the functions of vitamins as coenzymes. (20.6)

Practice Test for Chapter 20

1. Enzymes (20.1)
   - **A.** are biological catalysts
   - **B.** are polysaccharides
   - **C.** are insoluble in water
   - **D.** always contain a cofactor
   - **E.** are named with an *ose* ending

For questions 2 through 5, classify each enzyme as requiring a cofactor (C) or not requiring a cofactor (N). (20.6)

2. _____ an active enzyme that contains amino acids and a magnesium ion

3. _____ an active enzyme consisting of protein only

4. _____ an active enzyme requiring zinc ion for activation

5. _____ an active enzyme containing vitamin K

For questions 6 through 10, select answers from the following (E = enzyme; S = substrate; P = product): (20.1)

A. $S \longrightarrow P$ **B.** $EP \longrightarrow E + P$ **C.** $E + S \longrightarrow ES$

D. $ES \longrightarrow EP$ **E.** $EP \longrightarrow ES$

6. _____ the enzymatic reaction occurring at the active site

7. _____ the release of product from the enzyme

8. _____ the first step in the enzyme reaction

9. _____ the formation of the enzyme–substrate complex

10. _____ the final step in the enzyme reaction

For questions 11 through 15, match each enzyme with the reaction it catalyzes: (20.2)

A. decarboxylase   **B.** isomerase   **C.** dehydrogenase
D. lipase   **E.** sucrase

11. _____ $CH_3-\overset{OH}{\underset{|}{CH}}-\overset{O}{\overset{||}{C}}-OH \longrightarrow CH_3-\overset{O}{\overset{||}{C}}-\overset{O}{\overset{||}{C}}-OH$

12. _____ sucrose + $H_2O \longrightarrow$ glucose and fructose

13. _____ $CH_3-\overset{O}{\overset{||}{C}}-\overset{O}{\overset{||}{C}}-OH \longrightarrow CH_3-\overset{O}{\overset{||}{C}}-OH + CO_2$

14. _____ fructose $\longrightarrow$ glucose

15. _____ triacylglycerol + $3H_2O \longrightarrow$ fatty acids and glycerol

For questions 16 through 20, select your answers from the following: (20.3)

A. increases the rate of reaction   **B.** decreases the rate of reaction
C. denatures the enzyme, and no reaction occurs

16. _____ setting the reaction tube in a beaker of water at 100 °C

17. _____ adding substrate to the reaction vessel

18. _____ running the reaction at 10 °C

19. _____ adding ethanol to the reaction system

20. _____ adjusting the pH to optimum pH

For questions 21 through 25, identify each description of inhibition as one of the following: (20.4)

A. competitive   **B.** noncompetitive

21. _____ This alteration affects the overall shape of the enzyme.

22. _____ A molecule that closely resembles the substrate interferes with enzymatic activity.

23. _____ The inhibition can be reversed by increasing substrate concentration.

24. _____ The heavy metal ion, Pb^{2+}, bonds with an —SH side group.

25. _____ The inhibition is not affected by increased substrate concentration.

Answers to the Practice Test

1. A	**2.** C	**3.** N	**4.** C	**5.** C
6. D	**7.** B	**8.** C	**9.** C	**10.** B
11. C	**12.** E	**13.** A	**14.** B	**15.** D
16. C	**17.** A	**18.** B	**19.** C	**20.** A
21. B	**22.** A	**23.** A	**24.** B	**25.** B

20

Enzymes and Vitamins

Learning Goals

- Describe enzymes and their role in enzyme-catalyzed reactions.
- Classify enzymes and give their names.
- Describe the effect of changes of temperature, pH, concentration of enzyme, and concentration of substrate on enzyme activity.
- Describe the role of allosteric enzymes, feedback control, and covalent modification in regulating enzyme activity.
- Describe competitive and noncompetitive inhibition, and reversible and irreversible inhibition.
- Describe the types of cofactors found in enzymes.

Chapter Outline

Chapter Opener: Physician Assistant

20.1 Enzymes and Enzyme Action

20.2 Classification of Enzymes

Chemistry Link to Health: Isoenzymes as Diagnostic Tools

20.3 Factors Affecting Enzyme Activity

Explore Your World: Enzyme Activity

20.4 Regulation of Enzyme Activity

20.5 Enzyme Inhibition

20.6 Enzyme Cofactors and Vitamins

Clinical Update: Noah's Diet for Lactose Intolerance

⚛ Core Chemistry Skills

- Describing Enzyme Action (20.1)
- Classifying Enzymes (20.2)
- Identifying Factors Affecting Enzyme Activity (20.3)
- Describing the Role of Cofactors (20.6)

Selected Answers and Solutions to Text Problems

20.1 Chemical reactions in the body can occur without enzymes, but the rates are too slow at the relatively mild conditions of normal body temperature and pH. Catalyzed reactions, which are many times faster, provide the amounts of products needed by the cell at a particular time.

20.3 **a.** An enzyme (2) has a tertiary structure that recognizes the substrate.
b. The combination of an enzyme with the substrate is the enzyme–substrate complex (1).
c. The substrate (3) has a structure that fits the active site of the enzyme.

20.5 **a.** The equation for an enzyme-catalyzed reaction is:

$$E + S \rightleftharpoons ES \longrightarrow EP \longrightarrow E + P$$

E = enzyme, S = substrate, ES = enzyme–substrate complex

EP = enzyme–product complex, P = products

b. The active site is a region or pocket within the tertiary structure of an enzyme that accepts the substrate, aligns the substrate for reaction, and catalyzes the reaction.

20.7 **a.** Oxidoreductases catalyze oxidation–reduction reactions.

b. Transferases move (or transfer) groups, such as amino or phosphate groups, from one substance to another.

c. Hydrolases use water to split bonds in molecules (hydrolysis) such as carbohydrates, peptides, and lipids.

20.9 **a.** A hydrolase would catalyze the hydrolysis of sucrose.

b. An oxidoreductase would catalyze the addition of oxygen (oxidation).

c. An isomerase would catalyze the conversion of glucose to fructose.

d. A transferase would catalyze the transfer of an amino group from one molecule to another.

20.11 **a.** A lyase such as a decarboxylase removes CO_2 from a molecule.

b. The transfer of an amino group to another molecule would be catalyzed by a transferase.

20.13 **a.** Succinate oxidase catalyzes the oxidation of succinate.

b. Glutamine synthetase catalyzes the combination of glutamate and ammonia to form glutamine.

c. Alcohol dehydrogenase removes 2H from an alcohol.

20.15 **a.** PSA is the abbreviation for the enzyme prostate-specific antigen.

b. CK is the abbreviation for the enzyme creatine kinase.

c. CE is the abbreviation for the enzyme cholinesterase.

20.17 Isoenzymes are slightly different forms of an enzyme that catalyze the same reaction in different organs and tissues of the body.

20.19 A doctor might run tests for the enzymes CK and LDH to determine if the patient had a heart attack.

20.21 **a.** Decreasing the substrate concentration decreases the rate of reaction.

b. The reaction will slow or stop because the enzyme will be denatured at low pH.

c. The reaction will slow or stop because the high temperature will denature the enzyme.

d. The reaction will go faster as long as there are polypeptides to react.

20.23 From the graph, the optimum pH values for the enzymes are approximately: pepsin, pH 2; lactase, pH 6; sucrase pH 6; trypsin, pH 8.

20.25 When a regulator molecule binds to an allosteric site, the shape of the enzyme is altered, which makes the active site more reactive or less reactive and thereby increases or decreases the rate of the reaction.

20.27 In feedback control, the product binds to the first enzyme in a series, changing the shape of the active site. If the active site can no longer bind the substrate effectively, the reaction will stop.

20.29 **a.** (3) covalent modification

b. (2) a zymogen

c. (1) an allosteric enzyme

20.31 In order to conserve material and energy and to prevent clotting in the bloodstream, thrombin is produced from prothrombin only at a wound site.

20.33 **a.** If the inhibitor has a structure similar to the structure of the substrate, the inhibitor is competitive.

b. If adding more substrate cannot reverse the effect of the inhibitor, the inhibitor is non-competitive.

c. If the inhibitor competes with the substrate for the active site, it is a competitive inhibitor.

d. If the structure of the inhibitor is not similar to the structure of the substrate, the inhibitor is noncompetitive.

e. If adding more substrate reverses the inhibition, the inhibitor is competitive.

20.35 a. Methanol has the condensed structural formula $CH_3—OH$, whereas ethanol is $CH_3—CH_2—OH$.

b. Ethanol has a structure similar to methanol and could compete for the active site.

c. Ethanol is a competitive inhibitor.

20.37 a. Thiamine or vitamin B_1 is a cofactor (coenzyme), which is required by this enzyme for activity.

b. The Zn^{2+} is a cofactor, which is required by this enzyme for activity.

c. If the active form of an enzyme consists of only polypeptide chains, a cofactor is not required.

20.39 a. Pantothenic acid (vitamin B_5) is part of coenzyme A.

b. Tetrahydrofolate (THF) is a reduced form of folic acid.

c. Niacin (vitamin B_3) is a component of NAD^+.

20.41 a. A deficiency of vitamin D (cholecalciferol) can lead to rickets.

b. A deficiency of vitamin C (ascorbic acid) can lead to scurvy.

c. A deficiency of vitamin B_3 (niacin) can lead to pellagra.

20.43 Vitamin B_6 is a water-soluble vitamin, which means that any excess of vitamin B_6 is eliminated from the body each day.

20.45 a. At 60 min, the baseline level of breath hydrogen is approximately 20 ppm.

b. At 60 min, the level of hydrogen in Noah's breath is approximately 40 ppm.

20.47 Heating the milk in the hot chocolate will denature the protein enzyme, lactase. Since the enzyme is no longer active, Noah will suffer from the symptoms of lactose intolerance.

20.49 a. The enzyme bromelain found in fresh pineapple breaks down protein, which means that the gelatin dessert would not turn solid upon cooking. The high temperatures used to prepare canned pineapple denature the enzyme so it no longer catalyzes the hydrolysis of protein.

b. The enzyme in fresh pineapple juice can be used to tenderize tough meat because the enzyme breaks down proteins.

20.51 a. The oxidation of a glycol to an aldehyde and carboxylic acid is catalyzed by an oxidore-ductase.

b. Ethanol competes with ethylene glycol for the active site of the alcohol dehydrogenase enzyme, saturating the active site, which allows ethylene glycol to be removed from the body without producing oxalic acid.

20.53 The many different reactions that take place in cells require different enzymes because enzymes react with only a certain type of substrate.

20.55 In chemistry laboratories, reactions are often run at high temperatures using catalysts that are strong acids or bases. Enzymes, which function at physiological temperatures and pH, are proteins that are denatured rapidly if high temperatures or acids or bases are used.

20.57 Enzymes lower the activation energy of a reaction, thereby requiring less energy to convert reactants to products. They also bind the substrate in the active site of the enzyme in a position that is more favorable for the reaction to proceed.

20.59 In the lock-and-key model, the substrate sucrose fits the exact shape of the active site in the enzyme sucrase, but lactose does not.

20.61 **a.** The disaccharide lactose is a substrate (S).
  b. The suffix *ase* in lactase indicates that it is an enzyme (E).
  c. The suffix *ase* in lipase indicates that it is an enzyme (E).
  d. Trypsin is an enzyme that hydrolyzes polypeptides (E).
  e. Pyruvate is a substrate (S).
  f. The suffix *ase* in transaminase indicates that it is an enzyme (E).

20.63 **a.** Urea is the substrate for urease.
  b. Succinate is the substrate for succinate dehydrogenase.
  c. Aspartate is the substrate for aspartate transaminase.
  d. Phenylalanine is the substrate for phenylalanine hydroxylase.

20.65 **a.** The transfer of an acyl group is catalyzed by a transferase.
  b. Oxidases are classified as oxidoreductases.
  c. A lipase, which uses water to split ester bonds in lipids, is classified as a hydrolase.
  d. A decarboxylase is classified as a lyase.

20.67 The optimum temperature for an enzyme is the temperature at which the enzyme is fully active and most effective.

20.69 **a.** The rate of catalysis will slow and stop as a high temperature denatures the enzyme.
  b. The rate of the catalyzed reaction will slow or stop when the reaction mixture is placed in ice.
  c. The reaction will slow or stop because pH 2 is much lower than the optimum pH of the enzyme.

20.71 **a.** An enzyme is saturated if adding more substrate does not increase the rate of reaction.
  b. When increasing the substrate concentration increases the rate of reaction, the enzyme is not saturated.

20.73 An allosteric enzyme contains sites for regulators that alter the structure of the active site of the enzyme, which speeds up or slows down the rate of the catalyzed reaction.

20.75 In feedback control, the end product of the reaction pathway binds to the enzyme to slow down or stop the first reaction in the reaction pathway. It acts as a negative regulator.

20.77 In reversible inhibition, the inhibitor can dissociate from the enzyme, whereas in irreversible inhibition, the inhibitor forms a strong covalent bond with the enzyme and does not dissociate. Irreversible inhibitors act as poisons to enzymes.

20.79 **a.** (3) An irreversible inhibitor forms a covalent bond with an R group in the active site.
  b. (1) A competitive inhibitor has a structure similar to the substrate.
  c. (1) The addition of more substrate reverses the inhibition of a competitive inhibitor.
  d. (2) A noncompetitive inhibitor bonds to the surface of the enzyme, causing a change in the shape of the enzyme and active site.

20.81 **a.** The Mg^{2+} is a cofactor, which is required by this enzyme for activity.
  b. A protein that is catalytically active as a tertiary protein structure does not require a cofactor.
  c. Folic acid is a cofactor (coenzyme), which is required by this enzyme for activity.

20.83 **a.** Coenzyme A (3) requires pantothenic acid (B_5).
  b. NAD^+ (1) requires niacin (B_3).
  c. TPP (2) requires thiamine (B_1).

20.85 A vitamin combines with an enzyme only when the enzyme and coenzyme are needed to catalyze a reaction. When the enzyme is not needed, the vitamin dissociates for use by other enzymes in the cell.

20.87 **a.** A deficiency of niacin can lead to pellagra (3).
  b. A deficiency of vitamin A can lead to night blindness (1).
  c. A deficiency of vitamin D can lead to weak bone structure (2).

20.89 A heart attack may be the cause. Normally the enzymes LDH and CK are present only in low levels in the blood.

20.91 When designing an inhibitor, the substrate of an enzyme usually is known even if the structure of the enzyme is not. It is easier to design a molecule that resembles the substrate (competitive) than to find an inhibitor that binds to a second site on an enzyme (noncompetitive).

20.93 **a.** Antibiotics such as ampicillin are irreversible inhibitors.
    b. Antibiotics such as ampicillin inhibit enzymes needed to form cell walls in bacteria, not humans.

20.95 **a.** When pepsinogen enters the stomach, the low pH cleaves a peptide from its protein chain to form pepsin.
    b. An active protease would digest the proteins of the stomach rather than the proteins in the foods.

20.97 **a.** The reactants are lactose and water, and the products are glucose and galactose.
    b.

    c. By lowering the energy of activation, the enzyme furnishes a lower energy pathway by which the reaction can take place.

20.99 **a.** In this reaction, oxygen is added to an aldehyde. The enzyme that catalyzes this reaction would be an oxidoreductase.
    b. In this reaction, a dipeptide is hydrolyzed. The enzyme that catalyzes this reaction would be a hydrolase.
    c. In this reaction, water is added to a double bond. The enzyme that catalyzes the addition of a group without hydrolysis would be a lyase.

20.101 Cadmium would be a noncompetitive inhibitor because increasing the substrate and cofactor has no effect on the rate. This implies that the cadmium is binding to another site on the enzyme.

21
Nucleic Acids and Protein Synthesis

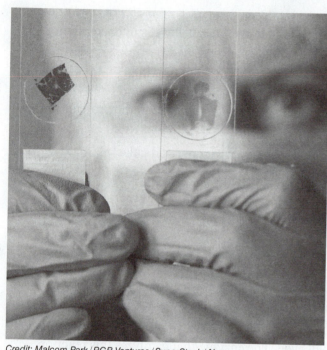

Ellen, who was diagnosed with breast cancer, has had a lumpectomy. Tissue samples from the tumor and lymph nodes were prepared for a pathologist by placing a thin section, 0.001 mm thick, on a microscope slide. The tissues, which tested positive for estrogen receptor, confirmed that Ellen's breast cancer tumors required estrogen for their growth. The bonding of estrogen, an activator, to the estrogen receptor increases the production of mammary cells and potential mutations that can lead to cancer. The tissues were also tested for altered genes BRCA1 and BRCA2. The normal genes suppress tumor growth, whereas the mutated genes lose their ability to suppress tumor growth, which increases the risk for breast cancer. Ellen's test results for a BRCA mutation were negative. How does tamoxifen reduce the risk of breast cancer?

Credit: Malcom Park / RGB Ventures / SuperStock / Alamy

CHAPTER READINESS*

⚛ Core Chemistry Skills

- Forming Amides (18.5)
- Drawing the Zwitterion for an Amino Acid (19.1)

- Identifying the Primary, Secondary, Tertiary, and Quaternary Structures of Proteins (19.4, 19.5)
- Identifying Factors Affecting Enzyme Activity (20.3)

*These Core Chemistry Skills from previous chapters are listed here for your review as you proceed to the new material in this chapter.

21.1 Components of Nucleic Acids

Learning Goal: Describe the bases and ribose sugars that make up the nucleic acids DNA and RNA.

- Nucleic acids are composed of bases, five-carbon sugars, and phosphate groups.
- In DNA, the bases are adenine, thymine, guanine, and cytosine. In RNA, uracil replaces thymine.
- In DNA, the sugar is deoxyribose; in RNA, the sugar is ribose.
- A nucleoside is composed of a base and a sugar.
- A nucleotide is composed of a base, a sugar, and a phosphate group.
- Deoxyribonucleic acid (DNA) and ribonucleic acid (RNA) are polymers of nucleotides.

♦ Learning Exercise 21.1A

1. Write the names and abbreviations for the bases in each of the following:

DNA _____

RNA _____

2. Write the name of the sugar in each of the following:

DNA _____ RNA _____

Answers   **1.** DNA: adenine (A), thymine (T), guanine (G), cytosine (C)
RNA: adenine (A), uracil (U), guanine (G), cytosine (C)
2. DNA: deoxyribose; RNA: ribose

◆ **Learning Exercise 21.1B**

Name each of the following, and classify it as a purine or a pyrimidine:

a.

b.

c.

d.

Answers   **a.** cytosine; pyrimidine
c. guanine; purine

b. adenine; purine
d. thymine; pyrimidine

◆ **Learning Exercise 21.1C**

Identify the nucleic acid (DNA or RNA) in which each of the following are found:

1. _____ adenosine monophosphate

2. _____ guanosine monophosphate

3. _____ dCMP

4. _____ cytidine monophosphate

5. _____ deoxythymidine monophosphate

6. _____ UMP

7. _____ dGMP

8. _____ deoxyadenosine monophosphate

Answers   **1.** RNA   **2.** RNA   **3.** DNA   **4.** RNA
5. DNA   **6.** RNA   **7.** DNA   **8.** DNA

◆ **Learning Exercise 21.1D**

Draw the condensed structural formula for deoxyadenosine monophosphate. Indicate the 5′ and the 3′ carbon atoms on the sugar.

Answer

Deoxyadenosine monophosphate (dAMP)

21.2 Primary Structure of Nucleic Acids

Learning Goal: Describe the primary structures of RNA and DNA.

- Nucleic acids are polymers of nucleotides in which the —OH group on the 3′ carbon of a sugar in one nucleotide bonds to the phosphate group attached to the 5′ carbon of a sugar in the adjacent nucleotide.

♦ **Learning Exercise 21.2A**

Draw the structure of a dinucleotide that consists of cytidine monophosphate (free 5′ phosphate) bonded to guanosine monophosphate (free 3′ hydroxyl). Identify each nucleotide, the phosphodiester bond, the free 5′ phosphate group, and the free 3′ hydroxyl group.

Answer

Copyright © 2015 Pearson Education, Inc.

♦ **Learning Exercise 21.2B**

Consider the following sequence of nucleotides in RNA: A G U C

1. Write the names of the nucleotides in this sequence. _____

_____

2. Which nucleotide has the free 5′ phosphate group? _____

3. Which nucleotide has the free 3′ hydroxyl group? _____

Answers   1. adenosine monophosphate, guanosine monophosphate,
                   uridine monophosphate, cytidine monophosphate
                2. adenosine monophosphate   3. cytidine monophosphate

21.3   DNA Double Helix

Learning Goal: Describe the double helix of DNA.

- The two strands in DNA are held together by hydrogen bonds between complementary base pairs, A with T and G with C.
- One DNA strand runs in the 5′ to 3′ direction, and the other strand runs in the 3′ to 5′ direction.

♦ **Learning Exercise 21.3A**

Complete the following statements:

1. The structure of the two strands of nucleotides in DNA is called a _____.

2. In one strand of DNA, the sugar–phosphate backbone runs in the 5′ to 3′ direction, whereas the opposite strand goes in the _____ direction.

3. On the DNA strands, the free phosphate group is at the _____ end and the free hydroxyl group is at the _____ end.

4. The only combinations of base pairs that connect the two DNA strands are _____ and

_____.

5. The base pairs along one DNA strand are _____ to the base pairs on the opposite strand.

Answers   1. double helix   2. 3′ to 5′   3. 5′; 3′
                4. A—T; G—C   5. complementary

♦ **Learning Exercise 21.3B**

Complete each DNA section by writing the complementary strand.

1. 5′ A A A T T T C C C G G G 3′

2. 5′ A T G C T T G G C T C C 3′

3. 5′ G C G C T C A A A T G C 3′

⚛ CORE CHEMISTRY SKILL

Writing the Complementary DNA Strand

Answers   **1.** 3′ T T T A A A G G G C C C 5′   **2.** 3′ T A C G A A C C G A G G 5′
             3. 3′ C G C G A G T T T A C G 5′

21.4   DNA Replication

Learning Goal: Describe the process of DNA replication.

• During replication, polymerase makes new DNA strands along each of the original DNA strands that serve as templates.

• Complementary base pairs ensures the correct pairing of bases to give identical copies of the original DNA.

♦ **Learning Exercise 21.4A**

Essay: Describe the process by which DNA replicates to produce identical copies.

Answer   In the replication process, the bases in each strand of the separated parent DNA are paired with their complementary bases. Because each complementary base is specific for a base in the parent strand of DNA, the new DNA strands are exact duplicates of the original strands of DNA.

♦ **Learning Exercise 21.4B**

Match each of the following terms with the correct description below:

    a. replication forks   **b.** Okazaki fragments   **c.** DNA polymerase
    d. helicase   **e.** leading strand   **f.** lagging strand

1. _____ the enzyme that catalyzes the unwinding of a section of the DNA double helix

2. _____ the points in open sections of DNA where replication begins

3. _____ the enzyme that catalyzes the formation of phosphodiester bonds between nucleotides

4. _____ the short segments produced in the formation of the 3′ to 5′ daughter DNA strand

5. _____ the new DNA strand that grows in the 5′ to 3′ direction during the formation of daughter DNA

6. _____ the new DNA strand that is synthesized in the 3′ to 5′ direction

Answers   **1.** d   **2.** a   **3.** c   **4.** b   **5.** e   **6.** f

21.5   RNA and Transcription

Learning Goal: Identify the different types of RNA; describe the synthesis of mRNA.

• The three types of RNA differ by their function in the cell: ribosomal RNA makes up most of the structure of the ribosomes and is the site of protein synthesis; messenger RNA carries information from the DNA to the ribosomes; and transfer RNA places the correct amino acids in the protein.

• Transcription is the process by which RNA polymerase produces mRNA from one strand of DNA.

- The bases in the mRNA are complementary to the DNA, except U in RNA is paired with A in DNA.
- The RNA polymerase enzyme moves along an unwound section of DNA in a 3′ to 5′ direction.
- In eukaryotes, initial RNA includes noncoding sections, which are removed before the RNA leaves the nucleus.
- The production of mRNA occurs when certain proteins are needed in the cell.
- Transcription factors bind to the promoter to activate the RNA polymerase for the transcription of a particular mRNA.

♦ **Learning Exercise 21.5A**

⚛ **CORE CHEMISTRY SKILL**

Writing the mRNA Segment for a DNA Template

Match each of the following characteristics with mRNA, tRNA, or rRNA:

1. is most abundant in a cell _____

2. has the shortest chain of nucleotides _____

3. carries information from DNA to the ribosomes for protein synthesis _____

4. is the major component of ribosomes _____

5. carries specific amino acids to the ribosome for protein synthesis _____

6. consists of a large and a small subunit _____

Answers 1. rRNA 2. tRNA 3. mRNA 4. rRNA 5. tRNA 6. rRNA

♦ **Learning Exercise 21.5B**

Fill in the blanks with a word or phrase that answers each of the following questions:

1. Where in the cell does transcription take place? _____

2. How many strands of a DNA molecule are involved in transcription? _____

3. What is the name of the sections in genes that code for proteins? _____

4. What is the name of the sections in genes that do not code for proteins? _____

5. What are the abbreviations for the four nucleotides in mRNA? _____

6. What is the corresponding section of an mRNA produced from each of the following?

   a. 3′ C A T T C G G T A 5′

   b. 3′ G T A C C T A A C G T C C G 5′

Answers 1. nucleus 2. one 3. exons 4. introns 5. A, U, G, C
6. a. 5′ G U A A G C C A U 3′   b. 5′ C A U G G A U U G C A G G C 3′

21.6 The Genetic Code and Protein Synthesis

Learning Goal: Use the genetic code to write the amino acid sequence for a segment of mRNA.

- The genetic code consists of a sequence of three nucleotides (triplets) called codons that specify the amino acids in a protein.
- The 64 codons for 20 amino acids allow several codons for most amino acids.

- The codon AUG signals the start of transcription, and codons UAG, UGA, and UAA signal the end of transcription.
- Proteins are synthesized at the ribosomes in a translation process that includes three steps: initiation, elongation, and termination.
- During translation, the appropriate tRNA brings the correct amino acid to the ribosome, where the amino acid is bonded by a peptide bond to the growing peptide chain.
- When the polypeptide is released, it takes on its secondary and tertiary structures to become a functional protein in the cell.

◆ **Learning Exercise 21.6A**

⚛ **CORE CHEMISTRY SKILL**

Give the three letter abbreviation for each of the amino acids coded for by the following mRNA codons:

Writing the Amino Acid for an mRNA Codon

1. UUU _____

2. GCG _____

3. AGC _____

4. CCA _____

5. GGA _____

6. ACA _____

7. AUG _____

8. CUC _____

9. CAU _____

10. GUU _____

Answers	**1.** Phe	**2.** Ala	**3.** Ser	**4.** Pro	**5.** Gly
	6. Thr	**7.** Start/Met	**8.** Leu	**9.** His	**10.** Val

◆ **Learning Exercise 21.6B**

Match the components **a** to **e** of the translation process with the correct description **1** to **5** below:

   a. initiation   **b.** activation   **c.** anticodon   **d.** translocation   **e.** termination

1. _____ the three bases in tRNA that complement a codon on the mRNA

2. _____ the combining of an amino acid with a specific tRNA

3. _____ the placement of methionine on the large ribosomal subunit

4. _____ the shift of the ribosome from one codon on mRNA to the next

5. _____ the process that occurs when the ribosome reaches a UAA, UGA, or UAG codon on mRNA

Answers   **1.** c   **2.** b   **3.** a   **4.** d   **5.** e

◆ **Learning Exercise 21.6C**

Write the mRNA that forms for each of the following sections of DNA. For each codon in the mRNA, write the amino acid that would be placed in the protein by a tRNA.

1. DNA: 3′ CCC   TCA   GGG   CGC 5′

mRNA: _____   _____   _____   _____

Amino acid: _____   _____   _____   _____

2. DNA: 3′ ATA   GCC   TTT   GGC   AAC 5′

mRNA: _____ _____ _____ _____ _____

Amino acid: _____ _____ _____ _____ _____

Answers   **1.** mRNA: 5′ GGG AGU CCC GCG 3′
                         Gly   Ser   Pro   Ala
           2. mRNA: 5′ UAU CGG AAA CCG UUG 3′
                         Tyr   Arg   Lys   Pro   Leu

◆ **Learning Exercise 21.6D**

A segment of DNA that codes for a protein contains 270 nucleotides. How many amino acids would be present in the protein for this DNA segment?

Answer   Assuming that the entire segment codes for a protein, there would be 90 $(270 \div 3)$ amino acids in the protein produced.

21.7 Genetic Mutations

Learning Goal: Identify the type of change in DNA for a point mutation, a deletion mutation, and an insertion mutation.

- A genetic mutation is a change of one or more bases in the DNA sequence that may alter the structure and ability of the resulting protein to function properly.
- In a point mutation, one base is changed, which may result in a different amino acid being placed in the protein.
- In an addition or deletion mutation, the insertion or deletion of one base alters all of the codons following the base change, which affects the amino acid sequence that follows the mutation.
- Mutations result from X-rays, overexposure to UV light, chemicals called mutagens, and some viruses.

◆ **Learning Exercise 21.7**

Consider the following segment of a DNA template strand: 3′ AAT CCC GGG 5′:

1. Write the mRNA produced.

_____ _____ _____

2. Write the amino acid order for the mRNA codons.

_____ _____ _____

3. A point mutation replaces the thymine in this DNA template strand with guanine. Write the mRNA produced.

_____ _____ _____

4. Write the new amino acid order.

_____ _____ _____

5. Why is this mutation called a point mutation?

6. How is a point mutation different from a deletion mutation?

7. What are some possible causes of genetic mutations?

Answers
1. 5′ UUA GGG CCC 3′   **2.** Leu–Gly–Pro
3. 5′ UUC GGG CCC 3′   **4.** Phe–Gly–Pro
5. One base is replaced with another.
6. In a point mutation, only one codon is affected and only one amino acid may be different. In a deletion mutation, all of the codons that follow the mutation are shifted by one base, which causes a different amino acid order in the remaining sequence of the protein.
7. X-rays, UV light, chemicals called mutagens, and some viruses are possible causes of genetic mutations.

21.8 Recombinant DNA

Learning Goal: Describe the preparation and uses of recombinant DNA.

- Recombinant DNA is synthesized by opening a piece of DNA and inserting a DNA section from another source.
- Much of the work with recombinant DNA is done with small circular DNA molecules called plasmids found in *E. coli* bacteria.
- Recombinant DNA is used to produce large numbers of copies of foreign DNA that are useful in genetic engineering techniques.

♦ **Learning Exercise 21.8**

Match the following terms with the correct description below:

a. plasmids   b. restriction enzymes   c. polymerase chain reaction
d. recombinant DNA   e. Human Genome Project

1. _____ a synthetic form of DNA that contains a piece of foreign DNA

2. _____ research that determined the DNA sequence of all the genes in a human cell

3. _____ small, circular, DNA molecules found in *E. coli* bacteria

4. _____ a process that makes multiple copies of DNA in a short amount of time

5. _____ enzymes that cut open the DNA strands in plasmids

Answers   **1.** d   **2.** e   **3.** a   **4.** c   **5.** b

21.9 Viruses

Learning Goal: Describe the methods by which a virus infects a cell.

- Viruses are small particles of 3 to 200 genes that cannot replicate unless they invade a host cell.
- A viral infection involves using the host cell's machinery to replicate the viral nucleic acid.
- A retrovirus contains RNA as its genetic material.

Key Terms for Sections 21.2–21.9

Match the following key terms with the correct phrase below:

a. DNA **b.** RNA **c.** double helix **d.** mutation **e.** virus **f.** recombinant DNA
g. transcription

1. _____ the formation of mRNA to carry genetic information from DNA to allow for protein synthesis

2. _____ the genetic material that contains the bases adenine, cytosine, guanine, and thymine

3. _____ the shape of DNA with a sugar–phosphate backbone and base pairs linked in the center

4. _____ the combination of DNA from different organisms which forms new DNA

5. _____ a small particle containing DNA or RNA in a protein coat that requires a host cell for replication

6. _____ a change in the DNA base sequence that may alter the shape and function of a protein

7. _____ a type of nucleic acid with a single strand containing the nucleotides adenine, cytosine, guanine, and uracil

Answers   **1.** g   **2.** a   **3.** c   **4.** f   **5.** e   **6.** d   **7.** b

♦ Learning Exercise 21.9

Match the terms with the correct description below:

a. host cell   **b.** retrovirus   **c.** vaccine   **d.** protease   **e.** virus

1. _____ the enzyme inhibited by drugs that prevent the synthesis of viral proteins

2. _____ a small, disease-causing particle that contains either DNA or RNA as its genetic material

3. _____ a type of virus that must use reverse transcriptase to make a viral DNA

4. _____ required by viruses to replicate

5. _____ inactive form of a virus that boosts the immune response by causing the body to produce antibodies

Answers   **1.** d   **2.** e   **3.** b   **4.** a   **5.** c

Checklist for Chapter 21

You are ready to take the Practice Test for Chapter 21. Be sure that you have accomplished the learning goals for each of the sections in this chapter. If not, review the section listed at the end of each goal. Then apply your new skills and understanding to the Practice Test.

After studying Chapter 21, I can successfully:

_____ Identify the components of the nucleic acids RNA and DNA. (21.1)

_____ Describe the nucleotides contained in DNA and RNA. (21.1)

_____ Describe the primary structure of nucleic acids. (21.2)

_____ Describe the structures of RNA and DNA; show the relationship between the bases in the double helix. (21.3)

_____ Explain the process of DNA replication. (21.4)

_____ Describe the structure and characteristics of the three types of RNA. (21.5)

_____ Describe the synthesis of mRNA (transcription). (21.5)

_____ Describe the function of the codons in the genetic code. (21.6)

_____ Describe the role of translation in protein synthesis. (21.6)

_____ Describe some ways in which DNA is altered to cause mutations. (21.7)

_____ Describe the process used to prepare recombinant DNA. (21.8)

_____ Explain how retroviruses use reverse transcription to synthesize DNA. (21.9)

Practice Test for Chapter 21

1. A nucleotide contains (21.1)
   A. a base
   B. a base and a sugar
   C. a phosphate group and a sugar
   D. a base and deoxyribose
   E. a base, a sugar, and a phosphate group

2. The double helix in DNA is held together by (21.3)
   A. hydrogen bonds
   B. ester linkages
   C. peptide bonds
   D. salt bridges
   E. disulfide bonds

3. The process of producing DNA in the nucleus is called (21.4)
   A. complementation
   B. replication
   C. translation
   D. transcription
   E. mutation

4. Which occurs in RNA but *NOT* in DNA? (21.1)
   A. thymine
   B. cytosine
   C. adenine
   D. phosphate
   E. uracil

5. Which type of molecule determines protein structure in protein synthesis? (21.6)
   A. DNA   B. mRNA   C. tRNA   D. rRNA   E. ribosomes

6. Which type of molecule carries amino acids to the ribosomes? (21.5)
   A. DNA   B. mRNA   C. tRNA   D. rRNA   E. protein

For questions 7 through 15, select answers from the following nucleic acids: (21.1, 21.3, 21.4, 21.5, 21.6)
   A. DNA   B. mRNA   C. tRNA   D. rRNA

7. _____ Along with protein, it is a major component of the ribosomes.

8. _____ This is a double helix consisting of two chains of nucleotides held together by hydrogen bonds between bases.

9. _____ This is a nucleic acid that uses deoxyribose as the sugar.

10. _____ This is a nucleic acid produced in the nucleus that migrates to the ribosomes to direct the formation of a protein.

11. _____ It places the proper amino acid into the peptide chain.

12. _____ It contains the bases adenine, cytosine, guanine, and thymine.

13. _____ It contains the codons for the amino acid order.

14. _____ It contains a triplet called an anticodon loop.

15. _____ This nucleic acid is replicated during cellular division.

For questions 16 through 20, select answers from the following: (21.4, 21.5, 21.6)

A. 5′ A G C C T A 3′
⋮ ⋮ ⋮ ⋮ ⋮ ⋮
3′ T C G G A T 5′

B. 5′ A U U G C U C 3′

C. 5′ A G T U G U 3′
⋮ ⋮ ⋮ ⋮ ⋮ ⋮
5′ T C A A C A 5′

D. G U A

E. 5′ A T G T A T 3′

16. _____ a section of an mRNA

17. _____ a strand of DNA that is not possible

18. _____ a codon

19. _____ a section from a DNA molecule

20. _____ a single strand that would not be possible for mRNA

For questions 21 through 25, indicate the correct order of protein synthesis: (21.5, 21.6)
A. tRNA assembles the amino acids at the ribosomes.
B. DNA forms a complementary copy of itself called mRNA.
C. Protein is formed and breaks away.
D. tRNA picks up specific amino acids.
E. mRNA goes to the ribosomes.

21. _____ first step

22. _____ second step

23. _____ third step

24. _____ fourth step

25. _____ fifth step

For questions 26 through 28, match each term with the correct description: (21.6, 21.7)
A. mutation

B. intron

C. exon

26. _____ an error in the transmission of the base sequence of DNA

27. _____ a section of DNA that codes for the synthesis of protein

28. _____ a section of DNA that does not code for the synthesis of protein

Answers to the Practice Test

1. E	2. A	3. B	4. E	5. A
6. C	7. D	8. A	9. A	10. B
11. C	12. A	13. B	14. C	15. A
16. B, D	17. C	18. D	19. A	20. E
21. B	22. E	23. D	24. A	25. C
26. A	27. C	28. B		

21

Nucleic Acids and Protein Synthesis

Learning Goals

- Describe the bases and ribose sugars that make up the nucleic acids DNA and RNA.
- Describe the primary structures of RNA and DNA.
- Describe the double helix of DNA.
- Describe the process of DNA replication.
- Identify the different types of RNA; describe the synthesis of mRNA.
- Use the genetic code to write the amino acid sequence for a segment of mRNA.
- Identify the type of change in DNA for a point mutation, a deletion mutation, and an insertion mutation.
- Describe the preparation and uses of recombinant DNA.
- Describe the methods by which a virus infects a cell.

Chapter Outline

Chapter Opener: Histology Technician

21.1 Components of Nucleic Acids

21.2 Primary Structure of Nucleic Acids

21.3 DNA Double Helix

21.4 DNA Replication

21.5 RNA and Transcription

21.6 The Genetic Code and Protein Synthesis

Chemistry Link to Health: Many Antibiotics Inhibit Protein Synthesis

21.7 Genetic Mutations

Explore Your World: A Model for DNA Replication and Mutation

21.8 Recombinant DNA

21.9 Viruses

Chemistry Link to Health: Cancer

Clinical Update: Ellen's Medical Treatment Following Breast Cancer Surgery

❀ Core Chemistry Skills

- Writing the Complementary DNA Strand (21.3)
- Writing the mRNA Segment for a DNA Template (21.5)
- Writing the Amino Acid for an mRNA Codon (21.6)

Selected Answers and Solutions to Text Problems

21.1 Purine bases (e.g., adenine, guanine) have a double-ring structure; pyrimidines (e.g., cytosine, thymine, uracil) have a single ring.

    a. Thymine is a pyrimidine base.

    b. This single-ring base is the pyrimidine cytosine.

21.3 DNA contains two purines, adenine (A) and guanine (G), and two pyrimidines, cytosine (C) and thymine (T). RNA contains the same bases, except thymine (T) is replaced by the pyrimidine uracil (U).

   a. Thymine is a base present in DNA only.

   b. Cytosine is a base present in both DNA and RNA.

21.5 Nucleotides contain a base, a sugar, and a phosphate group. The nucleotides found in DNA would all contain the sugar deoxyribose. The four nucleotides are deoxyadenosine monophosphate (dAMP), deoxyguanosine monophosphate (dGMP), deoxycytidine monophosphate (dCMP), and deoxythymidine monophosphate (dTMP).

21.7 **a.** Adenosine is a nucleoside.

   b. Deoxycytidine is a nucleoside.

   c. Uridine is a nucleoside.

   d. Cytidine monophosphate is a nucleotide.

21.9 **a.** Phosphate is present in (3) both DNA and RNA.

   b. Ribose is present in (2) RNA only.

   c. Deoxycytidine monophosphate is present in (1) DNA only.

   d. Adenine is present in (3) both DNA and RNA.

21.11

21.13

21.15 The nucleotides in nucleic acid polymers are held together by phosphodiester linkages between the 3′ OH group of a sugar (ribose or deoxyribose) and the phosphate group on the 5′ carbon of another sugar.

21.17 The backbone of a nucleic acid consists of alternating sugar and phosphate groups.

   —sugar—phosphate—sugar—phosphate—

21.19 The free 5′ end is determined by the free phosphate group on the 5′ carbon of ribose or deoxyribose of a nucleic acid.

21.21

Guanosine (G)

Cytidine (C)

21.23 Structural features of DNA include that it is shaped like a double helix, it contains a sugar–phosphate backbone, the nitrogen-containing bases are hydrogen bonded between strands, and the strands run in opposite directions. A forms two hydrogen bonds to T, and G forms three hydrogen bonds to C.

21.25 The two DNA strands are held together by hydrogen bonds between the complementary bases in each strand.

21.27 a. Since T pairs with A, if one strand of DNA has the sequence 5′ A A A A A A 3′, the second strand would be 3′ T T T T T T 5′.

  b. Since C pairs with G, if one strand of DNA has the sequence 5′ G G G G G G 3′, the second strand would be 3′ C C C C C C 5′.

  c. Since T pairs with A, and C pairs with G, if one strand of DNA has the sequence 5′ A G T C C A G G T 3′, the second strand would be 3′ T C A G G T C C A 5′.

  d. Since T pairs with A, and C pairs with G, if one strand of DNA has the sequence 5′ C T G T A T A C G T T A 3′, the second strand would be 3′ G A C A T A T G C A A T 5′.

21.29 The enzyme helicase unwinds the DNA helix so that the parent DNA strands can be replicated into daughter DNA strands.

21.31 First, the two DNA strands separate in a way that is similar to the unzipping of a zipper. Then the enzyme DNA polymerase begins to copy each strand by allowing the pairing of each of the bases in the strands with its complementary base: A pairs with T and C with G. Finally, a phosphodiester bond joins the base to the new, growing strand. This process produces two exact copies of the original DNA.

21.33 a. Helicase (2) unwinds the DNA helix.

  b. Primase (3) synthesizes primers at the replication fork.

  c. The replication fork (4) is the point in DNA where nucleotides add to the daughter DNA strand.

  d. Daughter DNA is synthesized from short sections called Okazaki fragments on the lagging strand (1).

21.35 a. 5′ C G A G G T A C 3′

  b. No; since the template strand runs from 3′ to 5′, the new DNA segment can be synthesized continuously in the 5′ to 3′ direction.

21.37 The three types of RNA are messenger RNA (mRNA), ribosomal RNA (rRNA), and transfer RNA (tRNA).

21.39 A ribosome consists of a small subunit and a large subunit that contain rRNA combined with proteins.

21.41 In transcription, the sequence of nucleotides on a DNA template strand is used to produce the base sequences of a messenger RNA. The DNA unwinds, and one strand is copied as complementary bases are placed in the mRNA molecule. In RNA, U (uracil) is paired with A in DNA.

21.43 To form mRNA, the bases in the DNA template strand are paired with their complementary bases: G with C, C with G, T with A, and A with U. The strand of mRNA would have the following sequence: 5′ GGC UUC CAA GUG 3′.

21.45 In eukaryotic cells, genes contain sections called exons that code for proteins and sections called introns that do not code for proteins.

21.47 5′ GGC GGA UCG 3′

21.49 A transcription factor is a molecule that binds to DNA and regulates transcription.

21.51 An activator binds to transcription factors and increases the rate of RNA transcription.

21.53 A codon is a three-base sequence (triplet) in mRNA that codes for a specific amino acid in a protein.

21.55 a. The codon CUU in mRNA codes for the amino acid leucine (Leu).
   b. The codon UCA in mRNA codes for the amino acid serine (Ser).
   c. The codon GGU in mRNA codes for the amino acid glycine (Gly).
   d. The codon AGG in mRNA codes for the amino acid arginine (Arg).

21.57 At the beginning of an mRNA, the codon AUG signals the start of protein synthesis; thereafter, the AUG codon specifies the amino acid methionine.

21.59 A codon is a base triplet in the mRNA template. An anticodon is the complementary triplet on a tRNA for a specific amino acid.

21.61 The three steps in translation are initiation, chain elongation, and termination.

21.63 a. The codons ACC, ACA, and ACU in mRNA all code for threonine: Thr–Thr–Thr, TTT.
   b. The codons UUU and UUC code for phenylalanine, and CCG and CCA both code for proline: Phe–Pro–Phe–Pro, FPFP.
   c. The codon UAC codes for tyrosine, GGG for glycine, AGA for arginine, and UGU for cysteine: Tyr–Gly–Arg–Cys, YGRC.

21.65 The new amino acid is joined by a peptide bond to the growing peptide chain. The ribosome moves to the next codon, which attaches to a tRNA carrying the next amino acid.

21.67 a. The mRNA sequence would be: 5′ CGA AAA GUU UUU 3′.
   b. The tRNA triplet anticodons would be: GCU, UUU, CAA, and AAA.
   c. From the table of mRNA codons, the amino acids would be: Arg–Lys–Val–Phe, RKVF.

21.69 a. 5′ AAA CAC UUG GUU GUG GAC 3′
   b. Lys–His–Leu–Val–Val–Asp, KHLVVD

21.71 In a point mutation, a base in DNA is replaced by a different base.

21.73 In a deletion mutation caused by the deletion of a base, all the codons from the mutation onward are changed, which changes the order of amino acids in the rest of the polypeptide chain.

21.75 The normal triplet TTT in DNA forms the codon AAA in mRNA. AAA codes for lysine. The mutation TTC in DNA forms the codon AAG in mRNA, which also codes for lysine. Thus, there is no effect on the amino acid sequence.

21.77 a. Thr–Ser–Arg–Val is the amino acid sequence produced by normal DNA.
  b. Thr–Thr–Arg–Val is the amino acid sequence produced by a mutation.
  c. Thr–Ser–Gly–Val is the amino acid sequence produced by a mutation.
  d. Thr–STOP; protein synthesis would terminate early. If this mutation occurs early in the formation of the polypeptide, the resulting protein will probably be nonfunctional.
  e. The new protein will contain the sequence Asp–Ile–Thr–Gly.
  f. The new protein will contain the sequence His–His–Gly.

21.79 a. Both codons GCC and GCA code for alanine.
  b. The polar acidic amino acid glutamate is replaced by valine, which is nonpolar. This changes how individual hemoglobin molecules interact with each other, causing them to link together into long fibers that distort the shape of the red blood cells.

21.81 *E. coli* bacterial cells contain several small circular plasmids of DNA that can be isolated easily. After the recombinant DNA is formed, *E. coli* multiply rapidly, producing many copies of the recombinant DNA in a relatively short time.

21.83 The cells of the *E. coli* are soaked in a detergent solution that disrupts the plasma membrane and releases the cell contents including the plasmids, which are then collected.

21.85 When a gene has been obtained using restriction enzymes, it is mixed with the plasmids that have been opened by the same enzymes. When mixed together in a fresh *E. coli* culture, the sticky ends of the DNA fragments bond with the sticky ends of the plasmid DNA to form a recombinant DNA.

21.87 In DNA fingerprinting, restriction enzymes cut a sample of DNA into fragments, which are sorted by size by gel electrophoresis. A radioactive probe that adheres to specific DNA sequences exposes an X-ray film placed over the gel and creates a pattern of dark and light bands known as a DNA fingerprint.

21.89 The bold sections represent the "sticky ends" of the cleaved bases.

$5'$ A A   **C G** T T $3'$
$3'$ T T **G C**   A A $5'$

21.91 a. $3'$ C C G A $5'$ **b.** $3'$ T T A C G C $5'$ **c.** $3'$ A A G G C T $5'$

21.93 A virus contains either DNA or RNA, but not both, inside a protein coat.

21.95 a. An RNA-containing virus must make viral DNA from the RNA to produce proteins for the protein coat, which allows the virus to replicate and leave the cell to infect new cells.
  b. A virus that uses reverse transcription is called a retrovirus.

21.97 Nucleoside analogs such as AZT and ddI are similar to the nucleosides required to make viral DNA in reverse transcription. When they are incorporated into viral DNA, the lack of a hydroxyl group on the $3'$ carbon in the sugar prevents the formation of the sugar–phosphate bonds and stops the replication of the virus.

21.99 Estrogen receptors are transcription factors that bind to DNA and increase the production of mammary cells, which can lead to mutations and cancer.

21.101 Tamoxifen blocks the binding of estrogen to the estrogen receptor, which prevents binding and activation of the gene.

21.103 a. 5′ ACC UUA AUA GAC GAG AAG CGC 3′
  b. Thr–Leu–Ile–Asp–Glu–Lys–Arg, TLIDEKR
  c. There is no change, Asp is still the fourth amino acid residue.

21.105 a.

Parent strand: | A | G | G | T | C | G | C | C | T |

New strand: | T | C | C | A | G | C | G | G | A |

  b.

| A | G | G | U | C | G | C | C | U |

  c. (Arg)—(Ser)—(Pro)

21.107 DNA contains two purines, adenine (A) and guanine (G), and two pyrimidines, cytosine (C) and thymine (T). RNA contains the same bases, except thymine (T) is replaced by the pyrimidine uracil (U).
  a. Cytosine is a pyrimidine base.　　**b.** Adenine is a purine base.
  c. Uracil is a pyrimidine base.　　　**d.** Thymine is a pyrimidine base.
  e. Guanine is a purine base.

21.109 a. Deoxythymidine contains the base thymine and the sugar deoxyribose.
  b. Adenosine contains the base adenine and the sugar ribose.
  c. Cytidine contains the base cytosine and the sugar ribose.
  d. Deoxyguanosine contains the base guanine and the sugar deoxyribose.

21.111 Thymine and uracil are both pyrimidines, but thymine has a methyl group on carbon 5.

21.113

21.115 Both RNA and DNA are polymers of nucleotides connected through phosphodiester bonds between alternating sugar and phosphate groups with bases extending out from each sugar.

21.117 Because A bonds with T, DNA containing 28% A will also have 28% T. Thus the sum of A + T is 56%, which leaves 44% divided equally between G and C: 22% G and 22% C.

21.119 There are two hydrogen bonds between A and T in DNA.

21.121 a. 3′ C T G A A T C C G 5′
  b. 5′ A C G T T T G A T C G A 3′
  c. 3′ T A G C T A G C T A G C 5′

21.123 DNA polymerase synthesizes the leading strand continuously in the 5′ to 3′ direction. The lagging strand is synthesized in small segments called Okazaki fragments because it must grow in the 3′ to 5′ direction and DNA polymerase can only work in the 5′ to 3′ direction.

21.125 One strand of the parent DNA is found in each of the two copies of the daughter DNA molecule.

21.127 a. Transfer RNA (tRNA) is the smallest type of RNA.
  b. Ribosomal RNA (rRNA) makes up the highest percentage of RNA in the cell.
  c. Messenger RNA (mRNA) carries genetic information from the nucleus to the ribosomes.

21.129 a. ACU, ACC, ACA, and ACG are all codons for the amino acid threonine.
  b. UCU, UCC, UCA, UCG, AGU, and AGC are all codons for the amino acid serine.
  c. UGU and UGC are codons for the amino acid cysteine.

21.131 a. AAG codes for lysine.　　　　　　**b.** AUU codes for isoleucine.
  c. CGA codes for arginine.

21.133 The anticodon on tRNA consists of the three complementary bases to the codon in mRNA.
  a. UCG　　　　　　　　　　**b.** AUA　　　　　　　　　　**c.** GGU

21.135 Using the genetic code, the codons indicate the following amino acid sequence:

START–Tyr–Gly–Gly–Phe–Leu–STOP

21.137 The codon for each amino acid contains three nucleotides, plus the start and stop codon consisting of three nucleotides each, which makes a minimum total of $(9 \times 3) + 3 + 3 = 33$ nucleotides.

21.139 A DNA virus attaches to a cell and injects viral DNA that uses the host cell to produce copies of the DNA to make viral RNA. A retrovirus injects viral RNA from which complementary DNA is produced by reverse transcription.

21.141 a. Okazaki fragments occur in replication of DNA (1).
  b. mRNA is synthesized from nuclear DNA during transcription (2).
  c. Some viruses use reverse transcription (5).
  d. Restriction enzymes are used to make recombinant DNA (4).
  e. tRNA molecules bond to codons during translation (3).

CI.41 a. The functional groups in aromasin are ketone, alkene, and cycloalkene.

b. The functional groups in testosterone are ketone, cycloalkene, and alcohol.

c. The functional groups in estrogen are phenol and alcohol.

d. The enzyme aromatase converts a six-carbon cycloalkene into an aromatic ring.

e. Aromasin has a steroid structure similar to that of testosterone, which binds with aromatase at the active site.

f. Molar mass of aromasin $(C_{20}H_{24}O_2)$
$= 20(12.01 \text{ g}) + 24(1.008 \text{ g}) + 2(16.00 \text{ g}) = 296.4 \text{ g/mole} \ (4 \text{ SFs})$

g. $30 \text{ tablets} \times \dfrac{25 \text{ mg aromasin}}{1 \text{ tablet}} \times \dfrac{1 \text{ g aromasin}}{1000 \text{ mg aromasin}} \times \dfrac{1 \text{ mole aromasin}}{296.4 \text{ g aromasin}}$

$= 2.5 \times 10^{-3} \text{ mole of aromasin} \ (2 \text{ SFs})$

CI.43 a. Glu–His–Trp–Ser–Tyr–Gly–Leu–Arg–Pro–Gly

b. EHWSYGLRPG

c. a point mutation

d. serine is replaced with phenylalanine

e. Serine has a polar —OH group, whereas phenylalanine is nonpolar. The polar serine would have been on the outside of the normal peptide, whereas the phenylalanine will move to the inside of the mutated GnRF. This could change the tertiary structure of the decapeptide, and possibly cause a loss in biological activity.

f. feedback control

CI.45 a. 5′ UGU AUA AAA CGU UUA AAA CGU ACG 3′

b. The respective anticodons on tRNA would be ACA, UAU, UUU, GCA, AAU, UUU, GCA, and UGC.

c. Cys–Ile–Lys–Arg–Leu–Lys–Arg–Thr

22
Metabolic Pathways for Carbohydrates

When Philip was 8 months old, he was taken to the hepatology unit with symptoms that included lethargy, difficulty breathing, and diarrhea. Blood tests indicated that Philip had very low blood glucose and high liver glycogen. He also had a doll-like face from fat deposits and an extended abdomen caused by a enlarged liver. Because of the large amount of glycogen in his liver, Philip was diagnosed with a glycogen storage disease (GSD) known as *von Gierke's disease* in which a genetic disorder produces a defective form of the enzyme *glucose-6-phosphatase*. As a result, glycogen in his liver could not be degraded to glucose for energy but was stored in the liver. Because Philip could not produce sufficient glucose, he was hypoglycemic and weak. After nursing began to feed him with small amounts of glucose or starch by nasogastric tube to raise his blood glucose levels, he showed a rapid improvement in physical behavior. During the day, he was fed cornstarch, which is easily digested to provide small, continuous, amounts of glucose in the blood. Now as a young child, Philip continues to thrive. Why did Philip's condition require him to be fed cornstarch every few hours?

Credit: KatarzynaBialasiewicz / Getty Images

CHAPTER READINESS*

⚛ Core Chemistry Skills

- Identifying D- and L-Fischer Projections (15.2)
- Describing Enzyme Action (20.1)

- Classifying Enzymes (20.2)
- Identifying Factors Affecting Enzyme Activity (20.3)
- Describing the Role of Cofactors (20.6)

*These Core Chemistry Skills from previous chapters are listed here for your review as you proceed to the new material in this chapter.

22.1 Metabolism and Energy

Learning Goal: Describe the three stages of catabolism, the structure of ATP, and the role of ATP.

- Metabolism is all of the chemical reactions that provide energy and substances for maintenance of life and for cell growth.
- Catabolic reactions degrade large molecules to produce energy.
- Anabolic reactions utilize energy in the cell to build large molecules for the cell.
- In cells, different organelles contain the enzymes and coenzymes for the various catabolic and anabolic reactions.
- Energy obtained from catabolic reactions is stored primarily in adenosine triphosphate (ATP), a high-energy compound.
- The hydrolysis of ATP, which releases energy, is linked with many anabolic reactions in the cell.

502   Copyright © 2015 Pearson Education, Inc.

♦ **Learning Exercise 22.1A**

Match each of the following components of a cell with its description or function:

    a. lysosomes   **b.** ribosomes   **c.** mitochondria
    d. cytosol   **e.** cell membrane

1. _____ separates the contents of a cell from the external environment

2. _____ contain enzymes that catalyze energy-producing reactions

3. _____ the fluid of the cell, which is an aqueous solution of electrolytes and enzymes

4. _____ are the sites of protein synthesis

5. _____ contain hydrolytic enzymes that digest old cell structures

Answers   **1.** e   **2.** c   **3.** d   **4.** b   **5.** a

♦ **Learning Exercise 22.1B**

Identify the stages of metabolism for each of the following processes:

    a. Stage 1   **b.** Stage 2   **c.** Stage 3

1. _____ involves the oxidation of two-carbon acetyl CoA

2. _____ polysaccharides undergo digestion to form monosaccharides, such as glucose

3. _____ digestion products such as glucose are degraded to two- or three-carbon compounds

Answers   **1.** c   **2.** a   **3.** b

♦ **Learning Exercise 22.1C**

Fill in the blanks with one of the following terms: phosphate groups, adenine, hydrolysis, ribose, high-energy, P_i, phosphate group(s), energy, anabolic, $ATP + H_2O \rightarrow ADP + P_i + energy$ (7.3 kcal/mole)

The ATP molecule is composed of the nitrogen base (1) _____, a (2) _____ sugar, and three (3) _____. ATP undergoes (4) _____, which cleaves a (5) _____ and releases (6) _____. For this reason, ATP is called a (7) _____ compound. The resulting phosphate group, called inorganic phosphate, is abbreviated as (8) _____. The equation for the hydrolysis of ATP is written as (9) _____. The energy from ATP is linked to cellular reactions that are (10) _____.

Answers   **1.** adenine   **2.** ribose   **3.** phosphate groups   **4.** hydrolysis
              5. phosphate group   **6.** energy   **7.** high-energy   **8.** P_i
              9. $ATP + H_2O \rightarrow ADP + P_i + energy$ (7.3 kcal/mole)   **10.** anabolic

22.2 Important Coenzymes in Metabolic Pathways

Learning Goal: Describe the components and functions of the coenzymes NAD^+, $NADP^+$, FAD, *and coenzyme A.*

- Coenzymes such as NAD^+, $NADP^+$, and FAD pick up hydrogen ions and electrons during oxidative processes.

- Coenzyme A is a coenzyme that carries acetyl (two-carbon) groups produced when glucose, fatty acids, and amino acids are degraded.

♦ **Learning Exercise 22.2**

Select the coenzyme(s) that matches each of the following descriptions:

    a. NAD^+ **b.** NADH   **c.** $NADP^+$ **d.** FAD   **e.** $FADH_2$ **f.** coenzyme A

1. _____ participates in reactions that convert a $C=O$ group to a hydroxyl group

    ⚛ **CORE CHEMISTRY SKILL**

    Identifying Important Coenzymes in Metabolism

2. _____ contains riboflavin (vitamin B_2)

3. _____ is the oxidized form of nicotinamide adenine dinucleotide

4. _____ contains the vitamin niacin

5. _____ is the oxidized form of flavin adenine dinucleotide

6. _____ contains the vitamin pantothenic acid, ADP, and an aminoethanethiol

7. _____ participates in oxidation reactions that produce a carbon–carbon ($C=C$) double bond

8. _____ transfers acyl groups such as the two-carbon acetyl group

9. _____ is the reduced form of flavin adenine dinucleotide

10. _____ is the oxidized form of NADPH

Answers   **1.** b   **2.** d, e   **3.** a   **4.** a, b   **5.** d
                6. f   **7.** d   **8.** f   **9.** e   **10.** c

22.3 Digestion of Carbohydrates

Learning Goal: Give the sites and products of the digestion of carbohydrates.

- Digestion is a series of reactions that break down large molecules into smaller molecules that can be absorbed and used by the cells.
- The end products of digestion of polysaccharides are the monosaccharides glucose, fructose, and galactose.

♦ **Learning Exercise 22.3**

Complete the table by providing sites, enzymes, and products for the digestion of carbohydrates:

Carbohydrate	Digestion Site(s)	Enzyme	Products
1. Amylose			
2. Amylopectin			
3. Maltose			
4. Lactose			
5. Sucrose			

Answers

Carbohydrate	Digestion Site(s)	Enzyme	Products
1. Amylose	**a.** mouth **b.** small intestine (mucosa)	**a.** salivary amylase **b.** pancreatic amylase	**a.** smaller polysaccharides (dextrins), some maltose and glucose **b.** maltose, glucose
2. Amylopectin	**a.** mouth **b.** small intestine (mucosa)	**a.** salivary amylase **b.** pancreatic amylase	**a.** smaller polysaccharides (dextrins), some maltose and glucose **b.** maltose, glucose
3. Maltose	small intestine (mucosa)	maltase	glucose and glucose
4. Lactose	small intestine (mucosa)	lactase	glucose and galactose
5. Sucrose	small intestine (mucosa)	sucrase	glucose and fructose

22.4 Glycolysis: Oxidation of Glucose

Learning Goal: Describe the conversion of glucose to pyruvate in glycolysis.

- Glycolysis is the primary anaerobic pathway for the degradation of glucose to yield pyruvate. Glucose is converted to fructose-1,6-bisphosphate, which is then split into two triose phosphate molecules.
- Oxidation of each three-carbon compound yields one NADH and 2 ATP.
- The pentose phosphate pathway is an alternative pathway for the oxidation of glucose, which produces the coenzyme NADPH and five-carbon pentoses.

♦ **Learning Exercise 22.4**

⊛ CORE CHEMISTRY SKILL

Identifying the Compounds in Glycolysis

Match each of the following terms associated with glycolysis with the best description(s):

a. 2 NADH	**b.** anaerobic	**c.** glucose	**d.** two pyruvate
e. 2 NADP$^+$	**f.** energy generated	**g.** 2 ATP	**h.** 4 ATP

1. _____ the starting material for glycolysis

2. _____ reduced in the pentose phosphate pathway

3. _____ operates without oxygen

4. _____ net ATP energy produced

5. _____ number of reduced coenzymes produced

6. _____ reactions 6 to 10 of glycolysis

7. _____ end products of glycolysis

8. _____ number of ATP required

Answers   **1.** c   **2.** e   **3.** b   **4.** g
             5. a   **6.** f   **7.** d, a   **8.** g

22.5 Pathways for Pyruvate

Learning Goal: Give the conditions for the conversion of pyruvate to lactate, ethanol, and acetyl coenzyme A.

- In the absence of oxygen, pyruvate is reduced to lactate and NAD^+ is regenerated for the continuation of glycolysis.
- Under aerobic conditions, pyruvate is oxidized in the mitochondria to acetyl CoA, which enters the citric acid cycle.

♦ Learning Exercise 22.5A

Fill in the blanks with the following terms:

lactate	NAD^+	fermentation
NADH	anaerobic	acetyl CoA

When oxygen is available during glycolysis, the three-carbon pyruvate may be oxidized to form
(1) _____ + CO_2. The coenzyme (2) _____ is reduced to (3) _____. Under
(4) _____ conditions, pyruvate is reduced to (5) _____. In yeast, pyruvate forms
ethanol in a process known as (6) _____.

Answers   **1.** acetyl CoA   **2.** NAD^+ **3.** NADH
4. anaerobic   **5.** lactate   **6.** fermentation

♦ Learning Exercise 22.5B

Essay: Explain how the formation of lactate from pyruvate during anaerobic conditions allows glycolysis to continue.

Answer   Under anaerobic conditions, the oxidation of pyruvate to acetyl CoA to regenerate NAD^+ cannot take place. Pyruvate is reduced to lactate using NADH in the cytosol and regenerating NAD^+.

22.6 Glycogen Synthesis and Degradation

Learning Goal: Describe the synthesis and breakdown of glycogen.

- Glycogen, the storage form of glucose, is synthesized when blood glucose levels are high.
- In the *glycogenesis* pathway, glucose units are added to a glycogen chain.
- *Glycogenolysis*, the breakdown of glycogen, occurs when blood glucose levels are depleted and glucose is required for energy by muscles and the brain.

♦ Learning Exercise 22.6

Associate each of the following descriptions with the correct
pathway in glycogen metabolism:

a. glycogenesis   **b.** glycogenolysis

⚛ CORE CHEMISTRY SKILL

Identifying the Compounds and
Enzymes in Glycogenesis and
Glycogenolysis

1. _____ breakdown of glycogen to glucose   **2.** _____ activated by glucagon

3. _____ starting material is glucose-6-phosphate   **4.** _____ synthesis of glycogen from glucose

5. _____ activated by insulin   **6.** _____ UDP activates glucose

Answers   **1.** b   **2.** b   **3.** a   **4.** a   **5.** a   **6.** a

22.7 Gluconeogenesis: Glucose Synthesis

Learning Goal: Describe how glucose is synthesized from noncarbohydrate molecules.

- In *gluconeogenesis*, glucose is synthesized from noncarbohydrate precursors such as lactate, pyruvate, citric acid cycle intermediates, and the carbon atoms of amino acids.

- Most of the enzymes used in gluconeogenesis are the same as the enzymes used in glycolysis except for hexokinase, phosphofructokinase, and pyruvate kinase.

- In the *Cori cycle*, lactate formed in the muscles is transported to the liver, where it is converted to pyruvate and then to glucose, which is used again by the muscles.

Key Terms for Sections 22.1–22.7

Match the following key terms with the correct definition below:

   a. ATP   **b.** glycogen   **c.** glycolysis
   d. catabolic reaction   **e.** gluconeogenesis   **f.** mitochondria

1. _____ the storage form of glucose in the muscle and liver

2. _____ a metabolic reaction that produces energy for the cell by degrading large molecules

3. _____ a high-energy compound produced from energy-releasing processes that provides energy for energy-requiring reactions

4. _____ the synthesis of glucose from noncarbohydrate compounds

5. _____ the degradation reactions of glucose that yield two pyruvate molecules

6. _____ the part of the cell where energy-producing reactions take place

Answers   **1.** b   **2.** d   **3.** a   **4.** e   **5.** c   **6.** f

♦ **Learning Exercise 22.7**

Match each of the following terms with the correct description below:

   a. gluconeogenesis   **b.** pyruvate   **c.** pyruvate kinase
   d. pyruvate carboxylase   **e.** Cori cycle

1. _____ an enzyme in glycolysis that cannot be used in gluconeogenesis

2. _____ a typical noncarbohydrate source of carbon atoms for glucose synthesis

3. _____ a process whereby lactate produced in muscle is used for glucose synthesis in the liver and used again by the muscle

4. _____ a metabolic pathway that converts noncarbohydrate sources to glucose

5. _____ an enzyme used in gluconeogenesis that is not used in glycolysis

6. _____ a metabolic pathway that is activated when glycogen reserves are depleted

Answers   **1.** c   **2.** b   **3.** e   **4.** a   **5.** d   **6.** a

Checklist for Chapter 22

You are ready to take the Practice Test for Chapter 22. Be sure that you have accomplished the learning goals for each of the sections in this chapter. If not, review the section listed at the end of each goal. Then apply your new skills and understanding to the Practice Test.

After studying Chapter 22, I can successfully:

_____ Associate catabolic and anabolic reactions with organelles in the cell. (22.1)

_____ Describe the role of ATP in catabolic and anabolic reactions. (22.1)

_____ Describe the coenzymes NAD^+, $NADP^+$, FAD, and coenzyme A. (22.2)

_____ Describe the sites, enzymes, and products of the digestion of carbohydrates. (22.3)

_____ Describe the conversion of glucose to pyruvate in glycolysis. (22.4)

_____ Give the conditions for the conversion of pyruvate to lactate, ethanol, and acetyl coenzyme A. (22.5)

_____ Describe the formation and breakdown of glycogen. (22.6)

_____ Describe the reactions in which noncarbohydrate sources are used to synthesize glucose. (22.7)

Practice Test for Chapter 22

1. The main function of the mitochondria is (22.1, 22.5)
   A. energy production   **B.** protein synthesis   **C.** glycolysis
   D. genetic instructions   **E.** waste disposal

2. ATP is a(n) (22.1)
   A. nucleotide unit in RNA and DNA   **B.** end product of glycogenolysis
   C. end product of transamination   **D.** enzyme
   E. energy storage molecule

Match each of the substances in questions 3 through 6, with one or more of the correct enzymes and the end product(s) of its digestion: (22.3)
   A. maltase   **B.** glucose   **C.** fructose   **D.** sucrase
   E. galactose   **F.** lactase   **G.** pancreatic amylase

3. _____ sucrose   **4.** _____ lactose

5. _____ amylose   **6.** _____ maltose

For questions 7 through 11, match each term or phrase with the correct cellular component: (22.1)
   A. mitochondria   **B.** lysosomes   **C.** cytosol
   D. ribosomes   **E.** cell membrane

7. _____ protein synthesis   **8.** _____ fluid part of the cell

9. _____ separates cell contents from external fluids   **10.** _____ energy-producing reactions

11. _____ degradation by hydrolytic enzymes of old cell structures

12. Glycolysis (22.4)
    A. requires oxygen for the catabolism of glucose
    B. represents the aerobic sequence for glucose anabolism and ATP production
    C. represents the splitting off of glucose residues from glycogen
    D. represents the anaerobic catabolism of glucose to pyruvate
    E. produces acetyl units and ATP as end products

13. Which does *not* appear in the glycolysis pathway? (22.4)
    A. dihydroxyacetone phosphate   B. pyruvate   C. NAD^+
    D. acetyl CoA   E. lactate

For questions 14 through 18, match each description with one of the following metabolic pathways: (22.4, 22.6, 22.7)
    A. glycolysis   B. glycogenolysis   C. gluconeogenesis
    D. glycogenesis   E. fermentation

14. _____ conversion of pyruvate to alcohol

15. _____ breakdown of glucose to pyruvate

16. _____ formation of glycogen

17. _____ synthesis of glucose

18. _____ breakdown of glycogen to glucose

For questions 19 through 25, match each description with the correct coenzyme: (22.2)
    A. NAD^+ B. NADH   C. FAD   D. $FADH_2$ E. coenzyme A

19. _____ converts a hydroxyl group to a $C{=}O$ group

20. _____ reduced form of nicotinamide adenine dinucleotide

21. _____ oxidized form of flavin adenine dinucleotide

22. _____ contains the vitamin pantothenic acid, ADP, and an aminoethanethiol

23. _____ participates in oxidation reactions that produce a carbon–carbon $(C{=}C)$ double bond

24. _____ transfers acyl groups such as the two-carbon acetyl group

25. _____ reduced form of flavin adenine dinucleotide

For questions 26 through 28, answer the following for glycolysis: (22.4)

26. _____ number of ATP invested for the oxidation of one glucose molecule

27. _____ number of ATP (net) produced from one glucose molecule

28. _____ number of NADH produced from the degradation of one glucose molecule

Answers to the Practice Test

1. A	2. E	3. D, B, C	4. F, B, E	5. G, A, B
6. A, B	7. D	8. C	9. E	10. A
11. B	12. D	13. D, E	14. E	15. A
16. D	17. C	18. B	19. A	20. B
21. C	22. E	23. C	24. E	25. D
26. 2	27. 2	28. 2		

22

Metabolic Pathways for Carbohydrates

Learning Goals

- Describe the three stages of catabolism, the structure of ATP, and the role of ATP.
- Describe the components and functions of the coenzymes NAD^+, $NADP^+$, FAD, and coenzyme A.
- Give the sites and products of the digestion of carbohydrates.
- Describe the conversion of glucose to pyruvate in glycolysis.
- Give the conditions for the conversion of pyruvate to lactate, ethanol, and acetyl coenzyme A.
- Describe the synthesis and breakdown of glycogen.
- Describe how glucose is synthesized from noncarbohydrate molecules.

Chapter Outline

Chapter Opener: Hepatology Nurse

22.1 Metabolism and Energy

Chemistry Link to Health: ATP Energy and Ca^{2+} Needed to Contract Muscles

22.2 Important Coenzymes in Metabolic Pathways

22.3 Digestion of Carbohydrates

22.4 Glycolysis: Oxidation of Glucose

22.5 Pathways for Pyruvate

22.6 Glycogen Synthesis and Degradation

Chemistry Link to Health: Glycogen Storage Diseases (GSDs)

22.7 Gluconeogenesis: Glucose Synthesis

Clinical Update: Philip's Diet for von Gierke's Disease

⚛ Core Chemistry Skills

- Identifying Important Coenzymes in Metabolism (22.2)
- Identifying the Compounds in Glycolysis (22.4)
- Identifying the Compounds and Enzymes in Glycogenesis and Glycogenolysis (22.6)

Selected Answers and Solutions to Text Problems

22.1   The digestion of polysaccharides takes place in stage 1.

22.3   In metabolism, a catabolic reaction breaks apart large molecules, releasing energy.

22.5   **a.** The synthesis of large molecules requires energy and involves anabolic reactions.
b. The addition of phosphate to glucose requires energy and is an anabolic process.
c. The breakdown of ATP releases energy and is a catabolic reaction.
d. The breakdown of large molecules involves catabolic reactions.

22.7   When ATP is hydrolyzed, sufficient energy is released for energy-requiring processes in the cell.

22.9   **a.** PEP $\longrightarrow$ pyruvate + P_i + 14.8 kcal/mole
    b. ADP + P_i + 7.3 kcal/mole $\longrightarrow$ ATP
    c. Combined: PEP + ADP $\longrightarrow$ ATP + pyruvate + 7.5 kcal/mole

22.11 $2100 \text{ kJ} \times \dfrac{1000 \text{ J}}{1 \text{ kJ}} \times \dfrac{1 \text{ cal}}{4.184 \text{ J}} \times \dfrac{1 \text{ kcal}}{1000 \text{ cal}} \times \dfrac{1 \text{ mole ATP}}{7.3 \text{ kcal}} \times \dfrac{507 \text{ g ATP}}{1 \text{ mole ATP}}$
    $= 3.4 \times 10^4 \text{ g of ATP (2 SFs)}$

22.13   **a.** Pantothenic acid is a component of coenzyme A.
    b. Niacin is the vitamin component of NAD^+ and $NADP^+$.
    c. Ribitol is the sugar alcohol that is a component of riboflavin in FAD.

22.15   In biochemical systems, oxidation is usually accompanied by the gain of oxygen or loss of hydrogen. Loss of oxygen or gain of hydrogen usually accompanies reduction.
    a. The reduced form of NAD^+ is abbreviated NADH.
    b. The oxidized form of $FADH_2$ is abbreviated FAD.

22.17   When a carbon–carbon double bond is formed, the coenzyme that picks up hydrogen is FAD.

22.19   Hydrolysis is the main reaction involved in the digestion of carbohydrates.

22.21   **a.** Lactose + H_2O $\longrightarrow$ galactose + glucose
    b. Sucrose + H_2O $\longrightarrow$ glucose + fructose
    c. Maltose + H_2O $\longrightarrow$ glucose + glucose

22.23   Glucose is the starting compound of glycolysis.

22.25   In the initial steps of glycolysis, ATP molecules are required to add phosphate groups to glucose (phosphorylation reactions).

22.27   When fructose-1,6-bisphosphate splits, the three-carbon intermediates glyceraldehyde-3-phosphate and dihydroxyacetone phosphate are formed.

22.29   ATP is produced directly in glycolysis in two places. In reaction 7, a phosphate group from 1,3-bisphosphoglycerate is transferred to ADP and yields ATP. In reaction 10, a phosphate group from phosphoenolpyruvate is transferred directly to ADP to yield another ATP molecule.

22.31   **a.** In glycolysis, phosphorylation is catalyzed by the enzyme hexokinase in reaction 1 and by phosphofructokinase in reaction 3.
    b. In glycolysis, direct transfer of a phosphate group is catalyzed by the enzyme phosphoglycerate kinase in reaction 7 and by pyruvate kinase in reaction 10.

22.33   **a.** One ATP is required in the phosphorylation of glucose to glucose-6-phosphate.
    b. One NADH is produced in the conversion of glyceraldehyde-3-phosphate to 1,3-bisphosphoglycerate.
    c. Two ATP and two NADH are produced when glucose is converted to pyruvate.

22.35   **a.** In reaction 1 of glycolysis, a hexokinase uses ATP to phosphorylate glucose.
    b. In reactions 7 and 10 of glycolysis, phosphate groups are transferred from 1,3-bisphosphoglycerate and phosphoenolpyruvate directly to ADP to produce ATP.
    c. In reaction 4 of glycolysis, the six-carbon molecule fructose-1,6-bisphosphate is split into two three-carbon molecules, glyceraldehyde-3-phosphate and dihydroxyacetone phosphate.

22.37 In a series of enzymatic reactions, galactose is phosphorylated to yield glucose-1-phosphate, which is converted to glucose-6-phosphate, which enters glycolysis in reaction 2. In the muscles, fructose is phosphorylated to fructose-6-phosphate, which enters glycolysis in reaction 3, where its movement through glycolysis is regulated by the enzyme phosphofructokinase. In the liver, fructose is phosphorylated to fructose-1-phosphate, which is converted to glyceraldehyde-3-phosphate, which enters glycolysis at reaction 6.

22.39 **a.** Low levels of ATP will activate phosphofructokinase and increase the rate of glycolysis.
   b. High levels of ATP will inhibit phosphofructokinase and slow or stop glycolysis.

22.41 Glucose-6-phosphate is the initial substrate for the pentose phosphate pathway.

22.43 The pentose phosphate pathway produces NADPH required for anabolic reactions.

22.45 Sucrose contains the monosaccharides glucose and fructose. Once hydrolyzed during digestion, glucose directly enters glycolysis at step 1, and fructose enters glycolysis either at step 3 in the muscle and kidney or step 6 in the liver.

22.47 A cell converts pyruvate to acetyl CoA only under aerobic conditions; there must be sufficient oxygen available.

22.49 The oxidation of pyruvate converts NAD^+ to NADH and produces acetyl CoA and CO_2.

$$CH_3-\overset{\overset{\displaystyle O}{\|}}{C}-COO^- + NAD^+ + HS-CoA \xrightarrow{\underset{\text{dehydrogenase}}{\text{Pyruvate}}} CH_3-\overset{\overset{\displaystyle O}{\|}}{C}-S-CoA + CO_2 + NADH$$

Pyruvate   Acetyl CoA

22.51 **a.** (3) ethanol
   b. (1) acetyl CoA
   c. (2) lactate
   d. (1) acetyl CoA, (3) ethanol

22.53 During fermentation, the three-carbon compound pyruvate is reduced to ethanol while decarboxylation removes one carbon as carbon dioxide, CO_2.

22.55 During strenuous exercise, under anaerobic conditions, pyruvate is converted to lactate. The accumulation of lactate causes the muscles to tire and become sore.

22.57 $$CH_3-\overset{\overset{\displaystyle O}{\|}}{C}-\overset{\overset{\displaystyle O}{\|}}{C}-O^- + NADH + H^+ \longrightarrow CH_3-\overset{\overset{\displaystyle OH}{|}}{C}H-\overset{\overset{\displaystyle O}{\|}}{C}-O^- + NAD^+$$

Pyruvate   Lactate

22.59 Glycogenesis is the synthesis of glycogen from glucose molecules.

22.61 Muscle cells break down glycogen to glucose-6-phosphate, which enters glycolysis.

22.63 Glycogen phosphorylase cleaves the glycosidic bonds at the ends of glycogen chains to remove glucose monomers as glucose-1-phosphate.

22.65 **a.** activates
   b. inhibits
   c. inhibits

22.67 The movement of glucose out of the bloodstream and into the cells is regulated by insulin, whereas fructose is not. Fructose can move into the cells and be degraded in glycolysis.

22.69 When the glycogen phosphorylase enzyme in the liver is defective, glycogen in the liver cannot be broken down to glucose.

22.71 When there are no glycogen stores remaining in the liver, gluconeogenesis synthesizes glucose from noncarbohydrate compounds such as pyruvate and lactate.

22.73 The enzymes in glycolysis that are also used in their reverse directions for gluconeogenesis are phosphoglucose isomerase, aldolase, triose phosphate isomerase, glyceraldehyde-3-phosphate dehydrogenase, phosphoglycerate kinase, phosphoglycerate mutase, and enolase.

22.75 **a.** Low glucose levels activate glucose synthesis (gluconeogenesis).
   b. Glucagon, produced when glucose levels are low, activates gluconeogenesis.
   c. Insulin, produced when glucose levels are high, inhibits gluconeogenesis.
   d. AMP inhibits gluconeogenesis.

22.77 People on low carbohydrate diets do not store normal amounts of glycogen and therefore lose this weight and the water weight used to hydrolyze the glycogen.

22.79 Some of the symptoms of von Gierke's disease are: liver enlargement due to glycogen accumulation, and hypoglycemia, which can lead to a shortened life expectancy.

22.81 Glycogen cannot be degraded completely to glucose, causing low blood glucose. Glycogen accumulates as stored glycogen in the liver. Lower insulin levels inhibit glycolysis and activate gluconeogenesis.

22.83 $2.5 \; \cancel{h} \times \dfrac{350 \; \cancel{kcal}}{1 \; \cancel{h}} \times \dfrac{1 \; mole \; ATP}{7.3 \; \cancel{kcal}} = 120$ moles of ATP (2 SFs)

22.85 **a.** Pyrophosphorylase is utilized in (1) glycogenesis but not glycogenolysis.
   b. Phosphoglucomutase is utilized in (3) both glycogenesis and glycogenolysis.
   c. Glycogen phosphorylase is utilized in (2) glycogenolysis but not glycogenesis.

22.87 **a.** Glucose-6-phosphatase is utilized in (2) gluconeogenesis but not glycolysis.
   b. Aldolase is utilized in (3) both glycolysis and gluconeogenesis.
   c. Phosphofructokinase is utilized in (1) glycolysis but not gluconeogenesis.
   d. Phosphoglycerate mutase is utilized in (3) both glycolysis and gluconeogenesis.

22.89 Metabolism includes all the reactions in cells that provide energy and material for cell growth.

22.91 Stage 1 involves the digestion of large food polymers, such as polysaccharides and proteins.

22.93 A eukaryotic cell has a nucleus, whereas a prokaryotic cell does not.

22.95 ATP is the abbreviation for adenosine triphosphate.

22.97 $ATP \longrightarrow ADP + P_i + 7.3$ kcal/mole (or 31 kJ/mole)

22.99 High energy is the reduced form, $FADH_2$; low energy is the oxidized form, FAD.

22.101 High energy is the reduced form, NADH; low energy is the oxidized form, NAD^+.

22.103 The reduced forms of these coenzymes include hydrogen obtained from an oxidation reaction.
   a. The reduced form of FAD is abbreviated $FADH_2$.
   b. The reduced form of NAD^+ is abbreviated $NADH + H^+$.
   c. The reduced form of $NADP^+$ is abbreviated $NADPH + H^+$.

22.105 Lactose undergoes digestion in the mucosal cells of the small intestine to yield glucose and galactose.

22.107 Glucose is the reactant and pyruvate is the product of glycolysis.

22.109 **a.** Reactions 1 and 3 of glycolysis involve phosphorylation of hexoses with ATP.
   b. Reactions 7 and 10 of glycolysis involve direct substrate phosphorylation that generates ATP.

22.111 Reaction 4, catalyzed by aldolase, converts fructose-1,6-bisphosphate into two three-carbon intermediates.

22.113 Phosphoglucose isomerase converts glucose-6-phosphate to the isomer fructose-6-phosphate.

22.115 Pyruvate is converted to lactate when oxygen is not present in the cell (anaerobic conditions) to regenerate NAD^+ for glycolysis.

22.117 Phosphofructokinase is an allosteric enzyme that is activated by high levels of AMP and ADP because the cell needs to produce more ATP. When ATP levels are high due to a decrease in energy needs, ATP inhibits phosphofructokinase, which reduces its catalysis of fructose-6-phosphate.

22.119 The rate of glycogenolysis increases when blood glucose levels are low and glucagon has been secreted, which accelerates the breakdown of glycogen.

22.121 The breakdown of glycogen (glycogenolysis) in the liver produces glucose.

22.123 a. A low blood glucose level increases the rate of glycogenolysis in the liver.
  b. Insulin, secreted when glucose levels are high, decreases the rate of glycogenolysis in the liver.
  c. Glucagon, secreted when glucose levels are low, increases the rate of glycogenolysis in the liver.
  d. High levels of ATP decrease the rate of glycogenolysis in the liver.

22.125 a. High blood glucose levels decrease the rate of gluconeogenesis.
  b. Insulin, secreted when glucose levels are high, decreases the rate of gluconeogenesis.
  c. Glucagon, secreted when glucose levels are low, increases the rate of gluconeogenesis.
  d. High levels of ATP decrease the rate of gluconeogenesis.

22.127 The cells in the liver, but not skeletal muscle, contain a phosphatase enzyme needed to convert glucose-6-phosphate to free glucose that can diffuse through cell membranes into the bloodstream. Glucose-6-phosphate, which is the end product of glycogenolysis in muscle cells, cannot diffuse easily across cell membranes.

22.129 Insulin increases the rate of glycogenesis and glycolysis and decreases the rate of glycogenolysis. Glucagon decreases the rate of glycogenesis and glycolysis and increases the rate of glycogenolysis.

22.131 The Cori cycle is a cyclic process that involves the flow of lactate and glucose between muscle and the liver. Lactate produced during anaerobic exercise is transported to the liver where it is oxidized to pyruvate, which is used to synthesize glucose. Glucose enters the bloodstream and returns to the muscle to rebuild glycogen stores.

22.133 a. $2.0 \times 10^3 \text{ kcal} \times \dfrac{1 \text{ mole ATP}}{7.3 \text{ kcal}} \times \dfrac{507 \text{ g ATP}}{1 \text{ mole ATP}} \times \dfrac{1 \text{ kg ATP}}{1000 \text{ g ATP}} = 140 \text{ kg of ATP (2 SFs)}$

  b. $250 \text{ g ATP} \times \dfrac{1 \text{ mole ATP}}{507 \text{ g ATP}} \times \dfrac{7.3 \text{ kcal}}{1 \text{ mole ATP}} \times \dfrac{1 \text{ day}}{2.0 \times 10^3 \text{ kcal}} \times \dfrac{24 \text{ h}}{1 \text{ day}} \times \dfrac{60 \text{ min}}{1 \text{ h}}$

  $= 2.6 \text{ min (2 SFs)}$

Metabolism and Energy Production

Since Natalie's diagnosis of mild emphysema due to secondhand cigarette smoke, she has been working with Angela, an exercise physiologist. Natalie's workouts started with low-intensity exercises that use smaller muscles. Now that Natalie has increased the oxygen concentration in her blood, Angela has added some exercises that use larger muscles, which need more O_2. Today Natalie had a stress test and an ECG to assess and evaluate her progress. Her results show that her heart is functioning more efficiently and that she needs less oxygen. Her doctor told her that she has begun to reverse the progression of emphysema. Why is oxygen required during aerobic exercise?

Credit: Javier Larrea / AGE Fotostock

CHAPTER READINESS*

⚛ Core Chemistry Skills

- Writing Equations for Hydrogenation, Hydration, and Polymerization (12.7)
- Classifying Enzymes (20.2)
- Identifying Important Coenzymes in Metabolism (22.2)
- Identifying the Compounds in Glycolysis (22.4)

These Core Chemistry Skills from previous chapters are listed here for your review as you proceed to the new material in this chapter.

23.1 The Citric Acid Cycle

Learning Goal: Describe the oxidation of acetyl CoA in the citric acid cycle.

- Under aerobic conditions, pyruvate is oxidized in the mitochondria to acetyl CoA, which enters the citric acid cycle.
- At the start of the citric acid cycle, acetyl CoA combines with oxaloacetate to yield citrate.
- In one turn of the citric acid cycle, the oxidation of acetyl CoA yields two CO_2, one GTP, three NADH, and one $FADH_2$. The phosphorylation of ADP by GTP yields ATP.

⚛ CORE CHEMISTRY SKILL

Describing the Reactions in the Citric Acid Cycle

♦ Learning Exercise 23.1A

Match each enzyme (**a** to **h**) with the equation(s) (**1** to **9**):

a. isocitrate dehydrogenase

b. α-ketoglutarate dehydrogenase

c. fumarase

d. succinate dehydrogenase

e. malate dehydrogenase   f. aconitase

g. succinyl CoA synthetase   h. citrate synthase

1. _____ acetyl CoA + oxaloacetate $\longrightarrow$ citrate   2. _____ citrate $\longrightarrow$ isocitrate

3. _____ isocitrate $\longrightarrow$ α-ketoglutarate   4. _____ α-ketoglutarate $\longrightarrow$ succinyl CoA

5. _____ succinyl CoA $\longrightarrow$ succinate   6. _____ succinate $\longrightarrow$ fumarate

7. _____ fumarate $\longrightarrow$ malate   8. _____ malate $\longrightarrow$ oxaloacetate

9. _____ allosteric enzymes that regulate the citric acid cycle

Answers   **1.** h   **2.** f   **3.** a   **4.** b   **5.** g   **6.** d   **7.** c   **8.** e   **9.** a, b

♦ **Learning Exercise 23.1B**

For each of the following steps in the citric acid cycle, indicate whether oxidation occurs (yes/no) and identify any coenzyme or direct phosphorylation product produced ($NADH + H^+$, $FADH_2$, GTP):

Step in Citric Acid Cycle	Oxidation	Coenzyme
1. acetyl CoA + oxaloacetate $\longrightarrow$ citrate	_____	_____
2. citrate $\longrightarrow$ isocitrate	_____	_____
3. isocitrate $\longrightarrow$ α-ketoglutarate	_____	_____
4. α-ketoglutarate $\longrightarrow$ succinyl CoA	_____	_____
5. succinyl CoA $\longrightarrow$ succinate	_____	_____
6. succinate $\longrightarrow$ fumarate	_____	_____
7. fumarate $\longrightarrow$ malate	_____	_____
8. malate $\longrightarrow$ oxaloacetate	_____	_____

Answers   **1.** no   **2.** no   **3.** yes, $NADH + H^+$ **4.** yes, $NADH + H^+$

               5. no, GTP   **6.** yes, $FADH_2$ **7.** no   **8.** yes, $NADH + H^+$

23.2 Electron Transport and ATP

Learning Goal: Describe the transfer of hydrogen ions and electrons in electron transport and the process of oxidative phosphorylation in ATP synthesis.

- The reduced coenzymes from glycolysis and the citric acid cycle are oxidized to NAD^+ and FAD by transferring hydrogen ions and electrons to electron transport.
- In electron transport, electrons are transferred to electron carriers, including coenzyme Q and cytochrome *c*.
- The final acceptor, O_2, combines with hydrogen ions and electrons to yield H_2O.
- The flow of electrons in electron transport pumps hydrogen ions across the inner mitochondrial membrane, which produces a high-energy hydrogen ion gradient that provides energy for the synthesis of ATP.
- The process of using the energy of electron transport to synthesize ATP is called oxidative phosphorylation.

♦ **Learning Exercise 23.2A**

Write the oxidized and reduced forms of each of the following electron carriers:

1. coenzyme Q   oxidized _____   reduced _____

2. cytochrome *c*   oxidized _____   reduced _____

3. flavin adenine dinucleotide   oxidized _____   reduced _____

4. nicotinamide adenine dinucleotide oxidized _____   reduced _____

Answers
   1. oxidized: CoQ   reduced: $CoQH_2$
   2. oxidized: cyt *c* (Fe^{3+})   reduced: cyt *c* (Fe^{2+})
   3. oxidized: FAD   reduced: $FADH_2$
   4. oxidized: NAD^+ reduced: $NADH + H^+$

♦ **Learning Exercise 23.2B**

1. Write an equation for the transfer of hydrogen from $FADH_2$ to CoQ.

2. What is the function of coenzyme Q in electron transport?

3. What are the end products of electron transport?

Answers
   1. $FADH_2 + CoQ \longrightarrow FAD + CoQH_2$
   2. CoQ accepts hydrogen atoms from NADH or $FADH_2$. From $CoQH_2$, the hydrogen atoms are separated into hydrogen ions and electrons, with the electrons being passed on to cytochrome *c*.
   3. H_2O and ATP

♦ **Learning Exercise 23.2C**

Match the following terms with the correct description below:

   a. oxidative phosphorylation   **b.** ATP synthase
   c. hydrogen ion pump   **d.** hydrogen ion gradient

1. _____ the complexes I, III, and IV, through which hydrogen ions move out of the matrix into the intermembrane space

2. _____ the protein complex through which hydrogen ions flow from the intermembrane space back to the matrix to generate energy for ATP synthesis

3. _____ use of energy from electron transport to form a hydrogen ion gradient that drives ATP synthesis

4. _____ the accumulation of hydrogen ions in the intermembrane space that lowers pH

Answers   **1.** c   **2.** b   **3.** a   **4.** d

23.3 ATP Energy from Glucose

Learning Goal: Account for the ATP produced by the complete oxidation of glucose.

- The oxidation of NADH yields 2.5 ATP molecules, whereas the oxidation of $FADH_2$ yields 1.5 ATP molecules.
- The complete oxidation of glucose yields a total of 32 ATP from direct phosphorylation and the oxidation of the reduced coenzymes NADH and $FADH_2$ from electron transport and oxidative phosphorylation.

Key Terms for Sections 23.1–23.3

Match the following key terms with the correct definition:

    a. citric acid cycle   **b.** oxidative phosphorylation   **c.** coenzyme Q
    d. cytochrome *c*   **e.** hydrogen ion pump

1. _____ a mobile carrier that passes electrons from NADH and $FADH_2$ to cytochrome *c* in complex III

2. _____ a mobile carrier that transfers electrons from $CoQH_2$ to oxygen

3. _____ moves hydrogen ions from the matrix into the intermembrane space

4. _____ the synthesis of ATP from ADP and P_i using energy generated from electron transport

5. _____ oxidation reactions that convert acetyl CoA to CO_2, producing reduced coenzymes for energy production via electron transport

Answers   **1.** c   **2.** d   **3.** e   **4.** b   **5.** a

⊛ CORE CHEMISTRY SKILL

Calculating the ATP Produced from Glucose

♦ **Learning Exercise 23.3**

Complete the following:

Substrate	Reaction	Products	Amount of ATP Produced
1. glucose	glycolysis (aerobic)		
2. pyruvate	oxidation		
3. acetyl CoA	citric acid cycle		
4. glucose	complete oxidation		

Answers

Substrate	Reaction	Products	Amount of ATP Produced
1. glucose	glycolysis (aerobic)	2 pyruvate	7
2. pyruvate	oxidation	acetyl CoA + CO_2	2.5
3. acetyl CoA	citric acid cycle	$2CO_2$	10
4. glucose	complete oxidation	$6CO_2 + 6H_2O$	32

Checklist for Chapter 23

You are ready to take the Practice Test for Chapter 23. Be sure that you have accomplished the learning goals for each of the sections in this chapter. If not, review the section listed at the end of each goal. Then apply your new skills and understanding to the Practice Test.

After studying Chapter 23, I can successfully:

_____ Describe the oxidation of acetyl CoA in the citric acid cycle. (23.1)

_____ Identify the electron carriers in electron transport. (23.2)

_____ Describe the process of electron transport. (23.2)

_____ Explain oxidative phosphorylation whereby ATP synthesis is linked to the energy of electron transport and a hydrogen ion gradient. (23.2)

_____ Account for the ATP produced by the complete oxidation of glucose. (23.3)

Practice Test for Chapter 23

1. Which is true of the citric acid cycle? (23.1)
   A. Acetyl CoA is converted to CO_2 and H_2O.
   B. Oxaloacetate combines with acetyl units to form citric acid.
   C. The coenzymes are NAD^+ and FAD.
   D. ATP is produced by direct phosphorylation.
   E. All of the above.

For questions 2 through 6, match the description with each of the following: (23.1)
   A. malate   B. fumarate   C. succinate
   D. citrate   E. oxaloacetate

2. _____ This compound is formed when oxaloacetate combines with acetyl CoA.

3. _____ H_2O adds to the double bond of this compound to form malate.

4. _____ FAD removes hydrogen from this compound to form a double bond.

5. _____ This compound is formed when the hydroxyl group in malate is oxidized.

6. _____ This compound is regenerated in the citric acid cycle.

7. One turn of the citric acid cycle produces (23.1, 23.3)
   A. 3 NADH   B. 3 NADH, 1 $FADH_2$ C. 3 $FADH_2$, 1 NADH, 1 ATP
   D. 3 NADH, 1 $FADH_2$, 1 ATP   E. 1 NADH, 1 $FADH_2$, 1 ATP

8. The citric acid cycle is activated by (23.1)
   A. high ATP levels   B. NADH   C. high ADP levels
   D. low ATP levels   E. succinyl CoA

9. The end product(s) of electron transport is (are) (23.2)
   A. H_2O + ATP   B. CO_2 + H_2O C. NH_3 + CO_2 + H_2O
   D. H_2 + O_2 E. urea (NH_2CONH_2)

10. How many complexes in electron transport provide electrons for ATP synthesis? (23.2)
    A. none   **B.** 1   **C.** 2   **D.** 3   **E.** 4

11. Electron transport (23.2, 23.3)
    A. produces most of the ATP in the body
    B. carries oxygen to the cells
    C. produces $CO_2 + H_2O$
    D. is involved only in the citric acid cycle
    E. operates during fermentation

For questions 12 through 20, match the metabolic processes with the correct component of electron transport: (23.2)
    A. NAD^+ **B.** FAD   **C.** CoQ   **D.** cytochrome c **E.** ATP synthase

12. _____ a mobile carrier that picks up electrons from $FADH_2$

13. _____ the coenzyme that accepts hydrogen atoms from NADH

14. _____ a mobile carrier that picks up electrons from $CoQH_2$

15. _____ the coenzyme used to remove hydrogen atoms from two adjacent carbon atoms to form carbon–carbon double bonds

16. _____ protein complex that returns hydrogen ions to the matrix to generate ATP

17. _____ coenzyme that contains flavin

18. _____ the reduced form of this coenzyme that generates 2.5 molecules of ATP

19. _____ the reduced form of this coenzyme that generates 1.5 molecules of ATP

20. _____ electron acceptor containing iron

For questions 21 through 25, indicate the number of ATPs produced: (23.3)
    A. 2.5 ATP   **B.** 5 ATP   **C.** 7 ATP   **D.** 10 ATP   **E.** 32 ATP

21. _____ from one turn of the citric acid cycle (acetyl CoA $\longrightarrow 2CO_2$)

22. _____ from complete reaction of glucose (glucose + $6O_2 \longrightarrow 6CO_2 + 6H_2O$)

23. _____ produced for each NADH that enters electron transport

24. _____ produced from glycolysis (glucose + $O_2 \longrightarrow$ 2 pyruvate + $2H_2O$)

25. _____ from oxidation of 2 pyruvate (2 pyruvate $\longrightarrow$ 2 acetyl CoA + $2CO_2$)

Answers to the Practice Test

1. E	**2.** D	**3.** B	**4.** C	**5.** E
6. E	**7.** D	**8.** C, D	**9.** A	**10.** D
11. A	**12.** C	**13.** C	**14.** D	**15.** B
16. E	**17.** B	**18.** A	**19.** B	**20.** D
21. D	**22.** E	**23.** A	**24.** C	**25.** B

Metabolism and Energy Production

Learning Goals

- Describe the oxidation of acetyl CoA in the citric acid cycle.
- Describe the transfer of hydrogen ions and electrons in electron transport and the process of oxidative phosphorylation in ATP synthesis.
- Account for the ATP produced by the complete oxidation of glucose.

Chapter Outline

Chapter Opener: Exercise Physiologist

23.1 The Citric Acid Cycle

23.2 Electron Transport and ATP

Chemistry Link to Health: Toxins: Inhibitors of Electron Transport

Chemistry Link to Health: Uncouplers of ATP Synthase

23.3 ATP Energy from Glucose

Chemistry Link to Health: Efficiency of ATP Production

Clinical Update: Improving Natalie's Overall Fitness

⚛ Core Chemistry Skills

- Describing the Reactions in the Citric Acid Cycle (23.1)
- Calculating the ATP Produced from Glucose (23.3)

Selected Answers and Solutions to Text Problems

23.1 The citric acid cycle is also known as the Krebs cycle and the tricarboxylic acid cycle.

23.3 One turn of the citric acid cycle converts 1 acetyl CoA to $2CO_2$, $3NADH + 3H^+$, $FADH_2$, GTP (ATP), and HS—CoA.

23.5 a. Two reactions, reactions 3 and 4, involve oxidation and decarboxylation which reduces the length of the carbon chain by one carbon in each reaction.
  b. There is a dehydration in reaction 2. Citrate is dehydrated to aconitate, which is then hydrated to isocitrate.
  c. NAD^+ is reduced by the oxidation reactions 3, 4, and 8 of the citric acid cycle.

23.7 a. The six-carbon compounds in the citric acid cycle are citrate and isocitrate.
  b. Decarboxylation reactions remove carbon atoms as CO_2, which reduces the number of carbon atoms in the chain (reactions 3 and 4).
  c. The five-carbon compound in the citric acid cycle is α-ketoglutarate.
  d. Secondary alcohols are oxidized in reactions 3 and 8.

23.9 a. Citrate synthase joins acetyl CoA to oxaloacetate.
  b. Succinate dehydrogenase and aconitase form a carbon–carbon double bond.
  c. Fumarase adds water to the double bond in fumarate.

23.11 a. NAD^+ accepts a hydrogen from the oxidation and decarboxylation of isocitrate.
  b. FAD accepts two hydrogens from the oxidation of succinate.

23.13 Isocitrate dehydrogenase and α-ketoglutarate dehydrogenase are allosteric enzymes, which increase or decrease the flow of materials through the citric acid cycle.

23.15 High levels of ADP means there are low levels of ATP. To provide more ATP for the cell, the reaction rate of the citric acid cycle increases.

23.17 Since malate builds up, the deficient enzyme is malate dehydrogenase.

23.19 Cyt c (Fe^{3+}) is the abbreviation for the oxidized form of cytochrome c.

23.21 a. The loss of H^+ and $2\ e^-$ is oxidation.
  b. The gain of $2H^+$ and $2\ e^-$ is reduction.

23.23 NADH molecules provide the hydrogen ions and electrons for electron transport at complex I.

23.25 Their order in electron transport is: $FADH_2$, CoQ, cytochrome c (Fe^{3+}).

23.27 The mobile carrier coenzyme Q transfers electrons from complex I to complex III.

23.29 When NADH transfers electrons to complex I, NAD^+ is produced (oxidation).

23.31 a. $NADH + H^+ + \underline{CoQ} \longrightarrow \underline{NAD^+} + CoQH_2$
  b. $CoQH_2 + 2cyt\ c\ (Fe^{3+}) \longrightarrow CoQ + \underline{2cyt\ c\ (Fe^{2+}) + 2H^+}$

23.33 In oxidative phosphorylation, the energy from the oxidation reactions in electron transport is used to synthesize ATP from ADP and P_i.

23.35 As hydrogen ions return to the lower-energy environment in the matrix, they pass through ATP synthase, where they release energy to drive the synthesis of ATP.

23.37 Glycolysis and the citric acid cycle produce the reduced coenzymes **NADH** and $FADH_2$, which enter electron transport where they release hydrogen ions and electrons that are used to generate energy for the synthesis of ATP.

23.39 If CN^- binds to the heme of a cytochrome, electrons cannot reduce Fe^{3+} to Fe^{2+} and will not be transported, thus stopping electron transport.

23.41 Because dinitrophenol induces thermogenesis and inhibits ATP synthase, it raises body temperature to unsafe levels and can cause constant sweating.

23.43 Two. In glycolysis, one glucose molecule forms two pyruvate, which oxidize to give 2 acetyl CoA to enter the citric acid cycle.

23.45 a. 2.5 ATP are produced from the oxidation of NADH in electron transport.
  b. 7 ATP are produced in glycolysis when glucose degrades to two pyruvate molecules.
  c. 5 ATP are produced when two pyruvate molecules are oxidized to 2 acetyl CoA and $2CO_2$.

23.47 Electron transport requires oxygen. A low level of oxygen will decrease the activity of electron transport and the formation of ATP.

23.49 Normally cells are 33% efficient at converting the energy stored in glucose to ATP energy; Natalie's cells are 24% efficient:

$$25 \text{ g glucose} \times \frac{1 \text{ mole glucose}}{180.2 \text{ g glucose}} \times \frac{32 \text{ moles ATP}}{1 \text{ mole glucose}} \times \frac{24\% \text{ efficiency}}{33\% \text{ efficiency}}$$

$= 3.2$ moles of ATP (2 SFs)

23.51 a. Succinate is part of the citric acid cycle.
  b. $CoQH_2$ is part of electron transport.

    c. FAD is part of both the citric acid cycle and electron transport.

    d. Cyt c (Fe^{2+}) is part of electron transport.

    e. Citrate is part of the citric acid cycle.

23.53 citrate $\longrightarrow$ <u>isocitrate</u>

    succinyl CoA $\longrightarrow$ <u>succinate</u>

    malate $\longrightarrow$ <u>oxaloacetate</u>

23.55 a. reactant: citrate   product: isocitrate

    b. reactant: succinate   product: fumarate

    c. reactant: fumarate   product: malate

23.57 a. Aconitase uses H_2O.

    b. Succinate dehydrogenase uses FAD.

    c. Isocitrate dehydrogenase uses NAD^+.

23.59 a. Aconitase catalyzes a hydration (4) reaction.

    b. Succinate dehydrogenase catalyzes an oxidation (1) reaction.

    c. Isocitrate dehydrogenase catalyzes an oxidation (1) and decarboxylation (2) reaction.

23.61 When one NADH undergoes oxidation via electron transport, a total of $10H^+$ are pumped across the inner mitochondrial membrane: $4H^+$ at complex I, $4H^+$ at complex III, and $2H^+$ at complex IV.

23.63 A maximum of 2.5 ATP can be produced by energy generated when electrons flow from NADH to oxygen (O_2).

23.65 The oxidation reactions of the citric acid cycle produce a source of reduced coenzymes for electron transport and ATP synthesis.

23.67 The oxidized coenzymes NAD^+ and FAD needed for the citric acid cycle are regenerated by electron transport, which requires oxygen.

23.69 a. Citrate and isocitrate are six-carbon compounds in the citric acid cycle.

    b. α-Ketoglutarate is a five-carbon compound.

    c. The compounds α-ketoglutarate, succinyl CoA, and oxaloacetate have keto groups.

23.71 a. In reaction 4, α-ketoglutarate, a five-carbon keto acid, is decarboxylated.

    b. In reactions 2 and 7, carbon–carbon double bonds in aconitate and fumarate are hydrated.

    c. NAD^+ is reduced in reactions 3, 4, and 8.

    d. In reactions 3 and 8, a secondary hydroxyl group in isocitrate and malate is oxidized.

23.73 a. NAD^+ is the coenzyme for the oxidation of a secondary hydroxyl group in isocitrate to a keto group in α-ketoglutarate.

    b. The coenzymes NAD^+ and CoA are needed in the oxidation and decarboxylation of α-ketoglutarate to succinyl CoA.

23.75 a. High levels of NADH inhibit isocitrate dehydrogenase and α-ketoglutarate dehydrogenase to slow the rate of the citric acid cycle.

    b. High levels of ATP inhibit isocitrate dehydrogenase to slow the rate of the citric acid cycle.

23.77 The transfer of electrons by complexes I, III, and IV generates energy to pump hydrogen ions out of the matrix into the intermembrane space.

23.79 a. Amytal and rotenone block electron flow from complex I to coenzyme Q.

    b. Antimycin A blocks the flow of electrons from complex III to cytochrome c.

    c. Cyanide and carbon monoxide block electron flow from cytochrome c to complex IV.

23.81 In the chemiosmotic model, energy is released as hydrogen ions flow through ATP synthase back to the mitochondrial matrix and is utilized for the synthesis of ATP.

23.83 In the intermembrane space, there is a higher concentration of hydrogen ions, which reduces the pH and forms an electrochemical gradient. As a result, hydrogen ions flow into the matrix, where the H^+ concentration is lower and the pH is higher.

23.85 ATP synthase is a protein complex that spans the inner mitochondrial membrane and protrudes into the mitochondrial matrix.

23.87 The oxidation of glucose to pyruvate produces 7 ATP, whereas the oxidation of glucose to CO_2 and H_2O produces a maximum of 32 ATP.

23.89 As hydrogen ions from the hydrogen ion gradient move through the ATP synthase to return to the matrix, energy is released and used to synthesize ATP by ATP synthase.

23.91 A hibernating bear has more brown fat which can be used during the winter to generate heat rather than ATP energy.

23.93 a. $7 \text{ moles ATP} \times \dfrac{7.3 \text{ kcal}}{1 \text{ mole ATP}} = 51 \text{ kcal (2 SFs) (from glycolysis)}$

   b. $5 \text{ moles ATP} \times \dfrac{7.3 \text{ kcal}}{1 \text{ mole ATP}} = 37 \text{ kcal (2 SFs) (2 pyruvate molecules to 2 acetyl CoA)}$

   c. $20 \text{ moles ATP} \times \dfrac{7.3 \text{ kcal}}{1 \text{ mole ATP}} = 150 \text{ kcal (2 SFs) (2 acetyl CoA in the citric acid cycle)}$

   d. $32 \text{ moles ATP} \times \dfrac{7.3 \text{ kcal}}{1 \text{ mole ATP}} = 230 \text{ kcal (2 SFs) (complete oxidation of glucose to } CO_2 \text{ and } H_2O)$

23.95 If the combustion of glucose produces 690 kcal in a calorimeter, but only 230 kcal (from 32 ATP) in cells, the efficiency of glucose use in the cells is 230 kcal/690 kcal or 33%.

23.97 a. weight = 115 lb; height = 5 ft 4 in. = $(5 \times 12) + 4 = 64$ in.; age = 21 y

   BMR $= 655 + (4.35 \times 115) + (4.70 \times 64) - (4.70 \times 21)$

   $= 1360$ kcal (rounded to nearest 10 kcal)

   b. $1360 \text{ kcal} \times \dfrac{1 \text{ mole ATP}}{7.3 \text{ kcal}} \times \dfrac{507 \text{ g ATP}}{1 \text{ mole ATP}} \times \dfrac{1 \text{ kg ATP}}{1000 \text{ g ATP}} = 94 \text{ kg of ATP (2 SFs)}$

24

Metabolic Pathways for Lipids and Amino Acids

Credit: Tyler Olson / Fotolia

Luke is a paramedic. Recently, blood work from a physical examination indicated a plasma cholesterol level of 256 mg/dL, which is elevated. Luke's doctor ordered a liver profile that showed elevated liver enzymes: *aspartate transaminase* (AST) of 226 units/L (the normal AST is 5 to 40 units/L) and *alanine transaminase* (ALT) of 282 units/L (the normal ALT is 5 to 35 units/L).

During Luke's career as a paramedic, he was exposed several times to blood and was accidentally stuck by a needle containing infected blood. A hepatitis profile showed that Luke was positive for antibodies to both hepatitis B and C. His doctor diagnosed Luke with *chronic hepatitis C virus* (HCV) infection. Hepatitis C is an infection caused by a virus that attacks the liver and leads to inflammation. Hepatitis C is usually passed by contact with contaminated blood or by needles shared during illegal drug use. Most people infected with the hepatitis C virus have no symptoms. As part of his treatment, Luke attended a class given by a public health nurse on living with hepatitis C. How many ATP molecules are produced from the beta oxidation of capric acid, the 10-carbon saturated fatty acid?

CHAPTER READINESS*

🎛 Core Chemistry Skills

- Identifying Fatty Acids (17.2)
- Drawing the Zwitterion for an Amino Acid (19.1)
- Identifying Important Coenzymes in Metabolism (22.3)
- Identifying the Compounds in Glycolysis (22.4)
- Identifying the Compounds and Enzymes in Glycogenesis and Glycogenolysis (22.6)
- Describing the Reactions in the Citric Acid Cycle (23.1)
- Calculating the ATP Produced from Glucose (23.3)

*These Core Chemistry Skills from previous chapters are listed here for your review as you proceed to the new material in this chapter.

24.1 Digestion of Triacylglycerols

Learning Goal: Describe the sites and products obtained from the digestion of triacylglycerols.

- Dietary fats begin digestion in the small intestine, where they are emulsified by bile salts.
- Pancreatic lipases catalyze the hydrolysis of triacylglycerols to yield monoacylglycerols and free fatty acids.
- Triacylglycerols reform in the intestinal lining, where they combine with proteins to form chylomicrons for transport through the lymphatic system and bloodstream.
- In the cells, triacylglycerols are hydrolyzed to glycerol and fatty acids, which can be used for energy.

♦ **Learning Exercise 24.1**

Match each of the following terms with the correct description below:

    a. chylomicrons   **b.** lipases   **c.** fat utilization

    d. monoacylglycerols and fatty acids   **e.** emulsification

1. _____ the hydrolysis of triacylglycerols in adipose tissues to produce energy

2. _____ lipoproteins formed when triacylglycerols are coated with proteins

3. _____ the breakup of fat globules in the small intestine by bile salts

4. _____ enzymes released from the pancreas that hydrolyze triacylglycerols

5. _____ the products of lipase hydrolysis of triacylglycerols in the small intestine

Answers   **1.** c   **2.** a   **3.** e   **4.** b   **5.** d

24.2 Oxidation of Fatty Acids

Learning Goal: Describe the metabolic pathway of β oxidation.

- When needed for energy, fatty acids bond to coenzyme A for transport to the mitochondria, where they undergo β oxidation.
- In β oxidation, an acyl chain is oxidized to yield a shortened fatty acid, acetyl CoA, and the reduced coenzymes NADH and $FADH_2$.

♦ **Learning Exercise 24.2A**

Match each of the following terms with the correct description:

    a. activation   **b.** carnitine   **c.** β oxidation

    d. NAD^+ and FAD   **e.** mitochondria

1. _____ coenzymes needed for β oxidation

2. _____ site in the cell where β oxidation of fatty acids takes place

3. _____ combination of a fatty acid with HS—CoA to form fatty acyl CoA

4. _____ carrier that moves the acyl group into the mitochondrial matrix

5. _____ the sequential removal of two-carbon sections from fatty acids

Answers   **1.** d   **2.** e   **3.** a   **4.** b   **5.** c

♦ **Learning Exercise 24.2B**

1. Write the equation for the activation of myristic (C_{14}) acid: $CH_3-(CH_2)_{12}-\overset{\overset{\textstyle O}{\|}}{C}-OH$

2. Write the equation for the first oxidation of myristoyl CoA.

3. Write the equation for the hydration of the double bond.

4. Write the equation for the second oxidation of myristoyl CoA.

5. a. How many cycles of β oxidation are needed for complete oxidation?

b. How many acetyl CoA units will be produced by complete oxidation?

1. $CH_3-(CH_2)_{12}-\overset{\overset{\displaystyle O}{\|}}{C}-OH + HS-CoA + ATP \longrightarrow CH_3-(CH_2)_{12}-\overset{\overset{\displaystyle O}{\|}}{C}-S-CoA + AMP + 2P_i + H_2O$

2. $CH_3-(CH_2)_{12}-\overset{\overset{\displaystyle O}{\|}}{C}-S-CoA + FAD \longrightarrow CH_3-(CH_2)_{10}-CH=CH-\overset{\overset{\displaystyle O}{\|}}{C}-S-CoA + FADH_2$

3. $CH_3-(CH_2)_{10}-CH=CH-\overset{\overset{\displaystyle O}{\|}}{C}-S-CoA + H_2O \longrightarrow CH_3-(CH_2)_{10}-\overset{\overset{\displaystyle OH}{|}}{CH}-CH_2-\overset{\overset{\displaystyle O}{\|}}{C}-S-CoA$

4. $CH_3-(CH_2)_{10}-\overset{\overset{\displaystyle OH}{|}}{CH}-CH_2-\overset{\overset{\displaystyle O}{\|}}{C}-S-CoA + NAD^+ \longrightarrow$

$CH_3-(CH_2)_{10}-\overset{\overset{\displaystyle O}{\|}}{C}-CH_2-\overset{\overset{\displaystyle O}{\|}}{C}-S-CoA + NADH + H^+$

5. a. 6 cycles   **b.** 7 acetyl CoA units

24.3 ATP and Fatty Acid Oxidation

Learning Goal: Calculate the total ATP produced by the complete oxidation of a fatty acid.

⚛ **CORE CHEMISTRY SKILL**

Calculating the ATP from Fatty Acid Oxidation (β Oxidation)

- The energy obtained from a particular fatty acid depends on the number of carbon atoms.
- Two ATP are required for activation. Then each acetyl CoA produces 10 ATP via the citric acid cycle; each NADH gives 2.5 ATP and each $FADH_2$ gives 1.5 ATP from electron transport.

♦ **Learning Exercise 24.3**

Lauric acid is a 12-carbon saturated fatty acid: $CH_3-(CH_2)_{10}-\overset{\overset{\displaystyle O}{\|}}{C}-OH$

1. How many ATP are needed for activation? _____

2. How many cycles of β oxidation are needed for complete oxidation? _____

3. How many NADH and $FADH_2$ are produced during β oxidation? _____

4. How many acetyl CoA units are produced? _____

5. What is the total number of ATP produced from the citric acid cycle and electron transport? _____

Answers

1. 2 ATP   2. 5 cycles
3. Five cycles produce 5 NADH and 5 $FADH_2$.   4. 6 acetyl CoA units
5. 5 NADH $\times$ 2.5 ATP/NADH $= 12.5$ ATP; 5 $FADH_2 \times$ 1.5 ATP/$FADH_2 = 7.5$ ATP;
   6 acetyl CoA $\times$ 10 ATP/acetyl CoA $= 60$ ATP;
   Total ATP $= 12.5$ ATP $+ 7.5$ ATP $+ 60$ ATP $- 2$ ATP (for activation) $= 78$ ATP

24.4 Ketogenesis and Ketone Bodies

Learning Goal: Describe the pathway of ketogenesis.

- When the oxidation of large amounts of fatty acids causes high levels of acetyl CoA, the acetyl CoA undergoes ketogenesis.
- Two molecules of acetyl CoA form acetoacetyl CoA, which is converted to the ketone bodies acetoacetate, β-hydroxybutyrate, and acetone.

♦ **Learning Exercise 24.4**

Match each of the following terms with the correct description:

⚛ **CORE CHEMISTRY SKILL**

Describing How Ketone Bodies are Formed

    a. ketone bodies   **b.** ketogenesis   **c.** ketosis

    d. liver   **e.** acidosis

1. _____ high levels of ketone bodies in the blood

2. _____ a metabolic pathway that produces ketone bodies

3. _____ β-hydroxybutyrate, acetoacetate, and acetone

4. _____ the condition whereby ketone bodies lower the blood pH below 7.4

5. _____ site where ketone bodies form

Answers **1.** c **2.** b **3.** a **4.** e **5.** d

24.5 Fatty Acid Synthesis

Learning Goal: Describe the biosynthesis of fatty acids from acetyl CoA.

- When all energy needs have been met and glycogen stores are full, excess acetyl CoA is used to synthesize fatty acids that are stored in the adipose tissue.
- Two-carbon acetyl CoA molecules link together to form palmitic (C_{16}) acid and other fatty acids.

♦ Learning Exercise 24.5

Indicate whether each of the following is characteristic of lipogenesis (L) or β oxidation (O):

1. _____ occurs in the matrix of mitochondria **2.** _____ occurs in the cytosol of mitochondria

3. _____ activated by insulin **4.** _____ activated by glucagon

5. _____ starts with fatty acids **6.** _____ starts with acetyl CoA units

7. _____ produces fatty acids **8.** _____ produces acetyl CoA units

9. _____ requires NADPH coenzyme **10.** _____ requires FAD and NAD^+ coenzymes

11. _____ activated by HS—CoA **12.** _____ activated by HS—ACP

Answers **1.** O **2.** L **3.** L **4.** O

      5. O **6.** L **7.** L **8.** O

      9. L **10.** O **11.** O **12.** L

24.6 Degradation of Proteins and Amino Acids

Learning Goal: Describe the hydrolysis of dietary protein and reactions of transamination and oxidative deamination in the degradation of amino acids.

- Proteins begin digestion in the stomach, where HCl denatures proteins and activates peptidases that hydrolyze peptide bonds.
- In the small intestine, trypsin and chymotrypsin complete the hydrolysis of peptides to amino acids.
- Amino acids are normally used for protein synthesis.
- Amino acids are degraded by transferring an amino group from an amino acid to an α-keto acid to yield a different amino acid and α-keto acid.
- In oxidative deamination, the amino group in glutamate is removed as an ammonium ion, NH_4^+.

♦ Learning Exercise 24.6A

Match each of the following terms with the correct description:

  a. nitrogen-containing compounds **b.** protein turnover **c.** stomach
  d. nitrogen balance   **e.** small intestine

1. _____ HCl activates enzymes that hydrolyze peptide bonds in proteins.

2. _____ Trypsin and chymotrypsin convert peptides to amino acids.

3. _____ These compounds include amino acids, amino alcohols, proteins, hormones, and nucleic acids.

4. _____ The process of synthesizing proteins and breaking them down.

5. _____ The amount of protein hydrolyzed is equal to the amount of protein used in the body.

Answers   **1.** c   **2.** e   **3.** a   **4.** b   **5.** d

♦ Learning Exercise 24.6B

Match each of the following descriptions with transamination (T) or oxidative deamination (D):

1. _____ produces an ammonium ion, NH_4^+

2. _____ transfers an amino group to an α-keto acid

3. _____ usually involves the degradation of glutamate

4. _____ requires NAD^+

5. _____ produces another amino acid and α-keto acid

6. _____ usually produces α-ketoglutarate

Answers   **1.** D   **2.** T   **3.** D   **4.** D   **5.** T   **6.** D

♦ Learning Exercise 24.7C

1. Write an equation for the transamination reaction of serine and oxaloacetate.

2. Write an equation for the oxidative deamination of glutamate.

Answers

1. $HO-CH_2-\overset{\overset{+}{N}H_3}{\underset{|}{C}H}-COO^- + {}^-OOC-\overset{\overset{O}{\|}}{C}-CH_2-COO^- \xrightarrow{\text{Aminotransferase}}$

$HO-CH_2-\overset{\overset{O}{\|}}{C}-COO^- + {}^-OOC-\overset{\overset{+}{N}H_3}{\underset{|}{C}H}-CH_2-COO^-$

2. ${}^-OOC-\overset{\overset{+}{N}H_3}{\underset{|}{C}H}-CH_2-CH_2-COO^- + NAD^+ + H_2O \xrightarrow{\substack{\text{Glutamate} \\ \text{dehydrogenase}}}$

${}^-OOC-\overset{\overset{O}{\|}}{C}-CH_2-CH_2-COO^- + NH_4^+ + NADH + H^+$

24.7 Urea Cycle

Learning Goal: Describe the formation of urea from an ammonium ion.

- The ammonium ion, NH_4^+, from amino acid degradation is toxic if allowed to accumulate.
- The urea cycle converts ammonium ion to urea, which forms urine in the kidneys.

♦ **Learning Exercise 24.7**

Arrange the following reactions in the order they occur in the urea cycle:

Reaction 1. _____   Reaction 2. _____   Reaction 3. _____   Reaction 4. _____

   a. Argininosuccinate is split to yield arginine and fumarate.

   b. Aspartate condenses with citrulline to yield argininosuccinate.

   c. Arginine is hydrolyzed to yield urea and regenerates ornithine.

   d. Ornithine combines with the carbamoyl group from carbamoyl phosphate.

Answers   **Reaction 1.** d   **Reaction 2.** b   **Reaction 3.** a   **Reaction 4.** c

24.8 Fates of the Carbon Atoms from Amino Acids

Learning Goal: Describe where carbon atoms from amino acids enter the citric acid cycle or other pathways.

- α-Keto acids resulting from transamination can be used as intermediates in the citric acid cycle or in the synthesis of lipids or glucose or oxidized for energy.

♦ **Learning Exercise 24.8**

Match each of the following terms with the correct description:

   a. glucogenic   b. ketogenic   c. oxaloacetate

   d. acetyl CoA   e. α-ketoglutarate   f. pyruvate

1. _____ amino acids that generate pyruvate or oxaloacetate, which can be used to synthesize glucose

2. _____ keto acid obtained from carbon atoms of alanine and serine

3. _____ keto acid obtained from carbon atoms of glutamine and glutamate

4. _____ keto acid obtained from carbon atoms of aspartate and asparagine

5. _____ amino acids that generate compounds that can produce ketone bodies

6. _____ compound obtained from carbon atoms of leucine and isoleucine

Answers   1. a   2. f   3. e   4. c   5. b   6. d

24.9 Synthesis of Amino Acids

Learning Goal: Illustrate how some nonessential amino acids are synthesized from intermediates in the citric acid cycle and other metabolic pathways.

- Humans synthesize only 11 amino acids. The other 9, called essential amino acids, must be obtained from the diet.

Key Terms for Sections 24.1–24.9

Match the following key terms with the correct description:

a. essential amino acid   **b.** transamination   **c.** lipogenesis
d. ketosis (acidosis)   **e.** β oxidation

1. _____ a reaction cycle that oxidizes fatty acids by removing acetyl CoA units

2. _____ the synthesis of fatty acids by linking two-carbon acetyl units

3. _____ a condition in which high levels of ketone bodies lower blood pH

4. _____ an amino acid that must be obtained from the diet

5. _____ the transfer of an amino group from an amino acid to an α-keto acid

Answers   1. e   2. c   3. d   4. a   5. b

♦ **Learning Exercise 24.9**

🔬 **CORE CHEMISTRY SKILL**
Distinguishing Anabolic and Catabolic Pathways

Match each of the following terms with the correct description:

a. essential amino acids   **b.** nonessential amino acids
c. transamination   **d.** phenylketonuria (PKU)

1. _____ amino acids synthesized in humans

2. _____ a genetic condition in which phenylalanine is not converted to tyrosine

3. _____ amino acids that must be supplied by the diet

4. _____ reaction that produces some nonessential amino acids

Answers   1. b   2. d   3. a   4. c

Checklist for Chapter 24

You are ready to take the Practice Test for Chapter 24. Be sure that you have accomplished the learning goals for each of the sections in this chapter. If not, review the section listed at the end of each goal. Then apply your new skills and understanding to the Practice Test.

After studying Chapter 24, I can successfully:

_____ Describe the sites, enzymes, and products for the digestion of triacylglycerols. (24.1)

_____ Describe the oxidation of fatty acids via β oxidation. (24.2)

_____ Calculate the number of ATP produced by the complete oxidation of a fatty acid. (24.3)

_____ Explain ketogenesis and the conditions in the cell that form ketone bodies. (24.4)

_____ Describe the biosynthesis of fatty acids from acetyl CoA. (24.5)

_____ Describe the sites, enzymes, and products for the digestion of dietary proteins. (24.6)

_____ Explain the role of transamination and oxidative deamination in degrading amino acids. (24.6)

_____ Describe the formation of urea from ammonium ion. (24.7)

_____ Explain how carbon atoms from amino acids are prepared to enter the citric acid cycle or other pathways. (24.8)

_____ Show how nonessential amino acids are synthesized from substances used in the citric acid cycle and other pathways. (24.9)

Practice Test for Chapter 24

1. The digestion of triacylglycerols takes place in the _____ by enzymes called _____. (24.1)
   A. small intestine; peptidases   **B.** stomach; lipases   **C.** stomach; peptidases
   D. small intestine; lipases   **E.** all of these

2. The products of the digestion of triacylglycerols are (24.1)
   A. fatty acids   **B.** monoacylglycerols   **C.** glycerol
   D. diacylglycerols   **E.** all of these

3. The function of bile salts in the digestion of fats is (24.1)
   A. emulsification   **B.** hydration   **C.** dehydration
   D. oxidation   **E.** reduction

4. Chylomicrons formed in the intestinal lining (24.1)
   A. are lipoproteins
   B. are triacylglycerols coated with proteins
   C. transport fats into the lymphatic system and bloodstream
   D. carry triacylglycerols to the cells of the heart, muscle, and adipose tissues
   E. all of these

5. Glycerol obtained from the hydrolysis of triacylglycerols enters glycolysis when converted to (24.1)
   A. glucose   **B.** fatty acids   **C.** dihydroxyacetone phosphate
   D. pyruvate   **E.** glycerol-3-phosphate

6. Fatty acids are prepared for β oxidation by forming (24.2)
   A. carnitine   **B.** acyl carnitine   **C.** acetyl CoA
   D. acyl CoA   **E.** pyruvate

7. The fatty acids in the β oxidation cycle do *not* undergo (24.2)
    A. reduction   **B.** hydration   **C.** dehydrogenation
    D. oxidation   **E.** formation of acetyl CoA

For questions 8 through 11, consider the β oxidation of palmitic (C_{16}) acid: (24.2, 24.3)

8. The number of β oxidation cycles required to oxidize palmitic (C_{16}) acid is
    A. 16   **B.** 9   **C.** 8   **D.** 7   **E.** 6

9. The number of acetyl CoA units produced by the β oxidation of palmitic (C_{16}) acid is
    A. 16   **B.** 9   **C.** 8   **D.** 7   **E.** 6

10. The number of NADH and $FADH_2$ produced by the β oxidation of palmitic (C_{16}) acid is
    A. 16   **B.** 9   **C.** 8   **D.** 7   **E.** 6

11. The total ATP produced by the β oxidation of palmitic (C_{16}) acid is
    A. 96   **B.** 106   **C.** 126   **D.** 134   **E.** 136

12. The oxidation of large amounts of fatty acids can produce (24.4)
    A. ketone bodies   **B.** glucose   **C.** low pH level in the blood
    D. acetone   **E.** pyruvate

13. The metabolic pathway of lipogenesis requires (24.5)
    A. fatty acids   **B.** acetyl CoA   **C.** FAD and NAD^+
    D. glucagon   **E.** ketone bodies

14. The digestion of proteins takes place in the _____ by enzymes called _____. (24.6)
    A. small intestine; peptidases   **B.** stomach; lipases   **C.** stomach; peptidases
    D. small intestine; lipases   **E.** stomach and small intestine; proteases and peptidases

15. The process of transamination (24.6)
    A. is part of the citric acid cycle   **B.** converts α-amino acids to β-keto acids
    C. produces new amino acids   **D.** is not used in the metabolism of amino acids
    E. is part of the β oxidation of fats

16. The oxidative deamination of glutamate produces (24.6)
    A. a new amino acid   **B.** a new α-keto acid   **C.** ammonia, NH_3
    D. ammonium ion, NH_4^+ **E.** urea

17. The purpose of the urea cycle in the liver is to (24.7)
    A. synthesize urea
    B. convert urea to ammonium ion, NH_4^+
    C. convert ammonium ion, NH_4^+, to urea
    D. synthesize new amino acids
    E. take part in the β oxidation of fats

18. The urea cycle begins with the conversion of NH_4^+ to (24.7)
    A. aspartate   **B.** carbamoyl phosphate
    C. citrulline   **D.** argininosuccinate
    E. urea

19. The carbon atoms from a ketogenic amino acid can be used to (24.8)
    A. synthesize ketone bodies
    B. convert urea to ammonium ion, NH_4^+
    C. synthesize fatty acids
    D. produce energy
    E. synthesize proteins

20. The carbon atoms from various amino acids can be used (24.8)
    A. as intermediates in the citric acid cycle
    B. in the formation of pyruvate
    C. in the synthesis of glucose
    D. in the formation of ketone bodies
    E. for all of these

21. Essential amino acids (24.9)
    A. are not synthesized by humans
    B. are required in the diet
    C. are excreted if in excess
    D. include leucine, lysine, and valine
    E. all of these

22. When the quantity of amino acids in the diet exceeds the needs of the cells, the excess amino acids are (24.9)
    A. stored for use at a later time
    B. used to synthesize glycogen
    C. excreted
    D. converted to fat
    E. used to make more protein

23. Phenylketonuria is a condition (24.9)
    A. that is abbreviated as PKU
    B. in which a person does not synthesize tyrosine
    C. that can be detected at birth
    D. that can cause severe mental retardation if untreated
    E. all of these

Answers to the Practice Test

1. D	**2.** E	**3.** A	**4.** E	**5.** C
6. D	**7.** A	**8.** D	**9.** C	**10.** D
11. B	**12.** A, C, D	**13.** B	**14.** E	**15.** C
16. B, D	**17.** C	**18.** B	**19.** A, C	**20.** E
21. E	**22.** C	**23.** E		

24

Metabolic Pathways for Lipids and Amino Acids

Learning Goals

- Describe the sites and products obtained from the digestion of triacylglycerols.
- Describe the metabolic pathway of β oxidation.
- Calculate the total ATP produced by the complete oxidation of a fatty acid.
- Describe the pathway of ketogenesis.
- Describe the biosynthesis of fatty acids from acetyl CoA.
- Describe the hydrolysis of dietary protein and the reactions of transamination and oxidative deamination in the degradation of amino acids.
- Describe the formation of urea from an ammonium ion.
- Describe where carbon atoms from amino acids enter the citric acid cycle or other pathways.
- Illustrate how some nonessential amino acids are synthesized from intermediates in the citric acid cycle and other metabolic pathways.

Chapter Outline

Chapter Opener: Public Health Nurse (PHN)

24.1 Digestion of Triacylglycerols

Explore Your World: Digestion of Fats

24.2 Oxidation of Fatty Acids

24.3 ATP and Fatty Acid Oxidation

Chemistry Link to Health: Stored Fat and Obesity

Explore Your World: Fat Storage and Blubber

24.4 Ketogenesis and Ketone Bodies

Chemistry Link to Health: Diabetes and Ketone Bodies

24.5 Fatty Acid Synthesis

24.6 Degradation of Proteins and Amino Acids

24.7 Urea Cycle

24.8 Fates of the Carbon Atoms from Amino Acids

24.9 Synthesis of Amino Acids

Chemistry Link to Health: Phenylketonuria (PKU)

Clinical Update: Treatment of Luke's Hepatitis C

⚛ Core Chemistry Skills

- Calculating the ATP from Fatty Acid Oxidation (β Oxidation) (24.3)
- Describing How Ketone Bodies Are Formed (24.4)
- Distinguishing Anabolic and Catabolic Pathways (24.9)

Selected Answers and Solutions to Text Problems

24.1 The bile salts emulsify fat to give small fat globules for lipase hydrolysis.

24.3 Fats are released from fat stores when blood glucose and glycogen stores are depleted.

24.5 Glycerol is converted to glycerol-3-phosphate, and then to dihydroxyacetone phosphate, an intermediate of glycolysis.

24.7 The enzyme glycerol kinase would be defective.

24.9 Fatty acids are activated in the cytosol at the outer mitochondrial membrane.

24.11 The coenzymes FAD, NAD^+, and HS—CoA are required for β oxidation.

24.13 The designation β-carbon is based on the common names of carboxylic acids in which the α-carbon is the carbon adjacent to the carboxyl group.

a. $CH_3-CH_2-CH_2-CH_2-CH_2-\underset{\beta}{CH_2}-CH_2-\overset{\overset{\textstyle O}{\|}}{C}-S-CoA$

b.

24.15 a.

b. $CH_3-(CH_2)_6-\underset{\underset{\textstyle H}{|}}{C}=\overset{\overset{\textstyle H}{|}}{C}-\overset{\overset{\textstyle O}{\|}}{C}-S-CoA$

24.17 a. and **b.** $CH_3-(CH_2)_4-\underset{\beta}{CH_2}-\underset{\alpha}{CH_2}-\overset{\overset{\textstyle O}{\|}}{C}-S-CoA$

c. Three β oxidation cycles are needed.
d. Four acetyl CoA units are produced from a C_8 fatty acid.

24.19 The hydrolysis of ATP to AMP involves the hydrolysis of ATP to ADP, and then ADP to AMP, which provides the same amount of energy as the hydrolysis of two ATP to two ADP.

24.21 Analyze the Problem

Number of Carbon Atoms	Number of β Oxidation Cycles	Number of NADH	Number of FADH$_2$	Number of Acetyl CoA
22	10	10	10	11

a. A C_{22} fatty acid will go through 10 β oxidation cycles.
b. The β oxidation of a chain of 22 carbon atoms produces 11 acetyl CoA units.
c. **ATP Production from Behenic Acid (C$_{22}$)**

Activation	-2 ATP
$10 \text{ NADH} \times \dfrac{2.5 \text{ ATP}}{\text{NADH}}$ (electron transport)	25 ATP
$10 \text{ FADH}_2 \times \dfrac{1.5 \text{ ATP}}{\text{FADH}_2}$ (electron transport)	15 ATP
$11 \text{ acetyl CoA} \times \dfrac{10 \text{ ATP}}{\text{acetyl CoA}}$ (citric acid cycle)	110 ATP
Total	148 ATP

24.23 Analyze the Problem

Number of Carbon Atoms	Number of β Oxidation Cycles	Number of NADH	Number of FADH$_2$	Number of Acetyl CoA
18	8	8	8	9

a. A C_{18} fatty acid will go through eight β oxidation cycles.

b. The β oxidation of a chain of 18 carbon atoms produces nine acetyl CoA units.

c. The energy from the oxidation of unsaturated fatty acids is slightly less than the energy from saturated fatty acids. For simplicity, we will assume that the total ATP production is the same for both saturated and unsaturated fatty acids.

ATP Production from Oleic Acid (C_{18})

Activation	-2 ATP
$8 \text{ NADH} \times \dfrac{2.5 \text{ ATP}}{\text{NADH}}$ (electron transport)	20 ATP
$8 \text{ FADH}_2 \times \dfrac{1.5 \text{ ATP}}{\text{FADH}_2}$ (electron transport)	12 ATP
$9 \text{ acetyl CoA} \times \dfrac{10 \text{ ATP}}{\text{acetyl CoA}}$ (citric acid cycle)	90 ATP
Total	120 ATP

24.25 Ketogenesis is the synthesis of ketone bodies from excess acetyl CoA from fatty acid oxidation, which occurs when glucose is not available for energy, particularly in starvation, low-carbohydrate diets, fasting, alcoholism, and diabetes.

24.27 Acetoacetate undergoes reduction using $NADH + H^+$ to yield β-hydroxybutyrate.

24.29 High levels of ketone bodies lead to ketosis, a condition characterized by acidosis (a drop in blood pH values), excessive urination, and strong thirst.

24.31 Fatty acid synthesis takes place in the cytosol of cells in the liver and adipose tissue.

24.33 Fatty acid synthesis starts when acetyl CoA, HCO_3^-, and ATP produce malonyl CoA.

24.35 a. (3) Malonyl CoA transacylase converts malonyl CoA to malonyl ACP.
　　b. (1) Acetyl CoA carboxylase combines acetyl CoA with bicarbonate to yield malonyl CoA.
　　c. (2) Acetyl CoA transacylase converts acetyl CoA to acetyl ACP.

24.37 a. A C_{10} fatty acid requires the formation of 4 malonyl ACP, which uses 4 HCO_3^-.
　　b. Four ATP are required to produce 4 malonyl CoA.
　　c. Five acetyl CoA molecules are needed to make 1 acetyl ACP and 4 malonyl ACP.
　　d. A C_{10} fatty acid requires 4 malonyl ACP and 1 acetyl ACP.
　　e. A C_{10} fatty acid chain requires 4 cycles with 2 NADPH/cycle or a total of 8 NADPH.
　　f. The four cycles remove a total of 4 CO_2.

24.39 a. Reaction 4, the reduction of the double bond to a single bond, is catalyzed by enoyl ACP reductase.
　　b. If fatty acid synthesis is inhibited, the bacteria cannot form cell walls and will not thrive.

24.41 The digestion of proteins begins in the stomach and is completed in the small intestine.

24.43 Hormones, heme, purines and pyrimidines for nucleotides, proteins, nonessential amino acids, amino alcohols, and neurotransmitters require nitrogen obtained from amino acids.

24.45 The reactants are an amino acid and an α-keto acid, and the products are a new amino acid and a new α-keto acid.

24.47 In transamination, an amino group is transferred from an amino acid to an α-keto acid, creating a new amino acid and a new α-keto acid.

$$\text{a. } H-\underset{\underset{\displaystyle O}{\|}}{C}-COO^- \qquad \text{b. } HS-CH_2-\underset{\underset{\displaystyle O}{\|}}{C}-COO^- \qquad \text{c. } CH_3-\underset{\underset{\displaystyle CH_3}{|}}{CH}-\underset{\underset{\displaystyle O}{\|}}{C}-COO^-$$

24.49 In oxidative deamination, the amino group in an amino acid such as glutamate is removed as an ammonium ion. The reaction requires NAD^+.

$$\overset{\overset{\displaystyle +}{NH_3}}{\underset{|}{}}$$
$$^-OOC-\overset{|}{CH}-CH_2-CH_2-COO^- + H_2O + NAD^+ \xrightarrow[\text{dehydrogenase}]{\text{Glutamate}}$$
Glutamate

$$^-OOC-\underset{\underset{\displaystyle O}{\|}}{C}-CH_2-CH_2-COO^- + NH_4^+ + NADH + H^+$$
α-Ketoglutarate

24.51 $H_2N-\underset{\underset{\displaystyle O}{\|}}{C}-NH_2$

24.53 The carbon atom in urea is obtained from the CO_2 produced by the citric acid cycle.

24.55 The body converts NH_4^+ to urea because NH_4^+ is toxic if allowed to accumulate in the liver.

24.57 If there is a deficiency of argininosuccinate synthetase, citrulline will accumulate.

24.59 Glucogenic amino acids can be used to produce intermediates for gluconeogenesis (glucose synthesis).

24.61 a. Carbon atoms from alanine form the citric acid cycle intermediate oxaloacetate.
  b. Carbon atoms from asparagine form the citric acid cycle intermediate oxaloacetate.
  c. Carbon atoms from valine form the citric acid cycle intermediate succinyl CoA.
  d. Carbon atoms from glutamine form the citric acid cycle intermediate α-ketoglutarate.

24.63 The amino acids that humans can synthesize are called nonessential amino acids.

24.65 Glutamine synthetase catalyzes the addition of an amino group to glutamate to form glutamine using energy from the hydrolysis of ATP.

24.67 PKU is the abbreviation for **p**henyl**k**eton**u**ria.

24.69 $CH_3-\underset{\underset{\displaystyle O}{\|}}{C}-COO^- + {}^-OOC-\overset{\overset{\displaystyle +}{NH_3}}{\underset{|}{CH}}-CH_2-CH_2-COO^-$
  Pyruvate Glutamate

24.71 a. and **b.**

Analyze the Problem

Number of Carbon Atoms	Number of β Oxidation Cycles	Number of NADH	Number of FADH$_2$	Number of Acetyl CoA
12	5	5	5	6

c. Five cycles of β oxidation are needed.

d. Six acetyl CoA units are produced.

e. **ATP Production from Lauric Acid (C_{12})**

Activation	−2 ATP
$5 \text{ NADH} \times \dfrac{2.5 \text{ ATP}}{\text{NADH}}$ (electron transport)	12.5 ATP
$5 \text{ FADH}_2 \times \dfrac{1.5 \text{ ATP}}{\text{FADH}_2}$ (electron transport)	7.5 ATP
$6 \text{ acetyl CoA} \times \dfrac{10 \text{ ATP}}{\text{acetyl CoA}}$ (citric acid cycle)	60 ATP
Total	78 ATP

24.73 Triacylglycerols are hydrolyzed to monoacylglycerols and fatty acids in the small intestine, which reform as triacylglycerols in the intestinal lining for transport as lipoproteins to the tissues.

24.75 Fats can be stored in unlimited amounts in adipose tissue compared with the limited storage of carbohydrates as glycogen.

24.77 The fatty acids cannot diffuse across the blood–brain barrier.

24.79 a. Glycerol is converted to glycerol-3-phosphate and then to dihydroxyacetone phosphate, which can enter glycolysis or gluconeogenesis.

b. Activation of fatty acids occurs in the cytosol at the outer mitochondrial membrane.

c. The energy cost is equal to two ATP.

d. Only acyl CoA can move into the intermembrane space for transport by carnitine into the matrix.

24.81 a. NAD^+ is involved in β oxidation.

b. β Oxidation occurs in the mitochondrial matrix.

c. Malonyl ACP is involved in fatty acid synthesis.

d. Cleavage of a two-carbon acetyl group occurs in β oxidation.

e. Acyl carrier protein is involved in fatty acid synthesis.

f. Acetyl CoA carboxylase is involved in fatty acid synthesis.

24.83 a. High blood glucose stimulates fatty acid synthesis.

b. Secretion of glucagon stimulates fatty acid oxidation.

24.85 Ammonium ion is toxic if allowed to accumulate in the liver.

24.87 a. Citrulline reacts with aspartate in the urea cycle.

b. Carbamoyl phosphate reacts with ornithine in the urea cycle.

24.89 a. Carbon atoms from serine form the citric acid cycle intermediate oxaloacetate.

b. Carbon atoms from lysine form the citric acid cycle intermediate acetyl CoA.

c. Carbon atoms from methionine form the citric acid cycle intermediate succinyl CoA.

d. Carbon atoms from glutamate form the citric acid cycle intermediate α-ketoglutarate.

24.91 Serine is degraded to pyruvate, which is oxidized to acetyl CoA. The oxidation produces $NADH + H^+$, which provides 2.5 ATP. In one turn of the citric acid cycle, the acetyl CoA produces 10 ATP. Thus, serine can provide a total of 12.5 ATP.

24.93 a. first oxidation   **b.** cleavage (thiolysis)

c. activation

24.95 a. $CH_3 - \overset{\overset{\displaystyle CH_3}{|}}{CH} - \overset{\overset{\displaystyle \overset{+}{N}H_3}{|}}{CH} - \overset{\overset{\displaystyle O}{\|}}{C} - O^-$ Valine   **b.** $CH_3 - CH_2 - \overset{\overset{\displaystyle CH_3}{|}}{CH} - \overset{\overset{\displaystyle \overset{+}{N}H_3}{|}}{CH} - \overset{\overset{\displaystyle O}{\|}}{C} - O^-$ Isoleucine

CI.47 a. GTP is part of the citric acid cycle.
   b. $CoQH_2$ is part of electron transport.
   c. $FADH_2$ is part of both the citric acid cycle and electron transport.
   d. Cyt c is part of electron transport.
   e. Succinate dehydrogenase is part of both the citric acid cycle and electron transport.
   f. Complex I is part of electron transport.
   g. Isocitrate is part of the citric acid cycle.
   h. NAD^+ is part of both the citric acid cycle and electron transport.

CI.49 a. The components of acetyl CoA are aminoethanethiol, pantothenic acid (vitamin B_5), and phosphorylated ADP.
   b. Coenzyme A carries an acetyl group to the citric acid cycle for oxidation.
   c. The acetyl group links to the sulfur atom ($-S-$) in the aminoethanethiol part of CoA.
   d. Molar mass of acetyl CoA ($C_{23}H_{38}N_7O_{17}P_3S$)

$$= 23(12.01\ g) + 38(1.008\ g) + 7(14.01\ g) + 17(16.00\ g) + 3(30.97\ g) + 32.07\ g$$

$$= 810.\ g/mole$$

   e. $1.0\ mg\ \cancel{acetyl\ CoA} \times \dfrac{1\ g\ \cancel{acetyl\ CoA}}{1000\ mg\ \cancel{acetyl\ CoA}} \times \dfrac{1\ mole\ \cancel{acetyl\ CoA}}{810.\ g\ \cancel{acetyl\ CoA}} \times \dfrac{10\ moles\ ATP}{1\ mole\ \cancel{acetyl\ CoA}}$$

$$= 1.2 \times 10^{-5}\ mole\ of\ ATP\ (2\ SFs)$$

CI.51 a.

$$
\begin{array}{l}
CH_2-O-\overset{\displaystyle O}{\overset{\|}{C}}-(CH_2)_{14}-CH_3 \\[4pt]
\quad\quad\quad O \\[-2pt]
\quad\quad\quad \| \\[-2pt]
CH-O-C-(CH_2)_{14}-CH_3 \\[4pt]
\quad\quad\quad O \\[-2pt]
\quad\quad\quad \| \\[-2pt]
CH_2-O-C-(CH_2)_{14}-CH_3
\end{array}
\ +\ 3H_2O \longrightarrow
\begin{array}{l}
CH_2-OH \\[4pt] \\
CH-OH \\[4pt] \\
CH_2-OH
\end{array}
\ +\ 3\ HO-\overset{\displaystyle O}{\overset{\|}{C}}-(CH_2)_{14}-CH_3
$$

   b. Molar mass of glyceryl tripalmitate ($C_{51}H_{98}O_6$)

$$= 51(12.01\ g) + 98(1.008\ g) + 6(16.00\ g) = 807.3\ g/mole\ (4\ SFs)$$

   c. Analyze the Problem

Number of Carbon Atoms	Number of β Oxidation Cycles	Number of NADH	Number of $FADH_2$	Number of Acetyl CoA
16	7	7	7	8

ATP Production from Palmitic Acid (C$_{16}$)

Activation	−2 ATP
7 NADH $\times \dfrac{2.5 \text{ ATP}}{\text{NADH}}$ (electron transport)	17.5 ATP
7 FADH$_2 \times \dfrac{1.5 \text{ ATP}}{\text{FADH}_2}$ (electron transport)	10.5 ATP
8 acetyl CoA $\times \dfrac{10 \text{ ATP}}{\text{acetyl CoA}}$ (citric acid cycle)	80 ATP
Total	106 ATP

∴ 1 mole of palmitic acid will yield 106 moles of ATP.

d. $0.50 \text{ oz butter} \times \dfrac{1 \text{ lb}}{16 \text{ oz}} \times \dfrac{454 \text{ g}}{1 \text{ lb}} \times \dfrac{80. \text{ g glyceryl tripalmitate}}{100. \text{ g butter}} \times \dfrac{1 \text{ mole glyceryl tripalmitate}}{807.3 \text{ g glyceryl tripalmitate}}$

$\times \dfrac{3 \text{ moles palmitic acid}}{1 \text{ mole glyceryl tripalmitate}} \times \dfrac{106 \text{ moles ATP}}{1 \text{ mole palmitic acid}} \times \dfrac{7.3 \text{ kcal}}{1 \text{ mole ATP}} = 33 \text{ kcal (2 SFs)}$

e. $45 \text{ min} \times \dfrac{1 \text{ h}}{60 \text{ min}} \times \dfrac{750 \text{ kcal}}{1 \text{ h}} \times \dfrac{0.50 \text{ oz butter}}{33. \text{ kcal}} = 8.5 \text{ oz of butter (2 SFs)}$

CI.53 a. The disaccharide maltose will produce more ATP per mole than the monosaccharide glucose.

b. The C$_{18}$ fatty acid stearic acid will produce more ATP per mole than the C$_{14}$ fatty acid myristic acid.

c. The six-carbon molecule glucose will produce more ATP per mole than two two-carbon molecules of acetyl CoA.